Fodor's 2nd Edi

MW00644267

Vietnam

The complete guide, thoroughly up-to-date

Packed with details that will make your trip

The must-see sights, off and on the beaten path

What to see, what to skip

Mix-and-match vacation itineraries

City strolls, countryside adventures

Smart lodging and dining options

Essential local do's and taboos

Transportation tips, distances and directions

Key contacts, savvy travel tips

When to go, what to pack

Clear, accurate, easy-to-use maps

Books to read, videos to watch, background essay

dor's Travel Publications • New York, Toronto, London, Sydney, Auckland
ww.fodors.com

II

Fodor's Vietnam

EDITOR: Deborah Kaufman

Editorial Contributors: Jim Barnhart, Andrew Chilvers, Pilar Guzman, Michael Mathes, Elka Ray, William Richardson, Craig Thomas, Jim Spencer

Editorial Production: Stacey Kulig

Maps: David Lindroth, *cartographer*; Rebecca Baer and Bob Blake, *map editors*

Design: Fabrizio La Rocca, *creative director*; Guido Caroti, *art director*; Jolie Novak, *senior picture editor*; Melanie Marin, *photo editor*

Cover Design: Pentagram

Production/Manufacturing: Yexenia M. Markland

Cover Photograph: Owen Franken

Copyright

Second Edition

ISBN 0–679–00295–2

ISSN 1520–4979

Special Sales

Fodor's Travel Publications are available at special discounts for bulk purchases for sales promotions or premiums. Special editions, including personalized covers, excerpts of existing guides, and corporate imprints, can be created in large quantities for special needs. For more information, contact your local bookseller or write to Special Markets, Fodor's Travel Publications, 280 Park Avenue, New York, NY 10017. Inquiries from Canada should be directed to your local Canadian bookseller or sent to Random House of Canada, Ltd., Marketing Department, 2775 Matheson Boulevard East, Mississauga, Ontario L4W 4P7. Inquiries from the United Kingdom should be sent to Fodor's Travel Publications, 20 Vauxhall Bridge Road, London SW1V 2SA, England

PRINTED IN THE UNITED STATES OF AMERICA

10 9 8 7 6 5 4 3 2 1

Important Tip

Although all prices, opening times, and other details in this book are based on information supplied to us at press time, changes occur all the time in the travel world, and Fodor's cannot accept responsibility for facts that become outdated or for inadvertent errors or omissions. So **always confirm information when it matters**, especially if you're making a detour to visit a specific place.

CONTENTS

Maps

ON THE ROAD WITH FODOR'S

EVERY VACATION is important. So here at Fodor's we've pulled out all stops in preparing *Fodor's Vietnam*. To guide you in putting together your travel experience, we've created multiday itineraries and neighborhood walks. And to direct you to the places that are truly worth your time and money, we've rallied the team of endearingly picky know-it-alls we're pleased to call our writers. Having seen all corners of Vietnam, they're real experts on the subjects they cover for us. If you knew them, you'd poll them for tips yourself.

Andrew Chilvers, who spent most of his life in London and Hong Kong and some years in Ho Chi Minh City, is a freelance journalist. He has written for newspapers and magazines in England, New Zealand, Vietnam, Thailand, and Japan, and hopes to extend his global reach. Andrew updated the Ho Chi Minh City and the Mekong Delta chapters.

Pilar Guzman, a freelance writer and illustrator, did much of the original research for *Fodor's Vietnam*. After visiting the country, she is now devoting all of her spare time to accurately recreating the dishes she ate there.

Michael Mathes, expert on exploring Hanoi and the northernmost reaches of Vietnam, is a freelance writer based in Hanoi. Vietnam has been his home since 1994, minus a brief hiatus in San Francisco. He is brave (or crazy) enough to travel around Hanoi by motorbike—wearing a helmet, of course—especially in search of the city's best *pho*, Vietnam's delicious noodle soup.

Elka Ray, a freelance writer and editor, resides in Hanoi and contributed to the Hanoi Dining, Lodging, Nightlife and the Arts, Outdoor Activities and Sports, and Shopping sections, as well as to Smart Travel Tips A to Z. Elka edits Vietnam Airlines magazine, *Heritage,* and is currently at work on a series of travel booklets about Vietnamese culture. Past writing assignments have involved touring Vietnam's luxury beach resorts, taking a behind-the-scenes look at the Miss Vietnam beauty pageant, and interviewing some of the country's best-known pop divas.

William Richardson updated the Portraits of Vietnam chapter. An environmental scientist by profession and a businessman by necessity, William has been living in Hanoi since 1994. He has worked as a consultant on small business investments and on environmental conservation in Vietnam. But he prefers to risk life and limb while touring the back roads of Vietnam on a Minsk motorcycle.

Craig Thomas, a recovering lawyer, is a freelance journalist based in Ho Chi Minh City. Craig, who writes for a number of regional newspapers and magazines, expanded the Central Coast and the South-Central Coast and Highlands chapters. Committed to one day speaking fluent Vietnamese, he spends his spare time pestering his Vietnamese friends to teach him new and obscure words.

Don't Forget to Write

Keeping a travel guide fresh and up-to-date is a big job. So we love your feedback—positive and negative—and follow up on all suggestions. Contact the Vietnam editor at editors@fodors.com or c/o Fodor's, 280 Park Avenue, New York, NY 10017. And have a wonderful trip!

Karen Cure
Editorial Director

World Time Zones

Numbers below vertical bands relate each zone to Greenwich Mean Time (0 hrs.).
Local times frequently differ from these general indications,
as indicated by light-face numbers on map.

Southeast Asia

- CHINA
- Guangzho
- Macau
- HONG KC
- Mandalay
- Hanoi
- LAOS
- Luang Prabang
- Haiphong
- BURMA (MYANMAR)
- HAINAN
- Pegu
- Vientiane
- Chiang Mai
- Rangoon (Yangon)
- Hue
- Danang
- THAILAND
- Korat
- Bangkok
- VIETNAM
- Andaman Sea
- Siem Riep
- CAMBODIA
- Isthmus of Kra
- Phnom Penh
- Ho Chi Minh City (Saigon)
- Gulf of Thailand
- Phuket
- South China Sea
- Songkhla
- Kota Kinabalu
- George Town
- WEST MALAYSIA
- MALAYSIA
- BRUNEI
- SA
- Medan
- Strait of Malacca
- Kuala Lumpur
- SARAWAK
- Kuching
- BORNEO
- SINGAPORE
- Karimata
- KALIMANTAN
- SUMATRA
- Jambi
- INDONESI
- INDIAN OCEAN
- KEPULAUAN
- Strait
- Palembang
- Banjarmasin
- GREATER SUNDA I
- Jakarta
- Java Sea
- Bandung
- Surabaya
- Yogyakarta
- JAVA
- BALI
- LOM
- 0 — 500 miles
- 0 — 750 km
- N

Taipei

TAIWAN

PACIFIC OCEAN

Laoag
LUZON
Baguio

Manila

INDORO

PHILIPPINES

VISAYAS *SAMAR*

Iloilo City
PANAY

NEGROS

Cebu City

AN

Sulu Sea

MINDANAO

Davao

PALAU

Celebes Sea

Strait

HALMAHERA

BIAK

**PAPUA-
NEW GUINEA**

ULAWESI
(he Celebes)

M O L U C C A S

SERAM

BURU

IRIAN JAYA

N D S

Ujung
Pandang

Banda Sea

KEPULAUAN
ARU

Flores Sea

R S U N D A   I S L A N D S

KEPULAUAN
TANIMBAR

FLORES

TIMOR

Timor Sea

MBA

AUSTRALIA

x

Vietnam

CHINA

Ha Giang

Nanning

CHINA

Lao Cai

Hong River

THAI
NGUYEN

Cao
Bang

Sapa

Yen Bai

Tuyen
Quang

Thai
Nguyen

Lang
Son

Dien
Bien Phu

VINH PHUC

Son
La

Viet Tri

Bac
Giang

Bac Ninh

Cam Pha

Hanoi

BAC NINH

Hoa
Binh

HUNG
YEN

Halong

Haiphong

HA Nam

TAY

THAI
BINH

HA NAM

Nam Dinh

Nam Binh

NINH BINH

*Gulf of
Tonkin*

Thanh Hoa

Hainan

L A O S

Vinh

Ha Tinh

Vientiane

Dong Hoi

Mekong River

Dong Ha
Hue

T H A I L A N D

Danang

Hoi An

Tam Ky

Quang Ngai

Kontum

Pleiku

Quy Nhon

Siem Riep
(Angkor Wat)

C A M B O D I A

Buon Me
Thuat

Tuy Hoa

Dalat

Nha Trang

Phnom Penh

Dong

Phan Rang

*Gulf of
Thailand*

Tay Ninh

Thu Dau
Mot

Bien Hoa

Phan Thiet

N

Chau Doc

My
Tho

Ho Chi Minh City (Saigon)

TIEN
GANG

Long Xuyen

VINH
LONG

Ben Tre

Vung Tau

Phu Quoc

Rach Gia

Can
Tho

Tra Vinh

South China Sea

0   100 miles

CAN THO

Soc Trang

0   150 km

Bac Lieu

Ca Mau

SMART TRAVEL TIPS A TO Z

Basic Information on Traveling in Vietnam, Savvy Tips to Make Your Trip a Breeze, and Companies and Organizations to Contact

ADDRESSES

To find addresses in Vietnam, it helps to know a few local practices. You may see addresses with numbers separated by a slash, such as "361/8 Nguyen Dinh Chieu St." This means you should head for No. 361 on Nguyen Dinh Chieu Street, and then look for an alley next to the building; you want No. 8 in this alley. When you see addresses with a number followed by a letter, such as "97A," this means there is more than one No. 97 on the street and you need to find the one numbered specifically with an "A." If you see "54bis," look for a building adjacent to No. 54; this is a leftover from the French that means 54½.

The English word *street* (abbreviated St.) is used throughout the book rather than the Vietnamese words: *pho* or *duong*. This was done to make sure street names are clear; in Vietnamese, the words pho and duong come before the names of the streets, which can prove very confusing when trying to find your way around. In addition, many Vietnamese refer to streets only by name (without adding pho or duong), so you may only see these words on street signs and maps.

AIR TRAVEL

International flights into Vietnam typically connect through hubs such as Bangkok, Singapore, Manila, Hong Kong, Kuala Lumpur, and Taipei and fly into Ho Chi Minh City and Hanoi. The airport in Danang, in central Vietnam, opened to international flights in 1999, but to date the traffic has been limited to charters from regional countries. Although negotiations to offer direct U.S.–Vietnam service are ongoing, at present there are no direct flights between Vietnam and North America. There are also no direct flights to Vietnam from the United Kingdom.

Note that two airlines may jointly operate a connecting flight from an Asian hub, so **ask if your airline operates every segment of your flight**—you may find that your preferred carrier flies only part of the way. For instance, if you purchased a ticket through an international carrier such as Air France, Cathay Pacific, or Thai International Airways, but are not flying directly to Hanoi or Ho Chi Minh City, it is possible that your connecting flight into Vietnam will be on Vietnam Airlines. Vietnam Airlines itself has direct routes from cities such as Paris (via Dubai) as well as Moscow and Sydney into Vietnam.

Some airlines' layovers are short; others, particularly those offering discounted fares, require an overnight stay in a connecting city. Before buying your ticket, **check to see who covers the cost of the hotel—you or the airline—if you have to stay overnight.**

For domestic air travel, major transportation hubs are Ho Chi Minh City, Hanoi, and Danang, but there is also service to Ban Me Thuot, Dalat, Dien Bien Phu, Haiphong, Hue, Nha Trang, Phu Quoc Island, Pleiku, Qui Nhon, and Vinh.

It's a good idea to **confirm both domestic flights and flights out of Vietnam two days in advance.** Flights are occasionally delayed or canceled altogether. Also, **be sure to arrive at the airport early**: 45 minutes to 1 hour before domestic flights or 2 hours before international flights.

During rainy season avoid flying in late afternoon and early evening, when storms generally occur.

CARRIERS

Domestic routes in Vietnam are flown by Vietnam Airlines and its smaller semiprivate competitor, Pacific Airlines. Despite the appearance of competition, however, ticket prices for both airlines are set by the government. At press time (winter 2000) both Vietnam Airlines and Pacific Airlines were charging about $135 for a one-way ticket to Hanoi from Ho Chi Minh City. Combined, these airlines will get you to all major destinations and many smaller airports in the country. Breaking up a Ho Chi Minh City–Hanoi flight by stopping in, say, Hue or Danang for a few days will cost you only $10 extra.

Note that since the fatal air crash in Phnom Penh, Cambodia, in September 1997, Vietnam Airlines has grounded all remaining Russian-made aircraft in its fleet. Planes now include 10 Airbus A320s, 3 Boeing 767s, and a few German Fokker 70s and French ATR 72s.

From the United States, Continental, Northwest, and United Airlines have flights into Tokyo, Singapore, and Bangkok, which then connect with regional carriers. Although there's no direct service from the United Kingdom, British Airways, Cathay Pacific, and Thai Airways fly to Bangkok and Hong Kong, from which there are two daily flights to Ho Chi Minh City, and one daily to Hanoi.

➤ MAJOR AIRLINES: **Asiana** (☎ 800/227–4262). **Cathay Pacific Airways** (☎ 800/233–2742 in the U.S.; 800/268–6868 in Canada).**China Airlines** (☎ 800/227–5118). **Korean Air** (☎ 800/438–5000). **Singapore Airlines** (☎ 800/742–3333).

➤ TO AND FROM THE U.S.: **Continental** (☎ 800/231–0856). **Northwest** (☎ 800/225–2525). **United Airlines** (☎ 800/241–6522).

➤ TO AND FROM THE U.K.: **British Airways** (☎ 0345/222–111). **Cathay Pacific** (☎ 0345/581–581). **Thai Airways** (☎ 020/7491–7953).

➤ DOMESTIC AIRLINES: **Pacific Airlines** (✉ 100 Le Duan St., Dong Da District, Hanoi, ☎ 04/518–1503; ✉ 177 Vo Thi Sau St., District 1, Ho Chi Minh City, ☎ 08/820–0978). **Vietnam Airlines** (✉ 1 Quang Trung St., Hoan Kiem District, Hanoi, ☎ 04/825–0888 or 04/832–0320; ✉ 116 Nguyen Hue St., District 1, Ho Chi Minh City, ☎ 08/829–2118 or 08/823–0696).

CHECK-IN & BOARDING

Assuming that not everyone with a ticket will show up, airlines routinely overbook planes. When everyone does, airlines ask for volunteers to give up their seats. In return, these volunteers usually get a certificate for a free flight and are rebooked on the next flight out. If there are not enough volunteers, the airline must choose who will be denied boarding. The first to get bumped are passengers who checked in late and those flying on discounted tickets, so **get to the gate and check in as early as possible,** especially during peak periods.

Vietnam Airlines closes its check-in counters 30 minutes before boarding, so **check in early.** Even if other passengers have yet to clear customs, it's still nearly impossible to get on the flight if you show up at the counter less than 30 minutes before your flight. And since most of the flights are overbooked, you are probably looking at a long, dreary wait.

Always **bring a government-issued photo ID to the airport.** You may be asked to show it before you are allowed to check in.

CUTTING COSTS

The least expensive airfares to Vietnam must usually be purchased in advance and are nonrefundable. It's smart to **call a number of airlines, and when you are quoted a good price, book it on the spot**—the same fare may not be available the next day. Always **check different routings** and look into using different airports. Travel agents, especially low-fare specialists (☞ Discounts & Deals, *below*), are helpful.

Consolidators are another good source. They buy tickets for scheduled international flights at reduced rates from the airlines, then sell them at prices that beat the best fare available directly from the airlines, usually without restrictions. Sometimes you can even get your money back if you need to return the ticket. Carefully read the fine print detailing penalties for changes and cancellations, and **confirm your consolidator reservation with the airline.**

When you **fly as a courier,** you trade your checked-luggage space for a ticket deeply subsidized by a courier service. There are restrictions on when you can book and how long you can stay.

➤ CONSOLIDATORS: **Cheap Tickets** (☎ 800/377–1000). **Discount Airline Ticket Service** (☎ 800/576–1600). **Unitravel** (☎ 800/325–2222). **Up & Away Travel** (☎ 212/889–2345). **World Travel Network** (☎ 800/409–6753).

ENJOYING THE FLIGHT

For more legroom, **request an emergency-aisle seat.** Don't sit in the row in front of the emergency aisle or in front of a bulkhead, where seats may not recline. If you have dietary concerns, **ask for special meals when booking.** These can be vegetarian, low-cholesterol, or kosher, for example. On long flights, try to maintain a normal routine, to help fight jet lag. At night, **get some sleep.** By day, **eat light meals, drink water** (not alcohol), and **move around the cabin** to stretch your legs.

Bear in mind that Vietnam Airlines does not offer in-flight movies. Bring a book or some other means of keeping yourself occupied.

FLYING TIMES

Flying time from Los Angeles to the Southeast Asian hub of Bangkok is approximately 18 hours, Chicago to Bangkok is 20 hours, and New York to Bangkok is 22 hours. Bangkok to Ho Chi Minh City takes 1 hour.

HOW TO COMPLAIN

If your baggage goes astray or your flight goes awry, complain right away. Most carriers require that you **file a claim immediately.**

➤ AIRLINE COMPLAINTS: U.S. Department of Transportation **Aviation Consumer Protection Division** (✉ C-75, Room 4107, Washington, DC 20590, ☎ 202/366–2220, airconsumer@ost.dot.gov, www.dot.gov/airconsumer). **Federal Aviation**

Administration Consumer Hotline (☎ 800/322–7873).

RECONFIRMING

In Vietnam both domestic and international flights should be reconfirmed 48 hours before departure.

AIRPORTS

The major gateways to Vietnam are Ho Chi Minh City's Tan Son Nhat Airport and Hanoi's Noi Bai Airport. Tan Son Nhat Airport was the U.S. military airport in Saigon and was once the busiest landing strip in the world. As the main gateway for thousands of *Viet Kieu,* returning overseas Vietnamese who still raise suspicion among the country's government workers, Ho Chi Minh City's airport has procedures that can involve more in-depth immigration checks and baggage searches—if customs (☞ Customs & Duties, *below*) has any cause for suspicion.

Hanoi's Noi Bai Airport, despite the aging Soviet MiGs resting on the runway, feels less like an airport serving the capital of a nation of 80 million people and more like a regional landing strip. Although work on a new two-story terminal began years ago, the project was virtually at a standstill from 1996 until early 2000. The latest, somewhat optimistic, predictions call for its completion by the end of 2001. In the meantime, you'll find 1970s-style utilitarian Soviet chic, but at least the arrival procedures are relatively painless.

In general, at both airports you are more than likely to get through immigration, pick up your waiting bags, and breeze in and out of customs before you break a sweat.

➤ AIRPORT INFORMATION: **Noi Bai International Airport** (✉ 35 km [22 mi] north of Hanoi, ☎ 04/886–5318). **Tan Son Nhat Airport** (✉ Hoang Van Thu Blvd., Tan Binh District, 7 km [4 mi] from central Ho Chi Minh City, ☎ 08/844–3179).

DUTY-FREE SHOPPING

There is a limited selection of alcohol, cigarettes, snack foods, and souvenirs in both Tan Son Nhat and Noi Bai airports. High prices and second-rate goods mean that you're better off not leaving your gift shopping to the last minute.

TRANSFERS

Figuring out how to get into Hanoi or Ho Chi Minh City from the airport can be a little overwhelming when you first arrive. There are a few options: either **have your hotel or tour company arrange to pick you up, or take a taxi or shuttle bus** into the city center. Airport Taxi has recently established a booth inside the terminal at Noi Bai in Hanoi. Buying a ticket here ($10 to central Hanoi) allows you to avoid the crush of freelance drivers who lurk outside. The minibus from Noi Bai costs $4. In Ho Chi Minh City, a metered cab will get you to the city center for less than $5. *See* Chapters 2 and 6 for more information about traveling between the airport and the city center.

BIKE TRAVEL

In scenic cities such as Hanoi and Hue, biking can be an ideal way to get around town, see the sights, and in the case of Hoi An and Nha Trang, head to the beach. However, you should **avoid bicycling in Ho Chi Minh City** because of the smog and heavy traffic; the city is also much more spread out than others in Vietnam. You can usually rent Vietnamese-made bicycles or the sturdier Phoenix bicycles from China for 25,000d to 35,000d per day from most tourist cafés and some hotels and tourist agencies. Make sure the bike has an attached wheel lock, or borrow a lock from the owner.

Hardy travelers have been known to bring their own mountain bikes and cycle the length of the country. Bikes can be placed on ferries, buses, and trains at an added cost, which varies by destination. A few tour operators organize bike trips across the country (☞ Tours & Packages, *below*).

➤ BIKE RENTALS: Many of the tourist cafés on **De Tham Street, District 1,** in Ho Chi Minh City rent bicycles and scooters. The **Memory Café** (✉ 33bis Tran Hung Dao St., Hoan Kiem District, ☎ 04/826–5854) in Hanoi rents bikes and motorcycles.

BIKES IN FLIGHT

Most airlines accommodate bikes as luggage, provided they are dismantled and boxed. For bike boxes, often free at bike shops, you'll pay about $5 from airlines (at least $100 for bike bags). International travelers can sometimes substitute a bike for a piece of checked luggage at no charge; otherwise, the cost is about $100. Domestic and Canadian airlines charge $25–$50.

BOAT & FERRY TRAVEL

For many riverside or seaside towns in Vietnam, boat rides are a natural attraction, sometimes the only way to get around, and a great way to get a view of life on, in, or near the water. Areas like the Mekong Delta are only worthwhile if you travel by boat. Even if you do not go through a travel agency or tourist office, cheap boats for hire will certainly find you—probably before you even get to the water's edge. With a bit of bargaining you can negotiate a deal, and apart from paying more than the locals for the same trip, you can count on being delivered safely back to your starting point. Just **make absolutely sure you agree on a price before you set off.** In northern Vietnam and in the Mekong Delta ferries are often the only way to get to destinations where bridges have not yet been built or have been destroyed, or to get to islands such as Cat Ba. Bicycles, cars, and motorbikes can usually be brought on board for a fee.

FARES & SCHEDULES

See individual chapters for travel agencies and other tourist cafés that provide information on boat routes, fares, and schedules.

BORDER CROSSINGS

Air travel is the recommended way to go between Vietnam and other points in Asia. You must **get a visa to visit most countries near Vietnam**—Laos, Cambodia, and China—which can be difficult; you're best off trying to make visa arrangements before you go to Vietnam. The exception is Thailand, which generally automatically grants short-term-stay visas to most Western visitors.

Going overland from Vietnam to other points is neither easy nor comfortable, although border crossings with China have been simplified in the past few years. To go to China you need to get a standard tourist visa for entry into the country from Vietnam. Vietnam–China border crossings include Mong Cai, Huu Nghi, and Lao Cai (near Sapa). Two trains per week run from Hanoi to Beijing, crossing at Dong Dang. The trip takes 55 hours. Although traveling overland into Laos is inadvisable due to rebel activity and banditry, many travelers make the trip via the Lao Bao border crossing, located 85 km (53 mi) from Dong Ha in central Vietnam.

➤ VISA OFFICES: **Chinese Embassy Visa Section** (⊠ 520 12th Ave., New York, NY, 10036 USA, ☎ 212/330–7409; ⊠ 46 Hoang Dieu St., Ba Dinh District, Hanoi, ☎ 04/845–3736, FAX 04/823–2826). **Cambodia** (⊠ 4500 16th St. NW, Washington, DC 20011 USA, ☎ 202/726–7742); ⊠ 71 Tran Hung Dao St., Hoan Kiem District, Hanoi, ☎ 04/825–3788, FAX 04/826–5225).

BUS TRAVEL

Although an extensive and dirt-cheap public bus system services every nook and cranny of the country, these buses are the most uncomfortable way to travel in Vietnam. Buses are often cramped, unbearably hot, packed with chain-smokers, and notoriously loud. Roads can be rough. Buses also break down like clockwork and operate under arbitrary schedules. Departure times depend on when they fill up, and arrival times depend on how many times they stop to pick up passengers—who are sometimes carrying pigs, chickens, snakes, goats, or fish—by the roadside.

Air-conditioned minibuses are a better alternative and are only slightly more expensive than regular buses; these are often available at or near most bus stations. Tourist minibuses between Hanoi and Ho Chi Minh City depart daily, usually in the early morning. An even better option is to **take the more convenient, reliable, and infinitely more comfortable privately run tour buses** organized by travel agencies, tourist offices, and travel cafés to most destinations. Even the most budget-conscious backpackers opt for the minivans or the reasonable tourist buses.

CUTTING COSTS

Sinh Café Travel, based in Ho Chi Minh City, has created a niche market with its privately run, open tour bus schedules. For $38 heading north and $33 going south, you can purchase an open-ended ticket on the Sinh Café bus that enables you to break your journey at several points—Nha Trang, Dalat, Hoi An, Hue, and Ninh Binh—en route to Hanoi or Ho Chi Minh City. You can stay for as much time as you can spare at each stop on this tour itinerary; the Sinh Café's 45-seat air-conditioned bus leaves daily from these stops. Service is run in partnership with several smaller agencies that have their own buses. Since the service is not a tour but a private means of transportation, you have the flexibility to stay (or not) in any of the stops for any number of days before hooking up with the next available seat arranged by the Sinh Café office at each of these points. The buses also stop at various sights along the way. Another reliable bus and tour company, based in Hanoi, is Rainbow Services, which charges $30 for air-conditioned buses between Hanoi and Ho Chi Minh City.

PAYING

Tour companies that run bus services accept dollars and dong. Public buses require dong.

RESERVATIONS

Although it's usually possible to get a seat a day before departure, you should **book your tickets as early as possible** to be on the safe side.

➤ BUS INFORMATION: **Rainbow Services** (⊠ 42 Nha Chung St., Hoan Kiem District, Hanoi, ☎ 04/826–8752). **Sinh Café Travel** (⊠ 246–248 De Tham St., District 1, Ho Chi Minh City, ☎ 08/836–7338, 08/835–5601, or 08/836–9420). *See* individual chapters for information on travel agencies and other tourist cafés that organize bus trips around the country; you can also find information on state-run bus companies and their services.

BUSINESS GROUPS & COMMERCE OFFICES

Many international business groups and chambers of commerce have opened offices in Hanoi and Ho Chi Minh City to serve the growing community of foreigners living in Vietnam and doing business here. You're usually welcome at monthly meetings, forums, and business lunches put on by these organizations. There may be a fee for certain functions, especially if a meal is involved.

➤ LOCAL GROUPS: **American Chamber of Commerce** (✉ 59A Ly Thai To St., 5th floor, Hoan Kiem District, Hanoi, ☎ 04/934–2790, FAX 04/934–2787; ✉ New World Hotel, 76 Le Lai St., Room 323, District 1, Ho Chi Minh City, ☎ 08/824–3562, FAX 08/824–3572. **British Business Group** (✉ British Embassy, 31 Hai Ba Trung St., Hoan Kiem District, Hanoi, ☎ 04/826–6306, FAX 04/934–4196; ✉ 25 Le Duan St., District 1, Ho Chi Minh City, ☎ 08/829–8433, FAX 08/822–1971). **Canadian Vietnam Business Association** (✉ IMAC, 103 Pasteur St., District 1, Ho Chi Minh City, ☎ 08/822–9632, FAX 08/822–9633). **United States Foreign Commercial Office** (✉ 6 Ngoc Khanh St., Ba Dinh District, Hanoi, ☎ 04/824–2422, FAX 04/831–4540).

BUSINESS HOURS

Vietnam has a tradition of afternoon siestas (especially in the countryside), which means that all activities except eating tend to stop during lunch, between 11:30 and 2. Urban life is changing rapidly in Vietnam, however, and as free-market economics affects Ho Chi Minh City and Hanoi, more and more businesses are staying open during lunchtime to accommodate the increasing number of tourists and office-bound Vietnamese who use their midday break as a time to catch up on shopping or chores.

BANKS & OFFICES

Vietnam is moving toward an official five-day workweek. Whereas some offices remain open on Saturday mornings, many do not. Most government agencies and foreign-invested companies take the weekend off.

Banks are only open on weekdays, usually from 8 AM to 4:30 PM. Post offices are open seven days a week. Cafés and restaurants are open all day, almost every day. Most sidewalk stalls serving breakfast and lunch finish by 2 and don't reopen for dinner until 4. By 10 PM in Hanoi and 11 PM in Ho Chi Minh City, activity starts slowing down; smaller cities die down even earlier. In bigger cities more popular venues stay open much later. You can always find late-night noodle stands. Bars and nightclubs usually close at about 1 AM or whenever the last customer leaves.

GAS STATIONS

If you cannot find a gas station, look for a glass bottle on a street corner, topped with a cone of paper. Vendors sell gas at many intersections in the cities, although you will have trouble finding gas after 10 PM.

MUSEUMS & SIGHTS

Most museums in Vietnam are closed on Sunday and Monday. Some are also closed on Saturday or are only open Saturday morning. Pagodas are generally open from dawn to dusk and later if it's the first or fifteenth day of the lunar month.

SHOPS

Small family-run shops seem to stay open indefinitely, primarily because living and working quarters are often one and the same.

CAMERAS & PHOTOGRAPHY

For photographers, the best time of year to visit Vietnam is from September to November, when the skies in the north are blue and the light has a wonderful golden quality. In the winter months, the central and northern regions of Vietnam are gray, while the spring and summer months bring heavy rains. If you plan to photograph the northern mountains, visit in the spring when the fruit trees are in bloom.

➤ PHOTO HELP: **Kodak Information Center** (☎ 800/242–2424). *Kodak Guide to Shooting Great Travel Pictures,* available in bookstores or from Fodor's Travel Publications (☎ 800/533–6478; $16.50 plus $5.50 shipping).

EQUIPMENT PRECAUTIONS

Always **keep your film and tape out of the sun.** Carry an extra supply of batteries, and **be prepared to turn on your camera or camcorder** to prove to security personnel that the device is real. Always **ask for hand inspection of film,** which becomes clouded after repeated exposure to airport X-ray machines, and **keep videotapes away from metal detectors.**

FILM & DEVELOPING

Print film is widely available in Vietnam, but be sure to **check the expiration dates** before you buy it. Slide film is hard to find. Getting film developed in Vietnam is cheap; each 4″ by 6″ print costs about 1,800d. Although many places do a fine job on prints, having slide film developed in Vietnam is a risky undertaking.

CAR RENTAL

At present, **you (as a tourist) are not permitted to drive a car yourself,** although you can rent motorbikes and scooters in major cities (☞ Transportation Around Vietnam, *below*). The only foreigners allowed to drive are those with business or diplomatic visas who have registered with the Ministry of Transportation and obtained a Vietnamese driver's license (exceptions are made for Laotian and Chinese nationals). These cumbersome procedures—and the hectic state of the country's traffic—assure that very few foreigners find themselves behind the wheel. A few American car-rental companies, such as Hertz, Thrifty, and Avis, have been negotiating with authorities to set up car-rental agencies in Hanoi and Ho Chi Minh City, but as yet no licenses have been signed. Even if a deal is inked, the first step is likely to be chauffeur-driven rental cars, not self-driven ones.

A rented car automatically comes with a driver who will, hopefully, speak some English. Cars and minivans with drivers are readily available from private and state-run travel agencies, tourist offices, and through most hotels in bigger cities such as Ho Chi Minh City, Hanoi, Hue, Danang, Nha Trang, and Vung Tau. You are charged either by the kilometer or by the day, or both. A daily rate runs anywhere from $30 to $60 per day, depending on the city in which you rent the vehicle, whether the vehicle has air-conditioning, the make of the car, and your bargaining skills. The agreed-on price should include gas and tolls (but clarify all this before you set off). Travel agencies can also arrange for English-speaking guides to accompany you and the driver.

The most common type of vehicles for rent are Japanese-made sedans and minivans, although some older Russian Volgas and small, new Korean Kias are available from smaller agencies. Four-wheel-drive vehicles such as Toyota Land Cruisers and Mitsubishi Pajeros are ideal for major forays into river deltas, highlands, or mountains, but there aren't many of these available for rent, and they are often twice the price of a sedan. Note that most rental cars lack seat belts. Remember that you must **negotiate a price in advance and check out the vehicle before you rent it.** Note that the name *Land Cruiser* is overused in Vietnam, especially in Hanoi. Too many people consider a Land Cruiser—made only by Toyota—to be any four-wheel-drive vehicle that's not a Russian jeep. For more information on getting around by car in Vietnam, *see* Car Travel, *below.*

CAR TRAVEL

As a tourist you are currently not allowed to drive cars yourself, although you may drive motorbikes (☞ Transportation Around Vietnam, *below*). For more information on renting a car with a driver, *see* Car Rental, *above.*

EMERGENCY SERVICES

If you have hired a car and driver for the day or longer and the car breaks down, you should not be held responsible for the cost of repairs. Make sure everyone is clear about this before you take off on a long journey. Your exemption from financial responsibility may be little consolation when your vehicle does break down, however. Mechanical and engine problems with Japanese-made sedans, Toyota Land Cruisers, or Mitsubishi Pajeros, for instance, are rare. But expect breakdowns in Russian-made jeeps and cars. Most mechanical problems can be fixed, and there are mechanics on virtually every block in the cities.

As for motorbikes, the Japanese-made ones are quite dependable. Repair shops for these are also ubiquitous throughout the cities. In the country-side old East German Simsons and Soviet-era Minsk motorcycles are the standards. They break down regularly, but everyone claims to know how to fix them (although it's not always true), and parts—at least for the Minsks—are readily available.

In case of a traffic accident, remember that the foreigner is always at fault. So, in minor accidents, even if you are not at fault it's a good idea to stay in the car and let your driver do the talking or to try to get out of the situation as quickly as possible without involving the police. Unless the case is crystal clear, you'll likely be fighting a losing battle and will probably be asked to pay damages immediately even if you are not to blame.

In general, Vietnam's traffic police—easily recognizable by their peach-color jumpsuits—are best avoided.

GASOLINE

Unleaded gasoline is sold by the liter in Vietnam. (There are about 4 liters to the gallon.) Gas stations sell at a government-regulated price of about 4,800d per liter. But **be careful: some gas station pumps issue a gas-oil mixture** (between 2% and 4% oil) for two-stroke motorcycles such as Minsks. Make sure you are getting the right gas for your vehicle. If communication proves impossible, find someone with a similar vehicle and watch what they pump into their vehicle. Gas is also sold by vendors on the street and at just about every corner in the cities—a fortunate option when stations are closed. Their price is slightly higher, however, and it's not unheard of for watered-down gas to be sold on the street.

PARKING

Any traveling by car you do will be with a hired driver, so he (drivers are rarely women) will be the one responsible for finding adequate parking.

On many streets in Ho Chi Minh City and Hanoi it is now illegal to leave an unattended car; the streets are simply too narrow or crowded. Instead, cars—and motorbikes and bicycles—are often parked in guarded lots, driveways, even on roped off pieces of sidewalk. A few streets now have marked automobile parking, and some of the newer high-rises in Ho Chi Minh City and Hanoi have underground or elevated garages.

ROAD CONDITIONS

The backbone of Vietnam's road system is Highway 1 or, as its French builders called it, La Route des Mandarins. This narrow, crumbling road, which is in the throes of never-ending upgrades, extends from near the Chinese border, north of Hanoi, through Ho Chi Minh City and to the heart of the Mekong Delta in the south. Other major roadways include: the recently upgraded Highway 5 from Hanoi to Haiphong; Highway 6 out to Dien Bien Phu; Route 70, which bisects the northwest; Highway 7, the Nghe An Province route into Laos; Route 14 through the central highlands; Route 22, west out of Ho Chi Minh City toward Tay Ninh and the Cambodian capital of Phnom Penh; and Route 80, through the upper Mekong Delta. In early 2000 construction began on a second north–south route, the Truong Son Highway. Following the famed wartime supply route known as the Ho Chi Minh Trail, this ambitious project will cut through Vietnam's western mountains, extending from the northern province of Ha Tay to Ho Chi Minh City.

Vietnam's major roads are for the most part paved. But all roads, except for a few spots such as the 16-km (10-mi) stretch on Highway 5, are slow going—96 km (60 mi) takes about 90 minutes to 2 hours, depending on the condition of the road. Thoroughfares labeled national roads cover only 12,000 km (7,500 mi) of Vietnam's transportation system; only 60% of these roads are paved. The lowest category of roads, called provincial or district roads, account for 40,000 km (25,000 mi) of the system. Only 8% of these are paved. Most dirt roads turn to mud during the rainy season and become impassable.

Highways are the main transport route for cars, public buses, transport trucks, tractors, motorbikes, bicycles, pedestrians, oxcarts, and a host of farm animals. Highway 1, for example, is the primary north–south commercial route.

Road conditions in the north are far worse than in the south, where the U.S. war effort built or paved many of the roads. But even these routes are suffering due to lack of maintenance or repair. Since the embargo was lifted on Vietnam, however, the World Bank and the Asian Development Bank have approved soft loans to upgrade much of Highway 1 and other roadways. Major progress has been made on certain stretches of Highway 1 and Highway 5.

When driving around the country, **try to travel during the day.** Driving at night can be hazardous because many vehicles don't have lights and it is difficult to see bad spots in the road.

ROAD MAPS

City maps and maps of Vietnam and Southeast Asia can be purchased from sidewalk vendors, hotel gift shops, bookstores, tourist cafés, and the ubiquitous postcard sellers who roam the city streets seeking out visitors. Detailed road atlases and topography maps of rural regions are, however, rare; they're also notoriously inaccurate.

RULES OF THE ROAD

Bicyclists, motorcyclists, and pedestrians take note: the romantic notion that Vietnamese city traffic is a crowded but mysterious ballet dance in which all parties approach each other in a calculated frenzy and then magically weave through to safety is, in a word, nonsense. Vietnam's traffic fatalities per capita are among the highest in the world. Yes, there seems to be a vague understanding among riders, drivers, and pedestrians that they're all in it together. But this doesn't make the streets much safer.

In the past few years traffic lights have sprung up all over Hanoi and Ho Chi Minh City. Don't put too much faith in them, though; red lights are often ignored, especially at night and especially in Hanoi. Right turns on red are forbidden, although you'd never realize this by watching an intersection. One-way streets are also dangerous, as there is usually a trickle of traffic flowing the wrong way. And although the Vietnamese technically drive on the right side of the road, the concept of lanes has yet to catch on.

When riding a motorbike or bicycle, **use your skills of prediction, timing, weaving, and of course honking.** And *always* give trucks, army jeeps, and buses the right-of-way. It's not that they won't necessarily *want* to stop for you—they just might not have any brakes. The best way to get through traffic on foot is to **walk at a steady pace across the street and, of course, watch out**; the oncoming vehicles will have a better chance of avoiding you if the drivers can get a sense of where you will be going next. If you stop suddenly, it's harder for drivers to judge where you are in relation to them.

CHILDREN IN VIETNAM

Traveling with very young children to Vietnam is not recommended, largely because of health considerations: young children's immune systems are not as developed as those of adults, and Vietnam doesn't have emergency children's medical care up to international standards. One hospital that does treat children, however, is the Hanoi Family Medical Practice in the Van Phuc Diplomatic Compound, in Hanoi (☞ Hanoi A to Z *in* Chapter 2).

If you do travel to Vietnam with young ones, brace yourself—and your child—for an interesting trip. Foreign youngsters, particularly Caucasians and especially blonds, are the center of attention almost everywhere they go in Vietnam, even in the major cities. People may want to hold your baby and may even take him or her across the street to show a friend—often without asking. Toddlers get pinched, poked, hugged, squeezed, and even grabbed between the legs or, worse, have their pants pulled down to see if they're "cut from the same cloth" as Vietnamese children. Of particular annoyance is the regularity with which fawning bystanders or complete strangers touch Western babies, especially on the face and mouth. Intestinal parasites can be transmitted by hands, so be sure people's fingers are clean before they start poking and prodding. No malice is intended by any of this, but it can be stressful.

FLYING

If your children are two or older, **ask about children's airfares.** As a general rule, infants under two not occupying a seat fly at greatly reduced fares or even for free. When booking, **confirm carry-on allowances** if you're traveling with infants. In general, for babies charged 10% of the adult fare you are allowed one carry-on bag and a collapsible stroller; if the flight is full, the stroller may have to be checked or you may be limited to less.

Experts agree that it's a good idea to use safety seats aloft for children weighing less than 40 pounds. Airlines set their own policies: U.S. carriers usually require that the child be ticketed, even if he or she is young enough to ride free, since the seats must be strapped into regular seats. Do **check your airline's policy about using safety seats during takeoff and landing.** And since safety seats are not allowed just everywhere in the plane, get your seat assignments early.

When reserving, **request children's meals or a freestanding bassinet** if you need them. But note that bulkhead seats, where you must sit to use the bassinet, may lack an overhead bin or storage space on the floor.

LODGING

Hotels, particularly those of international standard, are usually happy to add a cot or small bed to your room to accommodate children. Some hotels offer this service free for children under 12 and at only 10% to 20% of the room rate for those older than 12 years. Separate rooms for children are likely to be cheaper; when making reservations **ask if you can get a discount for your children and what the cutoff age is for these.**

PRECAUTIONS

Food hygiene is the most pressing concern when traveling with children. Be especially cautious with fruit shakes or juices, which may be made with contaminated ice. (Well-run city restaurants use boiled water and should be fine.) For more information on food safety, *see* Precautions *in* Food and Drink, *below.*

Transportation is another issue. Most taxis, rental cars, and buses in Vietnam don't have seat belts—let alone car seats for infants. And although trains are a safer option, the toilets are usually filthy and without running water.

SIGHTS & ATTRACTIONS

Places that are especially appealing to children are indicated by a rubber duckie icon in the margin.

SUPPLIES & EQUIPMENT

Few restaurants have high chairs, although diapers, baby bottles, and canned milk are available at minimarkets. Vietnam is also a great place to buy embroidered baby clothes and linens.

COMPUTERS ON THE ROAD

If you're bringing a laptop, check to see whether your computer's adapter can take 220 volts, the electrical voltage used in Vietnam. It is also advisable to **use an electrical surge protector** because power surges can cause permanent damage to your computer. Internal modems are particularly susceptible to power surges, especially when electricity returns after a power cut. Also, be sure to unplug your equipment after use. For longer stays, consider investing in a voltage stabilizer.

CONSUMER PROTECTION

Whenever shopping or buying travel services in Vietnam, **pay with a major credit card** so you can cancel payment or get reimbursed if there's a problem. If you're doing business with a particular company for the first time, **contact your local Better Business Bureau and the attorney general's offices** in your state and the company's home state, as well. Have any complaints been filed? Finally, if you're buying a package or tour, always **consider travel insurance** that includes default coverage (☞ Insurance, *below*).

> BBBs: **Council of Better Business Bureaus** (⊠ 4200 Wilson Blvd., Suite 800, Arlington, VA 22203, ☎ 703/276–0100, 𝖥𝖠𝖷 703/525–8277 www.bbb.org).

CUSTOMS & DUTIES

When shopping, **keep receipts** for all purchases. Upon reentering the country, **be ready to show customs officials what you've bought.** If you feel a duty is incorrect or object to the way your clearance was handled, note the inspector's badge number and ask to see a supervisor. If the problem isn't resolved, write to the appropriate authorities, beginning with the port director at your point of entry.

Keep in mind that **it is illegal to export antiques and wooden furniture** unless you get special permission to do so (☞ Shopping, *below*). If you purchase an item that looks like an antique, be sure to get a note from the store owner stating that it is not.

IN AUSTRALIA

Australian residents who are 18 or older may bring home $A400 worth of souvenirs and gifts (including jewelry), 250 cigarettes or 250 grams of tobacco, and 1,125 ml of alcohol (including wine, beer, and spirits). Residents under 18 may bring back $A200 worth of goods. Prohibited items include meat products. Seeds, plants, and fruits need to be declared upon arrival.

> INFORMATION: **Australian Customs Service** (Regional Director, ⊠ Box 8, Sydney, NSW 2001, ☎ 02/9213–2000, 𝖥𝖠𝖷 02/9213–4000).

IN CANADA

Canadian residents who have been out of Canada for at least 7 days may bring home C$500 worth of goods duty-free. If you've been away less than 7 days but more than 48 hours, the duty-free allowance drops to C$200; if your trip lasts 24–48 hours, the allowance is C$50. You may not pool allowances with family members. Goods claimed under the C$500 exemption may follow you by mail; those claimed under the lesser exemptions must accompany you. Alcohol and tobacco products may be included in the 7-day and 48-hour exemptions but not in the 24-hour exemption. If you meet the age requirements of the province or territory through which you reenter Canada, you may bring in, duty-free, 1.14 liters (40 imperial ounces) of wine or liquor *or* 24 12-ounce cans or bottles of beer or ale. If you are 16 or older you may bring in, duty-free, 200 cigarettes and 50 cigars. Check ahead of time with Revenue Canada or the Department of Agriculture for policies regarding meat products, seeds, plants, and fruits.

You may send an unlimited number of gifts worth up to C$60 each duty-free to Canada. Label the package UNSOLICITED GIFT—VALUE UNDER $60. Alcohol and tobacco are excluded.

> INFORMATION: **Revenue Canada** (⊠ 2265 St. Laurent Blvd. S, Ottawa, Ontario K1G 4K3, ☎ 613/993–0534; 800/461–9999 in Canada, 𝖥𝖠𝖷 613/957–8911, www.ccra-adrc.gc.ca).

IN NEW ZEALAND

Homeward-bound residents 17 or older may bring back $700 worth of souvenirs and gifts. Your duty-free allowance also includes 4.5 liters of wine or beer; one 1,125-ml bottle of spirits; and either 200 cigarettes, 250 grams of tobacco, 50 cigars, or a combination of the three up to 250 grams. Prohibited items include meat products, seeds, plants, and fruits.

> INFORMATION: **New Zealand Customs** (Custom House, ⊠ 50 Anzac Ave., Box 29, Auckland, New Zealand, ☎ 09/359–6655, 𝖥𝖠𝖷 09/359–6732).

IN THE U.K.

From countries outside the EU, including Vietnam, you may bring home, duty-free, 200 cigarettes or 50 cigars; 1 liter of spirits or 2 liters of fortified or sparkling wine or liqueurs; 2 liters of still table wine; 60 ml of perfume; 250 ml of toilet water; plus £136 worth of other goods, including gifts and souvenirs. If returning from outside the EU, prohibited items include meat products, seeds, plants, and fruits.

> INFORMATION: **HM Customs and Excise** (⊠ Dorset House, Stamford St., Bromley, Kent BR1 1XX, ☎ 020/7202–4227).

SMART TRAVEL TIPS A TO Z

IN THE U.S.

U.S. residents who have been out of the country for at least 48 hours (and who have not used the $400 allowance or any part of it in the past 30 days) may bring home $400 worth of foreign goods duty-free.U.S. residents 21 and older may bring back 1 liter of alcohol duty-free. In addition, regardless of your age, you are allowed 200 cigarettes and 100 non-Cuban cigars. Antiques, which the U.S. Customs Service defines as objects more than 100 years old, enter duty-free, as do original works of art done entirely by hand, including paintings, drawings, and sculptures.

You may also send packages home duty-free: up to $200 worth of goods for personal use, with a limit of one parcel per addressee per day (except alcohol or tobacco products or perfume worth more than $5); label the package PERSONAL USE and attach a list of its contents and their retail value. Do not label the package UNSOLICITED GIFT or your duty-free exemption will drop to $100. Mailed items do not affect your duty-free allowance on your return.

➤ INFORMATION: **U.S. Customs Service** (✉ 1300 Pennsylvania Ave. NW, Washington, DC 20229, www.customs.gov; inquiries ☎ 202/354–1000; complaints c/o ✉ Office of Regulations and Rulings; registration of equipment c/o ✉ Resource Management, ☎ 202/927–0540).

IN VIETNAM

When you enter Vietnam you will be given a yellow customs declaration slip and a blue departure slip. You need these to get out of the country, so **do not lose your customs forms** (if you do, a customs search, a fine, and a long delay are likely when you try to leave the country). Do not attempt to bring any weapons, pornographic materials, or anything that could be considered subversive into Vietnam, as you may receive a hefty fine, be detained, or in extreme cases, jailed. It is a good idea to **declare cameras, camcorders, laptop computers, and any other expensive electronics** that you want to take out of the country again, although it's not required.

DISABILITIES & ACCESSIBILITY

Very few places in Vietnam, including hotels, restaurants, sights, and office buildings, are fully wheelchair accessible. In many hotels makeshift ramps provide sufficient access into the building, but service areas such as restaurants, business centers, and rest rooms are up or down flights of stairs not serviced by elevators.

Health-care issues for travelers with disabilities should be well thought out before coming to Vietnam. Equipment of international-standard quality is for the most part unavailable, and hygiene is a concern.

➤ LOCAL RESOURCES: **Bright Futures for People with Disabilities** (✉ 190 Lo Duc St., Hanoi, ☎ 04/971–2894). **Vietnam Blind Association** (✉ 139 Nguyen Thai Hoc St., Hanoi, ☎ 04/845–2060, FAX 04/845–2682). **Vietnam Sports Association for the Disabled** (✉ 1B Le Hong Phong St., Hanoi, ☎ 04/823–2287, FAX 04/825–3172).

LODGING

Most elevators in larger hotels can accommodate wheelchairs, but very few guest rooms are equipped with large enough bathrooms or sufficient grab bars. Vietnam's newer hotels are the ones most likely to conform somewhat to international standards regarding wheelchair access and services for guests with disabilities.

RESERVATIONS

When discussing accessibility with an operator or reservations agent, **ask hard questions.** Are there any stairs, inside *or* out? Are there grab bars next to the toilet *and* in the shower/tub? How wide is the doorway to the room? To the bathroom? For the most extensive facilities meeting the latest legal specifications, **opt for newer accommodations.**

SIGHTS & ATTRACTIONS

Many of Vietnam's most famous sights are all but inaccessible to people with mobility problems. Pagodas often have stairs or narrow entrances, and ramps are unheard of.

TRANSPORTATION

City planning has largely ignored the requirements of the wheelchair-bound: there are virtually no curb cuts or permanent ramps, public transportation is inaccessible, and most office buildings have no elevators or escalators (some new office buildings, where many expatriates conduct business, have large elevators and temporary ramps). Taxi drivers often help passengers get from chair to backseat and back again. Cyclo drivers can also be helpful.

Vietnam Airlines claims it has the facilities and equipment to handle passengers using wheelchairs. The reality proves otherwise, however. When flying Vietnam Airlines, call ahead to be sure the appropriate equipment will be available at your departure and arrival points.

➤ COMPLAINTS: **Disability Rights Section** (✉ U.S. Department of Justice, Civil Rights Division, Box 66738, Washington, DC 20035-6738, ☎ 202/514–0301 or 800/514–0301; TTY 202/514–0301 or 800/514–0301, FAX 202/307–1198) for general complaints. **Aviation Consumer Protection Division** (☞ Air Travel, *above*) for airline-related problems. **Civil Rights Office** (✉ U.S. Department of Transportation, Departmental Office of Civil Rights, S-30, 400 7th St. SW, Room 10215, Washington, DC 20590, ☎ 202/366–4648, FAX 202/366–9371) for problems with surface transportation.

TRAVEL AGENCIES

In the United States, the Americans with Disabilities Act requires that travel firms serve the needs of all travelers. Some agencies specialize in working with people with disabilities.

➤ TRAVELERS WITH MOBILITY PROBLEMS: **Access Adventures** (✉ 206 Chestnut Ridge Rd., Rochester, NY 14624, ☎ 716/889–9096, dltravel@prodigy.net), run by a former physical-rehabilitation counselor. **Flying Wheels Travel** (✉ 143 W. Bridge St., Box 382, Owatonna, MN 55060, ☎ 507/451–5005 or 800/535–6790, FAX 507/451–1685, thq@ll.net, www.flyingwheels.com). **Hinsdale Travel Service** (✉ 201 E. Ogden Ave., Suite 100, Hinsdale, IL 60521, ☎ 630/325–1335, FAX 630/325–1342, hinstrvl@interaccess.com).

DISCOUNTS & DEALS

Be a smart shopper and **compare all your options** before making decisions. A plane ticket bought with a promotional coupon from travel clubs, coupon books, and direct-mail offers may not be cheaper than the least expensive fare from a discount ticket agency. And always keep in mind that what you get is just as important as what you save.

DISCOUNT RESERVATIONS

To save money, **look into discount reservations services** with toll-free numbers, which use their buying power to get a better price on hotels, airline tickets, even car rentals. When booking a room, always **call the hotel's local toll-free number** (if one is available) rather than the central reservations number—you'll often get a better price. Always ask about special packages or corporate rates.

When shopping for the best deal on hotels and car rentals, **look for guaranteed exchange rates,** which protect you against a falling dollar. With your rate locked in, you won't pay more, even if the price goes up in the local currency.

➤ AIRLINE TICKETS: ☎ 800/FLY–4–LESS.

➤ HOTEL ROOMS: **Travel Interlink** (☎ 800/888–5898, www.travelinterlink.com). **VacationLand** (☎ 800/245–0050, sales@vacationasia.com, www.vacation-land.com).

PACKAGE DEALS

Don't confuse packages and guided tours. When you buy a package, you travel on your own, just as though you had planned the trip yourself.

ECOTOURISM

Although a few nongovernmental organizations have been set up to recycle waste (one Hanoi project turns corks from wine bottles into place mats), most recycling is done on an ad hoc basis. This being said, not much in Vietnam goes to waste. The moment you set down a water bottle or soda can, someone will collect it for resale.

ELECTRICITY

To use your U.S.-purchased electric-powered equipment, **bring a converter and adapter.** The electrical current in Vietnam is 220 volts, 50 cycles alternating current (AC); in the north and other parts of the country, wall outlets take the continental European type, with two round plugs; they use the flat-pin type in much of the south. Many of the international hotels can provide you with converters and adapters.

If your appliances are dual-voltage, you'll need only an adapter. Don't use 110-volt outlets marked FOR SHAVERS ONLY for high-wattage appliances such as blow-dryers. Most laptops operate equally well on 110 and 220 volts and so require only an adapter and a surge protector (☞ Computers on the Road, *above*).

Blackouts sometimes occur, especially in summer, when everyone uses fans and air conditioners. Upscale hotels usually have generators, but you may want to keep a flashlight handy if you're staying in a minihotel.

E-MAIL & THE INTERNET

Vietnam has had e-mail service since 1992, when the Hanoi-based Institute of Information Technology linked up with a dial-back system at Coombs University in Australia. Full-scale Internet access finally became a reality in December 1997. Today Vietnam has five Internet service providers, all of which rent lines from the same Internet access provider, the Vietnam Data Corporation (VDC).

Business centers in larger international hotels provide Internet access, as do a growing number of Internet cafés in Hanoi, Ho Chi Minh City, and some smaller tourist centers such as Hoi An, Nha Trang, and even Sapa.

➤ INTERNET HOOK-UP: **Corporation for Financing and Promoting Technology, FPT** (✉ 75 Tran Hung Dao St., Hoan Kiem District, Hanoi, ☎ 04/822–3100; ✉ 75 Le Thi Hong Gam St., District 1, Ho Chi Minh City, ☎ 08/821–4160).

➤ INTERNET CAFÉS: **Emotion Cybernet Cafe** (✉ 52 Ly Thuong Kiet St., Hanoi, ☎ 04/934–1066). **Sinh Café Internet** (✉ 246 De Tham St., District 1, Ho Chi Minh City, ☎ 08/836–7338). **Tin Tin Internet Club** (✉ 2A Bao Khanh La., Hanoi, ☎ 04/928–5089).

EMBASSIES & CONSULATES

If your passport is stolen or lost or you are in need of any other kind of emergency assistance, contact your country's embassy or consulate. Embassies are in Hanoi and consulates in Ho Chi Minh City.

➤ CONSULATES: **Australia** (✉ 5B Ton Duc Thang St., District 1, Ho Chi Minh City, ☎ 08/829–6035, FAX 08/829–6031). **Canada** (✉ 203 Dong Khoi St., Room 102, District 1, Ho Chi Minh City, ☎ 08/824–2000, ext. 1209, FAX 08/829–4528). **New Zealand** (✉ 41 Nguyen Thi Minh Khai St., 5th floor, District 1, Ho Chi Minh City, ☎ 08/822–6907, FAX 08/822–6905). **United Kingdom** (✉ 25 Le Duan Blvd., District 1, Ho Chi Minh City, ☎ 08/823–2604, FAX 08/822–1971). **United States** (✉ 4 Le Duan Blvd., District 1, Ho Chi Minh City, ☎ 08/822–9433, FAX 08/822–9434).

➤ EMBASSIES: **Australia** (✉ 8 Dao Tan St. Van Phuc Quarter, Hanoi, ☎ 04/831–7755, FAX 04/831–7711). **Canada** (✉ 31 Hung Vuong St., Ba Dinh District, Hanoi, ☎ 04/823–5500, FAX 04/823–5333). **New Zealand** (✉ 32 Hang Bai St., Hoan Kiem District, Hanoi, ☎ 04/824–1481, FAX 04/824–1480). **United Kingdom** (✉ 31 Hai Ba Trung St., Hoan Kiem District, Hanoi, ☎ 04/825–2510, FAX 04/826–5762). **United States** (✉ 7 Lang Ha St., Ba Dinh District, Hanoi, ☎ 04/843–1500, FAX 04/843–1510).

EMERGENCIES

If something has been stolen from you, contact the police or your embassy (☞ Embassies & Consulates, *above*), especially regarding more costly items such as expensive jewelry or laptop computers. Also contact your embassy if your passport has been stolen or lost. For medical emergencies, seek assistance from local hospitals or clinics or from your hotel in more rural areas; *see* Health, *below, and* Emergencies *in* individual chapters.

➤ CONTACTS: **Ambulance** (☎ 115). **Police** (☎ 113).

ENGLISH-LANGUAGE MEDIA

To get a clear idea of what's happening in Vietnam, you're better off skipping local media in favor of regional publications such as the *South China Morning Post* or the *Far Eastern Economic Review.* The *Los Angeles Times* and *San José Mercury News* also have correspondents in Hanoi.

BOOKS

Hotel gift shops and bookstores in Hanoi and Ho Chi Minh City have a nice selection of coffee table photo books on Vietnam. For books dealing with Vietnam's history or politics, or for English-language translations of Vietnamese fiction, you'll find more choices abroad. For more information on books about Vietnam, *see* Books and Videos *in* Chapter 8.

➤ BOOKSTORES: **Bookazine** (✉ 28 Dong Khoi St., District 1, Ho Chi Minh City, ☎ 08/829–7455). **The Cat** (✉ 243 De Tham St., District 1, Ho Chi Minh City, ☎ 08/836–0016). **Foreign Language Bookshop** (✉ 61 Trang Tien St., Hoan Kiem District, Hanoi, ☎ 04/824–8914). **Tien Phong** (✉ 175 Nguyen Thai Hoc St., Ba Dinh District, Hanoi, ☎ 04/943–2337).

NEWSPAPERS & MAGAZINES

Vietnam News, the state-owned English-language daily, contains a mind-numbing mix of investment features and calls for foreign aid. Visitors may find it useful for the movie and art exhibitions listings.

Vietnam Investment Review, a weekly, is the English-language mouthpiece of the Ministry of Planning and Investment. The monthly *Vietnam Economic Times* is both better written and more entertaining, with some enlightening in-depth features. *The Guide,* a supplement to the *Vietnam Economic Times,* is packed with tips about Vietnamese culture as well as news briefs about upcoming cultural events. Passengers flying on Vietnam Airlines should take a look at *Heritage,* the glossy in-flight magazine filled with features about Vietnamese culture and tourist destinations.

RADIO & TELEVISION

Most hotels and minihotels in Vietnam have satellite TV. CNN, CNBC Asia, Star TV, and MTV Asia are standard; some hotels also offer the BBC, Discovery Channel, and French and German channels.

ETIQUETTE & BEHAVIOR

Vietnamese people rarely say "no." Usually they answer in the positive to avoid confrontational situations. If a situation is unpleasant, most people simply stay quiet and ignore it until it passes. Anger is generally viewed as a sign of weakness, and its display in public is considered ill-mannered. It is better to **remain calm and good-natured while trying to work out a disagreement with someone.**

Keep in mind that pointing at people and beckoning to them with your hand facing up is thought to be the height of rudeness. So remember to **call people with your hand facing down.** Crossing your fingers for good luck is also a sure way to embarrass yourself in Vietnam. Patting children on the head is considered a bad omen and is best avoided. In many pagodas you are required to remove your shoes before entering.

When hosting Vietnamese guests, be sure to offer drinks and food as soon as they arrive. It's considered impolite simply to ask if they would like anything. Also, Vietnamese women seldom drink beer or coffee, so have some green tea or soft drinks on hand. Don't be surprised if a social event ends quickly; they usually don't drag on too long in Vietnam unless you have gone out drinking or are doing business.

Giving gifts to Vietnamese can be an unfulfilling affair for someone from the West. Often the recipient simply acknowledges the gift and carries on as before. But this is not a sign of disrespect; any gift is always highly appreciated.

Public displays of affection are frowned upon in Vietnam. It's fine to put your arm around someone of the same sex, but refrain from touching

SMART TRAVEL TIPS A TO Z

people of the opposite sex—beyond a handshake in a business setting. Respect for elders is a key value in Vietnam; invite older people to sit down before you do so.

BUSINESS ETIQUETTE

In Vietnam, business meetings often start slowly, with both parties exchanging chitchat over a cup of tea. Don't rush in and expect to get down to business right away.

No matter what your line of work, there is one thing that no businessperson in Vietnam can do without: name cards. If you don't have business cards already, printers in any bigger town can whip them up overnight for pennies apiece. When it comes time to give them out, use both hands—it is more respectful. Accept incoming name cards with both hands, too.

FOOD & DRINK

The restaurants we list are the cream of the crop in each price category. A variety of eateries exists in Vietnam: small, basic Western-style restaurants serving Vietnamese food; upscale Western-style restaurants (including hotel restaurants), which can be surprisingly elegant and hip, serving Vietnamese, Chinese, Japanese, French, American, Italian, or other international cuisines; tourist cafés, which cater primarily to budget travelers, serving mediocre Western and Vietnamese dishes; stalls or stands on the street, surrounded by small plastic stools, serving very cheap and often quite good rice and noodle dishes; and peddlers selling food or coconut milk from their handcarts or shoulder poles.

If you eat at hotel restaurants, expect to pay international prices. Smaller restaurants—even those serving international cuisines—are surprisingly cheap. And if you stick to local restaurants, food will constitute a minor part of your travel costs.

For information on the types of cuisine available in Vietnam, *see* Pleasures and Pastimes *in* Chapter 1.

CATEGORY	COST*
$$$$	over $25
$$$	$15–$25
$$	$7–$15
$	$2–$7
¢	under $2

per person for a three-course dinner, including 10% tax and 5% service but not drinks

MEALS & SPECIALTIES

Com, the Vietnamese word for "food," is also the word for "rice." Plan to eat a lot of it in Vietnam, either steamed, fried, or made into rice paper or noodles. The most famous Vietnamese dish, especially in the north, is *pho*, a clear broth containing chicken or beef and soft rice noodles. Very popular at breakfast, pho is also served day and night. Spring rolls, known as *cha gio* in the south and *nem* in the north, are another Vietnamese classic. Stuffed with pork, shrimp, or crab, these rice paper rolls are deep-fried until golden. The central city of Hue is said to have the best food in Vietnam. Here you can try a local delicacy, *banh khoai*, a thin, crispy yellow pancake that is stuffed with shrimp, pork, and bean sprouts and served with peanut sauce and slices of star fruit, green banana, and mint.

MEALTIMES

Breakfast is served beginning at 6 at most sidewalk stalls and 7 at most restaurants, lunch is served anywhere between 11:30 and 2, and dinner is available any time after 5 and usually before 8. Restaurants are generally open daily (except major holidays), and although Vietnamese eat dinner fairly early, most restaurants remain open well into the night, even after they are supposed to close.

PAYING

As a rule the only restaurants that accept credit cards and perhaps traveler's checks are the more upscale places. However, if you do pay with plastic, these places may add a 4%–5% service charge to your bill.

PRECAUTIONS

It's important to **be careful of what you eat and drink** in Vietnam. Fresh, leafy vegetables are known to carry parasites, so avoid those of dubious origin or those likely to have been washed in tap water. Also, try to eat only fruit that you peel yourself. If you don't want some ingredient to be included, just ask (or gesture) for it not to be added.

That said, dining at street-side food stands can be as safe or safer than eating in restaurants, especially in cities. The stands often serve fresher food than many restaurants because they have a faster turnover; they also prepare the food in front of you. Be more careful of food stalls once you are out of urban areas. Most of all, use common sense when choosing where to eat: pick a food stand, restaurant, or café that looks clean, is crowded, and has fresh food.

It is imperative that you **avoid drinking tap water as well as beverages with ice,** which is often made from local water. Most decent restaurants either make their own ice using boiled water or buy ice in bulk from huge freezer warehouses. Your best bet is to **drink bottled water,** particularly the La Vie and Evian brands.

Keep in mind that monosodium glutamate (MSG) is used in many dishes in Vietnam, particularly in the ubiquitous pho. If you don't want MSG in your food, ask—the cooks may not have already added it to the dish. Many people are unfamiliar with the term MSG, so try referring to it by a popular brand name, Aji-nomoto.

RESERVATIONS & DRESS

Reservations are always a good idea: we mention them only when they're essential or not accepted. Book as far ahead as you can, and reconfirm as soon as you arrive.

WINE, BEER & SPIRITS

Along with locally owned breweries, a number of joint ventures operate in Vietnam. You'll find Heineken, Carlsberg, Tiger, and San Miguel, along with local beers such as Saigon Beer in the south and Halida in the north. *Bia hoi,* a watery draft beer, is available on many city street corners; look for low plastic stools occupied by jovial, red-faced men. Imported French, Italian, and even Chilean

wines are available in Ho Chi Minh City and Hanoi. Brave souls may want to pop open a bottle of Russian, Bulgarian, or Vietnamese bubbly—one of the latter bears the label "Product of the Thanh Ha Fertilizer Company"—or try the ubiquitous *ruou,* a highly inebriating rice whiskey.

GAY & LESBIAN TRAVEL

It is not uncommon for people of the same sex to hold hands or link arms in Vietnam. However, public displays of affection—whether between gay or straight couples—are socially unacceptable.

➤ GAY- & LESBIAN-FRIENDLY TRAVEL AGENCIES: **Different Roads Travel** (✉ 8383 Wilshire Blvd., Suite 902, Beverly Hills, CA 90211, ☎ 323/651–5557 or 800/429–8747, FAX 323/651–3678, leigh@west.tzell.com). **Kennedy Travel** (✉ 314 Jericho Turnpike, Floral Park, NY 11001, ☎ 516/352–4888 or 800/237–7433, FAX 516/354–8849, main@kennedytravel.com, www.kennedytravel.com). **Now Voyager** (✉ 4406 18th St., San Francisco, CA 94114, ☎ 415/626–1169 or 800/255–6951, FAX 415/626–8626, www.nowvoyager.com). **Skylink Travel and Tour** (✉ 1006 Mendocino Ave., Santa Rosa, CA 95401, ☎ 707/546–9888 or 800/225–5759, FAX 707/546–9891, skylinktvl@aol.com, www.skylinktravel.com), serving lesbian travelers.

HEALTH

As with any trip to a developing country, you should **check with the Centers for Disease Control and Prevention and your physician** about current health risks in Vietnam and recommended vaccinations before you go.

A first-aid kit with antacids, antidiarrheal, cold medicine, Band-Aids, antiseptics, aspirin, and other items you may need is a good idea. Also, know your blood type and **bring enough medication to last the entire trip;** you may be able to get common prescription drugs in Vietnam, but don't count on their availability or their quality. Just in case, however, have your doctor write you a prescription using the drug's generic

SMART TRAVEL TIPS A TO Z

name because brand names vary from country to country.

FOOD & DRINK

Contamination of drinking water and fresh fruit and vegetables by fecal matter poses a major health risk in Vietnam; this contamination causes the common intestinal ailment known as traveler's diarrhea and sometimes is responsible for visitors contracting typhoid fever, hepatitis A, and parasites. Traveler's diarrhea can also be caused simply by a change of diet. It usually only lasts a few days; **if symptoms persist or worsen, seek medical assistance.** Two drugs recommended by the National Institutes of Health for mild cases of diarrhea can be purchased over the counter in larger pharmacies: Pepto-Bismol and loperamide (Imodium).

If you come down with the malady, rest as much as possible and **drink lots of fluids** (such as tea without milk, especially herbal tea). In severe cases rehydrate yourself with a salt-sugar mixture added to purified water (½ teaspoon of salt and 4 tablespoons of sugar per quart or liter of purified water). It's recommended you **avoid eating unpeeled fruit and uncooked vegetables or those you suspect have been washed in unboiled water** and drinking unbottled or unboiled water or ice made from unbottled or unboiled water. **Drink bottled water** such as Evian or La Vie; it's even a good idea to brush your teeth with it.

MEDICAL CARE

Vietnam's medical infrastructure is not up to international standards. Hospitals and pharmacies are often undersupplied and out of date. Only a handful of Vietnamese doctors have top-quality Western training. Foreign insurance is very rarely accepted, so you should **expect to pay immediately in cash on completion of treatment.** The larger hospitals in Hanoi and Ho Chi Minh City have experience treating foreigners (mainly due to motorcycle accidents, the biggest cause of injury or death of Westerners in Vietnam), but there are few, if any, Western physicians based at these institutions. Blood supply is a serious problem in Vietnam: the nation's blood banks are small and, say Western doctors, insufficiently screened.

Foreign-run medical clinics offering basic treatment and 24-hour on-call services can guide you to local hospitals for more serious operations and can arrange for emergency medical evacuation to better hospitals in other countries in the region—Medevac planes dedicated to Vietnam are on standby in Singapore. Embassies have duty officers on call who can assist with logistics. If you get sick outside Hanoi or Ho Chi Minh City, get yourself to those cities as soon as possible. For more information on medical care, *see* individual chapters.

MEDICAL PLANS

No one plans to get sick while traveling, but it happens, so **consider signing up with a medical-assistance company.** Members get doctor referrals, emergency evacuation or repatriation, hot lines for medical consultation, cash for emergencies, and other assistance.

➤ MEDICAL-ASSISTANCE COMPANIES: **International SOS Assistance** (✉ 31 Hai Ba Trung St., Hoan Kiem District, Hanoi, Vietnam, ☎ 04/934–0555; ✉ 65 Nguyen Du St., District 1, Ho Chi Minh City Vietnam, ☎ 08/829–8520; ✉ 8 Neshaminy Interplex, Suite 207, Trevose, PA 19053, ☎ 215/245–4707 or 800/523–6586, FAX 215/244–9617, www.internationalsos.com; ✉ 12 Chemin Riantbosson, 1217 Meyrin 1, Geneva, Switzerland, ☎ 4122/785–6464, FAX 4122/785–6424, www.internationalsos.com; ✉ 331 N. Bridge Rd., 17-00, Odeon Towers, Singapore 188720, ☎ 65/338–7800, FAX 65/338–7611, www.internationalsos.com).

OVER-THE-COUNTER REMEDIES

Pharmacies are almost as common as tea stalls in Vietnam, and many pharmacists in cities speak English. Look for a shop with a green sign that reads *Nha Thuoc*. These usually stock pain killers (such as Panadol); eye, nose, and ear drops (such as Polydexa); cold remedies (such as Tiffy); and various antibiotics—for which no prescription is needed in Vietnam. Remember to check the expiration date when buying any sort of medication.

PESTS & OTHER HAZARDS

Malaria- and dengue-bearing mosquitoes bite at dusk and at night. No matter where you go, it's a good idea to protect yourself from mosquito-borne illnesses with a good insect repellent containing deet, and if you're in susceptible regions, use aerosol insecticides indoors, wear clothing that covers the body, and bring mosquito nets. If you're staying for a month or more and are traveling to rural areas, you should be vaccinated against Japanese encephalitis; for six months or more, against hepatitis B as well. Some of these vaccinations require staggered treatments, so plan ahead.

SHOTS & MEDICATIONS

Tetanus-diphtheria and polio vaccinations should be up-to-date—if you haven't been immunized since childhood, **consider bolstering your tetanus and polio vaccinations.** If you have never contracted measles, mumps, or rubella, you should also be immunized against them. Also note: **immunizations for hepatitis A and typhoid fever are advised.** According to the Centers for Disease Control and Prevention (CDC), there is a risk of contracting malaria only in rural areas of Vietnam, except in the Red River Delta and the coastal plain north of Nha Trang, which are safe. The CDC recommends taking mefloquine (brand name Larium) for malaria. Dengue fever occurs in Vietnam, although the risk for travelers is small, except during periods of epidemic-size transmission; there is no vaccine to prevent it, therefore you should **take precautions against mosquito bites.**

➤ HEALTH WARNINGS: **Centers for Disease Control and Prevention** (CDC; National Center for Infectious Diseases, Division of Quarantine, Traveler's Health Section, ✉ 1600 Clifton Rd. NE, M/S E-03, Atlanta, GA 30333, ☎ 888/232–3228, ⅏ 888/232–3299, www.cdc.gov).

HOLIDAYS

The traditional lunar new year, known as Tet in Vietnam and celebrated throughout much of Southeast Asia, falls in January or February, depending on the lunar calendar. Note that accommodations are scarce, and museums, offices, and shops tend to shut down for days at a time during Tet. Other national holidays include New Year's Day, the anniversary of the founding of the Vietnamese Communist Party (February 3); Liberation Day (April 30), commemorating the day the North Vietnamese army took Saigon; International Workers Day, or May Day (May 1, the date following Liberation Day, which means a two-day holiday); Ho Chi Minh's birthday (May 19); National Day (September 2); and Christmas Day.

INSURANCE

The most useful travel insurance plan is a comprehensive policy that includes coverage for trip cancellation and interruption, default, trip delay, and medical expenses (with a waiver for preexisting conditions).

Without insurance you will lose all or most of your money if you cancel your trip, regardless of the reason. Default insurance covers you if your tour operator, airline, or cruise line goes out of business. Trip-delay covers expenses that arise because of bad weather or mechanical delays. Study the fine print when comparing policies.

If you're traveling internationally, a key component of travel insurance is coverage for medical bills incurred if you get sick on the road. Such expenses are not generally covered by Medicare or private policies. U.K. residents can buy a travel insurance policy valid for most vacations taken during the year in which it's purchased (but check pre-existing-condition coverage). British and Australian citizens need extra medical coverage when traveling overseas. Always **buy travel policies directly from the insurance company;** if you buy them from a cruise line, airline, or tour operator that goes out of business you probably will not be covered for the agency or operator's default, a major risk. Before making any purchase, **review your existing health and homeowner's policies** to find what they cover away from home.

➤ TRAVEL INSURERS: In the U.S.: **Access America** (✉ 6600 W. Broad St., Richmond, VA 23230, ☎ 804/285–3300 or 800/284–8300, FAX 804/673–1583, www.previewtravel.com), **Travel Guard International** (✉ 1145 Clark St., Stevens Point, WI 54481, ☎ 715/345–0505 or 800/826–1300, FAX 800/955–8785, www.noelgroup.com). In Canada: **Voyager Insurance** (✉ 44 Peel Center Dr., Brampton, Ontario L6T 4M8, ☎ 905/791–8700; 800/668–4342 in Canada).

➤ INSURANCE INFORMATION: In the U.K.: **Association of British Insurers** (✉ 51–55 Gresham St., London EC2V 7HQ, ☎ 020/7600–3333, FAX 020/7696–8999, info@abi.org.uk, www.abi.org.uk). In Australia: **Insurance Council of Australia** (☎ 03/9614–1077, FAX 03/9614–7924).

LANGUAGE

Vietnamese, or *kinh*, is written in a Roman-based script, called *quoc ngu*, created by a French Jesuit scholar in the 17th century. Before that the Vietnamese created their own system, called *nom*, which drew on the Chinese system of characters. Although letters may look familiar, the language is tonally based and therefore quite foreign to Western ears. Barring a few exceptions in tones and words, written Vietnamese is homogeneous throughout the country. However, accents differ dramatically, particularly between north and south. *See* the Vocabulary and Menu Guide at the end of this book for more information.

It's best to **use a phrase book as a point-and-show device,** although a little Vietnamese goes a long way. With a few Vietnamese words, you may find daily interchange—such as bargaining with cyclo drivers—much easier, so **attempt to learn at least numbers and some important pronouns and verbs.** (Some helpful phrases and words are listed in our Vocabulary and Menu Guide.) In large cities English is practically a second language; in the countryside, particularly outside tourist spots, communicating your desires or intentions can be difficult if you don't speak any Vietnamese. French is still spoken among an elite but shrinking crowd of older Vietnamese. A surprisingly large number of Hanoians can speak Russian, although there is hardly any opportunity for most of them to use it these days. English is by far the most widely used language in Vietnam's tourist trade.

LODGING

Graham Greene did much to romanticize hotel life in Vietnam in his book *The Quiet American*. But aside from the Continental Hotel in Ho Chi Minh City, immortalized in Greene's book, and a handful of other older institutions including the Metropole Hotel Sofitel in Hanoi, hotels in Vietnam have little old-world mystery. The focus today is on newness; the vast majority of joint-venture, international-standard hotels in the nation are less than five years old. And unfortunately many of the older hotels that have survived the wrecking ball have fared poorly from years of neglect, bad management, and lack of funds.

Although hotel staffers are generally enthusiastic and some have received training in Korea or the West, really good service is still a rarity. A few hotels, however, are as luxurious and have as high standard of service as any international establishment in the world. Beach resorts are being developed along the coast, and two particular standouts are in Nha Trang and China Beach near Danang; another resort option is the majestically restored Sofitel Dalat Palace in the mountain town of Dalat.

In Hanoi, Ho Chi Minh City, and other major tourist destinations, the hotel industry continues to grow, and more and more international and smaller-size hotels are opening up. Many of the larger, international hotels often aren't fully booked and may be ready to give you a better room rate than listed; when calling to make reservations, **ask if you can get a deal on the price of a room.**

Besides the surprisingly pricey international properties, Vietnam has a selection of other accommodations. Midsize, midlevel hotels and guest houses are generally state run and are usually perfectly acceptable for a night's sleep, especially in cities and popular tourist areas. Yet another good option is minihotels.

In smaller towns or rural areas expect much more basic accommodations. Phones, televisions, and fax machines are the norm at most hotels outside the major cities, even the smaller ones, but don't expect luxury in anything but the country's most popular destinations. If you are going to very off-the-beaten-path places, you may not have much choice in the kind of place in which you stay—the one or two guest houses in town, which may not be up to your usual standard, may be your only lodging option.

The lodgings we list are the cream of the crop in each price category. We always list the facilities that are available—but we don't specify whether they cost extra: when pricing accommodations, always ask what's included and what costs extra. Properties indicated by an ✕⌂ are lodging establishments whose restaurants warrant a special trip.

Assume that hotels operate on the **European Plan** (EP, with no meals) unless we specify that they use the **Continental Plan** (CP, with a Continental breakfast), **Modified American Plan** (MAP, with breakfast and dinner), or the **Full American Plan** (FAP, with all meals).

The rates quoted below are for accommodations in summer. Reservations are recommended during July and August and during Tet, the lunar new year (January or February); prices sometimes fluctuate at that time.

CATEGORY	COST*
$$$$	over $200
$$$	$100–$200
$$	$50–$100
$	$25–$50
¢	under $25

All prices are for a standard double room, including 10% tax and 5% service.

HOTELS

All hotels listed in this book have private bath or shower unless otherwise noted. Most hotels listed, and especially those in major tourist

centers, have air-conditioning or fans, satellite TV, and international direct-dial (IDD) phones, which you need to make international calls.

The Vietnam National Administration of Tourism has instituted its own rating system, which vaguely conforms to international standards of quality. Yet hotels billed as five star in Vietnam are often more like three- or four-star hotels in the United States.

➤ MINIHOTELS: Unique to Vietnam, these privately owned, often family-run operations range from the utilitarian to the plush; they usually provide friendly service, spotless if basic rooms, and a homey environment. Although such facilities as swimming pools and exercise facilities are rare at these minihotels and their restaurants are often bland and lifeless, guest rooms generally have air-conditioning and usually include satellite TV, IDD telephones, refrigerators, and bathtubs. Unfortunately, sometimes they also include lots of street noise.

SERVICED APARTMENT RENTALS

If you want a home base that's roomy enough for a family and comes with cooking facilities **consider a furnished rental.** These can save you money, especially if you're traveling with a group. Home-exchange directories sometimes list rentals as well as exchanges.

In the past few years a number of international-standard serviced apartments have opened in Hanoi and Ho Chi Minh City. Most of these are underused, and agents are only too happy to cut deals with short-term occupants.

➤ SERVICED APARTMENTS: **Landmark Building** (✉ 5B Ton Duc Thang St., District 1, Ho Chi Minh City, ☎ 04/822–2098). **Oriental Park** (✉ 33 Quang An St., Tay Ho District, Hanoi, ☎ 04/829–1200). **Somerset Grand Hanoi** (✉ 49 Hai Ba Trung St., Hoan Kiem District, Hanoi, ☎ 04/934–2342).

MAIL & SHIPPING

When mailing packages into and out of Vietnam, be aware that your parcels will probably be scrutinized at the post office. **Note that videotapes, books, and compact discs are especially sensitive items to ship or mail** to and from Vietnam. Delivery times for mail going into and out of the country have been shortened substantially in the last few years. Expect about two weeks, sometimes longer, for mail to arrive in the West from Vietnam.

OVERNIGHT SERVICES

The U.S. Postal Service, DHL, FedEx, and UPS all have express mail services to Vietnam. Unfortunately the service isn't always that fast: it can take from four to seven days, depending on how long the package sits in customs.

➤ MAJOR SERVICES: **DHL** (✉ 778 Lang Rd., Dong Da District, Hanoi, ☎ 04/775–3999; ✉ 4 Huynh Huu Bac St., Tan Binh District, Ho Chi Minh City, ☎ 08/844–6303). **FedEx** (✉ 6B Dinh Le St., Hoan Kiem District, Hanoi, ☎ 04/826–4952; ✉ 26 Truong Son St., Tan Binh District, Ho Chi Minh City, ☎ 08/848–5888). **UPS** (✉ 4C Dinh Le St., Hoan Kiem District, Hanoi, ☎ 04/824–6483; ✉ 80F Nguyen Du St., District 1, Ho Chi Minh City, ☎ 08/829–4321).

POSTAL RATES

Postage is based on weight. On average, a postcard or letter to the United States costs about 16,000d; one to Europe costs about 13,000d. Stamps are sold at post office (*buu dien*) branches, which are generally open daily 6 AM–8 PM, and at many hotels and shops. Usually the postal clerk will cancel the stamps on your letter and give it back to you to put into the mail slot. This policy exists in part to eliminate any possibility of stamps being peeled off your letter for resale and your letter thrown away.

RECEIVING MAIL

Don't be surprised if you receive an already-opened parcel—just be grateful it arrived at all. Most parcels are opened as a matter of course, and sometimes the recipient in Vietnam is charged for the "service" of checking the parcel. In lieu of the parcel, you may receive a note providing information on where to collect a particular piece of mail. Sending items such as videos, books, compact discs, and

cassettes through the mail is risky. Because such packages make many stops along the way, they often become too tempting to resist, and opportunities abound for theft or loss. If they do arrive, they're sometimes confiscated or checked for subversive material. Such "quarantines" for videos sometimes provide opportunity for replication by unscrupulous postal clerks or customs officials before they're handed over to you. Most letters and postcards will arrive within about two weeks of being mailed from abroad.

The main post offices in Hanoi and Ho Chi Minh City (☞ individual chapters for addresses) have poste restante, where you can have mail sent to you from abroad.

SHIPPING PARCELS

To ship your treasures home, take unwrapped items to the post office between 8 AM and 4:30 PM. You can buy packing boxes and large envelopes there. Customs employees at the post office will check all items being sent out of the country.

It is not unheard of for parcels to go missing. **Tape boxes securely** to discourage prying fingers. Finally, cultivate patience; it can take up to three months for parcels from Vietnam to reach North America.

MONEY MATTERS

Although Vietnam is not as much of a bargain as other Southeast Asian countries, it is still a relatively inexpensive destination. However, some upscale international hotels in Ho Chi Minh City and Hanoi command prices exceeding $200 per night. But this is far from average. Reasonably priced minihotels and guest houses (☞ Lodging, *above*) are abundant and can run less than $20 per night in Hanoi or Ho Chi Minh City. Elsewhere they're even cheaper.

Food can be a steal. If you eat at small local restaurants, street-side cafés, food stalls, or markets, you'll pay between $1 and $5 and save hundreds over your counterparts. A meal at an upscale restaurant, including wine, costs an average of $15–$20.

Be aware that Vietnam has an official dual-pricing system, so **foreigners often are expected to pay more than double what locals do** for trains, buses, flights, and other goods and services. In 1999 an official decree banned dual pricing at temples and tourist sites; despite this rule, higher entrance fees for foreigners remain the norm.

Sample costs: a cup of coffee in a street café will cost you 2,500d (20¢); a cyclo ride will generally cost from 5,000d to 10,000d (from 35¢ to 70¢) per kilometer; a liter of *bia hoi* (fresh draft beer) is 2,500d (20¢); bottled beer goes for between 12,000d and 25,000d (about 85¢–$1.75); and a bowl of noodles from a food stall is 5,000d (35¢).

Prices throughout this guide are given for adults. For information on taxes, *see* Taxes, *below.*

ATMS

Although rare, you can find a few ATMs in Hanoi and Ho Chi Minh City. For information about specific bank and ATM locations, *see* individual chapters.

CREDIT CARDS

Credit cards have yet to catch on as a form of payment by Vietnamese, but they are accepted at most large international hotels, upscale restaurants, better shops, large tour operators such as Saigon Tourist, and airline agencies. Hotels and shops sometimes insist on a service charge of up to 4% if you pay by credit card, however. MasterCard and Visa are the most widely accepted cards. Some locations also accept American Express and Diners Club.

Throughout this guide, the following abbreviations are used: **AE,** American Express; **DC,** Diner's Club; **MC,** MasterCard; and **V,** Visa.

Keep a record of the contact phone number on the back of your card, the issuing bank's name and address, and your credit card number in a safe place, separate from your card. Should you lose your credit card in Vietnam and be unable to reach the issuing bank, contact ANZ Bank in Hanoi or Ho Chi Minh City for help.

➤ REPORTING LOST CARDS: **ANZ Bank** (✉ 14 Le Thai To St., Hoan Kiem District, Hanoi, ☎ 04/825–8190, FAX 04/825–8189; ✉ 11 Me Linh Sq., District 1, Ho Chi Minh City, ☎ 08/829–9316).

CURRENCY

The Vietnamese unit of currency is the dong (abbreviated as *d* throughout this guide), which comes in 100d, 200d, 500d, 1,000d, 2,000d, 5,000d, 10,000d, 20,000d, and 50,000d notes. Since a 50,000d note is worth about $3.50, you have to lug around quite a few notes. It's a good idea to **keep plenty of 5,000d, 10,000d, and 20,000d notes handy for cyclos, cabs, and snacks.** Pulling out 50,000d for a bowl of noodles that costs 5,000d is viewed by many Vietnamese like paying with gold bullion. Familiarize yourself with the 5,000d and 20,000d notes, as they are both blue. The many zeros on bills sometimes makes it difficult to see the difference between 5,000d and 50,000d notes, as does the appearance of Ho Chi Minh's countenance on every banknote.

CURRENCY EXCHANGE

Technically it is illegal for many smaller establishments to receive payments in anything but Vietnamese dong, but such rules are widely ignored. U.S. dollars are accepted at almost every private business, but many state enterprises—including trains—only accept dong. It's recommended that you **carry both dong and dollars** with you at all times. Twenty- and fifty-dollar bills are good for exchanging money and for paying hotel bills, although you will get a lower exchange rate on these bills than you would for hundred-dollar bills.

The official exchange rate at press time was about 14,400d to the U.S. dollar, 9,200d to the Canadian dollar, and 20,500d to the British pound. The Vietnamese dong has been impressively stable for the last few years, although perhaps artificially so. Between 1994 and mid-1997 the value of the dong changed less than 5% against the U.S. dollar. But in late 1997 the dong dropped 5% in four weeks. In August 1998 the value of

SMART TRAVEL TIPS A TO Z

the dong fell from 11,615 to the dollar to almost 13,000. It took another dive in February 1999, dropping to just under 14,000. Since then, the rate has remained stable, but you should **keep tabs on the exchange rate.**

Although traveler's checks are accepted for exchange at many places, cash—in the form of U.S. dollars or dong—is much more widely accepted. It's best to **bring at least a few hundred dollars in cash** or as much as you feel comfortable carrying. A money belt is a good idea.

For the most favorable rates, **change money through banks.** The Bank for Foreign Trade of Vietnam, or Vietcom Bank, has numerous branches all over the country and gives the official government rate. International banks have a presence in Vietnam and offer extensive banking services, including currency exchange, cash transfers, and cash advances on credit cards. Although they don't often have the best exchange rates, hotels are convenient places to change money. You can usually get the highest exchange rates in gold or jewelry shops, which are eager to convert their business profits into dollars. Although there was no visible police crackdown on black marketers in Hanoi or Ho Chi Minh City at press time, using the services of black-market money changers is a high-risk option. Not only do they often fail to give you the best rate, some of these freelance money changers are out to cheat customers. Note that at many places you may **get a better exchange rate using higher-denomination bills** (i.e., a $50 instead of a $10).

➤ EXCHANGE SERVICES: **International Currency Express** (☎ 888/278–6628 for orders, www.foreignmoney.com). **Thomas Cook Currency Services** (☎ 800/287–7362 for telephone orders and retail locations, www. us.thomascook.com).

TRAVELER'S CHECKS

Traveler's checks are accepted in Vietnam but not by every place and especially not in rural areas and small towns. You should **ascertain from an individual establishment whether it accepts traveler's checks,** particularly the type you are carrying, before assuming you can use them. (Banks that issue traveler's checks will tell you every place should take them, which may be correct but isn't always true.) Banks in Vietnam charge a fee, usually 1%–2%, for cashing traveler's checks into dollars. The fee is lower if you cash the checks for dong. If your checks are lost or stolen, they can usually be replaced within 24 hours. To ensure a speedy refund, buy your checks yourself (don't ask someone else to make the purchase). When making a claim for stolen or lost checks, the person who bought the checks should make the call.

OUTDOORS & SPORTS

Sports such as badminton, martial arts, and Ping-Pong remain popular pastimes in Vietnam. In line with the old Soviet imperative of athletic prowess, Vietnamese schools stress gymnastics. The uneven parallel bars doesn't pack in the crowds, however, like Vietnam's new sport to watch: soccer. A national semiprofessional league fills stadiums during its autumn-to-spring season. There is a local team in almost every city and town in the nation. Vietnam considers the Southeast Asian Games, held every two years, to be a gauge of their success and competitiveness in the international sports arena.

Hanoi and Ho Chi Minh City have plenty of tennis courts, although none of them are free. Golf courses are more popular in the south, although there is a course outside Hanoi and a driving range in the capital's suburbs. Swimming pools can be found at many luxury hotels—inquire about one-day memberships. Some sports clubs in the cities also have pools, but they are not always clean or adequately treated—or even full of water.

Tourist cafés in Hanoi and Ho Chi Minh City have begun organizing trekking tours. Mountain biking has a bright future as an adventure activity, but in-country orchestration has proven difficult so far. A few companies in Hanoi also organize kayaking tours of Halong Bay, using inflatable rubber kayaks. Contact tour organizations for more information (☞ Travel Agencies, *below*).

The coast has good spots for surfing, particularly Danang (the site of an international surfing competition in 1994). But for now, with the exception of hotel-affiliated diving clubs in China Beach near Danang and in Nha Trang, you need to bring your own surfboarding, snorkeling, and scuba-diving gear. Jet-skiing and paragliding clubs have opened in the resort towns of Vung Tau and Nha Trang, which also have a few scuba-diving schools.

For information on outdoor activities and sports in particular cities and regions, *see* individual chapters.

PACKING

Since you never know where you will have to lug your bags, it is always a good idea to **pack light.** Bring luggage that is easy to carry and makes the most sense for your travel plans, whether that means a backpack (especially one that doubles as a bag), rolling suitcase, or duffle bag. Be sure to leave room in your suitcase or bring expandable totes for all your bargain purchases. A lock for your suitcase can come in handy, as can a cable lock if you are planning to travel by train (to secure your bag).

For warm weather, bring cotton, linen, and any other natural-fiber clothing that allows your skin to breathe and is easy to wash. (You can get your laundry done very inexpensively at most hotels, although you may not want to give them your delicate items—they've been known to get ruined.) Avoid synthetic or other hard-to-clean fabrics, as you may have difficulty getting them laundered. Pack a light raincoat or umbrella during the rainy season, and warmer clothing in winter and early spring. Dress in Vietnam is generally informal, except during meetings. Shorts are acceptable for both men and women, although women may feel more comfortable in longer shorts or skirts.

Sandals, nylon or canvas sneakers, and walking shoes are fine for the cities and more developed parts of the country. Hiking boots are recommended if you're going to head into the hills or onto trails or if you are traveling during the rainy season. Keep in mind that you must remove your shoes when entering most temples, so you may want to bring ones that are hassle-free. A hat and sunblock are always good ideas.

In your carry-on luggage, **pack an extra pair of eyeglasses or contact lenses,** plus contact lens solution, and **enough of any medication you take** to last the entire trip. You may also ask your doctor to write a spare prescription using the drug's generic name, since brand names may vary from country to country. In luggage to be checked, **never pack prescription drugs or valuables.** To avoid customs delays, carry medications in their original packaging.

And **don't forget mosquito repellent and a first-aid kit** (with, perhaps, antacids, antidiarrheal, cold medicine, Band-Aids, antiseptics, etc.). Other items to consider are a Swiss-army knife, prophylactics, feminine hygiene products, packs of tissues (toilet paper is not always supplied in public places), moist towelettes, and your favorite toilet articles (in plastic containers, to avoid breakage and reduce the weight of luggage). Finally, be sure to bring the addresses of offices that handle refunds of lost traveler's checks.

CHECKING LUGGAGE

How many carry-on bags you can bring with you is up to the airline. Most allow two, but not always, so make sure that everything you carry aboard will fit under your seat or in the overhead bin, and get to the gate early. Note that if you have a seat at the back of the plane, you'll probably board first, while the overhead bins are still empty.

If you are flying internationally, note that baggage allowances may be determined not by piece but by weight—generally 88 pounds (40 kilograms) in first class, 66 pounds (30 kilograms) in business class, and 44 pounds (20 kilograms) in economy.

Airline liability for baggage is limited to $1,250 per person on flights within the United States. On international flights it amounts to $9.07 per pound or $20 per kilogram for checked baggage (roughly $640 per 70-pound bag) and $400 per passenger for unchecked baggage. You can buy additional coverage at check-in for about $10 per $1,000 of coverage, but it excludes a rather extensive list of items, shown on your airline ticket.

Before departure, **itemize your bags' contents** and their worth, and label the bags with your name, address, and phone number. (If you use your home address, cover it so potential thieves can't see it readily.) Inside each bag, **pack a copy of your itinerary.** At check-in, **make sure that each bag is correctly tagged** with the destination airport's three-letter code. If your bags arrive damaged or fail to arrive at all, file a written report with the airline before leaving the airport.

PASSPORTS & VISAS

To get into Vietnam, **a passport is required and a visa is generally necessary,** although it depends on your country of origin; check with the Vietnam Embassy. **Make two photocopies of the data page** (one for someone at home and another for you, carried separately from your passport). If you lose your passport, promptly call the nearest embassy or consulate and the local police.

ENTERING VIETNAM

American citizens are required to have a passport and a visa to enter Vietnam. You can obtain a visa from the Vietnamese embassy. The standard processing fee is $65 for a two-week turnaround and $80 for a four- or five-day rush turnaround. Although officially the embassy is only supposed to grant 30-day visas (that you may be able to extend once you're in Vietnam), persistent callers have been known to receive two-month visas.

➤ INFORMATION: **Office of Passport Services** (☎ 202/647–0518). **Vietnam Embassy** (✉ 1233 20th St. NW, Suite 400, Washington, DC 20036 USA, ☎ 202/861–0694, FAX 202/861–1297, www.vietnamembassy-usa.org/).

PASSPORT OFFICES

The best time to apply for a passport or to renew is in fall and winter.

Before any trip, check your passport's expiration date, and, if necessary, renew it as soon as possible.

➤ AUSTRALIAN CITIZENS: **Australian Passport Office** (☎ 131–232, www.dfat.gov.au/passports).

➤ CANADIAN CITIZENS: **Passport Office** (☎ 819/994–3500 or 800/567–6868, www.dfait-maeci.gc.ca/passport).

➤ NEW ZEALAND CITIZENS: **New Zealand Passport Office** (☎ 04/494–0700, www.passports.govt.nz).

➤ U.K. CITIZENS: **London Passport Office** (☎ 0990/210–410) for fees and documentation requirements and to request an emergency passport.

➤ U.S. CITIZENS: **National Passport Information Center** (☎ 900/225–5674; calls are 35¢ per minute for automated service, $1.05 per minute for operator service).

REST ROOMS

Hotels, guest houses, and restaurants that cater to tourists usually have Western-style toilets, at least in bigger towns. In bus and train stations, on trains themselves, and in restaurants in the countryside, you are more likely to find squat toilets. Most of these do not flush; use the plastic ladle to splash water around. Many public toilets charge a 500d entry fee, which entitles you to a scrap of toilet paper, usually kept in a basket near the front door. Unless you are really desperate, avoid the public toilets in parks and on street corners.

In remote areas the "bathroom" may actually be a small room with a sloped cement floor or a rickety platform perched over a pond.

SAFETY

Although it is widely accepted that Vietnam is safe for tourists, pickpocketing and bag snatching are becoming serious problems in Ho Chi Minh City, and even Hanoi is beginning to see more petty crime. You may want to **remove any jewelry that stands out.** The rest of Vietnam's cities are safer—the biggest hassles are being stared at and being overcharged for purchases. You should take standard precautions, however.

S M A R T   T R A V E L   T I P S   A   T O   Z

In the big cities **do not walk with your bag or purse on your street-side shoulder or leave it at your feet in a cyclo,** as the snatch-and-ride (on a motorbike or bicycle) is a common stealing method. Put your wallet in your front pocket or in a zipped-up bag or purse, and be extra alert when you enter busy markets or crowds. Also, watch out for children or elderly people who may be acting as decoys or pickpocketing you themselves. When sitting in a street café or in a cyclo, make sure you **either hold your bag in your lap with your hands through the straps or put the straps around your neck**; if you do put it at your feet, wrap its handles around your ankles so no one can grab it. If someone does steal your bag, don't pursue the thief—assailants often carry knives. As for cyclos, be sure to negotiate a price before you get in, don't go with a driver you don't feel comfortable with, and don't travel by cyclo after dark, especially in cities.

You want to **avoid leaving passports, cameras, laptop computers, and other valuables in your hotel room,** except if the room has a safe. If it doesn't, consider leaving your valuables in the hotel's safe or with the front desk. It is advised that you leave your passport in your hotel safe and carry only a photocopy with you while out exploring. A lock for your luggage can come in handy—even one for other purposes such as for added protection on doors and windows.

Minihotels in popular tourist areas such as Halong Bay seem to be thief magnets, so **always be sure your doors and windows are locked.** If you've hired a boat for a tour of the bay, have someone trustworthy watch your things if you take a dip in the water. And be extra cautious if you decide to spend the night on the boat.

Dozens of Vietnamese are killed every year by unexploded war ordnances. However, it is very unlikely you will visit any area where there are still unexploded ordnances. If you are going someplace where you believe you may be in danger, be sure to travel with a very experienced guide.

LOCAL SCAMS

When changing money, always count the received bills carefully. If you choose to change money on the street, count the Vietnamese dong before handing over your American money. Some black-market money changers try to shortchange customers. For instance, if the total should be 1,390,000d they will give you 1,300,009d.

WOMEN IN VIETNAM

Vietnam is a relatively safe place for women travelers. Since Vietnamese women, especially in rural areas, do not wear shorts or sleeveless tops, you may feel more comfortable following suit. Female travelers seem to encounter more hassles—such as grabbing and heckling—in central Vietnam than in other areas. Women who drink and smoke are frowned upon, and these activities may provoke criticism in rural areas. Walking alone or taking a solo cyclo ride at night is best avoided; if you're taking a taxi alone at night, sit in the back seat. Finally, don't venture too far down deserted beaches alone, and as you would anywhere, use your common sense.

SHOPPING

Bone up on your bargaining skills before your trip. The fixed-price standard of America and Western Europe is out the window in Vietnam, where paying the asking price on the street is just not done. Major exceptions include state department stores, restaurants, post offices, and transportation tickets—basically, the government-run businesses. Also, plenty of Western-style shops have opened, such as minimarts and even small supermarkets, and prices in these are usually marked and nonnegotiable. However, in other shops and markets and in minihotels, motorbike rental agencies, and some art galleries, **bargaining is almost always expected**; when dealing with anybody selling goods on the street (postcard and coconut sellers, boys who want to shine your shoes, cyclo drivers, etc.), it's positively de rigueur.

It's important to **keep the bargaining process good natured**; shopkeepers

SMART TRAVEL TIPS A TO Z

generally don't respond kindly to aggressive haggling. If you have time, comparison-shop for similar items in several stores to get a feel for prices. The final price will depend on your bargaining skill and the shopkeeper's mood but generally will range from 10% to 40% off the original price. If you don't have much time or really like an item, don't hesitate to buy it—you may not see it again (or you may see it for half the price, although you probably won't have paid that much for it to begin with). Also, **don't assume that all tourist-oriented shops are a rip-off**—some actually sell very nice items, but you need to use your judgment about whether a shop seems good.

Knowing numbers in the Vietnamese language puts you in a better position than if you go in armed with nothing but English and cash; they'll respect your attempt at learning the language, and/or they'll think you've been in Vietnam more than 20 minutes. One expression that's good to know if you're going on a buying spree is *dat qua!* It means "too expensive," and it's a good opening to negotiations if someone's quoted you a steep price. Step 2: shake your head and feign disinterest. Step 3: express interest in *another* shop or person selling the same item. If that doesn't get the price down, start walking away. If they've gone as low as they can you won't hear from them; if they haven't, they'll call you back. One trick the Vietnamese are not fond of is "testing" the price: seeing how low the merchant will lower his or her price but then not buying. If you name a price, be prepared to honor it if or when they agree to sell.

It's very important to **make sure an item can be legally taken out of the country before you buy it**. If you are interested in buying antiques, be aware that many items of historic or cultural value to Vietnam may not be exported. Wooden furniture also may not be exported. If you do buy antiques, you will need approval from the Ministry of Culture to take any pieces out of the country; this can sometimes be arranged by the merchant for a fee. Also check on customs and shipping fees to make sure your bargain doesn't turn costly.

With any purchase **make sure to get a receipt** for the amount paid, both for potential returns and for customs. If you are purchasing an item that looks like it could be an antique, be especially sure to get a receipt stating when it was made. Many lacquer and stone statues are designed to resemble antiques but are relatively new. The best of these replicas should have a Ministry of Culture label affixed to them that states they are not antiques; or get a note and bill from the shop stating the same thing. Note that some of the Vietnam War memorabilia for sale in Ho Chi Minh City is real, but much of it is mass produced in Vietnam or China. There are very few antiques in Vietnam's tourist shops.

KEY DESTINATIONS

The best place to shop in Vietnam is in Ho Chi Minh City, where souvenirs from throughout the country are sold at very competitive prices. You'll find wonderful embroidered linens, beaded shoes and bags, and stylish ready-to-wear clothes. Southern tailors are also reputed to be the most skilled cutters in the country, so you may want to have a suit or a traditional Vietnamese *ao dai* (straight-cut silk gowns worn over flowing pants) made here.

Hanoi has Vietnam's best selection of silks and velvets. Hang Gai Street in the Old Quarter is the place to have a padded velvet jacket made to measure. Other Hanoi specialties are blue-and-white pottery from nearby Bat Trang village and lacquer vases, bowls, and plates.

In the northern mountain town of Sapa, you can buy cloth and clothing embroidered by women of the Dao and H'mong ethnic minority groups. Or you can ask them to add embroidered designs to your favorite jeans or jacket.

Hoi An is famous for its hundreds of tailor shops. The selection of fabrics is limited, but these tailors can't be beat for speed or price. It's possible to have a whole new wardrobe made for less than the price of a single brand-name shirt. Just be sure to double-check the quality of the stitching.

Hue is known for its conical "poem hats", or *non bai tho*. Made of palm fronds, these hats have cut-out designs, only visible when held up to the light, or an inner rim embroidered with flowers and symbols.

SMART SOUVENIRS

If T-shirts bearing Vietnam's flag or printed with "Good Morning, Vietnam!" don't appeal, there are plenty of other unique souvenir options. On Hang Quat Street in Hanoi's Old Quarter, several shops carve wonderful wood-block stamps. For a few dollars you can have these customized with images and words of your choosing. Also in Hanoi, on Hang Gai Street, many shops sell thin silk sleeping bags for between $10 and $15. They won't keep the chill away but they do make luxurious liners for padded sleeping bags.

In Hoi An many of the houses have a pair of "eyes" over their doors—reputedly to keep ghosts and evil spirits away. Each eye is actually a circle of wood with a yin-yang symbol in the center, surrounded by carved petals. A pair costs about $2. Hoi An is also the place to buy colorful silk lanterns. Ranging from $2 to $15, these lanterns have light wooden frames that are collapsible for easy packing.

WATCH OUT

What seemed like a bargain in the shop might prove otherwise. When buying custom-made clothes, always **check that the seams are double-stitched and without raw edges.** Vietnamese color silks often run, as do the indigo-dyed fabrics made by some of the ethnic minority groups. Unless you live somewhere with cheap dry cleaners and no rain, **don't go overboard when buying silk.** And be aware that much of what gets called "silk" in Vietnam contains a high percentage of synthetic fibers.

You're better off without some things. Getting antiques out of the country requires official permission from the Ministry of Culture. Bear in mind that the counterfeit CDs and DVDs that are sold throughout the cities may be confiscated by customs when you get home. Souvenirs made from tortoiseshell or bits and pieces from other endangered creatures should also be shunned, unless you *want* bad karma for adding to the plight of Vietnam's beleaguered wildlife.

SIGHTSEEING GUIDES

In Hanoi and Ho Chi Minh City, travel agencies can provide English-speaking guides for about $15 a day. You may also be approached on the street by former interpreters or by cyclo drivers who want to make 50,000d for a full day's work guiding you around the city. Although this is just as viable an option as any, make sure you understand their English by conducting an informal interview before you agree on an amount.

At places like Marble Mountain, near Danang, you may encounter children who will attach themselves to you as unofficial—and often unwanted—guides. Some of them are charming and informative; others are plain annoying. Your best defense is to tell them up front how much you will—or won't—tip them.

STUDENTS IN VIETNAM

Vietnam's small population of university students is not as well organized as in America or Europe. But the average student group is very interested in learning English or studying abroad. The result is a community of intelligent young locals who for the most part are thrilled to practice their English with you.

➤ IDs & SERVICES: **Council Travel** (CIEE; ✉ 205 E. 42nd St., 14th floor, New York, NY 10017, ☎ 212/822–2700 or 888/268–6245, 🖷 212/822–2699, info@councilexchanges.org, www.councilexchanges.org) for mail orders only, in the U.S. **Travel Cuts** (✉ 187 College St., Toronto, Ontario M5T 1P7, ☎ 416/979–2406 or 800/667–2887, www.travelcuts.com) in Canada.

TAXES

AIRPORT TAX

Every time you fly into or out of an airport in Vietnam, whether on a domestic or international flight, you must pay an airport tax. The airport tax is 20,000d for domestic flights and $10 or 140,000d for interna-

SMART TRAVEL TIPS A TO Z

tional flights. You must get your boarding pass and airport tax receipt before going through the security check.

VALUE-ADDED TAX

Vietnam introduced a VAT tax at the start of 2000. It runs 20% on luxury items such as alcohol, cigarettes, and cars; 10% for hotels, bars, and nightclubs; and 5% for most other goods and services. Larger hotels, especially state-owned and joint-venture operations, often add another 5% service tax. **Ask about added taxes before checking in or ordering.**

TAXIS

Metered taxis are common in Hanoi and Ho Chi Minh City and are becoming more common in Vietnam's smaller cities. In Hanoi, the moment you step into a cab the meter reads 14,000d or 15,000d—the rate for the first 2 km or any part thereof; after that the rate runs about 6,000d per kilometer. Taxis in Ho Chi Minh City are slightly less expensive: the meter starts at 12,000d and then costs 6,000d per kilometer. Fares are always quoted in dong, and many drivers will complain if you try to pay with U.S. one-dollar bills. Although tipping is not required, some cabbies have developed a habit of "not having change" in the hope you'll tell them to keep it.

Although many cabbies act like reckless kings of the road, taxis are the safest way to get around Vietnam's cities. For information about specific cab companies, *see* individual chapters. A faster but less safe option is motorbike taxis (☞ Transportation Around Vietnam, *below*).

TELEPHONES

The days when you had to go to the post office to place a call in Vietnam are long gone. Although phone booths are rare and can only be operated with phone cards, public phones are common in shops and even people's homes.

Long-distance calls can be made from most hotels and guest houses, as well as from post offices. You cannot place collect calls from Vietnam.

AREA & COUNTRY CODES

The country code for Vietnam is 84. When dialing a Vietnamese number from abroad, drop the initial 0 from the local area code. Some city codes follow:

Dalat, 063; Danang, 0511; Hoi An, 0510; Haiphong, 031; Halong Bay, 033; Hanoi, 04; Ho Chi Minh City, 08; Hue, 054; Nha Trang, 058; Phan Thiet, 062; Vung Tau, 064.

When making international calls from Vietnam, use the following country codes: 1 for the United States and Canada, 61 for Australia, 64 for New Zealand, and 44 for the U.K.

CELL PHONES

Cell phones in Vietnam operate on the GSM900 system. Cell-phone users from Europe, Australia, and Asia can receive and place roaming calls in Vietnam. Another option is to buy a prepaid phone card that allows you to use your cell phone here. It's also possible to rent cell phones from Mobifone.

➤ CELL-PHONE RENTAL AND SERVICES: **VMS Mobifone** (✉ 54 Lang Ha St., Ba Dinh District, Hanoi, ☎ 04/833–4448; ✉ 123 Hai Ba Trung St., District 1, Ho Chi Minh City, ☎ 08/822–8171).

DIRECTORY & OPERATOR ASSISTANCE

Vietnam has an incredibly efficient operator service. Call **116** for local directory assistance. Calling **1080** will put you in touch with an information service staffed partly by English-speaking women who can tell you everything from the current time to what percentage of Vietnam's population is under the age of 20. If they don't know the answer offhand, they will take your number and call you back.

INTERNATIONAL CALLS

To call overseas from Vietnam, dial 00 + the country code (1 for the United States) + the area code + the number. Remember that the time difference between Eastern Standard Time (i.e., in New York) and Vietnam is 12 hours ahead, and the time difference between Pacific Standard Time and Vietnam is 15 hours ahead.

International phone calls from Vietnam cost a small fortune. Many hotels have international direct-dial (IDD), which they advertise as a selling point and which you need in order to call overseas. The connection can be surprisingly clear. The hotel will charge you for your call when you check out.

LOCAL CALLS

You can make local calls for free from most hotels. Even if your hotel room doesn't have a phone, you can usually make calls from the reception desk. Once in a while you will be charged around 1,000d–2,000d to make a call.

LONG-DISTANCE CALLS

To make an intercity or interregional telephone call, dial the city's area code + the number. For instance, to call Danang from Hanoi, dial 0511 + the number. When making a local call, omit the area code.

LONG-DISTANCE SERVICES

As of press time, **access numbers for reaching U.S. long-distance operators do not work in Vietnam,** although the phone companies claim otherwise. It's worth a try, but don't count on being successful. The hope is that this situation will change in the near future.

➤ Access Codes: **AT&T Direct** (☎ 800/222–0300). **MCI WorldPhone** (☎ 800/444–4444). **Sprint International Access** (☎ 800/793–1153).

PHONE CARDS

You can purchase phone cards at the telephone companies that are usually in or near post offices. These phone cards can be used on special phones inside the phone company offices or in hotel lobbies. Cards are available in the following denominations: 30,000d, 60,000d, 150,000d, and 300,000d. Card calls to the United States, Europe, and Canada cost about $4 for the first minute and about $3 for each additional minute.

➤ Phone Card Sales: **Mobicard Sales** (✉ 32 Lang Ha St., Ba Dinh District, Hanoi, ☎ 04/835–3850); ✉ 123 Hai Ba Trung St., District 1, Ho Chi Minh City, ☎ 08/822–8171).

PUBLIC PHONES

Most public phones are located in people's shops or homes. Look for a blue sign that reads **Dien Thoai Cong Cong.** Local calls cost 1,000d–2,000d.

TIME

Vietnam is seven hours ahead of Greenwich Mean Time. Vietnam is 15 hours ahead of Los Angeles, 12 hours ahead of New York, 7 hours ahead of London, and 3 hours behind Sydney. Daylight saving time is not observed.

TIPPING

Tipping at restaurants is not common in Vietnam, although many upscale places are starting to add a service charge and/or 10% gratuity to bills. If this hasn't been done and the service is good, you might **consider leaving 5%–10%.** You might also consider tipping other people in the service industry, including bellhops and cyclo drivers. As you go farther north, however, you may find that some hotel employees will refuse tips, waving them off with a perplexed grin. Others, especially those working for the private sector, are learning to appreciate gratuities. Although it's not necessarily expected, tour guides are more than happy to receive a tip if you enjoyed their services.

A common ploy among taxi drivers is to claim they don't have the 2,000d or 5,000d note you're expecting as change. Whether you challenge them on this scheme is up to you. Many cyclo drivers will request in English a "souvenir" after you've paid the agreed amount, to which you might feel compelled to answer, "But *I'm* the tourist." Of course, they're really requesting a tip.

TOURS & PACKAGES

Because everything is prearranged on a prepackaged tour or independent vacation, you'll spend less time planning—and often get it all at a good price.

A number of small, international companies have offices in Vietnam or are based there. Others have offices elsewhere in Southeast Asia or work with Vietnamese partner agencies. These companies can also arrange nationwide tours or one-day excursions for you from overseas, or they can make arrangements for you once you arrive (☞ Travel Agencies, *below*). The trips vary from upscale to rugged, backpacker-oriented travel.

Another option is to have one of the state-run tourist agencies, which are in every city and almost every province of Vietnam, organize a tour or even just a few day trips for you from abroad or in Vietnam. Unfortunately, these state-run agencies are often overpriced and not that helpful (☞ Travel Agencies, *below*).

Note that most tour operators can arrange all kinds of customized tours for groups of four or more.

BOOKING WITH AN AGENT

Travel agents are excellent resources. But it's a good idea to collect brochures from several agencies as some agents' suggestions may be influenced by relationships with tour and package firms that reward them for volume sales. If you have a special interest, **find an agent with expertise in that area**; ASTA (☞ Travel Agencies, *below*) has a database of specialists worldwide.

Make sure your travel agent knows the accommodations and other services of the place they're recommending. Ask about the hotel's location, room size, beds, and whether it has a pool, room service, or programs for children, if you care about these. Has your agent been there in person or sent others whom you can contact?

Do some homework on your own, too: local tourism boards can provide information about lesser-known and small-niche operators, some of which may sell only direct.

BUYER BEWARE

Each year consumers are stranded or lose their money when tour operators—even large ones with excellent reputations—go out of business. So **check out the operator.** Ask several travel agents about its reputation, and try to **book with a company that has a consumer-protection program.** (Look for information in the company's brochure.) In the United States, members of the National Tour Association and the United States

Tour Operators Association are required to set aside funds to cover your payments and travel arrangements in the event that the company defaults. It's also a good idea to choose a company that participates in the American Society of Travel Agents' Tour Operator Program (TOP); ASTA will act as mediator in any disputes between you and your tour operator.

Remember that the more your package or tour includes the better you can predict the ultimate cost of your vacation. Make sure you know exactly what is covered, and **beware of hidden costs.** Are taxes, tips, and transfers included? Entertainment and excursions? These can add up.

➤ TOUR-OPERATOR RECOMMENDATIONS: **American Society of Travel Agents** (☞ Travel Agencies, *below*). **National Tour Association** (NTA; ✉ 546 E. Main St., Lexington, KY 40508, ☎ 606/226–4444 or 800/682–8886, www.ntaonline.com). **United States Tour Operators Association** (USTOA; ✉ 342 Madison Ave., Suite 1522, New York, NY 10173, ☎ 212/599–6599 or 800/468–7862, ℻ 212/599–6744, ustoa@aol.com, www.ustoa.com).

LOCAL OPERATORS

Most state- and privately run travel agencies in Vietnam organize tours of the whole country. Privately run companies are more likely to be able to customize trips, have better English-speaking guides, and offer you a wider range of restaurant and hotel choices. The state-run operators are generally much less flexible and provide fewer options. The main drawback to organizing your trip through tour operators in Vietnam is that you generally don't have the same recourse to consumer protection as you do with many larger, American-based companies. *See* Travel Agencies, *below,* and individual chapters for more information on local tour operators and travel agencies.

GROUP TOURS

Among companies that sell tours to Vietnam, the following are nationally known, have a proven reputation, and offer plenty of options. The classifications that follow represent different price categories, and you'll probably encounter these terms when talking to a travel agent or tour operator. The key difference is usually in accommodations, which run from budget to better, and better-yet to best.

➤ SUPER-DELUXE: **Abercrombie & Kent** (✉ 1520 Kensington Rd., Oak Brook, IL 60521-2141 USA, ☎ 630/954-2944 or 800/323-7308, FAX 630/954-3324). **Travcoa** (✉ Box 2630, 2350 S.E. Bristol St., Newport Beach, CA 92660 USA, ☎ 714/476-2800 or 800/992-2003, FAX 714/476-2538).

➤ FIRST CLASS: **Global Spectrum** (✉ 1901 Pennsylvania Ave. NW, Suite 204, Washington, DC 20006 USA, ☎ 800/419-4446 or 202/293-2065, FAX 202/296-0815). **Mountain Travel-Sobek** (✉ 6420 Fairmount Ave., El Cerrito, CA 94530 USA, ☎ 510/527-8100 or 800/227-2384, FAX 510/525-7710). **Orient Flexi-Pax Tours** (✉ 630 3rd Ave., New York, NY 10017 USA, ☎ 212/692-9550 or 800/545-5540, FAX 212/661-1618). **Pacific Bestour** (✉ 228 Rivervale Rd., River Vale, NJ 07675 USA, ☎ 201/664-8778 or 800/688-3288, FAX 201/722-0829). **Pacific Delight Tours** (✉ 132 Madison Ave., New York, NY 10016 USA, ☎ 212/684-7707 or 800/221-7179, FAX 212/532-3406).

PACKAGES

Like group tours, independent vacation packages are available from major tour operators and airlines. The companies listed below offer vacation packages in a broad price range.

➤ AIR/HOTEL/SIGHTSEEING: **Orient Flexi-Pax Tours** (☞ Group Tours, *above*). **Pacific Bestour** (☞ Group Tours, *above*). **Pacific Delight Tours** (☞ Group Tours, *above*). **United Vacations** (☎ 800/328-6877).

➤ FROM THE U.K.: **Abercrombie & Kent** (✉ Sloane Square House, Holbein Pl., London SW1W 8NS UK, ☎ 020/7730-9600). **Kuoni Travel** (✉ Kuoni House, Dorking, Surrey RH5 4AZ UK, ☎ 01306/740500). **Imaginative Traveller** (✉ 14 Barley Mow Passage, London W4 4PH UK, ☎ 020/8742-8612).

THEME TRIPS

➤ ADVENTURE: **Asian Pacific Adventures** (✉ 826 S. Sierra Bonita Ave., Los Angeles, CA 90036 USA, ☎ 213/935-3156 or 800/825-1680, FAX 213/935-2691). **Green Bamboo** (2B Trang Thi St., Hoan Kiem District, Hanoi, Vietnam, ☎ 04/824-9179, FAX 04/826-4949, vietnamonline.com/green-bamboo). **Himalayan Travel** (✉ 110 Prospect St., Stamford, CT 06901 USA, ☎ 203/359-3711 or 800/225-2380, FAX 203/359-3669).

➤ BICYCLING: **Backroads** (✉ 801 Cedar St., Berkeley, CA 94710-1800 USA, ☎ 510/527-1555 or 800/462-2848, FAX 510/527-1444). **Butterfield & Robinson** (✉ 70 Bond St., Toronto, Ontario M5B IX3, Canada, ☎ 416/864-1354 or 800/678-1147, FAX 416/864-0541). **Global Spectrum** (☞ First-Class, *above*). **Green Bamboo** (☞ Adventure, *above*).

➤ CUSTOMIZED PACKAGES: **Absolute Asia** (✉ 180 Varick St., New York, NY USA, ☎ 212/627-1950 or 800/736-8187, FAX 212/627-4090). **CBS Tour** (✉ Charna Issara Tower, 3rd floor, 942/114 Rama IV Rd., Bangkok, ☎ 02/268-1280, FAX 66 02/268-1288). **Global Spectrum** (☞ First-Class, *above*). **Green Bamboo** (☞ Adventure, *above*). **Pacific Experience** (✉ 185 Spring St., Newport, RI 02840 USA, ☎ 800/279-3639, FAX 203/618-0121).

➤ LEARNING VACATIONS: **Myths and Mountains** (✉ 976 Tee Ct., Incline Village, NV 89541-9004 USA, ☎ 800/670-6984). **Smithsonian Study Tours and Seminars** (✉ 1100 Jefferson Dr. SW, Room 3045, MRC 702, Washington, DC 20560 USA, ☎ 202/357-4700, FAX 202/633-9250).

➤ VIETNAM VETERANS: **Global Spectrum** (☞ Group Tours, *above*). **Vietnam Veterans of America Foundation** (✉ 8605 Cameron St., Ste. 400, Silver Spring, MD 20910 USA, ☎ 301/585-4000, FAX 301/585-0519) organizes tours to Vietnam at least once a year.

TRAIN TRAVEL

The 2,600-km (1,612-mi) rail system, built by the French, goes north–south, servicing coastal towns between Hanoi and Ho Chi Minh City. The trains' main drawback is that they're slow. The quickest train from Ho Chi Minh City to Hanoi, the Reunification Express, takes about 36–44 hours, depending on how many stops it makes. Train travel is better for the shorter hops between Hanoi and Hue; Hanoi and Lao Cai, which gets you to Sapa; or Ho Chi Minh City and Nha Trang.

Bear in mind that Vietnam's trains are not luxurious. Regardless of what class ticket you hold, the bathrooms are often dirty. Noise is another problem; day and night, when the train stops, vendors may pop into your compartment to try to sell you soda, beer, and cigarettes. Smoking is permitted in all compartments.

Security is another concern. At all times **keep the metal grille over the window shut,** as kids sometimes throw rocks and debris at passing trains. Do not place any valuables near the windows: when the train stops, people may try to grab items through the windows.

Finally, you probably want to **bring food and water with you,** although you can sometimes get some on the trains or from vendors in stations.

CLASSES

Train travel through Vietnam can be an enjoyable experience, not to mention a time saver if you take overnight trips, provided you can get a soft sleeper or at least a soft chair. There are several seating and sleeping options on the train: the best are soft-berth sleepers, which generally have comfortable, 4-inch-thick mattresses and contain only four bunks; next are the mid-range soft sleepers, which also have only four bunks but with 2-inch-thick mattresses (Vietnamese nationals are allowed in these cabins but not in the soft-berth sleepers); then come hard-berth sleepers, which have reed mats instead of mattresses and six bunks (the top ones are cheapest); after that are soft seats, which are wooden seats with a soft cushion but no space to lie down; and finally, hard seats, which are just what they sound like. Don't skimp: **when traveling long distances by train, always reserve the soft-berth sleeper.**

The Victoria Sapa Hotel in the mountain town of Sapa offers luxurious train service, complete with plush carriages, for those traveling between Hanoi and Lao Cai and staying at the hotel. If you want to travel in style and can spare the cash, this is the way to go.

FARES & SCHEDULES

Fares vary based on the length of trip and the class of travel, and you'll need separate tickets for each destination. You can purchase tickets at train stations; travel agencies can also help you book tickets.

Train service runs daily between Hanoi and Hue (12–14 hours, $57 for a soft berth); daily between Hanoi and Lao Cai (11 hours; $10–$20 for soft sleeper, available only on Friday night); and daily between Ho Chi Minh City and Nha Trang (15–22 hours, $25–$35). It's also possible to take a train from Hanoi to Beijing (twice weekly, 55 hours, $58–$88). The northeastern border crossing is at Dong Dang, just north of Lang Son.

The Victoria Sapa's deluxe train carriages leave Hanoi on Monday, Wednesday, and Friday evenings. They depart from Lao Cai on Tuesday and Thursday mornings and on Sunday evenings. A four-berth compartment costs $50 on Mondays, Wednesdays, and Thursdays; a two-berth compartment costs $80. On weekends, tickets for the four-berth and two-berth sleepers cost $70 and $120, respectively.

➤ TRAIN INFORMATION: **Hanoi Railway Station** (Ga Hanoi; ✉ Le Duan St. at Tran Hung Dao St., Hoan Kiem District, ☎ 04/825–3697 or 04/825–3949). **Saigon Railway Station** (Ga Saigon; 1 Nguyen Thong St., District 3, Ho Chi Minh City, ☎ 08/846–8704). **Victoria Sapa Hotel** (☎ 020/871–522, FAX 020/871–539).

PAYING

Train tickets must be paid for in dong, unless you book through a tour company. Foreigners are charged higher fares than Vietnamese nationals. Once you disembark you may need to show your ticket again, so **don't throw away your ticket stub.** If you discard your ticket on the train you may face a major hassle when trying to leave the station and may even be forced to pay again.

RESERVATIONS

It's a good idea to **book ahead,** especially for overnight travel, although for some trips you can only reserve a few days in advance. Tickets can either be booked at the train station or through a local tour company.

TRANSPORTATION
AROUND VIETNAM

There are no subways in Vietnam, nor is there much of a mass transit system to speak of. Public bus service is spotty and unreliable, and the buses are generally unsafe and overcrowded. They do go almost everywhere, however. Nonetheless, you are better off taking one of the private tour buses run by travel agencies and tourist cafés (☞ Bus Travel, *above*). The train is a better option as a mode of public transportation for getting across the country, or at least from north to south (☞ Train Travel, *above*). But the easiest way to get around the country is on tourist buses, minivans, or in a car with a driver (☞ Car Rental, *above*).

Cyclos (pedicabs), the bicycle-drawn buggies that are unfortunately on the verge of becoming outlawed, provide the most entertaining and cheapest means of transportation in Vietnam. In Ho Chi Minh City the cyclos are too narrow to seat two healthy Westerners; in Hanoi the cyclos are wider and may be able to accommodate more than one person. Although cyclo drivers are supposed to charge 2,000d per kilometer, they definitely deserve more since many double as informed English-speaking tour guides. Plan to pay 10,000d–25,000d per hour. Bargaining is advised, but it's worth giving the guys a break (and a tip).

One of the quickest ways to get around Vietnam's major cities is to ride on the back of a motorbike taxi, known as a *Honda om* or a *xe om*. This service usually costs about 20,000d. Motorbike drivers are often ex-cyclo drivers who have saved up enough money for a bike. They'll drive up alongside you and ask where

you're going and whether you're interested in a ride. It's relatively safe to travel on motorbikes; unfortunately, the same can't be said for the roads, especially at rush hour.

You can also rent motorbikes and scooters in major cities at most tourist cafés and some hotels and guest houses for about 45,000d to 80,000d a day. A deposit is usually required along with a passport or a photocopy of one. Although automobile driving is off-limits for tourists, motorbike riding by tourists is generally accepted by the police; it is technically illegal, but few Vietnamese police seem to enforce this rule. Temporary insurance for tourists is basically nonexistent, and your own auto insurance generally does not apply. It's a good idea, however, to **make sure your medical insurance covers you in case of a motorbike accident,** even if you are only a passenger.

Driving a motorbike in Hanoi is easier than doing so in hectic Ho Chi Minh City, but traffic skills remain poor throughout the country. Traffic lights are often ignored, traffic police are treated with contempt, pedestrians seem oblivious to the flow—and danger—of vehicles, late-night construction workers play cards in the intersections, and children have been known to dart into streets without warning. It is imperative that you **use the horn** since most drivers rarely glance around before changing lanes. Unfortunately, since everyone uses the horn at every opportunity, it has become less of a warning and more of an announcement of one's status as a motorcycle rider. You should **wear a helmet.**

TRAVEL AGENCIES

A good travel agent puts your needs first. Look for an agency that has been in business at least five years, emphasizes customer service, and has someone on staff who specializes in your destination. In addition, **make sure the agency belongs to a professional trade organization.** The American Society of Travel Agents (ASTA), with 27,000 agents in some 170 countries, is the largest and most influential in the field. Operating under the motto "Integrity in Travel," it maintains and enforces a strict code of ethics and will step in to help mediate any agent-client disputes if necessary. ASTA also maintains a Web site that includes a directory of agents. (If a travel agency is also acting as your tour operator, *see* Buyer Beware *in* Tours & Packages, *above*.)

➤ LOCAL AGENT REFERRALS: **American Society of Travel Agents** (ASTA; ☎ 800/965–2782 24-hr hot line, FAX 703/684–8319, www.astanet. com). **Association of British Travel Agents** (✉ 68–71 Newman St., London W1P 4AH, ☎ 020/7637–2444, FAX 020/7637–0713, information£abta. co.uk, www.abtanet.com). **Association of Canadian Travel Agents** (✉ 1729 Bank St., Suite 201, Ottawa, Ontario K1V 7Z5, ☎ 613/521–0474, FAX 613/521–0805, acta.ntl@ sympatico.ca). **Australian Federation of Travel Agents** (✉ Level 3, 309 Pitt St., Sydney 2000, ☎ 02/9264–3299, FAX 02/9264–1085, www.afta.com. au). **Travel Agents' Association of New Zealand** (✉ Box 1888, Wellington 10033, ☎ 04/499–0104, FAX 04/ 499–0827, taanz@tiasnet.co.nz).

TRAVEL AGENCIES IN VIETNAM

Almost every city and province has a state-run tourist agency that does everything from book trains, planes, and automobiles to arrange guided tours and extend visas. These state-run agencies are often pricey, slow, and not that helpful, but in some smaller provinces they're the only game in town. Hotels, big and small, are frequently affiliated with a state-run or private agency, or they have their own travel services that can organize excursions for you.

The larger firms (Vietnam Tourism, Saigon Tourist, Hanoi Tourism) are huge state-owned agencies with fingers in many pies. If you book a tour outright through, for example, Saigon Tourist, expect to be shuttled every step of the way from the Saigon Tourist hotel to the Saigon Tourist bus to the Saigon Tourist restaurant to the Saigon Tourist reed boat that floats down the river at Perfume Pagoda. And you'll pay for the privilege: for example, Hanoi Tourism's

superior-class 15-day/14-night nationwide bonanza costs $3,150 per person. These companies are not known for their flexibility; they *are* known as cash cows for the Vietnamese government, and many people find that their services and accommodations don't match their prices. On the other hand, they've got connections absolutely everywhere.

In organizing travel around the country, don't write off "Backpackerville" completely. In Ho Chi Minh City, you'll find numerous, well-informed, privately owned travel agencies that cater to budget travelers around Pham Ngu Lao Street in District 1, including those run out of tourist-oriented restaurants such as Sinh Café or Kim Café (☞ Chapter 6). There is no specific congregation of such agencies in Hanoi, but some are in the Old Quarter, around Hang Be Street and Hang Bac Street (☞ Chapter 2).

These tourist cafés, as they're called, have many of the services large travel agencies do and generally some of the best information, the widest selection of adventure tours and day trips, and the lowest prices. Some extend visas; a number double as hotels and restaurants. (Tourist cafés are referred to throughout this guide in this context—primarily as good travel agencies but also as good spots to meet other travelers over a cup of coffee.) Most are not equipped to handle tour bookings from overseas; they're mainly walk-in establishments.

Tourist cafés have their travel itineraries posted on the walls, with photographs of the destinations, prices of each tour, and departure days clearly visible. Accommodations are usually in average minihotels. Occasionally you may want to question their policies: Queen Café's five-day/four-night jeep adventure through the northwest is $65 per person with a "good driver" but $75 per person with an "experienced driver"—makes you wonder what the terms mean.

Tourist agencies in cities like Hue, Danang, Halong Bay, and Haiphong all claim they can provide English-speaking guides. But outside the main cities, it's definitely hit or miss.

See individual chapters for specific information on local travel agencies and tourist cafés.

VIETNAM VETERANS

The office of the Vietnam Veterans of America Foundation (VVAF) in Vietnam is involved in building long-lasting ties and increasing understanding between Vietnamese and Americans. VVAF organizes cultural exchange programs and a prosthetics clinic. Veterans returning to Vietnam are encouraged to contact VVAF, either in Hanoi or at its Maryland office. At least once a year VVAF organizes tours to Vietnam; contact the Maryland office for information.

➤ VETERANS' RESOURCE: **Vietnam Veterans of America Foundation** (✉ 8605 Cameron St., Ste. 400, Silver Spring, MD 20910 USA, ☎ 301/585–4000, FAX 301/585–0519; ✉ 51 Ly Thai To St., Hanoi, ☎ 04/934–1607, FAX 04/934–1606).

VISITOR INFORMATION

As of yet, there is no official source of tourist information abroad, but you might try calling the Vietnam embassy or consulate (☞ Passports & Visas, *above*). There are a couple of business magazines available internationally, such as the *Vietnam Economic Times*, which provides some business information of interest to tourists. The local Vietnamese papers provide slanted news coverage with little emphasis on the arts or leisure. In Vietnam, privately and state-run travel agencies, tourist cafés, and hotels are your best sources of information.

➤ U.S. GOVERNMENT ADVISORIES: **U.S. Department of State** (✉ Overseas Citizens Services Office, Room 4811 N.S., 2201 C St. NW, Washington, DC 20520, ☎ 202/647–5225 for interactive hot line, 301/946–4400 for computer bulletin board, FAX 202/647–3000 for interactive hot line); enclose a self-addressed, stamped, business-size envelope.

WEB SITES

Do check out the World Wide Web when you're planning. You'll find everything from current weather forecasts to virtual tours of famous cities. Fodor's Web site, www.fodors. com, is a great place to start your on-line travels. When you see a 🐾 in this book, go to www.fodors.com/urls for an up-to-date link to that destination's site.

There are dozens of Web sites dedicated to Vietnam and issues of interest to visitors. Check out www.vietnamnow.com and www.vietnamadventures.com for information on specific destinations, restaurants, and hotels. The *Vietnam Business Journal* site, www.viam.com, may be of interest to tourists and business travelers alike.

WHEN TO GO

Vietnam has a number of annual festivals and holidays (☞ Holidays, *above, and* Festivals and Seasonal Events *in* Chapter 1). The biggest, Tet, the lunar new year, falls in January or February, depending on the lunar calendar. Although it is a very picturesque and lively time of year in Vietnam, accommodations are scarce; museums, offices, and shops tend to close for days at a time; and the weather in the north can be cold and drizzly.

CLIMATE

Vietnam's climate varies widely from region to region during different times of the year. The best time of year in northern Vietnam is from October to December, when the weather is cool and the least rainy. Chilly, wet weather starts in December and continues through March, when a clammy mist descends on the region; the northern mountains get even colder. Sweltering heat is common from May to early October. Flooding can be expected during the rainy summer months.

The central highlands are fairly cool year-round and dry from December to March. Along the central coast, the rainy season brings wet weather from December to February; dry heat is the norm from June to October.

In the south the best weather is from December to April, when it is dry. May to November generally brings the wet season and sporadic showers, usually during lunchtime. The rain shouldn't discourage you from visiting the south during this time (espe-

SMART TRAVEL TIPS A TO Z

cially in late fall), although flooding in the Mekong Delta can make traveling there difficult.

Overall, the best time of year to visit all of Vietnam is from late September to December and from March to April.

➤ FORECASTS: **Weather Channel Connection** (☎ 900/932–8437), 95¢ per minute from a Touch-Tone phone.

The following are average daily maximum and minimum temperatures for Hanoi and Ho Chi Minh City.

HANOI

Jan.	66F	19C	May	84F	29C	Sept.	82F	28C
	54	12		72	22		68	20
Feb.	66F	19C	June	88F	31C	Oct.	81F	27C
	55	13		73	23		68	20
Mar.	70F	21C	July	86F	30C	Nov.	75F	24C
	59	15		73	23		63	17
Apr.	77F	25C	Aug.	84F	29C	Dec.	70F	21C
	66	19		73	23		59	15

HO CHI MINH CITY

Jan.	84F	29C	May	88F	31C	Sept.	88F	31C
	74	23		74	23		74	23
Feb.	84F	29C	June	88F	31C	Oct.	88F	31C
	74	23		74	23		74	23
Mar.	85F	30C	July	88F	31C	Nov.	85F	30C
	74	23		74	23		74	23
Apr.	86F	30C	Aug.	88F	31C	Dec.	85F	30C
	74	23		74	23		74	23

1 DESTINATION: VIETNAM

VIETNAM TODAY: MOTORBIKES AND WATER BUFFALOS

VIETNAM is a country on the move. The introduction of economic reforms—known as *doi moi*—more than 10 years ago acted as a catalyst, releasing the energies of the nation left behind after decades of war and isolation. Now wherever you travel in Vietnam—in the towns, the cities, and the countryside—you will see people on the go.

From the rows of *pho* (noodle soup) stalls lining the sidewalks to the numerous vendors selling postcards to the huge neon signs advertising Western chic, it is apparent that this drive to make it in this new era cuts across social boundaries. Billboards hawk everything from Lifebuoy soap to Heineken beer to the newest luxury apartments, and they tower above streets jammed with motorbikes, bicycles, and more and more cars.

It seems as if, once the sun rises, the entire population is up within an hour rushing headlong into another day. The roads are often gridlocked with motorbikes by 6:30 AM, making you wonder just where so many people are going so early in the morning. The answer is in frantic pursuit of advancement, which ends each day only when everyone is too exhausted to continue. Most Vietnamese are in bed by 10 PM. All this goes on despite the continued presence of the old Communist Party cadres, who have by no means completely embraced the gung ho, American-style capitalism that they themselves initiated.

It is especially in the main cities—Hanoi, Haiphong, Danang, and most of all Ho Chi Minh City (Saigon)—that you see this rush to make money. But travel just 30 mi from the heart of downtown Ho Chi Minh City or Hanoi and you still see farmers sowing rice seeds with water buffalos, and duck herders wooing their flocks across roads where the only hazards are passing bicycles. These scenes are no less exhilarating than those in the booming cities.

Vietnam is a country of stunning beauty, with a pristine coastline of golden beaches stretching 3,226 km (2,000 mi) from tip to tail along the South China Sea. To the north, Vietnam borders China along the rugged Hoang Lien mountain chain, a breathtaking landscape of deep valleys and tall, mysterious peaks shrouded in mist. Down the country's enormous arched spine are forest-covered highlands, which can be as deliciously cool as a European spring. These mountains, as well as those in the north, are home to Vietnam's ethnic minority groups—the Black Thai, Flower H'mong, Ede, and Muong—whose traditional way of life has been basically preserved despite the passing centuries and the ravages of war. The majority of Vietnamese, however, live along the coast, and in the country's two major deltas—the Red River Delta in the north and the Mekong Delta in the south. Here the land fans out into patchworks of vivid-green, wet rice paddies, fruit orchards, and fishing hamlets inhabited by a thousand generations of farmers and fisherfolk.

In the midst of this beautiful country, stark reminders of the high price paid by the Vietnamese people for their independence is never far away. Although few visible signs of the damage sustained by Vietnam remain, every town has its monument to war, be it a captured American jet fighter or a victorious North Vietnamese tank. And dotting the cities and countryside are huge Soviet-style memorials recording the millions who died in the country's most recent struggle against outside forces.

For 2,000 years the country has been fending off foreign invaders, most notably the Chinese, French, Japanese, and Americans (☞ Vietnam at a Glance: A Chronology *in* Chapter 8 for more information on Vietnam's history). The Chinese were the first to invade, and by the time they were driven out by Ngo Quyen in AD 938, they had ruled the country for 1,000 years. During the following centuries the Vietnamese migrated south in ever-increasing numbers, battling with the kingdoms of Champa and Angkor as they went. These expansionist ambitions led to conflicts between competing Vietnamese lords—the Nguyen and the Trinh—vying for control of the country.

The French initially entered the scene at the beginning of the 19th century by invitation from the Nguyen lords, who sought assistance in crushing a rebellion against them. But by the mid-19th century, the French had taken over by force, annexing large parts of Vietnam to create the colony of Cochin China. The Japanese occupation during World War II interrupted the French monopoly, briefly. With Japan's surrender, the French returned to rule Vietnam, but not without conflict: by 1946 anti-French sentiments developed into the French-Indochina War.

The French were defeated at Dien Bien Phu in 1954, and the country was split into two under the Geneva Accords that same year. Cold War concerns drew the American military into Vietnam, which led to full-scale U.S. involvement in the Vietnam War. But American firepower only reinforced the conviction among many Vietnamese that they would not be defeated. And the 1968 Tet Offensive was the turning point. By 1973 most U.S. troops had left the country, and the Saigon regime soon fell.

But strife did not end there for the Vietnamese. Following Khmer Rouge border incursions in 1978, Vietnam became involved in armed conflict with Cambodia until 1989, effectively ending the "killing fields" of Pol Pot. In response to Vietnam's involvement in Cambodia, the Chinese invaded northern Vietnam in 1979, devastating much of the countryside and many towns and villages. But the Vietnamese army repulsed the Chinese, and for the first time in decades, the Vietnamese people lived in relative peace. They were not, however, without a new set of visitors: the Soviets.

Now that the Soviets have departed, what becomes evident is the Vietnamese people's amazing resilience after so many thousands of years of conflict. From each of their foreign rulers they have taken what appealed to them and melded the most dissonant elements of foreign cultures into a way of life uniquely their own. When you visit Vietnam you can't help but marvel at the Vietnamese people's endurance. Waiflike, silk-clad women bear yokes hung with baskets of rice weighing twice their own weight. Or they build roads, protected only by a conical hat and a perfectly white handkerchief tied over nose and mouth. You also can't help but

admire their panache: don't be surprised to encounter a pair of bareheaded men careening on a motorbike through city traffic at the height of a midday downpour, the driver tooting his horn with a soggy cigarette in his mouth, his companion, arms outstretched, balancing a large pane of glass on his knees. That mixture of practicality and bravado is in some ways the essence of Vietnam, and it is what's taking the country into the future.

NEW AND NOTEWORTHY

From the days of the colonizing French to those of the occupying American troops, Saigon's hotels and restaurants have a history of catering to foreigners, and today Vietnam is surprisingly travel-friendly. Even the government in Hanoi, zealous guardian of all things Vietnamese, has reversed its famed xenophobia and virtually eliminated domestic travel restrictions at the same time it has beefed up travel facilities and agreed to a number of joint-venture hotels with foreign companies and investors. The result is the current boom in **new high-rise luxury hotels** and the development of more beach resorts along the coast, although the frenetic results can be unsightly. The international chains going up overnight seem to homogenize the cityscapes—but they also lower the average hotel rates, as does any fluctuation in currency. Some luxury properties have officially dropped their rates by 30% or more. If you have not yet booked your trip, consider calling the hotels directly to see if they'll make you a deal. All but the busiest hotels will probably be willing to listen to an offer.

The **currency crisis** that beset Southeast Asia in 1997 seriously affected all economies in the region. Although Vietnam has no convertible currency, its economy inevitably suffered as a result of the region's downturn. This slump will probably continue for a few years as the region slowly recovers. However, what this means for you, the traveler, is that you may be able to negotiate with hotels for significant discounts on the price of rooms.

Most hotels—from mom-and-pop mini-hotels to five-star palaces—have a wide range of **travel services.** Tours in particular are widely available, as everyone from the central government bureaucrat to the corner café owner runs or organizes excursions. The result? Nearly every attraction in every corner of the country is accessible—provided, of course, you have a wide-open schedule and heaps of patience.

Although the country is undergoing a **major road-improvement program,** precarious road conditions and suicidal driving habits persist, making car travel nerve-racking. A road in the central highlands may wash out, stranding villagers (or you) for a week. A typhoon, or even the threat of one, could shut down Halong Bay or Mekong Delta tourism for days. Construction began in early 2000 on a major north–south route, the Truong Son Highway, which will follow the wartime supply route known as the Ho Chi Minh Trail. Phase 1 is scheduled for completion by 2003.

The government's various **campaigns against corrupting foreign influences,** known by the appellation "social evils," seem to take hold of the nation and then gradually release. Foreign advertisements in vogue one month are deemed offensive or inappropriate the next and are removed. A month later they're back. Nightclubs steer clear of trouble for 18 months, then a dozen are raided. This cycle isn't fixed, but it isn't random either: crackdowns often coincide with official gatherings, such as Communist Party congresses and international conferences. These conferences also bring good results: before a 1997 meeting in Hanoi of representatives of French-speaking countries, the Vietnamese government beautifully renovated the glorious opera house, built in 1911.

The government has put a lot of money into **reliable air service,** and state-run Vietnam Airlines has seen considerable improvements. Planes seem to run efficiently and frequently to destinations throughout Vietnam and to certain international cities.

WHAT'S WHERE

Central Coast

Two of Vietnam's finest cities, Hue and Hoi An, are in the central coast region.

Both places provide a fascinating look into Vietnam's past. Hoi An is an ancient trading and fishing town with a heavy Chinese influence. Ancient homes, temples, and meeting houses remain as they were 200 years ago. Hue, the former capital of Vietnam, was once the home of the country's emperors. Although much of Hue was destroyed during the Vietnam War, its Imperial City and palatial royal tombs are still impressive reminders of Vietnam's regal past. In between Hue and Hoi An is Danang, the region's major transportation hub and home to the splendid Cham Museum.

Hanoi

Quieter and more reserved than brash, bustling Ho Chi Minh City, Hanoi is the self-appointed capital of Vietnamese culture. This city of majestic lakes, wide tree-lined boulevards, and hauntingly familiar colonial French architecture is one of the most charming cities in Southeast Asia. Hanoi oozes history and legend: Ho Chi Minh declared Vietnamese independence here in 1945 in Ba Dinh Square; the Old Quarter, a dense 15th-century collection of the original 36 Streets, beckons you into its maze; the Lake of the Restored Sword—the physical, emotional, and legendary heart of the capital—enthralls; and the many makeshift sidewalk cafés invite you to sip green tea and share your tales of the city. Hanoi is the home base for touring parts of the north; use it as a jumping-off point to other sites in the area, such as the Perfume Pagoda or Halong Bay, and destinations farther afield, such as Sapa or Dien Bien Phu.

Ho Chi Minh City (Saigon)

Ho Chi Minh City, still called Saigon by most (and both names are used interchangeably throughout this book), is a lively—some might say hectic—city with French colonial architecture, broad boulevards, and a busy waterfront on the Saigon River where barges and sampans load up with freight. It is also a city that is changing overnight: new high-rises are rapidly transforming the skyline, and an ever-increasing number of motorbikes compete for space on the streets with a sea of bicycles. The city is filled with history—from the French-built Notre Dame Cathedral to the War Remnants Museum and the Reunification Palace. And its streets are alive with activity. For a good view of it all, head up to the rooftop bar at the Hotel Caravelle Delta or Hotel Majestic. The city also offers a wide range of cuisines—not only Vietnamese but also French, American, Russian, and Thai. It makes a good base for daylong excursions to the northernmost part of the Mekong Delta and the infamous Cu Chi Tunnels.

Mekong Delta

The Mekong Delta is a patchwork of waterways, tropical fruit orchards, mangrove swamps, and brilliant green rice paddies that run their way into the emerald-color South China Sea. It's a land touched by ancient and modern cultures, from the Funanese to the Khmer, Cham, and Vietnamese, all living side by side today after centuries of strife. Running through the upper delta is the Mekong River, dotted with small fertile islands where fruit grows in abundance. In the lower delta are crocodile-infested swamps and cajeput forests teeming with monkeys and wild pigs. The farther south you go, the more untamed the delta becomes. If you're looking for wild frontiers, take time to explore the farthest reaches of the Mekong Delta—it doesn't get much more isolated than this.

The North

A world away from Hanoi, the rest of northern Vietnam is home to more than 50 ethnic minorities, most of whom live in the fiercely beautiful highlands of the Tonkinese Alps. Take the overnight train to the enchanting trading outpost of Sapa and spend a long weekend in Montagnard country, trekking to the remote villages of the Dao, the H'mong, and the Thai. Jump into a jeep for a bumpy weeklong circuit through the idyllic valley village of Mai Chau and out to Dien Bien Phu, site of the doomed French garrison that surrendered to the Vietminh in 1954. To the east lies the grandeur of Halong Bay, a dramatic region of limestone islets and secluded coves that has earned official World Heritage status. Northeast of Hanoi up Highway 1 is Lang Son, a frontier town where Vietnamese and Chinese residents have put aside the animosity generated by a brief but fierce border war in 1979 in order to proceed with the business of doing business. Here is where people gather to buy and sell everything from monkeys to Mercedes Benzes.

South-Central Coast and Highlands

If you want to take time out to relax, make sure to visit the south-central coast and highlands. Here you'll find Vietnam's two main resort towns—Nha Trang, by the ocean, and Dalat, in the mountains. On the South China Sea, Nha Trang has a glorious palm-lined boulevard running the length of its beach, flanked by hotels and ocean-side restaurants. Although not as developed as other beach resorts in Southeast Asia, it is a nice place to spend a couple of days. If it's mountains and lakes you're after, head to temperate Dalat, the country's number one destination for Vietnamese newlyweds. In Dalat the pace is slow, and activities include strolling along the lake, visiting waterfalls, paddleboating on the lake, playing a round of golf, touring Emperor Bao Dai's summer palace, and sipping the local specialty—artichoke tea. Also in the region are the highland towns of Pleiku and Kontum—good jumping-off points for treks into Vietnam's remaining forests and for visits to the villages of the country's hill-tribe minorities.

PLEASURES AND PASTIMES

Architecture

Vietnamese architecture is as eclectic as its culture. A host of invading and vanquished civilizations—the Cham, the Chinese, the French, the Americans, and the Russians—have left their marks on the nation in a hodgepodge of contrasting styles.

Historically, the Vietnamese themselves were not big builders. The oldest existing buildings in the country are temples built by the Cham, the Indianized Hindu culture occupying south-central Vietnam around the area of present-day Nha Trang from the 4th to the 15th centuries (many Vietnamese from this region are descendants of the Cham people). Temple sites such as the Po Ro Me Tower and the Ra Thap Towers outside Phan Rang on the central coast are still centers of annual Cham pilgrimages. Khmer influence (descendants of the Kingdom of Angkor, now Cambodia) can be seen in the Po Klong Garai Towers built in the 13th century at Thap Cham.

Most temples and pagodas around the country reflect the Chinese influence on Vietnamese culture. But because the Vietnamese mainly built using wood, many ancient pagodas and temples "still standing" have actually been rebuilt, often many times. The layout and foundations of the Temple of Literature in Hanoi, for example, may be 900 years old, but many of the wooden structures of the pagoda and entrance gate are renovations. In Hue, the citadel surrounding the impressive Imperial City, although modeled on its Chinese counterpart, the Forbidden City in Beijing, is actually relatively modern—it was constructed in the early 19th century by French architect Olivier de Puymanel. Sadly, much of this exquisite palace was destroyed during the 1968 Tet Offensive. Hue also has an incredible collection of tombs—vast and beautiful temples to emperors, constructed in an array of architectural styles reflecting the wealth of Vietnam's royal families. Some structures, such as the 10th-century capital of Hoa Lu, southeast of Hanoi, have been around for centuries.

French architecture has probably had the most pervasive foreign influence on Vietnamese building. In Hanoi you still find such classic French colonial architectural treasures as the Presidential Palace, the National Assembly, and the exquisite Opera House, modeled on its counterpart in Paris. The city also possesses treasure troves of various styles that would excite any student of architecture; for example, beautiful Art Deco blocks seem to step straight out of 1920s Le Corbusier–influenced designs.

In the south much of the French architecture was bulldozed to make way for American-style urban planning, although some of it still exists. Many colonial villas were demolished in the 1960s for what has been irreverently described as "bunker architecture"—buildings reflecting a city under siege. The best example of this in Ho Chi Minh City is the Reunification Palace (formerly the Presidential Palace)—a model of '60s-style building design. However, classic colonial buildings such as the ornate and rather flamboyant Hôtel de Ville (now the People's Committee Building) and the Central Post Office are vivid reminders of the romance of what the French once called the "Paris of the East."

One of the last architectural influences to take hold in Vietnam was, unfortunately, that of the Soviet Union. Apart from an imposing monolith, the Ho Chi Minh Mausoleum in Hanoi, there is very little to commend about most Soviet-era structures, which generally dominate the suburbs of most towns and cities. They usually are residential tower blocks that would not be out of place in a Moscow suburb.

Both Hanoi and Ho Chi Minh City have an amalgam of this overwrought Communist bloc nostalgia, early 20th-century Art Deco, French colonialist chic, mandarin Chinese elegance, and a fast-growing array of high-rises, all sprinkled with a healthy dose of kitsch. In Hanoi's Old Quarter and Ho Chi Minh City's Cholon district, a certain rhythm and style are at least maintained. But as residents turn to remodeling or rebuilding their homes, chaos has come to rule in the once-uniform 36 Streets that make up the Old Quarter and the old, Chinese-style houses of Cholon. Tacky plastic and aluminum-framed house exteriors now abut 100-year-old wooden homes or pagodas. Those who don't have the cash to renovate add to their century-old storefronts a hideous blinking neon sign advertising pho, or iron smelting, or gas cookers.

The race for space and the astronomical rise in real estate values are forcing new builders to head skyward with the funkiest and most foul of plans. This is also true in the areas outside the old quarters of both cities, where newfound wealth (or more accurately, newfound nonpoverty) is precipitating a residential construction boom that has even the most avid reformers worried about the new Hanoi and the new Ho Chi Minh City. The soothing ochre-color walls of the French villas are being replaced with cheap concrete, aluminum, and plate glass. The result is houses that look centuries old about three months after they're built. You'll also see these old-looking new houses along the highways throughout the country—just look for the date of construction on top of the house. Only time will tell what a new Vietnam will look like—but no one can deny that the architectural face of the country is rapidly changing.

Art

Whether you're a seasoned collector or just like pretty pictures, you can appreciate the explosion of Vietnamese art splashed onto canvases throughout the country. Much of the work is derivative (copies of French masters, for instance) or clichéd, but some is truly unique and impressive. A handful of painters, including members of the loosely knit but hiply and cleverly named "Gang of Five" (Ha Tri Hieu, Hong Viet Dung, Dang Xuan Hoa, Pham Quang Vinh, and Tran Luong), are treated as conquering heroes by expatriates, collectors, and international artists. The undisputed art capital is Hanoi, where dozens of galleries line their walls with the latest by Vietnam's rising stars. An afternoon meandering through the galleries is a must. Lacquerware (a Chinese creation, which the Vietnamese have embraced as their own) and stone and wood sculptures are for sale everywhere. Many pieces are painstaking replicas of ancient figures or statues, whereas others are chintzy knockoffs. A trained eye will easily distinguish the trash from the treasure. And if you're in the country to make major art purchases, it is crucial you work with a respected dealer; fakes of the more famous artists are sprouting like weeds.

Beaches

Unlike Thailand and other Southeast Asian countries, Vietnam's beach culture is still largely undeveloped. The country's endless stretch of pristine coast is still a working shoreline, home to thousands of fishing families who row daily into the surf in tiny, oval-shape boats woven from reed and rattan. Some towns along the coast, however, are beginning to be developed to accommodate the influx of tourists. Nha Trang is home to the Thai-style Ana Mandara resort, and China Beach, near Danang, has the Furama Resort, an international hotel opened in 1997. Other new resorts are opening in Phan Thiet and Vung Tau.

These resorts are so new they still retain an air of glorious isolation, and it will be a few years yet before they attract the international tourist set. For now, for the most part, there are few restaurants or bars along the waterfront, no boutiques selling designer surf wear, and no lifeguards. And although the coral reefs and sea life are incredible and the surf is excellent, particularly in Danang (the site of an international surfing competition in 1994), very few places, if any, rent gear or give lessons. Check with your hotel or bring

your own snorkeling, scuba diving, boating, or surfing equipment. Jet skiing and paragliding clubs have opened in Vung Tau and Nha Trang, which also has a scuba diving club, as does China Beach. For some of the most beautiful, untouched beaches in Vietnam, you'll need to head north to Halong Bay or south to Phu Quoc Island.

Dining

Although it may not look it at first glance, Vietnam is a nation obsessed with its culinary traditions. Rule 1: Vietnamese food is not "Chinese food without the spices." Sophisticated cuisine, distinct from what is north of its border, has evolved in Vietnam over the last few thousand years. Soy sauce is not as common in Vietnam as in China, for instance; instead, the nearly universal seasoning of choice in the country is *nuoc mam*—inadequately translated as fish sauce—a clear amber liquid pressed out of large barrels of anchovies and salt. This exquisitely complex condiment submerges itself in the flavors of other ingredients—it's truly a remarkable concoction. Don't be put off by the smell of this potent liquid; skeptical foreigners have been known to become converts after a couple of experiences. But do take care not to overdo it, as a little bit goes a long way.

The cuisines in south, central, and north Vietnam differ subtly. Southern Vietnamese cooking uses a great variety of greens, fruits, meats, and seafood. The French, ever the gourmands, left their mark on the region in the form of elaborate vegetable dishes (French transplants such as asparagus are still grown in the southern highlands). The Indian influence is also apparent in the south, judging by the number of curries.

Central Vietnam is known almost as much for its culinary presentation—exquisitely displayed dishes are small but varied and numerous—as for its use of spices. Here the seafood and fresh fish are adorned with plenty of chili. Shrimp sauce is also a favorite, as are different forms of *banh*, rice pancakes with all kinds of fillings.

In the more temperate latitudes of the north, dishes are traditionally lighter and consist of fewer ingredients. Stir-fry is more popular in the north than elsewhere—understandable given China's proximity. But the dish that reigns supreme in Hanoi and the north (although also commonly found in the south) is *pho*, the ubiquitous noodle soup that can safely be called Vietnam's national dish. Served at all hours but especially at breakfast, this chicken (or beef or pork or shrimp) soup for the soul is a work of art that perfectly balances texture and taste.

To taste pho and other favorites, you need only step out of your hotel and into the streets. Vietnam's best eating isn't found in elegant restaurants or hotel dining rooms but at stalls on every street corner and in every marketplace. These soup, rice, noodle, and seafood kitchens are usually run by several generations of a single family, and sitting down on the low plastic chairs at one of these self-contained sidewalk operations for a bowl of *bun cha* (chopped grilled meat over vermicelli-style rice noodles) feels like joining in a family gathering.

In addition to pho, noodles, and spring rolls (called *nem* in the north and *cha goi* in the south), rice is another staple, served with anything and everything. In Vietnam, rice is food, food is rice. There is one word for both: *com*. Seafood is also delicious, abundant, and cheap all over Vietnam, but particularly in coastal towns such as Nha Trang, Danang, and Halong Bay, where large crabs and prawns are grilled to perfection. Beef and pork are also generally of high quality, but chicken tends to be somewhat tough in Vietnam. Dog meat isn't as inexpensive or plentiful as you might think, and the chance of encountering it shouldn't deter you from exploring Vietnam's back-alley food scene; just watch out for dishes that contain *thit cho*. Be sure to wander the markets in search of the dozens of incredible indigenous fruits, including rambutans, litchis, kumquats, papayas, pineapples, star fruit, and the spiky olfactory overload known as durian.

As for international cuisine, Vietnam's major cities have reentered the modern age. Upscale restaurants to suit nearly every palate have opened in Ho Chi Minh City and Hanoi. The nation's top hotels are winning over expatriate clientele with their superb cuisine. French, Italian, Indian, Chinese, Korean, Mexican, Middle Eastern, Thai, and, yes, certain configurations of fast food are all represented in the northern and southern hubs. And if *onigiri* are your favorite, you're in luck; Ho Chi Minh City alone has more than 20 Japanese restaurants. As soon as you venture outside Hanoi and Saigon, finding top-notch Western food is difficult. However, family-run restaurants and cafés with fresh seafood offerings, delicious meats, and tasty *an chay* (vegetarian dishes) are nearly everywhere.

Drinks include local beers—Ba Ba Ba (333), Halida, and Tiger—and rice wine (similar to sake), although you may want to skip the snake rice wine (with a cobra in the bottle) made "especially for men." You can also get French, Australian, and Californian wines at the better international restaurants, as well as beers such as Heineken (made in Vietnam) and Foster's. Tap water—and ice—are not potable for foreigners, so be sure to ask for bottled water like La Vie or Evian, which are widely available. Another option is a Coca-Cola or 7Up (both also now made in Vietnam). Good, strong coffee and Vietnamese tea are served with breakfast, after dinner, and any time of day at local cafés.

Golf

With the influx of international businesspeople and tourists, golf courses have been opening—or reopening, as the case may be—after a long period of "anti-bourgeois" dormancy. These days most fairways are in the south. There are two 18-hole golf courses outside Saigon: the Vietnam Golf and Country Club, in the outlying district of Thu Duc, 10 km (6 mi) north of Saigon, and the Song Be Golf Resort, 20 km (12 mi) outside the city. Another delightful course is in Phan Thiet, 200 km (125 mi) east of Saigon. In the north, there is one golf course 40 km (25 mi) from Hanoi. One of the nicest, and oldest, courses in the country (dating from the 1920s) is in Dalat, in central Vietnam.

Shopping

There is plenty to buy in Vietnam, although perhaps not of as high quality as elsewhere in Asia. Custom-made clothing in silks and linens, and unique handicrafts, such as delicate blue-and-white ceramics, elegant black-and-red lacquerware, colorful textiles made by ethnic minority groups, and intricate wood carvings of Buddhas and animals, can be found at rock-bottom prices. You can also find all kinds of items at the local markets, from aluminum kitchenware, straw baskets, and lacquer chopsticks to plastic barrettes, velvet slip-on shoes, conical hats, and baseball caps. In addition, Vietnam—particularly Hanoi—has a booming contemporary arts scene, although paintings can get pricey. The asking price might be as little as $30, but don't be surprised if it's $1,000.

Hanoi is less expensive than Ho Chi Minh City and is a better place to find silks and have clothes tailor-made. Ho Chi Minh City, however, has better markets and choicer shops filled with more contemporary-looking goods appealing to expatriates and Vietnam's growing moneyed class. In the rest of the country, shopping is more tourist oriented and is centered around the major sights in the towns. One exception is the colorful outdoor weekend market in Sapa, in northern Vietnam. Here hill tribes from around the area convene to sell and exchange their beautifully embroidered, indigo-dyed clothing, as well as other handicrafts and food staples.

GREAT ITINERARIES

The itineraries that follow suggest ways in which destinations can be combined and give an idea of reasonable (minimum) amounts of time needed in various destinations. Other suggested itineraries are in every chapter.

Hanoi to Ho Chi Minh City

Length of Stay: 1–2 Weeks

If you have one to two weeks in Vietnam, you can divide your time between the country's two major urban centers, Hanoi and Ho Chi Minh City, and take short trips to the surrounding areas. For instance, from Ho Chi Minh City you could make a daylong foray into the Mekong Delta or to the Cu Chi Tunnels and the Caodai Holy See in Tay Ninh. From Hanoi you could take a day trip to the Perfume Pagoda or make an overnight excursion to beautiful Halong Bay.

With two weeks you can probably also fit in a visit to one or maybe two destinations in the middle of the country—Hue, Danang, Dalat, or Nha Trang, for instance. You might begin in Ho Chi Minh City, fly to Danang, take a train, bus, or car to Hue, and from there fly to Hanoi. Or fly directly to Hue for a night and then fly on to Hanoi. Another option is to stop briefly in Danang, then drive to China Beach and on to beautifully preserved Hoi An for a day. This itinerary doesn't give you much time to explore each region, but it does give you a chance to see more of the country.

TRANSPORTATION➤ Air travel to Ho Chi Minh City, Danang or Hue, and Hanoi is the best way to make use of limited time. Note that not all routes are flown every day and that Vietnam Airlines does not have service between every city (for instance, there is no service between Dalat and Nha Trang, between Danang and Hue, or between Hanoi and Haiphong). Check with your travel agent and confirm the availability of flights with Vietnam Airlines as soon as you are in the country. Once at your destination, rent a car and driver to get to places that are close enough to be easily reached by road.

Length of Stay: 3 Weeks or More

If you have three weeks or longer, you can travel the length of the country; plan on spending even more time in Vietnam if you want to get to more off-the-beaten-path spots. Seeing the whole country will give you a sense of its diversity—from the Mekong Delta's floating markets to the beaches of central Vietnam, from the former imperial capital of Hue to northern Vietnam's rugged highlands. Start either in Hanoi or in Ho Chi Minh City—and spend a couple of days exploring. Then use the city as a base for making one- to three-day excursions to points nearby (to the Mekong Delta in the south, for instance, or to Halong Bay in the north). After seeing the region, head north or south, depending on the city you began in; along the way, stop in such places as Dalat, Nha Trang, Danang, and Hue. Two or three days in each destination should be sufficient to see the sights, but who knows: you may find a delightful hotel on a secluded beach and decide to stay much longer.

TRANSPORTATION➤ If you're set on seeing as much as possible in the shortest amount of time, it makes the most sense to fly between major cities and towns—just be prepared to either backtrack a bit or skip a city or two since Vietnam Airlines doesn't fly between every destination in the country (☞ Transportation *in* Length of Stay: 1–2 Weeks, *above*). A series of flights from town to town up the coast from Ho Chi Minh City to Hanoi doesn't take much longer than a direct flight between the two. Only one destination in the northwest—Dien Bien Phu—is serviced by Vietnam Airlines. The rest you'll have to cover by land unless you'd like to charter a helicopter (☞ Chapter 2 for more information). To get to more inaccessible areas like the central highlands and the DMZ (Demilitarized Zone), be prepared to brave the roads with a jeep and driver or minibus tour (☞ Chapter 5 for more information).

A slower and less comfortable but perhaps more romantic way to get across the country is by train. The Reunification Express (☞ Train Travel *in* Smart Travel Tips A to Z) travels the length of the country from Ho Chi Minh City to Hanoi (and vice versa), stopping at most major towns along the coast. The scenery is often spectacular, sometimes drab, but the experience itself is never boring. (Depending on how long you wish to stay in each place, this trip could even be managed in two weeks or less.) You can also quite easily combine air travel with your train journey. For example, from Ho Chi Minh City you could fly to Nha Trang, then to Danang, and from there take a train or bus or hired car to Hue. From Hue fly to Hanoi, and from there explore northern Vietnam.

A third option is to hire a car or minibus with a driver to drive you the length of the country from Ho Chi Minh City to Hanoi, or vice versa (☞ Car Rental *in* Smart Travel Tips A to Z). Keep in mind that when driving around Vietnam you should set aside more time than you think to get from place to place. A distance of 100 km (62 mi) can take from 90 minutes to two hours, depending on road conditions.

FODOR'S CHOICE

No two people agree on what makes a perfect vacation, but it's fun and helpful to know what others think. We hope you'll have a chance to experience some of Fodor's Choices yourself in Vietnam. For detailed information about each entry, refer to the appropriate chapter.

Cultural Landmarks

★ **Central Post Office, Ho Chi Minh City.** Completed in 1891, this classic colonial building, with a huge map of old Indochina inside, is one of the best examples of the French architectural presence in Vietnam.

★ **Cham Museum, Danang.** Savor the glories of the ancient kingdom of Champa at the impressive Cham Museum.

★ **Emperor's Tombs, Hue.** Vietnam's emperors were laid to rest in these elaborately constructed, extraordinarily beautiful, and peaceful tombs.

★ **Hotel Continental, Ho Chi Minh City.** The setting for Graham Greene's *The Quiet American* and the meeting place for journalists and diplomats during the Vietnam War, the Continental is one of most historic hotels in town.

★ **Temple of Literature, Hanoi.** An oasis in the middle of Hanoi, the country's first university is an example of 11th-century Vietnamese architecture.

Dining

★ **Le Camargue, Ho Chi Minh City.** Unique Eurasian cuisine is accented by an elegant open-air villa setting. *$$$$*

★ **Lemongrass, Ho Chi Minh City.** Masterful Vietnamese standards and tasteful Franco-Viet decor make this an expat standard. *$$$*

★ **Hoa Sua, Hanoi.** The food is good, but what makes this place really special is the terra-cotta patio surrounded by palms—a great place for a calm lunch or brunch. *$$*

★ **Khazana, Hanoi.** Surprisingly delicious Indian cuisine made in a real tandoor oven is served in an opulent setting. *$$*

⭐ **Ngoc Suong, Nha Trang.** Try some of the world's freshest and finest seafood while dining in a delightful garden. $$

⭐ **Seasons of Hanoi, Hanoi.** Delicious and artfully presented Vietnamese dishes are served in an antiques-filled villa. $$

⭐ **Café des Amis, Hoi An.** Five heavenly courses of seafood or vegetarian ambrosia are served nightly; come again the next night, as the unwritten menu changes daily. $

Lodging

⭐ **Hotel Caravelle Delta, Ho Chi Minh City.** The most popular hotel in the city has the best location and luxurious rooms with great city views. $$$$

⭐ **Metropole Hotel Sofitel, Hanoi.** Its beautifully renovated French colonial architecture and central location make this one of the most popular hotels in Hanoi. $$$$

⭐ **Sofitel Dalat Palace, Dalat.** On the cool slopes of rolling green hills, this perfectly restored old-world resort is an ideal retreat, especially for golfers. $$$$

⭐ **Hotel Majestic, Ho Chi Minh City.** One of Vietnam's great colonial hotels offers a slice of colonial Saigon in its heyday. $$$

⭐ **Auberge Hotel, Sapa.** Until recently the only game in town, this expanded yet delightful hotel has hardwood floors, grand views, and great prices. ¢

⭐ **Stilt house, ethnic minority villages.** A night in a traditional stilt house (such as those in Mai Chau or outside Sapa), a world away from fax machines and honking Honda Dreams, may be your most relaxing downtime in Vietnam. ¢

The Natural World

⭐ **Hai Van Pass, north of Danang.** This stretch of Highway 1, perched on top of the Truong Son mountain range, has an unforgettable panorama of the startlingly limpid South China Sea.

⭐ **Halong Bay, northern Vietnam.** Jutting dramatically out of the South China Sea, Halong Bay's limestone archipelago is a water-bound sculpture garden.

⭐ **Mekong Delta, southern Vietnam.** Traveling along Mekong River tributaries on a boat to a tropical fruit orchard may

be one of your most memorable excursions in Vietnam.

⭐ **Nha Trang, south-central coast.** Catch this beautiful resort beach on the South China Sea before it becomes overdeveloped.

⭐ **Sapa, northern Vietnam.** Hill-tribe cultures thrive in the magnificent verdant highlands shadowed by Vietnam's tallest mountain, Fansipan.

Shrines and Places of Worship

⭐ **Caodai Holy See, Tay Ninh.** South of Ho Chi Minh City, this colorfully decorated temple is devoted to Caodaism, a religion based on an amalgamation of Eastern and Western thought.

⭐ **Emperor Jade Pagoda, Ho Chi Minh City.** A Vietnamese "It's a Small World," this pagoda is lined with carnival-like sculptures and reliefs of gods and mythical figures.

⭐ **Marble Mountains, south of Danang.** Remarkable cave temples house dozens of statues of the Buddha, some said to have magical powers.

⭐ **Perfume Pagoda, near Hanoi.** This holy temple complex and mountaintop cavern inspire all who enter.

Shopping

⭐ **Co, Hanoi.** You can order custom-designed linen clothing and fine embroidery here.

⭐ **Heritage, Ho Chi Minh City.** The beautiful contemporary-looking lacquerware and outstanding replicas of antique Buddhas and statuary will leave you wishing you had bought more.

⭐ **Hoi An.** The whole town, a perfectly preserved ancient port, is dedicated to seamstress boutiques and to souvenir shops that sell pottery and paintings by local artists.

⭐ **Tax Department Store, Ho Chi Minh City.** Some of the city's best bargains—from designer clothes to handmade bags to custom-made clothes—can be found at this huge store.

⭐ **Saturday market, Sapa.** Hill tribes from around Sapa convene at this colorful outdoor market to sell and exchange their beautiful handicrafts and food staples.

FESTIVALS AND SEASONAL EVENTS

There are nearly 400 major festivals throughout the country and countless smaller celebrations. Every festival is dedicated to something: a legendary event, a supernatural being, or quite often a famous ancestor. Most of Vietnam's festivals originated in the north and central regions and migrated southward; many events are celebrated differently in each locale. The dates of most festivals are based on the lunar calendar, as are weddings, funerals, and other important occasions. For exact festival dates, check with your tour operator or travel agency.

EARLY–MID-JAN.:➤ **Ong Tao,** the Festival of the Kitchen God, falls on the 23rd day of the 12th and last month of the lunar year, right before Tet. During this festival, every family buys a carp for the kitchen god, who watches over the house throughout the year, so he can ride to heaven on it. For a bon voyage, houses are cleaned and gifts offered. When the kitchen god returns home, new year celebrations begin.

MID-JAN.–MID-FEB.:➤ By far Vietnam's largest and most important festival, **Tet,** the celebration of the lunar new year, takes place for a week usually between mid-January and mid-February. Many travelers to Vietnam plan

their trips around Tet—either they come for the holiday or try to avoid it. Tet is a complex weeklong holiday whose themes are renewal, spiritual growth, ancestral reverence, and family ties. It's like Christmas, New Year's, Thanksgiving, Easter, Rosh Hashanah, and Yom Kippur all rolled into one. In many cases entire communities shut down, and people take a few days off from their busy lives. Many museums, markets, restaurants, shops, and offices are closed for a four- or five-day weekend. Major hotels stay open; some fine dining establishments may be closed for the first day of Tet but will open on Day 2 or 3.

Traditional Tet food, particularly *banh chung* (gelatinous sticky rice cakes with fatty pork), is consumed by the pound. Peach blossom branches ornament newly cleaned homes, and *mung tuoi* (small red envelopes of money) are presented to youngsters for good luck. Vietnamese love asking, "Where will you *an Tet*?"—literally, "Where will you eat Tet?" If you say you've got no plans, don't be surprised if you receive half a dozen invitations to celebrate at someone's house.

But passing Tet with some new friends is more than throwing on a pair of slacks and rapping on the door. Timing is crucial. It is not advisable for you to be the first person to cross the threshold of a Vietnamese house as the clock strikes midnight and ushers in the new year.

This role of honor is reserved, usually well in advance, for a distinguished guest such as a party official, a university professor, or a successful businessperson. If the wrong person stumbles through the door first, it could mean disaster for the household.

House calls are positively required during Tet. Day 1 is reserved for close family relatives. Day 2 is for distant relatives, intimate relations, and important colleagues or bosses. Days 3 and 4 are for friends and newer acquaintances. If you are invited to *an Tet*, it is generally understood that you will show up on one of these days. A gift such as fruit or flowers and mung tuoi for the children will be greatly appreciated. But if you are going to sit down for a meal, you'll score major points with a bottle of cognac.

MAR.–APR.:➤ Early spring, in the middle of the second lunar month, is the time of the Buddhist **pilgrimage to the Perfume Pagoda** near Hanoi. The crowds at this time can clog the winding river with rowboats and make ascending the slippery stairs to the mountaintop a bit of a traffic nightmare, but you'll be welcomed with open arms by the thousands of pilgrims.

APR.:➤ **Thanh Minh** is celebrated on the fifth day

of the third month and is a day of ancestor worship; ceremonies usually involve burning incense over the graves of diseased loved ones. The **H'mong Spring Festival** is celebrated in the northwest mountain town of Sapa.

SUMMER

LATE MAY–EARLY JUNE:➤ A three-day celebration in the fourth lunar month brings some colorful and oversize mythology to the village of **Phu Dong,** just across the Red River from Hanoi. The event commemorates the legendary exploits of the genie Thanh Giong, an ancient warrior born in Phu Dong who helped ward off Chinese invaders. Two hundred men hoist a massive centuries-old likeness of the local hero—he was said to be gargantuan—in a spectacular procession on the final day, when a Giong-led victory over the Chinese is reenacted.

Tet Doan Ngu, the celebration of the summer solstice, falls on the fifth day of the fifth month. Historically the festival takes place during the hottest time of the year, when fevers and malaria are most common. Fruit, rice, cakes, and liquor are served to ward off these diseases, and effigies are burned to satisfy the god of death.

AUG.–SEPT.:➤ **Tet Trung Nguyen or Vu Lan,** the second most important festival after Tet, takes place on the 14th or 15th day of the seventh lunar month. It is a time to give thanks and praise to parents and ancestors. But its most important function is to help lost souls by pardoning and looking after them. These homeless spirits, Buddhists believe, include those who died unnatural deaths: soldiers killed in war, murder victims, and ancestors whose graves are not properly tended by the living.

On **Ram Thang Bay,** the 15th day of the seventh lunar month, the portals of hell are allegedly thrown open, and its souls ascend to the material world for a day, where offerings of fruit, sticky-rice cakes, flowers, and sweetened rice cookies are intended to ease their transition to heaven. Captured animals, in particular birds and fish, are released to signify the liberation of lost souls, and it is not uncommon to see a Vietnamese throw a cupped bird skyward or let a carp slither out of his or her hands into a lake or stream. Burning paper models of material objects, called *hang ma,* is also common, and although this tradition has ancient origins, modern times are providing a curious twist—paper models of motorcycles, mobile phones, luxury cars, and even new homes are set ablaze in the hope of providing comfort for the damned. This festival is a favorite for parents, who bring children to the pagodas to teach them about gratefulness, piety, and respect. On the night before Vu Lan, big pagodas in Hanoi and Saigon are packed with people.

AUTUMN

A 4,000-year dependence on the rice harvest has generated an abundance of harvest festivals. Each region celebrates differently, so you may want to ask your tour guide or operator about specific harvest festivals.

SEPT.:➤ Ten thousand screaming, chanting, gambling Vietnamese gather in the northern town of Do Son in the eighth lunar month for the **Do Son Buffalo Fighting Festival.** Hordes attend for the deep reverberating thud of 2,000-pound beasts racing toward each other from a distance of 250 yards and, perhaps more than anything, for the glory that comes with a victory. The hometown of the winning buffalo and its trainers earns bragging rights for an entire year. A buffalo meat feast follows the competition.

SEPT.–OCT.:➤ **Trung Thu, or the Mid-Autumn Festival** (also known as the Moon-Watching Festival), on the 14th or 15th day of the eighth lunar month, is especially for children. Families throw parties for their children and friends. Parading around with gongs and drums and doing dragon dances is the order of the day, as is eating fruits and cakes.

NOV.–DEC.:➤ **Trung Thap,** which falls on the 10th day of the 10th lunar month, is a festival surrounding the traditional harvesting of herbal plants.

2 HANOI

Ancient lore and postmodern kitsch collide in Vietnam's capital. Experience both in the sensory feast of Hanoi's Old Quarter, where traditional guilds are juxtaposed with modern glitter. Wander around the city's lakes and along its wide, tree-lined boulevards, where French colonial architecture and age-old temples meet. Explore its lively art and café scenes, and breeze through its quirky museums. Then head out of town on excursions to some of northern Vietnam's highlights.

By Michael
Mathes,
Elka Ray, and
Felicity Wood

H ANOI, THE SELF-APPOINTED STRONGHOLD of "true" Vietnamese, anti-imperialist culture, has learned to covet satellite TV and blue jeans. The country's leaders let in a flood of overseas investment from China, Malaysia, Singapore, Taiwan, and even the United States and Australia, and now the capital of the Socialist Republic of Vietnam relishes its newfound economic liberalization despite itself. Although Western fashions, music, and food have managed to elbow their way into the once-impenetrable north, Hanoi is appealing because it retains its ancient culture, French colonial architecture, broad tree-lined boulevards, and beautiful lakes.

The city dates to the 7th century, when Chinese Sui dynasty settlers occupied the area and set up a capital called Tong Binh. In 1010 King Ly Thai To is said to have seen a golden dragon ascending from Hoan Kiem Lake. The dragon is a traditional Chinese symbol of royal power, and the king took the omen literally: he relocated his capital to the shores of the lake, the site of present-day Hanoi, and named his new city Thang Long, or "City of the Ascending Dragon." During the 11th century the old citadel was built, and 36 villages, each with its own specialized vocation, sprang up to service the royal court. This is the origin of the 36 streets that define the city's Old Quarter.

In 1428 King Le Loi is said to have driven Vietnam's Chinese overlords from the country with the help of a magic sword from heaven. Celebrating his success after the war with a boating excursion on a lake, Le Loi was confronted by a gigantic golden tortoise that retrieved the sword for its heavenly owner. Thus the lake became known as the Lake of the Restored Sword, or Ho Hoan Kiem. In 1789 the Chinese reconquered Hanoi, but not for long. Nguyen Huc, leader of a rebellion in Tay Son (in the south), drove the Manchu invaders out of the country and crowned himself Emperor Quang Trung. Officially, however, by then the country was led by the Nguyen dynasty, which moved the capital to Hue under the rule of Gia Long in 1802. This chapter in northern Vietnam's history was in part orchestrated by the French, who began to play a stronger role in the political and commercial fabric of the country.

The French usurped more and more control, setting up the protectorate of Annam in 1883–84, which meant the Hue royalty held the reins but only under the auspices of French rule. In the following years the French set up its administration and used Hanoi as the Eastern Capital, or Dong Kinh (the origin of *Tonkin*), of French Indochina. The Chinese character of the city was basically eliminated as the French filled in canals between Hanoi's many lakes and created a plain on which to remake the capital in its own mold. They constructed the large villas and administrative buildings that cluster in the streets around the present-day Presidential Palace and the Ho Chi Minh Mausoleum and that continue to give the city a somewhat dilapidated but still striking colonial-era feel.

In 1954 the French were defeated by the Vietminh at Dien Bien Phu, and France, Britain, the United States, and the Soviet Union decided at the Geneva Accords to divide the country at the 17th parallel. From 1954 until 1975, Hanoi served as the capital of the Democratic Republic of Vietnam, or North Vietnam, from which Ho Chi Minh initiated his struggle to reunify the country. Despite American attempts to smash the Communist administration by bombing it from the air, the city survived the war with most of its grandeur remarkably intact. The post-1975 socialist order sought to seal off the city and, after the war with China in 1979, expelled ethnic Chinese from Vietnam, although many of these predominantly mercantile families had lived in Vietnam for generations.

In the decades after 1975, relations with the Soviet Union were strengthened. Tens of thousands of Russian advisers came to live in Hanoi and other parts of the country, leaving their mark in such buildings as the Viet Xo Cultural Palace. But the '80s were a tough time for Hanoians and everyone else. Natural disasters and international isolation led to near mass starvation. Then in 1986 the government proclaimed *doi moi*, the move to a market economy. Foreign investors started preliminary explorations, and the Soviet Union dissolved, taking with it foreign assistance to Vietnam. But more and more foreign investment started coming, especially after the American embargo was lifted in 1994.

More than a decade of economic reforms has changed the attitudes of the ruling party members considerably, and reformist city leaders are learning the ways of capitalism quickly—perhaps too quickly, according to some of the aging Communist Party cadres and conservative critics who pride themselves on their city's being the seat of Vietnam's socialist revolution. Although they are loath to admit it, their once-firm hold on the past and its ideals of solidarity are loosening quickly. The sanctimonious concept known as market socialism is intended to strike a delicate balance between socialist ideals and economic prosperity, but although most young Hanoians are familiar with the former, it is the latter they crave.

Few can argue that the last decade of change in Hanoi has been anything short of a godsend. Hanoi in the 1990s welcomed billions of dollars of foreign investment and the many international visitors eager to see this city (and nation) in the midst of renewal. In the past three years, however, the economy has slowed its overheated pace, in part due to lingering effects of the Asian financial crisis that rocked Vietnam's regional neighbors and prompted a conservative rethink by the powers that be. Nevertheless, despite continued grumblings by foreign investors, the economy has continued to open, and the people have increasing amounts of disposable income. The city has modernized rapidly: less than a decade ago the predominant sound at an intersection was the delicate ring of bicycle bells; today motorcycles and cars are taxing the city's antiquated road system. Life for a pedestrian is, in short, dangerous. But the chaos has its own attraction. Dust hangs heavy in the air as a side effect of the construction boom, and you can see changes that took years to happen in the West occurring literally before your eyes. Where the prison commonly referred to by U.S. soldiers as the Hanoi Hilton once stood is now a 20-story office building. Where once a small lake sat is now a gas station.

Nonetheless, Hanoi remains a city of academics, artists, diplomats— and contradictions. Although you will see people carrying their new TVs on the back of their Honda Dream motorbikes, you will also see people carrying hundreds of pounds of rice on bicycles. People may zoom around all day doing business, but they also take time out for discussions over a cup of coffee in a café. Pete Peterson, once a prisoner in the Hanoi Hilton, has been the U.S. ambassador to Vietnam since 1997. On a Sunday you may see him strolling to his favorite noodle stand with his Australian-Vietnamese wife, whom he met and married in Hanoi. Octogenarian General Vo Nguyen Giap, commander of the Vietminh forces at Dien Bien Phu, is involved in Vietnam's developing telecommunications industry. Like everyone else in Hanoi and all over Vietnam, General Giap is aware of his history but is moving on with the times.

Pleasures and Pastimes

Art Galleries

Hanoi is Vietnam's undisputed fine arts capital, with dozens of art galleries happily partaking in an artistic renaissance. At least half a dozen are serious venues and not just wall space for souvenir art. A tour of the finer galleries—showing the works of young painters like Dinh Y Nhi, Truong Tan, and Le Thiet Cuong—offers a glimpse into the modern Vietnamese psyche. Exhibits at government-sponsored galleries show Vietnam's awkward transformation from communism to "free-market socialism." Here, idyllic portraits of village life hang next to political propaganda posters. The burnished inlay of lacquer, a Chinese creation embraced by Vietnam as its own; extraordinary watercolors on rice paper; the multifarious weavings of the ethnic minority groups—all have emerged from hibernation to create a national oeuvre surprisingly palatable to Western sensibilities. (Perhaps too palatable, say critics, who have voiced their disdain for the wall candy that says little about the strains or surges in Vietnamese society.) With the burgeoning reputation of Vietnamese art in both domestic and international circles, however—and perhaps due to tourists' predilection for wall candy—prices have risen remarkably in the past five years.

Cafés

More than any other city in Vietnam, Hanoi has a flourishing café society, a legacy of French colonial days. Now historic haunts compete with trendy cafés serving imported coffee to the sounds of jazz and MTV. At the humbler end of the spectrum, myriad sidewalk spots—often consisting of just a few tiny stools and tables—play host to students, artists, Communist Party cadres, and philosophical types who sip *ca fe den,* or black coffee, sometimes with a whipped egg on top. Park yourself at one of these places, and—who knows—you could find yourself sitting beside the next Vietnamese Hemingway or Einstein, or the chairman of the Hanoi People's Committee.

Dining

Hanoi's cuisine offers plenty of excitement if you're an adventurous diner. What it doesn't have in color or spice, it makes up for in unusual offerings—from eight-course meals of dog meat (*thit cho*) to barbecued songbirds and snake-penis wine. (In the outlying snake village of Le Mat, your dinner is skinned alive and its blood mixed with rice wine for a 100-proof shot of virility!)

If you're looking for a dinner a bit less provocative, you should know that Hanoi is also home to Vietnam's most famous dish—*pho* (rice noodles in chicken or beef broth). This and other northern specialties are best enjoyed at the bustling sidewalk food stalls lining many streets. Hanoi also has a wide array of good international restaurants, and new ones are opening all the time. (They also close frequently, so some listings may be gone by the time you get to Hanoi; check in advance before setting out.)

Cuisine options range from Vietnamese to Japanese, French, and Italian. Prices range from the incredibly cheap to the just plain inexpensive—even in more upscale restaurants you'll pay less than in other big cities around the world (except perhaps at the big international hotels). In Hanoi, restaurants usually close by 10 PM. Sidewalk eateries stop serving breakfast and lunch by 2 and usually reopen for dinner around 4. You can always find a late-night noodle stand.

The capital is also a city for beer drinkers. Pints of *bia hoi* (fresh but weak draft beer) are enjoyed from late morning, with snack foods like boiled peanuts, dried squid, and pork rolls. Hundreds of bia hoi sites

dot the city, providing ample opportunity for you to experience this
quintessential Hanoi pastime.

Lakes

Hanoi's network of lakes is perhaps its most romantic asset. In the
evenings groups of Vietnamese of all ages line the shores of Hanoi's
biggest lake, West Lake (Ho Tay), and central Hoan Kiem Lake to soak
up the calming breeze off the water. With such an abundance of water,
it's surprising that boating is not really part of Hanoi life. Apart from
the canoes used by fishermen and a few low-budget paddleboats popular with courting couples, the lakes are free of nautical traffic. You
can, however, hire cruise boats on West Lake for large parties. And with
the opening of the upscale Hanoi Club on the lake's southeast fringe,
speedboats, Jet Skis, and catamarans have begun to appear.

Lodging

In the last seven or eight years, many luxurious joint-venture international hotels have opened in Hanoi—too many, it appears, and the resulting price war means good news for visitors. Some of these hotels
are in the early years of their existence, which is reflected in the sometimes haphazard service. Patience may be required. Minihotels, which
are reasonably priced and generally have such amenities as cable TV,
IDD telephones, and air-conditioning, are another good option. These
smaller properties are often a better option than the huge state-run hotels, many of which were built in the '60s and haven't been properly
maintained or renovated since.

Most hotels are in the historic, crowded, and central Hoan Kiem District, which includes the bustling Old Quarter, or in the Ba Dinh District, around Ho Chi Minh's Mausoleum and on West Lake. Although
hotels in the Ba Dinh District may seem a little far away (you may need
to take a taxi to get into the center of town), they are out of the hustle and bustle of downtown and closer to most of the embassies and
some corporate offices.

Unless otherwise noted, all hotels have IDD phones and private bathrooms.

Shopping

It is often said the average working Hanoi woman spends more than
50% of her salary on clothing. And judging by the activity around the
vendors selling both bolts of cloth and ready-to-wear fashions, it's
more than just an urban myth. The Vietnamese—both men and women—
are generally sharp dressers (if they can afford to be), mixing classic European style and retro '70s items. You can easily get clothing—in silk
linen, or any other fabric—tailor-made in a day or two. Hanoi offers
some of Vietnam's best selections of silver jewelry, pottery, hand-woven
textiles, embroidery, and art, as well as traditional prints, bright wooden
water puppets, pottery, and baskets from nearby villages. Finding quality gifts may take some hunting, however, as standards of work vary
greatly. Unlike many Asian cities, Hanoi has markets that are generally
better for sightseeing than for finding a treasure trove of souvenirs.

EXPLORING HANOI

Hanoi is divided into four main districts, or *quan*. The **Hoan Kiem Di**
trict, named after the lake at its center, stretches from the railwa
tracks to the river, north of Nguyen Du Street, and is the hub of a
local and tourist activity. Just north of the lake is the Old Quarter,
charming cluster of ancient streets. South of the lake you'll find th
modern city center, once the French Quarter, which houses grand col

nial-style villas that have been turned into hotels and offices; the best examples of French-era architecture are around Dien Bien Phu Street and Le Hong Phong Street, where embassies line the road.

The **Ba Dinh District** includes the zoo, Ho Chi Minh's Mausoleum, and areas around West Lake. Stately buildings, fine hotels, and open spaces define the area. North of both Ba Dinh and Hoan Kiem is picturesque West Lake. The **Hai Ba Trung District,** which covers the southeast part of Hanoi, is a calm, elegant residential area; the primary attraction here is Lenin Park, in the northwest corner of the district. The **Dong Da District,** to the southwest, is where the Temple of Literature can be found (along its northern edge).

Unlike Ho Chi Minh City, Hanoi does offer a few places where you can have a very pleasant stroll, particularly around the edges of its many lakes. The escalating traffic congestion along its narrow streets, where the footpaths are already crowded with sidewalk vendors, often forces you back out into the melee, however. Anyone thinking to take a wistful walk along the banks of the Red River should take a taxi toward the Thang Long Bridge (the road to the airport) and get off just south of the imposing concrete span, where there is a small green fringe bordering the waterway.

Getting around Hanoi on foot can be tiring, so if you intend to stick within the Old Quarter or elsewhere in Hoan Kiem District, break up your walks with a cyclo ride or two. Otherwise consider taking taxis, or if the weather is good and you're feeling a little more gung ho, hop on the back of a *xe om* (motorcycle taxi). Although the traffic may look a little daunting, once you learn to trust your driver, you will (perhaps) realize there actually is a knack for navigating what seems like streams of vehicular anarchy. If you're feeling really brave, consider renting a Chinese bicycle for a day and pedaling yourself around.

Once you have seen the sights in Hanoi, it's time to jump off into the "real" Vietnam—the countryside. Less than an hour out of Hanoi in any direction brings you to stretches of rice paddies interrupted only by villages and jagged rocky outcrops, which makes taking day trips, with the capital as a base, a very viable option.

Great Itineraries

IF YOU HAVE 2 DAYS

If you'll just be passing through, your time would be best spent exploring the Old Quarter and visiting Ho Chi Minh's Mausoleum and the adjacent museum. On your second day take in a show at the water-puppet theater and browse the city's many art galleries.

IF YOU HAVE 5 DAYS

Spend two days wandering the Old Quarter and exploring the Ba Dinh District, where you'll find such interesting sights as the Ho Chi Minh Mausoleum, One-Pillar Pagoda, and the Temple of Literature. Then devote your remaining time to side trips from the city: to Halong Bay (☞ Chapter 3), where you can easily spend two days exploring the limestone grottoes by boat; or a one-day trip to the Perfume Pagoda (☞ Side Trips from Hanoi, *below*); or an overnight stay in a Thai minority family's stilt house in Mai Chau Valley (☞ Chapter 3).

IF YOU HAVE 10 DAYS

Spend a few days seeing the major sights described above while making arrangements to travel to Sapa (☞ Chapter 3) by car or train (allow a day or an overnight for traveling either way). Sapa's mountain trails and ethnic minority villages will occupy you for at least two full days. Upon your return to Hanoi, take in the sights you may have missed,

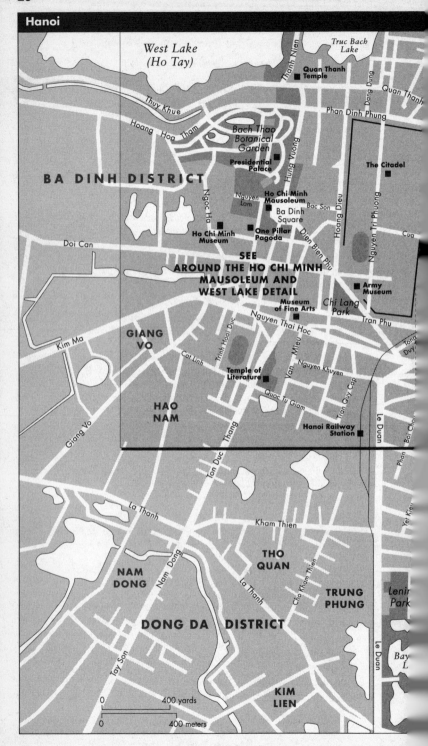

West Lake (Ho Tay)

Truc Bach Lake

Thanh Nien

Quan Thanh Temple

Bung Dung

Quan Thanh

Thuy Khue

Phan Dinh Phung

Hoang Hoa Tham

Bach Thao Botanical Garden

The Citadel

Hung Vuong

Presidential Palace

BA DINH DISTRICT

Nguyen Lam

Ho Chi Minh Mausoleum

Bac Son

Ba Dinh Square

Ngoc Ha

Hoang Dieu

Nguyen Tri Phuong

Cua

Ho Chi Minh Museum

One Pillar Pagoda

Dien Bien Phu

Doi Can

SEE AROUND THE HO CHI MINH MAUSOLEUM AND WEST LAKE DETAIL

Army Museum

Kim Ma

GIANG VO

Museum of Fine Arts

Nguyen Thai Hoc

Chi Lang Park

Tran Phu

Tong Duy

Trinh Hoai Duc

Cat Linh

Van Mieu

Nguyen Khuyen

Tran Quy Cap

Le Duan

Phan Boi Chau

Giang Vo

Temple of Literature

HAO NAM

Quoc Tu Giam

Hanoi Railway Station

Ton Duc Thang

La Thanh

Kham Thien

Yet Kieu

Nam Dong

THO QUAN

Cho Kham Thien

TRUNG PHUNG

Lenin Park

NAM DONG

La Thanh

DONG DA DISTRICT

Tay Son

KIM LIEN

Le Duan

Bay L

0   400 yards

0   400 meters

Yen Phu

Long Bien Bridge

Hang Dau

H. Giay Gam Cau

Hang Khoai

Tran Nhat Duat

Phuc Tan

Hang Chieu

H. Luoc D. Xuan Hang Duong

Hang Chieu

Hang Ma Cha Ca

H. Buom

SEE THE OLD QUARTER DETAIL

Chuong Duong Bridge

H. Vai

P. Lan Ong

Luong Ngoc Quyen

H. Can Hang Dao

Hang Bo

Hang Bac Hang Mam

Tran Quang Khai

H. Non

Cau Go

Hang Thung

Bach Dang

Red River (Song Hong)

Hang Gai Le Thai To

Lo Su

Hoanng

Le Thai To

Hoan Kiem Lake

Tran Nguyen Han

Chuong Duong

HOAN KIEM DISTRICT

Dinh Tien

Hang Khay

Indira Gandhi Park

Ly Thai To

Museum of the Revolution

Trang Tien

Ngo Quyen

Hai Ba Trung

Opera House

Museum of History

Thuong Kiet

Ba Trieu

SEE THE FRENCH QUARTER DETAIL

Bach Dang

Tran Hung Dao

Hang Bai

Phan Chu Trinh

Le Thanh Tong

Tran Khanh Du

Tran Quoc Toan

Nguyen Du

Hang Chuoi

Tran Thanh Tong

Nguyen Khoai

Ba Trieu

Hue

Tran Xuan Soan

Hoa Ma

Luong Yen

Nguyen Cong Tru

Lo Duc

Yec Xanh

Nguyen Cao

To Hien Thanh

Doan Tran Nghiep

Tho Lao

Le Dai Hanh

Hue

HAI BA TRUNG DISTRICT

Tran Khat Chan

Dai Co Viet

Lang Yen

such as Lenin Park or the Opera House and the nearby History and Revolutionary museums. Your next excursion could be to the mist-covered islets of Halong Bay or a shorter trip to the Perfume Pagoda or the ancient Vietnamese capital of Hoa Lu. If you have time, make your way to the nearby professional craft villages such as Bat Trang, just 12 km (7 mi) on the east side of the Red River, the source of most ceramics sold in Hanoi.

When to Tour Hanoi

The ideal time to visit Hanoi weatherwise is between October (with temperatures averaging 80°F) and mid-December (with temperatures ranging from the upper 60s to mid-70s), when the heat and humidity are not so oppressive. But be prepared for cold snaps and chilly nights. The brief spring from March to April is also a pleasant time. From January to March a layer of clammy mist—the infamous *mua phun*—hovers over Hanoi. The city begins its summer swelter in May and sweats through August, when the monsoons bring heavy downpours and sudden flooding. This continues until late September, so if you choose to brave the elements at this time, bring rubber footwear and rain pants or buy them in Hanoi—because you could be in it up to your knees. Temperatures range from the mid-70s to the high 90s.

Late January to early February is a good time to visit if you want to breathe in the excitement of Tet, the lunar new year, a movable date based on the Chinese lunar calendar. In preparation for Vietnam's largest festival, the Old Quarter comes alive with floor-to-ceiling displays of moon cakes, red banners, joss sticks, and red envelopes for giving lucky money (*mung tuoi*) to children. Beware: when Tet does arrive, many shops and restaurants close for up to a week—although some restaurants have discovered the financial benefits of staying open. If you're planning to conduct any business, this is definitely not the time to do it.

February is also the time to join the mass Buddhist pilgrimage to the Perfume Pagoda, but be prepared to deal with serious crowds—many thousands each day—if you make the trip during this peak season. Smaller religious festivals take place at Hanoi's temples and outlying villages in March and April. Because all Vietnamese festivals follow the lunar calendar, check with your tour operator or travel agency for exact dates.

The Old Quarter

Hoan Kiem Lake, Long Bien Bridge, a former city rampart, and a citadel wall surround the oldest part of Hanoi. The area was unified under Chinese rule, when ramparts were built to encircle the city. When Vietnam gained its independence from China in the 11th century, King Ly Thai To built his palace here, and the area developed as a crafts center. Artisans were attracted from all over the northern part of the country and formed cooperative living and working situations based on specialized trades and village affiliation. In the 13th century the various crafts—silversmiths, metalworkers, potters, carpenters—organized themselves into official guilds.

This area is referred to as the 36 Streets—actually there are nearly 70. To this day the streets are still named after the crafts practiced by the original guilds, and they maintain their individual character despite the encroachment of more-modern lifestyles. Note the slim buildings called tunnel or tube houses—with narrow frontage but deceiving depth—which combine workshops and living quarters. They were built this way because each business was taxed according to the width of its store front. In addition to the specialty shops you'll still find here, each street has religious structures reflecting the beliefs of the village from which

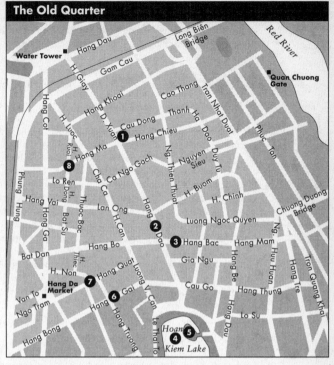

The Old Quarter

its original guilds came. Some are temples dedicated to the patron saint of a particular craft. Hang Bong and Hang Dao, for example, each have five of these pagodas and small temples. Many are open to the public and offer welcome relief from the intensity of the streets.

Numbers in the text correspond to numbers in the margin and on the Old Quarter map.

A Good Walk

Begin your walking tour of the Old Quarter in the northern section of the Hoan Kiem District, at the **Dong Xuan Market** ① on Hang Chieu Street. From here you can dive right into the bustle of the ancient streets—but be careful in the traffic! These streets are narrow, and the main road-ways are clogged with motorbikes, street sweepers, endless mercantile activity, and more. Also be aware that many streets in Hanoi—and throughout Vietnam—bear different names in different sections. The main artery north through the Old Quarter, for example, is 1½ km (1 mi) long and changes its name six times. This is the street on which you'll start.

From the intersection of Hang Chieu and Dong Xuan streets, head south on Dong Xuan, which immediately turns into Hang Duong (Sugar) Street and then into Hang Ngang Street. Spare a moment for 48 Hang Ngang Street, where President Ho Chi Minh wrote his country's Declaration of Independence. Continue south, to **Hang Dao Street** ②. Hang Dao Street divides the Old Quarter and serves as a convenient corridor from which to venture down any of the appealing side streets. Once you come to busy **Hang Bac Street** ③, turn left.

Turning right down Hang Be Street brings you to the historic boat-building district. The bamboo rafts, called *cai mang,* that you see here were designed especially for the shallow rivers, lakes, and swamps of Hanoi. From Hang Be Street take a right on Cau Go Street, the southeast border of the Old Quarter. This neighborhood was known for its flower market in colonial times, a vestige of which can be found before the intersection with Hang Dao Street. Just beyond this flower mart and to the left is the northern tip of **Hoan Kiem Lake** ④, the focal point for legends surrounding King Le Loi's encounter with the Ho Guom tortoise. On the left, or east, side is the distinctive red footbridge that leads to **Ngoc Son Temple** ⑤. This is a good place to have a rest and enjoy the lake.

Walk back to Cau Go Street and through the chaotic intersection here. To the west of this roundabout, Cau Go Street becomes **Hang Gai Street** ⑥, where you can wander through some art galleries or shop for embroidery, silk, or other souvenirs. From here turn north onto Hang Hom Street, which leads to **Hang Quat Street** ⑦. This area is home to a few of the oldest musical instrument shops still standing in the Old Quarter. A quick jog to the left on Hang Non Street will bring you to Hang Thiec Street, where utilitarian tin chests and utensils dangle from every doorway. Farther north, this street becomes Thuoc Bac Street. The street has maintained quite a bit of its French-era Art Deco frontage. Eventually this street intersects **Hang Ma Street** ⑧, which gets its name from the paper goods and fake money made for burning to appease and comfort ancestral spirits. East on Hang Ma Street leads you back to Hang Chieu Street and the Dong Xuan Market. At the end of Hang Chieu is the O Quan Chuong, the last remaining of the five gates of ancient Hanoi.

TIMING

One walk will not be enough to acquaint you with the various specialties of the mazelike Old Quarter. Be prepared to get distracted by the activity, honked at by motorbikers, approached by beggars, hounded by cyclo drivers, repulsed by the food stalls vending all kinds of dishes, and accept that you will lose your way at least twice—no matter what time of day. Since the Old Quarter is filled with shops, this is the kind of walk that could take two hours or 10, depending on how much of a browser you are. If you use a landmark such as Dong Xuan or Hang Da (☞ Shopping, *below*) market, or the northern edge of Hoan Kiem Lake, you could complete a circuit in two to three hours.

Sights to See

①   **Dong Xuan Market.** Once conveniently accessible by riverboat, this market, the oldest and largest in the city, has seen trading with the whole of Southeast Asia. The huge structure, to which the French added a number of features including a new facade, was destroyed by a massive fire in 1994—ironically enough on July 14, Bastille Day. The fire displaced 3,000 workers, caused millions of dollars in damage and losses, and took five human lives, not to mention the lives of thousands of exotic and endangered animals. The market reopened in December 1996 with a bit of a stir: hundreds of women, livid over unfair stall allocations, took to the streets in anger, inducing the prime minister's office to intercede. Today the market looks more like a concrete shopping mall but continues to offer all manner of local and foreign goods. ✉ *Dong Xuan and Hang Chieu Sts., Hoan Kiem District.* ◷ *Daily 6–6.*

③   **Hang Bac Street.** This street was originally dominated by silversmiths and money changers and still has a wide variety of jewelry shops. The Dong Cac jewelers' guild was established here in 1428, and it later erected a temple (now gone) in tribute to three 6th-century brothers whose jewelry skills, learned from the Chinese, made them the patron saints of Vietnamese jewelry.

②   **Hang Dao Street.** Since the 15th century, when it was one of the original silk-trading centers, Hang Dao Street has been known for its textiles. It first specialized in lovely pink silk, always in particular demand because the color symbolizes the Vietnamese lunar new year. By the 18th century the street had branched out into a whole spectrum of colors. When the French colonized Vietnam, Hang Dao Street became the center for all traffic in silk, with massive biweekly trade fairs. Indians who settled here at the turn of the 20th century introduced textiles from the West, and today the street features ready-made clothing in addition to bolts of silk.

★ ❻ **Hang Gai Street.** The Street of Hemp now offers a variety of goods, including ready-made silk, lovely embroidery, and silver products. With plenty of art galleries, crafts stores, and souvenirs, this is ground zero for tourists on foot.

❽ **Hang Ma Street.** Here you can find delicate *ma,* paper replicas of material possessions made to be burned in tribute to one's ancestors. These faux luxury villas and Honda Dream motorbikes can be found alongside more practical merchandise such as imported party decorations.

★ ❼ **Hang Quat Street.** The Street of Fans now features a stunning array of religious paraphernalia, including beautiful funeral and festival flags. It is one of the most atmospheric streets in Hanoi.

★ ❹ **Hoan Kiem Lake** (Ho Hoan Kiem or Ho Guom). The spiritual, legendary, and social heart of Hanoi, Hoan Kiem Lake, the Lake of the Restored Sword, is one of the most enchanting spots in the city. In the early morning mist locals come to the lakeshore to swing their arms and legs in exercise, play a little badminton, and practice tai chi. The lake serves as a gathering point during major festivals such as Tet and for holidays like National Day, but it's also a relaxing lunchtime escape or evening rendezvous point for friends and lovers. Vietnamese of all ages delight in recounting the legend of how the Lake of the Restored Sword got its name: 15th-century war hero Le Loi used a magic golden sword from heaven to vanquish Chinese invaders. While Le Loi was boating on the lake in celebration of his successful martial exploits, a gigantic tortoise rose from the depths and retrieved the blade for its heavenly owner. The legend may owe some of its universal popularity to the real turtles still living in the lake. The apparently unique species, known as *Rafetus swimhoei,* are a city favorite—some estimate they're the largest freshwater turtles on earth, but no one knows for sure. Huge crowds gather at the water's edge whenever one of these near-mythical creatures comes up for air, which herpetologists (yes, they're the reptile experts) say is happening with increasing frequency as the lake becomes more polluted.

❺ **Ngoc Son Temple** (Den Ngoc Son). Quiet and well-manicured, this 18th-century shrine, whose name means "jade mountain," sits on an island in Hoan Kiem Lake and is one of Hanoi's most picturesque temples. This shrine is dedicated to 13th-century military hero Tran Hung Dao, scholar Van Xuong, and to Nguyen Van Sieu, a Confucian master who assumed responsibility for repairs made to the temple and the surrounding areas in 1865. He helped build both Pen Tower (Thap But), a 30-ft stone structure whose tip resembles a brush, and the nearby rock hollowed in the shape of a peach, known as the Writing Pad (Dai Nghien). To get to the temple, walk through Three-Passage Gate (Tam Quan) and across the Flood of Morning Sunlight Bridge (The Huc). The island temple opens onto a small courtyard where old men, oblivious to visitors, are engrossed in spirited games of *danh co tuong,* or Chinese chess. In the pagoda's anteroom is a 6-ft-long stuffed tortoise that locals pulled from Hoan Kiem Lake in 1968. ⊠ *Dinh Tien Hoang St., Hoan Kiem District.* ⊡ *12,000d.* ☉ *Daily 8–8, later for festivals and 1st and 5th days of every lunar month.*

The French Quarter

Regardless of your opinion of their colonial policies, the French certainly can be applauded for thoroughly transforming this once-swampy southern suburb of Hanoi. In order to reflect the grandeur and aesthetic befitting the capital of their protectorate (the French called it Tonkin, from the Vietnamese *Dong Kinh,* or Eastern Capital), French developers rebuilt much of southern Hanoi from the ground up. The wide tree-lined boulevards combine with the majesty of Parisian-style villas and the shuttered elegance of government buildings to form an unusually handsome seat of colonial power. The French have long gone, of course, and for decades Hanoians lacked the affluence to renovate or further build on the architectural contributions of the colonialists. Villas fell into disrepair, and only those buildings appropriated for state offices were even moderately maintained. This part of the city was caught in a 1920s- and '30s-style time warp.

Although much of the French Quarter's appeal lies in its grand but aging architecture, the area is fast becoming a leading diplomatic and commercial section of the city. As you walk through this airy, surprisingly green district, note the considerable international presence here: more than a dozen embassies occupy renovated villas or compounds in the grid of avenues south of Hoan Kiem Lake, and 20-story office buildings have begun to shadow the streets of this lovely part of town.

Numbers in the text correspond to numbers in the margin and on the French Quarter map.

A Good Walk

This 3- to 4-km (2- to 2½-mi) walk, beginning southeast of Hoan Kiem Lake, ends on the west side of the lake. If you've arranged for a driver to pick you up afterward, tell him to meet you in front of the Nha Tho Lon, the Grand Cathedral, also known as St. Joseph's.

Start on the steps of the downtown area's grandest building, the restored **Opera House** ⑨. In front of you is Trang Tien Street, which leads straight out to the southern edge of Hoan Kiem Lake. The area behind and to the south of the Opera House is Nhuong Dia, site of the original Thang Long naval base, which protected the city from enemies attacking via the Red River. By 1875 the French had filled this area with their own military barracks and hospitals. From the Opera House steps turn sharply to the right and follow Trang Tien Street east to its end. Here, at No. 1, is the **Museum of History** ⑩, which houses some of Vietnam's dearest artifacts. This often empty landmark is in a tranquil garden whose only fault is its proximity to the honking, smoke-belching trucks on Tran Quang Khai Boulevard. Just up Trang Tien Street, at 25 Tong Dan Street, is the **Museum of the Revolution** ⑪.

Return to the huge intersection in front of the Opera House. From here head south on Phan Chu Trinh Street—that's the second road on the left if you're looking west from the Opera House steps. As you walk down this street, you'll pass buildings housing the Algerian embassy (⊠ 12 Phan Chu Trinh St.) and its stately ambassador's residence, the Union of Vietnamese Youth, and the Vietnam Students Association.

Turn right onto **Tran Hung Dao Street** ⑫. A leisurely 1-km (½-mi) walk will bring you to Quan Su Street and past an embassy row of sorts.

At the intersection of Tran Hung Dao and Quan Su streets, on your right-hand side very close to the police headquarters, is a large shuttered building that houses the Ministry of Transportation and Communication. To the left is the **Viet Xo Cultural Palace** ⑬, the Soviet Union's

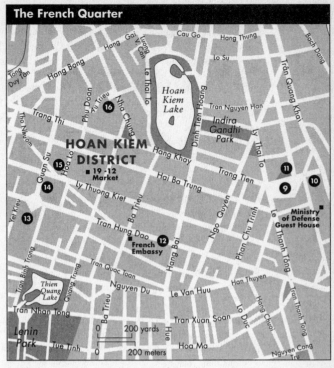

The French Quarter

most striking architectural contribution to this district of the city. Opposite the west side of the Viet Xo Cultural Palace, at 17 Yet Kieu Street, is the Fine Arts College. Founded by the French as an Indochina-wide arts academy in 1924, the college has regained its fine reputation and today trains many of Vietnam's best young artists. Next door to the college is the Alliance Française, a popular center for learning French and a vibrant western cultural hub.

Now travel north on Quan Su Street to the nearby **Ambassador's Pagoda** ⑭. At Ly Thuong Kiet Street, turn right, then left about 300 ft later at Hoa Lo Street. This is the site of what's left of the infamous **Hoa Lo Prison** ⑮, the late-19th-century "fiery furnace" that the French euphemistically called La Maison Centrale and that American prisoners of war sardonically nicknamed the Hanoi Hilton.

From Hoa Lo continue east on Ly Thuong Kiet Street for another block and a half. On the left is the entrance to a bustling market with CHO 19–12 (19–12 Market or December 19th Market) on rusting iron gates. Some of Hanoi's most intense street commerce goes on in here, especially in the early morning. (If you want to skip the market, continue down Ly Thuong Kiet Street and take a left on Quang Trung Street.) The market spills out onto Hai Ba Trung Street, named after the rebellious and heroic Trung sisters, who led a short-lived revolt against the Chinese in AD 40. Turn right on this street and then left on Quang Trung Street. Beyond Trang Thi Street, the road merges with Nha Chung Street. Heading north on Nha Chung brings you to the Hoan Kiem District Culture Center (Nha Van Quan Hoan Kiem), a Soviet-style dance hall. Another 650 ft or so and you've reached **St. Joseph's Cathedral** ⑯, a proud but tired-looking stone-and-cement edifice that fronts a small square. From here it's just a two-block walk east to Hoan Kiem Lake or two blocks north to busy Hang Gai Street in the Old Quarter.

TIMING

This is a full-morning walk that could extend into the afternoon if you're keen on Vietnamese history or would like to comb through the many photographs and other exhibits outlining Vietnam's modern-day revolutions. The museums, including the one at Hoa Lo Prison, are closed on Monday and at lunchtime. If you *must* see all three museums on this walk and you have other afternoon plans, then start early: go to the Revolutionary Museum first, as it opens at 8. The History Museum opens its doors at 8:45. You can also save time by hopping in a cyclo or taxi on Phan Chu Trinh Street, at the Opera House, and going straight to the Viet Xo Cultural Palace. The December 19th Market slows down in mid-afternoon, but by 5 it's lively again with an after-work crowd. Rush hour is not the loveliest of times to roam the city, however, as the mass of motorbikes in narrow arteries like Nha Chung Street turns pedestrians into second-class citizens.

If you're in Hanoi on a Sunday night, you may want to wind up at the cathedral by 7 or 7:30, when Mass lets out and throngs of churchgoers, particularly elderly Vietnamese women in traditional outfits, throng the streets and the square in front.

Sights to See

OFF THE
BEATEN PATH

AIR FORCE MUSEUM – The Air Force Museum is a predominantly outdoor affair, with Soviet MiG fighters, helicopters, and more. The nearby Anti-aircraft Museum (⊠ 176 Truong Chinh St., ☎ 069/533–086) has anti-aircraft equipment and other weaponry. The museums are in Dong Da District, and you'll likely need a rented car or taxi to reach them. ⊠ 86 Truong Chinh St., ☎ 069/552–323. ☞ 10,000d. ☉ Tues.–Sat. 7:30–11:30 and 1–4:30.

⓮ **Ambassador's Pagoda** (Chua Quan Su). This stately prayer house once served the many ambassadors who called on the Le kings. A hall named Quan Su was built in the 15th century to receive these guests, mostly Buddhists, and a pagoda was built for them in which they could comfortably worship. The hall burned to the ground, but the pagoda was saved. The Ambassador's Pagoda escaped destruction a second time, as it was the only pagoda not burned or ransacked in the final chaotic days of the Le dynasty. This pagoda sees more action than most in town, as it serves as headquarters for the official Vietnam Buddhist Association. It's also in part dedicated to a monk who is said to have saved King Ly Than Tong from his deathbed, so many older women come here to pray for good health. Dozens of young monks come here for daily study in the classrooms directly behind the pagoda. ⊠ 73 Quan Su St., Hoan Kiem District, ☎ 04/825–2427. ☞ Free. ☉ Daily 7:30–11:30 and 1:30–5:30.

⓯ **Hoa Lo Prison (Hanoi Hilton).** There's not much left of the infamous "Hanoi Hilton," the prison that once housed captured American servicemen during the Vietnam War, including U.S. Air Force pilot Douglas "Pete" Peterson, who at press time was rounding out his tenure as the first U.S. ambassador to Hanoi. These days it's the focal point of what the government plans as the central business district of the emerging metropolis of Hanoi—much to the chagrin of local residents: the Somerset Grand Hanoi, a twin-tower structure that now occupies the site, is not one of the world's more aesthetically pleasing buildings. What does remain, however, is a small section of the old prison, which is now a museum, and the tree under which Do Muoi, the aging former General Secretary of the Communist Party, used to sit while writing on the backs of leaves during his imprisonment by the French during the years of Vietminh resistance.

Opened in late 1997, the **Hoa Lo Prison Museum** is a blunt reminder of the horrors of colonialism and wartime imprisonment. Here, through the front gates of the old French Maison Centrale (Central House, or Prison), built in 1896, you can get a handle on what life was like for Vietnamese prisoners held during France's occupation of Vietnam. (The number of prisoners under the French grew from 615 in 1913 to 2,000 in 1953.) Several small cells still exist, although many—particularly on the north side of the museum, where political prisoners were held—are repainted in a dull, inauthentic black and gray. The real thing can be found in the southern hall, beyond the grisly guillotine and body basket, where death row prisoners, including Hoang Van Thu, Tran Dan Ninh, and Nguyen Van Cu (who escaped and became a powerful early leader of modern Vietnam), were held. These cells are dank, dark, and anything but welcoming.

On exhibit upstairs are Vietnamese propaganda photos of American POWs, including U.S. Senator John McCain and Ambassador Peterson, cheerily shooting pool, cooking, and writing letters. You won't be able to see the building where the American pilots were kept since it has been torn down, as has the cell from which Do Muoi escaped in 1945 with 100 prisoners. This was accomplished through the maze of sewers that ran under the prison, parts of which are on display in the courtyard. Also on display are present-day photos of some of the last prisoners held by the French before their defeat in 1954, when the government of the newly formed Democratic Republic of Vietnam took over the prison.

If you're looking for historical detail about the prison, bring your own well-informed guide; those available at the museum are far more inclined to talk about the size of the cells than reveal any nuggets about what once took place behind the musty yellow walls. Note, too, that there's little information in English at the museum. ⌧ *1 Hoa Lo St., Hoan Kiem District,* ☎ *04/824–6358.* ⊡ *10,000d.* ⊙ *Tues.–Sun. 8:30–11:30 and 1:30–4:30.*

⑩ **Museum of History** (Bao Tang Lich Su). Opened in 1932 as the museum of the École Française d'Extrême Orient, this building has served in its present capacity since 1958, when the French finally handed it back to Hanoi authorities. It houses treasures from early history, particularly Vietnam's Bronze Age. Of special interest are the Ngoc Lu bronze drums, vestiges of this period some 3,000 years ago that have become enduring national Vietnamese symbols. Tools from the Paleolithic Age are on display, as are ceramics from the Ly and Tran dynasties. Painstakingly elaborate but somewhat corny dioramas depict various Vietnamese victories over hostile invaders. Note the representations of the victory of Ngo Quyen over Nam Han troops in 938 and the 1861 attack on the French ship *L'Espérance (The Hope)*. Upstairs are a few sparse exhibits focusing on more modern Vietnamese culture: standouts include a beautiful 18th-century sedan chair made of lacquered wood and inlaid with gold and a model of a Tay Nguyen stilt house. The museum was undergoing a major renovation at press time, so look for new exhibits.

Visiting the Museum of History can be a frustrating experience. You get the impression that preserving Vietnam's distinct identity is the focus here—like in so many institutions in this country—despite the looming and often invasive presence of foreign cultures, particularly China. There is far too little explanatory text, even in Vietnamese, and English-language translation is lacking. You would be best served accompanied by a translator and, if possible, a historian. The English-language brochure is often out of print, and English-speaking guides are only occasionally available. ⌧ *1 Trang Tien St., Hoan Kiem District,* ☎ *04/825–3518.* ⊡ *10,000d.* ⊙ *Tues.–Sun. 8:45–11:45 and 1:15–4:30.*

⑪ **Museum of the Revolution** (Bao Tang Cach Mang). History buffs will do better here, at the Museum of the Revolution, than at the Museum of History, just across the street. Built in 1926 to house the French tax office, this cavernous museum opened its doors in 1959 and now has 29 halls, individual rooms that focus on specific events or periods in Vietnam's arduous road to independence. The focus naturally lands on the country's efforts against French colonialism, Japanese fascism, and American imperialism. The photographs from the August 1945 Revolution are particularly interesting. Fortunately, just about all the exhibits have English and French commentary, so a few hours in here can be a great learning experience. On the other hand, it may be difficult to swallow some of the museum section titles, such as "The Peaceful Struggle for National Reunification, 1954–1957." English-language guided tours must be arranged in advance. ✉ *25 Tong Dan St., Hoan Kiem District,* ☎ *04/825–4151.* 🎫 *10,000d.* ⊙ *Sat. 8–11:30, Tues.– Fri. and Sun. 8–11:30 and 1–4.*

⑨ **Opera House** (Nha Hat Lon). The centerpiece of French architecture in Hanoi and one of the grandest buildings in the city, the Hanoi Opera House is a small-scale version of the Paris Opéra designed by Charles Garnier and completed in 1875. The Hanoi structure, finished in 1911, incorporates the same grand elements of Napoleonic architectural style. Despite (or because of) the theater's French history, its steps were the site of frequent denunciations against colonial rule. Immediately following World War II, in August 1945, Vietminh troops commandeered the Opera House and announced from its balcony the triumph of the August Revolution.

Today the Opera House is positively glowing after a three-year restoration. Complete with an enhanced orchestra pit for 60 musicians and a movable stage, the 400-seat, three-tier theater once again hosts national celebrations, ballet, symphonies, pop and rock concerts, and opera. The renovation included extensive redesign of the surrounding gardens. Seeing a show may be the only way to get into the Opera House, however, as its doors are usually closed. ✉ *1 Trang Tien St., Hoan Kiem District,* ☎ *04/824–8029.*

⑯ **St. Joseph's Cathedral** (Nha Tho Lon). The imposing square towers of this century-old cathedral rise up from a small square near Hoan Kiem Lake on the edge of the Old Quarter. French missionaries built the cathedral in the late 19th century and celebrated the first Mass here on Christmas Day 1886; it feels as though absolutely nothing's changed since then—the liturgy has not been modernized since the cathedral was built. The small but beautiful panes of stained glass were created in Paris in 1906. Also of note is the ornate altar, with its high gilded side walls.

Septuagenarian Father Do Tong presides here; he conducts Mass mostly in Vietnamese but will attempt to intersperse English or French when he sees foreigners in attendance. Sunday Mass is a popular event, and the pews—men and women are separated—are often full. On major holidays like Christmas and Easter it can be positively chaotic, with 5,000 people either trying to cram their way in or trying to follow along with the service from the front steps. The creaky wooden front doors open for Mass, but if you're visiting at midday, you'll have to walk through the iron gates to the left of the main entrance and enter through the side door, which is up the steps near the back of the structure. ✉ *Nha Tho St., Hoan Kiem District,* ☎ *04/828–5967.* ⊙ *Mass Sun. at 4:30, 5:30, 7, and 10 AM, and 6 PM; Mon.–Tues. and Thurs. at 5:30 AM; Wed. and Fri.–Sat. at 5:30 AM and 6 PM.*

NEED A
BREAK?

Café Moca (✉ 14–16 Nha Tho St., ☎ 04/825–6334), opposite St. Joseph's Cathedral, offers excellent international coffees at reasonable prices. The striking two-story brick interior—those wrought-iron chandeliers were custom made—could belong to a student coffeehouse in Cambridge or Berkeley.

⑫ **Tran Hung Dao Street.** Once called rue Gambetta, Tran Hung Dao Street is now named after the revered 13th-century Vietnamese warrior who repulsed Kublai Khan's Mongol hordes at a legendary battle on the Bach Dang River, near present-day Haiphong. This long tree-lined boulevard is the southern border of the French Quarter and a marked example of the stateliness with which the French imbued these east–west streets. Today the boulevard is lined with a number of diplomatic missions; among them, fittingly, is the massive **French embassy** (No. 57), which takes up an entire city block. Because an imposing wall has been erected around the compound, little can be seen of the glorious embassy garden with centuries-old banyan trees. You'll also pass by the Indonesian embassy at the corner of Ngo Quyen Street (taking a right here brings you up to the Metropole Hotel Sofitel and the Government Guest House, the former Palace of the Governor of Tonkin), as well as the Finnish and German ambassadors' residences. Also here are the embassies of Cambodia, at 71A Tran Hung Dao Street; India, at Nos. 58–60; and Iraq, at No. 66.

⑬ **Viet Xo Cultural Palace** (Cung Van Hoa Viet-Xo). Never one to downplay its influence, the Soviet Union assisted with the design and construction of this "workers' cultural palace." Inaugurated September 1, 1985, the rigid 120-room white colossus stretches from Yet Kieu Street to Tran Binh Trong Road. The palace is actually three structures: the performance building houses a 1,200-seat concert hall; the study and technology buildings contain a library, a conference hall, and an observatory. The palace is noted for hosting a variety of clubs where Hanoians gather to share ideas on everything from biochemistry and chess to billboard usage in the Old Quarter. Most documents in the library are in either Vietnamese or Russian and have particular relevance to labor and trade issues, as it was specifically the Soviet Trade Union that contributed aid in honor of its Vietnam counterpart. The Vietnam Trade Union headquarters is just across the street, next to the Ministry of Transportation and Communication. The broad open space here known as May 1 Square is conducive to commemorating the past and present glories of the Communist Party, and you'll invariably see propaganda posters and waves of dangling street lights consisting of blinking yellow stars and red hammers and sickles. ✉ *91 Tran Hung Dao St., Hoan Kiem District*, ☎ *04/825–3787.* ▦ *Free.* ☉ *Daily 8–noon and 1–4:30.*

Around Ho Chi Minh's Mausoleum

Ask a cyclo or taxi driver to take you from Hoan Kiem Lake to the Ho Chi Minh Mausoleum, in Ba Dinh District. This once-forested area west of the citadel—which is still a military base—is an expansive and refreshingly tranquil district whose stalwart buildings and monuments seem to revel in the glories of Ho Chi Minh and the communist cause. As you travel northwest on Dien Bien Phu Street, you'll leave the tightly woven fabric of the Old Quarter behind and find yourself surrounded by sweeping French-era villas and massive ochre-color government buildings, most newly painted and all well protected from the sun by a phalanx of tall tamarind trees. Many of these villas house the embassies of socialist (or once-socialist) nations that have stood fast by Vietnam during the last few decades. Scattered among these gems are occasional anomalies of Soviet-era architecture.

At the end of Dien Bien Phu Street is the minimally landscaped Ba Dinh Square, in the center of which flutters Hanoi's largest Vietnamese flag. One can almost hear the echoes of Ho Chi Minh's voice ringing out over loudspeakers to the half million northern Vietnamese who gathered to hear Uncle Ho's Declaration of Independence on September 2, 1945. A quarter century later, six days after Ho's death in 1969 (also on September 2), another 100,000 Hanoians gathered here to pay homage to their late president. On the west side of the square is the mausoleum itself, a cold and squat cubicle that's nonetheless arresting in its simplicity and grandeur. In the days leading up to Vietnam National Day (September 2) and Ho Chi Minh's birthday (May 19), thousands of curious citizens—many of them students from nearby districts and provinces—and loyal party members line up to pay their respects to the patriarch, preserved for eternity behind bullet-proof glass.

Across the square from the mausoleum and slightly to the left is Ba Dinh Meeting Hall, the four-story headquarters of the Communist Party and where the National Assembly convenes. Across the square and to the right, where Dien Bien Phu Street meets the square, stands the huge and graceful Ministry of Foreign Affairs. Directly opposite the mausoleum and at the end of short Bac Son Road is the monument to Vietnam's revolutionary martyrs. A palm- and willow-shaded mansion to the right of the monument is the home of former minister of defense and national treasure General Vo Nguyen Giap, who orchestrated the brilliant siege at Dien Bien Phu in 1954. Behind the mausoleum are the Ho Chi Minh Museum and One-Pillar Pagoda; directly to the north is Ho's house on stilts, and beyond that the Presidential Palace and then West Lake (Ho Tay). The underrated Fine Arts Museum as well as the Army Museum and the famed Temple of Literature are also within easy walking distance.

Numbers in the text correspond to numbers in the margin and on the Around the Ho Chi Minh Mausoleum and West Lake map.

A Good Walk

Start at the **Ho Chi Minh Mausoleum** ⑰, in the heart of the Ba Dinh District. Once you have passed by the unflinching guards and through the mausoleum itself, you'll be directed through large iron gates toward **Ho Chi Minh's Residence** ⑱, which is in the tranquil wooded compound of the **Presidential Palace** ⑲. Although visitors are welcome to Uncle Ho's house, the palace itself is off-limits, as is much of the surrounding parkland. Behind the Presidential Palace, however, is the large **Botanical Gardens** ⑳, which *is* open to the public, although the entrance is a bit far away, on Hoang Hoa Tham Street. A short pathway leads from Ho Chi Minh's house to **One-Pillar Pagoda** ㉑, the reconstructed Buddhist tower in the center of a small square lake. To the left is Dien Huu Pagoda; this charming but seldom-visited temple sits in the shadow of the architecturally disorienting **Ho Chi Minh Museum** ㉒.

From the museum walk out the front doors and down the steps toward Ba Dinh Square. Turn right on Hung Vuong Street, the road in front of the mausoleum, then left on Le Hong Phong Street. This wide, shaded boulevard leads back to Dien Bien Phu Street, where you should bear right. In about 200 yards you'll reach shady Chi Lang Park, once a small lake bordering the southern edge of the citadel but later filled in by the French. Here, set back behind a wide square of polished marble, is a sight you are not likely to find elsewhere in the world: a statue of Vladimir Ilyich Lenin. Although long discredited in his home country, Lenin still looms large in Vietnam, and Hanoi's aging party cadres continue to place flowers here in celebration of Lenin's October Revolution.

Around the Ho Chi Minh Mausoleum and West Lake

West Lake
(Ho Tay)

Truc Bach
Lake

TO WEST LAKE SPORTS
AND CULTURE CLUB

Thuy Khue

Hoang Hoa Tham

Thanh Nien

Dang Tai

Nam Trang

Ngu Xa

Duc Chinh

Yen Phu

Khac Nhu

Pham Hong Thai

Nguyen Truong To

Chau Long

Cua Bac

Quan Thanh

Dang Dung

Hang Bun

Hoe Nhai

Phan Dinh Phung

Ministry of
Planning &
Investment

THE CITADEL

BA DINH DISTRICT

Ngoc Ha

Hung Vuong

Hoang Van Thu

Ba Dinh
Meeting Hall

Ba Dinh
Square

Bac Son

Hoang Dieu

Nguyen Tri Phuong

Hang Cot

Ly Nam De

H. Vai

Hang Ga

Nguyen Lam

Ngoc Ha

Doi Can

Chua Mot Cot

Dien Bien Phu

Cua Dong

Phung Hung

Bat Dan

Ong Ich Khiem

Le Hong Phong

Hung Vuong

Chu Van An

Son Tay

Flag
Tower

Ly Nam De

Kim Ma

Giang V. Minh

Trinh Hoai Duc

Kim Ma
Bus Station

Nguyen Thai Hoc

Chi Lang
Park

Tran Phu

Tong Duy Tan

Hang Bong

Hang Da

GIANG
VO

National
Stadium

Van Mieu

Nguyen Khuyen

Tho Nhuom

Trang

Quan Su

Quan Thi

Cat Linh

Giang Vo

Ton Duc Thang

Quoc Tu Giam

Tran Quy Cap

Le Duan

Hoa Lo Prison
(Hanoi Hilton)

HAO
NAM

Hanoi
Railway Station

Phan Boi Chau

Ly Thuong

Kiet

Lenin appears to be leaning resolutely toward the **Army Museum** ㉓, just across Dien Bien Phu Street. To the left is the 100-ft tower known as the Flag Pillar, the surviving remnant of the Nguyen dynasty citadel, which has become a historic symbol of the city. From the Army Museum, retrace your steps to the intersection of Le Hong Phong, Dien Bien Phu, and Hoang Dieu streets. Turn left on Hoang Dieu Street and continue, going past the Chinese embassy on your right, until you reach very busy Nguyen Thai Hoc Street. One block to the right is the **Fine Arts Museum** ㉔, set back in a courtyard. From here the **Temple of Literature** ㉕ is just across the street, secluded behind a low stone wall. To get to the entrance, proceed south down Van Mieu Street, opposite the art museum, and turn right on Quoc Tu Giam Street. You can't miss the entrance, on the right.

TIMING

Taking in all these sights within a comfortable time frame depends on your preferences and how long you want to spend traversing through museums or gazing at architectural anomalies. Three hours should be enough to get from Ho Chi Minh's Mausoleum to the Fine Arts Museum, provided you don't venture over to the Botanical Gardens. Leave at least another 30 to 40 minutes for the Temple of Literature. Or conversely, you could start at the Temple of Literature—it opens in the summer at 7:30, in winter at 8—and make your way up to the Botanical Gardens or to West Lake, taking in the sights along the way. Generally speaking, this walk is more pleasant during the week, but so long as there's no special holiday, weekends are quite fine, too. The only real delay is lining up to view Uncle Ho (keep in mind, too, that his mausoleum is closed in the afternoons). If you are an early riser, consider catching the dawn patrol of people doing calisthenics and tai chi in front of the mausoleum in Ba Dinh Square.

Sights to See

㉓ **Army Museum** (Bao Tang Quan Doi). Although not as provocative as its Ho Chi Minh City counterpart, the Army Museum is nonetheless an intriguing example of Vietnam's continuing obsession with publicizing its past military exploits. At the southern edge of what was once the Thang Long citadel, which housed the imperial city, the museum buildings were once used as French military barracks. In the courtyard of the museum, Chinese- and Soviet-made weaponry—including MiG fighters, antiaircraft guns, and what is said to be the tank that smashed through the gates of the Presidential Palace in Saigon on April 30, 1975—surround the wreckage of an American B-52 and F-4 fighter jet shot down over Hanoi. (Regardless of how you feel about the bombastic zeal behind such a display, standing next to this mountain of twisted metal is a humbling experience.) Other, far-less-arresting displays include depictions of the Trung sisters' revolt against Chinese overlords in AD 40, sound-and-light shows highlighting battles and troop movements during the wars against the French and Americans, bicycles known as steel horses that were used on the Ho Chi Minh Trail, captured French and American firearms and uniforms, field maps and tables of major attacks, and the dreaded *pungee* sticks.

Adjacent to the museum is the **Hanoi Flag Pillar,** a 100-ft tapered hexagonal guard tower atop a three-tier square base. Built in 1812, the pillar escaped destruction by the French when they leveled much of the citadel; instead they used the tower as an observation and communication station—much like the Vietnamese military before them. The intricate fan- and flower-shape holes allow light into the tower, which has a crisp red-and-yellow Vietnamese flag fluttering from its flagpole.

⊠ *28 Dien Bien Phu St., Ba Dinh District,* ☎ *04/823–4264.* ▨ *10,000d.* ☉ *Tues.–Thurs. and weekends 8–noon and 1:30–4:30.*

☁ ㉑ **Botanical Gardens** (Vuon Bach Thao). This 50-acre park behind the Presidential Palace was designed by French landscape engineers in 1890. After defeating the French in Hanoi in late 1954, the state rebuilt the gardens and opened the grounds and its extensive network of cement trails to the public. Athletes in search of exercise congregate here for pickup soccer games, badminton, tai chi, and jogging. Lovers looking for seclusion cross the bridge to an island in the middle of the lake. Between dusk and closing time—10 PM—this island retreat is definitely rated R. ⊠ *Entrance on Hoang Hoa Tham Rd., Ba Dinh District.* ▨ *2,000d.* ☉ *Daily 7 AM–10 PM.*

★ ㉔ **Fine Arts Museum** (Bao Tang My Thuat). The evolution of Vietnamese art is sparingly, if not lovingly, chronicled in this musty three-story museum, which opened in 1966 after serving as a boarding house for French girls living in Indochina. The architecture, sculpture, drawing, and fine arts of Vietnam are displayed in a series of exhibits, mainly organized chronologically, starting with Stone Age and Bronze Age artifacts on the third floor. You'll also find examples of lacquer and wood sculpture, including a fantastical bodhisattva with 1,000 eyes and arms, a 16th-century statue from the Hoi Ha Pagoda.

Several yard-high stone statues and wooden sculptures lining the open-air hallways reflect the wide range of artistic styles incorporated into Vietnamese art. Note the intrusion of the Soviet aesthetic on mid-20th-century sculpture: the martial, even superhuman, forms are a far cry from the elegance and lightheartedness of the Dong Ho village folk art or the centuries-old evocative lacquered-wood depictions of *arhats* (enlightened monks) from the Tay Phuong Pagoda. On the lower floors are oil and watercolor paintings by such Vietnamese masters as Nguyen Tu Nghiem, Bui Xuan Phai, and To Ngoc Van. The central exhibition rooms on the first floor contain some of Vietnam's most stunning lacquer painting, much of it excellent examples of socialist realism and so-called combat art—these should not be missed.

Conspicuously absent are the most recent works of art from Vietnam's bold young painters. The unfortunate reality is that these artists are busy showing their works in stylish Hanoi and Saigon galleries and selling to eager collectors, while the Ministry of Culture, which is ultimately responsible for the art museum, doesn't have the financial resources to buy their works. Note that many of the exhibits are in a state of perpetual rearrangement and may be closed to visitors at any time. ⊠ *66 Nguyen Thai Hoc St., Ba Dinh District,* ☎ *04/823–3084.* ▨ *10,000d.* ☉ *Daily 9:15–6.*

★ ⑰ **Ho Chi Minh Mausoleum** (Lang Chu Tich Ho Chi Minh). It is hard to overstate Ho Chi Minh's heroic stature among the Vietnamese and how significant his mausoleum and the surrounding area are in Vietnam's ideological consciousness. Respected as a determined revolutionary patriot and loved as a public figure who empathized with the people, particularly of the North, Ho Chi Minh has reached icon status in the minds of most Vietnamese. Perhaps it's because schools throughout the country focus almost exclusively on the man's positive exploits, deferring any responsibility for failed economic policies or mismanagement onto Ho's successors, that the youth of Vietnam, although often frustrated by the limitations of the rigid communist system, continue to admire and venerate the man. Many of the faithful who visit the tomb are, in fact, school children on field trips; some of them walk past Ho's reclining body with tears in their eyes, others suppress giggles, but mostly they appear mystified at the pinkish-yellow glow that seems to emanate from the frail, wispy-bearded corpse. Although the number of citizens queuing up to see their late president has dropped significantly in the last few years, thousands of Vietnamese still visit the revered site—and Ba Dinh Square, where independence was declared in 1945—each year to pay homage to "Uncle Ho." During the country's major national holidays, Vietnam's power troika—the general secretary of the Communist Party, the prime minister, and the president—line up in front of the mausoleum with other national leaders to review columns of parading ethnic minorities, rolling tanks, and goose-stepping soldiers.

Had officials followed the president's wishes, this structure would never have been built, as Ho Chi Minh had expressed in his will his desire to be cremated. But the preservation of the Vietnamese leader and his memory has gone the way of such other communist figureheads as Lenin, Stalin, and Mao. Ho's embalmed body, touched up now and again in Russia, is virtually the only thing inside the mausoleum. Just inside the entrance is Ho's famous quotation, "Nothing is more precious than independence and freedom," etched in bright gold lettering, followed by his signature. The structure itself is a squat, cold, gray cubicle ringed by columns and topped by a flat, square frieze adorned with the words "Chu Tich (President) Ho Chi Minh" in red plum marble. Built using materials native to Vietnam, such as marble from Marble Mountain outside Danang, the mausoleum stands out as an exception to the graceful architectural environment that is Hanoi.

When you enter the mausoleum, be aware of the strict propriety expected of visitors. Although you will see Vietnamese pilgrims moving in a solemn single-file procession, foreigners must sign in at an office at No. 8 Hung Vuong Street, south of the mausoleum, then leave their possessions at another checkpoint closer to the actual tomb, where uninformative brochures are for sale. Your purchase of them amounts to your entrance donation. No cameras, hats, or bags of any kind may be brought in the building, and you are expected to behave respectfully. This means not wearing shorts or tank tops or putting your hands in your pockets while inside. Talking is also forbidden, and once inside the chilly room containing Ho's corpse you are discouraged from lingering for more than a few moments in front of the glass. ⊠ *Enter at corner of Hung Vuong and Le Hong Phong Sts., ☎ 04/845–5128. ▣ 4,000d donation expected. ☉ Tues.–Thurs. and weekends 8–11; usually closed Oct. and/or Nov., when Ho's body is in Russia for maintenance.*

㉒ **Ho Chi Minh Museum** (Bao Tang Ho Chi Minh). Opened on May 19, 1990, on what would have been Ho's 100th birthday, this complex was established, in the language of the brochure that you can take on entering, "to satisfy the Vietnamese people's desire to express their deep gratitude to the President." In 1997 officials finally scraped together funding to add English commentary to the bizarre exhibits, making this museum a must-see—if only for 15 minutes—on the Uncle Ho circuit. A collection of manifestos, military orders, correspondence, and photographs from the Communist Party's early days to the present are mixed with historical exhibits covering the October and August revolutions, the fight against fascism, Ho's revolutionary world movement, and Vietnam's struggle against imperialism.

You're encouraged to start at the top and wind your way down. The centerpiece on the top floor is a gargantuan gold lotus flower that itself contains smaller exhibits about Ho's revolutionary activities. Labyrinthine murals and installations lead from the section called

MEET UNCLE HO

ORIGINALLY NAMED NGUYEN Sinh Cung, Ho Chi Minh (literally "bringer of light") is the final and most memorable pseudonym in a series of more than 50 that Vietnam's intrepid leader acquired during the course of his remarkable life. Born in 1890 in the central Vietnamese province of Nghe An, Ho received traditional French schooling and became a teacher. However, he inherited from his father (who abandoned the family early on) a wanderlust that became fueled by a lifelong obsession with Vietnamese independence.

In 1911 Ho signed on to the crew of a French freighter; two years later a stint aboard another French ship took him to the United States, where he settled for a year in Brooklyn, New York, and found work as a laborer. Ho then left for London, where he became an assistant pastry chef. He mastered several languages—among them English, French, German, Russian, Cantonese, and Japanese. He moved to Paris for six years and became increasingly active in socialist, communist, and nationalist movements. After helping to found the French Communist Party, Ho left for Moscow in 1924. It soon became clear that to successfully foment a workers' revolution in Vietnam, he would have to dedicate himself to organizing his countrymen.

By the end of the 1920s, a number of poorly organized revolts had incited aggressive French retaliation, which was only compounded by economic depression. In 1930, while based in Hong Kong, Ho consolidated a number of rebellious factions under the umbrella of the Indochinese Communist Party. However, it was not until 1941—after escaping arrest in Hong Kong, forging documentation "proving" his death, shuttling between China

and the Soviet Union, and disguising himself as a Chinese journalist—that he was able to sneak back into Vietnam.

Shortly thereafter Ho founded the Vietminh Independence League. In July 1945, U.S. OSS officers met with Ho; impressed with Ho's operation, they agreed to supply him with arms. In August, Ho called for a general uprising, known as the August Revolution. Ho proclaimed himself president of the Democratic Republic of Vietnam in the north. The following year, Ho, in order to rid northern Vietnam of Chinese troops, agreed to an accord with the French: Vietnam would be a "free state" within the French Union and 25,000 French troops would be stationed there. Tensions between the Vietminh and the French escalated, however, and soon led to the French-Indochina War.

By 1950 the United States was supplying military aid to the French, and Ho's government was recognized by the Soviet Union and China. The French-Indochina War ended in 1954 with the Vietminh's defeat of the French at Dien Bien Phu. American involvement in Vietnam escalated rapidly.

Ho died of natural causes in September 1969 at the age of 79. After his death the fighting continued, although in 1970 Henry Kissinger began secret talks with the North Vietnamese. By 1975 the Vietnam War had ended, and the country was reunited.

Ho never married—he asserted that the Vietnamese people were his family—thus he preferred the familiar "Uncle Ho." Although he died more than 30 years ago, Uncle Ho is still present, from his embalmed body in the Ho Chi Minh Mausoleum to his portrait on Vietnamese currency.

"Past" into the "Future," where you'll find everything from space-age conceptual representations of peace to models of automobiles symbolizing America's military failure. A red "volcano" surrounded by national totems symbolizes the various national liberation movements. Under the banner "Ho Chi Minh and Young People," huge plastic fruit sits atop a slanting table framed by a backdrop black-and-white photo of nuclear reactors, a display that would look more at home on the set of *Dr. Strangelove*. At one point you stumble into a small but disorienting house of mirrors. Dark TV screens hang from the corners. The few Vietnamese who wander the floors seem less interested in the exhibits and more curious about the specifics of the overwrought Soviet architecture. It is indeed eerie.

You must leave your cameras and bags at the reception area. You'll also find an interesting gift shop in the museum. ⊠ *3 Ngoc Ha St., Ba Dinh District (also accessible from Chua Mot Cot St.),* ☎ *04/846–3752.* 🎫 *5,000d.* ⏱ *Tues.–Thurs. and weekends 8–11 and 1:30–4.*

OFF THE BEATEN PATH

HO CHI MINH TRAIL MUSEUM – The elaborate network of paths of the Ho Chi Minh Trail was used by North Vietnam to transport supplies to Vietcong strongholds in South Vietnam during the Vietnam War. The newly opened Ho Chi Minh Trail Museum provides color on the trail, one of the war's most riveting symbols of dedication and perseverance. Hire a taxi or car and driver to visit the museum. ⊠ *Hwy. 6, 20 km (12 km) south of Hanoi, Ha Tay Province,* ☎ *034/820–889.* 🎫 *10,000d.* ⏱ *Tues.–Sun. 7:30–11 and 1:30–4:30.*

⓲ **Ho Chi Minh's Residence** (Nha Bac Ho). After 1954 Ho Chi Minh had the run of the Presidential Palace, but the ostentation was too much for the ascetic president, who openly shunned luxury and preferred the humble former home of the palace's electrician, where he lived for four years. Then, the story goes, in 1958 Ho Chi Minh moved to this simple but tastefully designed wooden house on stilts, which served as his living quarters and work space until his death in 1969. An elegant but spare study—some books, his small typewriter, a few newspapers, and an electric fan presented to him by a group of Japanese communists are visible—adjoins his equally spare bedroom. Downstairs he received his guests: foreign dignitaries, Politburo members, army cadres, and schoolchildren. The well-manicured gardens surrounding the house are home to flame trees, willows, mango trees, and the aromatic milkweed. Cyprus trees thrive on the edge of the pond, which Ho had stocked with carp. A crisp clap of the hands apparently still brings the fish to the surface.

Regardless of Ho Chi Minh's faith in the accuracy of the city's anti-aircraft gunners, some doubt must be thrown on the claim that Ho Chi Minh spent so much time in this open-air sanctum, with only the various trees, his wooden house, and a trusty old war helmet as protection. American bombers targeted Hanoi during the war, and they surely would have emptied their loads on Ba Dinh District had they known their archenemy was feeding fish and conferring with his generals in the unprotected confines of his stilt house. Indeed, Ho's Politburo ordered the construction of a nearby bomb shelter, later dubbed House No. 67. Legend holds that Uncle Ho refused to use the shelter as a home, preferring to confer with the Politburo in this fortified bunker but to sleep in his stilt house.

Before visiting Ho's residence, wait for the rest of the group that accompanied you through the mausoleum to go on ahead; it's much more enjoyable to walk through the jasmine-scented compound unhurried and without the inevitable chatter of other tourists. You may want to purchase a 20,000d booklet entitled *The Living Quarters and Working Place of President Ho Chi Minh,* available at the entrance gate to the house. Although overwrought, it's actually quite informative.

The area around Ho's house is serene; linger by the carp-filled pond lined with blossoming flame and cypress trees and take in the strains of traditional music often played here during the day. You'll exit this area via a pebbled pathway to the south of the mausoleum. As if they were themselves sights on the tour, older Vietnamese intellectuals wearing bifocals and striped cotton pajamas sit on park benches and read the Communist Party mouthpiece, *Nhan Dan (The People)*, or sip green tea and smoke cigarettes. ⊠ *Hung Vuong St., Ba Dinh District.* 🖃 *3,000d.* ⊙ *Daily 7:30–11 and 1:30–4.*

OFF THE
BEATEN PATH

THE MUSEUM OF ETHNOLOGY – The museum recounts the history and traditions of Vietnam's numerous ethnic minorities and the Kinh majority. You'll need to hire a taxi or rent a car to get to the museum, which is about 8 km (5 mi) west of the city center. ⊠ *Dich Vong St., Cau Giay,* ☎ *04/836–0350.* 🖃 *10,000d.* ⊙ *Tues.–Sun. 8:30–5:30.*

㉑ **One-Pillar Pagoda** (Chua Mot Cot). The French destroyed this temple, once known as Lien Hoa Tower but now exclusively referred to as One-Pillar Pagoda, on their way out in 1954. It was reconstructed by the new government and still commemorates the legend of Emperor Ly Thai Tong. It is said that the childless emperor dreamed that Quan Am, the Buddhist goddess of mercy and compassion, seated on a lotus flower, handed him a baby boy. Sure enough, he soon met and married a peasant woman who bore him a male heir, and in 1049 he constructed this monument in appreciation. The distinctive single pillar is meant to represent the stalk of the lotus flower, a sacred Vietnamese symbol of purity. The pillar was originally a single large tree trunk; today it's made of more durable cement. The tiny 10-square-ft pagoda is covered by an ornate curved roof and rises out of a square pond. Steps leading to the pagoda from the south side of the pond are usually blocked off, but if there aren't too many people around, a monk may invite you into this miniature prayer room.

Just a few yards from the One-Pillar Pagoda is **Dien Huu Pagoda,** a delightful but often-overlooked temple enclosing a bonsai-filled courtyard. A tall and colorful gate opens out onto the path leading to the Ho Chi Minh Museum, but the entrance is opposite the steps to the One-Pillar Pagoda. ⊠ *Ong Ich Kiem St., Ba Dinh District.* 🖃 *Free.* ⊙ *Daily 7–5:30.*

⑲ **Presidential Palace** (Phu Chu Tich). This imposing three-story palace just north of the Ho Chi Minh Mausoleum testifies to France's dedication to architectural elegance in Indochina. Constructed from 1900 to 1906, the bright, mustard-yellow building served as the living and working quarters of Indochina's governors-general. When Ho Chi Minh returned to Hanoi after the defeat of the French in 1954, he refused to live in the palace itself but chose the more modest quarters of the palace electrician. He did, however, offer use of the palace to distinguished guests during their visits to the capital. Today the building is used for formal international receptions and other important government meetings. You can view the structure from the outside but cannot go into the palace. Surrounding the building are extensive gardens and orchards, as well as the famed Mango Alley, the 300-ft pathway from the palace to Ho Chi Minh's stilt house (☞ *above*). ⊠ *Hung Vuong St. and Hoang Van Thu St., Ba Dinh District.*

★ ㉕ **Temple of Literature** (Van Mieu). An unusually well-preserved example of Vietnamese architecture, this monument to Confucius was built
in 1070 by Emperor Ly Thanh Tong and is widely considered the most
important historic site in the Dong Da District of Hanoi. Soon after
its construction, it became the site of Vietnam's first university, Quoc
Tu Giam, which specialized in training students—many of them sons
and daughters of emperors and other high-ranking dignitaries—to
pass the rigorous examinations for government and civil service posts.
The achievements of several centuries of the university's doctoral re-
cipients are recorded on 82 stelae (stone slabs), which rest on stone
tortoises. The oldest of these, the Dai Bao Stela, dates to 1442. It was-
n't until 1802 that Emperor Gia Long moved his capital and the national university to Hue. The French later used the building as,
appropriately, their school of civil administration, dubbing it the Temple of the Crows because of the birds that tended to gather here.

Van Mieu is divided into five courtyards. The first two, now bare of
buildings, used to house the wooden hostels and dormitories for students. A central walkway once reserved for the king runs down the
center of these open sections between two square lotus-flower ponds.
Separating these courtyards from the middle section of the compound
is an elaborate two-story gate, the second floor of which is called the
Poet's Balcony. University examinations eventually came to include poetry competitions, introduced by Emperor Le Loi, and poetry readings
still take place from this balcony on special occasions—as do concerts
of traditional and classical music. The gate opens onto a large square
fish pond, which is bracketed on either side with the stone stelae.
Through an ancient wooden doorway is the fourth area, containing
the temple dedicated to Confucius and his disciples. On the far side of
this temple is the site of what was the Van Mieu Library, destroyed by
bombing raids in 1954.

If you come before 3:20, there is a water-puppet show that's worth
seeing. Traditional music plays throughout the day. Several stalls sell
books, temple trinkets, and ethnic minority handicrafts. At press time
restoration was underway for the library, lecture halls, and a small museum. ⊠ *Quoc Tu Giam St., Ba Dinh District,* ☎ *04/845–2917 or 04/*
823–5601. 🔁 *12,000d; 20,000d for an English-speaking guide.* ☉ *Summer, daily 7:30–6; winter, daily 8–5.*

West Lake

About 3 km (2 mi)—10 minutes by taxi or motorbike—northwest of
Hoan Kiem Lake is West Lake (Ho Tay), a body of water that's steeped
in legend. It is said a giant golden calf from China followed the peal
of a monk's bronze bell to this spot. When the ringing stopped, the calf
lost its direction and kept walking in circles, creating the basin of West
Lake. Like Hoan Kiem's tortoise, the calf is said to still dwell in the lake.
If so, it likely feeds on the snails that are considered a local delicacy.

West Lake's wealth of history takes a more tangible form in the temples and war memorials that line its shores. Development is changing
the face of the shore, however, as luxury hotels and high-rent villas eat
away at the land of traditional flower villages like Nghi Tam, where
wealthy expatriates seclude themselves behind walls of bougainvillea.

The lake itself is a weekend boating spot for Vietnamese families,
which paddle around the murky waters in boats shaped like ducks and
dragons, or in the relatively new rubber dinghies for rent on Than
Nien Street. Afterward they stop in one of the floating restaurants for
snails boiled in lemon leaves or *banh tom* (deep-fried shrimp cakes

You can also rent boat houses made of bamboo for an afternoon of fishing (although eating what you catch is not recommended). A major new attraction is the West Lake Sports and Culture Club water park.

Numbers in the text correspond to numbers in the margin and on the Around Ho Chi Minh's Mausoleum and West Lake map.

A Good Walk

Start your walk at the beginning of the wide causeway of Thanh Nien Street that divides West Lake from the smaller Truc Bach Lake, created when fishermen closed off the southeast section of West Lake. Thanh Nien means "youth"; the causeway was so named in honor of the young "volunteers" who helped build this roadway between the two lakes. Along the way note the floating seafood restaurants and the neon signs of the times—billboards for beer and computers. At the very beginning of Thanh Nien duck into ornate **Quan Thanh Temple** ㉖. Sidewalk vendors in front will offer you incense and flowers. This is a marvelous spot to take a rest and soak up the atmosphere; try to ignore the street noise beyond the walls.

Staying on the same side of the street, walk for about five minutes to reach an unnamed **War Memorial** ㉗ to antiaircraft gunners stationed on the roof of a nearby factory who shot down 10 American planes in 1967. Walk about 650 ft, then cross the street to Hanoi's oldest pagoda, the delightful **Tran Quoc Pagoda** ㉘, on an islet jutting into West Lake. The West Lake side of the causeway is often crowded with picnicking students, many of whom may make attempts at communicating in English with you. (The Truc Bach Lake side is more of a lovers' lane in the evenings, with couples nuzzling on motorbikes or benches.) From the pagoda it's a 10- to 15-minute walk back to the beginning of Thanh Nien Street, where you will find a small flower garden (*vuon hoa*) bearing the name of Ly Tu Trong, a revolutionary martyr whose white-plaster statue faces the Presidential Palace to the south. Older women gather here to exercise and perform tai chi, while the busy park across the street plays host to badminton games.

If you're up for walking back into the center of town from here, or at least want to walk part of the way before getting a cyclo or taxi, then head east along the beautiful and shaded **Phan Dinh Phung Street** ㉙. The street ends about 1 km (½ mi) from the edge of West Lake, near a rectangular park and Hanoi's own version of the Leaning Tower of Pisa: the old water tower and critical military fortification built by the French. This is the northern edge of the Old Quarter, and cyclos are everywhere. Some taxis should be waiting near the Galaxy Hotel, to the right of the park.

TIMING

The causeway can be traversed in about 20 minutes, but allow for an hour or more if you want to peek around the temples. Allow 90 minutes if you want to rent a paddleboat from the quay on the Truc Bach side. The walk along Phan Dinh Phung Street to the water tower is another 15 to 25 minutes.

Sights to See

㉙ **Phan Dinh Phung Street.** This beautiful shaded avenue leads past sprawling French villas and Chinese mandarin mansions (many occupied by long-serving party members) as well as the gracious but seldom-used **Gothic North Door Cathedral** (Cua Bac), at the corner of Phan Dinh Phung and Hang Bieu streets. The large wheel of stained glass at the cathedral is reminiscent of Renaissance-era artwork in Europe and is enchanting from the inside; try the large front doors or ask around for a caretaker to let you in. On the right side of the street are

the tall ramparts of the **citadel,** the military compound that once protected the Imperial Palace of Thang Long. In a surprising move, army
officials in 1999 opened to the public a road that runs straight through
the once-secretive space.

㉖ Quan Thanh Temple (Chua Quan Thanh or Chan Vu Quan). A 4-ton,
13-ft-tall black bronze statue of the Taoist god Tran Vu is housed here.
Built by King Ly Thai To in the 11th century, this much-made-over temple was once known as the Temple of the Grand Buddha. An important collection of 17th-century poems can be seen in the shrine room.
Above the ornamented main gate is a 1677 replica of the bronze bell
that supposedly lured the West Lake's legendary golden calf from
China. Huge trees drape over the courtyard, keeping the temple and
its environs cool and somewhat dark, even in midday. On your way
out note that the rock formation in the goldfish pond hosts a number
of very loud cicadas. A pair of brightly painted plaster tigers protects
the entrance. ⊠ *Quan Thanh and Thanh Nien Sts., Ba Dinh District,*
☎ *04/823–4378.* ▱ *5,000d donation.* ☉ *Daily 8–4:30.*

㉘ Tran Quoc Pagoda (Chua Tran Quoc). Hanoi's oldest temple dates from
the 6th century, when King Ly Nam De had a pagoda, named Khai
Quoc, built on the bank of the Red River. More than a thousand years
later excessive erosion of the riverbank caused King Le Kinh Tong to
move the pagoda to Goldfish Islet (Ca Vang) on West Lake, and a sub-
sequent Le king renamed it Tran Quoc. This modest temple is noted
for its stela dating from 1639, which recounts the history of the pagoda
and its move from the Red River, and the lovely brick stupa adjacent
to the main temple. Tran Quoc is an active monastery where resident
monks in brown robes hold daily services. Architecturally distinct
from other Hanoi pagodas, Tran Quoc maintains a visitors hall in front
and various statues, including a gilded wooden depiction of Shakya-
muni Buddha. In the main courtyard is a giant pink-and-green planter
holding a bodhi tree, purportedly a cutting from the original bodhi tree
beneath which the Buddha reached his enlightenment. The bodhi was
a gift from the president of India, who visited the pagoda in 1959. The
Vietnamese government recognized the site as a national historic relic
in 1989. It is a popular spot for Vietnamese tourists and Hanoi couples, and street vendors and photographers gather here to cash in on
the business. ⊠ *Thanh Nien St., Tay Ho District.* ▱ *5,000d donation.*
☉ *Daily 8–4:30.*

㉗ War Memorial. If you're interested in Vietnam War history, head for
this small memorial between West Lake and Truc Bach Lake; it marks
the capture of one of the war's most famous POWs. On October 26,
1967, Navy lieutenant commander John McCain's jet fighter was shot
down, sending him parachuting into Truc Bach Lake. Suffering from
badly broken bones and severe beatings, he was imprisoned in the "Hanoi
Hilton" and other North Vietnamese prisons for more than five years.
He went on to become an Arizona senator and a vocal advocate of rec-
onciliation between the United States and his former captors. In 1997
he traveled to Hanoi to meet the old man who allegedly plucked him
from the lake and near-certain death. McCain's bid for the Republi-
can nomination in the 2000 presidential race sparked renewed interest in the man among Hanoi's intelligentsia, not to mention a flurry
of activity at the lake itself when McCain made a return visit in April
2000, just ahead of the 25th anniversary of the end of the Vietnam War.
The red-sandstone memorial features a bound and suspended prisoner
with his head hanging low and the letters U.S.A.F. (the memorial is in-
correctly labeled, as McCain belonged to the Navy and not the Air Force).
⊠ *Thanh Nien St., Ba Dinh District.*

West Lake Sports and Culture Club. Still under construction at press time, this large complex will have three parts when complete: a water park, a sports club, and an amusement park with roller coasters and a Ferris wheel offering a charming nighttime panorama of the lake and city. The water park, opened in May 2000, has giant water slides, a wave pool, a children's pool, and more. ✉ *614 Lac Long Quan St., Tay Ho District,* ☎ *04/753–2753.* 🎫 *50,000d.* ☼ *Daily 9–9.*

DINING

Most of Hanoi's international restaurants are found in the Hoan Kiem District, as are many places serving Vietnamese cuisine. Local specialties, such as *banh cuon* (a rice pancake with savory stuffing) and *mi xao* (Chinese egg noodles), can be found on Ngo Cam Chi Street (off Hang Bong Street) in the Old Quarter. Goat meat is the specialty of Lang Ha Street, south of the U.S. embassy, and dog meat (if you're really an adventurous eater) is served in restaurants on Nghi Tam Road between West Lake and the Red River.

Tong Duy Tan Street, where the king's food was cooked in ancient times, and the junction of Dien Bien Phu and Hang Bong streets are busy with noodle shops serving seafood dishes and *ga tan,* a chicken soup cooked with eight Chinese herbs, including lotus seed; it is considered especially good for women's health. Men may want to try *pin tan,* the same soup made with bull parts, instead, for the same effect. Toasted bread soaked in honey is served with the soup—you are charged by the slice. Make sure to avoid dishes with "scallops"; they are actually tough, bitter periwinkles. Eat upstairs at the restaurants in this area for a better view of the street.

Another excellent food street, known as "Xoi Alley," tees off Tong Duy Tan Street toward Trang Thi Street. *Xoi,* or sticky rice, is a glutinous grain served with sausage, boiled egg, dried shredded pork, or cucumbers and fish sauce. Here you can find sticky rice, fried noodles, or pho any time of day and late into the night. The "fast food" advertised in café windows actually means cheap rice, omelets, and noodle dishes.

Keep in mind that Hanoi's dining scene is in constant flux. Although the establishments listed below have staying power, it is recommended that you call before heading out to a particular restaurant, as places may close as suddenly as they open. In addition, it's not uncommon for owners and managers to change, transforming the whole restaurant for better or worse.

Hoan Kiem District

American
$$ ✕ **Red Onion Bistro.** Hanoi's most gregarious chef, American Bobby Chin, dishes up California-style cuisine on the fourth floor of a newly built office and residential tower. Favorites include pan-fried tuna with wasabi mashed potatoes, nachos, and a tray of Mediterranean appetizers. Homesick cowboys will appreciate Bobby's meat loaf as well as the Red Onion's generic, could-be-anywhere-on-earth decor, complete with large booths and a pool table. The attached bar, Fat Jax, stays open past midnight—late by Hanoi standards. ✉ *4th floor, Somerset Grand Hanoi, 49 Hai Ba Trung St., Hoan Kiem District,* ☎ *04/934–2342. AE, MC, V.*

Cafés
$$ ✕ **Au Lac Café.** On a sunny day this outdoor café across the street from the Metropole Hotel is the best lunch or breakfast spot in town. Cap-

Hanoi Dining and Lodging

(Hoy Tay)

Dining

Al Fresco	**27**
Au Lac Café	**32**
Bangkok-Hanoi	**12**
Brother's Cafe	**3**
Café des Arts	**22**
Cafe Que Huong	**37**
Café 252	**5**
Cha Ca La Vong	**24**
Che Thap Cam Cu	**10**
Chilli	**29**
Dac Kim Bun Cha	**21**
La Dolce Vita	**23**
Edo	**1**
Emperor Restaurant	**36**
Fanny's Ice Cream	**15**
Hoa Sua	**11**
Hue Restaurant	**35**
Il Grillo	**8**
Il Padrino	**16**
Khazana	**26**
Ky Y	**38**
Luna D'Autunno	**4**
Mediterraneo	**17**
Moca Café	**20**
Nam Phuong	**31**
Nha Hang Gio Moi	**7**
129 Mai Hac De	**30**
Press Club	**33**
Red Onion Bistro	**13**
Restaurant Benkay	**6**
Saigon Sakura	**14**
La Salsa	**18**
Seasons of Hanoi	**2**
Soho	**28**
Tandoor	**25**
Van Anh Thai Food	**19**
Vegetarian Restaurant	**9**
The Verandah	**34**

Lodging

Camellia II Hotel	**18**
Chains First Eden	**21**
Dan Chu Hotel	**24**
Dragon Hotel	**6**
Eden Hotel	**11**
Galaxy Hotel	**22**
Green Park Hotel	**9**
Guoman Hotel	**13**
Hanoi Club	**4**
Hanoi Daewoo	**1**
Hanoi Horison	**2**
Hilton Hanoi Opera	**26**
Ho Tay Villas	**3**
Hoa Binh Hotel	**23**
Hotel Nikko Hanoi	**8**
Lavender Hotel	**16**
Melia Hanoi	**10**
Meritus Westlake	**5**
Metropole Hotel Sofitel	**25**
Phan Thai Hotel	**20**
Planet Hotel	**7**
Prince Hotel	**12**
Saigon Hotel	**14**
Thuy Nga Hotel	**15**
Vinh Quang Hotel	**19**
Win Hotel	**17**

Thuy Khue

Hoang Hoa Tham

Bach Thao Botanical Garden

BA DINH DISTRICT

Phan Dinh Phung

Dang Dung

Quan Tha...

The Citadel

Presidential Palace

Ho Chi Minh Mausoleum

Ba Dinh Square

Nguyen Lam

Nguyen Lam

Hoang Dieu

Nguyen Tri Phuong

Ngoc Ha

Ho Chi Minh's Museum

One Pillar Pagoda

Dien Bien Phu

Le Hong Phong

Army Museum

Kim Ma

Museum of Fine Arts

Chi Lang Park

Tran Ph...

Trinh Hoai Duc

Cat Linh

Nguyen Thai Hoc

Nguyen Khuyen

Tong Duy

Temple of Literature

Quoc Tu Giam

Tran Quy Cap

GIANG VO

HAO NAM

Hang Bot

Hanoi Railway Station

Le Duan

Cultur...

La Thanh

Nam Dong

La Thanh

Kham Thien

Cho Kham Thien

THO QUAN

TRUNG PHUNG

Phan Bội...

DONG DA DISTRICT

Le Duan

Ba...

HANOI
OLD QUARTER

Hoan
Kiem
Lake

Hoa Lo
Prison
(Hanoi
Hilton)

HOAN KIEM DISTRICT

Indira
Gandhi
Park

Museum
of the
Revolution

Museum
of History

Opera
House

Thien
Quang
Lake

Hong River

Long Bien Bridge

Chuong Duong Bridge

Hoe Nhai
Yan Phu
Hang Dau
Gam Cau
Hang Khoai
H. Giay
Phung Hung
Hang Cot
Hang Ga
H. Luoc
D. Xuan
Cha Ca
Hang Ma
H. Vai
P. Lan Ong
H. Can.
Bat Dan
Hang Bo
H. Non
Hang Gai
Hang Bong
ng Thi
Hang Chieu
Hang Giay
H. Buom
Luong Ngoc Quyen
Hang Bac
Hang Mam
Hang Dao
Hang Bo
Luong V. Can
Cau Ga
Hang Trung
Le Thai To
Dinh Tien Hoang
Hang Thung
Lo Su
Tran Nguyet Han
Trang Tien
Hai Ba Trung
Ngo Quyen
Ly Thai To
Tran Quang Khai
Bach Dang
Hang Bong
Ba Trieu
Ly Thuong Kiet
Tran Hung Dao
Hang Bai
Pho Phan Chu Trinh
Le Thanh Tong
Tran Quoc Toan
Quang Trung
Ba Trieu
Nguyen Du
Tran Xuan Soan
Hang Chuoi
Tran Thanh Tong
Nguyen Khoai
Hoa Ma
Hue
Nguyen Cong Tru
To Hien Thanh
Doan Tran Nghiep
Tinh
n Tong
Phuc Tan
Tran Nhat Duat
Minh Khai

KEY
① Hotels
● Restaurants

0   400 yards
0   400 meters

puccinos, pastas, tasty salads, and even bagels are served on an outdoor terrace. Don't confuse it with the look-alike next door, Diva
Café. ⊠ *57 Ly Thai To St., Hoan Kiem District,* ☎ *04/825–7807. No
credit cards.*

$$ ✕ **Moca Café.** Thanks to this two-story café, the street facing St.
Joseph's Cathedral is infused with the smell of roasting coffee beans.
An airy interior, good coffee, and a huge menu of Western, Vietnamese,
and Indian dishes keep this café packed. Your best bet is the Indian
food. ⊠ *14–16 Nha Tho St., Hoan Kiem District,* ☎ *04/825–6334.
MC, V.*

¢ ✕ **Café 252.** This is the famous breakfast spot where Catherine Deneuve
hung out while filming *Indochine.* It's strictly no-frills but serves good
pastries and the best yogurt in town. ⊠ *252 Hang Bong St., Hoan Kiem
District,* ☎ *04/825–0216. No credit cards.*

¢ ✕ **Che Thap Cam Cu.** This hole-in-the-wall serves only one thing, *che*—
a sweet green bean concoction that is part drink, part pudding. Espe-
cially popular with Vietnamese women, che is a typical treat on sultry
summer afternoons. A number of imitators have sprung up following
the success of this old Hanoi institution. Walk to the end of the alley
and look for the shop on your left. ⊠ *72G Tran Hung Dao St., Hoan
Kiem District,* ☎ *04/824–5642. No credit cards.*

¢ ✕ **Fanny's Ice Cream.** Set across the street from Hoan Kiem Lake, this
charming, French-managed café dishes up the best ice cream in town.
The offerings, all made with natural ingredients and no preservatives,
include unique local flavors like young rice or tamarind, along with
old favorites such as coffee, rum raisin, and coconut. Try the refresh-
ing lemon or, if you're determined to sin, a double scoop of raspberry
and dark, wickedly rich chocolate. ⊠ *48 Le Thai To St., Hoan Kiem
District,* ☎ *04/828–5656. No credit cards.*

Eclectic

$$ ✕ **Al Fresco.** This colorful south-of-the-border-cum-pizza restaurant-
bar a block south of Hoan Kiem Lake gets high marks from expats
and travelers. Run by a friendly Aussie and a Canadian, the eclectic
East-meets-West dining is coupled with a casual open-air ambience. The
Mexican rolls, filled with avocado and chicken, are highly recommended. Al Fresco's may be the most popular foreign restaurant in Hanoi
because of its jumbo portions of ribs, pasta, T-bone steak, Mexican
salad, and pizza. ⊠ *23L Hai Ba Trung St., Hoan Kiem District,* ☎ *04/
826–7782. No credit cards.*

$$ ✕ **The Verandah.** This restaurant, straight out of a George Orwell novel,
seems a bit past its prime, but remains a pleasant spot for a lazy brunch
or late-afternoon drink. Create your own breakfast, picking from all
sorts of greasy British favorites such as baked beans, or sausages and
fried tomatoes, or opt for one of the more healthful Greek or smoked-
salmon salads. Housed in a villa near the center of town, this eatery
has attentive staff, high ceilings, and minimal but elegant decor. The
namesake verandah provides for breezy al fresco dining. ⊠ *Nguyen
Khac Can St., Hoan Kiem District,* ☎ *04/825–7220. AE, MC, V.*

French

$$ ✕ **Café des Arts de Hanoi.** Run by an amiable Frenchman, this cozy
★ restaurant is popular with Hanoi's French expatriates. Terra-cotta
floors, wooden tables, and regularly changing exhibits of paintings by
local artists give the place a homey feel. At night the long wooden bar
is a fine place to stop for a drink. The menu features such typical French
fare as *croque monsieur* (ham and cheese sandwich dipped in egg and
sautéed in butter), beefsteak with fries, and a delicious pastis-flavored
shrimp dish. The eggplant Parmesan is a good vegetarian option. ⊠ *11
Bao Khanh La., Hoan Kiem District,* ☎ *04/828–720. AE, MC, V.*

$$ ✕ **Hoa Sua.** Walk through a front courtyard off the street to find a quiet
★ terra-cotta terrace, shaded by umbrellas and palms. More than a
restaurant, Hoa Sua is a humanitarian project: young people in need
of assistance are trained as waiters and cooks. The latter project seems
to have turned out better than the former, as service can be erratic. But
the food—both French and Vietnamese—is decent. Try the goat cheese
on toast, the avocado salad, or the vegetable terrine (skip the chicken);
save room for the fruit crumble or chocolate mousse. It's best to re-
serve a table for lunch on the terrace, or head into the air-conditioned
interior, also charmingly decorated with wrought-iron furniture. The
adjoining pastry shop has a mouthwatering selection of breads, cakes,
and pastries for takeout. ⊠ *81 Tho Nhuom St., Hoan Kiem District,*
☎ *04/824–0448. No credit cards.*

Indian

$$ ✕ **Khazana.** This restaurant in the center of town is an opulent trib-
★ ute to North Indian cuisine. Indian art and music add color to the el-
egant dining room, but it is manager Shankar Dutta's eye for detail
that has earned this place its excellent reputation. For example, Khazana offers rock sugar and aniseed instead of after-dinner mints. The
tandoori chicken is outstanding, while the mutton dishes—actually made
with goat meat (the traditional Indian recipes use mutton)—melt in your
mouth. For vegetarian options, try the *malai kofta* (sweet, deep-fried,
gravy-covered cottage cheese balls filled with nuts) or the *baghar-e-baigan*
(baby eggplant in a mildly spiced coconut gravy). The slightly higher-
than-average prices are justified both by the quality and quantity of
food; the set lunches are an excellent value. ⊠ *41B Ly Thai To St.,*
Hoan Kiem District, ☎ *04/824–1166. MC, V. No lunch Sun.*

$ ✕ **Tandoor.** This small Indian restaurant in the Thuy Loi minihotel
makes up for its lack of ambience with a wonderful yet inexpensive menu.
Food is prepared fresh, with hand-ground spices. You can't go wrong
with anything here, but fluffy garlic nan bread, tender chicken *masala,*
and eggplant curry are particularly good. The fish *tikka* in red sauce and
the chicken kebab marinated in yogurt are also sensational. Service is very
friendly, although it can become chaotic at dinnertime. They also deliver.
⊠ *24 Hang Be St., Hoan Kiem District,* ☎ *04/824–5359. MC, V.*

Italian

$$ ✕ **Il Padrino Wine Bar and Delicatessen.** This peppy, Italian-run eatery
is a pleasant spot to cool down and fuel up. Floor-to-ceiling windows
face Hoan Kiem Lake. After having an espresso brewed on the Rizen-
erazione machine, you may feel up to seeing all of Hanoi's sights in a
day. The iced coffee, yogurt, good-size sandwiches, tasty pasta carbonara,
and midnight closing time may keep you coming back. ⊠ *42 Le Thai*
To St., Hoan Kiem District, ☎ *04/828–8449. AE, V.*

$$ ✕ **La Dolce Vita Bat Dan Cafe.** Best known for its sweet and savory
crepes, this Italian-run eatery also has hearty pastas and a warm, wel-
coming atmosphere. If you're really hungry, try the filling cheese-
slathered lasagna. Open late, this café, which offers patrons the use of
various board games and chess sets, is also a good place to go for a
drink. ⊠ *10 Bat Dan St., Hoan Kiem District,* ☎ *04/828–6411. AE,*
MC, V.

$$ ✕ **Mediterraneo.** Delicious, reasonably priced Italian food is served in
the bright, California-like atmosphere of this central eatery. Along
with the best *bruschetta* (toasted bread with olive oil and various top-
pings) in town, the Italian hosts serve excellent cappuccinos, thin-
crust pizzas cooked in a wood-burning oven, and an interesting array
of homemade grappas—try licorice or peach. ⊠ *23 Nha Tho St.,*
Hoan Kiem District, ☎ *04/826–6288. MC, V.*

Japanese

$$$ ✕ **Saigon Sakura.** Frequented by expats, this take-off-your-shoes Japanese restaurant has clean Zen decor and good-value fixed-price lunches. Try the excellent calamari with vinegar marinade or the unbeatable $15 sushi deal. Service is enthusiastic—staff members yell a traditional Japanese greeting to approaching customers. The sushi bar is a nice option if you're dining alone. ✉ *17 Trang Thi St., Hoan Kiem District,* ☎ *04/825–7565. MC, V.*

Mediterranean

$$$$ ✕ **Press Club, The Dining Room.** Modern Mediterranean cuisine and
★   fine wines are served at this elegant restaurant evoking the 1930s. Eat inside in the tasteful, wood-paneled dining room or outside on the terrace surrounded by palms. International managers and chefs, including visiting chefs from many of the region's finest hotels, ensure consistently excellent food and service. The pepper squid is a refreshing appetizer, as is the marinated seafood. For dessert try homemade ice cream or a juicy apple tart. In late 1999 a poll among Hanoi residents by *The Guide*, a local arts and leisure magazine, found that the Press Club won hands down in the "fine dining" category. ✉ *59A Ly Thai To St., Hoan Kiem District,* ☎ *04/934–0888. AE, D, MC, V.*

Spanish

$$ ✕ **La Salsa Tapas Bar and Restaurant.** A Canadian and Frenchman run Hanoi's latest Friday-night hot spot. Nibble on small servings of seviche, zesty meatballs, and marinated mushrooms, or choose an entrée of warm duck salad, pan-fried salmon, or lamb tenderloin. If you're not in the mood to see and be seen, avoid the cozy downstairs bar and hide out in the quieter upstairs dining room. To wash down your meal, try some of La Salsa's Spanish wines or the house sangria, which is made according to a secret family recipe. ✉ *25 Nha Tho St., Hoan Kiem District,* ☎ *04/828–9052. AE, MC, V.*

Thai

$ ✕ **Bangkok-Hanoi.** The Bangkok-Hanoi feels authentic: the chef is from Thailand, Thai decorations and music fill the little eatery, and you'll even find ice-cold Singha beer. The spicy salads are excellent. For dessert try a dish of sweet taro or pumpkin in coconut milk. The 40,000d set lunches make this a popular afternoon-dining spot. ✉ *52A Ly Thuong Kiet St., Hoan Kiem District,* ☎ *04/934–5598. No credit cards.*

¢ ✕ **Van Anh Thai Food.** Although there's no decor to speak of, this small restaurant has gained a cult following among Hanoi's expats. Run by a Thai man, Wijit Lekkhumpoon, and his Vietnamese wife, Van Anh, this spick-and-span eatery offers incredibly cheap Thai delights such as spicy seafood soup, leaf-wrapped chicken, fried fish cakes, and spicy papaya salad. It's very clean and, thanks to all the fluorescent lights, very bright. ✉ *5A Tong Duy Tan St., Hoan Kiem District,* ☎ *04/928–5163. No credit cards.*

Vegetarian

$$ ✕ **Vegetarian Restaurant Com Chay Nang Tam.** An unusual array of vegetarian dishes, many prepared to resemble meat, are served in a dimly lighted villa. The warm corn squares are a pleasing starter, and the "ginger fish," made of tofu, is a good main course. The restaurant fills up so reservations are recommended, especially for larger parties. ✉ *79A Tran Hung Dao St., Hoan Kiem District,* ☎ *04/826–6140. No credit cards.*

Vietnamese

$$$ ✕ **Emperor Restaurant.** Located off the street in a renovated French villa, the Emperor provides arguably the most beautiful and romantic setting in all of Hanoi. Climb the curved wooden staircase and enter the elegant, high-ceiling Vietnamese-style dining room; downstairs the resident jazz band plays in the Emperor Pub (☞ Nightlife and the Arts, *below*). The food is as impressive as the decor, with plenty of seafood dishes and Hue specialties, including the delectable Hue spring rolls. ✉ *18B Le Thanh Tong St., Hoan Kiem District,* ☎ *04/826–8801. AE, MC, V.*

$$ ✕ **Cha Ca La Vong.** Right in the thick of the Old Quarter is Hanoi's most famous purveyor of *cha ca* (grilled boneless fish cubes marinated in dill and served with rice noodles and peanuts). Watch out: you cook cha ca at your table on a brazier that can send hot grease flying. (On a warm evening, you may feel as though you're being grilled along with the fish.) Portions are small, but that doesn't seem to dissuade the tourists who pack the upstairs restaurant. Fewer people sit downstairs. The grease-covered walls add to the authentic, pungent experience. ✉ *14 Cha Ca St., Hoan Kiem District,* ☎ *no phone. No credit cards.*

$$ ✕ **Nam Phuong.** Definitely aimed more at tourists than at a local clientele, this restaurant offers a good introduction to Vietnamese cuisine. Just bear in mind that portions of the tasty and beautifully presented dishes, such as beef in coconut milk, are disappointingly scanty. The ambience, on the other hand, is lovely, with musicians playing traditional Vietnamese instruments and waitstaff dressed in traditional outfits. The restaurant is housed in a nicely renovated French villa. ✉ *19 Phan Chu Trinh St., Hoan Kiem District,* ☎ *04/824–0926. AE, MC, V.*

$ ★ ✕ **Dac Kim Bun Cha.** After souvenir shopping on Hang Bac Street, consider having lunch at this four-story Old Quarter institution. The first floor is tiny and used for food preparation, but staff members will eagerly lead you up . . . and up . . . and up the winding tiled stairs until enough empty plastic stools can be found for your party. You may be planted cozily among other customers. Ordering shouldn't be hard: the restaurant offers only two dishes, and locals say both are tops: *bun cha* (grilled pork patties with rice noodles) are served with heaping plates of herbs and lettuce; as a side, try the huge pork- and crab-filled spring rolls. Wash both down with *bia lanh* (cold beer) or *che da* (iced Vietnamese tea). ✉ *1 Hang Manh St., Hoan Kiem District,* ☎ *no phone. No credit cards. No dinner.*

$ ★ ✕ **Hue Restaurant.** Come here for imperial Hue cuisine and other traditional Vietnamese fare in a rustic outdoor-indoor setting. Pork Pie is a poor translation for culinary nirvana—a some-assembly-required platter of sugarcane-wrapped ground pork that you roll with greens and vegetables in rice paper and dip into a delicious peanut sauce. For those who wince at this carnivorous frenzy, vegetarian delights are plentiful. If you are sensitive to MSG, beware: the chefs use it liberally. ✉ *6 Ly Thuong Kiet St., Hoan Kiem District,* ☎ *04/826–4062. No credit cards.*

Around Lenin Park

Cafés

¢ ✕ **129 Mai Hac De.** Both locals and visitors flock to this closet-size café to perch on knee-high stools and sip smooth, creamy fruit shakes. The basic café menu features pastries, baked potatoes, some rather mediocre rice and noodle dishes, and a selection of excellent grilled sandwiches. This is a fine place to stop for a snack and some much-needed caffeine after a tour of Lenin Park. ✉ *129 Mai Hac De St., Hai Ba Trung District,* ☎ *no phone. No credit cards.*

Chinese

$$ ✕ **Nha Hang Gio Moi.** The best part about this plain-looking restaurant is its lovely location overlooking a lake in Lenin Park. The Chinese and Vietnamese dishes are good, although not superb. Try the hot-and-sour soup, the chili prawns, or the sweet-and-sour chicken. Eat here if you're in the area, but don't make a special trip. ⊠ *63 Le Duan St., Lenin Park, Hai Ba Trung District,* ☎ *04/822–9839. No credit cards.*

Italian

$$$ ✕ **Il Grillo.** This very popular Italian-run eatery serves authentic prosciutto and grappas. The rib-eye steak is highly recommended, as are the homemade pasta dishes. Ask Luca, the proprietor, for the day's specials. The restaurant has cheerful, cozy decor—like a cabin in the Dolomites. It's the perfect place for a hearty meal and a well-earned beer after a day of sightseeing. Reservations are recommended, especially for Sunday night. ⊠ *116 Ba Trieu St., Hai Ba Trung District,* ☎ *04/822–7720. AE, MC, V.*

Japanese

$$$$ ✕ **Restaurant Benkay.** You'll find high standards, along with accompanying high prices, at this elegant hotel restaurant. The traditional Japanese decor is as elegantly understated as the service, and the food will transport you straight to Tokyo. Set lunches, such as breaded pork or chicken, start at just $7, although once here it's all too tempting to go for the five-course, $88 *kaiseki* menu of seafood specialties or the divine $60 sushi dinner. Be forewarned that portions are small. ⊠ *Hotel Nikko Hanoi, 84 Tran Nhan Tong St., Hai Ba Trung District,* ☎ *04/822–3535. AE, DC, MC, V.*

$$ ✕ **Ky Y.** The Japanese equivalent of your friendly neighborhood diner, this cozy restaurant is always packed with Japanese businesspeople. Astonishingly low prices encourage overindulgence in sushi or sashimi; the lunch specials are a steal at less than $6. Seating is at low, take-your-shoes-off tables or at a long polished bar. ⊠ *29 Phu Dong Thien Vuong St., Hai Ba Trung District,* ☎ *04/978–1386. AE, DC, V.*

Pan-Asian

$ ✕ **Chilli.** Terra-cotta tiles, cheery checked tablecloths, and bright-yellow walls tempt passersby into this simple little restaurant. Service is friendly, and the Singaporean chef dishes up some of the most reasonably priced Pan-Asian cuisine in town. Don't miss the chicken with chili and cashew nuts, or the pungent fish in black bean sauce. This is also a reliable option for delivery. ⊠ *53A Le Van Huu St., Hai Ba Trung District,* ☎ *04/943–2698. No credit cards.*

Vietnamese

$$ ✕ **Soho.** A sister restaurant of Seasons of Hanoi (☞ *below*), this establishment exudes the same aura of casual elegance. Set in a small but airy villa decorated with antiques and old black-and-white photographs, Soho offers seating at the bar, in an intimate upstairs dining room, or on a terrace. Although portions can be small, the food is superb, with such southern favorites as the delectable crab cakes. The duck spring rolls, a variation on traditional Vietnamese spring rolls, are a favorite here. Flambéed bananas are an exciting way to end the meal. A victim of its own success, this restaurant is occasionally invaded by tour groups; if you prefer peace and quiet, it's worth phoning to check. Come dark, the terrace is a fine place for a drink as it offers a view of Hanoi youngsters out cruising on Ba Trieu Street. Reservations are required for large parties. ⊠ *57 Ba Trieu St., Hai Ba Trung District,* ☎ *04/826–6555. AE, MC, V.*

$ ✕ **Cafe Que Huong.** Popular with both locals and foreigners, this relaxed restaurant serves typical Vietnamese fare in a villa with an attached courtyard. On warm summer nights sit at an outside table beneath a roof of thatched palm and order the excellent, tender fried squid; wash it down with a cold beer. Other good bets include the tofu with tomato sauce and the fried greens with garlic—guaranteed to keep Dracula away. ✉ *42 Tang Bat Ho St., Hai Ba Trung District,* ☎ *04/ 971–1444. No credit cards.*

Around the Ho Chi Minh Mausoleum/Ba Dinh District

Italian

$$$ ✕ **Luna D'Autunno.** Hanoi's newest Italian eatery offers covered outdoor seating on a terra-cotta terrace, as well as indoor tables. The layout feels a bit like a cafeteria, but the food is excellent. Try one of their fat sandwiches or the exquisite platter of marinated vegetables with feta cheese, or go all out with a four-cheese pizza. On Friday nights there's a jazz band, followed by live piano on Saturday evenings. Delivery is free. ✉ *11B Dien Bien Phu St., Ba Dinh District,* ☎ *04/823–7338. AE, MC, V.*

Japanese

$$$–$$$$ ✕ **Edo.** Located in the Hanoi Daewoo Hotel, this is one of Hanoi's better and more expensive restaurants. The grilled salmon is especially good, and, come noon, the $11 sushi lunch buffet lures in hordes of hungry businesspeople. ✉ *Hanoi Daewoo Hotel, 360 Kim Ma St., Ba Dinh District,* ☎ *04/831–5000. AE, MC, V.*

Vietnamese

$$ ✕ **Brother's Cafe.** Entering this beautiful restaurant is like stepping back in time. The front room, decorated with carved wooden beams and Buddha statues, is an old, tile-roof pagoda that backs onto a large, quiet courtyard. Outside, tables are shaded by potted palms and cooled by antique brass fans, and at night the courtyard is lighted by candles. With no à la carte menu, diners help themselves to a large buffet of hot and cold dishes, including lots of seafood, pork, and chicken, plus five kinds of Vietnamese salads. The $5 lunch buffet includes a glass of juice, whereas the $10 dinner buffet includes a glass of wine. ✉ *26 Nguyen Thai Hoc St., Ba Dinh District,* ☎ *04/733–3866. MC, V. No lunch Sun.*

Around West Lake

Vietnamese

$$ ✕ **Seasons of Hanoi.** In a beautifully restored villa dating from 1902,
★ Seasons is filled with antiques from Indochina. Young British expatriate Justin Wheatcroft has given his restaurant a classic feel, with French elegance meeting Vietnamese charm. The coconut and lemongrass chicken curry is a rich choice, and the fish baked in a clay pot is tasty but salty. Highly recommended are the soft-shell crab tempura and the divine eggplant in a clay pot. Sunday brunch is popular. ✉ *95B Quan Thanh St., Ba Dinh District,* ☎ *04/835–5444. AE, MC, V.*

LODGING

Never before have visitors to Hanoi had so many choices of places to stay. Whatever your budget, there's no longer any need to accept musty rooms and indifferent service. Hotels range from charming and idiosyncratic to some of the most luxurious in the region (although even the swankiest properties tend to have spotty service; managers are working hard to develop more professional staffs, but for the time being, it's a good idea to cultivate patience). The general character of hotels varies somewhat by district: Ba Dinh District and the shores of West Lake are home to larger and more upscale facilities. The central Hoan Kiem District has it all, with swank new business hotels, old state-run places, and hundreds of minihotels. Since a number of upscale international joint-venture hotels have opened in the past two years, increased competition has led to across-the-board price cuts. Not only can you get terrific deals at these high-end hotels, but even minihotels have been forced to renovate and slash prices. Many hotels suffer from low occupancy rates so be sure to ask about discounts.

Hoan Kiem District

$$$$ ⊞ **Metropole Hotel Sofitel.** The exquisitely renovated Metropole, built
★ by the French in the early 1900s, combines old-world European grandeur with modern convenience. And you can't beat the central location in the heart of Hanoi. The bar-side pool is a nice option on a sunny day or warm evening, and the lobby bar is a good bet any day of the week. You're better off going out for meals, however. The impeccably decorated rooms with French-style shuttered windows are luxurious, if not incredibly spacious. Just keep in mind that although this is an internationally managed hotel, service is not always up to par. ⊠ *15 Ngo Quyen St., Hoan Kiem District,* ☎ *04/826–6919,* 𝔽𝔸𝕏 *04/826– 6920. 244 rooms. 2 restaurants, 2 bars, air-conditioning, in-room safes, minibars, room service, pool, health club, dry cleaning, laundry service, concierge, business services, meeting rooms, travel services, airport shuttle, car rental. AE, DC, MC, V.*

$$$ ⊞ **Hilton Hanoi Opera.** So convincingly does the design of this hotel complement that of the nearby Opera House that many newcomers take it for an original French building. Sadly, this elegance gives way to an ostentatious lobby inside. The rooms, on the other hand, are both tasteful and comfortable. Within the hotel are a bakery, a fancy Chinese restaurant, and a French bistro that offers a massive if somewhat uninspired Sunday brunch. What really makes this hotel stand out, however, is its location. Where else can you relax in the swimming pool and look out at the Opera House? ⊠ *1 Le Thanh Tong St., Hoan Kiem District,* ☎ *04/933–0500,* 𝔽𝔸𝕏 *04/933–0530. 269 rooms. 3 restaurants, 2 bars, air-conditioning, in-room safes, minibars, room service, pool, health club, dry cleaning, laundry service, concierge, business services, meeting rooms. AE, D, MC, V.* 🐾

$$–$$$ ⊞ **Guoman Hotel.** Since opening in 1997, this well-run and centrally located hotel has become very popular with business travelers. The rooms are pleasant, and the service is efficient. The main restaurant, Café Paradise, has an American chef who turns out good and reasonably priced international fare. An outdoor café features nightly barbecues. ⊠ *83A Ly Thuong Kiet St., Hoan Kiem District,* ☎ *04/822–2800,* 𝔽𝔸𝕏 *04/822– 2822. 149 rooms. 3 restaurants, bar, air-conditioning, in-room safes, minibars, room service, health club, laundry services. AE, DC, MC, V.*

$$–$$$ ⊞ **Hoa Binh Hotel.** In a grand old building, the Hoa Binh is poised to accommodate an upscale crowd but seems to be lacking an experienced staff. The spacious rooms are clean and have high ceilings, but they betray sloppy renovations. However, the hotel is efficient, well maintained, and wins points for nostalgic charm. It also has a decent French restaurant and a massage service (with staff trained at the Institute of Traditional Medicine) that is one of the best deals in town at just 50,000₫ per hour. Ask about discount room rates for longer stays. ⊠ *27 L Thuong Kiet St., Hoan Kiem District,* ☎ *04/825–3315,* 𝔽𝔸𝕏 *04/826*

9818. 88 rooms. Restaurant, bar, air-conditioning, minibars, massage, sauna, dry cleaning, laundry service, business services, car rental. AE, MC, V.

$$–$$$ 🏨 **Melia Hanoi.** Although many of Hanoi's newly opened luxury hotels have low occupancy rates, this new, glitzy, 23-floor hotel tower is consistently busy. The secret? What it lacks in charm it makes up for in price. After discounts, guests receive top-notch facilities and service at minihotel prices. One restaurant serves international cuisine; the other specializes in Chinese and Thai food and hosts a popular nightly Thai dinner buffet. ✉ *44B Ly Thuong Kiet St., Hoan Kiem District,* ☎ *04/ 934–3343,* ℻ *04/934–3344. 308 rooms. 2 restaurants, air-conditioning, in-room safes, minibars, room service, pool, health club, dry cleaning, laundry service, concierge, business services, meeting rooms. AE, D, MC, V.*

$$ 🏨 **Chains First Eden Hotel.** Located in the Old Quarter, this hotel is an excellent point of departure for walking tours. You can start by checking out the chaos in the streets from the hotel's top-floor restaurant, which serves Vietnamese and Western fare. The rooms themselves have all the amenities, but unfortunately also have darkly oppressive furniture and curtains that may induce flashbacks to the 1970s. Deluxe rooms contain individual fax machines. All in all, although it was built in 1996, this hotel feels a bit faded. ✉ *3A Phan Dinh Phung St., Hoan Kiem District,* ☎ *04/828–3896,* ℻ *04/828–4066. 42 rooms. Restaurant, air-conditioning, minibars, laundry service, travel services. AE, DC, MC, V. CP.*

$$ 🏨 **Dan Chu Hotel.** Contrasted with the freshly painted exterior and shining new lobby, the rooms in this colonial-era hotel are disappointingly drab—some lack windows and all have frightful synthetic bedspreads. On the plus side, the rooms are spacious and have high ceilings. Furthermore, the location is great, and an airy, verdant backyard commands a certain serene elegance. ✉ *29 Trang Tien St., Hoan Kiem District,* ☎ *04/825–4937,* ℻ *04/826–6786. 56 rooms. Restaurant, bar, air-conditioning, minibars, room service, dry cleaning, laundry service, concierge, business services, travel services, car rental. AE, DC, MC, V.*

$$ 🏨 **Planet Hotel.** The Planet offers plush rooms and a great location in the Old Quarter overlooking West Lake. Wooden touches offset the ultraslick modern edge and the profusion of granite. ✉ *120 Quan Thanh St., Hoan Kiem District,* ☎ *04/843–5888,* ℻ *04/843–5088. 53 rooms. Restaurant, 2 bars, air-conditioning, in-room safes, minibars, refrigerators, room service, hot tub, sauna, health club, dry cleaning, laundry service, concierge, business services, travel services, car rental. AE, DC, MC, V.*

$$ 🏨 **Saigon Hotel.** A joint venture between Saigon Tourist (which manages the Rex Hotel in Ho Chi Minh City) and the Hanoi Railway Service, this property offers friendly service and, despite the concrete '60s architecture, a pleasant ambience. Rooms are standard. The rooftop garden is a terrific place for an evening drink; from here you can see the Hanoi Towers office complex, on the site of the former "Hanoi Hilton" prison. The hotel is not far from the train station, opposite the United Nations Vietnam headquarters, and near the Fansland Cinema, which sometimes shows movies in English. The professionally run restaurant serves Vietnamese, French, and American food. ✉ *80 Ly Thuong Kiet St., Hoan Kiem District,* ☎ *04/826–8499,* ℻ *04/826–6631. 44 rooms. Restaurant, 2 bars, air-conditioning, in-room safes, minibars, room service, massage, sauna, dry cleaning, laundry service, business services, meeting rooms, travel services, car rental. AE, D, MC, V.*

$–$$ ☆ 🏨 **Galaxy Hotel.** Built in 1918, this granite-face hotel has been fully renovated to accommodate business travelers and seems wholly modern. The comfortable rooms have typical hotel decor and are quieter than you'd suspect given the hotel's proximity to the bustling Old Quarter; some have garden views. ✉ *1 Phan Dinh Phung St., Hoan Kiem District,* ☎ *04/828–2888,* 𝔽𝔸𝕏 *04/828–2466. 60 rooms. 2 restaurants, bar, air-conditioning, in-room safes, minibars, room service, laundry service, dry cleaning, concierge, business services, meeting rooms, travel services, car rental. AE, DC, MC, V.*

$–$$ 🏨 **Thuy Nga Hotel.** Just a stone's throw from the central Hoan Kiem Lake, this upscale minihotel is a gem. Service is efficient and friendly, and the rooms are tastefully decorated with wooden furniture and plush carpeting. Some of the standard rooms lack windows so be sure to ask. It's worth splurging on the top-floor $70 VIP suite, which has a large terrace with a stunning view over the lake. ✉ *4 Ba Trieu St., Hoan Kiem District,* ☎ *04/934–1256,* 𝔽𝔸𝕏 *04/934–1262. 20 rooms. Restaurant, air-conditioning, in-room safes, minibars, laundry service. AE, DC, MC, V. CP.*

$ 🏨 **Prince Hotel** (Hoang Tu). This posh minihotel offers comfortable and elegant rooms, very nice bathrooms with tubs, and a very enthusiastic English-speaking staff. Balconies afford views that range from a peek at the beautiful Hai Ba Trung Pagoda to the havoc of apartments to the Somerset Grand Hanoi. Conveniently located near the train station, the Prince is also not too far from the city center. ✉ *96A Hai Ba Trung St., Hoan Kiem District,* ☎ *04/824–8314,* 𝔽𝔸𝕏 *04/824–8323. 20 rooms. Bar, air-conditioning, fans, minibars, dry cleaning, laundry service, car rental. AE, MC, V.*

¢–$ 🏨 **Phan Thai Hotel.** Modern minihotel conveniences, inoffensive decor, balconies, and a friendly staff make this a very decent accommodation. Conveniently located in the Old Quarter, it's near Hoan Kiem Lake on a candy-selling street. The top floors provide a fabulous view of Old Quarter roofs and the Long Binh train and bicycle bridge. Also upstairs is a family altar, featuring tiled dragons and a many-armed goddess. ✉ *44 Hang Giay St., Hoan Kiem District,* ☎ *04/824–3667,* 𝔽𝔸𝕏 *04/826–6677. 16 rooms. Restaurant, air-conditioning, minibars, laundry service, travel services, car rental. AE, DC, MC, V.*

¢–$ ☆ 🏨 **Win Hotel.** At the top end of the budget accommodations, the Win is immaculate and homey all at once. On a quiet street just off Le Thai To Street, it's also just a short skip from Hoan Kiem Lake. Floor-to-ceiling one-way windows let Hanoi in, or you can keep the light out with lace and red-velvet curtains. Carved hardwood furniture, tastefully arranged artificial flowers, high ceilings, clean baths, satellite television, and a fluffy dog in the lobby make you feel at home. An added bonus is its location next to Café Nhan, which is the size of a mansion and is famous for its avocado shakes and rocket-fuel coffee. ✉ *34 Hang Hanh St., Hoan Kiem District,* ☎ *04/828–7371 or 04/828–7150,* 𝔽𝔸𝕏 *04/824–7448. 8 rooms. Air-conditioning, fans, minibars, laundry service, travel services, car rental. MC, V.*

¢ 🏨 **Camellia II Hotel.** This well-run, well-maintained minihotel, located near Hang Da Market in the thick of the Old Quarter, has clean, bright rooms and a friendly staff. There's a glossy feel to everything here—shiny new bathrooms, lots of glazed wood, and an abundance of satin. Although the hotel is not exactly tasteful, given the price, it's hard to quibble. The $25 rooms are slightly larger, but offer no real advantage over the $20 ones. ✉ *31 Hang Dieu St., Hoan Kiem District,* ☎ *04/828–5704,* 𝔽𝔸𝕏 *04/828–5777. 12 rooms. Air-conditioning, fans, minibars, laundry service. MC, V. CP.*

¢ 🏨 **Lavender Hotel.** It's hard to find fault with this cheery minihotel located around the corner from Xoi Alley—a street lined with noodle and rice shops that stay open late. The friendly manager, Mr. Thang speaks great English and runs a tight ship: the rooms are clean and bright with big windows and sparkling bathtubs. Rooms in the front have balconies. Guests have access to the hotel e-mail account. ⊠ *3D Tong Duy Tan St., Hoan Kiem District,* ☎ *04/828–6723,* ℻ *04/828–6046. 12 rooms. Air-conditioning, fans, minibars. AE, MC, V. CP.*

¢ ⊞ **Vinh Quang Hotel.** This hotel is on Hang Quat, or Fan Street, one of the most charming and lively streets in the Old Quarter. Now, instead of selling fans, stores here specialize in red-velvet banners with messages like GOOD LUCK IN YOUR NEXT LIFE. Aside from the cheap East-West fusion decor, the Vinh Quang offers neat, efficient rooms and a great central location. Front rooms have balconies overlooking the color and activity of Hang Quat Street. Some of the smaller back rooms are windowless. ⊠ *24 Hang Quat St., Hoan Kiem District,* ☎ *04/824–3423,* ℻ *04/825–1519. Restaurant, bar, air-conditioning, fans, minibars, laundry service, travel services. AE, MC, V.*

Around Lenin Park

$$–$$$ ⊞ **Hotel Nikko Hanoi.** With its sleek and airy lobby offering a peek into a tiny Japanese garden, this 15-story hotel is a shining example of understated Japanese elegance. The rooms are both simple and luxurious, with plenty of light, tasteful wooden furniture, and large closets. The corner suites have spacious bathrooms that overlook Lenin Park across the street. Standard and deluxe rooms are the same size, but the latter have more windows. Three restaurants serve Japanese, Chinese, or French food: the Chinese dining room does an excellent Sunday dim sum, and Restaurant Benkay (☞ Dining, *above*) offers the most authentic—and most expensive—Japanese food in town. ⊠ *84 Tran Nhan Tong St., Hai Ba Trung District,* ☎ *04/822–3535,* ℻ *04/822–3555. 260 rooms. 3 restaurants, bar, air-conditioning, in-room safes, minibars, room service, pool, sauna, health club, dry cleaning, laundry service, concierge, business services, meeting rooms. AE, DC, MC, V. CP.*

$$ ⊞ **Green Park Hotel.** This hotel's exterior, painted a terrifying shade of
★ green, must scare off many potential guests. Ignore the paint job and you'll discover a truly charming hotel, where the marble-floor lobby is always full of fresh flowers, and staff members will go out of their way to make you feel at home. The rooms—some of which look toward nearby Lenin Park—are spacious, quiet, and, given the hotel's exterior, surprisingly tasteful. Front rooms have larger windows and are slightly bigger than back ones, but all rooms are pleasant. The corner suites are especially wonderful, with light streaming in from all directions and large, luxurious bathrooms. The top-floor restaurant serves Asian and Western food and has a lovely view over Lenin Park and Thuyen Quang Lake. A breakfast buffet is included in the room rate. ⊠ *48 Tran Nhan Tong St., Hai Ba Trung District,* ☎ *04/822–7725,* ℻ *04/822–5977. 40 rooms. Restaurant, air-conditioning, in-room safes, minibars, room service, massage, dry cleaning, laundry service, concierge, business services, meeting room, travel services. AE, DC, MC, V.*

$ ⊞ **Eden Hotel.** The Eden—not to be confused with the Chains First Eden Hotel on Phan Dinh Phung Street—offers top-rate minihotel service in a decent location near Thuyen Quang Lake. Bright rooms with carved-wood furniture have all of the conveniences—carpeted floors, big baths, and 10 television channels. Happily absent are neon and nylon, especially in the low-lighted, wood-paneled dining area. In the lobby, birds sing over a tremendous fish tank, and an altar is stacked with fake gold, oranges, beer, and Cokes for the ancestors. ⊠ *78 Tho Nhuom St., Hoan Kiem District,* ☎ *04/824–5273,* ℻ *04/822–8235. 25 rooms. Restaurant, air-conditioning, minibars, dry cleaning, laundry service, concierge, travel services, car rental. AE, DC, MC, V.*

Around the Ho Chi Minh Mausoleum/Ba Dinh District

$$$$ ☒ **Hanoi Daewoo Hotel.** The pool here—the longest in Southeast Asia—
★   is just one example of how over the top this hotel is. Even its impres-
      sive collection of more than 1,000 paintings by contemporary Vietnamese
      artists, hanging in public spaces and guest rooms, is worthy of a book.
      Space is abundant—from the open marble lobby that spills into a large
      two-story lounge overlooking the pool to the four restaurants serving
      Chinese, Japanese, Vietnamese, and Western cuisine. Rooms are big and
      lavishly decorated in better-than-average hotel-style furnishings; some
      overlook the zoo, West Lake, or downtown Hanoi. The main drawback
      is that you need to take a taxi to get downtown; although there is a
      shuttle service, it doesn't run very frequently. ☒ *360 Kim Ma St., Ba
      Dinh District,* ☎ *04/831–5000,* FAX *04/831–5010. 411 rooms. 4 restau-
      rants, 2 bars, air-conditioning, in-room safes, minibars, room service,
      pool, hot tub, sauna, aerobics, exercise room, dance club, dry cleaning,
      laundry service, concierge, business services, meeting rooms, travel ser-
      vices, car rental. AE, DC, MC, V.*

$$ ☒ **Hanoi Horison Hotel.** Known as the "Emerald City" because of its
      impressive green glass-fronted facade, the Horison is a joint Viet-
      namese-Indonesian project. In the spacious lobby, which has a marble
      floor and Indonesian artwork, there is a bakery that serves good pas-
      tries. Rooms are luxurious, if not overly large, and are done in sooth-
      ing pastels. There is an international restaurant, and the Chimney Pub
      features occasional live music. ☒ *40 Cat Linh St., Ba Dinh District,*
      ☎ *04/733–0808,* FAX *04/733–0688. 350 rooms. Restaurant, bar, lobby
      lounge, air-conditioning, in-room safes, minibars, room service, pool,
      tennis court, exercise room, laundry service, business services, meet-
      ing rooms, travel services. AE, DC, MC, V.*

Around West Lake

$–$$$ ☒ **Ho Tay Villas.** If you crave complete silence, these villas, 5 km (3
      mi) outside Hanoi on West Lake, offer peaceful accommodations that
      feel like a cross between an elegant estate and a socialist summer
      camp. The grounds are gorgeous, with lots of flowering trees and wild
      birds. Rooms are clean, with all the amenities, although perhaps a lit-
      tle musty from age and proximity to the lake. For $140 you can stay
      in a suite that has its own meeting room—perfect if a socialist head of
      state should happen to drop by. ☒ *Dang Thai Mai St., Quan Tay Ho,*
      ☎ *04/845–2393,* FAX *04/823–2126. 75 rooms. Restaurant, bar, air-con-
      ditioning, fans, minibars, tennis court, laundry service, meeting rooms,
      travel services. MC, V.*

$$ ☒ **Hanoi Club.** Well-appointed rooms at this swank private sports club
      offer spectacular sunset views over West Lake and include the use of
      the club's plush facilities. The only drawback? With two tennis courts,
      squash courts, a huge gym, a golf driving range, an outdoor pool, and
      sailboats to keep you busy, you'll have trouble finding time to sight
      see. Moreover, the hotel has Western, Chinese, and Japanese restau-
      rants, so you won't even need to go out for food. ☒ *76 Yen Phu St.,
      Tay Ho District,* ☎ *04/823–8115,* FAX *04/823–8390. 12 rooms. 3
      restaurants, bar, air-conditioning, in-room safes, minibars, room ser-
      vice, pool, massage, driving range, 2 tennis courts, health club, squash,
      boating, dry cleaning, laundry service, meeting rooms. AE, MC, V. CI*

$$ ☒ **Meritus Westlake Hotel.** Stunning views of Truc Bach and West lake
      and a central location are two of the highlights of this luxury hotel. I
      takes only a few minutes to drive into central Hanoi, plus it's a shor
      hop to the Ho Chi Minh Mausoleum and diplomatic district. The gues
      rooms are both comfortable and tasteful, but what makes this hote

stand out is its swimming pool. Set on the fourth floor with a view over the neighboring lakes, the pool has a retractable roof, making it the only hotel pool in Hanoi that can be used year-round. At present there are two restaurants serving Chinese and Western food, as well as a top-floor bar with a great view of the city. Future plans call for a Japanese restaurant and a 19th-floor Italian eatery. A full breakfast is included in the room rate. ⊠ *1 Thanh Nien St., Ba Dinh District,,* ☎ *04/823–8888,* 𝖥𝖠𝖷 *04/829–3888. 322 rooms. 2 restaurants, bar, air-conditioning, in-room safes, minibars, room service, pool, massage, health club, dry cleaning, laundry service, concierge, business services, meeting rooms, travel services. AE, DC, MC, V.*

$ 🖳 **Dragon Hotel.** It's hard to imagine Mother Theresa, who stayed here in 1996, surrounded by so much extravagance—a many-armed statue of the Goddess of Mercy, carp-filled pools, gold dragon statues—and that's before you get into the room. With ornately carved wooden furniture, institutional carpeting, and mirrors beside the beds, the rooms are a tribute to tackiness. It's not all in bad taste, however; the staff is friendly, and the rooms do overlook a leafy canal. There's also a lovely terra-cotta patio strung with birdcages. A full breakfast is included in the room rate. ⊠ *9 Tay Ho Rd., Ba Dinh District,* ☎ *04/829–2954,* 𝖥𝖠𝖷 *04/829–4745. 23 rooms. Air-conditioning, in-room safes, laundry service, travel services. AE, MC, V.*

NIGHTLIFE AND THE ARTS

The Arts

The arrival of television has dealt a serious blow to Hanoi's once-vibrant performing-arts scene, and it is unclear whether or not it will ever recover. Throughout the city, once-thriving movie houses have gone dark as Hanoians tune in to Vietnam Television and satellite TV, and for the past few years, VCRs have been flying out of the stores, further jeopardizing the fate of film and performing arts in Vietnam.

Nonetheless, some Hanoians remain firm in their belief that nothing beats a live performance. With the multi-million dollar restoration of the Opera House finally finished, Hanoi's performing-arts scene may reemerge. The imposing French-built arts palace features Vietnam's top traditional musicians and pop stars as well as the occasional Western performer. Elsewhere in the city, you can catch a performance of Vietnamese folk opera, traditional music, or enchanting water puppetry. If you want a peek at the results of years of Eastern European physical training, go to the circus at the northern edge of Lenin Park.

To find out about upcoming cultural events, pick up a copy of *The Guide,* a useful arts and entertainment monthly available at many hotels, including the Metropole.

Circus

☾ **Vietnam Circus** (Rap Xiec; ⊠ Tran Nhan Tong and Tran Binh Tong Sts., at north end of Lenin Park, Hoan Kiem District, ☎ 04/822–0268) was founded 45 years ago in the mountains, along with the Communist Party. The troupe's jovial director, Nguyen Quang Vinh, has spent time in Las Vegas with Ringling Brothers and Barnum & Bailey Circus, with which the Vietnam Circus has an exchange program. Besides an evening of guaranteed entertainment—the elephants and monkeys are accompanied by the antics of 160 human performers—the circus is also a significant bit of architecture, with its distinctive 1,500-seat, round-top building. In winter, bring a jacket. Shows are two hours and are held from Wednesday through Sunday at 8 PM; ticket prices range from 15,000d to 30,000d.

Film

Alliance Française (⊠ 42 Yet Kieu St., Hoan Kiem District, ☎ 04/826–6970) sponsors weekly viewings of French films, as well as art exhibits.
Fansland Cinema (⊠ 84 Ly Thuong Kiet St., Hoan Kiem District, ☎ 04/825–7484) occasionally shows non-Vietnamese films; check the listings outside the theater to see if an English-language movie is playing. Screenings are usually at 5:30 PM and 8 PM.
New Age Cinema (⊠ Hang Bai St., Hai Ba Trung District, ☎ 04/825–3911) often shows non-Vietnamese movies; check the listings outside the theater.

Theater and Opera

Hanoi's performing-arts legacy is impressive. As in Europe, the emperors often kept acting guilds and musicians in or around the Imperial Palace. Roving drama and musical troupes entertained citizens in the countryside. The arrival of the French and the 20th century saw an explosion of theater culture in the capital, the lingering remnants of which can be experienced at a handful of small drama houses that host troupes performing traditional folk arts.

Tuong is a classical art form developed in central Vietnam. It uses very few stage props, and the actors must conform to age-old rules of behavior concerning their specific characters. Content usually focuses on Vietnamese legends, and music is minimal. The northern folk art known as *cheo* is more of a "people's opera," incorporating both comic and tragic elements. Music and singing are prominent, as cheo developed into a loud and lively art form in order to outdo the noise and distractions of the marketplace, where it was originally performed. *Cai luong*, the "renovated opera" that emerged in the early 20th century, is more similar to Western dramas and operas than the other styles. Music and singing are an important feature of these performances. Although cai luong is a southern creation, the form has endeared itself to Hanoians. The Hanoi theaters listed below stage productions (none prints schedules in English, so call or drop by the theater to see if there's something on for an evening when you're in town).

Chuong Vang Theater of Hanoi (⊠ 72 Hang Bac St., Hoan Kiem District, ☎ 04/825–7823) has performances of cai luong- and tuong-style shows on Saturday evenings.
Hanoi Opera House (Nha Hat Lon; ⊠ 1 Trang Tien St., Hoan Kiem District, ☎ 04/993–0113), whose Vietnamese name translates literally to "House Sing Big," is worth a visit, no matter what happens to be showing. This beautifully restored French building hosts regular classical music concerts, ballets, and Western and Vietnamese operas, plus a variety of singers. The nearby Hilton Hanoi Opera often has information on upcoming performances, or check *The Guide* or *Vietnam News*. Tickets usually cost between 80,000d and 150,000d.
Hanoi National Opera (⊠ 15 Nguyen Dinh Chieu St., Ba Dinh District, ☎ 04/826–7361), a tiny, simple drama house, seats 50 guests. Cheo operas and traditional music concerts are usually staged on Monday, Wednesday, and Friday at 8 PM, but call or stop by to confirm. This theater will arrange special performances for groups of 1 or more. Tickets cost 50,000d.
Traditional Music Club (⊠ 15B Nguyen Dinh Chieu St., Hai Ba Trung District, ☎ 04/826–7361) features traditional cheo operas, folk songs, and traditional dancing. Shows start at 8 PM on Monday, Wednesday, and Friday and cost $4.

Youth Theater (Nha Hat Tuoi Tre; ✉ 11 Ngo Thi Nham St., Hoan Kiem District, ☎ 04/825–4673), a 650-seat facility, is one of the larger theaters in the city and focuses mainly on contemporary drama, although music and dance are sometimes performed. About a dozen foreign theater groups perform here annually. From Thursday through Sunday the theater hosts comedy acts aimed at children, for which tickets cost 30,000d.

Traditional Music

As much of Vietnam's dramatic performances are closely linked with the strains of Vietnamese music, there are very few concerts of exclusively traditional music in the city. Your best bet is to see a water-puppet performance or go to the theater to watch cheo, tuong, or cai luong (☞ Theater and Opera, *above*).

If you happen across an old man or woman on the street who's playing a one-stringed instrument in an impromptu fashion, consider yourself extremely lucky. *Xam,* a type of melancholy folk music, is a dying art in Vietnam—and not because it's the music played at funerals, although xam artists are often invited to perform at such functions. Xam artists are simply dying off, and no one's replacing them. Four professional xam musicians were on hand throughout the day and evening at Hoan Kiem Lake in Hanoi—one at each corner—in the xam heyday of the early 1940s. A half century later there's not a single true xam master plying his or her trade on the streets of the capital. One aging xam professional, the unflagging Hoang Thi Cau of Ninh Binh Province, has done much to save her art from extinction by teaching xam to some cheo performing groups in and around Hanoi and by recording her performances for future generations. But the prospects for this ancient art are bleak; cheo artists are understandably concerned with preserving their own beloved art, and experts say that true xam music cannot be performed by anyone but a bona fide xam master.

Water Puppetry

The thousand-year-old art of *roi nuoc,* or water puppetry, is unique to northern Vietnam and easily ranks as one of Southeast Asia's most beautiful and complex art forms. Long considered an art of the common people, water puppetry gained acceptance at royal celebrations and was often performed for reigning emperors and kings. Water puppetry is performed on—and under, in particular—a small pond whose surface conceals the flurry of action beneath it. Through the near-magical use of bamboo rods and a system of pulleys and levers, master puppeteers stand waist deep at the back of the pond (usually behind a curtain) and make their lacquered marionettes literally walk on water. Shows usually depict scenes from rural life and Vietnamese legend, and the experience is positively delightful.

Central Puppet Theater (✉ 361 Truong Chinh St., Dong Da District, ☎ 04/853–4545) holds water-puppet shows Saturday at 8 PM. Tickets cost 30,000d.

♻ **Municipal Water Puppet Theater** (✉ 57 Dinh Tien Hoang St., on northeast shore of Hoan Kiem Lake, Hoan Kiem District, ☎ 04/825–5450) is the best place to see water puppetry performed in Hanoi. From seven to eight puppeteers pull the strings from behind elaborate stage sets while half a dozen musicians play soothing traditional folk music. The resident Thang Long Water Puppet Troupe is the only troupe that has toured Europe and North and South America in the past. If you're in Hanoi on a package tour, it's highly likely you're already scheduled for a show here. If not, get your tickets early, as they do sell out. Tickets are 40,000d, including a cassette of the music, or 20,000d without. The curtain goes up at 8 every night but Monday, and there's a 9:45 AM matinee on Sunday. Occasionally there are 6 PM shows as well.

There's a 10,000d fee to use your camera; videotaping costs 50,000d. Souvenir puppets are available to buy.

Nightlife

Hanoi has enough bars and clubs to keep you busy. They range from the low-key Met Pub to the eclectic R&R Tavern to the popular Apocalypse Now dance club. Because many ventures are short-lived—Hanoi's nightclubs are curiously prone to electrical fires and other mysterious disasters—it's wise to call ahead when possible.

Bars and Pubs

Emotion Cybernet Cafe (⊠ 52 Ly Thuong Kiet St., Hoan Kiem District, ☎ 04/934–1066) offers Internet access, cheap food and drinks, and a large-screen TV that's regularly tuned in to soccer matches.

Emperor Pub (⊠ 18B Le Thanh Tong St., Hoan Kiem District, ☎ 04/826–8801) is the latest place for Hanoi's expat yuppies to see and be seen, thanks to its classy villa setting, cushy couches, pool table, and resident jazz band.

Fat Jax Bar (⊠ 4th floor, Somerset Grand Hanoi, 49 Hai Ba Trung St., Hoan Kiem District, ☎ 04/934–2342), located in the Red Onion Bistro (☞ Dining, *above*), attracts a mellow crowd of expats and businesspeople. It stays open late and has a pool table.

GC (⊠ 5 Ngo Bao Khanh St., Hoan Kiem District, ☎ 04/825–0499) draws a mainly expat crowd with its low lights, alternative and techno music, and upstairs pool table. Most patrons alternate between this bar and the neighboring—and almost identical—Polite Pub (☞ *below*).

Jazz Club (⊠ 31 Luong Van Can St., Hoan Kiem District, ☎ 04/828–7890) is owned by one of Hanoi's best-known jazz musicians, Quyen Van Minh. Nightly live jazz, performed by both local and foreign musicians, is the big draw here.

Library Bar, Press Club (⊠ 59A Ly Thai To St., Hoan Kiem District, ☎ 04/934–0888) has plush couches, unobtrusive staff, and a menu of fancy (and expensive) cocktails and Cuban cigars. On Friday evenings the attached terrace hosts an after-work happy hour popular with Hanoi's expats; a live jazz band plays Friday nights.

Le Maquis (⊠ 2A Ta Hien St., Hoan Kiem District, ☎ 04/828–2598), a tiny, casual, bar that opens onto the street in the heart of Hanoi's backpacker district, is easy to find thanks to the number of Russian Minsk motorcycles parked out front (this is the official headquarters of Hanoi's Minsk motorcycle club). This a fine place to go for a drink, a snack, and some travel advice.

Met Pub (⊠ 15 Ngo Quyen St., Hoan Kiem District, ☎ 04/826–6919), on the Ly Thai To Street side of the Metropole Hotel, is where high-rolling businesspeople watch satellite TV at the wood-panel bar and middle-aged expats drink martinis and listen to live jazz. An after-work crowd comes for the lively happy hour, despite the rather pricey snack foods and drinks. Nightly dinner buffets have changing themes.

Polite Pub (⊠ 5 Ngo Bao Khanh St., Hoan Kiem District, ☎ 04/825–0959) is the hangout of choice for Hanoi's young, groovy expats, who lounge at the bar listening to rock or alternative tunes or challenge each other to games of Foosball or pool. On weekends, the Polite Pub is often packed from 9 PM to midnight, before Apocalypse Now goes into full swing.

R&R Tavern (⊠ 38A Cua Dong St., Hoan Kiem District), run by a mellow American and his Vietnamese wife, is a Hanoi institution. The pub offers an all-American menu of nachos and burgers, draft beer, darts, and Grateful Dead classics.

S Bar and Tex Mex Restaurant (⊠ 112K1 Hao Nam St., Dong Da District, ☎ 04/851–4479) dishes up good bar snacks—including some rea

sonably successful interpretations of Mexican food—plus the best
blended margaritas in town.

Spotted Cow (✉ 23C Hai Ba Trung St., Hoan Kiem District, ☎ 04/
824–1028) is the bar of choice for committed frat-brother types. Cheap
draft beer, darts, and plenty of rowdy fun can be found at this small,
Australian-run joint.

Dance Clubs

Apocalypse Now (✉ 338 Ba Trieu St., Hai Ba Trung District, ☎ 04/
821–6416) trades on the mystique of the Francis Ford Coppola movie
with Vietnam War props—fake blood dripping from the lamps, a helicopter coming out of one wall, murals of choppers, and more. Black
paint and no windows add to the bomb-shelter atmosphere, where expatriates hunker down for drinking and dancing until almost dawn.
Until 11 PM you'll be blasted with rock oldies, which give way to
dance hits and techno as the night wears on. Despite—or because of—
its sweaty, meat market feel, this club is very popular on weekends after
11 PM. On weeknights, play a game on the free pool tables.

Club Q (✉ Daewoo Hotel, 360 Kim Ma St., Ba Dinh District, ☎ 04/
831–5000) has high-tech sound and lighting, plus live music nightly.
Sing in English in one of the five very private karaoke rooms—a truly
Vietnamese (and Asian) experience. The club could do with some more
clientele to fill up the dance floor, however.

Dong Da Magic (✉ 3 Thai Thinh St., Dong Da District, ☎ 04/563-
0257) is not just a nightclub: it also features a 100-seat cinema, a video
arcade, a high-tech disco, a party room, cheap beer and drinks, and
lots of hyped-up teenagers. Multiple levels of glitzy dance rooms will
keep your adrenaline pumping until the bread vendors start shouting,
"Banh me nao!"

Metal Night Club (✉ 57 Cua Nam St., Dong Da District, ☎ 04/824-
1975) has the stainless-steel panels and rivets to back up its name. The
music, however, is not metal but Asian techno and dance hits. Local
young people pack the place on weekends.

New Century (✉ 10 Trang Thi St., Hoan Kiem District, ☎ 04/928-
5285) is Hanoi's hippest new nightspot, thanks to slick industrial
decor, dry ice, lasers, and the best light show in town. The latest dance
hits plus techno keep the mainly local crowd bopping on the dance floor.
On weekends, getting a table here—especially one with a view over
the dance floor—can be tough.

OUTDOOR ACTIVITIES AND SPORTS

Participant Sports

Basketball

U.S. citizens in Hanoi hoop it up on the half-court of the **American Club**
(✉ 19–21 Hai Ba Trung St., Hoan Kiem District, ☎ 04/824–1850) on
Wednesday evenings around 7. The club has a membership policy, but
Americans passing through town are more than welcome.

Somewhat serious full-court action can be found at the **Hanoi Sports
Center** (Trung Tam The Duc The Thao Hanoi; ✉ 115 Quang Thanh
St., at the southeast corner of West Lake, Ba Dinh District, ☎ 04/845–
5193) most days, particularly weekends, from 2 to 4. You might end
up being paired with someone from the Vietnam women's team, which
practices here regularly. As referees are used, small monetary contributions are expected.

Biking

Memory Café (✉ 33bis Tran Hung Dao St., Hoan Kiem District) rent bicycles. Ms. CoCo will show you on a map where to go. One of the best trips is simply to head south along the river. Another more ambitious trip takes you over the Long Bien Bridge into the countryside. Go south from the bridge, under the car bridge, and continue south along the river. After two hours you should reach Bat Trang, a village where pottery is sold.

Boating

In Hanoi, sailing—and water- and jet-skiing—are, for the most part, reserved for members of the elite **Hanoi Club** (✉ 76 Yen Phu St., Tay Ho District, ☎ 04/823–8115), a once-troubled international project that has finally opened its doors and docks. If you're not a member or the guest of a member, the only way you'll be able to use the club's catamarans and other goodies (including tennis, racquetball, squash, and exercise facilities and a swimming pool) is if you stay at the hotel or apartment facilities managed by the club (☞ Lodging, *above*).

Paddleboating and sculling are the en vogue forms of boating in Hanoi. You can rent dragon-shape paddleboats on **Truc Bach Lake** at a few spots, one on the southwest corner of the lake and another on the causeway. Thien Quang Lake, just north of Lenin Park, also has paddleboats for rent. Go to the **Student Culture Center** (Nha Van Hoa Hoc Sinh Sinh Vien) on the small island that is connected by bridge to Tran Nhan Tong Street. Boats are from 6,000d to 10,000d per half hour. The newer plastic boats are more expensive than the rusting metal hulks.

A **boat house** on the southern edge of Bay Mau Lake, in the middle of Lenin Park, rents old racing sculls for 12,000d per hour. There are also swan-shape paddleboats that cost 8,000d per hour. Access is via Da Co Viet Road.

Bowling

Bowling is the latest craze to strike Vietnam's trendy young urbanites. If your image of bowling includes older folks in matching shirts, you're in for a surprise: pumping music, lights, and attached bars add a little extra excitement to this wholesome pursuit. Call ahead to reserve a lane.

Cosmos Bowling Centre (✉ 8B Ngoc Khanh St., Ba Dinh District, ☎ 04/831–8668) is a popular spot that charges 10,000d per game on Sunday; 15,000d on Monday, Wednesday, and Friday; and 30,000d on Tuesday, Thursday, and Saturday.

Hanoi Starbowl Centre (✉ 2 Pham Ngoc Thach St., Dong Da District ☎ 04/574–1614), housed in a trendy shopping mall, offers 30 lanes of high-tech fun for 15,000d per game during the day, 25,000d from 4 to 7 PM, and 40,000d from 7 PM on.

Hanoi Superbowl (✉ Fortuna Hotel, 6B Lang Ha St., Ba Dinh District, ☎ 04/831–3333) has 24 lanes. Games cost 10,000d on weekday mornings and 25,000d at other times.

Golf

King's Island Golf & Country Club (✉ Dong Mo, Son Tay town, Ha Tay Province, about 45 km, or 28 mi, west of Hanoi, ☎ 034/834–666) is a gorgeous 18-hole lakeside course surrounded by the beautiful Tan Vien Mountain. Greens fees are $50 for guests on weekdays and $80 on weekends. Caddy fees add an extra $8, and renting clubs will set you back another $20. Guests reach the club via a scenic boat trip across a reservoir.

Lang Ha Golf Driving Range (✉ 16A Lang Ha St., Ba Dinh District, ☎ 04/835–0909) charges diehards $10 for a chance to practice their shots.

Health Clubs

A few major hotels in Hanoi allow you to purchase one-day memberships to their exercise facilities, even if you aren't staying at the hotel.

Clark Hatch Fitness Center (✉ Metropole Hotel Sofitel, 15 Ngo Quyen St., Hoan Kiem District, ☎ 04/826–6919, ext. 8881) has all your basic workout equipment—weights, a few machines, treadmills, and stationary bicycles—which you can use while watching the activity on the street below. They also have the best trainers in town as well as whirlpools and saunas. A one-day membership costs $17.

Daewoo Hotel Fitness Center (✉ Hanoi Daewoo Hotel, 360 Kim Ma St., Ba Dinh District, ☎ 04/831–5000, ext. 3309) has treadmills, stationary bikes, and machines, plus yoga and aerobics classes. You can also use the 50-meter pool and the saunas, all for $20 a day.

Guoman Hotel Fitness Center (✉ 83A Ly Thuong Kiet St., Hoan Kiem District, ☎ 04/822–2800) has treadmills, stationary bikes, a stair climber, and some machines. The $8 fee includes use of the sauna.

Jogging

The best place to run in the city is around spacious **Lenin Park** (✉ Main entrance on Tran NhanTong St., Hai Ba Trung District), a favorite sports and exercise locale for Vietnamese and foreigners tired of the exhibitionist nature of a Hoan Kiem Lake workout (although that's not a bad place for a run, too).

The **Botanical Garden** (✉ Entrance on Hoang Hoa Tham Rd., Ba Dinh District) is another place to run. Or, if you're an early riser, join the throngs of runners that pack the city streets at 5 AM. It is understood by everyone that runners are off the roads by 6:30 AM, however. Jogging is definitely not recommended in the streets of Hanoi during the day or evening, even though you may see some expatriates huffing and puffing through the center of town.

The **Hash House Harriers** (ask at the Metropole Hotel Sofitel for locations and times) run every Saturday afternoon around 2 PM. The throngs of expatriates running through the capital's suburbs always garner lots of attention.

Swimming

Army Hotel pool (✉ 33A Pham Ngu Lao St., Hoan Kiem District, ☎ 04/826–5540) is a clean and well-run saltwater pool that charges $4 for a day pass.

Hanoi Daewoo Hotel pool (✉ 360 Kim Ma St., Ba Dinh District, ☎ 04/831–5000) is an arched 80-meter affair that costs $20 for a day pass, including use of the gym, sauna, and whirlpool.

Meritus Lifestyle Club (✉ Meritus Westlake Hotel, 1 Thanh Nien St., Ba Dinh District, ☎ 04/823–8888) has the best pool in town, with a retractable roof and breathtaking views over West Lake. A day pass costs $15 and includes use of the hotel's well-equipped gym, Jacuzzi, and sauna.

Thang Loi Hotel pool (✉ Yen Phu St., Ba Dinh District, ☎ 04/829–4211), out near West Lake, is an inviting place to swim; Fidel Castro stays at the hotel when he visits. Entrance to the pool, open from 6 AM to 10 PM, runs 20,000d.

Tennis

Hanoi Daewoo Hotel (✉ 360 Kim Ma St., Ba Dinh District, ☎ 04/766–0912) has two courts that are open to visitors. The cost is $6 per hour before 4 PM and $10 in the evenings.

Hanoi Horison Hotel (✉ 40 Cat Lin St., Dong Da District, ☎ 04/733–0808) charges $4 per hour until 4 PM and $6 per hour thereafter.

Thang Loi Hotel (✉ Yen Phu St., Ba Dinh District, ☎ 04/829–4211, ext. 391) has two courts out on West Lake that you can rent for 40,000d to 66,000d per hour, depending on the time of day (evening is most costly due to the lights). Hours of operation are 6 AM–10 PM.

Spectator Sports

Sports have been an integral and institutionalized part of the Hanoi educational system for years. Competition on an international level, however, has only recently taken off, although financial strains severely limit the number of meets or tournaments in which Vietnam can participate. Many resources are still committed to the study and improvement of martial arts such as tae kwon do and *wushu,* two disciplines in which Vietnam is world renowned. Ping-Pong and badminton are also determinedly pursued.

The **General Department of Physical Culture and Sports of Vietnam** (✉ 36 Tran Phu St., Ba Dinh District, ☎ 04/825–3158) and the **Hanoi Sports Department** (✉ 10 Trinh Hoai Duc St., Ba Dinh District, ☎ 04/826–4639) can provide information on sporting events in the city, including dates of charity races, major tournaments, and so on.

Soccer

No sport captures the attention and hearts of the Vietnamese quite like soccer. The game's biggest crowds are down in Saigon, but the religiously followed semi-professional national league packs them in at the 20,000-seat capacity **National Stadium** (✉ corner of Nguyen Thai Hoc and Trinh Hoai Duc Sts., Ba Dinh District). The season runs roughly from October to May, and when the Hanoi Police face off against the Ho Chi Minh City Police in the capital, you can bet the stadium is rocking. Smaller matches are held at the Army Stadium, in the southern portion of the citadel, with access from Hoang Dieu Street. Nearly every Vietnamese bar in town has a soccer schedule, and with a bit of gesturing and pointing you'll be able to figure out whether or not a huge match is going to be played while you're in town.

SHOPPING

Hanoi offers plenty of shopping options: the area north of Hoan Kiem Lake is bustling with tiny shops carrying everything from shoes to clothes to antique timepieces. Hanoi is Vietnam's fine arts capital, and running along the southern part of Hoan Kiem Lake, where Hang Khay Street turns into Trang Tien Street, are a number of arts-and-crafts galleries and antiques shops (note, however, that it is illegal to take antiques out of the country without permission from the government; ☞ Shopping *in* Smart Travel Tips A to Z for more information). You can find paintings and watercolors, as well as crafts such as lacquerware and puppets, on Trang Tien and Hang Khay streets in Hoan Kiem District. Any number of shops along Hang Gai and Duc Loi streets, not far from Hoan Kiem Lake, can inexpensively produce custom-made clothes. Hang Gai is also good for souvenirs and antiques. If you fancy beautiful hand-embroidered linens, check out Hang Gai Street, which turns into Hang Bong Street. Many shops on Hang Gai Street sell inexpensive silk linens that make nice liners for padded sleeping bags. Most souvenir and silk shops in the tourist area of the Old Quarter are open to about 10 PM on weekends. Note: a 1997 law designed to protect Vietnam's forests made it illegal to export wooden furniture.

Markets

Hang Da Market (⊠ Hang Da St., Hoan Kiem District) is a sprawling two-story market. The outer stalls sell imported liquor and foodstuffs; flower vendors are on the south side. Also to the south, several inside stalls sell blue-and-white pottery at very reasonable prices. On the northern edge of this market, you'll find a colorful bird market.

Hom Market (Cho Hom; ⊠ Pho Hue and Tran Xuan Soan Sts., Hai Ba Trung District) is one of the biggest and most crowded markets in town. Upstairs is a Western-style market with air-conditioning, and downstairs is a Vietnamese-style open market. If you need plastic tubs, candles, or padded bras, this is the place to go.

19–12 Market (Cho 19–12; ⊠ Ly Thuong Kiet St. between Hoa Lo and Quang Trung Sts., Hoan Kiem District), the December 19th Market, has items for everyday use: vegetables, meat (even dog meat), poultry, clothes, pots and pans, toilet paper, etc.

Specialty Shops

Art

When buying art in Vietnam, be careful of fakes. Paintings by Vietnam's most famous painters—Bui Xuan Phai, Nguyen Tu Nghiem, and Le Thiet Cuong—are the most widely copied. Serious art collectors should consult the well-respected high-end galleries. If you're serious about seeing Hanoi's art scene, consider contacting fine arts consultant **Suzanne Lecht** (☎ 04/862–3184, FAX 04/862–3185), who can lead you on studio tours and advise you on major purchases.

Apricot Gallery (⊠ 40B Hang Bong St., Hoan Kiem District, ☎ 04/828–8965) displays works by the country's most famous contemporary artists. Even if you have no intention of shelling out thousands of dollars for a painting, this beautiful gallery will give you a great introduction to modern Vietnamese art.

Co Xanh (Green Palm Gallery; ⊠ 51 Hang Gai St., Hoan Kiem District, ☎ 04/826–7116) is the top end of souvenir art galleries, with a good selection of paintings by graduates of the Hanoi Fine Arts College. Prices are determined by the stature of the painter and size of the piece, but can easily run into the hundreds. Mr. Ha, the owner, is very reputable and easygoing and speaks excellent English.

Hanoi Studio (⊠ 13 Trang Tien St., Hoan Kiem District, ☎ 04/934–4433) houses works by many of Vietnam's well-known contemporary artists. The manager, Ms. Hang, speaks good English and is very informative.

Mai Gallery (⊠ 3B Phan Huy Chu St., Hoan Kiem District, ☎ 04/825–1225) is run by the daughter of Vietnam's leading art critic, Duong Tuong. Down an alley, it is largely a showcase for Hanoi painters and is very popular with serious collectors.

Red River Gallery (⊠ 71A Nguyen Du St., Hai Ba Trung District, ☎ 04/822–9064) is the gallery that put the Gang of Five painters—Ha Tri Hieu, Hong Viet Dung, Dang Xuan Hoa, Pham Quang Vinh, and Tran Luong—on the map. Red River exhibits the most established Vietnamese artists and is a must-see for serious art collectors willing to shell out thousands of dollars.

Salon Natasha (⊠ 30 Hang Bong St., Hoan Kiem District, ☎ 04/826–1387), the avant-garde hub of Hanoi's art scene, is run by a Russian expatriate and her husband, artist Vu Dan Tan. It exhibits and sells some of the most provocative art in Vietnam today. Natasha, a respected and trusted art dealer, sells painted vases and unframed oil paintings by well-known artists at reasonable prices.

Trang An Gallery (⊠ 15 Hang Buom St., Hoan Kiem District, ☎ 04/826–9480), housed in a gorgeous colonial-era structure, is an impressive, well-designed gallery with three rooms and a courtyard. The gallery hosts regular exhibits of the latest paintings and avant-garde installations of Vietnam's internationally recognized young artists.

Van Gallery (⊠ 25–27 Trang Tien St., Hoan Kiem District, ☎ 04/825–1532), located near the Opera House, has a good selection of high-end souvenir art, plus some works by Hanoi's big-name painters.

Clothing and Accessories

It's possible to have clothes made to order with enough time (one day to three weeks, depending on what you want made and how busy the tailor is). You may also need to return a couple of times to have the clothes fitted.

La Boutique and The Silk (⊠ 10F Dinh Liet St., Hoan Kiem District, ☎ 04/934–323; ⊠ 6 Nha Tho St., Hoan Kiem District, ☎ 04/928–5368) has a colorful selection of woven silk scarves imported from Laos, as well as shirts, jackets, and trousers made from embroidered and woven ethnic minority fabrics. The shop also sells some silver jewelry made by various ethnic-minority groups.

Cao Minh (⊠ 47 Tran Hung Dao St., Hoan Kiem District, ☎ 04/824–2727) is a good but expensive tailor from Saigon, where tailors are generally considered to be more talented.

Co (⊠ 18 Nha Tho St., Hoan Kiem District, ☎ 04/828–9925) stocks some ready-to-wear linen clothing and provides quality custom-made garments. Owing to this store's popularity, it may take more than a week to have clothes made.

Duc Loi Silk (⊠ 76 Hang Gai St., Hoan Kiem District, ☎ 04/826–8758) has a colorful selection of ready-made silk shirts and scarves. This shop has a wide choice of printed silk fabrics and can make clothes quickly.

Ipa-Nima (⊠ 30B Nguyen Huu Huan St., Hoan Kiem District, ☎ 04/934–0876) is the place to get beautifully designed, funky, and fashionable handbags made of rattan, brocade, crochet, beads, and all kinds of other materials. It also sells accessories like cuff links.

Jade (⊠ 219 Hang Bong St., Hoan Kiem District, ☎ 04/828–8335) is managed by a French-Vietnamese woman trained in fashion design. Choose from ready-to-wear pieces or have them copied in your size.

Kenly Silk (⊠ 108 Hang Gai St., Hoan Kiem District, ☎ 04/826–7236) has good and relatively inexpensive silk and linen clothing.

Khai Silk (⊠ 121 Nguyen Thai Hoc St., Ba Dinh District, ☎ 04/823–3508; ⊠ 96 Hang Gai St., Hoan Kiem District, ☎ 04/825–4237) is where the Princess of Thailand shops for fine silk blouses, sweaters, scarves, lingerie, sheets, and more. Linen is also available, as are men's clothes.

Le Minh Silk (⊠ 79–111 Hang Gai St., Hoan Kiem District, ☎ 04/828–8723) offers the usual Hang Gai Street selection of ready-made silk shirts, ties, and padded velvet jackets. Upstairs you'll find the best selection of locally made and imported silk fabrics in Hanoi, including crepes and taffetas.

Phuong Anh (⊠ 56 Hang Hom St., Hoan Kiem District, ☎ 04/826–1556) is a small, crowded shop where you can get a dress and other clothes made for you in three days (even faster if you are really pressed for time and beg).

Song (⊠ 7 Nha Tho St., Hoan Kiem District, ☎ 04/828–9650) is a beautiful boutique stocked with women's clothing in silk, cotton, and linen. The French designer exports her clothes and has a second shop in Melbourne.

Thanh Ha (⊠ 114 Hang Gai St., Hoan Kiem District) does a nice job on women's suits. The store also stocks some pretty beaded handbags and satin slippers.

Embroidery

Tan My (⊠ 66 Hang Gai St., Hoan Kiem District, ☎ 04/825–1579) is the most famous embroidery shop in Hanoi. Employees from Thuong Tin Province, which is known for its rich embroidery tradition, adorn tablecloths, silk clothing, and wall hangings with intricate designs. Ready-made work depicts everything from traditional Vietnamese floral patterns and dragon designs to scenes from Western fairy tales, or you can custom-order. Ms. Huong, the manager, is very comfortable dealing with foreigners, and her English is excellent.

Tuyet Lan (⊠ 65 Hang Gai St., Hoan Kiem District, ☎ 04/825–7967) does beautiful embroidery, especially children's bed sheets. They do not offer discounts. This place is good competition to Tan My, but there's no air-conditioning.

Handicrafts

Craft Link (⊠ 43 Van Mieu St., Ba Dinh District, ☎ 04/843–7710) is a terrific place to buy local handicrafts. Proceeds go to the ethnic minority women who make these crafts.

Craft Window (⊠ 99 Nguyen Thai Hoc St., Ba Dinh District, ☎ 04/733–5286; ⊠ 6 Nha Chung St., Hoan Kiem District, ☎ 04/828–9477) has an excellent selection of crockery, ethnic minority crafts, beaded handbags, and beautiful embroidered greeting cards.

Co Xanh (Green Palm Gallery; ☞ Art, *above*) sells boxes and figurines made of silver. The owner, Tran Thanh Ha, speaks English and is very reputable.

KAF (⊠ 318 Ba Trieu St., Hoan Kiem District, ☎ 04/822–0022) sells quality reproductions of antique Buddha statues and lacquerware.

Lan Vietnamese Handicrafts (⊠ 26 Au Trieu St., Ba Dinh District, ☎ 04/828–9278) sells patchwork quilts made by youngsters with disabilities, who otherwise would have trouble earning a living.

Housewares and Furnishings

Delta Deco (⊠ 12 Nha Tho St., Hoan Kiem District, ☎ 04/828–9616) is a small boutique filled with stylish, Italian-designed and locally made housewares. You'll find beautiful wooden bowls and trays, mirrors, ceramics, candlesticks, and boxes.

DOME (⊠ 10 Yen The St., Ba Dinh District, ☎ 04/843–6036) has well-designed, modern home furnishings—linens, furniture, lamps, candles, and more. Simple, curved designs in wrought iron are a signature style, one you'll see in restaurants and hotels throughout town.

Indochine House (⊠ 13 Nha Tho St., Hoan Kiem District, ☎ 04/824–8071), across from St. Joseph's Cathedral, sells real and reproduction antique furnishings. This is the latest business venture of the British man who runs two elegant, antiques-filled Hanoi restaurants—Seasons of Hanoi and Soho (☞ Dining, *above*).

Nha Dep (⊠ 29 Trang Tien St., Hoan Kiem District, ☎ 04/934–5607) is a large showroom filled with high-quality wooden furniture, plush sofas, modern office furniture and supplies, and glassware.

Quang's Ceramics (⊠ 22 Hang Luoc St., Hoan Kiem District, ☎ 04/828–3440), a huge shop in the Old Quarter, sells colorful crockery and ceramic lamps made in the nearby pottery village of Bat Trang.

Musical Instruments

Hanoi Music Center (⊠ 42 Nha Chung St., Hoan Kiem District, ☎ 04/824–3058) sells guitars, metronomes, keyboards, and pianos.

Pham Bich Huong (⊠ 11 Hang Non St., Hoan Kiem District) carries a great selection of traditional Vietnamese instruments; the proprietor, however, speaks almost no English.

SIDE TRIPS FROM HANOI

Although Hanoi is the cultural and historic centerpiece of northern Vietnam, much of the city's history and many of its legends and traditions are rooted in the region surrounding the capital. Citadels, temples, art guilds, and festival focal points ring the city, and a few hours' drive in any direction will bring you to points of interest ranging from pagodas to idyllic valleys and national parks. Hanoi serves as a base for day trips or short excursions to the Perfume Pagoda, the Thay (Master's) Pagoda, Tam Dao hill station, the ancient capital of Hoa Lu, Phat Diem Cathedral, and the primeval beauty of Cuc Phuong National Park.

Tours organized by Hanoi's tourist cafés and travel agencies (☞ Travel Agencies *in* Hanoi A to Z, *below*) cover all of the sights and are the most time-efficient way to see this region. Tourist café tours are less expensive than those run by travel agencies: a group trip to Perfume Pagoda or Hoa Lu through a tourist café costs about $20 per person, including entrance tickets and meals. If a daily group tour isn't available to the site you want, these companies can arrange a private car and driver for the day. A good example is the "Suburbs of Hanoi" tour: this full-day trip goes to the silk-making village of Ha Dong, the Bat Trang pottery village, a snake farm in Gia Lam across the Red River, and the village of Dong Ho, where the ancient folk art of wood-block printing is still practiced. The trip averages $35 for an air-conditioned car and driver for the whole day. An English-speaking guide costs from $10 to $20 per day.

For history, religion, and a bit of hiking, head west to the Thay and Tay Phuong pagodas. Combine a trip here with Co Loa Citadel, and you've got a full day of exploring. Go with a group tour or rent a private car with a driver for between $30 and $50 for the trip.

Co Loa Citadel

❶ *15 km (9 mi) north of Hanoi.*

Less than 30 minutes north of Hanoi is a series of large earthen ramparts that once protected one of the country's earliest capitals from Chinese invaders. Co Loa, or "snail," so named for the spiral-shape protective walls and moats that resembled the spiral design of a nautilus, was built by An Duong Vuong more than 2,000 years ago and remains one of northern Vietnam's important historical relics.

At the end of the Bronze Age, in the 3rd century BC, King Vuong decided to move the power seat of the Lac Viets—a sophisticated society of indigenous northern Vietnamese, considered by many Vietnamese to be their direct ancestors, who eventually were incorporated into the Chinese empire. They relocated north of the Red River Delta to a fortress designed to be the ultimate protection from the invading Chinese. Nine large earthen ramparts guarded the inner palace of Co Loa. Carefully designed gates were built at angles to each other, and defense mounds created further obstacles for attackers. A series of moats fed by tributaries of the Red River lent an air of medieval invincibility to the place.

According to one of Vietnam's oldest legends, certain forces conspired against King Vuong and his well-protected citadel. After decades of failed attempts to defeat King Vuong's armies, Chinese general Trieu Da or

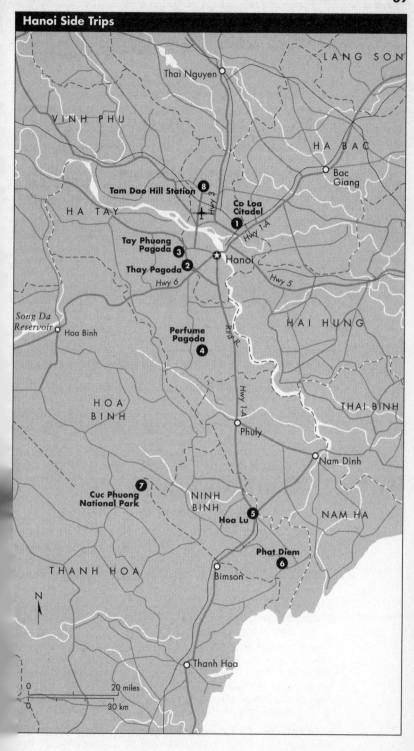

Hanoi Side Trips

LANG SON

Thai Nguyen

VINH PHU

HA BAC

Bac Giang

Tam Dao Hill Station ⑧

HA TAY

Co Loa Citadel ①

Hwy 3

Hwy 1-A

Tay Phuong Pagoda ③

Thay Pagoda ②

Hanoi

Hwy 5

Hwy 6

Song Da Reservoir

Hoa Binh

HAI HUNG

Perfume Pagoda ④

Red R.

Hwy 1-A

HOA BINH

THAI BINH

Phuly

Nam Dinh

Cuc Phuong National Park ⑦

NINH BINH

Hoa Lu ⑤

NAM HA

Phat Diem ⑥

THANH HOA

Bimson

N

0   20 miles
0   30 km

Thanh Hoa

dered his own son to surrender to King Vuong and then propose marriage to King Vuong's daughter, My Chau. Against the advice of his ministers, the king accepted. The new son-in-law lived harmoniously in his new home for three years, eventually coercing his wife into revealing defense secrets and helping him steal a magic crossbow—a gift to King Vuong from the gods, which held all the military secrets to the citadel. With their newfound knowledge, Trieu Da and his troops immediately invaded Co Loa and conquered the Lac Viets. King Vuong had his daughter beheaded. The son-in-law, Trong Thuy, realized his betrayal and threw himself into Ngoc Pond.

Only three of the earthen ramparts are extant today. The rectangular inner wall has a perimeter of 1½ km (1 mi), a middle rampart is in the shape of a polygon with a perimeter of 6½ km (4 mi), and the outer wall is 8 km (5 mi) long. You can explore the site of the ancient imperial palace. Nearby, under an old banyan tree, is Ba Chua, a temple dedicated to Princess My Chau. Inside, there is a headless stone statue of the princess. A temple to An Duong Vuong has also been built on the site of the inner palace. In front of this temple is Ngoc Pond, where the evil son-in-law, Trong Thuy, allegedly killed himself.

A large and colorful festival on the sixth day of Tet, the lunar new year, celebrates King An Vuong Duong, now considered the guardian spirit of Co Loa. Communists banned this and other festivals after taking power in 1954, proclaiming that such superstitious rituals had no place in the new socialist order. But by the late 1980s Hanoi was no longer so eager to squelch such celebrations, and the Co Loa Festival and others like it have enjoyed a revival of sorts in the past decade.

Arriving and Departing

You should be able to hire a car with driver for about $50 to go from Hanoi to Co Loa Citadel as well as the Thay Pagoda and Tay Phuong Pagoda (☞ *below*). A round trip and a visit to Co Loa alone takes about two hours. Tourist cafés and travel agencies can arrange minivan tours to the three sites if there is enough interest. This trip takes about two-thirds of a day, depending on how long you linger at the sites.

Thay Pagoda and Tay Phuong Pagoda

40 km (25 mi) southwest of Hanoi in Hay Tay Province.

Two lovely pagodas can be combined with the Co Loa Citadel to make an enjoyable day trip from Hanoi. (Admission to the pagodas is 10,000d each.)

❷ The **Thay Pagoda,** or Master's Pagoda, is named in honor of Tu Dao Hanh, a 12th-century monk. A statue of Master Hanh is to the left of a large central altar that supports the statues of 18 arhats, monks who have reached enlightenment. To the right is Ly Nhan Tong, a king who was the supposed reincarnation of Tu Dao Hanh. The Thay Pagoda is the site of one of two ancient water-puppetry stages remaining in Vietnam. Constructed during the 15th century, this small stage is set on stilts in the middle of a pond and was used during elaborate pagoda ceremonies and royal visits. Water-puppetry shows still take place here, particularly on the annual festival of the pagoda, which is from the fifth through the seventh days of the third lunar month.

Numerous caves provide opportunities for exploring around the hillsides near Thay Pagoda. A few hiking trails also crisscross the landscape. Twenty kilometers (12 miles) to the northwest is **Ba Vi Mountain**. This 4,250-ft peak affords a spectacular view of the Red River valley and the mountains to the west. Four guest houses offer lodging in the surprisingly relaxing and remote nature preserve; you can reserve rooms through travel agencies and tourist cafés in Hanoi.

3 The **Tay Phuong Pagoda,** or Western Pagoda, comprises three sanctuaries built into a hillside and surrounded by a square enclosure. Each ancient wooden structure is separated by a small pool of water that reflects an eerie soothing light into the temples. Begun in the 3rd century, the pagoda was rebuilt in the 9th century and eventually expanded to its present size. The centuries-old curved rooftops are particularly noteworthy, as are the masterpieces of wood sculpture. About six dozen figures carved from jackfruit wood are the pagoda's primary features. The pagoda's rafters are elaborately carved with bas-reliefs of dragons and lotuses, and ceramic animal statues grace the rooftops.

Arriving and Departing

Trips organized by tourist cafés and travel agencies usually cover the admission fees for these sites. It's easy to combine a trip to these two pagodas with a visit to Co Loa Citadel (☞ *above*), north of Hanoi.

Perfume Pagoda

★ **4** *60 km (37 mi) south of Hanoi.*

Considered Vietnam's most important Buddhist site, the Perfume Pagoda (Chua Huong) is the largest of a cluster of shrines carved into the limestone of the Huong Tich Mountains. In late spring the trails leading up to the shrines are clogged with thousands making their pilgrimage to pray to Quan Am, the goddess of mercy and compassion.

According to a Vietnamized version of the Chinese legend, Quan Am was a young wife falsely accused of trying to kill her newlywed husband. Thrown out of her mother-in-law's house, she took refuge in a monastery, posing as a monk. A reckless girl one day blamed her pregnancy on the monk, not knowing he was a she. Without a word of self-defense, the vilified monk took the child in and raised him. Only after Quan Am died did villagers discover her silent sacrifice. In the past, pilgrims came to the grottoes to pray for Quan Am's help in bearing sons and in fighting unjust accusations.

From the shores of the Yen River, you are ferried to the site, 4 km (2½ mi) away, on sampans that seem to be made of flimsy aluminum. It's a spectacular ride through the flooded valley, past boats laden with fruit and farmers at work in their fields. You'll be let off at Chua Tien Chu. From there, follow a stone path uphill to the various pagodas and shrines. Three kilometers (2 miles) later you'll reach the Perfume Pagoda. A steep set of stairs takes you inside the impressive cavern, where gilded Buddhas and bodhisattvas sit nestled in rocky recesses. The air is misty from incense and the cooking fires of the Buddhist monks who tend the shrines.

In early spring, from just after Tet to the middle of the second lunar month, thousands of Buddhists make their pilgrimage to the Perfume Pagoda. This is an intense—and sometimes stressful—time to visit, as the crowds of Vietnamese faithful clog the Yen River with extra boats and make navigating the slippery stairs more of an exercise in caution than a journey of discovery. The atmosphere at this time of year is positively electric with thousands of Buddhists crowding into the cavern to leave offerings, catch a droplet of water from a holy stalactite, or buy Buddhist trinkets and mementos from the dozens of stall owners.

Arriving and Departing

Day trips from Hanoi to the Perfume Pagoda, leaving at about 6:30 AM, are available from any number of travel agencies, such as Vietnam

Tourism and Vinatour, as well as from tourist cafés, such as the Green Bamboo Café (☞ Travel Agencies *in* Hanoi A to Z, *below*). These tours run as low as $12 per person, including all transport and entrance fees. You can also rent a car for about $30, and a guide for $10 to $20; you'll still have to pay the 33,000d per person entrance fee to get into the pagoda itself. If you're feeling brave, go by motorbike.

Hoa Lu

⑤ *113 km (70 mi) south of Hanoi.*

Hoa Lu, the first capital of independent Vietnam, is known as "Halong Bay without the water." Both the stunning natural surroundings and Hoa Lu's status as a former seat of power make for an interesting excursion.

After three decades of internal strife following the expulsion of the Chinese by Ngo Quyen in the year 938, Dinh Tien Hoang unified the country. (A colorful festival on the 12th day of the third lunar month commemorates this successful reunification.) The new king moved the capital to Hoa Lu, in a valley whose maze of narrow streams and inhospitable limestone outcroppings served as natural protection for the fledgling nation; he had numerous fortifications built around his citadel in order to avert another Chinese invasion, and word quickly spread of his ruthless treatment of prisoners. (The king reportedly fed enemies to tigers and then boiled their bones in ceremonial urns.) Despite such tactics, the Dinh dynasty was short-lived; Dinh Tien Hoang was assassinated by bodyguards in 979. The killers were discovered and put to death, and General Le Dai Hanh ascended to the throne, establishing the Early Le dynasty. Upon Le Dai Hanh's death in 1009, Ly Thai To became the first king of the Ly dynasty and moved the capital to Thang Long, the site of present-day Hanoi.

Much of the ancient capital of Hoa Lu has been destroyed or has succumbed to the forces of nature, but the two sanctuaries that do survive hint at the tastes of the king and his court. The first temple honors Dinh Tien Hoang and houses statues of the king and his three sons in the musty, dimly lighted back room. Outside, all that remains of an elaborate throne is the stone base. The main hall has been heavily restored, and much of the wood construction you'll see here is from renovations done in the 17th century. The second temple is named after Le Dai Hanh, the general who became the first emperor of the Le dynasty in 980. A series of elaborate swords and spears are arranged in front of incense bowls and corner altars. To the right, as you walk in, is a square fish pond bearing lovely oversize lotus flowers.

In an unforgivable affront to the historic atmosphere and environment of Hoa Lu, local officials have recently erected a nearby building housing artifacts unearthed during 1998 excavations that uncovered remnants of the original citadel. The artifacts are fine; it's the appallingly garish red metal roof for which someone should lose his or her job.

A short bus or car ride away—drivers and group tour operators know exactly where to go—from Hoa Lu is a **trio of caves** accessible by a traditional boat ride down the Hoang Long River, a peaceful stream that winds through rice paddies after cutting its path through the steep limestone cliffs around Hoa Lu. Village women row you the 2 km (mi) through Tam Coc, a series of three caves, one of which has a ce ment plaque on its far side commemorating Nguyen Cong Cay, a Vietnamese weapons maker who lived in Hoa Lu from 1947 to 1950 an plotted with other resisters against the French. At the far end of th boat ride, other women in similar boats are waiting to sell you so drinks, bananas, even embroidery. It's a hard sell and somewhat ruins the idyllic moment. Another cave, Bich Dong, is also reachable by boat; you can disembark to visit the 17th-century pagoda here.

Lodging

Most people treat Hoa Lu as part of a day trip and return to Hanoi by nightfall, but a growing number of adventure travelers are picking up on the charms of the region (it's all relative) and are choosing to spend the night in the town of Ninh Binh, a provincial capital that is aiming to flex its tourism muscles. If you're going to visit Hoa Lu or Phat Diem Cathedral, and don't mind a night away from the big city, consider staying in Ninh Binh. Accommodations are nothing to write home about, but this is a good jumping-off point for the area. Contact travel agencies in Hanoi (☞ Travel Agencies *in* Hanoi A to Z, *below*) to book a room at one of the area minihotels.

¢–$ ⊡ **Hoa Lu Hotel.** The largest hotel in Ninh Binh is a huge, drab affair. The rooms are adequate but overpriced. ⊠ *Tran Hung Dao St., Ninh Binh,* ☎ *030/871–217,* ℻ *030/874–126. 100 rooms. Air-conditioning, IDD phones. No credit cards.*

Arriving and Departing

Tourist cafés and travel agencies have minibus tours to Hoa Lu for about $20 per person—entry tickets, boat ride, and lunch included. You can also rent a car. It makes sense to combine an excursion to Hoa Lu with a trip to nearby Phat Diem, an enclave of Catholic churches (☞ *below*). This trip takes the good part of a day.

Phat Diem

❻ *121 km (75 mi) southeast of Hanoi.*

On your way back to Hanoi from Hoa Lu, take a 25-km (16-mi) detour to Phat Diem. You know you're headed in the right direction when you pass one stone church after another. Although tensions between organized religions and the Vietnamese central government still exist, relations have improved considerably between officials and Vietnam's Catholic order. Many of these structures have been built in the last few years with financial assistance from American organizations.

All these churches pale in comparison to the massive complex known as **Phat Diem Cathedral,** built in 1891 in Kim Son village, one of the first landfalls of Portuguese missionaries in the 16th century. The cathedral itself is a hulking stone edifice with an enormous bell atop its tallest tower; it's surrounded by a courtyard, which in turn is surrounded by a huge moat. The prayer hall itself is a wooden marvel, however. Almost the entire interior is made of Vietnamese (and surely Laotian) hardwood, with massive wooden pillars supporting arched ceiling beams in what is truly an artist's loving creation. The curved eaves are a nod to Sino-Vietnamese architecture, but the crosses and saints (all sitting in the lotus position) reflect the fervor of the 150,000-strong congregation. Many of Phat Diem's Catholics fled south in 1954, when Vietnam was divided into north and south.

Catholicism is definitely experiencing a comeback in these parts, and because a more liberal tone has been adopted by Hanoi, **Sunday Mass** is now extremely popular. Services are held at 5 and 9 AM; by 10 everyone's already out in the fields. On holidays such as Christmas and Easter, expect crowds of 10,000 or more.

The church is said to help provide shelter for the faithful who visit Phat Diem and wish to stay in charming Kim Son village, but there are no

genuine accommodations for visiting tourists. Consider Ninh Binh
(☞ Lodging *in* Hoa Lu, *above*) for a nearby stay.

Arriving and Departing

Some tours that go to Hoa Lu do not stop at Phat Diem, so ask ahead.
If you can't find one that stops on the day you wish to go, you should
be able to hire a car and driver—although finding one who will get
you there for 5 AM Mass might be tough. It shouldn't run more than
$60 round-trip.

Cuc Phuong National Park

❼ *140 km (87 mi) southwest of Hanoi. The park entrance is in Ninh Binh
Province, 40 km (25 mi) from Ninh Binh town.*

Outside the general loop of tourist traffic in the north is secluded and
prehistoric-looking Cuc Phuong, one of Vietnam's most important
protected areas. Established in 1962 by President Ho Chi Minh as Vietnam's first national park, Cuc Phuong is 54,320 acres (about 85 square
mi) of heavily forested subtropical lowlands that is home to 64 mam-
mal species, including the red-bellied squirrel, the pig-tailed macaque,
the three-striped palm civet, and a kind of barking deer called the munt-
jac. Leopards and tigers have also been spotted. More than 250 bird
species and 33 types of reptiles live here as well, along with an array
of nearly 2,000 species of flora.

The low-key Endangered Primate Rescue Center is in the park and can
be visited if the staff isn't too busy. Although this habitat would seem
to be the perfect place to see Vietnam's wildlife in full splendor, mam-
mal- and bird-watching are sadly not particularly successful pastimes
in the park. Despite Cuc Phuong's status as a protected preserve, the
primary forest habitat has been heavily denuded during the past few
decades, and officials believe the park's wildlife numbers are dwindling.
The conditions will worsen when the huge Ho Chi Minh Highway, already under construction, splits the park in two in violation of Vietnam's own environmental-protection laws. Rerouting of the highway
was under discussion at press time.

Despite the misfortunes of northern Vietnam's animals, Cuc Phuong
is absolutely beautiful. April is especially lovely, and the swarms of but-
terflies that gather here would have amazed Nabokov. Dozens of miles
of trails lead to such highlights as cascading Giao Thuy waterfall, a
1,000-year-old tree, and Con Moong Cave, the "cave of early man,"
where evidence of prehistoric humans has been discovered. Longer hikes
lead to some Muong villages. Many trails are well marked, but traveling this thick forest would be foolish without a guide. Admission to
the park is 70,000d; be sure to bring lots of mosquito repellent, especially if you plan to stay the night in the area.

Lodging

You'll probably end up in one of two areas: the **park headquarters** (☎
030/866–085), just beyond the main gates, or **Bong,** a tiny village 20
km (12 mi) into the park. Overnighters can stay at either location, but
tour operators usually guide guests to the facilities at park headquarters. Air-conditioned bungalows here are pricey at $40 per night
whereas rooms with air-conditioning and shared baths at a nearby guest
house run from $10 to $20. Call the park headquarters for information and reservations. The staff is quite helpful.

In Bong two stand-alone bungalows are available, for about $35, as
well as nine simple rooms in a guest house. These run from $10 to $20.
There are only four hours of electricity per night in Bong, and bath

rooms are shared. Reservations are recommended for either location. You may wish to consider going on a weekday, as Cuc Phuong's proximity to Hanoi makes it a favorite weekend retreat among Vietnamese student groups. Bong, secluded as it is, occasionally fills with a boisterous crowd of between 100 and 200 students. You can make reservations through travel agencies in Hanoi.

Arriving and Departing

Cuc Phuong is a three-hour drive down Highway 1 from Hanoi and can be visited as a day trip if you leave early in the morning. If you've rented a car, it's possible to drive with a guide into the center of the park and hike out to the road to the west of the park, where your driver will meet you. You then drop your guide off at the headquarters on your way back to Hanoi. Tour operators in Hanoi are loath to recommend this outright, claiming the road is too dangerous and difficulty in finding you should anything happen to you in the park, so you'll have to arrange it once at Cuc Phuong. Overnight cars to Cuc Phuong can be arranged for $70 to $90. Hanoi Tourism charges $118 for transportation and driver's expenses, as well as an overnight stay in a double room at park headquarters. Adventurous expats often pile onto their motorbikes for weekend runs to the park.

Tam Dao Hill Station

❽ *85 km (53 mi) northwest of Hanoi in Vinh Phuc Province.*

Up in the clouds, at an elevation of 3,050 ft, the damp hill station of Tam Dao feels like the mountain town that time forgot—almost. In 1907 French developers scaled the rugged 4,590-ft peaks (there are three of them) north of Hanoi and decided the cool weather of a nearby mountain retreat could serve the French well. The result was a graceful town of elegant villas surrounded by lush vegetation and sweeping views of the valley below. Since the French left in 1954, however, little grace has been bestowed on Tam Dao, whose chalet charm took a decided turn for the worse (perhaps it was the lack of oxygen up there) when Soviet-era architecture announced itself in the form of a monstrously square 40-room hotel. (You're welcome to stay here, but try one of the more intimate minihotels first.) Most villas—and the town church—have fallen into disrepair, although a few developers remain confident that Tam Dao could be resuscitated as a tourist resort; they've bought up some crumbling lodges and have begun to build.

Few people, even locals, realize that Tam Dao and the surrounding peaks are in a national park, which may be one reason why logging remains a problem for the area. But for the most part, a hike up to the radio transmitter above the town is a walk into dense jungle. Small Buddhist temples line the concrete steps up to the tower, and a spring bubbles up from beneath the underbrush and splays out into a small waterfall. If you're spending the night up in these mountains, bring a sweater and some rain gear.

A guard station has been set up at the base of the mountain, and vehicles are charged a few dollars to get up to the hill station. The 15-km (9-mi) climb is a fascinating ride from subtropical vegetation up to more temperate flora such as pine trees. People have been known to ride mountain bikes up to Tam Dao and spend the night, but the climb is extreme. Less active riders put their bikes in minivans on the way up and then career down the extremely winding and dangerous—but ultimately exhilarating—route to the guard station.

Lodging

$–$$ 🏨 **Mela Hotel.** This recently opened property is a sort of luxury mini-hotel-villa on the town's outskirts. Some rooms have views of the valley. Future plans call for a pool to be installed. ✉ *Near path to the Tam Dao waterfall, Tam Dao District,* ☎ *211/824–321,* FAX *211/824–352. 25 rooms. Restaurant, nightclub, conference room. MC, V.*

¢   🏨 **Hoa Hong Hotel.** Travelers who long for good old Soviet-era homeliness should try the Hoa Hong (Rose) Hotel. This faded, formerly state-owned hotel is the biggest eyesore in town, but has inexpensive rooms. Rooms lack phones, air-conditioning, and heating, but do have TVs and hot water. ✉ *Tam Dao District,* ☎ *211/824–263,* FAX *211/824–290. 50 rooms. Restaurant, meeting rooms. No credit cards.*

Arriving and Departing

There are no organized group tours to Tam Dao, but you can easily arrange a trip here on your own through a travel agency or tourist café.

HANOI A TO Z

Arriving and Departing

By Bus

Try to take minibuses (☞ *below*) instead of buses, as full-size buses are cramped, hot, and notoriously loud, uncomfortable, and unsafe. Bus schedules are quite arbitrary, and few station attendants speak any English or French. Buses leave when full, and arrival times depend on how many times a bus stops along the road to cool off its overheated engine or pick up more passengers. Contact the state-owned **Hanoi Bus Company** (✉ 32 Nguyen Cong Tru St., Hai Ba Trung District, ☎ 04/971–4590) for information.

The **BIC Bus Company** (✉ 2 Hoang Van Thu St., Haiphong, ☎ 031/820–800) is a Korean joint venture quickly making inroads in northern Vietnam. They offer service to and from Haiphong, Ninh Binh, and other points south. Lang Son in the far north may also soon be in their schedule. Pseudo-independent **minibus service,** particularly to Haiphong, is available from the alleyway called Hang Trung, adjacent to the Royal Hotel (✉ 20 Hang Tre St.). These buses are more expensive than their hulking counterparts, yet they're usually just as crowded.

Three major bus stations—none of which is in the center of town—serve the capital, in addition to a few express minibus services.

Giai Bat Bus Station (Ben Xe Giai Bat; ✉ Giai Phong St., Hai Ba Trung District, ☎ 04/864–1462) serves most southern routes, including Vinh, Hue, and ultimately Ho Chi Minh City. It's 7 km (4 mi) south of the Hanoi Railway Station, on Gia Phong Street, opposite the Giap Bat Railway Station.

Gia Lam Bus Station (Ben Xe Gia Lam; ✉ Ben Xe St., Gia Lam District, ☎ 04/827–1529) provides service in the north, to destinations such as Lang Son and Haiphong. It's best to buy your ticket ahead of time. The station is across the Red River and just beyond the tollbooth, 100 yards off Nguyen Van Cu Street on Ben Xe Street.

Kim Ma Bus Station (Ben Xe Kim Ma; ✉ Nguyen Thai Hoc and Gian Vo Sts., Ba Dinh District, ☎ 04/845–2846) is the closest of Hanoi's stations to downtown. It serves most routes to the northwest, including Dien Bien Phu.

By Car

As Hanoi is the largest city and tourist center in northern Vietnam and a major international gateway, few Western visitors actually arrive here by car. Those who do are usually coming from Ho Chi Minh City via Highway 1 or from Danang or Hue after flying there from Ho Chi Minh City. A much more common method is to tour the south by land, say, by car or train from Ho Chi Minh City to Hue and then fly from there to Hanoi.

It's quite easy to arrange leaving Hanoi by car for side trips (☞ Getting Around by Car, *below*). Only a few road tolls are charged, and the cost is minimal—about 5,000d per car.

By Minibus

Make arrangements for travel by minibus—either independently or with group tours—through travel agencies, tourist cafés, and hotels.

By Plane

Many international airlines fly into Hanoi (☞ Air Travel *in* Smart Travel Tips A to Z).

Pacific Airlines (✉ 100 Le Duan St., Dong Da District, ☎ 04/851–1503) is Vietnam's smaller domestic carrier; ticket prices are comparable to those of Vietnam Airlines.

Vietnam Airlines (✉ 1 Quang Trung St., Hoan Kiem District, ☎ 04/832–0320) has nonstop international flights between Hanoi and Bangkok, Seoul, Hong Kong, Taipei, Guangzhou, Dubai, Paris, Vientiane, and Phnom Penh. Domestic destinations served from Hanoi include Danang, Dien Bien Phu, Ho Chi Minh City, Hue, Nha Trang, and Vinh. Flight schedules are often different each day of the week. At press time Hanoi and Washington were aiming to resume long-delayed negotiations on a civil aviation deal that may see U.S. carriers flying direct to Vietnam in the near future.

AIRPORT

Noi Bai International Airport (☎ 04/821–6660) is about 35 km (22 mi) north of the city. For international flights you must pay an airport departure tax of 140,000d or $10 (you can pay in either currency) and for domestic flights 25,000d or $2. At press time a flashy new terminal was under construction and set to open by 2001.

BETWEEN THE AIRPORT AND THE CITY CENTER

By Bus: Vietnam Airlines runs a bus service into Hanoi; tickets are 45,000d per person, and it takes about 40 minutes. Buses leave when full, which can sometimes mean a wait. The bus usually drops people off at their hotel if it's not too far from the center of town. Buses to the airport depart from the Vietnam Airlines office (☞ *above*). Book a seat in advance for 45,000d per person.

By Taxi: The official Airport Taxi fare into town is $10. Pick up a voucher at the stand inside or outside the terminal, pay in advance (they'll let you pay on arrival if you complain about such a procedure), and you'll be escorted to your cab. Many unofficial taxi drivers also hover at the terminal's exit and will tug at your sleeve or luggage cart in order to get your business. They'll get you into town for less than the official taxis if you bargain well, but they don't offer receipts and often drive clunking, steering-challenged Russian Volgas. They'll also try to get you to pay for the tolls into town.

To get out to the airport, hire an official taxi for $10; they congregate in front of the Vietnam Airlines office and cruise about the city. You can also call for a taxi at 04/825–4250. Travelers looking to share taxis congregate in front of the Vietnam Airlines office, as do enterprising private drivers. Be prepared to bargain hard—it's hard to beat the official rate.

By Train

DOMESTIC TRAVEL

The ticket office at the main Hanoi train station, **Ga Hanoi** (✉ Opposite 115 Le Duan St., at west end of Tran Hung Dao St., Hoan Kiem District, ☎ 04/825–3549), is open 7:30 to 11:30 and 1:30 to 3:30. You'll find a special counter where foreigners buy tickets, and some of the schedules are even in English. Another, smaller train station, up the tracks from the main one, services northern routes; the foreign booking agents at the main station will direct you.

Trains leave four times daily for Ho Chi Minh City (soft berth $97 to $125, 40 hours), but only one is an express (32 hours). The express makes stops at most major cities, including Vinh, Hue, Danang, and Nha Trang. Purchase a day in advance if you want to ensure a seat. Other destinations include Lang Son ($4, twice daily, 5 hours); Lao Cai (hard berth $17, soft sleeper $22; once daily; 11 hours); and Haiphong ($4, four times daily, 2 hours).

INTERNATIONAL TRAVEL

Trains connect Beijing with Hanoi twice weekly; the trip takes about 55 hours. The northeastern border crossing is at Dong Dang, just north of Lang Son in the northeast (☞ Chapter 3). The closest Chinese city to the Vietnamese border crossing is Nanning, the capital of Guangxi Province. A second international route leads from Hanoi through the border town of Lao Cai, to the northwest, and on to the Chinese provincial capital of Qunming. This train departs every Friday and Sunday night and is the same sleeper train many tourists take to go to Sapa. Standard tourist visas to China allow entry into the country from any port but Nepal. On the Vietnamese side, however, you'll have to have the appropriate overland exit permit stamped into your visa. This should be done before you arrive in Vietnam, although it is feasible to have your visa amended after you've arrived.

Getting Around

By Bicycle

Bikes can be rented at hotels and cafés in the center of town for around 10,000d per day. Make sure the bike you get has a lock. You can get the tires pumped up at just about any street corner for 300d to 500d per tire.

By Car

These days in Hanoi it seems as if everybody with four wheels want to rent you their car. This has caused rental rates to drop slightly, but you can still count on paying from $30 to $35 per day in the city for an air-conditioned sedan and a driver. Expect to pay $40 or more per day for a minivan.

To hire a car and driver, contact any hotel, a large operator such as Vietnam Tourism, one of the tourist cafés, or any other travel agency (☞ Travel Agencies, *below*). If you play your cards right—i.e., don't rent from a large hotel—you can probably rent a coffin-black Russian Volga for $25 per day or less. These clunkers aren't so reliable, however, so you'd best not be heading off to sign a $20 million joint-venture agreement in one.

You can almost certainly arrange for a pickup at your hotel, although a deposit—usually 50% of the fare and some form of identification such as a photocopy of your passport—is often expected. There is need for you to leave your passport with the agency renting you the car. The general time frame for day rentals is from 8 AM until dusk. If you keep the car beyond 5:30 or 6, the rates will rise. Before you rent the car, make sure it is clear *exactly* how much the rate will rise if you keep the car longer.

See The Northwest A to Z *in* Chapter 3 for information on renting four-wheel-drive vehicles.

By Cyclo

Cyclo drivers in Hanoi are less likely to speak English than their Saigon counterparts, so definitely bring a map and be prepared to gesture. On the upside, cyclos here are wider than anywhere else in Vietnam, so two medium-size Westerners can squeeze into one; the fare is usually from 5,000d to 10,000d, depending on the distance. A cyclo driver will be more than happy to take you around for the whole day for as little as 40,000d to 50,000d. Make sure you're both on the same wavelength when you're talking money: unsuspecting travelers have been known to agree to a fare of 10,000d, only to have the cyclo driver later claim the agreed-upon figure was $10. *See* Transportation Around Vietnam *in* Smart Travel Tips A to Z for more information.

By Motorbike

Motorbike taxis, known as xe om or *Honda om,* are one way to get around the city—if you're brave. Although the traffic may look a little daunting, drivers (hopefully) know how to navigate the traffic.

If you decide to rent a motorbike yourself and drive around the city, realize the traffic *is* busy, loud, and crazy. And although the streets may be less intimidating in Hanoi than in Ho Chi Minh City, the consensus is that drivers are worse. And Westerners are paying the price: Vietnam's number one cause of injuries and death of foreigners is accidents involving a motorcycle. You can purchase helmets on Pho Hue and Lo Duc streets. Don't become a Vietnam traffic statistic—wear one. That said, many hotels and tourist cafés rent motorbikes. Prices start at about 70,000d per day. A deposit is usually required, as is a passport or a photocopy, and you sign a short-term contract (be sure you're aware of the stipulated value of the bike in the contract). And speaking of contracts, you would be wise to consult your insurance policy; many companies refuse to cover motorcycle drivers or riders.

Memory Café (⊠ 33bis Tran Hung Dao St., Hoan Kiem District, ☎ 04/826–5854) has motorcycles available. **Tourist Service Office** (⊠ 18C Ngo Quyen St., Hoan Kiem District, ☎ 04/824–7391) is a good place for rentals.

By Taxi

Although Hanoi's cabbies act like reckless kings of the road, taxis are still the safest way to get around town. The moment you step into a cab, the meter (all cabs in Hanoi should be metered) reads 14,000d; after that rates run about 5,600d per kilometer. A trip across town will cost you about 25,000d.

Taxis tend to congregate at the northwest corner of Hoan Kiem Lake, on Trieu Viet Vuong Street, and outside most major hotels. You can also call for a cab, as all taxi dispatchers speak English. Competition is intense; a cab will probably be at your doorstep in less than three minutes if you're somewhere downtown. And don't be surprised if the cab that shows up is from a different company than the one you called; it means they've intercepted your request. Order a taxi by phone from the following:

Airport Taxi (☎ 04/825–4250); **Hanoi Taxi** (☎ 04/853–5252); **Red Taxi** (☎ 04/856–8686); **Taxi CP** (☎ 04/824–1999); and **Taxi PT** (☎ 04/856–5656).

Contacts and Resources

Currency Exchange

The dollar has proven almighty, even in the capital of communist Vietnam, and exchanging greenbacks for Vietnamese dong is easy. Most major international banks in Hanoi have a currency exchange and other financial services such as money transfers, credit-card cash advances, and cashing traveler's checks. Vietnamese banks, such as Vietcom Bank and VID Public Bank, also have such services. The rates of exchange at the international banks are controlled by the State Bank of Vietnam, so you'll likely find one is as good as the other. Hotels, too, can change money.

The dong has been stable for the past six years, although the currency crisis that beset the rest of Southeast Asia in 1997 has had some effect. Your best bet is generally the gold and jewelry shops around town. Jewelry shops have exchange bureau licenses. Avoid the black-market money changers who gather around the General Post Office; they are illegal (though such rules are rarely enforced) and usually try to cheat customers.

Many of Hanoi's shops and upscale restaurants will accept both dollars and dong. Some shops, such as art galleries, list all their prices in U.S. dollars.

Major banks in Hanoi include the following:

ABN-AMRO Bank (✉ Daeha Business Center, 360 Kim Ma St., Ba Dinh District, ☎ 04/831–5250, FAX 04/831–6874), **ANZ Bank** (✉ 14 Le Thai To St., Hoan Kiem District, ☎ 04/825–8190, FAX 04/825–8189), **Bank of America** (✉ 27 Ly Thuong Kiet St., Hoan Kiem District, ☎ 04/824–9316, FAX 04/824–9322), **Citibank** (✉ 17 Ngo Quyen St., Hoan Kiem District, ☎ 04/825–1950, FAX 04/824–3960), **Credit Lyonnais** (✉ 10 Trang Thi St., Hoan Kiem District, ☎ 04/825–9625, FAX 04/826–0080), **Deutsche Bank** (✉ 53 Quang Trung St., Hoan Kiem District, ☎ 04/826–8554, FAX 04/826–8652), **Standard Chartered Bank** (✉ 49 Hai Ba Trung St., 8th floor, Hoan Kiem District, ☎ 04/825–8970, FAX 04/825–8880), **VID Public Bank** (✉ 2 Ngo Quyen St., Hoan Kiem District, ☎ 04/826–6953, FAX 04/826–8228), and **Vietcom Bank** (Bank for Foreign Trade of Vietnam; ✉ 23 Phan Chu Trinh St., Hoan Kiem District, ☎ 04/934–3137, FAX 04/824–1395).

Doctors and Hospitals

Medical facilities in Hanoi are not up to international standards. A few foreign-run medical clinics offer basic treatment—at Western prices—and can arrange for emergency medical evacuation in the region.

Emergency Viet Duc Hospital (Benh Vien Viet Duc; ✉ 40 Trang Th St., Hoan Kiem District, ☎ 04/825–5956) is open 24 hours for emergency surgery; the staff speaks English, French, and German.

Hanoi Family Medical Practice (✉ A-1 Bldg., Van Phuc Diplomatic Compound, Suite 109–112, Kim Ma Rd., Ba Dinh District, ☎ 04/843–074? 09/040–1919 for emergency mobile phone) is the creation of Israe Dr. Rafi Kot, who has one of the busiest practices in Hanoi. An expe staff of foreign doctors offers x-rays, ultrasound, blood screening dental work, inoculations, and pediatric care.

Institute of Traditional Medicine (✉ 26 Nguyen Binh Khiem St., Hoa Kiem District, ☎ 04/943–1018) specializes in herbal treatmen acupuncture, and massage, as well as the diagnosis and treatment of illness through various methods.

International SOS (✉ 31 Hai Ba Trung St., Hoan Kiem District, ☎ 04/934–0555), formerly AEA International, arranges emergency medical assistance, with referrals or evacuations. Routine health care and dentistry are also available.

Olaf Palme Swedish Hospital (Benh Vien Olop Panmo; ✉ Lang Trung St., Dong Da District, ☎ 04/834–3176) treats children and adults.

Vietnam International Hospital (Benh Vien Quoc Te Viet Nam; ✉ 1 Phuong Mai Rd., next to Bach Mai Hospital, Hai Ba Trung District, ☎ 04/574–0740; 04/574–1111 for emergencies) opened in 1997 with much fanfare and hope. Gynecology, dentistry, and accident and emergency treatment are among the services; English-speaking doctors are available.

Embassies

If you have passport problems while in Hanoi, have had something very expensive stolen, or are extremely ill, contact your embassy.

Australia (✉ 8 Dao Tan St., Van Phuc Quarter, Ba Dinh District, ☎ 04/831–7755, FAX 04/831–7711). **Canada** (✉ 31 Hung Vuong St., Ba Dinh District, ☎ 04/823–5500, FAX 04/823–5333). **New Zealand** (✉ 32 Hang Bai St., Hoan Kiem District, ☎ 04/824–1481, FAX 04/824–1480). **United Kingdom** (✉ 31 Hai Ba Trung St., Hoan Kiem District, ☎ 04/825–2510, FAX 04/826–5762). **United States** (✉ 7 Lang Ha St., Ba Dinh District, ☎ 04/843–1500, FAX 04/843–1510).

Emergencies

Ambulance (☎ 15). **Fire** (☎ 14). **Police** (☎ 13).

English-Language Bookstores

The selection of English-language reading material—or even Vietnamese-language books, for that matter—is notoriously bad in Hanoi. All bookstores are state-run, and censorship is heavy. But in some, particularly on Trang Tien Street, you will be able to find a selection of international newspapers and magazines, provided none has infuriated Xunhasaba, the state-owned book distributor that occasionally yanks an issue off the shelves if a story portrays Vietnam too harshly.

The Gioi Publishers Bookshop (✉ 46 Tran Hung Dao St., Hoan Kiem District, ☎ 04/825–1289) has a varied selection of books on Vietnamese history, language, culture, and military exploits.

Hieu Sach Hanoi (✉ 34 Trang Tien St., near the Metropole Hotel Sofitel, Hoan Kiem District, ☎ 04/824–1615) has a selection of books in English.

The **National Library** (✉ 31 Trang Thi St., Hoan Kiem District, ☎ 04/825–5397) is in a lovely compound. There are books in English, but you're not allowed to comb through the stacks; locate the book you want on one of the few computers on offer (you're allotted five minutes), and an assistant will bring it to you. You must show your passport to enter.

The **State Bookshop** (✉ 44 Trang Tien St., Hoan Kiem District, ☎ 04/825–4282) has a wide range of newspapers and magazines, as well as plenty of books about Vietnam.

Xunhasaba (✉ 32 Hai Ba Trung St., Hoan Kiem District, ☎ 04/826–0382), or the State Enterprise for the Import and Export of Books and Periodicals, has a wide selection of mainly technical titles, such as computer-instruction manuals. The staff is not helpful, and the store closes for lunch.

Film Developing and Camera and Watch Repair

For the best film developing, try the storefronts at 1 Trang Thi Street and 19 Ba Trieu Street. Cameras can be fixed at any of the many camera repair shops on Trang Thi Street, on the south side of Hoan Kiem Lake, but for serious repairs, you're better off buying a point-and-shoot camera in Hanoi and fixing your trusty SLR when you get home.

For watch repair, try **Phuc Hung** (✉ 13 Hang Phen St., Hoan Kiem District, ☎ 04/828–1247). Expect minimal English but fast service. **Tuan Dung** (✉ 61 Hang Dao St., Hoan Kiem District, ☎ 04/826–4758) has a good selection of unusual batteries.

Guided Tours
See Travel Agencies, *below.*

Late-Night Pharmacies
See Emergency Viet Duc Hospital *in* Doctors and Hospitals, *above.*

Post Office
The **General Post Office** (Buu Dien Trung Vong; ✉ 75 Dinh Tien Hoang St., Hoan Kiem District, ☎ 04/825–7036) occupies most of a city block across from Hoan Kiem Lake. Phone, fax, and telex services are available, as is express-mail service from companies such as Federal Express, DHL, and UPS. It's open daily from 6:30 AM to 8 PM. Dozens of other small post-office branches dot the city.

Precautions
See Safety *in* Smart Travel Tips A to Z.

Travel Agencies
The following travel agencies operate in Hanoi—some in many other parts of the country as well. They offer visitor information, transportation and hotel bookings, car and bus rentals, guided tours, private tour guides, and visa extensions. If you've signed on to a package tour from the United States, Europe, or Australia, it is highly likely you'll be cared for by one of these companies. *See* Tour's & Packages *and* Travel Agencies *in* Smart Travel Tips A to Z for a further discussion of your options.

Ann's Tourist (✉ 26 Yet Kieu St., Hoan Kiem District, ☎ FAX 04/822–0018, ✉), headquartered in Saigon but with another office in Hanoi, is a private company that coordinates package and private tours and can assist with air or train reservations and car rentals.

Buffalo Tours (✉ 11 Hang Muoi St., Hoan Kiem District, ☎ 04/828–0702, FAX 04/826–9370) is one of a handful of young upstart tour companies that have it together. They're quite handy with smaller and more quirky tours and services, such as dinner cruises on West Lake or kayaking trips.

Exotissimo Travel (✉ 26 Tran Nhat Duat St., Hoan Kiem District, ☎ 04/828–2150, FAX 04/828–2146, ✉) has rapidly become one of the biggest foreign names in the business in Hanoi. An international wholesale inbound tour operator for more upscale travelers, Exotissimo offers retail and walk-in services as well. It caters mainly to Francophone clientele but is expanding its English-language service.

Hanoi Toserco (✉ 8 To Hien Thanh St., Hai Ba Trung District, ☎ 04/878–0004, FAX 04/822–6055, ✉), a large state-run office, arranges travel services, books hotels, finds housing, and coordinates package tours.

Hanoi Tourism (✉ 18 Ly Thuong Kiet St., Hoan Kiem District, ☎ 04/826–6714, FAX 04/824–1101, ✉) is one of the city's biggest state-run travel agencies.

OSC Vietnam Tours (✉ 38 Yet Kieu St., Hoan Kiem District, ☎ 04/826–4500, FAX 04/825–9260) is the travel arm of the gargantuan Oil Services Company of Vietnam, headquartered in Vung Tau.

Saigon Tourist (✉ 55 Phan Chu Trinh St., Hoan Kiem District, ☎ 04/825–0923, FAX 04/825–1174 for tours), the largest tour agency in Vietnam, is based in Saigon but has an office in the capital. Service is sometimes impersonal, but they can arrange everything.

TF Handspan Travel (✉ 36 Nguyen Huu Huan St., Hoan Kiem District, ☎ 04/926–0444) is a small but reliable outfit specializing in the quirky and adventurous, such as kayaking trips on the Da River.

Vidotour (✉ 28 Hoa Ma St., Hoan Kiem District, ☎ 04/821–5682, FAX 04/972–1107), one of the largest private tour agencies in Vietnam, can provide many travel services, especially in the south.

Vietnam Tourism (✉ 30A Ly Thuong Kiet St., Hoan Kiem District, ☎ 04/825–6916, FAX 04/825–7583) is another one of the country's large state-run travel agencies.

Vinatour (✉ 54 Nguyen Du St., Hoan Kiem District, ☎ 04/825–5963, FAX 04/825–2707), one of Vietnam's first tour companies, is a midsize state-run agency.

TOURIST CAFÉS

These (mainly) private companies offer many of the services of large travel agencies but usually at lower prices. Many double as hotels and restaurants, and some have computers where you can check e-mail or surf the Internet. Most are not equipped to handle tour bookings from overseas; it's mainly a walk-in business.

Pricewise, the tourist cafés' group tours can't be beat. For instance, a full-day guided tour to the Perfume Pagoda, including transportation, entrance fees, and boat rides, costs as little as $10 per person. To Halong Bay it's an even better deal (from less than $20 per person for two boat rides, a guide, lunch, and an overnight stay), but the accommodations are usually in average minihotels. (*See* Travel Agencies *in* Smart Travel Tips A to Z for more discussion of tourist cafés.)

Green Bamboo Café (✉ 2B Trang Thi St., Hoan Kiem District, ☎ 04/824–9179, FAX 04/826–4949 ✉) had been the reigning café king for some time, but their new digs are a bit sterile. Their tour services are still hard to beat.

Meeting Cafe (✉ 59 Ba Trieu St., Hoan Kiem District, ☎ 04/825–8813) is good for arranging small tours.

Memory Café (✉ 33bis Tran Hung Dao St., Hoan Kiem District, ☎ 04/826–5854) is a tiny café run by a friendly couple.

Old Darling Cafe (✉ 7 Hang Quat St., Hoan Kiem District, ☎ 04/828–9977) was the second café run by the original owner of the Darling (☞ *below*); he's since left, but the café soldiers on, albeit in a less comfy space.

Queen Café (✉ 65 Hang Bac St., Hoan Kiem District, ☎ 04/826–0860, FAX 04/826–0300, ✉) is Hanoi's current mother of travel cafés. Backpackers stream in and out of the joint; if you feel like a number in here, it's because you *are* a number in here. Service, however, is among the best in town.

Real Darling Cafe (✉ 33 Hang Quat St., Hoan Kiem District, ☎ 04/826–9386, FAX 04/825–6562), the site of the original Darling organization, is far busier than the "Old" version (☞ *above*). They've been around for nearly a decade and provide full tour packages to northern Vietnam, among other things.

Sinh Café (✉ 56 Hang Be St., Hoan Kiem District, ☎ 04/824–2457, FAX 04/822–6055) is affiliated with the Saigon heavy hitter of the same name as well as state-owned Hanoi Toserco. There are (at least) four different branches of this cafe, whose specialty is the Sinh Café Open Tour, a bus service that runs the length of the country (☞ Bus Travel *in* Smart Travel Tips A to Z.)

Tin Tin Pub (✉ 14 Hang Non St., Hoan Kiem District, ☎ 04/826–0860, FAX 04/825–0000) was once one of the busiest tourist cafés in town, but business has slowed down somewhat.

Tourist Smiling Café (✉ 22 Cau Go St., Hoan Kiem District, ☎ 04/ 824–4554) is one tourist café option.

3 THE NORTH

HALONG BAY, SAPA, DIEN BIEN PHU

Northern Vietnam's stark beauty lies in its mist-shrouded islets and rice-terraced mountains. Fishing boats ply the magnificent waters of Halong Bay, while diligent farmers harvest crops on the steep slopes of the Tonkinese Alps, and fluttering rice stalks whisper the rhythm of Mai Chau Valley. In the shadow of Fansipan, the country's tallest peak, are the villages of northern Vietnam's ethnic minority groups. This region of imposing mountains bore witness to French ignominy at Dien Bien Phu—and at the same time nurtured Ho Chi Minh's revolution.

By Michael
Mathes

THE SPECTACULAR TOPOGRAPHY OF THE NORTH includes the Hoang Lien Mountains—or Tonkinese Alps, as they are commonly called—the sprawling Red River Delta, and Halong Bay's limestone islets jutting out of the South China Sea. Even though the region has borne the brunt of centuries of war—first the Chinese invaders, then the French colonialists, the Americans, and once again the Chinese—and bomb craters still pockmark the Red River Delta, much of northern Vietnam has maintained its austere beauty.

The Red River Delta is the most densely populated area of Vietnam, with more than 1,000 people per square mile, compared with approximately 400 per square mile in the Mekong Delta. Many of these inhabitants of the Red River Delta, and those in the mountains to the north and west, are very poor. Extreme weather patterns—too much rain and too many damaging storms in the wet season, too little rain in the dry season—make living off the land more difficult than in the south. Years of postcolonial isolation, xenophobia, and ruinous collectivization programs also drove the north to the brink of disaster. Although forced collectivization and other such socialist land schemes have been confined to the dustbins of history, there are new threats and concerns for the indigenous people of northern Vietnam.

In the remote highlands and valleys north and west of Hanoi, ethnic minority populations continue to live as they have for centuries—despite the government's attempts at cultural integration. The history of these unique ethnic minorities is still the subject of some dispute, but many anthropologists now believe the largest of these ethnic groups, the Muong, as well as smaller groups like the Kho-mu, the Khang, the Mang, and the La Ha, have been living in the Hoang Lien Mountains and the northern foothills for thousands of years, preceding even the arrival of the Kinh—the ethnic Vietnamese who now make up 87% of the country's population.

Most other groups migrated from China or Laos—some as late as the 19th century—as a result of war or lack of land. (Communities of a number of these ethnic minorities can still be found in the countries from which they came, including China, Laos, Thailand, Cambodia, and Burma; migration across national borders is common.) Living in the highest elevations, near the climatic limits of hill rice cultivation, are the H'mong and Dao (pronounced *zao*). The clothing and jewelry of these two groups, particularly the women, are among the most colorful and elaborate in the north. The Muong and Thai (with distinct Black Thai and White Thai subgroups) are two of the larger minorities, each numbering about a million. They practice wetlands cultivation on the middle and lower slopes and generally live in airy, comfortable stilt houses in village clusters ranging from a handful of houses to several dozen.

Slash-and-burn agriculture, the traditional mainstay of ethnic minority economies, was for centuries an ideal form of natural resource management. Over the last decade or more, however, as the land available for such cultivation shrinks, this method has begun to generate heated controversy in Vietnam and has been blamed for just about every natural calamity that has befallen the north. Indeed, northern Vietnam is the most deforested region of Indochina, with as much as 90% of its primary forests lost to human encroachment. Acres of trees are cut down every day for use as fuel or for wood for construction. A migration of Kinh Vietnamese from the Red River Delta farther inland and into the distant valleys is also displacing many nomadic farmers as land privatization plans take hold.

Vietnam's growing energy needs are also wreaking havoc on minority life. The Hoa Binh Dam, Vietnam's first hydroelectric power project, 70 km (43 mi) southwest of Hanoi, displaced 60,000 people from the Da River valley. Most were ethnic minorities who were pushed into higher elevations, geography in which they had little farming experience or expertise. Another, larger hydroelectric project, farther up the Da River in Son La Province, has already been approved. Feasibility studies estimate that 440 square km (170 square mi) of forest and farming area will be sacrificed, and anywhere from 110,000 to 143,000 people displaced.

From the mid-19th century until their departure in 1954, French colonialists had varied and extensive contact with these ethnic minority groups, all of whom they referred to as Montagnards (mountain people). Some of these groups sided with the French against the Kinh Vietnamese, whereas others helped foment rebellion against the French.

Only in the last few years have large numbers of tourists begun to seek out ethnic minority villages in northern Vietnam. For the villagers it has been a mixed blessing. A booming business of selling handicrafts, clothing, and textiles to tourists has sprung up in many communities, and around Sapa in particular. Increased contact between these ethnic minorities and tourists has created a flurry of interest in their cultures and lives but has also cost them some privacy. For instance, one unfortunate casualty has been the near disappearance of Saturday-night "love markets," where young Red Dao men and women in search of a spouse or lover would pair off for an evening of socializing and possible romance. In Sapa there is no sign of this market, which was once the highlight of the trip for visitors. Too many flashbulbs and curious foreign faces have driven the love market out of the spotlight and into more remote areas of the north.

Pleasures and Pastimes

Dining

Except for Hanoi and the coastal regions, dining in the north is more of a necessity than a delight. Seafood dishes in Haiphong, Cat Ba, Halong Bay, and farther up the coast are delicious. The mountains provide few opportunities for gourmands, however. Rice is a staple, of course, as well as corn, cassava, and green vegetables. Pond stocking ensures an ample fish supply. Although beef is now readily available in mountain towns, pork is the more common meat. Chicken, pork, and beef are usually tough, however, and little of the animals goes to waste. In the homes of poorer villagers especially, keep an eye out for meat dishes; they're usually accompanied by offal, and your hosts may not realize that most people from the West steer clear of such fare. By the same token, understand that meats are still a delicacy in many poor communities; as foreign visitors are still extremely rare in some areas, your hosts may splurge and butcher a pig or a few chickens in your honor. Deciding what to eat and what to pass up is an issue to treat with some sensitivity.

One "pleasure" that you most likely will be unable to avoid while traveling through the highlands is rice wine, or *ruou* (pronounced zeeoo). Distilled locally, ruou is everywhere, and is used as a welcoming drink. It is also drunk at lunch, before, during, and after dinner, while gathering with friends, when meeting with officials, at small and large celebrations, and as a good-luck send-off. Refusing it outright is difficult, stopping once you've started is nearly impossible, and getting sick from drinking too much is easy.

A communal twist on the ruou standard is *ruou can* (straw-rice wine), which is consumed by up to a dozen people at the same time through bamboo straws stuck into an earthenware jar. First half-filled with manioc and rice husks, the jar is sealed tight and left to ferment for 17 days. On the day of consumption, a water-sugar mixture is added. The sweet, slightly fetid alcohol is downed at weddings and other major celebrations—such as a couple of foreigners stepping into a remote village. It's beneficial that ruou can is more diluted than its bottled brother, which can be anywhere from 60 to 110 proof.

Hiking

One of the best ways to experience northern Vietnam is by tackling the trails that lead out of the towns and into more remote areas of the highlands. Whether you're stepping into a national park (Cuc Phuong [☞ Chapter 2], Ba Be, and Cat Ba Island national parks all have spectacular hiking) or onto a Montagnard trail, these footpaths lead through more pristine terrain than you would be able to see from the back seat of a bouncing jeep. Wildlife sightings are more likely (but still rare) the farther you are from busy roads and towns. Villages throughout the mountains are connected by trails, and it may not be long before someone produces a publication documenting and mapping a network of the best hiking trails in the north. Until then, however, your best bet is to pick up local maps when you arrive at a destination. Dozens of trails lead out of the hillside town of Sapa, for instance, and into H'mong villages. Minority peoples have a vast knowledge of local routes, but communication may be a problem. You may want to have a guide along, especially if you intend on trekking to the foot—or if you've got three or four days, to the top—of Mt. Fansipan, Vietnam's highest peak.

The tourist cafés in Hanoi (☞ Hanoi A to Z *in* Chapter 2) have begun organizing tours that combine four-wheel drive transportation and serious hiking. It won't exactly be a one-on-one experience with nature, but the tour operators have researched the hikes with knowledgeable locals and are pretty familiar with the needs and desires of Western travelers.

If you're going hiking but are concerned about land mines and unexploded ordnance in the north, keep in mind that there is little to fear if you stay on marked trails or on clear footpaths. However, unless you're with an experienced guide, you should not hike along Vietnam's border region with China, specifically in the area around Lang Son and Mong Cai. Mine laying was common during the 1979 border war, and it's best to skip unmarked hillside exploring.

Jeep Trips

Adventure awaits on the roads of the north. Mud slides, breakdowns, and teeth-rattling stretches of "highway" compete for your attentions with spectacular scenery, revolutionary history, and ethnic minority culture. Only in a rented Russian jeep—or in a far more civilized Toyota Land Cruiser or Mitsubishi Pajero—are you in complete control of where and when you stop. The no-nonsense drivers speak little English, but they're also quite familiar with the terrain and can lead you to sights left alone by the big tour companies. By far the most popular multiple-day jeep route is northwest from Hanoi, including overnight stops at Mai Chau, Dien Bien Phu, and Sapa. Some villages just a mile or two off the road haven't seen Westerners since the French left in 1954. Arrange a jeep tour of any length from a Hanoi hotel, tour operator, or tourist café (they can also book your hotels). You'll pay by the kilometer and by the number of nights your driver is away from home.

Lodging

Except in the major cities such as Hanoi and Haiphong and established tourist destinations like Halong Bay and Sapa, accommodations in the north lack many basic amenities. If you're looking for comfort, stick close to Hanoi. In other small cities and towns such as Dien Bien Phu, Lang Son, or Lao Cai, expect hot running water in your hotel room, but don't count on having IDD phones, heaters, or bathtubs. In more remote areas, such as ethnic minority villages near Yen Phu or small coastal communities in the far northeast, expect to share a mat or roll-away mattress in the living room of a host family—with a bathroom that's a curtained shack next to a well where you draw your own water. Don't write such an experience off, however; many of the stilt houses in ethnic minority villages are exquisitely built, cool, and comfortable, and you may find the owners to be your most gracious hosts.

Shopping

If you've got an eye for indigenous style, northern Vietnam can be your mecca. The region's ethnic minority communities, particularly the women of these groups, have developed sophisticated trading networks, not just among themselves but for tourists as well. And what's trading hands is positively beautiful: richly dyed textiles; hand-loomed silk scarves, headdresses, and broadcloth; brocaded vests and dresses; woven bamboo baskets of all shapes and sizes; and traditional silver jewelry. The "industry" has even internationalized, and savvy distributors in Hanoi and Saigon are scrambling to send Vietnam's ethnic minority styles to overseas markets.

Exploring the North

A trip to the north is difficult to rush because traveling around often takes a long time, and changing weather can make some roads quite dangerous—even impassable. Roads for the most part are in bad shape. The major highways of the lowlands (Highway 5 to Haiphong, Highway 1 to Lang Son, Highway 6 to Hoa Binh) are being continuously upgraded, and the construction itself slows down traffic flow. In the mountains of the north and northwest, heavily traveled routes are paved but are still in lousy condition. Routes to distant villages like Muong Te or remote destinations like Ha Giang town are rutted dirt roads that wash out with the first heavy rain. Traveling them can be physically exhausting.

With this in mind, there are two ways to travel through the north. The most challenging is to cover the region by car, from Hanoi to Son La to Dien Bien Phu to Lai Chau to Sapa and back to Hanoi. This route is adventurous and allows for some great exploring, but it's a challenge: five or more days on rutted mountain roads is not for everyone. Make a run to the Chinese border near Lang Son, or stop at Ba Be Lake on the way back to Hanoi for a leisurely few days in this stunningly remote nature preserve. You'll have to have some idea of your itinerary before leaving Hanoi, however; your driver will want to know how long he'll be away from home.

The easiest way to see the north is to base yourself in Hanoi (☞ Chapter 2) or Haiphong, from which you can take two- or three-day trips. Using this method is highly recommended because it gives you a way to appreciate northern Vietnam without the discomforts of one endless, grueling road trip. You can either arrange these trips yourself or sign up with one of a variety of tour operators. Some destinations are too far for day trips, but you can easily hire a car or jeep to head there and back, or to get to Sapa, you can hop on the relatively comfortable overnight train from Hanoi.

Tours organized by Hanoi's tourist cafés (☞ Hanoi A to Z *in* Chapter 2) cover the more popular destinations and are the most inexpensive and time-efficient way to see this region. Large travel agencies in Hanoi such as Vietnam Tourism, Saigon Tourist, and Exotissimo Travel (☞ Hanoi A to Z *in* Chapter 2) arrange tours that are more expensive and, perhaps, more comfortable. Lodging, transportation, entrance fees to sites, and most meals are usually included. If you don't want to be stuck with a group of strangers (tourist cafés usually fill up a minivan or larger—from 6 to 20 people; international tour companies and the large tour operators inside the country try to fill up coach buses—from 15 to 40 people), you're better off renting a car with a driver from your hotel or a tour agency. If you'd like to be in control of every single aspect of the trip, including driving, your best bet is to rent a motorbike.

Numbers in the text correspond to numbers in the margin and on The North map.

Great Itineraries

Destinations in the north can be grouped into two geographic categories: the lowland areas in and around the Red River Delta; and the Hoang Lien Mountains, or Tonkinese Alps. If you have more than four days, it's quite easy to venture into both the lowlands *and* the mountains. You can reach the delightful scenery on the coast, specifically Halong Bay and Cat Ba, from Hanoi in as little as four hours. Travel in the mountains is usually slower and requires more patience, but you'll soon discover that heading up into the northern highlands brings you into another world: a world of rugged and austere beauty, fascinating ethnography, and timeless traditions.

IF YOU HAVE 3 DAYS

If you don't have much time in the north, start with ⊞ **Halong Bay** ③. From Hanoi you can easily get to this jewel in northern Vietnam's topographical crown. Hire a car from the capital or go with an organized trip and head east to Halong City, where you can hop on one of dozens of tour boats that can shuttle you around the thousands of limestone islands. Stay in one of the many hotels in town, or if adventure is your modus operandi, spend the night on the boat. From there catch a ferry to **Cat Ba Island** ④, the largest in the Halong Bay region and site of one of Vietnam's most beautiful national parks. Either return to your car in Halong City or take the high-speed ferry back to Haiphong, where you can catch the train or a minibus back to Hanoi.

IF YOU HAVE 6 DAYS

Travel from Hanoi to ⊞ **Sapa** ⑫ and spend three days exploring the mountain trails that lead to ethnic minority villages. Head to the popular Saturday market, where members of ethnic groups such as the Red Dao and the H'mong gather to buy provisions and sell fabrics and clothing. You can see Sapa in a day's travel to and from Hanoi—or book a soft sleeper on the night train from the capital. If you've hired a four-wheel-drive vehicle to Sapa, consider an overnight side trip to the remote but incredibly beautiful ⊞ **Ba Be Lakes** ⑦.

IF YOU HAVE 9 DAYS

If you have more than a week and can stand being in a car for many hours on rough roads, traveling through the farthest reaches of the north can be a true adventure. Rent a four-wheel-drive vehicle (driver included) and do a circuit of this dramatic highland region. From Hanoi head for **Mai Chau** ⑨; you'll pass the impressive Hoa Binh Hydroelectric Power Dam on the way. Stay overnight in the lovely minority villages near Mai Chau or push on to ⊞ **Son La** ⑩. From here head through spectacular valleys to infamous ⊞ **Dien Bien Phu** ⑪, near the Laotian border, to e

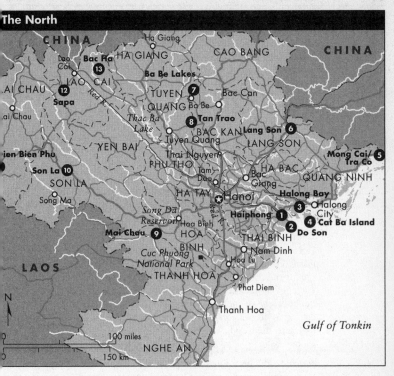

plore the ruins of the French garrison. Wind your way over the bumpy roads past scenic and laid-back Lai Chau to 🏔 **Sapa** ⑫ and **Bac Ha** ⑬, and then take a full day's drive back to Hanoi. Or break up the journey back by stopping at the 🏔 **Ba Be Lakes** ⑦. An alternative itinerary is to take the return train from Hanoi to Sapa, take a two-day jaunt to Mai Chau from the capital, and fly from Hanoi to Dien Bien Phu. For the last few days head to the crystal-clear waters of 🏔 **Halong Bay** ③.

When to Tour the North

The best time to tour the northern highlands is from late October to mid-December, after the August–October monsoons have abated and any mud slides are likely to have been cleared. As for Halong Bay, the season runs from early summer to mid-autumn. From July to September beware of tropical typhoons; flooding in Haiphong and Hanoi is common during these storms. The capital is hot and extremely humid in summer, which makes it a popular time for residents to head for the hills or the coast.

Beach season—which occurs mainly south of Haiphong at Do Son—is mid-summer, when hotels are filled with vacationing Hanoians who for some reason seem to love the extremely narrow and dirty beaches. The season culminates with the Do Son buffalo fights. By late October the place is virtually deserted. If you want the beach resort entirely to yourself, go to Do Son in November.

Northern Vietnam has a clearly defined winter, with a cold and clammy mist settling in for a few months starting in January. January and February are quite cold in the mountains, and Mt. Fansipan, Vietnam's highest peak, is occasionally dusted with snow. If you're heading into the highlands in winter and intend to do some trekking, come prepared: a light sweater, a waterproof jacket, a wool hat, long johns, and some insulated hiking boots should keep you warm.

During Tet, the lunar new year, you'll find northern Vietnam cold and drizzly but extremely festive. If you're coming during this time, make plane and hotel reservations very early. Also understand that many tour operations, such as trips to Halong Bay, are severely limited or suspended during this period.

THE NORTHEAST

Natural beauty and nationalized industry share the spotlight in Vietnam's northeast. Take Quang Ninh Province as an example. Halong Bay and the rest of coastal Quang Ninh are battling with the province's expanding coal-mining industry over precious natural resources. Designated a World Heritage Site by UNESCO in 1995, Halong Bay is a breathtaking collection of limestone islands and secluded coves that captured the imagination and the fancy of millions who saw the movie *Indochine,* starring Catherine Deneuve.

What was once a poor, struggling fishing village catering primarily to Communist Party officials has become the premier vacation spot in the north. Horsepower has long since replaced wind as the means of transport through the bay, and hotels have sprouted like weeds in Halong City, but the emerald waters and mysterious caves of this natural wonder continue to enchant. Just north of Halong Bay lies the gritty, soot-coated town of Cam Pha, the center of Vietnam's coal industry and a threat to the fragile ecosystem of the coast.

Similar destinies and dilemmas face Haiphong. Once the sleepy second cousin to the booming port of Saigon, Haiphong is emerging as more than just Vietnam's second-largest port. The city is awakening to the prospect of both tourism and the rapid development of import-export channels. Tree-lined boulevards, expansive green parks, and impressive if crumbling French colonial architecture fill the downtown. To the north of the city center, 10,000-ton freighters unload containers bound for Hanoi and load up with Vietnamese exports. A new deep-sea port, farther downstream from Haiphong, will be fully operational by 2005.

International trade of a slightly different sort dominates the Wild West atmosphere of Lang Son and Mong Cai, two boomtowns on the Chinese border northeast of Hanoi. Nearly abandoned after retreating Chinese troops leveled them during a brief border war in 1979, the towns have risen again. Little animosity seems to remain between the two nations, which have normalized relations and opened border crossings, and cross-border trade—much of it illicit—is bustling. East of Mong Cai is Tra Co, northern Vietnam's most pristine stretch of beach. It's well off the beaten path, but the unruffled serenity of this coastline makes it worth the trip.

Haiphong

1 *103 km (64 mi) east of Hanoi on Hwy. 5.*

Haiphong, today Vietnam's third-largest city, with a population of more than 1.6 million, has been a hub of the north's industrial activity for the last century and one of its most significant seaports since the Tran dynasty ruled (1225–1400). Because of its strategic location, this port city has seen the coming and going of many foreign invaders. The Bach Dang River, on the outskirts of present-day Haiphong, was the site of one of Vietnam's greatest victories over forces from China: Kublai Khan's 300,000-man army and navy were soundly trumped by Vietnamese under the command of Tran Hung Dao in 1288. Six hundred years later the French settled into Haiphong and began turning it into a major industrial and shipping center. Following the German occupation of France in World War II, the Japanese muscled into Haiphong and began directing valuable Vietnamese exports back to Japan. Once again in control of the port city after the war, the French bombed Haiphong over a bizarre customs dispute, killing up to 1,000 Vietnamese civilians and precipitating the eight-year war between the Vietminh and the French.

Haiphong figured prominently in the war against the Americans as well. Because of its strategic location on the northeast coast, the city was often bombed during the Vietnam War and suffered particularly devastating attacks during the 1972 holiday season that became known as the Christmas bombings. President Richard Nixon ordered the mining of Haiphong Harbor in May 1972. The U.S. Navy was asked to help clear the mines as part of the agreement between the U.S. government and Vietnam in the Paris peace talks of 1973.

In 1979, following conflicts between Vietnam and China, as many as 100,000 ethnic Chinese who had lived for generations in the Haiphong area piled into barely seaworthy boats and fled from what they expected to be deadly reprisals by their Vietnamese neighbors. Few acts of retribution took place, but the damage had been done. Haiphong has struggled to gain back much of its economic power lost because the large section of the merchant class that was Chinese left the city.

Now there is little visible evidence of Haiphong's troubled past, except perhaps the French architecture—much of it delightful—that can be spotted throughout the city center. The city's powerful People's Committee is too busy finding funding for its new deep-sea port and other massive projects to linger over past sentiments.

Haiphong's reputation as a dingy industrial port is not entirely justified. This is indeed the largest and busiest port in the north, and container trucks rumble through town on the way to Highway 5 and Hanoi. But the port itself is on the northern edge of the city and hugs the Cam River, away from the heart of the city. As you cross the Lac Long Bridge into the city center, you leave the dusty and bustling outskirts (where most of the industry with its factories is based) and slip into a quaint, clean downtown. Here huge banyan trees and blossoming magnolias line wide boulevards, and Vietnamese play badminton in the stately Central Square (Quang Truong). A walk through the city center feels like stepping into a time warp: portraits of revolutionary heroes, especially Ho Chi Minh, hang elegantly from the eaves of buildings; socialist realist propaganda posters announce the latest health-awareness campaign; and swarms of bicycles fill the streets.

Today you are most likely to use Haiphong as a transfer point to destinations like Cat Ba, Do Son (both actually part of greater Haiphong), and Halong Bay. Here you can catch a cyclo to the port, and take the first boat out. If you have time, however, settle into an enjoyable two-day stay in Haiphong before moving farther afield. Some say it is what Hanoi was like four years ago: a sleepy northern city with less traffic and less nightlife, but bursting with potential. Even if you're in town for a half day, make the best of your time by picking up the excellent Haiphong Tourist Map at one of the major hotels and then walking around downtown. Or head to Vietnam Tourism (☞ The Northeast A to Z, *below*), a somewhat helpful operation that can find you a hotel, hire a car and driver, and answer questions about ferry and train schedules.

It's very easy to navigate central Haiphong. Sidewalks on the main boulevards are wide, and the parks and gardens provide ample room to roam. If you've come to Haiphong by car and plan to spend a leisurely day sightseeing, have the driver park at a hotel and then go for a long walk.

🕒 Shady, green **Children's Park** (Cong Vien Thieu Nhi), framed by Tran Phu and Tran Hung Dao streets, is the site of tai chi classes in the morning, but children make the best of the playground during the day and the amusement park rides in the evening. At nighttime, strolling couples compete with roller skaters. Many locals come down to the park after dinner to sit at sidewalk stalls and drink fruit shakes or eat sweets.

At the intersection of Hoang Van Thu and Tran Hung Dao streets stands
★ one of the most beautiful buildings in Haiphong: the **City Theater** (Nha Hat Thanh Pho). Built by the French in 1907, this theater has all the exterior designs of a classic, except for its coat of splendidly pink paint. Once the site of lavish French and Vietnamese productions, the 400-seat theater was taken over by the Vietminh following World War II. President Ho Chi Minh addressed the world's youth in a June 1946 speech from the steps. A huge likeness of Uncle Ho now hangs above the wooden front doors—the painting is visible from hundred of yards away and feels eerily like the focal point of the city. In a way it is; the Haiphong People's Committee now holds its major meetings and assemblies here. Stage productions and concerts do take place, but they're rare. If you're not attending a show, you need written permission from the Department of Culture and Information (☎ 031/745–763) to step inside. ⊠ *Between Hoang Van Thu St. and Dinh Tien Hoang St.* ⊙ *Not open to public except for performances or with special permission.*

In the heart of the city, the **Haiphong Museum** (Bao Tang Thanh Pho Hai Phong)—an underrated gem of a building that rivals the City Theater in "pinkness"—is housed in a huge shuttered French villa with creaky wooden staircases, musty corners, and occasionally rotating ceiling fans. Although it attempts to cover all of the history, geography, archaeology, agriculture, and wildlife of the region (the stuffed owl with a rodent in its claws is rather macabre), the museum focuses on Vietnam's struggle for independence from various forces. Make sure you see the Bach Dang stakes, those sharp wooden poles driven into the riverbed that impaled Kublai Khan's boats in 1288, as well as the room dedicated to the Vietnam War. Here you can inspect a (presumably deactivated) MK-52 mine pulled from the waters of Haiphong Harbor in 1973, the lighthouse lantern that warned of impending bombing raids, and the antiaircraft gun that brought down a dozen U.S. planes. Little is in English, so bring a good guide or be prepared to do some guesswork. ⊠ *66 Dien Bien Phu St.* 🎫 *500d.* ⊙ *Daily 7:30 AM–10:30 AM, Wed. and Sun. also 7:30 PM–9:30 PM.*

Haiphong's pagodas are tucked into the city's alleyways or off in the suburbs; no major religious structures except the **Large Cathedral** (Nha Tho Lon; ⊠ 46 Hoang Van Thu St.) stand out in the middle of town. The cathedral was built in 1880 by Catholic missionaries from Spain.

Some beautiful pagodas are found in the southern and eastern districts
★ of the city. The most impressive and moving of these is the **Du Hang Pagoda** (Chua Hang). This 300-year-old temple is a good example of traditional Vietnamese architecture. A gate and three buildings surround a stone courtyard crowded with flowers, statues, and bonsai plants. In front and to the right of the compound is a round pond with lotus flowers encircled by white statues of the Buddha and scholars. One of the 10 monks who live here may be chanting his daily prayers and tapping on a round wooden drum in the richly gilded main sanctuary. Occasionally in the afternoons, the senior monk holds one-on-one healing sessions with the sick or mentally unbalanced. Hundreds of Buddhists fill the courtyard on the first and fifth of every lunar month. To get here follow Cat Cut Street south until you hit Chua Hang Street. After

a few alleyways you'll see the pagoda set back on the left. ✉ *Off Chua Hang St.* 🎫 *Free.* ☉ *Daily 6 AM–11:30 AM and 1 PM–6 PM.*

Quiet **Nghe Temple** (Den Nghe) is dedicated to Le Chan, a heroic peasant woman who helped organize the popular revolt against the Chinese that was led by the two Trung sisters in AD 40. Later Le Chan helped lay the foundation for the city of Haiphong. Ceramic reliefs at the top of the front wall depict the Trung sisters in royal carriages. Two huge red-and-gold wooden carriages (built in 1916), similar to those used by the Trung sisters and by royalty, are on display. Ancestral altars and chapels are to the right, through the courtyard. ✉ *Corner of Me Linh and Le Chan Sts.* 🎫 *Donation.* ☉ *Daily 8–11 and 2–5.*

Before repulsing invaders in AD 938, Emperor Ngo Quyen allegedly gathered his armies at the **Ve (Drawing) Pagoda** (Chua Ve). Similarly, General Tran Hung Dao spied on enemy Chinese troops from a perch on the pagoda grounds and then drew the battle maps that would help him orchestrate a commanding victory in 1288—hence the pagoda's name. ✉ *Behind Holiday Mansion Hotel on Danang St.*

Dining and Lodging

For a city of 1.6 million people, Haiphong doesn't have many upscale restaurants. Local seafood is excellent and cheap, however, and available at any number of nondescript, small, family-run establishments. A few of the better-known ones are listed here, as are the handful of international restaurants on Dien Bien Phu Street. Restaurants specializing in fish are clustered around the north end of Rau Bridge (Cau Rau), a few miles from the city center on the road south to Do Son. Most restaurants close by 10 PM.

Haiphong has little of the style or variety of accommodations available in Hanoi and Saigon—yet. A few international hotels have opened up, but a relative lack of choice makes it easy to decide where to stay (on Dien Bien Phu Street, most likely). It also increases the likelihood that your first choice may be booked. Call ahead if you know your travel dates. If you're shopping around for hotels in person, *definitely* ask to see the room before you hand over your cash; a peculiarly arbitrary pricing system seems to have taken hold in Haiphong, and smaller $20 rooms are often much more pleasant than larger $35 rooms in the same hotel. And keep in mind that almost none of the rates are written in stone (meaning: you may be able to make a deal). Unless noted otherwise, every room comes with a private bath.

$$ ✕ **Chie Japanese Restaurant.** The best Japanese food in the city can be had here. The 11-page menu makes ordering an ordeal, but the staff is patient and won't hesitate to suggest a favorite. Recessed tables and cushioned seating help make you feel a little closer to Tokyo than northern Vietnam. Take your shoes off and relax for a while. ✉ *64 Dien Bien Phu St.,* ☎ *031/821–018. MC, V.*

$$ ✕ **Quan Sake.** This Japanese restaurant cashes in on the growing market of Japanese expatriates living in Haiphong. Traditional fare—minus sushi—is served by a Vietnamese chef trained in Japan. Prix-fixe menus are available at lunch and dinner. As for ambience and decor, consider this: Quan Sake advertises take-out and delivery service. You may want to take them up on it. ✉ *55 Dien Bien Phu St.,* ☎ *031/823–659. No credit cards.*

$ ✕ **Saigon Thien Bao.** This lively restaurant north of the train station serves excellent seafood prepared by the Saigonese-born chef-proprietor. Salads are also a specialty. ✉ *6 Tran Binh Trong St.,* ☎ *no phone. No credit cards.*

$ ✕ **Trung Hoa Restaurant.** Dine on Chinese at this hotel restaurant serving the best Peking duck in town. ⊠ *Hoa Binh Hotel, 104 Luong Khanh Thien St.,* ☎ *031/846–909. No credit cards.*

$$$ 🏨 **Huu Nghi Hotel.** The decor in Haiphong's kitschy hotel of the moment ranges from dungeonlike to gaudy and is impersonal in character, yet the place is often full. Even during the day, anywhere but the ground and top floors can be spooky, dark, and even depressing—if only they'd turn on the lights. At $300, the Superior Suite is the most overpriced room in town. Rooms have IDD phones and satellite TVs. ⊠ *60 Dien Bien Phu St.,* ☎ *031/823–244 or 031/823–310,* FAX *031/ 823–245. 162 rooms. Restaurant, bar, air-conditioning, IDD phones, minibars, pool, tennis court, laundry service, business services, meeting rooms, travel services. AE, DC, MC, V.* ✺

$$$ 🏨 **Royal Garden Harbour View Hotel.** With its French colonial architecture—there's even a Citroën in the driveway—this hotel is Haiphong's one-and-only luxury lodging choice. Rooms here are spacious and tastefully decorated, offering plenty of delicate touches and welcome amenities such as in-room Internet access, IDD phones, and satellite TVs. Breakfast is included in the room rate. ⊠ *4 Tran Phu St.,* ☎ *031/ 827–827,* FAX *031/827–828. 127 rooms. Restaurant, bar, in-room data ports, minibar, massage, laundry service, business services, meeting rooms. AE, MC, V.*

$$ 🏨 **La Villa Blanche.** The three small buildings of this guest house, as well as the larger adjoining quarters run by the affiliated Navy Guest House, are unexciting and overpriced but clean. There is little distinction between the $50 standard room and the $70 superior, so you may want to opt for the less expensive room. Breakfast is included in the price, and rooms have IDD phones. ⊠ *5 Tran Hung Dao St.,* ☎ *031/842– 863 La Villa Blanche; 031/842–856 Navy Guest House,* FAX *031/841– 113. 100 rooms. Air-conditioning, in-room data ports, refrigerators, business services. AE, MC, V.*

$$ 🏨 **Tray Hotel.** Rooms are clean and spacious, but the decor is drab at this hotel popular with Taiwanese and Thai tourists. What the Tray lacks in character, however, it makes up for in amenities, such as IDD phones and satellite TVs, and service. ⊠ *47 Lach Tray St.,* ☎ *031/828– 555 or 031/828–222,* FAX *031/828–666. 78 rooms. Restaurant, bar, pool, barbershop, massage, sauna, laundry service. AE, MC, V.*

$ 🏨 **Dien Bien Hotel.** Despite the wedding banquets that are occasionally thrown in its cheesy restaurant, there's little excitement at this hotel. Rooms are small and clean, and the English-speaking staff is more than happy to help with anything you may need. ⊠ *67 Dien Bien Phu St.,* ☎ *031/842–264,* FAX *031/841–743. 20 rooms. Restaurant, air-conditioning, minibars, refrigerators. MC, V.*

$ 🏨 **Hotel du Commerce (Thuong Mai).** This creaky, aging hotel is run by Vietnam Tourism—nothing except the quirky French colonial exterior suggests otherwise. Most rooms have satellite TV. Rooms in front have nice views and arched hallways but let in too much street noise. Vietnamese food is served in the restaurant. ⊠ *62 Dien Bien Phu St.,* ☎ *031/842– 706,* FAX *031/842–560. 35 rooms. Restaurant, air-conditioning. MC, V.*

$ 🏨 **Thang Nam Hotel.** Two things stand out at the otherwise nondescript Thang Nam: the staff is quiet and thoughtful and knows what you need before you do; and one of the few tennis courts in town is right out back. It's not free, but hotel guests get a discount. ⊠ *55 Dien Bien Phu St.,* ☎ *031/823–460,* FAX *031/841–019. 20 rooms. Air-conditioning. No credit cards.*

Nightlife

If you've got a good set of lungs, you'll be the hit of Haiphong. Every block has its requisite half-dozen **karaoke clubs,** and many hotels are blessed with them as well.

Cola Disco (⊠ 53 Lach Tray St., ☎ 031/844–910) is the biggest and silliest disco going in Haiphong; there is a 40,000d cover for men, less for women. **Do Son Casino** (⊠ Zone 3, Do Son, ☎ 031/861–189) is close enough that you may want to make the trip (☞ Do Son, *below*). The dark **Haiphong Club** (⊠ 17 Tran Quang Khai St., ☎ 031/822–603) has live music. **Maxim's Bar** (⊠ 51 Dien Bien Phu St., ☎ 031/822–934) is a moody, murky spot that provides live music. The **Saigon Café** (⊠ 107 Dien Bien Phu St., ☎ 031/822–195) is Haiphong's version of the corner pub and is popular with locals, expatriates, and travelers.

Getting Around

For information on arriving and departing from Haiphong, *see* The Northeast A to Z, *below*.

BY BICYCLE

Seeing downtown Haiphong by bike is almost idyllic. Unfortunately there are few places to rent them. Try Dien Bien Phu Street or cross streets like Dinh Tien Hoang Street and Minh Khai Street. You could probably get a sturdy Chinese bicycle for the day for about a dollar. Ask at your hotel as a last resort.

BY CYCLO

Haiphong cyclos are often large enough for two Westerners. They're great during the calm of midday or later in the evening when the streets are empty; riding one in the hectic and slow evening rush hour is not advised. Cyclo riders will be happy to cart you around this flat city for an entire day for about 30,000d.

BY MOTORBIKE TAXI (XE OM)

If you're here without wheels and want to see some pagodas outside the city center, a lift on the back of a motorbike may be your best option—especially if you're pressed for time. Prices are comparable to fees for cyclos. You'll arrive quicker than in a three-wheeler but probably more frazzled.

BY TAXI

You probably won't need to take a taxi except to get from the train station to your hotel or to the ferry landing. Taxi companies have figured this out, and plenty wait outside the Haiphong Railway Station and at the ferry landing. Try **Taxi 84 Company** (☎ 031/848–484) or **Viet Phuong Taxi** (☎ 031/828–282 or ☎ 031/878–787) to arrange a ride by phone.

Do Son

❷ *21 km (13 mi) southeast of Haiphong, 124 km (77 mi) southeast of Hanoi.*

This rapidly overbuilt seaside resort was but a quaint fishing village just five years ago. Today the oceanfront is packed with dozens of hotels or what are soon to be hotels. Vietnamese, particularly Hanoians, flock to this resort in midsummer to escape the sweltering heat. Many come to soak up some sun, meander on the promenade, and feast on fresh seafood. Others come for what is euphemistically called "Thai massage," a growing industry in Do Son that has yet to be clamped down. And still others come to swim in the murky waters. The ocean here isn't so much polluted as it is discolored by river silt wash making its way down the coast from Haiphong. But it doesn't make for great beach bathing. Nevertheless, in June, July, and August rooms can be hard to come by. Nearly the entire town is booked up for one week in September during the buffalo fights (☞ *below*). By late autumn beachgoers have completely vacated the place.

The promontory that rises above the finger of land on which Do Son sits provides wonderful views of the fishing harbor on the inland side and of the village itself to the north. The major presence atop the hillside is the **Do Son Casino** (✉ Zone 3, ☎ 031/861–189), the only casino in a country where gambling is technically illegal. The way around this rule is to limit entry to only those with a foreign passport. Slot machines fill the first of two rooms. In the back hall, roulette, blackjack, baccarat, and *tai siiu* (big and small) are offered. There are few people playing; the staff usually outnumbers the guests.

Each year the village gears up for its famous **Do Son Buffalo Fighting Festival,** a semireligious festival honoring local patron saint Diem Tuoc Dai Vuong, also known as the Great Footprint King. The one-day event, obviously not for animal lovers, takes place on the ninth day of the lunar month, usually in about mid-September. Legend has it that on that date in the 1400s, two old men sat playing chess on nearby Nghe Mountain while two buffalos fought below. One of the men turned out to be a saint who left his birdlike footprint on an altar tray, thus identifying himself as the Great Footprint King. This tale may not have much to do with buffalos, but it was enough to start a tradition that draws thousands of visitors to Hai Phong and Do Son to gamble on the fights.

On the day of the fight, the buffalos are led into the stadium in a procession with gongs and drums. Two buffalos face off against each other, their masters releasing them so they can thunder toward each other from a distance of 650 ft. The fights last anywhere from 10 seconds (sometimes the hit from a first charge is deadly) to 15 minutes. This continues all day until only two bulls remain. The thousands of spectators place their own secret bets. Others are not so clandestine; entire villages, which come to see bulls groomed by their neighbors, may put communal bets of up to $10,000 on the line. After the final battle all the participating buffalos are slaughtered for a victory feast, and the winner's head is paraded around the town.

Dining and Lodging

The fresh seafood in Do Son is superb. Most family restaurants lining the beach road in Zones 1 and 2 serve the day's fresh catch. The same cannot yet be said for the hotels, which for the most part serve mediocre food. Most of the hotels were built quickly in the mid-'90s to accommodate growing numbers of visitors.

$　✕ **Tri Huong Restaurant.** Tri and his wife, Huong, run the best-placed restaurant in town, right at the northern edge of the promenade in Zone 1. The seafood is simple but tasty. A lively, almost crazed atmosphere exists in summer. Perversely, what would be the loveliest location for dining—a terrace that juts out into the sea—is actually the parking lot. ✉ *At the northern edge of the promenade in Zone 1,* ☎ *031/861–244. No credit cards.*

$$　☷ **The Garden Resort & Hotel.** Gambling may never be so easy in Vietnam once—or if—this hotel is completed. Set to open by mid-2001, this flashy spot is owned by the casino developers and is just down the hill from gambling central (☞ Do Son Casino, *above*). Plans originally called for a 350-room megacomplex, but the project has been toned down to a 100-room affair. Call the casino ☎ 031/861–189 for inquiries. ✉ *Zone 3, Do Son. 100 rooms. Pool, massage, tennis court, dance club.*

$$　☷ **Hai Au Hotel.** This uninspired structure is where the Do Son Casino currently shuttles its patrons after an evening of vice (you can continue your evil ways at the hotel by taking advantage of free karaoke) Rooms are musty, and it's never a good sign when the porter looks down and scans the floor the moment he turns on the lights. One plus: it's

only 150 yards from the beach. Breakfast is included in the room rate. ⊠ *Zone 2,* ☎ *031/861–272,* FAX *031/861–176. 54 rooms. Restaurant, air-conditioning. AE, DC, MC, V.*

$ ⚏ **Khu Biet Thu Garden Resort.** A five-villa complex from the 1970s sits across the street from the Hai Au Hotel. The most recently remodeled building is nearest the ocean. Ask for one of the second-floor rooms facing the water. Huge trees, a volleyball court, and no in-room phones give the place a pseudo-rustic feel. ⊠ *Zone 2,* ☎ *031/861–226,* FAX *031/ 861–186. 21 rooms. Air-conditioning. No credit cards.*

Halong Bay

★ ❸ *175 km (109 mi) east of Hanoi, 55 km (34 mi) northeast of Haiphong.*

Halong Bay's 3,000 islands of dolomite and limestone cover a 1,500-square-km (579-square-mi) area extending across the Gulf of Tonkin nearly to the Chinese border. According to Chinese legend this breathtaking land- and seascape (similar to the Guilin area of China) was formed by a giant dragon that came barreling out of the mountains toward the ocean. Geologists are more likely to attribute the formations to sedimentary limestone that formed here between 300 and 500 million years ago, in the Paleozoic Era. Over millions of years water receded and exposed the limestone to winds, rain, and tidal erosion.

Today the limestone formations are exposed to hordes of tourists—but don't let that discourage you. Hundreds of fishing trawlers and tour boats share space on these crystal waters, yet there seems to be room for everyone. The eons of erosion have left countless nooks and crannies to explore: secluded half-moon beaches lie at the base of steep untouched forest canopies, and grottoes of all shapes and sizes—some well-trampled, others virtually unknown—are open jaws of stalactites and stalagmites. One of the largest and most visited is the **Grotto of the Wooden Stakes** (Hang Dau Go), claimed to be the 13th-century storage spot for the stakes that General Tran Hung Dao planted in the Bach Dang River in order to repel the invasion of Kublai Khan. This cavernous grotto has three distinct chambers and is reached by climbing 90 steps. Another quite popular destination in the bay is the **Grotto of Bewilderment** (Sung Sot), a stalagmite cave, estimated to be 1 million years old, with 29 chambers inside.

Most people use the main population center, **Halong City,** as a base from which to venture into the bay. Although it's now officially one municipality, Halong City was until 1996 two separate towns: Bai Chay is now Halong City West, where Halong Road winds its way around the coast and past the lifeless central beach; Hon Gai is the grimier Halong City East, where a coal transportation station dominates the center of town and covers nearby roads and buildings with a sooty film. Locals still refer to the towns by their old names. A five-minute ferry ride (500d per person, 7,000d per car) across the mouth of a large inlet links the two communities. Plans for a bridge have been tossed around, but construction has yet to begin.

If you think the mouth of this inlet is a busy place now, just wait a few years, when construction is likely to be going full speed ahead on massive Cai Lan, a deep-water port to be built inside Bai Chay Bay. Millions of tons of coal will be delivered on barges through the straits of Bai Chay to a nearby thermal-power plant. It all sounds like an environmental nightmare, and there has been discussion about UNESCO possibly revoking Halong Bay's status as a World Heritage Site.

Boat trips through Halong Bay are the main attraction. Little of the majesty of this region can be found in the city, so head out onto the water and start exploring. Ten- and 30-ft fishing boats have been converted by the dozen into Halong Bay's tourist-boat fleet. Hotels or travel agencies in Halong Bay or Hanoi (☞ The Northeast A to Z *below, and* Hanoi A to Z *in* Chapter 2) can arrange boat trips for you (often they are part of organized tours from Hanoi), or you can go down to the wharf and bargain yourself onto a boat for the day—although this is becoming more and more difficult. Boats can be had for anywhere from $4 to $20 per hour; if you're going to be out on the bay all day, see if they'll knock 20% off the hourly rate. Unfortunately, if you are making arrangements yourself you may find it's not that simple. It seems an organized ring of boat masters does its best to guide you onto their boats of choice and charge you what they want—even if the creaky dinosaur looks like it's already seen its last three-hour tour. Self-sufficient travelers have fallen victim to the old bait-and-switch: they've arranged a next-day boat tour with local fishermen, only to be told in no uncertain terms the following morning that they could not board their chosen boat, but they could take a different one for quite a bit more money. You may have no choice in the end. Usually travel agencies, however, have their tried-and-true favorites.

Dining and Lodging

Few restaurants distinguish themselves in Halong. Restaurateurs figure you're a captive audience, and they all basically serve up the same dishes: boiled or grilled shrimp, sweet-and-sour fish, and fried squid, washed down with beer. Crabs, sautéed beef with vegetables, and chicken dishes are also readily available. Halong Road and the center of town are crowded with these nondescript eateries.

Halong City West is where most visitors bed down for an evening or two. The city appears to have divided its buildings into two main camps: minihotels and karaoke bars. The larger hotels, some of which are listed below, are slightly less tacky than the average downtown minihotel, which can be had for $20 or less. Sleeping on a fishing boat in Halong Bay is au courant among today's adventure travelers. Tourist companies are hesitant to arrange such overnight accommodations, however, as past incidents with bandits and extortion-happy police have tainted the image of this destination. These days tour groups need permission from the local police; a "permit" runs anywhere from $50 to $100, more if you've got a large group. Note that the posh hotels offer a 50% discount in summer.

$$$ 🏨 **Halong Plaza Hotel.** At this modern luxury hotel close to the ferry landing, a spacious front lobby has a glass-fronted entryway looking out onto the bay. Most of the rooms, too, have views of the bay, although some face the more industrial back side. Rooms are fairly large, have IDD phones, and are decorated with standard but tasteful hotel furnishings. The staff aims to please, but doesn't always quite get it right. ⊠ *8 Halong Rd.,* ☎ *033/845–810,* 𝔽𝔸𝕏 *033/846–867. 200 rooms. 2 restaurants, bar, air-conditioning, in-room safes, minibars, no-smoking rooms, pool, massage, exercise room, dance club, laundry service, business services, meeting rooms. AE, MC, V.*

$$$ 🏨 **Heritage Halong.** This eight-floor glitzy international hotel in front of a nondescript stretch of beach soaks up much of the package-tour business in Halong Bay. Rooms are clean and have IDD phones and satellite TVs; those on the top floors in front have lovely views of the distant islands. ⊠ *88 Halong Rd.,* ☎ *033/846–888,* 𝔽𝔸𝕏 *033/846–999. 101 rooms. Restaurant, café, air-conditioning, pool. AE, MC, V.*

$$ 🏨 **Halong I Hotel.** The grande dame of Halong properties, a French
★   colonial-period restoration, is evocative of a more sublime era. Pull up on the circular gravel driveway and walk down arched open-air pa-

sageways toward the reception area. The front verandas are great for sipping tea and playing cards after dinner. Don't expect fawning service here, however; thankfully the whole place is quiet—except for the strains of karaoke wafting up from the roadside below. Book the Catherine Deneuve Room if you can. The room that the French über-star stayed in while filming *Indochine* tops the price list, but it has an in-room fax and two toilets. A few dozen yards away is the affiliated Halong II Hotel, with less charm and lower prices; the two hotels share booking and reception. ✉ *Halong Rd.,* ☎ *033/846–320,* 𝐅𝐀𝐗 *033/846– 318. Halong I, 23 rooms; Halong II, 38 rooms. Restaurant, air-conditioning. AE, MC, V.*

$ 🏠 **Vuon Dao Hotel.** Ask for one of the top-floor rooms with a view of the sea at this three-story hotel run by Halong Tourist Company, the state-run travel agency. Rooms have IDD phones and satellite TVs. Breakfast is included in the room rate. ✉ *Halong Rd.,* ☎ *033/846–427,* 𝐅𝐀𝐗 *033/846–287. 77 rooms. Restaurant, air-conditioning. MC, V.*

Cat Ba Island

❹ *At southern end of Halong Bay, 30 km (19 mi) east of Haiphong by boat.*

One of Halong Bay's most remarkable formations is Cat Ba Island, 420 square km (162 square mi) of wildly steep spines of mountains, narrow valleys and waterfalls, lush wetlands, golden beaches, and one of Vietnam's most beautiful national parks. The park was established in 1986 to protect about two-thirds of the island. The sea life in much of the surrounding inshore waters is also protected. Included in these ecosystems are tropical evergreen forests, 15 kinds of mammals (including wild boars and hedgehogs), 200 species of fish, 21 species of birds, and 640 species of plants. Don't expect to see many wild mammals, such as the endangered monkeys that supposedly swing from the trees.

In 1938 a French archaeologist found traces of an ancient fishing culture on the island dating from the end of the Neolithic Era. Human bones alleged to be 6,000 years old were also found. More recently, American bombers targeted the military and naval station here, causing numerous casualties and forcing hospitals to set up in nearby caves on the island to avoid the bombings. An ethnic Chinese community numbering about 10,000 settled on Cat Ba over the years, only to leave en masse in 1979 after Chinese troops invaded Vietnam in the brief but bloody border war of that year. The ethnic Chinese, or Hoa, sailed in dinghies to Hong Kong or other Asian ports, many dying along the way. Few ethnic Chinese have returned to Cat Ba.

Today the population of more than 12,000 continues to subsist on fishing and rice and fruit cultivation, but tourism is quickly becoming Cat Ba's new cash crop. The beaches, particularly the lovely curved stretch of sand just over the hillside from the southeast corner of the wharf, are infinitely nicer than Do Son's, and Vietnamese tourists have begun to take note of them. Walk off your seafood dinner by heading to the nearest beach, where you can sip iced coffee and watch the shooting stars. Splendid caves, just off the road to the national park, offer great opportunities for exploring. One such spot is **Trung Tang cave,** a strategic haven for the North Vietnamese Army in the Vietnam War. Today, a wily old veteran tends to the cave and has some interesting stories to tell.

Tour packages usually include minibus transportation to the national park, where a guide leads a hike through it, down to a nearby village in a lovely cove, and over to a bay where a boat is waiting to bring you back to town. This runs about $10 per person, with lunch included.

Ask at your hotel; most can book this tour. Or you can head down to the wharf and arrange for a boat yourself—just make sure they know what you're asking, and you know what they're offering. Rates are not set in stone, so be sure to bargain.

Hiking through Cat Ba can be strenuous: the mountain ridges are steep, trails are poorly marked, and roads are narrow, making blind crests somewhat dangerous. Talk to your hotel owner or one of the many local tour operators about the best hiking trails for your level. A hike through the park—through the tropical forest to a rocky peak overlooking much of the island—is best done with a guide.

A high-speed ferry has been added to the schedule of two slower ferries to and from Haiphong, cutting the travel time by two-thirds. Minihotels are sprouting in the town of Cat Ba, the island's main commercial center, in order to accommodate the growing numbers of tourists. They're all relatively clean and incredibly cheap. New bars blare teeny-bop music and serve chilled margaritas. Just about any of the hotels can arrange for car or minibus tours of the island and rides to the national park. You can also get to the park on your own (rent a Soviet-era Minsk or take a motorbike taxi, if you're really adventurous) and hire a guide there. But it's much easier to go along on one of tours, where the park and guide fees are prepaid and a hike is mapped out. The park is also a favorite spot for Vietnamese tourists, many of whom seem to be able to scale the slippery rocks in stiletto heels.

Dining and Lodging

The sudden plethora of dining and lodging facilities in Cat Ba means one thing: cheap prices. The seafood here is simply prepared but incredibly fresh. Most restaurants and hotels are right in the middle of town and are easy to find. You may want to try one of the many new minihotels in town; they are all about the same. You'll be tempted to sleep with the room's windows open to allow in the cool ocean breezes. Be careful, though—you could also allow in some uninvited two-legged guests.

¢ ✕ **Huu Dong Restaurant.** A huge soft-drink sign on the roof makes this tiki house on stilts hard to miss. Seafood and vegetable dishes are served here. ⊠ *Le Thanh Tong St.,* ☎ *033/888–407. No credit cards.*

¢ ✕ **Luong Son Restaurant.** Seafood is the specialty here at Luong Son. Try the delectable fried squid. This restaurant also offers travel services. ⊠ *Le Thanh Tong St.,* ☎ *033/888–364. No credit cards.*

¢ ✕ **Restaurant Gaulois.** At this popular spot the proprietor will make special seafood dishes if the restaurant is not too busy and you ask nicely. Beware: Gaulois sort of keeps its own strange time schedule. ⊠ *Le Thanh Tong St.,* ☎ *no phone. No credit cards.*

¢ 🏨 **People's Committee Guest House** (Gieng Ngoc Hotel). On the southeastern tip of land at the end of the promenade (to the right as you face town), this old French resort was converted into a state-run hotel long ago, and it feels like it. Some of the rooms don't have air-conditioning, so be sure to ask. ⊠ *At the end of Le Thanh Tong St.,* ☎ *033/ 835–190. 47 rooms. No credit cards.*

Mong Cai and Tra Co

❺ *310 km (192 mi) northeast of Hanoi, 128 km (79 mi) northeast of Halong City.*

The relatively subdued coastal province of Quang Ninh explodes in flurry of trade and cross-border activity at **Mong Cai** (sometimes called Hai Ninh), a boomtown on the Chinese border that has literally risen from the ashes. There is little in this city that speaks of the Chinese invasion in 1979 that left Mong Cai a smoldering, mine-strewn waste land. Today it's a dusty but bustling city of 50,000, whose population nearly doubles every day as Chinese cross the border to do business with their southern neighbors.

Much of the activity in town centers around the customs quay on the Ka Long River, where porters heave boxes and bulging sacks onto small wooden boats bound for China on the opposite bank. The boats return with goods destined for Hanoi and ports south. A footbridge links Vietnam with the Chinese city of Dongxing; the Vietnamese border patrol has set up a checkpoint a few hundred yards south of the bridge. Chinese flash their identity cards and are waived into Vietnam, but the officials are reluctant to let Westerners past the guard station—even if it's just to look—without the appropriate exit permit or a valid visa into China. Vietnamese dong and Chinese renminbi are used interchangeably. Needless to say, Vietnam's antismuggling police units are very active here.

The main reason to make the trip into these far reaches of Quang Ninh Province is to experience the loveliest beach in northern Vietnam. Nine kilometers (6 miles) east of Mong Cai, on an island separated from the mainland by a sea channel, is **Tra Co,** a tiny fishing village on a largely uninhabited 16-km (10-mi) stretch of golden sand. You could conceivably walk up the beach into China; a few military guardhouses face the South China Sea just north of the fishing village, but the military personnel are often snoozing in hammocks strung between the knobby evergreens that come down to the beach. During the day most of the village is deserted; the men are offshore fishing in their boats, and the women and children are hauling in the catch from lengthy nets strung up along the coastline.

If you spend the night in Tra Co, wake up before sunrise and walk down to the water's edge to watch the fisherfolk slip into their boats. On the main north–south road an older man with a regal bearing builds and repairs the wooden fishing boats used by the village. Farther up the road is a once-resplendent Catholic church. A tacky red-tin roof replaced the one bombed out by the Chinese in 1979. A few miles farther south is Mui Ngoc, a beautiful spit of a beach known locally as a smuggler's haven.

Dining and Lodging

Hotels are cheap and basic in Mong Cai; the ones listed below have rooms with private bathrooms. The seedy Tra Co Hotel is right on the sand, while a few other guest houses line the north–south road. Some family homes double as restaurants on this stretch of asphalt. Many restaurants serve authentic southern Chinese dishes as well as fresh seafood. In the breezy evenings young couples and friends gather by the roadside at the Mong Cai Bridge to have fruit shakes, sticky-rice ice cream, or coffee.

¢   🏨 **Binh Minh Hotel.** Like most of the hotels in Mong Cai, this one is very basic. Rooms have private baths and IDD phones. ⊠ *Huu Nghi Rd.,* ☎ *033/881–185. 14 rooms. Air-conditioning. No credit cards.*

¢   🏨 **Dong A Hotel.** This no-frills place is one of the few hotels in town. Rooms have private baths. ⊠ *1 Hung Vuong Rd.,* ☎ *033/881–151. 18 rooms. Air-conditioning. No credit cards.*

₊ang Son

❻   *150 km (93 mi) northeast of Hanoi.*

North of Hanoi and the Red River Delta, Highway 1 weaves and wends its way through narrow valleys and past jagged cliffs into the mountains of Lang Son Province. Vietnam's major north–south artery officially ends at the provincial capital of Lang Son, another booming trade outpost near the Chinese border. Like Mong Cai, Lang Son was nearly destroyed by retreating Chinese troops in 1979, but the town has quickly regrown. Blinking neon lights advertise the central post office, new minihotels and trading companies abound, and Chinese can be heard in the markets.

Although there is little of beauty in Lang Son, the atmosphere is electric. Traders and smugglers convene in corner cafés and hammer out deals with everyone from local shop owners to border guards. Foot porters hustle down the dusty streets bound for rendezvous points farther south. Market stalls in the winding streets of central Lang Son are bursting with cheap Chinese goods, mostly plastic toys and appliances. Lang Son Province is home to many ethnic minorities, including the Nung and the Tay, who often come into town to load up on provisions.

Nineteen kilometers (12 miles) north of Lang Son is the border village of Dong Dang, the site of the **Friendship Gate.** Despite the name, there were sporadic exchanges of gunfire here between Vietnam and China until 1992. Relations are friendlier today, but smuggling is a major concern in this province (a vast network of foot trails makes monitoring border crossings extremely difficult), and the border guards here are serious and often surly. However, visiting the border at Friendship Gate is possible. You may have to leave your passport at the guardhouse on the Vietnamese side before you walk the few hundred yards to the border. Chinese and Vietnamese guards are separated by a 600-yard no-man's-land of sorts.

Numerous caves and grottoes a few miles from Lang Son are worth exploring. The most beautiful are in an area known as **Nhi Tam Thanh,** overlooking which is Waiting Woman Mountain. Legend says a woman waited here so long for her husband to return from battle that she turned to stone. A guard at the mouth of the caves can escort you through, or, if you want to go yourself, provide flashlights for a small fee.

About 30 km (19 mi) south of Lang Son on Highway 1, a spring—known locally as the **Pissing Cow Waterfall**—sputters out of the hillside. It is reached through a private garden and is a favorite spot for local children to play.

On the desolate plateau above Lang Son, southeast of the town on Route 4 heading toward Quang Ninh Province, is a **military cemetery.** The few hundred grave sites face ominously toward China and the ring of steep mountains to the north. The gates to the cemetery are usually locked, but the watchman will lead you up the 100 or so stairs to let you in.

The Northeast A to Z

Arriving and Departing
Haiphong serves as a departure point to places such as Cat Ba, Do Son, and Halong Bay, so you may end up traveling first to the city on your way to other destinations.

BY BUS
State-run public buses travel from Hanoi to Haiphong, Mong Cai, and other points in the area, but they are ancient, unsafe, and usually packed to the gills—basically, not worth your trouble. State-run buses to Hanoi leave from Gia Lam Station when full, mostly in the early morning or late afternoon. The fairly comfortable coaches of the privately owned **BIC Bus Company** (⊠ 2 Hoang Van Thu St., Haiphong ☎ 031/820–800) make the two-hour trip to Haiphong and back

Hanoi six times per day. No reservations are required, and tickets cost 25,000d each way; buses depart from Kim Ma Bus Station (☞ Hanoi A to Z *in* Chapter 2). At press time, the company had plans to add trips to Lang Son.

You can hitch a ride on a minivan that shuttles tourists to and from Haiphong on their way to Cat Ba Island or Halong Bay. Reserve your seat at one of the many tourist cafés in Hanoi (☞ Hanoi A to Z *in* Chapter 2).

BY CAR

Hiring a car and driver from one of the many travel agencies and tourist cafés in Hanoi (☞ Hanoi A to Z *in* Chapter 2) or going with an organized tour on a minivan are the easiest ways to get around the northeast. These aren't always the most pleasant means, however, as many of the roads are in bad condition.

To get to Haiphong from Hanoi, for instance, you must take Highway 5, one of the most hectic stretches of road in the north. The asphalt is just fine, but traffic is congested, and road rules get tossed out the window. Riding to Haiphong by motorbike is not recommended. Renting an air-conditioned car for a day's drive to Haiphong and back to Hanoi will run from $50 to $70 and will take about two hours. Of note on your way are the half-dozen pagodas set back in the rice fields along Highway 5. Cars or minivans traveling on to Halong Bay from Haiphong must cross the Cam River by ferry at Binh Station (Ben Binh), at the north end of Cu Chinh Lan Street. Access is easiest from Ben Binh Street, one block east. Ferries leave every 10 or 15 minutes. Passenger tickets cost 5,000d, more for cars.

Halong Bay is a three-and-a-half-hour drive from Hanoi. There are two routes, but your driver will most likely head east on Highway 5. Halfway to Haiphong, just before the city of Hai Duong, you'll turn left onto Highway 18. Much of this road is new or repaved and feels like the Autobahn compared to the rest of the country's roads. Renting an air-conditioned car with driver from Hanoi costs between $112 and $150 for a two-day, one-night trip to Halong, including all car and driver expenses. A travel agency such as Vietnam Tourism may charge more. If it's not the weekend or if it's in the dead of winter or heat of summer, bargain hard—you can usually get a better deal.

Hiring a car is really the only way to get to Mong Cai. To get there from Halong Bay, take the highway east from Halong City. The road winds up the coast 40 km (25 mi) to Cam Pha, a dingy coal-mining town. Beyond Cam Pha the road traverses gorgeous valleys and provides some majestic ocean views. About 60 km (37 mi) past Cam Pha, the road to Mong Cai turns to the right in the quiet trading post of Tien Yen. It's another 97 km (60 mi) or so to Mong Cai.

Lang Son is a relatively painless four or so hours from Hanoi. Road improvements on Highway 1 allow for easy access by car, although a four-wheel-drive vehicle is necessary if you're going beyond Lang Son, such as on a longer loop into Cao Bang Province (☞ The Far North, *below*) or east to Quang Ninh Province.

BY FERRY

There is no boat service from Hanoi to Haiphong, but ferries from Haiphong to other destinations abound. Five boats leave the Haiphong port for Halong each day. Four of them (the 6 AM, 11 AM, 1:30 PM, and 4 PM) dock in Halong East, and only one (the 9 AM) goes to Halong West. If you land on the east side, you'll want to catch the ferry across the inlet; it's only a five-minute ride (ferries depart every 10 minutes or so in the morning and early evening and less frequently at other times). The companies serving Halong East and Halong West are different, but they both charge 45,000d, and both trips take four hours.

Unless you're a guest of the Vietnamese military, the only way on and off Cat Ba Island is by boat. There is ferry service from Halong City to Cat Ba, but the more common route is from Haiphong. Three ferries leave Haiphong's Binh Station (Ben Binh) for Cat Ba town every day. The standard ferries leave at 6:30 AM and 1:30 PM and arrive in Cat Ba three hours later, after a brief stopover in Cat Hai. The fare is 55,000d. Don't take the 11 AM ferry, as it stops at Cat Hai and does not continue on to Cat Ba town; you'll be stuck at Cat Hai until the 1:30 ferry arrives a few hours later. The high-speed jet boat **Limbang Express** (✉ Binh Station Ferry Landing, Haiphong, ☎ 031/838–311 in Haiphong; 04/851–2918 in Hanoi) makes one trip per day from Haiphong to Cat Ba. It leaves at 9 AM, takes an hour, and costs 90,000d. On Saturday there's a second express as well at 2 PM. The Cat Ba–Haiphong return trip is at 4 PM every day (at 11:30 AM and 4 PM on Saturday). If you're coming from Hanoi, you could take the 6 AM train to Haiphong, catch a cyclo or taxi from the train station to the ferry landing, and take the 9 AM express to Cat Ba. This has become a popular alternative to the slow ferries, so you'll need a reservation. A warning: the Limbang Express is often overbooked, and some passengers holding tickets for the one air-conditioned cabin may be shifted back to the engine room.

BY HELICOPTER

If you want to be the first on your block to say you've flown in a Russian helicopter and lived to tell the tale, see Halong Bay in style on the MI70, the 20-seat chopper owned by state-run Northern Service Flight Company. The Hanoi–Halong Bay trip takes 50 minutes, and you get 10 minutes of bliss circling the emerald waters before the pilot touches down and ushers you onto a boat that cruises the bay. Seats on the bird run $175 each—with $20 extra for the boat, food, and an English-speaking guide. Departure is 7:15 AM Saturday from Hanoi; you'll be back in Hanoi by tea time. You can also rent the helicopter outright for $3,695, boat trip included. Inquire at the Metropole Hotel Sofitel in Hanoi (☞ Lodging *in* Chapter 2) about reservations.

BY ORGANIZED TOUR

A number of travel agencies and tourist cafés in Hanoi (☞ Hanoi A to Z *in* Chapter 2) organize trips to various points in the region. This is one of the best—and by far the easiest—ways to see the area.

BY PLANE

Vietnam Airlines (☞ Ho Chi Minh City A to Z *in* Chapter 6) flies to Haiphong from Ho Chi Minh City daily.

BY TRAIN

Four trains per day (from 6 AM to early evening) leave Hanoi bound for Haiphong from one of two stations: Hanoi Railway Station (Ga Hanoi) and Long Bien Station. Tickets for all trains can be purchased at the Hanoi Railway Station, but you must ask at the ticket booth whether your train leaves from there or from Long Bien Station. The cost is 52,000d. The unspectacular trip takes just over two hours. There are two stations in Haiphong. The first, Thuong Li Railway Station, is west of the city. You should detrain at the **Haiphong Railway Station** (☎ 031/846–433) which is the end of the line on the Hanoi route. In the Reception Room for Tourists, the attendant can book ferry tickets, explain the schedule to Cat Ba and Halong Bay and train times back to Hanoi, and even recommend a hotel or restaurant. There's also a left-luggage service.

One train per day departs from Hanoi for Lang Son. The picturesque ride takes six hours and costs 67,000d one-way. Two trains per week continue on to the Dong Dang border crossing and then into China. It's likely that you'll have to change trains in Pinxiang, 20 minutes north of the border, and then again in Nanning, the capital of China's Guangxi Province. To take advantage of this, you must have the appropriate exit permit, your Vietnam visa, and a visa to China.

Getting Around

Most likely you will be traveling around this area with an organized tour or with your own car and driver. Getting from place to place in this region by other means is not easy.

BY FERRY

See Arriving and Departing by Ferry, *above*.

BY MINIBUS

Air-conditioned minibuses travel from Haiphong to Halong Bay. These line up at the Binh Car and Bus Station (Ben O To Binh), which is just on the north side of the Cam River in Haiphong. (The ferry from the Haiphong port to the north bank is 5,000d and runs every 10 or 15 minutes.) The minibuses cost about 55,000d per person and leave when full (and they can get very full). Ask the ticket agent about minibuses back to Hanoi from Halong Bay, if that's where you're headed.

Contacts and Resources

CURRENCY EXCHANGE

Money can be exchanged at most hotels in larger towns in the area. If you're going to smaller towns, however, it's a good idea to exchange money before you go.

Major banks can exchange your dollars into dong, cash traveler's checks, and give cash advances on credit cards. **Asia Commercial Bank** (⊠ 69 Dien Bien Phu St., Haiphong, ☎ 031/823–389) can exchange money but cannot cash traveler's checks. **VID Public Bank** (⊠ 56 Dien Bien Phu St., Haiphong, ☎ 031/823–999). **Vietcom Bank** (⊠ 11 Hoang Dieu St., Haiphong, ☎ 031/842–658).

EMERGENCIES

There are no medical facilities of international standard in the region. In case of a major medical emergency, try to get to Hanoi or Saigon as quickly as possible. For immediate attention in Haiphong, try the **Vietnam-Czech Friendship Hospital** (Benh Vien Viet-Thiep), on Nha Thuong Street, or the **Traditional Medicine Hospital** (Benh Vien Dong Y), on Nguyen Duc Canh Street.

GUIDED TOURS

The easiest way to see northeast Vietnam is to arrange trips at a travel agency or tourist café in Hanoi (☞ Hanoi A to Z *in* Chapter 2). The trips generally include transport in a tour bus or minivan, accommodation (double occupancy; standard depends on price of tour), and an English-speaking guide. Tours to Halong Bay usually include a five-hour (or longer) boat trip and lunch on the boat. Tour packages to Cat Ba Island often include guided tours of the national park, a stop at a nearby village in a lovely cove, and a boat trip back to town.

POST OFFICE

Stamps can be bought at most hotels. In Haiphong the brightly painted main **Post Office** (⊠ Corner of Nguyen Tri Phuong and Dinh Tien Hoang Sts.) has IDD phones and mail and fax services.

See Hanoi A to Z *in* Chapter 2 for information about travel agencies and tourist cafés in Hanoi.

Haiphong Toserco (⊠ 40 Tran Quang Khai St., ☎ 031/841–415) and **Vietnam Tourism Haiphong** (⊠ 57 Dien Bien Phu St., ☎ 031/829–052) can get you a local English-speaking guide, hire a car, find you a hotel room, and arrange trips to Halong Bay, Cat Ba Island, and other points.

Halong Tourist Company (⊠ 1 Halong Rd., ☎ 033/846–272) and **Quang Ninh Tourism Company** (⊠ 7 Halong Rd., ☎ 033/846–350 or 033/846–320) are both government-owned, and although they have experience setting up boat trips in the bay, and guiding package tours to the hotels owned by their companies, they're not experts at dealing with actual people. They can provide an English-speaking guide for about $10 per hour; call ahead.

THE FAR NORTH

Ethnic minority villages and natural splendor abound in Vietnam's northernmost region. Cao Bang Province is home to the Dao and Tay groups; Ha Giang Province, the country's farthest north, is populated by the H'mong, the small but distinct group called the Bo Y, and the even smaller Pu Peo group. The terrain in this northernmost area is rugged, and it is one of Vietnam's poorest regions. In the remote districts near the Chinese border, the illiteracy rate surpasses 90%. The rocky, inhospitable mountains leave little room for rice cultivation. Corn and fruit are more common crops here, and honey production is on the rise. Although Ha Giang Province is extremely beautiful, there are still hardly any facilities for tourists. But if you're an adventurous traveler who delights in finding your own way—even if it means hitching a ride on an oxcart for eight hours—then Vietnam's far north is for you.

The provincial capital of Cao Bang is linked to Lang Son, 120 km (74 mi) to the east, by windy and rutted Highway 4. The road, which essentially follows the Chinese border from the coast westward, was the site of numerous skirmishes in the late 1940s between French colonial troops and Vietminh guerrilla forces. The French tried to maintain garrisons at Lang Son and Cao Bang, but by 1950 the Vietnamese had ousted them from the area.

Ba Be Lakes

➐ *240 km (149 mi) north of Hanoi.*

The idyllic Ba Be Lakes region, in Bac Can Province, is home to one of Vietnam's oldest national parks. The lake environs are beautiful and peaceful; occasionally you can even hear monkeys as you float down the lake in a wooden longboat. It's quite possible you'll find no other visitors here, which leaves you to explore the breathtaking mountains and caves, El Capitan–like limestone cliffs, gurgling streams, and rushing waterfalls all on your own.

The 9-km (6-mi) fjordlike lake is too big to explore in its entirety in one day, but you can see as much of it as possible if you start out early in the morning, before the mist has burned off, on a rented motorized wooden longboat. Foreign visitors are rare (for now, so the boatman may see dollar signs in his eyes. But you should be able to hire a boat for about 30,000d per hour. Pack a lunch and have the boatman head to the waterfall (*thac nuoc*), a lovely spot for a picnic. Toward the far end of the lake (a good three hours by boat) is the remarkable Ha

Puong Cave, where the Nam Nang River has carved a 300-ft grotto out of the hillside. Bats and swallows swoop through the darkness. At the far end of the lake are villages of the Thai ethnic minority, which could conceivably host visitors, although accommodations would be *very* rustic. Otherwise try the state-owned guest house (☞ Lodging, *below*).

Lodging

¢ ⊞ **Ba Be Guest House.** Before the Ba Be Hotel (☞ *below*) opened, this state-owned guest house beneath forested hills near the water's edge was the only game in town. Now there is also a hotel. If you stay here, you can choose between accommodations in one of the eight brick houses or in one of the eight stilt houses with attached bathrooms. ⊠ *Ask for directions in town,* ☎ *0281/876–127. 30 rooms. Air-conditioning. No credit cards.*

¢ ⊞ **Ba Be Hotel.** About 30 minutes away from Ba Be Lakes in Ba Be townlet is this hotel, where cheery manager Nguyen Quynh will set you up with a clean room with a private bathroom. ⊠ *In Ba Be town,* ☎ *0281/876–115. 9 rooms. No credit cards.*

Tan Trao

❽ *130 km (81 mi) north of Hanoi.*

The region's isolated mountains and once-lush jungles provided Ho Chi Minh and his forces with sufficient cover from the French and Japanese. In early 1945 Ho Chi Minh set up headquarters for the Communist Party in the remote village of Tan Trao, high in the mountains west of Thai Nguyen town. Tan Trao was also the birthplace in 1945 of what became known as the August Revolution, when General Vo Nguyen Giap led Vietminh troops eastward to attack a garrison occupied by the Japanese at Thai Nguyen. General Giap's attack inspired similar uprisings throughout the country. Nine years later he would lead the Vietminh to glory at Dien Bien Phu (☞ The Northwest, *below*).

Currently no organized tours visit Tan Trao. But if you do make it here, there are a few sights to see: a museum dedicated to Ho Chi Minh, a giant banyan tree where General Giap rallied his troops, Ho Chi Minh's simple jungle hut (*nha lua*), and the Tay minority communal house (*dinh*) where the first National Congress met. If you have hired a jeep or car to Ba Be Lakes (☞ *above*), have a day to spare, and don't mind bedding down in an amenityless guest house, consider an excursion to Tan Trao. But be sure to ask ahead about road conditions; the road west from Thai Nguyen can wash out during heavy rains.

he Far North A to Z

Arriving and Departing

BY CAR OR FOUR-WHEEL-DRIVE VEHICLE

The drive from Hanoi to Ba Be Lakes takes you past green-tea plantations, stunning mountain vistas, and ethnic minority stilt houses. The road was repaved in 1997, so a four-wheel-drive vehicle is no longer needed—unless you are planning to see more off-the-beaten-path areas such as Tan Trao. You should be able to hire a car and driver from travel agencies in Hanoi—including two nights' lodging for the driver—for about $180 (☞ Hanoi A to Z *in* Chapter 2).

BY TOURIST CAFÉ TOUR

A number of Hanoi tourist cafés have tours of north-central Vietnam, with Ba Be Lakes as the centerpiece. **Queen Café** (☞ Hanoi A to Z *in* Chapter 2) has a five-day, four-night tour that usually includes stops in Lang Son, Cao Bang, and the Ba Be Lakes region. The price of $65 includes a "normal" driver; it's $75 with an "experienced" one. The distinction doesn't exactly instill confidence, but the café has a good reputation.

THE NORTHWEST

Vietnam's staggering beauty and ethnic diversity are perhaps most evident in the northwest, where the imposing highlands are inhabited by dozens of ethnic minority groups as well as the Kinh, the ethnic majority. Physically and culturally removed from Hanoi, many communities in the remote far west have existed as they have for generations, harvesting terraced rice fields or practicing slash-and-burn agriculture on the rocky hillsides. Babbling mountain streams wind their way through deep, extended valleys.

Many of these streams join up with the Song Da, the once-rushing Da River that has been tamed by Hoa Binh Dam, Vietnam's first hydroelectric power project, about 74 km (46 mi) southwest of Hanoi. Here, in the shadow of this Soviet-built hydroelectric marvel, some farmers still live without electricity. The winding, hilly roads beyond Hoa Binh offer panoramic views. Dusty crossroads towns like Man Duc leave little to smile about, but there are exquisite nearby caves and brick homes built right into the limestone rock at the base of towering cliffs. Make sure your driver stops at the picturesque first view of Mai Chau. Here the valley spreads out before you in its remarkable greenness, and the tap-tap-tapping of carpentry signals the building frenzy currently enveloping the district.

Rising majestically above the region is Mt. Fansipan, Vietnam's tallest peak. In its shadow lies the sleepy hill town of Sapa, the tourist mecca of the northwest, where Dao and H'mong women converge at the local market to buy, sell, and trade.

The northwest is very conducive to adventurous four-wheel-drive tours. The Hanoi–Mai Chau–Son La–Dien Bien Phu–Lai Chau–Sapa-Hanoi loop is the most interesting of all, and it's the one followed by most tour operators. It's equally popular with small groups that have rented jeeps or Land Cruisers on their own and want a multiple-day excursion. If you're comfortable with the thought of a four- to seven-day jeep trek, you'll want to spend plenty of time here. If not, there are still some wonderful options to consider. Idyllic Mai Chau is only four to five hours by car from Hanoi; you could push off early one morning and be back the next evening. Sapa is accessible by a fairly comfortable overnight train ride from Hanoi; you may wish to head there for a weekend to see various ethnic minority groups. You can also fly here: Vietnam Airlines has three flights per week to Dien Bien Phu, the only northwestern town reachable by air.

Mai Chau

❾ *170 km (105 mi) southwest of Hanoi, south of Hwy. 6, in Hoa Binh Province.*

The Brigadoon of Vietnam, Mai Chau is nestled in a serene valley that has been called one of the most beautiful spots in the country. Like the fictitious town that rises every 100 years, Mai Chau appears out of the mist as if in a dream. The town itself is inhabited mainly by the majority Kinh Vietnamese. White Thai villages dot the paddy-rich valley, however, and this is where you're likely to spend most of your time

The White (and later the Black) Thai migrated to Vietnam from what is now Thailand about 2,000 years ago. Today they incorporate elements of both cultures. The Mai Chau Valley is home to a number of Thai villages whose hospitality is genuine and memorable. If you're staying overnight in a stilt house, expect your host family to offer you a roll-up mattress and mosquito net, unlimited use of a tobacco bong (*thuoc lao*), and giant vats of rice wine.

The Mai Chau market teems with villagers selling everything from hand-carved opium pipes to flayed pigs. Except for some women, most villagers have given up wearing traditional garb. Although many villagers still farm, tourism and panning for gold have become the most lucrative industries. A tourist alley of sorts has sprung up in the village, accessible from the dirt road just beyond the large guest house (☞ Lodging, *below*). The de facto mayor of the Thai villages lives on this road, and his house is frequented by visitors and villagers. Baskets, old crossbows, and lovely weavings are laid out on tables in front of the stilt houses. Many other silk scarves and textiles hang from the windows. And they're all for sale.

Buy some bottled water in town before heading out on a long hike through the green (or golden, depending on when you go) rice fields and into the nearby hills. Countless footpaths head off into the mountains from the main valley routes and are used by Montagnards (usually women) who gather wood for cooking fires or for construction. Their baskets are usually extremely heavy, and it takes great skill to balance more than 200 pounds using only shoulder straps or a head brace.

The mountainsides have been largely denuded of their primary forest cover, forcing the villagers to hike more than a day to reach the larger trees needed for building stilt houses. The White Thai villagers here are very friendly and will often invite you into their homes to watch TV together or to share some homemade rice wine or even lunch. Local children will often call out to passing hikers in Thai, "Pai la la?" (Hello, where are you going?) Your response: "Pa in!" (Just walking through!)

Lodging

¢ 🏠 **Mai Chau Guest House.** Just beyond the center of town is this large and unfortunate-looking guest house. Each of the 10 rooms is as sterile as the next; ask for one with a private bathroom. Although the place tries to create some atmosphere by hanging fabrics made by ethnic minorities (for sale, of course) throughout the lobby, it feels forced. ⊠ *Ask for directions in town,* ☎ *018/867–262. 10 rooms, 6 with bath. No credit cards.*

¢ 🏠 **White Thai Villages.** Many people enjoy staying in one of the White
★ Thai villages behind the guest house, where any of 60 households will put you up. Immaculately clean and surprisingly airy and comfortable, the traditional Thai longhouse sits on stilts about 7 ft up—with barely a nail used in the construction. The split-bamboo floor is soft, smooth, and springy under foot. The going rate is 50,000d per person per night. Your hosts would accept less, but a hefty portion of the money goes to district coffers. ⊠ *Ask for directions in village,* ☎ *no phone. No credit cards.*

En Route Northwest of Mai Chau in southern Son La Province, the road rises to a sheltered plateau. As the road sweeps downward, you'll see one of the few remaining primary forests in northern Vietnam. The old trees are huge, a sign of how the entire northern highlands once looked when tigers, leopards, and elephants reigned. This forest stretches for only a few hundred yards, and the drive through is eerie. Farther up Highway 6 are the rolling tea plantations and steep escarpments of the Moc Chau district in Son La Province. This area is famed for its tea as well as for the productive dairy industry, supported in part by UN assistance. But locals don't seem to ever enjoy the two together. Beyond Moc Chau the road sweeps down vast valleys and past Black Thai villages, through the town of Yen Chau and eventually to the town of Son La.

Son La

❿ *320 km (198 mi) west of Hanoi on Hwy. 6, 160 km (99 mi) northwest of Mai Chau.*

Son La is a convenient overnight stop on the journey to Dien Bien Phu (☞ *below*). Even if you're not bedding down in Son La, take some time to explore the immediate environs. Many hill tribes reside in the area, which until 1980 was considered part of the Tay Bac Autonomous Region. The Tay Bac's support of the French during the French-Indochina War led to repressive government measures against them.

For a commanding view of the town and the surrounding area, climb the stone steps to the lookout tower known as **Cot V3.** Just outside the town you can visit a former **French penal colony,** (☎ 10,000d) destroyed by American bombers but partially rebuilt. If you feel like soaking your tired bones for a while, have your driver or a motorbike taxi take you to the **hot springs** a few miles south of the main road. West of town are the small but intriguing **Tam Ta Toong Caves.**

Six kilometers (4 miles) southeast of Son La is the **Forestry Research Center,** which runs an animal-breeding program and studies deforestation and habitat loss. Son La is an ideal place to conduct such research; the province is one of the most deforested regions of the country, with more than 90% of its primary forests already destroyed. ☉ *Daily 7:30–11:30 AM and 1:30–4:30 PM.*

Dining and Lodging

¢ ✕ **Thit De Restaurant.** Goat meat—*thit de*—is the local delicacy here, so why not try some goat kebabs or *tiet canh* (goat's-blood curd soup) if you're really an adventurous eater? One of the better spots to enjoy such a culinary experience is this restaurant. ✉ *Dien Bien Rd.,* ☎ 022/852–394. *No credit cards.*

$ 🏨 **Hoa Ban Hotel.** More than a dozen minihotels are found in Son La, but one of the nicest is the Hoa Ban Hotel. Unfortunately, the staff can be unhelpful at times. ✉ *Hoa Ban Rd.,* ☎ 022/852–395. *23 rooms. No credit cards.*

¢ 🏨 **Phong Lan Hotel.** This is a very basic hotel, but the people working here are friendlier than those at the Hoa Ban Hotel (☞ *above*). ✉ *Ch Van Thinh Rd., Chuong Le District,* ☎ 022/853–516. *No credit cards.*

Dien Bien Phu

⓫ *470 km (291 mi) west of Hanoi, 150 km (93 mi) west of Son La, 1 km (10 mi) from Laos.*

The dream of reestablishing colonial rule throughout Indochina turned into an all-too-vivid nightmare for the French at Dien Bien Phu. History has documented General Vo Nguyen Giap's stunning victory over Colonel Christian de Castries and his 13,000 French and Vietnamese troops (as well as Foreign Legion volunteers) as one of the greatest military achievements of the modern era: a surprise 57-day siege culminating in the surrender of the French garrison on May 7, 1954. The Vietminh army had been on the offensive for much of 1953, and General Henri Navarre, commander of French forces in Indochina, was intent on regaining the initiative throughout the region by building up a series of bases from which his troops could mount offensive action. One of these bases, in the far northwest of Vietnam near the Laotian border, had been overrun by the Vietminh in 1952, but Navarre had ordered its recapture (the French took it back in 1953). The ethnic Thai minority called this centuries-old trading post on the Burma–China–Vietnam road Muong Thanh; the Vietnamese named it Dien Bien Phu.

Such a remote garrison ringed by inhospitable mountains would make it unlikely, thought the French, that General Giap would infiltrate the valley with ground troops. The French clearly controlled the skies and used two landing strips in the valley to shuttle in supplies, reinforcements, and batteries of howitzers and other field guns. But by late 1953 Giap had encircled the French garrison with 50,000 men and had accomplished a feat of near-impossible logistics: dragging into offensive position dozens of 105-millimeter artillery cannon and antiaircraft guns up steep and densely forested slopes, all under the nose of French surveillance planes and scout missions.

The surprise assault began on March 13. Two weeks later the airstrips were within Vietminh artillery range, forcing the French to turn to parachute drops for resupplying the base and cutting off the base from vital troop reinforcements. While the French were waiting, the Vietminh were digging. An elaborate tunnel system crisscrossed the valley and gave Giap's soldiers the necessary element of surprise over the French. The French solicited assistance from their longtime allies the Americans and the British, but to no avail. The defenders were steadily dwindling, and the injured began piling up in the French underground hospital. Morale collapsed, and on May 7, after a series of attacks by the Vietminh, the white flag was raised over the command bunker.

Coincidentally, the next day an international conference (whose initial purpose one month earlier was the completion of a peace treaty for the Korean conflict) opened in Geneva. The result was a declaration temporarily partitioning Vietnam along the 17th parallel until national elections could be held to determine a single government (they were never held). Tellingly, the agreement was never signed, partly because of the refusal by the United States to actively participate due to the presence of the Communist Chinese at the convention.

Today's Dien Bien Phu (population 29,000), in the immense Muong Thanh Valley, serves as the remote capital (since 1995) of westernmost Lai Chau Province. The shift in provincial power anticipated the erection of a second massive hydroelectric project on the Da River, which, if it ever gets built, will leave the former provincial seat of Lai Chau, 110 km (68 mi) north of Dien Bien Phu, at the bottom of an 800-ft deep reservoir. But Lai Chau is no stranger to water woes. Deforestation in the surrounding ring of mountains has caused catastrophic flooding of the Da River. This has meant major new construction in Dien Bien Phu, a district whose primary attraction for tourists is history. The gaudiest example of these new buildings is the ostentatiously ornate provincial party headquarters.

The informative **Dien Bien Phu Museum,** under renovation at press time, has been built on the site of the battle with the French. There is a section dedicated to the region's ethnic minority communities, but French ignominy and Vietnamese glory are the main topics here. The main hall recounts the events of the siege and the battle itself, with blinking maps and legends synchronized with a recorded loop outlining the battle's chronology. Outside is a collection of weapons used in and around the garrison: the Vietnamese tanks and guns look as if they were polished yesterday afternoon, the rusting French jeeps are riddled with bullet holes, and the remains of a French plane lie in a twisted heap. English-speaking guides are available. ⊠ *A1 St., Muong Thanh,* ☎ *023/826–298.* ☞ *5,000d.* ☉ *Daily 7–11 and 1:30–5.*

The **memorial cemetery,** across the street from the Dien Bien Phu Museum, is the final resting place for many unknown Vietminh soldiers. Here in bas-reliefs are scenes of the battle depicted in near life-size socialist realism. One of the most emotional aspects of Dien Bien Phu is here: the names of all the Vietminh casualties from the historic battle at Dien Bien Phu are carved on the backside of the front wall of the cemetery. ☞ *5,000d.* ☉ *Daily 7–11 and 1:30–5.*

The **command bunker** of Colonel de Castries, in walking distance of the Dien Bien Phu Museum, has been remade with makeshift sandbags filled with concrete. Overhead is a reproduction of the corrugated roof from which a lone Vietminh soldier waved a victory flag—the image, re-created several hours after the fact for a documentary film, became Vietnam's enduring symbol of victory over colonial oppression. ☞ *5,000d.* ☉ *Daily 7–11 and 1:30–5.*

Some of the battle's most intense combat took place at nearby Hill A1, a position labeled **Eliane** by the French. A monument to Vietminh troops now stands here. ☞ *5,000d.*

Dining and Lodging

More minihotels are opening in Dien Bien Phu; ask at travel agencies in Hanoi for the most up-to-date information (☞ *Hanoi A to Z in* Chapter 2).

$ ✕ **Lien Tuoi Restaurant.** Catering mostly to foreign tourists, this large restaurant has a wide array of Western dishes. The most popular item is chicken stewed with mushrooms. Menus are available in English and French. It's only a short walk away from Hill A1. ⊠ *27 Pho Muong St.,* ☎ *023/824–919. No credit cards.*

$ 🏨 **Muong Thanh Hotel.** This snazzy hotel complex has cornered the market in Dien Bien Phu. Rooms in the main building or Thai stilt house are clean, and service is friendly. The grounds feature a tourist office, a fitness room of sorts, karaoke, a sauna, and even a large pool out back. Breakfast is included in the room rate. Rooms don't have IDD phones, but there is one in the lobby. ⊠ *25 Phuong Him Lam St.,* ☎ *023/826–719,* 𝔽𝔸𝕏 *023/826–720. 40 rooms. Restaurant, air-conditioning, pool, massage, sauna, badminton, exercise room, travel services. No credit cards.*

Sapa

⑫ *35 km (22 mi) south of Lao Cai town, 170 km (105 mi) northeast of Dien Bien Phu, 350 km (217 mi) northwest of Hanoi.*

Ringed by Vietnam's tallest peaks, Sapa is an enchanting hill-tribe village that has become the de facto tourist capital of the northwest. Sapa is part of the province of Lao Cai (which means "town of sand") and is a 90-minute drive from the provincial capital (also known as Lao Cai). A pilgrimage to Sapa offers a glimpse of some of the country's most breathtaking mountain scenery as well as its ethnic minority cultures. The hill tribes cultivate rice and ginger and hunt wild game in traditional methods; they continue as they always have to worship the soul of rice, their ancestors, and the spirits of earth, wind, fire, river, and mountains. To see them in their traditional style of dress—layers of indigo-dyed, brilliantly embroidered cotton; elaborate headdresses and silver adornments—is to feel yourself caught in a time warp.

The French dubbed the area around Sapa the Tonkinese Alps. In 1922 colonial authorities displaced the minority residents and began building villas for themselves in the town, turning it into a kind of health resort and a retreat from the oppressive heat of Hanoi as well as having it serve a nearby ore mine. Between the end of French colonial rule in 1954 and national reunification 21 years later, the North Vietnamese government made weak attempts to grant the ethnic minorities political representation and the same constitutional rights as the majority Kinh population—provided they took up the struggle against the U.S.-backed Saigon regime. Since 1975 the government has pursued "integration" programs in which the state provides limited education and health care for free. At the core of these programs were and are settlement and resettlement strategies. Since the late 1980s Sapa has been one of the regions where the government is encouraging relocation.

The protection of Sapa's cultural diversity and the environment seems to have little place on the state agenda, however. Tourism may corrupt the integrity of the local populace and upset the area's fragile ecology. Some of the minority groups practice slash-and-burn agriculture, and along with the depredations of two centuries of outside interests, this has already reduced the virgin forest to a mere 12 square km (5 square mi). Further destruction would be tragic, considering the area's remarkable natural gifts.

The local population is made up of the H'mong, the Dao, the Tay, the Giay, the Muong, the Thai, the Hoa (ethnic Chinese), and the Xa Pho, and is divided into 18 local communes with populations of between 970 and 4,500 inhabitants. These hill tribes, known as Montagnards by the French, convene every Saturday in Sapa to exchange everything from staples and handicrafts to live snakes. Be sure to plan your trip to Sapa so that it coincides with this colorful weekend market.

Be prepared to be relentlessly pursued and targeted as a walking dollar sign. Women and children hawkers will be in your face from the moment you come into town. And it's not just in Sapa proper; children along the valley road long ago learned how desperate foreigners are to take cuddly snapshots of ethnic minority children. Try not to cringe the first time you hear one of them say "No money, no photo."

The town of Sapa is charming, but economic development has already put a strain on the small but growing community. Before 1954 there were 248 luxury villas throughout town and in the surrounding hillsides. The vast majority of these buildings have disappeared—they were either destroyed by invading Chinese troops during the 1979 border war (fires spread to the surrounding mountains, wreaking environmental havoc) or by the wrecking balls that are making way for new mini-hotels, marketplaces, a roller rink, and an international-style hotel. The lovely stone church has been spared, however, and services are still held here on Sunday morning and on Christian holidays.

The center of town is a street below the muddy soccer field, but here
★ you'll find the pulse of the community. The **Sapa Market** convenes on Saturday on the slippery stone stairway that crosses this narrow, bitumen-flecked street. A drab but roomy new marketplace-on-stilts has recently been completed, meaning that much of the buying and selling now takes place under a roof. H'mong and Red Dao women come into town with the rising sun. Most walk in from surrounding villages, while a few catch rides on the backs of motorcycles. They are often dressed in their finest traditional garb: richly embroidered vests and dresses, aqua-and-black cotton shirts, finely detailed silver

necklaces and bracelets, and elaborate headdresses that tinkle with every movement. These women are well aware of Westerners' fondness for ethnic minority wares and are eager to sell to you. Many have picked up a few French and English words or phrases. Part of the fun is bargaining with them, but don't express too much initial interest, or you may be labeled a sucker. Hold out for as long as you can, then ask to see the good stuff. Invariably an elderly Dao woman will understand what you're looking for, dig deep into her bamboo basket, and produce fabric of quality superior to what she'd been showing you only moments before.

Sapa is part of the **Nui Hoang Lien Nature Reserve** (☎ 020/871–433), a mountainous 7,400-acre landscape covered by temperate and sub-temperate forests. The reserve provides a habitat for 56 species of mammals—including tigers, leopards, monkeys, and bears—17 of which (the Asiatic black bear, for example) are considered endangered. An impressive 150 species of birds, including the red-vented barbet and the collared finch bill, can be found only in these mountains. Among the area's geological resources are minerals from sediments deposited in the Mesozoic and Paleozoic periods. From the Muong Hoa River to the peak of Mt. Fansipan, the eastern boundary of the reserve is formed by a ridge of marble and calcium carbonate. Also found in this region is kaolinite, or China clay, used in the making of porcelain.

Guided walking tours of the nature reserve are recommended and are easily arranged through hotels and guest houses in town. Pick up a very helpful copy of *Sapa,* which has detailed but somewhat crude maps outlining treks to nearby minority villages; these guides can be found at any hotel, post office, or tourist shop in town. Minsk or jeep drivers will be happy to take you down the rutted road from Sapa past the Auberge Hotel (☞ Dining and Lodging, *below*) for a full day of hiking, swimming in waterfall pools, and visiting H'mong and Thai villages. Hoteliers and tour companies can also make arrangements for you.

A **30-minute hike** from the center of town to the radio tower above Sapa gives you a spectacular panoramic view. Climb the stone steps from the main road. Next to the Ham Rong Hotel is a guard house where you may or may not have to pay 5,000d to hike to the top; it depends on the watchman's mood. The steps lead up past well-manicured gardens and through rocky fields. A path breaks off to the right and winds around boulders to the tower. The town of Sapa is laid out below, and across the valley is Mt. Fansipan.

Hiking **Mt. Fansipan,** Southeast Asia's tallest peak at 10,372 ft, requires little technical expertise. What it does take is three or four days, as you must depart from Sapa and hike *down* into the valley, then back up the other side. Bring your own tent and sleeping bag if you don't want to count on the hit-or-miss equipment available at some of the hotels or local tour agencies. You'll also want an experienced guide to help you navigate the wet, chilly mountainside and suggest the best route and places to camp. If you're serious about hiking Mt. Fansipan, contact Phuc Tinh Company (☞ The Northwest A to Z, *below*), which organizes four-day treks to the peak for about $220 per person. Or ask for more details at the Auberge Hotel or the Green Bamboo Hotel. It can get very cold in Sapa and even colder on the mountain, so you need to dress accordingly (☞ When to Tour the North, *above*).

Dining and Lodging

Although it may seem like two-thirds of Sapa's buildings are hotels, clearly compromising the town's rugged charm, the result is a wide range of options. You can find rooms here for as little as 45,000d pe night, although you may want to opt for something a bit more upscale. Note, however, that even most of the dirt-cheap minihotels have private bathrooms with hot water. Note that power cuts can sometimes be a problem at hotels; you may want to keep a flashlight handy just in case.

\$\$ ✕ **Delta Italian Restaurant.** It's a family affair at Sapa's only Italian restaurant, where hearty backpackers and other tourists gather for large portions of pasta. Amiable owner-chef Mr. Tung spent six months in Milan and, he says, has made the pasta fresh daily since the place opened in 1999; his wife is the waitress, his brother the kitchen manager. ✉ *Near the market,* ☎ *020/871–799. No credit cards.*

¢ ✕ **Camillia Restaurant.** This family-run operation does a brisk business with visitors to Sapa. Deer is on the menu here, as well as chicken, beef, and Vietnamese spring rolls. ✉ *Near the market,* ☎ *no phone. No credit cards.*

¢ ✕🏨 **Auberge Hotel.** A Hanoi transplant, owner Dang Trung has the
★ best thing going in Sapa: a lovely, popular hotel with exquisite views of the mountains. Rooms, particularly on the third floor, are cozy and clean and have functioning fireplaces. Breakfast is by far the best culinary event in the restaurant: you can feast on standard Vietnamese fare—and excellent spring rolls—while soaking up rays out on the terrace. Mr. Trung and his son can help with all sorts of travel information. Competition for these rooms is fierce, so reservations are a must. One major fault: Mr. Trung can't say "no," so overbooking is a serious problem. He rarely leaves anyone in the lurch, although you may find yourself with a room in an Auberge annex or in another minihotel altogether. ✉ *Main road,* ☎ *020/871–243,* 𝖥𝖠𝖷 *020/871–666. 12 rooms. Restaurant, laundry service, travel services, car rental. No credit cards.*

\$\$ ✕🏨 **Hotel Victoria Sapa.** The premier hotel in Sapa, the Victoria caters to the luxurious fancy of its guests. The hotel, a French-designed pleasure palace on a hilltop overlooking town, has spacious, clean, and tastefully decorated rooms with inviting bathtubs, satellite TVs, IDD phones, and heaps of amenities. A pricey restaurant adorns the main hall, as does a gift shop for those who don't want the hassle of bargaining for souvenirs. A sports complex includes a heated swimming pool, a bar, a sauna, and tennis courts. If all that isn't enough, the hotel also has its own tour package in which guests stay in private luxury sleeper and dining cars on the train to and from Hanoi. ✉ *Overlooking town,* ☎ *020/871–522. 77 rooms. Restaurant, bar, air-conditioning, room service, pool, sauna, tennis court, laundry service. AE, DC, MC, V.* ✆

¢ 🏨 **Cau May Hotel.** Overpriced but quiet, this out-of-the-way sleeper is a good place to find some solitude. Nothing but fruit orchards and mountains appear out the front windows. As you drive into town from Lao Cai, take a right as soon as you reach the end of the soccer field. Turn left after 100 yards; the hotel is on the right. ☎ *020/871–293. 8 rooms. No credit cards.*

¢ 🏨 **The Green Bamboo.** Run by the Green Bamboo Café in Hanoi, this mountainside accommodation sprang up almost overnight and already has taken much of the pressure off the Auberge Hotel (☞ *above*). The small, rather sunny rooms are decked out with televisions, new but simple furniture, and private bathrooms. If you're looking for a quiet getaway, stay elsewhere on the weekends. The Green Bamboo sends its backpacker tour groups here, and the bar downstairs is popular. The hotel is 100 yards past the Auberge on the main road. Reservations, which are suggested, can be made at the **Green Bamboo Café** in Hanoi (✉ 2B Trang Thi St., Hoan Kiem District, ☎ 04/824–9179). ✉ *Main road,* ☎ *020/871–411,* 𝖥𝖠𝖷 *020/871–214. 28 rooms. Bar, café, laundry service, travel services. No credit cards.*

¢ ⌂ **Ham Rong Hotel.** This imposing, faux château-style hotel is in a large compound 100 yards up the hill from the town church. There are two main buildings with clean double rooms that have televisions and decent bathrooms. Concrete is a recurring theme in the hotel's gardens. You'll need earplugs to block out the blare of the town's nearby loudspeaker, which doesn't get going until 7:30 AM or so. ⊠ *100 yards above the church,* ☎ *020/871–251,* FAX *020/871–303. 31 rooms. Restaurant, air-conditioning, travel services. No credit cards.*

Bac Ha

⓭ *100 km (62 mi) northeast of Sapa, 350 km (217 mi) northwest of Hanoi.*

Northeast of Sapa is Bac Ha, a small town built on a desolate highland plain northeast of Lao Cai. The main reason for venturing here is the century-old **Sunday-morning market,** one of the largest in the northwest. Ethnic minority villagers such as the Dao and the Flower H'mong (related to the H'mong but wearing brighter and more elaborate clothing) come from miles around to buy, sell, and trade everything from horses and dogs to medicinal herbs and beautiful handmade tapestries. Tourists are definitely in the background at this market; you'll be tolerated and respected, but rarely approached by sellers. One thankful deviation from this function-over-form mentality is the lovely, high-pitched songs performed by Flower H'mong singers. If the market manager hasn't been able to arrange singers for that day, he plays a cassette of their songs over the public address system. The market gets going at about 9 AM, but early birds can be seen setting up their stalls and sipping *pho* (noodle soup) for breakfast as the sun comes up. A 3- to 6-km (2- to 4-mi) walk up the road past the Sao Mai Hotel (turn left at the fork; ☞ *below*) brings you to some ethnic minority villages that will be more than happy to see you.

Many minihotels in Sapa (☞ *above*) arrange day trips to Bac Ha, which leave at about 6 AM. The going rate is $10 per person in a Russian jeep. The road is bumpy, and the trip takes three hours each way. If you're heading back to Hanoi, you may want to travel to Bac Ha on a Sunday morning and then get dropped off at the Lao Cai train station in the afternoon so that you can take the train that evening (☞ The Northwest A to Z, *below*).

Dining and Lodging

¢ ✕ **Cong Fu Restaurant.** This hole-in-the-wall does a brisk business with lunching tourists. Very basic Vietnamese fare, such as pho, and noodle, meat, and chicken dishes, is served. Service can be painfully slow—simple orders like a cold beer sometimes take more than five minutes to arrive. ⊠ *Off main road, about 200 yards from entrance to market,* ☎ *no phone. No credit cards.*

¢ ⌂ **Sao Mai Hotel.** If you're staying the night in Bac Ha, the Sao Mai is the ritziest accommodation in town—compared to local homes, that is—which isn't saying much. Rooms are in stilt houses or in a new annex with extensive wood paneling. ⊠ *On same road as market but on other side of highway,* ☎ *020/880–288. 25 rooms. No credit cards.*

The Northwest A to Z

Arriving and Departing

BY CAR OR FOUR-WHEEL-DRIVE VEHICLE

A sedan is a perfectly viable way to get around much of the northwest if you're traveling in the dry season. Cars, however, are not recommended for the remote and difficult stretches of road; you'll need a jeep or four-wheel-drive vehicle to get you through the trouble spots. You can rent cars in dozens of spots in Hanoi (☞ Hanoi A to Z *in* Chapter 2), and you'll be able to book a two-day, one-night car trip to Sapa for about $80, all driver's expenses included. A longer excursion in a four-wheel-drive vehicle is more expensive: the going rate for the popular six-day, five-night excursion through the northwest (Hanoi to Mai Chau to Son La to Dien Bien Phu to Sapa to Hanoi) in a Russian jeep is $200. A Toyota Land Cruiser can be rented for about $530 from the Green Bamboo Café in Hanoi and $600 from Vidotour (☞ Hanoi A to Z *in* Chapter 2) in Hanoi for the same tour. The price is a bit steep, but the more modern four-wheel-drive vehicles are safer and nicer.

The trip to Mai Chau from Hanoi can be treacherous in the rain, especially beyond Hoa Binh city, where the road rises into the steep mountains and sharp curves give way to long cliff drop-offs. However, the condition of the road is decent enough to manage without a four-wheel-drive vehicle.

Set aside at least five days to visit Dien Bien Phu from Hanoi: two days traveling each way and one full day to see what you came for—although the remarkable scenery makes the trip as interesting as the history of the place. If you're coming from Mai Chau and Son La, the natural next step is to continue clockwise: through the charming high lonesome of Lai Chau, on to Sapa, and then back to Hanoi. The Dien Bien Phu–Sapa road is in worse condition than the Hanoi–Dien Bien Phu road, so a high-clearance four-wheel-drive vehicle is necessary. The journey from Dien Bien Phu to Sapa is a hard day's trip on narrow, rutted roads through beautiful scenery. This round-trip route adds a day or two to your journey but is much more interesting than following the same route back and forth.

The 35-km (22-mi) stretch of road from Sapa to the border town of Lao Cai, to the north, is in better condition than the Dien Bien Phu–Sapa route. You may prefer to go directly to Sapa, bypassing Dien Bien Phu, Son La, and Mai Chau, and heading up and down Highway 2 and Route 70.

BY MOTORBIKE

The Hanoi–Dien Bien Phu–Sapa route is only for adventurous motorcyclists. You'll need a 150-cc engine or larger, and you should have some knowledge of engine mechanics, although locals are adept at fixing ailing Russian Minsks. Also, be prepared to get wet in mud puddles. At some larger washout spots, however, enterprising locals set up ferry services on small boats for motorcycles. These roads are very remote, and adequate emergency care is virtually nonexistent. Wear a helmet, take a sheet of important words and phrases (such as the Vietnamese expressions for "My clutch is broken"), and go with someone else. You'll need high clearance and maneuverability, however, so doubling up on bikes is not recommended.

If you drive a motorbike from Hanoi to Mai Chau, pay extra attention on the mountain roads: the trucks that run this route are notoriously stingy when it comes to giving adequate room to two-wheelers. For more information on renting motorbikes, *see* Hanoi A to Z *in* Chapter 2.

BY MOUNTAIN BIKE

If you've got the legs, lungs, and equipment, mountain biking is a formidable but fantastic way to experience the steep mountain ranges of Hoa Binh Province. Most people who do the Mai Chau route find alternative transportation to the provincial capital of Hoa Binh, such as an early morning public bus. From there it's about 100 km (62 mi) up and down two major sets of mountains. Hardy bikers reach Mai Chau by evening, exhausted. Slower riders spend the night in a home in one of many roadside villages.

BY PLANE

Dien Bien Phu is the only town in the northwest accessible by commercial jet. There is an 11:30 AM **Vietnam Airlines** (☞ Hanoi A to Z *in* Chapter 2) flight Monday, Wednesday, and Saturday from Hanoi. The one-way fare is $53.

Consider flying to Dien Bien Phu and returning to Hanoi via some form of ground transportation, either down Highway 6 or up to Sapa and down Route 70 and Highway 2. Talk with one of the travel agencies or tourist cafés in Hanoi to see if they have contacts in Dien Bien Phu who could book you a one-way trip back to the capital. They may insist, however, that you pay for the mileage for the driver's return to Dien Bien Phu.

BY TRAIN

If you don't want to lose a whole day driving to Sapa, take the overnight train from Hanoi to Lao Cai, a dreary border town of 33,000 people that was leveled when the Chinese stormed it in 1979. The most comfortable trip to Lao Cai is on Friday night, when you get a soft sleeper in a four-person compartment on the "luxury" train. The one-way ticket costs about $25. The train leaves the Hanoi railway station at 8:15 PM and takes 11 hours. Currently tickets *cannot* be purchased more than two days in advance (in order to prevent agents from selling them at inflated rates). So get to the Hanoi Railway Station (Ga Hanoi) by Thursday morning to be assured of getting on the Friday-night train.

Don't lose your ticket after boarding the train. You need to present it to the station guards in Lao Cai when arriving at the station and again when departing the station upon returning to Hanoi. You can purchase your return ticket in Sapa (and check train and bus schedules) at the small post office in the center of town. Unfortunately, the night train from Lao Cai back to Hanoi doesn't have soft sleepers, and the hard sleepers ($15) are basically straw mats on a slab of wood. There are six in one compartment, and the top bunks are cheapest.

Minibuses waiting at the Lao Cai train station can take you the 35 km (22 mi) to Sapa for 25,000d. The buses leave when full and usually drop you off in front of the Auberge Hotel. From Sapa buses return to the Lao Cai train station twice daily, at 6:30 AM and 2 PM, but you can join with other travelers and share a bus or jeep that will leave at the time you want. If you'd like to combine a one-way train to Sapa with a return to Hanoi by jeep or car, you can arrange that in Sapa at the Auberge Hotel or at one of the tour agencies dotting the main roads.

BY TRAVEL AGENCY OR TOURIST CAFÉ TOUR

Most travel agencies and tourist cafés in Hanoi (☞ Hanoi A to Z *in* Chapter 2) organize two kinds of trips to the northwest: an overnight to Mai Chau, and a six-day, five-night excursion loop by jeep (☞ By Car or Four-Wheel-Drive Vehicle, *above*). On the very popular Mai Chau tour, you travel either on a 12-seat minibus or in a 30-seat tour bus, and you generally stay at the White Thai village behind the guest house. This tour costs about $20 per person, lodging included. The six-day loop tour, which is also popular, costs about $80 per person, with a minimum of four people. That makes it pretty crowded in a Russian jeep. Lodging is not included on this tour, but you don't have to find it yourself. The driver does that for you; you just need to pay for it. Note that these tourist cafés often insist on full prepayment; don't let that go without a fight, as up-front payment may give the driver little incentive to perform ideally. If you're taking a jeep tour, remember to take the name and telephone number of the manager at the Hanoi agency where you arranged your trip.

Contacts and Resources

CAR AND MOTORBIKE RENTAL

Cars with drivers can be hired from travel agencies and tourist cafés in Hanoi. For more information, *see* Hanoi A to Z *in* Chapter 2.

CURRENCY EXCHANGE

It's best to exchange money in Hanoi before your trip; however, if you need to, you can usually exchange money (generally cash, not traveler's checks) at your hotel.

EMERGENCIES

In case of medical emergency, try to get to the larger towns in the region. If you are really ill, get to Hanoi as quickly as possible.

GUIDED TOURS

Guided tours of the region can be arranged through travel agencies and tourist cafés in Hanoi. For more information *see* Hanoi A to Z *in* Chapter 2.

The **Phuc Thinh Company** (✉ 20 Cau May St., Sapa, ☎ 020/871–331) conducts four-day hiking trips to Mt. Fansipan. The cost is $220, which includes food, tents, and tours of remote mountain villages. The company will also custom-design tours according to your interests.

PRECAUTIONS

Make sure you hire a good driver whom you can trust, as roads can be bad. Don't drink tap water or eat raw vegetables, and make sure meat is well cooked. Bring the right clothing; it gets chilly in the mountains—even in spring and autumn—and downright cold in winter.

4 THE CENTRAL COAST

HUE, HOI AN, DANANG

In Hue, explore the majestic tombs of emperors and the partially restored Imperial City, and absorb the almost eerie quiet of the long-gone ruling families' weighty presence. Perfectly preserved Hoi An lets you see how ordinary Vietnamese traders and fishermen lived in centuries past. In Danang, learn about the history and culture of the Cham people. Then take a trip to famous China Beach and to the ruins of the ancient Cham city at My Son. At all times, enjoy the unique and delicious cuisine for which this region is famous.

By Sherrie
Nachman

Updated by
Craig Thomas

EXTENDING FROM the 17th parallel, which once divided the country, to the former Imperial City of Hue, and south to the historically rich port town of Hoi An is Vietnam's scenic central coast. As you drive along National Highway 1—which, like most roads in Vietnam, is in rough shape—expect to catch glimpses of the emerald-green South China Sea and scenes of traditional Vietnamese rural life as they have appeared for centuries. The age-old rhythm of planting and harvesting continues undisturbed, and families dry their rice in their front yards only inches from the road. The dramatic peaks of the Truong Son Mountains seem to cascade into the sea, providing a stunning backdrop to the scene. For the beach lover there are numerous long sandy beaches, while the culture vulture can comb through ancient Cham ruins or visit tombs and pagodas. The highlights of the region are Hue and Hoi An, two of Vietnam's most interesting and hospitable cities. Although Hanoi and Ho Chi Minh City may give you a taste of contemporary Vietnam and its recent history, Hue and Hoi An put you in a seemingly mythical Vietnam of centuries past.

Once the capital of Vietnam and home to its emperors, Hue today is largely in ruins, the consequence of both French attacks in the late 19th century and American bombings during the Vietnam War. Only recently have efforts been made to restore Hue's imperial architecture. Despite the ruins, the Imperial City, as Hue is known, continues to evoke the grandeur of its royal past. In contrast, the tiny city of Hoi An, originally a Chinese trading village on the sea, is incredibly well preserved. Families live in 200-year-old homes—amazing landmarks incorporating architectural elements from traditional Chinese, Vietnamese, and Japanese styles, reflecting those who populated Hoi An over the centuries.

The third major city in this region is Danang, which may be familiar to you as an important U.S. Air Force base during the Vietnam War. Today it is a port town that offers little in the way of sights except for the fabulous museum of Cham culture. The ancient Kingdom of Champa existed from the 2nd to the 17th centuries around present-day Danang, Nha Trang, and Phan Rang, although its power was significantly weakened by the Viet and the Khmer in the 15th century. The city also has the region's largest airport, which makes it a convenient jumping-off point for visiting Hue (which itself has a small airport), Hoi An, and other points of interest in the region.

In between Danang and Hoi An are the Marble Mountains, where temples have been built in the caves, and China Beach, made famous by the television show of the same name. As you drive between Hue and Danang on National Highway 1, be sure to stop at Lang Co Beach and the dramatic Hai Van Pass, which runs across the Truong Son Mountain range and overlooks the South China Sea below. (Unfortunately, the mountains' natural beauty is slightly spoiled by the hordes of postcard vendors who try to sell you packets of coconut cookies and chewing gum.)

Pleasures and Pastimes

Art and Architecture

Because this area served as the seat of the Kingdom of Champa from the 2nd to the 17th centuries, it has the greatest concentration of Cham art and architecture in the country. Savor the glories of Champa at the excellent Cham Museum in Danang. Soak in the history of Vietnam's emperors while exploring the grand remnants of the Imperial City of Hue and the magnificent Imperial Tombs. Get a feel for 17th- and 18th-century Vietnamese life in Hoi An, where the well-preserved houses and pagodas have hardly changed in the last 200 years. Hoi An's streets are also lined with art galleries, small shops selling all kinds of artifacts, and small cafés.

Dining

Along the central coast you can find outstanding regional cuisine. Hoi An's specialties include White Roses, a delicious and beautiful shrimp dumpling that resembles a rose (if you squint a little), and the simple *com ga* (spicy rice and chicken). Imperial Hue's cuisine, distinguished by the elegant radial symmetry of its presentation, is said to be the most sophisticated in Vietnam. One specialty of Hue is *banh khoai,* a rice pancake filled with shrimp and pork and topped with sprouts, fresh mint, and spicy star fruit. Be sure to try the peanut dipping sauce that accompanies this dish. Another popular regional dish, served in both Hue and Hoi An, is *bun bo Hue,* a dish of rice noodles and broth topped with pork, beef, and pork rinds. There aren't many formal restaurants in this area, but there are plenty of small, pleasant family-run places with truly outstanding food. Imagine the Vietnamese version of a really good diner—nothing fancy, but decent portions of good, cheap food.

Almost all hotels and "real" restaurants post costs in dollars and accept both dollars and dong. Roadside cafés and smaller restaurants post prices in dong, but they also accept dollars. More and more establishments in this area are accepting credit cards—although a "service charge" of 3%–4% is generally added—and traveler's checks.

Lodging

You won't find many luxury hotels in this region, but there are several clean, comfortable accommodations, including some with tennis courts or swimming pools. Most have private bathrooms, unless otherwise noted. Hotel choices, especially in Hue and Hoi An, are numerous, and new minihotels are popping up regularly. Almost all hotels post costs in dollars and accept either dollars or dong.

Outdoor Activities

The entire region is excellent for bicycling and motorcycling because the traffic hysteria that reigns in Ho Chi Minh City does not exist here. There aren't many cars in Hoi An and there are relatively few in Hue; Danang is much more of a city with the concomitant traffic. The beaches in Hoi An, like everything about the town, are exceedingly pleasant places in which to relax. Close to Danang is the famous China Beach, which is pleasant but doesn't quite live up to its acclaimed glory from the eponymous television program. Rumors abound that diving facilities will soon be available in the Danang area.

Exploring the Central Coast

It's relatively easy to travel around the fascinating and culturally rich central coast region. Hue and Hoi An are only about three hours from each other by car; Hoi An is less than an hour south of Danang, and Hue is about two hours north. The best plan is probably to fly into Danang, travel to Hoi An, and leave from Hue. Trips to My Son and China Beach usually originate or end in Danang or Hoi An.

Numbers in the text correspond to numbers in the margin and on the Central Coast, Hue, Danang, and Hoi An maps.

Great Itineraries

IF YOU HAVE 3 DAYS

Fly from Hanoi, Ho Chi Minh City, or Nha Trang to Danang, but by-pass the city itself. Instead head straight for ⊞ **Hoi An** ㉒–㉟ and spend a day to a day and a half seeing the city and/or relaxing at nearby Cu

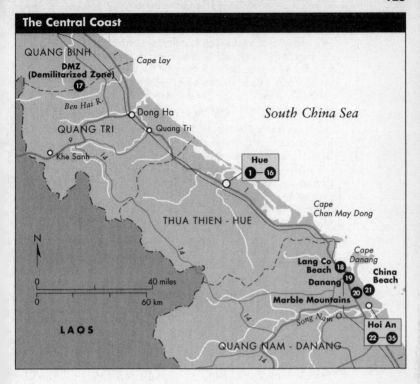

The Central Coast

QUANG BINH

Cape Lay

DMZ (Demilitarized Zone) 17

Ben Hai R.

Dong Ha

QUANG TRI

Quang Tri

South China Sea

Khe Sanh

Hue 1 — 16

Cape Chan May Dong

THUA THIEN - HUE

N

0 ——— 40 miles

0 ——— 60 km

Cape Danang

Lang Co Beach 18

Danang 19

China Beach

Marble Mountains 20 21

LAOS

Song Nam O

Hoi An 22 — 35

QUANG NAM - DANANG

Dai Beach. Have dinner overlooking the river at Café des Amis, and stay in the Hoi An Hotel, the city's largest and friendliest. From Hoi An it is a quick three-hour drive to ⊞ **Hue** ①–⑯; spend your remaining time exploring the Imperial City and the tombs and pagodas that line the banks of the Perfume River.

IF YOU HAVE 5 DAYS

Spend a half day in **Danang** ⑲ exploring the treasures of the Cham Museum. That same day head out to the **Marble Mountains** ⑳ and then continue on to ⊞ **Hoi An** ㉒–㉟ for a couple of nights. See Hoi An's historical and architectural treasures at a leisurely pace, but make sure to fit in a visit to Cua Dai Beach and to the Cham temples at My Son. You'll probably have time to have a shirt, dress, pants, or just about anything else you desire made in the silk shops that line Tran Phu and Le Loi streets; any clothing item can be made in less than 24 hours. Spend your last two days in **Hue** ①–⑯.

When to Tour the Central Coast

Unfortunately, the central coast is plagued by Vietnam's worst and most unpredictable weather. Rain can strike at any moment, especially in Hue. The official rainy season begins in November and ends in March, so the best time to go is from April to October (although it still may be rainy or overcast). Like the rest of the country, the area comes alive during Tet, the celebration of the lunar new year, which takes place in January or February.

HUE

Bisected by the Perfume River and 13 km (8 mi) inland from the South China Sea in the foothills of the Annimite Mountains (Truong Son Mountains), Hue (pronounced hway) stands as a reminder of Vietnam's imperial past. The seat of 13 Nguyen dynasty emperors between 1802 and 1945, Hue was once Vietnam's splendid Imperial City. Although it was devastated by the French in the 19th century and again by fighting between the Vietnamese Communists and the Americans in the 20th, the monument-speckled former capital has a war-ravaged beauty. One can still imagine its former splendor, despite gaping holes in its silhouette. UNESCO recently declared Hue a World Heritage Site, and the city's gems are slowly being restored.

As early as the 2nd century BC, Hue was home to rulers: it was the seat of command for the Chinese Han army and was called Tay Quyen. By the 2nd century AD, Hue was captured by local chieftains, who renamed it K'ui Sou. Between the 10th and 14th centuries, the Cham and the Vietnamese fought over control of the city. By the 15th century, the Vietnamese had successfully captured the city from the Cham and renamed it Phu Xuan. In 1558 the city became the capital of a region ruled by Lord Nguyen Hoang, which established control of South Vietnam by the Nguyen lords. (During this time, two warring factions—the Nguyen lords, who controlled South Vietnam, and the Trinh lords, who controlled North Vietnam—were fighting for control of the whole country.)

With the Tay Son Rebellion in the 18th century, the Nguyen lords were temporarily defeated. Led by the sons of a wealthy merchant, the Tay Son rebels were acting on a general sentiment of discontent with both Nguyen and Trinh rule. The Tay Son emperor, Quang Trung, was installed in Hue from 1786 to 1802, until the ousted Lord Nguyen Anh returned, with French backing. At the same time, Nguyen Anh captured Hanoi from the Tay Son rebels, who had defeated the Trinh and the Chinese-backed Ly Dynasty based in the northern capital. In 1802, Nguyen Anh anointed himself Emperor Gia Long and made Hue the capital of a newly united Vietnam. Twelve Nguyen dynasty emperors followed him to the throne until 1945, and their impressive tombs, Imperial City, and pagodas are reminders of the important role the city once played.

It was under Emperor Gia Long's rule that the city's architectural identity was established—and the prospect of French colonial rule in Vietnam initiated. With guidance, ironically, from the French architect Olivier de Puymanel, Gia Long designed and built the city's surrounding fortress in the style of the Forbidden City in Beijing. The result is a fairly modern structure that looks centuries old. Enclosed within the thick walls of the Chinese-style citadel is the Imperial City (Hoang Thanh), where all matters of state took place and which was off limits to all but mandarins and royal family. Within the Imperial City was the Forbidden Purple City (Tu Cam Thanh), where the emperor and his family lived; very little of it remains today.

In the 1830s, voices of dissent arose against the French presence in Vietnam. The French responded by attacking Hue in 1833 (they had been looking for an excuse to assert their claims to the country in exchange for assisting Gia Long to the throne) and making the country—particularly, Tonkin and Annam—into a protectorate. During this time, a Western-style city was established across the river from the citadel to accommodate the French forces; some of these old French colonial buildings are still standing. In 1885, after repeated disagreements between the French and the emperors of Hue, the French pillaged the Royal Court, burned the Royal Library, and replaced Emperor Ham Nghi with the more docile Emperor Dong Khanh.

It was the Tet Offensive of 1968, however, that really destroyed large parts of the Imperial City. During one of the fiercest battles of the Viet nam War, the North Vietnamese army occupied the city for 25 days, flying its flag in defiance and massacring thousands of supposed South Vietnamese sympathizers. The South Vietnamese and the Americans moved in to recapture the city with a massive land and air attack and in doing so further destroyed many of Hue's architectural landmarks. Overall, more than 10,000 people died in the fighting, many of them civilians.

Although much of the Imperial City was reduced to rubble, many sections still exist, and Hue's main draw continues to be the remnants of its glorious past. Today tourists keep the city thriving. There are many hotels and numerous cyclo drivers who can give you a tour of the Imperial City for only 50,000d. On top of it all, Hue is known for its outstanding cuisine.

Exploring Hue

Hue itself is quite small, and you can easily get around the Imperial City on foot. Within walking or biking distance, too, are the local market and the Imperial Museum. To visit the sprawling tombs and pagodas on the outskirts of Hue, you will need to hire a car and driver—or a motorbike if you're more adventurous. Several of the tombs and pagodas, most notably Minh Mang Tomb and Thien Mu Pagoda, sit along the banks of the Perfume River and can be reached by boat. Don't feel obligated, however, to take one of those slow-moving boat trips up the Perfume River—you may find the scenery far from spectacular and the pace very slow.

The Citadel

A GOOD WALK

You'll most likely be staying on the east bank of the Perfume River, so it's best to begin your walk at the Phu Xuan Bridge and Le Loi Street. Cross the Phu Xuan Bridge, making sure to notice the French-built Tran Tien Bridge, a symbol of Hue, off to your right. Once across the river, a right will take you down Tran Hung Dao Street to the **Central Market** ①. After you visit the market, head back along Tran Hung Dao Street to the Phu Xuan Bridge; the street will turn into Le Duan. Take the first right after the bridge, which will lead you across a moat and through the Ngan Gate (Cua Ngan) into **The Citadel** ②. After entering through the Ngan Gate, you will see four of the Nine Holy Cannons on your right. These bronze cannons depict the four seasons; the other five depict the Chinese elements—water, soil, wood, metal, and fire. Take the first left and make your way along 23 Thang 8 Street (it's not a specific address); on your right you will see the entrance of the Imperial City. Across from the entrance to the Imperial City is the 122-ft **Flag Tower** ③.

The **Imperial City** ④, once a large royal complex, is now mostly in ruins. Enter through the Noontime, or Royal Gate (Cua Ngo Mon), and take an immediate left toward the **Nine Dynastic Urns** ⑤, which symbolize the formidable Nguyen dynasty. Head back toward the entrance to the Imperial City and turn left across the Golden Water Bridge (Trung Dao Bridge), once used only by the emperor. Straight ahead is one of the few still-intact structures in the Imperial City: the intricately decorated **Palace of Supreme Harmony** ⑥.

Exit the palace through the back of the gift shop. On either side of the path leading to the entrance of the **Forbidden Purple City** ⑦ are the Halls of the Mandarins, where mandarins (court officials) dressed in special attire before paying homage to the emperor. Through the courtyard in front of the halls, you can see the vast empty expanse on the threshold of the Forbidden Purple City—a result of the Tet Offensive. To your right, the Royal Theater or Festival Hall is largely intact. Behind it is the intimate and partially restored **Royal Library** ⑧.

Hue

THE CITADEL

IMPERIAL CITY

Perfume River

Train Station

N

0   400 yards
0   400 meters

TO DANANG AND PHU BAI AIRPORT

Heading east from the Royal Theater, exit the Imperial Enclosure through the beautiful and ornate Eastern Gate (Hien Nhan Mon). Make a right on Doan Thi Diem Street and then take the first left on Le Truc Street to get to the **Imperial Museum** ⑨. In a beautifully preserved building that was formerly part of the palace, the museum houses a fine collection of imperial objects. Across the street are the unimpressive Military Museum and Hue's Archaeological Center, once a kind of prep school for male members of the royal court and now closed to the public.

Make a left out of the Imperial Museum and then another left onto Dinh Tien Hoang Street. Follow the street through what feels like a quiet suburban residential neighborhood for about 1 km (¾ mi). At the intersection with Tinh Tam Street is **Tinh Tam Lake** ⑩, overgrown with lotus flowers in spring and summer. On the other side of Dinh Tien Hoang Street, across from the footpath that bisects Tinh Tam Lake, is another lake, Tang Tau, with a small island; once the location of the Royal Library, this is the current home of the small Ngoc Huong Pagoda. It's a very peaceful place to take a break.

TIMING

This walk should take you about four hours at a very leisurely pace. Early morning and late afternoon are the best times to explore Hue because it can get quite warm in the middle of the day, especially from April to October. Also many tour guides insist they need a two- to three-hour break in the middle of the day.

SIGHTS TO SEE

❶ **Central Market** (Cho). Hue's large Central Market has the usual collection of fresh fruits, dried fish, and motor parts. It's the best place to pick up two local specialties: conical hats, which can be decorated to order, and sesame-seed candy. It's also a good spot to see Hue daily life or to have a delicious and inexpensive meal. ⊠ *On citadel side of riverfront, next to Tran Tien Bridge.* ⊙ *Daily 7:30–dusk.*

❷ **The Citadel** (Kinh Thanh). Seeking to secure his empire, Emperor Gia Long built this almost 4-square-km (1½-square-mi) citadel with a 65-ft-wide moat in the heart of Hue in 1805. Gia Long was assisted in the design by the French architect Olivier de Puymanel, and the result is a combination of French military architect Vauban's work and classic Chinese-style architecture. The citadel was initially built of earth and later reinforced by 6-ft-thick brick walls and fortified by 10 gates. Today much of the citadel is given over to residential and even agricultural use. Enclosed in the structure is the ☞ **Imperial City**, where official government activity once took place. Within it is the ☞ **Forbidden Purple City**, which was the private sanctuary of the emperors and their families. ▨ *Free.*

❸ **Flag Tower** (Cot Co). This 122-ft structure, Vietnam's tallest flagpole, is one of the symbols of Hue. It was originally built in 1809 to serve as the Imperial Palace's central observation post. Like much of Hue, it has a history of being destroyed. The Flag Tower was toppled during a typhoon in 1904. It was rebuilt in 1915, destroyed again in 1947, and rebuilt anew in 1949. When the city was occupied by the North Vietnamese during the Tet Offensive of 1968, the National Liberation Front flag flew from the Flag Tower. The interior is closed to the public. ⊠ *In front of 23 Thang 8 St., facing Ngo Mon Gate.*

❼ **Forbidden Purple City** (Tu Cam Thanh). Built at the beginning of the 19th century, the Forbidden Purple City, inside the ☞ **Imperial City**, was almost entirely destroyed during the Vietnam War; now it's largely a wide-open field. At its threshold is a vast expanse of spotty vegetation and rubble. In its glory days the Forbidden Purple City housed members of the imperial family and the concubines and eunuchs who served them. Anyone else who entered was executed. After the 1968 Tet Offensive, only the **Royal Theater,** on the right-hand side, and the intimate and partially restored Royal Library (☞ *below*) behind it remained intact. ⊠ *In Imperial City.* 🖾 *55,000d admission to Imperial City includes Forbidden Purple City.* ⊙ *Daily 7–5.*

❹ Imperial City (Hoang Thanh). The Imperial City, also known as the Imperial Enclosure, was once a complex of palaces and pavilions where civil and religious ceremonies took place. Inside it was the ☞ **Forbidden Purple City,** where the royal family lived. Now the Imperial City betrays disappointingly few remnants of its past glory beneath the sporadic vegetation that has taken over the ruins. Nonetheless, it still conveys a sense of splendor. There are four gateways into the enclosure: the **Gate of Peace** (Cua Hoa Binh), **the Gate of Humanity** (Cua Hien Nhan), the **Gate of Virtue** (Cua Chuong Duc), and the **South Gate** (Ngo Mon). You can only get to the Imperial City after you have entered the citadel. ⊠ *Inside citadel.* 🖾 *55,000d.* ⊙ *Daily 7–5.*

❾ Imperial Museum. This beautiful wooden structure was built in 1845 and houses miscellaneous royal knickknacks, such as wooden incense boxes, many inlaid with mother-of-pearl. The museum's walls are inscribed with Vietnamese poetry. There is also a good collection of ceramics, traditional musical instruments, and old weapons. ⊠ *Dinh Cong Trang St. at Doan Thi Diem St.* 🖾 *22,000d.* ⊙ *Daily 7–noon and 1:30–5.*

❺ Nine Dynastic Urns (Cuu Dinh O The-Mieu). Cast in 1835 and weighing approximately 5,000 pounds each, every one of these urns is dedicated to a ruler of the Nguyen dynasty. Emperor Gia Long, the founder of this dynasty, is featured on the central urn, the most elaborately decorated of the nine. The urns are covered with nature motifs, including the sun and moon, rivers and mountains, and various landscapes. Many of the designs are Chinese in origin, dating back 4,000 years. ⊠ *To left of entrance to Imperial City, when entering through Ngo Mon Gate.* 🖾 *55,000d admission to Imperial City includes Nine Urns.* ⊙ *Daily 7–5.*

❻ Palace of Supreme Harmony (Thai Hoa Dien). This richly decorated wooden palace painted gold and red was constructed in 1803. In its imperial glory in the 19th century, it was where the emperor held special events, ceremonies, and festivals for the new moon. This is also where the emperor received dignitaries. Throngs of mandarins paid their respects to his highness while he sat on his elevated throne. Now the palace houses a gift shop where 10,000d will get you an imperial tune from the authentically outfitted minstrels. ⊠ *In Imperial City.* 🖾 *55,000d admission to Imperial City includes Palace of Supreme Harmony.* ⊙ *Daily 7–5.*

❽ Royal Library (Thai Binh Lau). The Royal Library is one of the few largely intact buildings in the Imperial City. The wooden structure is on the right side of the Forbidden Purple City in a field of grass and rubble. The delicately carved architecture has survived, although there are no books or other library-like objects left. ⊠ *In Imperial City.* 🖾 *55,000d admission to Imperial City includes Royal Library.* ⊙ *Daily 7–5.*

❿ Tinh Tam Lake (Ho Tinh Tam). In spring and summer this little lake is covered with lotus flowers. Do as the emperors once did and walk across one of the bridges to the island for a brief respite. ⊠ *Dinh Tien Hoang and Tinh Tam Sts.*

The Imperial Tombs and the Thien Mu Pagoda

A GOOD BOAT RIDE OR DRIVE

Many of the prearranged boat rides organized through hotels or touris offices provide you with an all-day tour of the Imperial Tombs as we as of the Thien Mu Pagoda. These boat trips are worth taking if you have the time, although a faster way to visit the tombs is by car. The tombs and pagodas of Hue are beautiful and peaceful. At the tombs you won't just find a small tombstone: the emperors were laid to rest in elaborate pine forests and gardens with their own islands amid minilakes and pagodas. Boat tours generally stop at any combination of the following places: the Tomb of Tu Duc, the Tomb of Minh Mang, and the Thien Mu Pagoda. The Tomb of Khai Dinh and the Tomb of Duc Duc are more easily accessible by car. You can also get to each of the other tombs by car—or by motorbike or bicycle, if you are more adventurous.

The price of admission for each tomb and pagoda varies; some, such as the Thien Mu Pagoda, are free, whereas others, such as the Tomb of Tu Duc, cost as much as 50,000d. Many boat trips, such as those arranged through Thua Thien–Hue Tourism, DMZ Tour Office, and other government agencies (☞ Travel Agencies *in* Hue A to Z, *below*), are advertised at a cost of $15 or so. But the agencies neglect to inform you of the additional admission fees that you must pay at some stops. Other boats, holding up to 10 people, cost $10–$35, depending on whether you rent the boat yourself for only three or four people or join a preexisting group. You can arrange both options at the pier opposite the train station or through your hotel. The Huong Giang Tourist Company's tours give you the terrific option of going by boat and returning by car. Another option is to hire a car and driver to take you by land to the tombs.

Many boat tours follow this route down the Perfume River: heading west along the river, you approach the **Thien Mu Pagoda** ⑪ on the right-hand side. After about 6 km (4 mi), you come to the **Tomb of Tu Duc** ⑫. The **Tomb of Dong Khanh** ⑬ is a short walk northeast of the Tomb of Tu Duc. Once back on the boat you proceed another 5 km (3 mi) down the river and then on foot 1 km (½ mi) inland to the **Tomb of Minh Mang** ⑭, on the west side of the river.

To get to the **Tomb of Khai Dinh** ⑮, 1½ km (1 mi) inland on the other (east) side of the river, you're better off going by car on a separate trip, although some boat trips will take you here. The **Tomb of Duc Duc** ⑯, which lies within the city limits on the east bank of the river, is also most easily reached by car.

It takes about a day to visit most of the tombs and pagodas by boat. Going by car to all of the tombs will take you about half a day. You may, however, be happy to see just a couple of them; set aside about an hour for each (not including transportation time). Organized tours begin in the morning at about 8 and return at around 3. These trips are available daily throughout the year.

⑪ **Thien Mu Pagoda.** At this Mahayana Buddhist temple is one of Hue's most famous monuments, the seven-story, octagonal Phuoc Nguyen Tower. It was built in 1844 by Emperor Thieu Tri and is a peaceful spot, overlooking the Perfume River. Each of the tower's tiers is dedicated to a different human incarnation of Buddha. Across the temple's main entrance is the famed Austin car that in 1963 delivered the Buddhist monk Thich Quang Duc to Saigon, where he set himself on fire in an act of pacifist protest against President Diem's regime. The main sanctuary, behind the tower, houses a splendid, large Laughing Buddha; it's open daily 7–11 and 2–5. The temple is still a training center for monks, so you may see the young novices with their mostly shaved heads going about their daily activities. Behind the temple compound is a large cemetery stretching over the hills. ⊠ *About 2½ km (1½ mi) southwest of citadel on left bank of Perfume River.* ☎ *Free.* ⊙ *Daily 7–5.*

⑬ Tomb of Dong Khanh. Peace and quiet reign at this small tomb set among rice fields and fruit trees. More modest and less crowded than its grand neighbor, the Tomb of Tu Duc (☞ *below*), the Tomb of Dong Khanh has few interesting artifacts, but seduces with its pastoral setting. ⊠ *Follow the road that leads to the Tomb of Tu Duc about ½ km (⅓ mi) around the corner; this is northeast of Tu Duc on the right side of the river.* ☎ *22,000d.* ⊙ *Daily 7–5.*

⑯ Tomb of Duc Duc. This partially renovated tomb has a story that beats any soap opera. Be sure to take a guide who can explain the family history of exile, untimely death, and heartbreak of Emperors Thanh Tri, Duy Tan, and Duc Duc, as well as their many wives and children. Take the opportunity to meet the grandson of Duc Duc, who still lives on the premises. ⊠ *2 km (1 mi) from Le Loi St. on the right bank of the river.* ☎ *Free.* ⊙ *Daily 7–5.*

⑮ Tomb of Khai Dinh. An unbelievable concoction of glitzy elements, the Tomb of Khai Dinh, completed in 1931, is well worth a visit. Khai Dinh became emperor in 1916 at the age of 31 and died in 1925. Climb the few flights of steps, flanked by dragons, to enter a surprisingly colorful tomb heavily decorated with tile mosaics. Scenes from the four seasons welcome you into the main building. It's best to visit this tomb by car, since it's not directly on the river. ⊠ *About 16 km (10 mi) south of Hue and about 1½ km (1 mi) inland on right bank of Perfume River.* ☎ *50,000d.* ⊙ *Daily 8–5.*

⑭ Tomb of Minh Mang. Another Hue classic, the Tomb of Minh Mang, emperor from 1791 to 1841, was completed in 1843 by his successor. His tomb is one of the most palatial, with numerous pavilions and courtyards in a beautiful pine forest. The burial site is modeled after the Ming tombs in Beijing. Sculptures of mandarins, elephants, and lions border the route to the burial site. ⊠ *About 11 km (7 mi) south of Hue and 1½ km (1 mi) inland on left bank of Perfume River.* ☎ *50,000d.* ⊙ *Daily 8–5.*

★ ⑫ Tomb of Tu Duc. One of Hue's most visited tombs, the Tomb of Tu Duc has its own lake and pine forest. Built in 1867 by thousands of laborers, the tomb was once the second residence of Tu Duc, emperor from 1829 to 1883. Despite having more than 100 wives and numerous concubines, Tu Duc somehow found the time to escape here to relax and write poetry. One of his favorite spots was the Xung Khiem Pavilion on the pond filled with lotus blossoms. It's easy to see why he chose this place as a retreat—you may end up spending an hour just wandering around the grounds. ⊠ *About 5 km (3 mi) south of Hue, on right bank of Perfume River.* ☎ *50,000d.* ⊙ *Daily 8–5.*

OFF THE
BEATEN PATH

TU HIEU PAGODA – You have to walk through a junglelike path from the road and pass a crescent-shape pool to get to one of Hue's most beautiful and peaceful pagodas. This temple, built in 1843, houses a large gold Buddha flanked by gladiolus. It's a good place for quiet meditation. The monks live in simple rooms off to the side. ⊠ *About 3 km (2 mi) south of Hue.* ⊙ *Daily 8–5.*

Dining and Lodging

Most of Hue's hotels are on the east bank of the Perfume River. You have an excellent selection in all price ranges. The larger hotels even have (small) swimming pools and tennis courts. Most have travel se vices and can arrange for a car and driver for a customized tour. Hotels of all sizes arrange boat tours to the tombs and pagodas as well as guided tours in and around Hue.

$$$ ✕ **Century Riverside Hotel Restaurant.** Perhaps the most upscale din-
★ ing establishment in Hue, the Century is decorated in traditional Viet-
namese style with many Western touches, such as white-linen tablecloths.
Diners are usually guests of the Century Riverside or the adjacent
Houng Giang Hotel. Two particularly tasty dishes are the grilled fish
in banana leaves and the superb spring rolls. ✉ *49 Le Loi St.,* ☎ *054/
823–390. AE, MC, V.*

$$ ✕ **Club Garden.** A dimly lighted street leads you to the entrance of this
★ small restaurant, where a string of hanging lights welcomes you. One
of Hue's most upscale spots, the Club Garden is primarily filled with
tourists. Outside is a large garden, but the air-conditioned, fly-free interior is nicer. This is the place to get a fabulous fixed-price five-course
dinner for less than $10. A friendly family of waiters serves outstand-
ing Vietnamese and Chinese food. The seafood and fish dishes are particularly good, as are the pork buns. ✉ *12 Vo Thi Sau St.,* ☎ *054/826–
327. No credit cards.*

$$ ✕ **Huong Giang Hotel Restaurant.** From the windows of this spacious
third-floor restaurant you get great views of the Perfume River. Large
portions of very solid Vietnamese food and Western dishes, such as
chicken and french fries, are served. Make a reservation if you want a
seat by the window. The service is excellent; the only downside is the
occasional large tour group that takes over the place. ✉ *51 Le Loi St.,*
☎ *054/822–122. AE, MC, V.*

$ ✕ **Am Phu.** In operation for more than 80 years, this restaurant, a fa-
vorite with locals, serves excellent Vietnamese cuisine. The nonglam-
orous atmosphere keeps this place relatively free of Western tourists.
Everyone eats together at large tables covered with red plastic table-
cloths. Although there are no prices listed on the menu, most dishes
are about 30,000d, depending on how large a serving is requested. ✉
35 Nguyen Thai Hoc St., ☎ *054/825–259. No credit cards.*

$ ✕ **Lac Thanh Restaurant.** Packed with tourists and teeming with post-
card and cigarette vendors, this dive (and its next-door copycat) serves
the tastiest and cheapest meals in Hue. Some notable dishes include
Asian basics such as shrimp and vegetables over crispy noodles and
tofu or beef and vegetables wrapped in rice paper and dipped in peanut
sauce. For dessert, try the delicious coconut ice cream topped with choco-
late sauce and peanuts. ✉ *6A Dien Tien Hoang St.,* ☎ *no phone. No
credit cards.*

$ ✕ **Ngoc Anh.** This open-air restaurant—the Vietnamese version of a
sidewalk café—serves high-quality Vietnamese and Chinese food in a
relaxed atmosphere. The sizzling-hot clay-pot seafood special is ex-
ceptional. ✉ *29 Nguyen Thai Hoc St.,* ☎ *054/822–617. No credit cards.*

$ ✕ **Tong Phuoc Nen.** Although soup is the specialty of the house, you
can also order a variety of fish dishes. Different types of eel soup are
some of the more popular choices. Try *lau luon,* a tangy eel-and-veg-
etable concoction served over noodles, or *chao luon,* a more traditional
soup prepared with mushrooms and lotus seed. Upstairs, the terrace
seating has a kind of rustic charm with its whitewashed walls. Diners
include more adventurous tourists and lots of Vietnamese teenagers.
✉ *20 Ba Trieu St.,* ☎ *054/825–264. No credit cards.*

¢ ✕ **Banh Beo Ba Cu.** Don't be put off by the grungy interior of this restau-
rant. The quality of the decor is in inverse proportion to the quality
of the food. This favorite among locals serves only eight dishes, all spe-
cialties of the region. The price of 3,000d per dish should allow you
to try them all (if you're hungry enough). Particularly memorable is

the *banh uot thit nuong* (grilled meat rolled in pastry). ⊠ *47 Nguyen Hue St.,* ☎ *no phone. No credit cards.*

¢ ✕ **Banh Khoai.** This two-table, family-run food stall serves some of the best banh khoai in town. The meat-filled rice pancake (three for 10,000d) topped with bean sprouts comes to the table piping hot. Break it up with chopsticks into your small rice bowl, add the greens and sauce, and eat. This place is a great dining experience if you don't mind eating in what is essentially this family's kitchen. You may have to share your table with the cook, who could need the space to peel shrimp. ⊠ *2 Nguyen Tri Phuong St., off Hanoi St.,* ☎ *no phone. No credit cards.*

¢ ✕ **Bun Bo Hue.** Close to the center of Hue, this very downscale sidewalk food stall serves some of the best bun bo Hue, the Hue noodle specialty made with beef and pork. This is the only dish served, and there is no menu. ⊠ *11B Ly Kiet St.,* ☎ *no phone. No credit cards.*

¢ ✕ **Mai Huong.** Although it may not live up to your fantasy of a Parisian patisserie, this small "coffee shop" is still a good place for a slice of coconut or apple cake and a cup of tea. Just keep in mind that the ice cream doesn't even vaguely resemble Carvel's. ⊠ *14 Nguyen Tri Phuong St.,* ☎ *no phone. No credit cards.*

$$–$$$ 🏨 **Century Riverside Inn.** A large Western-style establishment on the river, the Century is the most luxurious hotel in town. Still, the hotel is not opulent by Western standards, but it is very clean and comfortable. The public rooms are tastefully decorated, and there's even a gift shop, albeit overpriced. About half the rooms, which are done in fairly standard hotel-style decor, have river views; all rooms have IDD phones. After a long day of sightseeing, relax by the small riverfront swimming pool. ⊠ *49 Le Loi St.,* ☎ *054/823–390,* FAX *054/823–399. 158 rooms. 4 restaurants, bar, air-conditioning, minibars, refrigerators, room service, pool, tennis courts, bicycles, shop, dry cleaning, laundry service, travel services. AE, MC, V.*

$$ 🏨 **Dong Da Hotel.** This spacious hotel on a quiet street corner falls somewhere between a minihotel—one of the new, privately owned small places popping up all over Vietnam—and a Western-style accommodation. Rooms are clean and modern and have simple Japanese-style furnishings, including rice-paper room dividers. All have TVs. ⊠ *15 Ly Thuong Kiet St.,* ☎ *054/823–071,* FAX *054/823–204. 37 rooms. 2 restaurants, bar, air-conditioning, laundry service, travel services, car rental. AE, MC, V.*

$$ 🏨 **Hoa Hong Hotel II.** Almost as comfortable as its more expensive neighbors, the Century Riverside and the Huong Giang, this hotel has similarly styled semiluxurious rooms. It's one of the tallest buildings in town and has the reassuring air of a Western Holiday Inn. The decor is nondescript, but everything is new and tasteful. All rooms have TVs and minibars. Although the hotel is not on the water, it's tall enough so that many rooms have excellent views of the river. Traditional music and dance are performed nightly in the hotel's restaurant. ⊠ *1 Pham Ngu Lao St,* ☎ *054/824–377,* FAX *054/826–949. 60 rooms. Restaurant, air-conditioning, minibars, dry cleaning, laundry service, travel services. MC, V.*

$$ 🏨 **Huong Giang Hotel.** Large rooms with traditional Vietnamese-style
★ decor and the most helpful staff in Hue make the Huong Giang, on the north end of the east bank, the most pleasant hotel in town. Bamboo furniture fills the rooms, and there is an almost palatial feel to the lobby. Ask for one of the renovated older rooms—they're better than the newer ones surrounding the pool. All rooms have IDD phones. The hotel also has a very good restaurant and rooftop bar-garden with panoramic views of the river. The travel office in the hotel is exceptional. ⊠ *51 Le Loi St.,* ☎ *054/832–220,* FAX *054/821–426. 102 rooms. 2 restaurants, 2 bars, outdoor café, air-conditioning, pool, tennis court, dry cleaning, laundry service, travel services. AE, MC, V.*

$–$$ ⌂ **Hue Hotel.** Run by and adjacent to Thua Thien–Hue Tourism, this refurbished property has two types of rooms. The more expensive rooms are clean but sparse and have superb air-conditioning. The cheaper rooms, which have fans only, are not as clean as the pricier ones, although they are still acceptable. Oddly, the cheaper rooms look out over the river, but the more expensive ones are set back closer to Le Loi Street. The staff speaks very little English and is not very helpful. ⊠ *15 Le Loi St.,* ☎ *054/822–369,* ℻ *054/824–806. 11 rooms. No credit cards.*

$ ⌂ **A Dong Hotel 1.** This pleasant, clean, and airy minihotel is a great budget alternative. There's nothing particularly charming about the place, but it does a great job of providing large, basic, immaculate rooms. It scores big, however, with fresh fruit and flowers delivered daily to your room. The staff speaks very little English but is eager to please. ⊠ *1 Chu Van An St.,* ☎ *054/824–148,* ℻ *054/828–074. 7 rooms. Restaurant, bar, air-conditioning, minibars, refrigerators, laundry service, travel services, car rental. No credit cards.*

$ ⌂ **A Dong Hotel 2.** The cheaper of the A Dong hotels, this one is a fine example of a small, clean, well-run minihotel. Rooms are plain, although all have a private bathroom. ⊠ *7 Doi Cung St.,* ☎ *054/822–765,* ℻ *054/828–074. 15 rooms. Restaurant, air-conditioning, laundry service, travel services, car rental. No credit cards.*

$ ⌂ **Binh Minh.** If you're traveling on a budget, the small Binh Minh may be for you. Rooms are sunny, and some have sliding doors that lead to balconies. The staff is very knowledgeable and speaks English. ⊠ *12 Nguyen Tri Phuong St.,* ☎ *054/825–526,* ℻ *054/828–362. 22 rooms. Restaurant, air-conditioning, fans, minibars, refrigerators, laundry service, travel services. No credit cards.*

$ ⌂ **Dong Duong (Indochina) Hotel.** It's just as clean and pleasant as its hotel counterpart, the Huong Giang Hotel (☞ *above*), but the Dong Duong has larger rooms and a more intimate environment. The cozy and sunny rooms are arranged in a horseshoe shape around a small garden; all are on the first or second floor. Staying here you sacrifice having access to a restaurant or recreational facilities, but you get the feel of a small inn and easy access to the center of town. ⊠ *3 Hung Vuong St.,* ☎ *054/826–070,* ℻ *054/826–074. 12 rooms. Air-conditioning, fans, minibars, refrigerators, laundry service, travel services, car rental. AE, MC, V.*

$ ⌂ **Dong Loi Hotel.** Although this hotel looks slightly worn, it is very reasonably priced and in the downtown area. Rooms are tidy, no-frills accommodations, with unmatched curtains, bedding, and towels. The staff will arrange city tours and excursions outside Hue for you. The adjoining restaurant serves French and Vietnamese dishes at reasonable prices. ⊠ *11A Pham Ngu Lao St.,* ☎ *054/822–296,* ℻ *054/826–234. 30 rooms. Restaurant, air-conditioning, minibars, refrigerators, laundry service, travel services. AE, MC, V.*

$ ⌂ **Duy Tan Hotel.** Despite its large and semigrand appearance, this hotel functions as a glorified minihotel. Rooms are bright and spacious, although the renovation job is pretty spotty. But the new bathrooms with tubs are a plus. ⊠ *12 Hung Vuong St.,* ☎ *054/825–001,* ℻ *054/826–477. 58 rooms. Restaurant, air-conditioning, minibars, refrigerators, laundry service, meeting rooms, travel services, car rental. No credit cards.*

$ ⌂ **Saigon Hotel.** Don't be put off by the strangely decorated restaurant (for instance, the neon-backlighted cow's head) in this fairly new minihotel. Rooms are sunny and squeaky clean, and the bathrooms are in excellent condition and have tubs. ⊠ *32 Hung Vuong St.,* ☎ *054/821–007,* ℻ *054/821–009. 20 rooms. Restaurant, air-conditioning, fans, laundry service, travel services, car rental. No credit cards.*

¢–$ 🏨 **Hoa Hong I.** The smaller and less luxurious of the Hoa Hong family of hotels, this place has comfortable rooms with IDD phones and bathrooms with tubs. Just ignore the fake-flower finishing touches and the overly cutesy pastel decor. ⊠ *46C Le Loi St.,* ☎ *054/824–377,* 𝔽𝔸𝕏 *054/826–949. 56 rooms. Restaurant, air-conditioning, minibars, refrigerators, laundry service, travel services. No credit cards.*

¢–$ 🏨 **Hung Vuong Hotel.** Both backpackers and nonbackpackers, especially those taking the Sinh Café Bus (☞ Arriving and Departing *in* Hue A to Z, *below*), which drops off and picks up passengers here, stay at the Hung Vuong because of the wide price range of rooms. All are clean, and the most expensive ones overlook the river. The hotel adjoins the Thua Thien–Hue Tourism office and is centrally located near downtown Hue. You can also get information from the Sinh Café representative here. ⊠ *2 Hung Vuong St.,* ☎ *054/823–866,* 𝔽𝔸𝕏 *054/ 825–910. 70 rooms. Restaurant, air-conditioning, minibars, refrigerators, laundry service, travel services, car rental. No credit cards.*

¢–$ 🏨 **Le Loi Hue Hotel.** A little run-down but passable, this hotel close to the train station has rooms with many amenities, including IDD phones. It often has vacancies when other places are booked. ⊠ *2 Le Loi St.,* ☎ *054/822–153,* 𝔽𝔸𝕏 *054/824–527. 150 rooms. Restaurant, air-conditioning, minibars, refrigerators, laundry service, travel services, car rental. No credit cards.*

¢   🏨 **Hoan My Hotel.** Slightly off the beaten path, this bright white minihotel has modest, clean rooms at decent though not exceptional prices. The staff speaks very little English, so you may have to make do with a little sign language. Those traveling on a budget will appreciate the nearby Banh Beo Ba Cu restaurant (☞ *above*). ⊠ *16 Dong Da St.,* ☎ *054/821– 560,* 𝔽𝔸𝕏 *054/821–561. 20 rooms. Restaurant, air-conditioning, fans, minibars, refrigerators, laundry service, travel services. No credit cards.*

Nightlife and the Arts

Compared to Ho Chi Minh City and Hanoi, Hue is a sleepy town with little in the way of nightlife. A number of new bars catering to the backpacker crowd have recently opened on Le Loi and Hung Vuong streets, however. Hue recently witnessed the opening of its own branch of the popular **Apocalypse Now** bar (⊠ 7 Nguyen Tri Phuong St., ☎ 054/ 820–152). Locals and visitors come here to shoot pool and listen to old and new rock music.

A culturally enlightening way to spend an evening in Hue is to take a **night cruise** on the Huong River. Boats featuring musical groups performing traditional Hue folk songs can be rented through most tourist agencies or directly at the river next to the Floating Restaurant (⊠ O⸱ Bach Dang St., near intersection with Nguyen Thai Hoc St.). If you still have the energy after a day visiting Hue's tombs and pagodas, you don't want to miss this enchanting experience.

Shopping

There aren't many places to shop in Hue, although you can pick u⸱ some nice souvenirs—including wood carvings and replicas of antiqu⸱ compasses and teapots—at the stands inside the Imperial City and alon⸱ Le Loi Street. The Central Market isn't filled with spectacular find⸱ except for conical hats with poems stitched inside (*non la tho*), dec⸱ rated to order, and sesame-seed candy—two Hue specialties.

Side Trip from Hue

Hue is a convenient location from which to visit the former Demili⸱ rized Zone (DMZ), which lies about 100 km (62 mi) north of the ci⸱

A trip here can be combined easily with a visit to the Vinh Moc Tunnels and to the numerous former battlefields of the war that dot the area.

DMZ and Environs

🕧 *90 km (56 mi) northwest of Hue.*

The origins of the **DMZ** date to the Geneva Accords of 1954—really just a cease-fire and interlude in the extensive fighting for control of Vietnam—which divided the country in half at the 17th parallel at the Ben Hai River. The northern half of the country became the Communist-led Democratic Republic of Vietnam, and the south became the Republic of Vietnam (led by Ngo Dinh Diem and supported by the United States). The DMZ, which consisted of an area extending 5 km (3 mi) on either side of the borderline, was supposed to have been a temporary measure, enforced only until the Democratic Republic of Vietnam and the Republic of Vietnam could be reunited following elections in 1956. The elections never took place, and the inaptly named DMZ was only abolished after many years of fighting that culminated in the victory of the North Vietnamese forces in 1975. Almost as soon as it was created, the DMZ was militarized, and by 1965 it had become a key battleground in the fight between north and south. The fighting forced virtually all the inhabitants of the area to flee and rendered the DMZ a wasteland.

The area south and west of the DMZ was the scene of some of the most bitter fighting of the war. Some names that may be familiar from the war are Con Thien, Camp Carroll, the Rockpile, Hamburger Hill, Quang Tri, and, above all, Khe Sanh.

One of the biggest battles of the war—and one of the most significant American losses—took place at **Khe Sanh,** the site of a U.S. Army base, in 1968. Khe Sanh lies in a highland valley not far from Highway 9, which links Vietnam with southern Laos. General William Westmoreland, the commander of U.S. forces in Vietnam from 1965 to 1968, became convinced in late 1967 that the North Vietnamese were massing troops in the area in preparation for a campaign to seize South Vietnam's northernmost provinces. Relying on an analogy with the French defeat at Dien Bien Phu (☞ Chapter 3), he reinforced Khe Sanh with thousands of marines and ordered the dropping of more than 75,000 tons of explosives on the surrounding area. The North Vietnamese suffered horrendous casualties—estimates are that as many as 10,000 North Vietnamese soldiers and hundreds of U.S. Marines lost their lives, a sacrifice that seems senseless given the abandoning of the base by the American forces in June 1968. Although the debate continues, many military experts believe that the battle at Khe Sanh was merely a feint designed to pull American forces away from the population centers of South Vietnam in preparation for a massive assault by the North Vietnamese in the Tet Offensive of early 1968.

Although there is only a small **museum** commemorating the battle at Khe Sanh, a visit to the base provides a sense of how isolated and besieged the U.S. Marines must have felt as they were bombarded from the surrounding mountains. In the museum, which opens whenever tours come through the area, there are a number of interesting pictures of the battle and a book for visitors' comments that demonstrates the continuing debate about the American presence in Vietnam.

About 20 km (12 mi) north of the DMZ are the 3-km-long (2-mi-long) **Vinh Moc Tunnels,** built by villagers in the area from 1966 to 1968 to escape American bombing and later used by the North Vietnamese army to transport goods to Con Co Island. Less claustrophobic than the tunnels at Cu Chi, they are nonetheless a testament to the determination and ingenuity of the Vietnamese people under extreme circumstances.

Make sure to be in the front of the line when you descend into the tunnels if you want to benefit from the guide's presentation.

ARRIVING AND DEPARTING
Virtually all the tour agencies in Hue (☞ Travel Agencies *in* Hue A to Z, *below*) can arrange trips to the DMZ, Khe Sanh, and the Vinh Moc Tunnels. Given the scattered locations of these sites, tours generally leave Hue early in the morning and return about 12 hours later.

Hue A to Z

Arriving and Departing

Hue is 108 km (67 mi) north of Danang, 140 km (87 mi) north of Hoi An, 1,097 km (680 mi) north of Ho Chi Minh City, and 689 km (427 mi) south of Hanoi.

BY BUS

The **Sinh Café Bus** (✉ At Hung Vuong Hotel, 2 Hung Vuong St., Hue, ☎ 054/822–121) stops in Hue on both its northbound and southbound routes. The one-way fare from Hanoi to Hue is $12, and the trip takes about 12 hours. One-way open tour tickets from Ho Chi Minh City to Hue, with stops in Dalat, Nha Trang, and Hoi An, can be purchased for less than $40 (☞ Bus Travel *in* Smart Travel Tips A to Z). The Sinh Café bus usually departs, both northbound and southbound, between 7 and 8 AM. Call for details, as the schedule changes.

BY CAR OR MINIBUS

You can rent a minibus with a driver to take you from Hue to Hoi An, Danang, or other points nearby; the cost is approximately $25–$50 for the trip, depending on the kind of vehicle, its age, and whether it has air-conditioning.

BY PLANE

Vietnam Airlines (✉ 7 Nguyen Tri Phuong St., ☎ 054/846–320) flies to Hue's **Phu Bai Airport**, 15 km (9 mi) south of the city center, from Ho Chi Minh City (1 hour; $70 one-way; twice a day) and Hanoi (50 minutes; $70 one-way; once or twice a day). The Vietnam Airlines office in Hue is open Monday–Saturday 7–11 and 1:30–4:40. The schedule changes frequently, so confirm departure times with your hotel travel agent or with the airline a day or two before your flight. **Taxis** are available at the airport to take you into town; the cost is generally about 80,000d.

BY TRAIN

Trains from all over Vietnam come into the **Hue Railway Station** (Ga Hue; ✉ On right bank at southwest end of Le Loi St.). The ticket office is open daily 7:30–5. Four trains depart daily for Ho Chi Minh City (24 hours, $40–$60 for a sleeping berth), and four depart daily for Hanoi (15 hours, $40–$50 for a sleeping berth).

Getting Around

BY BICYCLE

One of the easiest ways to get around Hue is by bicycle, which you can rent from the Century Riverside Inn (☞ Dining and Lodging *above*) or any number of places on Hung Vuong Street.

BY BOAT

Many hotels in Hue can arrange dragon-boat rides, which shuttle you from one tomb and pagoda to the next along the Perfume River. The boat companies are usually affiliated with the Thua Thien–Hue Tourist (☞ Travel Agencies, *below*), or they are run independently. You can also arrange for your own boat with guide at the pier across from the train station on Le Loi Street; a small boat, seating approximately si people, costs $15 a day. In addition, Lac Thanh Restaurant (☞ Dining and Lodging, *above*) has its own mini–tourist company, which rents boats. Make arrangements at the restaurant or at the pier.

BY CAR OR MINIBUS

Cars or minibuses with drivers can be rented through hotels, booking offices, and government-run travel agencies (☞ Travel Agencies, *below*) for $40 and up per day, depending on the condition of the car. A guide will cost about $25 a day above and beyond the cost of the car and driver. Keep in mind that some of the hard-to-reach monuments, such as the Tomb of Tu Duc, are more accessible if you hire a car and guide.

BY CYCLO

You can almost always find a cyclo outside hotels or cruising along the right bank. For 20,000d you should be able to get pretty much anywhere, although you will almost always have to negotiate to get down to this price. If you hate to bargain, the Century Riverside Inn (☞ Dining and Lodging, *above*) posts suggested cyclo prices, which the drivers follow.

BY TAXI

Taxis are metered. Expect to pay less than $5 for trips around town. Call **Hue Taxi ATC** (☎ 054/824–500 or 054/833–333) to arrange a ride, or just hail one on the street, although they are not always easy to find. Taxi drivers will also take you anywhere you want to go for a prearranged price. A one-hour taxi trip should cost about $10.

Contacts and Resources

CURRENCY EXCHANGE

The Thua Thien–Hue branch of **Vietcom Bank** (ICBV; ⊠ 46 Hung Vuong St., ☎ 054/822–281) changes money and gives cash advances on Visa and MasterCard. It's open weekdays 7–11 and 1:30–3:30. You can exchange money at most hotels in Hue.

DOCTORS AND HOSPITAL

If your illness is not life threatening, seek assistance through your hotel staff. In case of emergency, contact **Benh Vien Trung Uong Hue** (Hue General Hospital; ⊠ 16 Le Loi St., ☎ 054/822–325). They do not speak English.

GUIDED TOURS

Guided tours can be arranged through a number of different travel agencies (☞ Travel Agencies, *below*). Many hotels are affiliated with one of the government-run tourism agencies. The **DMZ Tour Office** (☞ *below*) arranges different types of tours: guided city tours for $15 per day include tours of the citadel and Imperial Tombs; excursions to surrounding areas include the DMZ and the Bru or Van Kieu ethnic minority village.

Several agencies organize **boat trips** on the Perfume River, which include stops at the tombs and the Thien Mu Pagoda (☞ Getting Around by Boat, *above*). Most depart at 8 AM daily and cost 40,000d, excluding tomb and pagoda entry fees, which can run as high as 50,000d each.

PHARMACY

The woman working at **Thuoc Tay** (⊠ 5 Hung Vuong St.) speaks better French than English, but she is very helpful, especially if you write down what you need. If she doesn't have what you're looking for, she will recommend someone else who does. On Hung Vuong Street there are a number of other pharmacies near this one. The sign claims the pharmacy stays open 7:30 AM–10 PM, but it closes for lunch.

The past several years have witnessed a proliferation of private tourist companies in Hue, primarily located on Le Loi and Hung Vuong streets. Most of these can arrange visits to Hue's tombs, pagodas, and other sights; they can also help you with bus, train, and air tickets.

DMZ Tour Office (⌧ 26 Le Loi St., ☎ 054/825–242) arranges minibus and car rentals that include a guide, tours of Hue by car, boat tours along the Perfume River, and trips to the DMZ. It also books train and air tickets. It's open daily 8–7.

Huong Giang Tourist Company (⌧ 17 Le Loi St., ☎ 054/832–220, FAX 054/833–588) is a first-class travel agency that gives excellent tours of Hue (including a boat tour of the tombs from which you return by car) and organizes trips to the DMZ. One special feature is its cooking tours, during which you can learn to cook Vietnamese food. The agency is affiliated with the Houng Giang Hotel (☞ Dining and Lodging, *above*) but is in a separate location. It's open daily 7–noon and 1:30–5, and they accept credit cards.

Thua Thien–Hue Tourism (Cong Ty Du Lich Thua Thien–Hue; ⌧ 30 Le Loi St., ☎ 054/822–369, 054/822–288, or 054/822–355) is a government-run tourism agency. It offers services similar to those of other agencies in town. It's open daily 8–5.

DANANG AND ENVIRONS

Although Danang was once an important port town and a critical U.S. Air Force base during the Vietnam War, today it is a dreary, slightly run-down city with only one tourist attraction: an impressive museum of Cham culture. It's not the biggest tourist destination, so there aren't many good hotels or restaurants, except for the Furama Resort in nearby China Beach. Danang has a major regional airport, however, which makes it the arrival point for Hue, Hoi An, and other nearby cities. (Hue also has a smaller airport.) South of the city, on the way to Hoi An, are China Beach and the cave-temples of the Marble Mountains.

There's really no reason to spend more than a morning in Danang visiting the Cham Museum. But just outside Danang, en route to Hoi An, are the Marble Mountains and China Beach. Both China Beach and the Marble Mountains can be seen as part of a single day trip from Danang (or Hoi An) or as stops on your way to Hoi An. A pilgrimage to My Son, Vietnam's most significant Cham ruins, also merits at least a half day, either from Danang or Hoi An.

Lang Co Beach

⑱ *35 km (22 mi) north of Danang, 73 km (45 mi) south of Hue.*

A convenient stopover on the trip from Hue to Danang, Lang Co is an idyllic hamlet on a peninsula jutting out into the South China Sea. Lang Co Beach is a good place to have lunch and spend the day, and for the true sun worshipper, it may be worth a night's stay. Take the turn off Highway 1 at the sign for the Thanh Tam Resort; this will lead you to the long sandy beach.

Danang

⑲ *108 km (67 mi) south of Hue, 30 km (19 mi) north of Hoi An, and 972 km (603 mi) north of Ho Chi Minh City.*

Danang became an important port city at the end of the 19th century when silt filling up the Thu Bon River eliminated neighboring Hoi An access to the sea. The French gained control of Danang (which they called Tourane) in 1888, taking it by force from Emperor Gia Long (he had promised it to them in exchange for their help but had reneged on his agreement). In its heyday, during the first half of the 20th century, the city was second only to Saigon as Vietnam's most cosmopolitan center.

During the Vietnam War the city played a significant role: it was the first place U.S. Marines landed in March 1965, and it subsequently became home to a large U.S. Air Force base. Only 200 km (124 mi) south of the DMZ, the city was an ideal location for launching bombing missions. The influx of army personnel brought enormous growth, numerous refugees, and all kinds of entertainment, including movie theaters, bars, and prostitution. Soldiers would take time off at the nearby R&R resort of China Beach (☞ *below*). By March 1975, Danang was in a state of total chaos as people tried to escape the fast-encroaching North Vietnamese army and had to fight for space on any boat or plane leaving the city. Today there are remnants of the American presence in the city, as well as vestiges of the French in the wide avenues and old villas. But Danang is not a place where you are likely to want to linger after visiting its highlight, the Cham Museum.

★ On display at the **Cham Museum** are artifacts from the Kingdom of Champa, which ruled this region for more than 1,000 years. The Cham religion combines native beliefs with elements of Indian culture and early Hindu thought (the god Shiva is often represented on Cham ruins). The Cham adopted many elements of Indian art and Sanskrit as their sacred language. Prevalent in an area stretching from the north of Hue south to the Mekong Delta in the 10th and 11th centuries, the Cham established a kingdom between the Khmer to the south and the Viet to the north. In the 12th century, the Cham were under frequent attack by the Khmer. In the 13th century, backed by the Chinese, the Viet attacked the northernmost Cham, but were defeated in 1377 when the Cham reached an agreement with the Chinese. The Cham had a substantial presence until the 1400s, when they were conquered by the Viet. After that, they had a much smaller presence in the area until they were finally completely overthrown by the Viet in the 1700s. Remnants of the sandstone-and-brick towers built for Hindu worship by the Cham can still be found along the central coast, and descendants of the Cham continue to live in the highlands.

The Cham Museum was founded by the French in 1915 to exhibit Cham sculptures and fragments of temples and towers found by archaeologists. Exhibits are arranged chronologically, reflecting the changing seats of power in the kingdom from Emperor Indrapura to Tra Kieu to My Son to Khuong My. The highly sensual, innovative, and expressive works from Tra Kieu's reign (7th century) and that of My Son (8th–9th centuries) and the abundant sandstone carvings of the god Shiva show the prosperity of the Kingdom of Champa.

As you walk through the museum, note that although Buddha is traditionally pictured seated in the lotus position, the Cham Buddha is displayed on a throne in an imperial pose, with his feet flat on the ground. This subtle difference in Buddha styles reflects the Cham belief in the spiritual continuum between crown and divinity: the nobility were thought to be "higher up" because they were more directly connected to God. The symbol of fertility, Uroja (meaning woman's breast or female breast), which you will also see throughout the museum, reveals the esteem afforded women in Cham culture.

Keep in mind the following cast of characters as you look at the Cham sculptures: Vishnu, god of conservation and life; Garuda, the holy bird;

Danang

Danang Bay

Tach Thang Lagoon

Thanh Son

Tran Quy Cap

Ly Thuong Kiet

Nguyen Du

Dong Da

Ly Tu Trong

Ong Inc Khiem

Ba Dinh

Le Lai

Nguyen Thi Minh Khai Thi

Quang Thi Trung

Le Loi

Nguyen Chi Thanh

Dinh Tien Hoang

Cao Van

Hai Phong

Pasteur

Ngo Gia Tu

Phan Dinh Phung

Ferry Station

Le Duan

Hung Vuong

Market

Trien Nu Vuong

Ly Thai To

Bus Station

Tran Quoc Toan

Thai Phien

Ong Inc Khiem

Nguyen Thai

Hoang Dieu

Hong Phong

Tran Phu

Bach Dang

Hoang Van Thu

Bamboo Green Hotel

Le Dinh

Duong

Le Dai Ha

Phan Chu Trinh

Truong Nu Vuong

Cham Museum

Han River

TO DANANG AIRPORT

Le Duo

Nguyen Tri Phuong

Hoang Dieu

Truong Nu Vuong

Nui Thanh

Nguyen Van Troi

N

0   400 yards

0   400 meters

TO CHINA BEACH, MARBLE MOUNTAINS, HOI AN

Rama, god of creation and birth; Sarasvati, Rama's wife and goddess of sacred language, whose animal counterpart is a swan; Laksmi, Vishnu's wife and goddess of prosperity; Shiva, god of the dead, who is represented in phallic form (*linga*); Skanda, god of war and son of Shiva and Uma, who is often depicted as a peacock; Ganesha, god of peace and the son of Shiva and Uma, whose disobedience prompted Shiva to cut off his head. When Uma prayed to the gods for forgiveness and for a new head for Ganesha, they gave her a consolation prize of the head of the first animal she spotted. Hence you have the omnipresent elephant-head-and-human-body motif.

The central **Tra Kieu Altar** (in the Tra Kieu Room)—in the middle gallery, opposite the entrance and across the courtyard—illustrates in relief sculpture part of the Hindu *Ramayana* epic story. This is the museum's best-preserved relief. Beginning on the left panel and working clockwise, the narrative runs as follows: Rama successfully breaks the sacred bow; Rudra is granted the right to marry King Janak's daughter Princess Sita; the fathers, King Videha and King Dasaratha, interact; and the wedding festivities follow.

Although you may be offered a guided tour of the Cham Museum, you should make sure you understand what your potential guide is saying and that he or she is truly knowledgeable about the museum's contents before wasting your time and money. ⊠ *Intersection of Tran Phu and Le Dinh Duong Sts.* ▦ *20,000d.* ☉ *Daily 8–6.*

OFF THE
BEATEN PATH

MY SON – About 70 km (43 mi) southwest of Danang, or 45 km (28 mi) due west of Hoi An, are the My Son Cham ruins: former temples and towers dedicated to kings and divinities, particularly Shiva, who was considered the founder of the Kingdom of Champa. Construction first began in the 4th century under the order of the Cham king Bhadresvara and continued until the 13th century. With more than 70 brick structures, of which some 20 remain in recognizable form today, My Son was the most important religious and architectural center of the Kingdom of Champa. Although extensively damaged by American bombing during the war, the My Son complex still retains vestiges of its former glory. Most of the statuary that formerly adorned the temples was taken to the Cham Museum (☞ *above*) in Danang by the French in the early 20th century. Seeing both the museum and the temples of My Son will enable you to fully appreciate the wonders of Cham culture. Make arrangements for a car and driver through the Danang Travel Information Center (☞ *Arriving and Departing in Danang and Environs A to Z, below*).

Lodging

$$ 🏨 **Bamboo Green.** A welcome addition to Danang's desultory lodging scene, this brand-new hotel is only a five-minute walk from the Cham Museum (☞ *above*). Rooms are large and tastefully decorated, and the satellite TVs, IDD phones, and efficient room service give you the feeling that you've briefly stepped out of Vietnam. ⊠ *158 Phan Chu Trinh St.,* ☎ *0511/822–997,* ℻ *0511/822–998. 46 rooms. Restaurant, bar, air-conditioning, minibars, refrigerators, room service, massage, dry cleaning, laundry service, business services, travel services, car rental. AE, MC, V.*

Shopping

If you find yourself stuck in Danang for the day, fabric shops and tailors along **Hung Vuong Street** can make clothes for you cheaply and quickly. Shirts and pants should cost less than $10 apiece.

Marble Mountains

★   *11 km (7 mi) southwest of Danang, 19 km (12 mi) north of Hoi An.*

Five beautiful limestone peaks, known as the Marble Mountains, rise above the beach south of Danang and north of Hoi An. Tours from Danang en route to Hoi An generally stop here, and a visit to the mountains can easily be combined with a trip to China Beach (☞ *below*). The five Marble Mountains have been equated with the five basic elements of Chinese philosophy: Tho Son (earth), Thuy Son (water), Hoa Son (fire), Moc Son (wood), and Kim So (metal). Over the centuries the *dong* (caves) in the Thuy Son Peak have been turned into temples and shrines. The first to use them were the Cham, who turned them into Hindu shrines. The Buddhists have since taken over, adorned, sanctified, and inhabited them.

Ever since the local government cracked down on solicitation—i.e., people hassling tourists for money—the Marble Mountains have become a very pleasant place to spend a few hours. The climb up the path leading to the various cave-pagodas is not particularly strenuous, unless attempted in the middle of a hot, sunny day. Polite children in traditional school uniforms (white shirt and blue trousers) may take you by the hand and give you a free guided tour of the various Buddhist cave sanctuaries. Since there is only one path, and there are enough people around, it's usually not a problem to have them accompany you. At the end of these tours, don't be surprised if they offer you the "best price . . . for you only" for marble souvenirs, such as miniature Marble Mountains. You shouldn't feel obliged to buy one, however.

After entering through **Ong Chon Gate,** the main entrance, you'll see the **Linh Ong Pagoda,** a Buddhist shrine inside a cave, filled with a large collection of Buddhas. The hole at the top of the cave filters in an ethereal sort of natural light. As you continue on the main path, you'll come to another temple, the **Tam Thai Tu Pagoda,** where monks still live. The path then leads to a spectacular view of the mountains and the surrounding countryside. ✉ *About 11 km (7 mi) south of Danang; 19 km (12 mi) north of Hoi An off Hwy. 1.* 💰 *Free, but donation may be requested at pagodas.*

China Beach

  12 km (7 mi) southeast of Danang, 25 km (16 mi) north of Hoi An.

Yes, the TV show *China Beach* was based on this place, but the China Beach that was an R&R resort spot for U.S. soldiers during the Vietnam War is actually 5 km (3 mi) north of what is now called China Beach (Bac My An). China Beach's pristine and quiet sandy stretches are a welcome change from Danang's portlike atmosphere. Stop here on your way to or from Hoi An, make it a day trip from Danang or Hoi An, or stay at the Furama Resort (☞ Dining and Lodging, *below*); you can make arrangements through travel agencies in either town or in Ho Chi Minh City.

Activity on China Beach is limited to lazing on the sand and surfing. Surfboards can be rented from the Furama Resort and China Beach Resort (☞ Dining and Lodging, *below*), where you can also rent surfing gear and bicycles. It's best to come between May and July, when the water is placid. Waves can be very large at other times—in fact, the first international surfing competition in Vietnam was held in China Beach in December 1992. With the opening of the Furama Resort, the atmosphere in China Beach is more inviting, and it means, thankfully, that there is somewhere to stay other than the state-run China Beach Resort.

ONE LAST TRAVEL TIP:

Pack an easy way to reach the world.

123 456 7891 2345
J.D. SMITH

Wherever you travel, the MCI WorldCom Card℠ is the easiest way to stay in touch. You can use it to call to and from more than 125 countries worldwide. And you can earn bonus miles every time you use your card. So go ahead, travel the world. MCI WorldCom℠ makes it even more rewarding. For additional access codes, visit **www.wcom.com/worldphone**.

EASY TO CALL WORLDWIDE

1. Just dial the WorldPhone® access number of the country you're calling from.

2. Dial or give the operator your MCI WorldCom Card number.

3. Dial or give the number you're calling.

China (A)	108-12
Hong Kong	800-96-1121
Indonesia ◆	001-801-11
Japan ◆	00539-121▶
Korea	00729-14
Malaysia ◆	1-800-80-0012
Philippines ◆	105-14
Singapore (A)	8000-112-112
Taiwan ◆	0080-13-4567
Thailand (A) ★	001-999-1-2001
Vietnam (A) ÷ ●	1201-1022

(A) Calls back to U.S. only. ◆ Public phones may require deposit of coin or phone card for dial tone.
▶ Regulation does not permit intra-Japan calls. ★ Not available from public pay phones. ÷ Limited availability.
● Local service fee in U.S. currency required to complete call.

EARN FREQUENT FLIER MILES

Bureau de change

Cambio

外国為替

In this city, you can find money on almost any street.

NO-FEE FOREIGN EXCHANGE

The Chase Manhattan Bank has over 80 convenient
locations near New York City destinations such as:

      Times Square
      Rockefeller Center
      Empire State Building
      2 World Trade Center
      United Nations Plaza

Exchange any of 75 foreign currencies

 CHASE

THE RIGHT RELATIONSHIP IS EVERYTHING.®

For those seeking to really get away from it all, one of the most beautiful and pleasantly deserted beaches in all of Vietnam can be found just a short stroll from the China Beach Resort. Walk south down the beach from the resort for about ½ km (⅓ mi) until you arrive at a pristine white-sand beach straight out of a tourist brochure.

Dining and Lodging

$ ✕⌂ **China Beach Resort** (Non Nuoc). At the foot of the Marble Mountains, this glorified motel on the water is one of only two lodging options in town. This ripe-for-the-wrecking-ball, 1960s concrete structure may be replaced by a new resort to be built by an American-Vietnamese joint venture at an unscheduled date in the future. If you must stay here, though, the resort has reasonably clean, utilitarian rooms with views of the sea. This is also one of the few places to eat in town with adequate Vietnamese food, although the environment is nondescript. ✉ *Non Nuoc, Danang,* ☎ *0511/836–216,* FAX *0511/836–335. 95 rooms. 2 restaurants, bar, air-conditioning, tennis court, beach, laundry service, travel service, car rental. No credit cards.*

$$$ ⌂ **Furama Resort.** Right on the beach, this international, joint-venture resort is made up of a group of French-Vietnamese–style villas surrounding an artificial tropical swimming lagoon. Rooms overlook either the lagoon or the ocean. The interior evokes the French colonial era, with a Vietnamese influence: shuttered windows, cane furniture, ceiling fans, and Vietnamese pieces. The resort has a shuttle service from Danang's airport and can organize tours for you to Danang, Hue, and Hoi An. ✉ *68 Ho Xuan Huong St.,* ☎ *0511/847–333; 08/821–1888 in Ho Chi Minh City,* FAX *0511/847–666. 200 rooms. 2 restaurants, 2 bars, air-conditioning, in-room safes, minibars, room service, pool, sauna, driving range, 2 tennis courts, health club, beach, surfing, bicycles, dry cleaning, laundry service, meeting rooms, travel services. AE, MC, V.*

Danang and Environs A to Z

Arriving and Departing

BY CAR

China Beach and the Marble Mountains are easily accessible by car from Danang, as is Hoi An. You can make arrangements at most hotels and through the **Danang Travel Information Center** (✉ 67A Quang Trung St., Danang, ☎ 0511/863–595). Depending on the type of car you rent, the round-trip price to Hoi An with a stop at the Marble Mountains should cost no more than $30.

BY PLANE

Vietnam Airlines (✉ 35 Tran Phu St., Danang, ☎ 0511/821–130, FAX 0511/832–759) flies to Danang's airport, 3 km (2 mi) southwest of the city, from Ho Chi Minh City (twice daily), Hanoi (twice daily), and Nha Trang (four times a week). To make arrangements in Danang, go to the Vietnam Airlines booking office; it's open 7–11 and 1:30–4:30. Booking offices in Hoi An, including those in your hotel, can also make plane reservations. A regular taxi to the airport should cost no more than 50,000d; to reserve one, call **Airport Taxis** (☎ 0511/825–555), Danang's most reliable taxi company.

Getting Around

BY CAR AND MOTORBIKE

See Arriving and Departing by Car, *above,* for information about renting cars with drivers; motorbikes can also be rented from many hotels and travel agencies.

BY TAXI

In Danang, the **taxi** drivers hanging out at the Cham Museum offer the cheapest rates in town—about $15 for the day. They also provide transportation to Hoi An for about $10. Taxis are preferable to cyclos since the roads are bad, even in town, and the scenery is grim.

Contacts and Resources

CURRENCY EXCHANGE

Changing money at your hotel is the easiest option. **Vietcom Bank** (✉ 140 Le Loi St.) is the only place in Danang that gives credit card cash advances; it's open weekdays 7:30–11 and 1–4.

EMERGENCIES

Contact your hotel for medical assistance or if something has been stolen.

Travel Agency

Danang Tourism Services Co. (✉ 76 Hung Vuong St., ☎ 0511/823-993 or 0511/825-653, ℻ 0511/821-312) is your best bet for travel services in Danang. In addition to travel arrangements and car rentals, they can handle visa extensions and can book you into one of their many affiliated hotels.

HOI AN

Perhaps the most delightful of all Vietnamese towns, enchanting riverside Hoi An, 30 km (19 mi) south of Danang, defies the insidious pace of modernization. Preserved in pristine condition are its 18th-century houses, pagodas, and assembly halls built by the early Fujian, Canton, Chaozhou, and Hainan—Chinese communities living in Hoi An. The many galleries selling the works of local artists and artisans and the numerous cafés give the town a strong bohemian feel. Hoi An offers great cuisine and is probably the most tourist-friendly town in the whole country, with many Internet cafés and with English being widely spoken. The whole town can easily be navigated by foot in an hour, but plan to spend more time in Hoi An than you think you'll need, since it's easy to fall in love with the place. Just outside of town is the pleasant Cua Dai Beach, which is arrived at by taking a 5-km (3-mi) ride through a picturesque slice of rural Vietnam. Also nearby are the My Son Cham ruins (☞ Danang and Environs, *above*), which evoke the ancient history of this region.

Hoi An, or Faifo as it was called in previous centuries, is a composite of many foreign influences. From the 2nd to 10th centuries AD, the city was under the control of the Kingdom of Champa and was an important port town. During the 14th and 15th centuries, the Cham and the Vietnamese fought for control of Hoi An, and as a consequence the city ceased to be a trading center. Peace between the Cham and the Vietnamese in the 16th century once again made possible the accommodation of ships from all over Asia and Europe, bringing merchants in search of silk, porcelain, lacquer, and medicinal herbs. During the Tay Son Rebellion in the 1770s, Hoi An was severely damaged by fighting.

After a speedy reconstruction the town managed to sustain a two-century tenure as a major international port town where Chinese, Japanese, Dutch, and Portuguese merchants came to trade. During the off-season seafaring merchants set up shop, and foreigners' colonies began to develop along Hoi An's riverfront. To this day, ethnic Chinese, who settled early in Hoi An, make up a significant portion of the population.

The French arrived in the late 1800s and made Hoi An an administrative post. They even built a rail line to Danang (then called Tourane). By this time, the Thu Bon River, which connected Hoi An to the sea had begun to fill up with silt, making navigation almost impossible. Danang gradually eclipsed Hoi An as the major port town in the area. Fortunately, Hoi An was not destroyed during the Vietnam War.

The old town combines Vietnamese, Japanese, and Chinese architectural styles, and is strictly reserved for pedestrians, bicycles, and the occasional motorbike. With ancient structures on almost every corner, it's the perfect place for a leisurely stroll. You can get a map from your hotel or from the local tourist office at the corner of Nguyen Hue and Phan Chu Trinh streets.

To get tickets to official monuments you must go to the central tourist office at the corner of Nguyen Hue and Phan Chu Trinh streets, rather than to the locations themselves. For 50,000d you get to choose from a "menu" of sights: one of three museums, one of three assembly halls, one of four old houses, and the Japanese Bridge or the Quan Cong Temple. Once you buy your first ticket from the tourist office, you may purchase an additional entry ticket there to any sight for 10,000d (these are also available at most hotels).

If at all possible, time your visit to Hoi An to coincide with the 14th day of the month according to the lunar calendar. On this night the streets of the old town are restricted to pedestrian traffic, and paper lanterns replace electric lights. The effect is magical.

A Good Walk

A good place to begin exploring Hoi An is at the tourist office, where you must purchase your ticket, on Nguyen Hue Street, close to the corner of Phan Chu Trinh Street. You can find an English- or French-speaking guide in the office for 50,000d.

After purchasing your ticket, start your walk at the small colonial-era **Museum of History and Culture** ㉒, approximately one block from the tourist office, at the corner of Tran Phu and Nguyen Hue streets. The entrance to the museum brings you to a collection of ancient ceremonial gongs and other religious objects. Walk across the courtyard filled with birdcages to get to **Quan Cong Temple** ㉓, dedicated to a deified Chinese general. Leave through the front entrance, and you'll find yourself directly in front of the **Central Market** ㉔, one of Vietnam's most pleasant and easy to navigate. Stay clear of the river unless you want to stumble onto the day's catch.

After exiting the market from where you came in, make a right onto Tran Phu Street and walk to No. 178, just before Hoang Dieu Street, the **Assembly Hall of the Hainan Chinese Congregation** ㉕. Continue east on Tran Phu Street, which turns into Nguyen Duy Hieu Street after it intersects with Hoang Dieu Street. Just past the intersection on the left, at No. 157, is the **Chaozhou Assembly Hall** ㉖, with its fine wood carvings. Turn around and start walking back down Tran Phu Street the way you came. Continue until you get to the corner of Tran Phu and Tran Quy Cap streets; cross over Tran Phu so that you are on the even-number side of the street. Almost immediately on your right, at No. 46, is the colorful **Assembly Hall of the Fujian Chinese Congregation** ㉗, now a temple devoted to Thien Hau, the goddess of the sea. Continue along Tran Phu Street until you come to No. 64, the **Chinese All-Community Assembly Hall** ㉘, on your right; as its name implies, it was used as a meeting place for all the Chinese communities in Hoi An. At No. 80 is the Diep Dong Nguyen House, which has been converted into the **Museum of Trade Ceramics** ㉙. Farther along on your left is the ancient **Quang Thang House** ㉚, at No. 77.

At the intersection of Tran Phu and Chau Thuong Van streets, on the north side, is the **Assembly Hall of the Cantonese Chinese Congregation** ㉛. Farther along Tran Phu Street, past a row of souvenir shops and the intersection with Nhi Trung Street, is the entrance to the red wooden **Japanese Bridge** ㉜. After visiting the bridge, keep going on Tran Phu Street, but note that the street name changes to Nguyen Thi Minh Khai Street. At No. 4 is the **Old House of Phung Hung** ㉝, where eight generations of one family have lived for more than 200 years. Turn around and head back east on Tran Phu Street. Take the small road that forks in front of the Japanese Bridge (Chau Van Thuong Street) to get to Nguyen Thai Hoc Street. At No. 101 is the **Old House of Tan Ky** ㉞. Continue east on Nguyen Thai Hoc Street and then make a left onto Le Loi Street. Cross Phan Chu Trinh Street; on the corner is the **Tran Family Chapel** ㉟, where you can get a tour from members of the Tran Family.

TIMING

This walk will probably take you about three or four hours at a very leisurely pace. Other sights outside of town (☞ Off the Beaten Path, *below*) will take about an hour each.

Sights to See

㉛ **Assembly Hall of the Cantonese Chinese Congregation.** The main altar of this hall, founded in 1786, is dedicated to Quan Cong, a revered General of the Chinese Han dynasty. ⊠ *176 Tran Phu St., at Nguyen Thi Hue St.* ☞ *Included in 50,000d tourist-office ticket.* ☉ *Daily 8–5.*

㉗ **Assembly Hall of the Fujian Chinese Congregation.** Built as a meeting place for Chinese residents of Hoi An, this hall later became a temple dedicated to the Fujian goddess of the sea and protector of fishermen Thien Hau. It's a reminder of how important fishing and trading were to the Chinese community in Hoi An. Thien Hau is represented in th mural near the entrance. Another mural depicts six Fujian families who fled from China to Hoi An in the 17th century. The gate is newer: it was constructed in 1975. ⊠ *Opposite 35 Tran Phu St.* 🖼 *Included in 50,000d tourist-office ticket.* ⊙ *Daily 8–5.*

㉕ Assembly Hall of the Hainan Chinese Congregation. This hall, founded by Chinese from Hainan, was constructed in 1883 in memory of more than 100 merchants who were mistakenly (some say purposefully) killed by a general in Emperor Tu Duc's army because they were thought to be pirates. ⊠ *178 Nguyen Duy Hieu St.* 🖼 *Included in 50,000d tourist-office ticket.* ⊙ *Daily 8–5.*

㉔ Central Market. Hoi An's Central Market is one of the most enjoyable markets in Vietnam. The merchants here are friendly, and a large selection of merchandise is available. The outer aisles of the market are lined with silk shops that can do custom clothing orders—pants, shirts, dresses, and even suits—all made for you in less than 24 hours. In the center aisles are fresh and dried fruit, flowers, and fresh tobacco. Walk toward the river to find the fish sellers with their daily catch. Miscellaneous items, such as batteries, pajamas, and bicycle pumps, pop up in stands throughout. ⊠ *Intersection of Tran Quy Cap and Tran Phu Sts.* ⊙ *Daily 6–dusk.*

㉖ Chaozhou Assembly Hall (Trieu Chau). Constructed by the Chaozhou Chinese community in 1776, this assembly hall exemplifies Chinese wood carving of this period at its finest. Note the carved ceiling and the depiction of Chinese women on the doors in the front of the altar. ⊠ *157 Nguyen Duy Hieu St.* 🖼 *Included in 50,000d tourist-office ticket.* ⊙ *Daily 8–5.*

㉘ Chinese All-Community Assembly Hall (Chua Ba). This assembly hall was built in 1773 as a meeting place for Cantonese, Chaozhou, Fujian, Hainan, and Hakka families living in Hoi An. ⊠ *64 Tran Phu St.* 🖼 *Included in 50,000d tourist-office ticket.* ⊙ *Daily 8–5.*

㉜ Japanese Bridge (Cau Nhat, or Lai Vien Kieu). One of the city's landmarks and one of its oldest structures, this red-painted, wooden bridge was originally built in 1593 by the Japanese to link their quarter of town to the Chinese quarter. It has been rebuilt a number of times since. At one end of the structure are statues of two dogs; at the other, statues of two monkeys—perhaps indicating the years when the bridge's construction was begun and completed. The small temple (Chua Cau) on the northern side of the bridge is dedicated to Tran Vo Bac De (God of the North), revered by sailors because he controls wind and rain. ⊠ *Tran Phu St., west of Nhi Trung St.* 🖼 *Included in 50,000d tourist-office ticket.* ⊙ *Daily 8–5.*

㉒ Museum of History and Culture. This small museum—housed in just one large room—provides a great introduction to Hoi An and its culture. On display are ancient bowls, cups, and other ceramics, many of them archaeological artifacts. There is also a collection of traditional Chinese objects, including pagoda bells and the "watchful eyes" placed above doorways for protection. The courtyard is filled with birdcages, which makes for a pleasant atmosphere. ⊠ *7 Nguyen Hue St..* 🖼 *Included in 50,000d tourist-office ticket.* ⊙ *Daily 8–5.*

★ **㉙ Museum of Trade Ceramics.** The ancient Diep Dong Nguyen House has been converted into a terrific small museum dedicated to the history of ceramics in Hoi An. The collection includes ancient wares, some of them recovered from shipwrecks in the surrounding waters, and a large assortment of household objects, such as bowls and vases. There are also detailed architectural drawings of the house, with an explanation of its design and its Chinese, Vietnamese, and Japanese influences. ⊠ *80 Tran Phu St.* 🎫 *Included in 50,000d tourist-office ticket.* ☉ *Daily 8–5.*

㉝ Old House of Phung Hung. Ask the owner to explain in French, or his granddaughter to explain in English, the architectural significance of this house built in 1780. Eight generations of the Phung Hung family have lived here since that time. Note the Japanese influences in the roof, the Chinese influences in the balcony, and the Vietnamese architectural style of the walls. On the second floor is a bowl containing dice: if you roll a red one, it is said, your journey will be lucky; if not, you should probably postpone your trip. ⊠ *4 Nguyen Thi Minh Khai St.* 🎫 *Included in 50,000d tourist-office ticket.* ☉ *Daily 8–5.*

㉞ Old House of Tan Ky. One of the oldest private houses in Hoi An, this structure has remained largely unchanged in the 200 years since it was built. Seven generations of the Tan Ky family have lived here. The house incorporates both Chinese and Japanese styles. Chinese poetry is engraved in mother-of-pearl on the walls. The back door was constructed to open onto the river so that water-borne goods could be easily transported into the house. ⊠ *101 Nguyen Thai Hoc St.* 🎫 *Included in 50,000d tourist- office ticket.* ☉ *Daily 8–5.*

NEED A BREAK?   Dine in a 200-year-old home at the **Yellow River (Hoang Ha) Restaurant** (⊠ 38 Tran Phu St.), where the owner serves Chinese specialties and will happily tell you about his family.

㉓ Quan Cong Temple. Founded in 1653 by the Chinese community, this temple is dedicated to Quan Cong, a revered general of the Chinese Han dynasty. Come here to contemplate life inside the bright-red interior of the temple or while watching the small school of fish that happily dart around in the pond out front. The carp, symbolic of patience in Chinese mythology, is displayed throughout. ⊠ *168 Tran Phu St.* 🎫 *Included in 50,000d tourist-office ticket.* ☉ *Daily 8–5.*

㉚ Quang Thang House. One of Hoi An's ancient family homes—built about 300 years ago—this house has some beautiful wood carvings on the walls of the rooms that surround the courtyard. ⊠ *77 Tran Phu St.* 🎫 *Included in 50,000d tourist-office ticket.* ☉ *Daily 8–5.*

㉟ Tran Family Chapel. Built in 1802, this house is dedicated to the worship of the Tran family's deceased ancestors. The altar in the house faces west, the direction the Vietnamese believe their ancestors face. Behind the altar stands a box with pictures and names of dead relatives. Tours are given in English by members of the Tran family. ⊠ *21 Le Loi St.* 🎫 *Included in 50,000d tourist-office ticket.* ☉ *Daily 8–5.*

OFF THE BEATEN PATH   **CHUC THANH PAGODA AND PHUOC LAM PAGODA –** If you are interested in seeing even more pagodas, head north on Nguyen Truang To Street for approximately 1 km (½ mi) to the end, turn left, and follow the path until you reach the Chuc Thanh Pagoda, the oldest pagoda in Hoi An. Founded in 1454 by Minh Hai, a Chinese Buddhist monk, the pagoda contains several ancient religious objects, including several bells and gongs made of both stone and wood. On the way back stop at the Phuoc Lam Pagoda, built in the mid-17th century. Note the interesting Chinese architecture and the large collection of ceramics on its roof. Both pagodas are open daily 8–5.

JAPANESE TOMBS – Hire a motorbike and a driver to take you 3 km (2 mi) north of the city to see the few surviving tombs of Hoi An's old Japanese community. (Cars are not recommended because the tombs are at the end of a narrow, rugged path, and it's best to hire a driver for the motorbike because the tombs are almost impossible to find on your own.) The tombs, erected in the 1600s, are reminders of the early Japanese presence in the area. Although the tombs—tombstones, really—are not nearly as grand as those in Hue, it's worth the trek if only to see the "suburbs" of Hoi An. En route you'll see families sitting in their front yards and field workers harvesting rice. Buried in the first tomb along the dirt path—clearly visible in the front yard of a family home, although there are no signs—is a Japanese merchant named Masai. About another 1,500 ft ahead is the most famous of Hoi An's Japanese tombs, the burial place of another Japanese merchant named Yajirobei, who died in 1647. Perched right in the middle of a working rice field, his tomb has an almost supernatural feel.

ining and Lodging

Reasonable rates for nice accommodations and delicious cuisine are even more incentive to extend your stay in this hospitable town.

$$ ✕ **Tam Tam Café.** This restaurant-cum-bar is the perfect place to unwind after a day of sightseeing. The French proprietor oversees the preparation of steaks, homemade pastas, and traditional French and Italian dishes. Set in a tastefully restored former tea warehouse, the Tam Tam is also a good spot to while away the warmer hours of the day playing pool or reading with a cold drink. ⊠ *110 Nguyen Thai Hoc St.,* ☎ *0510/862–212. No credit cards.*

$$ ✕ **Ving Hung Restaurant.** A peaceful oasis across the street from the Cantonese Assembly Hall, this restaurant serves superb seafood and local specialties such as White Roses, the delicious shrimp dumpling said to resemble a rose. Chinese lanterns and lacquered chairs decorate the place, which caters primarily to tourists. Sit outside on Chinese high-back wooden chairs and watch your fellow travelers walk by. ⊠ *147B Tran Phu St.,* ☎ *0510/862–203. AE, MC, V.*

$ ✕ **Café Can.** Café Can, located along the riverfront, serves fantastic meals at absurdly low prices. The seafood here is excellent, particularly the fish served in banana leaves and the steamed crab. The set meal includes five courses and is a good and inexpensive option for those with healthy appetites. ⊠ *74 Bach Dang St.,* ☎ *0510/861–525. No credit cards.*

$ ✕ **Café des Amis.** There is no menu at the Café des Amis. Instead, your
★ waiter will ask if you want to eat a seafood or vegetarian meal and then he will start bringing you food. Expect five or six excellent courses. Funky Western background music and a waterfront location make for a great atmosphere. Be warned: visitors who eat here on their first night in Hoi An have a tendency not to try anywhere else. ⊠ *52 Bach Dang St.,* ☎ *0510/861–616. No credit cards.*

$ ✕ **Faifoo.** Come here for refreshing fruit shakes, as well as a great multicourse sampler menu of chicken and pork dishes, all for next to nothing. You might want to avoid the "Pizza-Spaghetti-Guacamole," however; it's not one of Faifoo's better dishes. ⊠ *104 Tran Phu St.,* ☎ *0510/861–548. No credit cards.*

$ ✕ **Ly Cafeteria 22.** Catering mostly to backpackers, this very friendly spot serves tasty local specialties such as *cao lau* (a noodle dish topped with pork and bean sprouts) and White Roses. This is a great place for a cheap lunch; it's also open for dinner. ⊠ *22 Nguyen Hue St.,* ☎ *0510/861–603. No credit cards.*

$ ✕ **My Lac.** Excellent and inexpensive traditional Vietnamese and Chinese cuisine is served at this friendly, family-run establishment. ⊠ *106 Tran Phu St.,* ☎ *0510/861–591. No credit cards.*

$ ✕ **Restaurant Thanh.** This restaurant makes a splendid flounder (or whatever white fish happens to be fresh that day) cooked in banana leaves, as well as a refreshing squid salad prepared with lemon, onion, peanuts, and cucumber. Unfortunately the open-air, candlelighted riverfront ambience is frequently disrupted by persistent postcard vendors. ⊠ *76 Bach Dang St.,* ☎ *0510/861–366. No credit cards.*

$$$ 🏨 **Victoria Hoi An Resort.** Although not yet complete at press time, this resort, part of the Victorian Hotel & Resorts chain, is scheduled to open on Cua Dai Beach early in 2001. Most of the 100 bungalow units will have views of the sea. ⊠ *Ho Chi Minh City,* ☎ *08/990–1350. 100 bungalows. Restaurant, bar, pool, tennis court, business services, meeting rooms, travel services. ΛE, MC, V.* ✒

$$–$$$ 🏨 **Hoi An Hotel.** The most cheerful staff in all of Vietnam makes up for the lack of luxury in what is just about the only real hotel in Hoi An. Rooms are comfortable, spotless, and spacious, if basic (there are hair dryers, though). The outstanding Hoi An tourist office is in the lobby; it runs tours of the city and makes travel arrangements for your next destination. At press time the hotel was scheduled to open villas on the Cua Dai Beach by the middle of 2001. ⊠ *6 Tran Hung Dao St.,* ☎ *0510/ 861–445,* 🆏 *0510/861–636. 130 rooms. Restaurant, air-conditioning, fans, bicycles, laundry service, travel services, car rental. AE, MC, V.*

$–$$ 🏨 **Hai Yen Hotel.** One of a number of new hotels on the road to the beach, the Hai Yen has spacious and inexpensive suites and an almost rural setting, with rice fields just a few steps away. ⊠ *22A Cua Dai St.,* ☎ *0510/862–445,* 🆏 *0510/862–443. 33 rooms. Restaurant, bar, minibars, shop, travel services, car and motorbike rental. AE, MC, V.*

$ 🏨 **Cua Dai Hoi An Hotel.** One of the nicest accommodations in town, this plush minihotel has spotless, sunny rooms, many with balconies. It's between the beach and the town center, both of which are just a short bike ride away (you can rent bikes at the hotel). ⊠ *18A Cua Dai St.,* ☎ *0510/862–231. 17 rooms. Restaurant, air-conditioning, fans, bicycles, laundry service, travel services. No credit cards.*

$ 🏨 **Huy Hoang Hotel.** Close to the river and the Central Market, this hotel has a couple of brightly decorated, basic rooms with balconies overlooking the tree-lined street; ask for one these. Others don't have windows and aren't nearly as nice. ⊠ *73 Phan Boi Chau St.,* ☎ *0510/ 861–453. 20 rooms. Air-conditioning, fans, bicycles, motorbikes, travel services, car rental. No credit cards.*

$ 🏨 **Thanh Binh.** This centrally located hotel has clean rooms that get plenty of light. Get here early: the hotel often fills up by noon with budget travelers. ⊠ *1 Le Loi St.,* ☎ *0510/861–740. 14 rooms. Air-conditioning, fans, laundry service, travel services, car rental, free parking. No credit cards.*

$ 🏨 **Thanh Binh II (Peace Hotel).** This sister hotel to the original Thanh Binh Hotel (☞ *above*) offers squeaky-clean rooms only a few minutes' walk from Hoi An's main attractions. There is also a tailor's shop on the second floor of the hotel. ⊠ *1A Nhi Trung St.,* ☎ *0510/863–715. 32 rooms. Restaurant, air-conditioning, minibars, laundry services, car and motorbike rental. MC, V.*

$ 🏨 **Thien Trung.** Rooms are neat and bright at this hotel close to the bus station and only a short bike ride from the old town. ⊠ *63 Phan Ding Phung St.,* ☎ *0510/861–720 or 0510/861–769. 16 rooms. Restaurant, air-conditioning, fans, laundry service, travel services, car rental. No credit cards.*

$ 🏨 **Vinh Hung Hotel.** This Chinese-inspired hotel near the Japanese Bridge has dark wood carvings and a smiling Buddha in the lobby. Rooms are sunny and cheerfully decorated. ⊠ *142 Tran Phu St.,* ☎ *0510/861– 621,* 🆏 *0510/861–893. 12 rooms. Bar, air-conditioning, fans, laundry service, travel services. MC, V.*

Outdoor Activities and Sports

For a low-impact, highly scenic workout, rent a **bicycle** and ride 20 minutes from the center of town to Cua Dai Beach, a splendid place to catch a breeze and relax in the sun. Bikes can be rented from a number of places in town (☞ Getting Around *in* Hoi An A to Z, *below*). To get to the beach, go 5 km (3 mi) east of the town center along Tran Hung Dao Street, which turns into Cua Dai Street, all the way to the beach. The price for parking your bicycle is often as much as for a day-long rental, but it is easily negotiable; you shouldn't pay more than 1,000d.

Short **paddleboat trips** along the Thu Bon (Cai River) can be arranged at Hoang Van Thu Street or through young solicitors who hang out at the riverside cafés across from 50 Bach Dang Street. Hoi An Tourism (☞ Travel Agencies *in* Hoi An A to Z, *below*) arranges **motorized boat trips,** including visits to a ceramics factory and a shipyard. Full-day boat trips to Cham and Cam Kim islands and to My Son can also be arranged at the dock across from 62 Bach Dang Street.

Shopping

Because it's a low-key place, Hoi An is perhaps the most pleasant town in all of Vietnam in which to shop for souvenirs and clothes—and the quality of items here is generally pretty high. Along **Tran Phu Street** are numerous shops selling everything from works of art and ceramics to clothing and opium paraphernalia. Although most ceramic objects are billed as antiques, only some are the real thing. Unless you are an antiques expert or do some serious comparative shopping—which usually means being duped into buying an "antique" and then having another shop owner let you know that you were fooled—it is often impossible to tell a phony from a real antique by the price since they often cost the same (note that antiques can only be taken out of Vietnam with special permission; *see* Shopping *in* Smart Travel Tips A to Z. Bargaining is advisable as quoted prices are generally largely inflated, especially for fine art.

For cheap, casual clothing and same-day service on custom orders, try any one of the many tailoring shops on Le Loi or Tran Hung Dao streets. These shops are overflowing with endless yards of Vietnamese, Japanese, and Chinese silks and cottons. Prices will depend on the quality of the material you choose. For somewhat elaborate articles of clothing, such as fitted jackets and formal attire, tiny **Phuong Huy II** (✉ 25B Tran Phu St.) does an excellent job and can turn around any order in a day.

Hoi An A to Z

Arriving and Departing
BY CAR
The only way to get to Hoi An from Danang is by minibus or car, which takes about an hour due to poor road conditions, even though it's only a 30-km (19-mi) trip. The trip to Hoi An costs $5–$10, depending on the number of passengers, and is a very scenic drive through small towns and rice paddies. You can rent a car with a driver from **Danang Tourism Services Co.** (✉ 76 Hung Vuong St., Danang, ☎ 0510/823–993) or from any travel agency in Hoi An (☞ Travel Agencies, *below*).

BY PLANE
The closest **airport** to Hoi An is the one in Danang, 30 km (19 mi) north. To get to Hoi An, rent a car with a driver in Danang.

Getting Around

The most enjoyable and most convenient means of getting around H
An are on foot, by bicycle (for 7,000d per day), and by motorcycle (fe
about 70,000d per day). There are only a few cyclos, but the town
so small that you probably won't need to take one. **Hoi An Tourism** (u
Travel Agencies, *below*) has a wide variety of bicycles and motorc
cles for rent. You can also rent bikes from many hotels and cafés.

Contacts and Resources

CURRENCY EXCHANGE

Change money at your hotel or at the **Hoi An Bank** (⊠ 4 Hoang Di₆
St.), which also docs cash advances on Visa and MasterCard.

EMERGENCIES

Dr. Phuoc (⊠ 74 Le Loi St., ☎ 0510/861–419) is highly recommende
for his medical skills and his English-language ability. Serious illness
should be referred to **Hoi An's hospital** (⊠ Corner of Cua Dai and Hoar
Dieu Sts.).

PRECAUTIONS

The streets of Hoi An are very dark at night, but the city is general
safe. Consider bringing a flashlight to help you find your way aroun

TRAVEL AGENCIES

There are a number of booking offices along Le Loi and Tran Hu
Dao streets handling train and plane reservations, car rentals, hotel a
rangements, and excursions from Hoi An to the Marble Mountai
and China Beach.

Hoi An Tourism Office (⊠ 6 Tran Hung Dao St., ☎ 0510/861–373
0510/861–362, 🖷 0510/861–636), the state-run travel agency op
ated out of the Hoi An Hotel, organizes tours following several d
ferent itineraries of the city, as well as excursions to the Marl
Mountains and China Beach. The staff here speaks perfect English a
provides excellent services.

5 THE SOUTH-CENTRAL COAST AND HIGHLANDS

NHA TRANG AND DALAT

Set aside a few days to escape to two of Vietnam's best-known resort towns: seaside Nha Trang and the mountain village of Dalat. In Nha Trang, stroll along stretches of sandy beach and dance the night away at a waterfront nightclub. Head to Dalat for long walks and to visit Emperor Bao Dai's summer palace. If you have a little more time, include a trip to the rugged mountainous area around Kontum and Pleiku and visit the villages of Vietnam's hill tribes.

By Sherrie
Nachman
with Pilar
Guzman

Revised by
Craig Thomas

THE SPRAWLING BEACHES OF NHA TRANG and the cool mountain refuge of Dalat are two of the best reasons to come to south-central Vietnam. Nha Trang, the capital of Khanh Hoa Province, and Dalat are two of the country's oldest resorts. Nha Trang has long been a favorite destination for Vietnamese, who come to frolic in the sea. Dalat has been a popular retreat since the French first started visiting in the early 1900s. A mountain town in the midst of the central highlands, it has an abundance of natural beauty. Come here to catch a cool hilltop breeze, even in summer when the rest of the country is sweltering; play golf; hike; and visit the waterfalls along with the many Vietnamese who spend their honeymoons in Dalat. Don't expect untouched beaches or mountain terrain in either town, however. Both are established resort areas and are undergoing further development as new hotels are built and old ones are renovated. Although there are several attractions to keep you busy in Nha Trang and Dalat, there are few cultural or historic sights of note. Visit these towns only if you have some extra time and want to spend a few days relaxing in a pleasant environment.

For those with more time and a willingness to stray from the beaten path, south-central Vietnam has much to offer outside of Nha Trang and Dalat. The highland towns of Pleiku and Kontum are good jumping-off points for treks into Vietnam's remaining forests and for visits to the villages of the country's hill-tribe minorities. Near the coastal town of Quang Ngai lies the Son My Memorial for the victims of the My Lai massacre, a sobering reminder of the savage toll war often exacts on the innocent. Along the length of the coast you'll find spectacular scenery and beautiful beaches without the tourist clutter.

Pleasures and Pastimes

Beaches

Nha Trang's several miles of narrow, sandy beaches stretch from the center of town to its north end. Pick a spot to lounge on the beach, go swimming, and have a light meal at a waterfront café. Although the beaches are clean and pleasant, they are not isolated: along the beach is the road on which sit most of the town's hotels—a reminder that Nha Trang is a resort area.

All along the south-central coast from Quang Ngai south to Nha Trang are numerous small towns with inviting beaches, although with little in the way of facilities. If you have the time, consider heading outside of Nha Trang to the more isolated Dai Lanh or Doc Let beaches.

Dining

Nha Trang has numerous outstanding and reasonably priced seafood restaurants, including a few along the beachfront. Many serve whatever has been caught earlier in the day. Unusual for a town of its size, Nha Trang also has two restaurants serving Western-style food—which means you won't have any trouble finding burgers or spaghetti and meatballs here. Another good option is to buy fresh seafood from the vendors along the beach. They will prepare it for you in a matter of moments, and the prices are reasonable.

In contrast, the large agricultural center of Dalat has surprisingly poor and uninspiring restaurants. Dalat's only local specialties are dried deer meat, strawberry jam, and artichoke tea, although you can find plenty of basic Vietnamese food.

Lodging

Once the preserve of dreary and run-down hotels, Nha Trang has seen an enormous improvement in its lodging scene over the past few years,

The competition from new and privately owned hotels and minihotels has even forced some of the state-owned accommodations to spruce up their acts. Dalat has one of Vietnam's only true luxury hotels outside Ho Chi Minh City and Hanoi—the Sofitel Palace, which is reminiscent of a French château and has the added bonus of an adjacent tennis court and golf course. Other hotels in Dalat are clean and cheerful. Accommodations in the central highlands are much more limited than in the coastal areas, but efforts are underway to provide more facilities. Unless otherwise noted, hotels listed in this chapter have guest rooms with private bathrooms.

Nightlife

Nha Trang has quite an exciting nightlife for such a small Vietnamese city. Many bars and ice cream shops stay open well past midnight. You can play pool until breakfast time at the Nha Trang Sailing Club and dance until 4 AM at several bars and the local disco. Dalat, on the other hand, is an ideal place to crack open that book you've been carrying around, because there is really nothing else to do at night.

Outdoor Activities and Sports

As resort towns, both Nha Trang and Dalat provide myriad activities. In Nha Trang you can go swimming, diving, sailing, and snorkeling, as well as participate in many other water sports. Dalat's mountains and lakes provide an ideal setting for a long walk or a trip in a paddleboat. In the central highlands around Pleiku and Kontum, you can arrange hiking treks and elephant rides into some of Vietnam's best forests.

Waterfalls

Consistent with its image as a honeymoon resort town, Dalat is home to several gushing waterfalls, including Cam Ly Falls, Datania Falls, and Prenn Falls. Although they don't compare in size to Niagara Falls, they are good places to spend a couple of hours wandering around.

Exploring the South-Central Coast and Highlands

Dalat is only about 200 km (124 mi) southwest of Nha Trang, but the trip can easily take at least seven hours by car. The driving is slow because the roads connecting the towns are winding and narrow and head through a number of mountain passes. If you do go by car, you'll pass through lush countryside covered with rice fields and, closer to Dalat, coffee farms and strawberry fields. The easiest way to get to either city is to fly directly from Ho Chi Minh City; there are no direct flights between Nha Trang and Dalat.

Numbers in the text correspond to numbers in the margin and on the South-Central Coast and Highlands, Nha Trang, and Dalat maps.

Great Itineraries

IF YOU HAVE 3 DAYS

Choose either ⛴ **Nha Trang** ⑤–⑦ or ⛴ **Dalat** ⑧–⑳ as your destination; it takes too long and is too difficult to get to both in so short a time. And remember that this is the part of your trip when you get to relax, so you're probably better off visiting just one place. Spend one day sightseeing and the other days loafing around. With so little time, you would definitely want to fly here from either Hanoi or Ho Chi Minh City.

IF YOU HAVE 6 DAYS

With six days you could see both ⛴ **Nha Trang** ⑤–⑦ and ⛴ **Dalat** ⑧–⑳. Spend three days in Nha Trang, being sure to include as many of the city's restaurants as possible. If you're heading south from Hoi An

The South–Central Coast and Highlands

LAOS

QUANG
NGAI

KONTUM

1 Son My Memorial

Kontum
4

BINH DINH

Pleiku
3

GIA LAI

2 Qui Nhon

CAMBODIA

*Chao
Bay*

PHU YEN

○ Tuy Hoa

14   26

Buon Me Thuot

*Van Phong
Bay*

DAC LAC

KHANH HOA

Nha Trang
5 — 7

• Lat
Village

Dalat
8 — 20   ■ Prenn Falls

Cam Ranh
*Cam Ranh
Bay*

SONG BE

LAM DONG

NINH THUAN

Nam Cat Tien
National Park

22

20

23

Dambri Falls

21

**Po Klong Garai
Cham Towers**

Langa
Lake

*Padaran
Bay*

24

BINH THUAN

*Phan Ri
Bay*

South China Sea

N

DONG NAI

○ Phan Thiet

*Phan Thiet
Bay*

BA RIA -
VUNG TAU

0   50 miles

0   75 km

to Nha Trang, use one of the days to break the journey with a visit to the 🈁 **Son My Memorial** ①. Spend two days in Dalat and another day visiting the **southern central highlands** ㉑–㉔.

When to Tour the South-Central Coast and Highlands

The best time to come to Nha Trang is between April and September, during the dry season. It rains frequently in October and November and can be chilly. Dalat is worth visiting any time of the year but provides the most relief from June through August, when the rest of the country is really hot.

NORTH OF NHA TRANG

The portion of the south-central coast lying between Hoi An and Nha Trang is an area with few tourist attractions but often breathtaking scenery and seemingly endless white-sand beaches. If you're traveling by car between the two cities, don't miss the opportunity to visit the Son My Memorial, built in remembrance of the brutal My Lai massacre.

Farther inland, the central-highland towns of Pleiku and Kontum are good bases from which to explore the villages of the hill tribes.

Son My Memorial

❶ *110 km (68 mi) south of Hoi An.*

My Lai, a sleepy hamlet about 13 km (8 mi) east of the city of Quang Ngai in the Son My district, is a site infamous for the worst atrocity carried out by American forces during the war in Vietnam. On the morning of March 16, 1968, U.S. troops entered the Son My area (including My Lai, Thuan-Yen, and other hamlets) and massacred hundreds of Vietnamese civilians—mostly women and children—in an act that has come to symbolize the often senseless brutality that accompanied the conflict in Vietnam.

Although the full truth concerning the events of My Lai remains shrouded in controversy, what is known is that the area around Son My was considered by the U.S. military to be a stronghold of the Vietcong and that a number of American soldiers had been killed and wounded in the area in the days preceding March 16, 1968. (A note on the term Vietcong: Vietcong is used throughout this book to refer to the opposition movement in the South because it is the term that is probably the most familiar. However, the history of this term is a complex one; *see* Vietnam at a Glance: A Chronology *in* Chapter 8 for further explanation). In response, three platoons under Charlie Company exacted a terrible revenge that included pillaging, rape, and mass executions of civilians. The killing and destruction, which occurred under the at least tacit approval of a number of higher officers, took place over a number of hours, during which time the soldiers took a break for lunch before resuming their criminal acts.

Hundreds of Vietnamese civilians died; the only reported American casualty was a U.S. soldier who shot himself in the foot in order to avoid participating in the atrocities. Although a cover-up of the events of My Lai was attempted, a number of the participants went public; the resulting scandal contributed to the deterioration of American support for the war in Vietnam. Only one man, Lieutenant William Calley, who led Charlie Company's 1st Platoon—responsible for some of the worst atrocities—was ever convicted for the crimes that took place at My Lai. After serving three years of his sentence, Lieutenant Calley was paroled in 1974.

The Son My Memorial is dedicated to the victims of the massacre at My Lai and lies about 10 km (6 mi) east of National Highway 1A, just north of the town of Quang Ngai. The road leading to the memorial begins next to the My Tra Hotel (☞ Lodging, *below*). The memorial itself is set on the grounds of the former hamlet of Thuan-Yen, where many of the worst crimes took place. In striking contrast to the terrible events that took place here, the memorial is set against a quiet and pastoral backdrop.

Lodging

$–$$ ⊞ **My Tra Hotel.** This surprisingly modern and efficient hotel is conveniently located for visits to the Son My Memorial and nearby lovely Bien Khe Beach. The rooms are clean but simple, with watercolors of traditional scenes of rural Vietnamese life for decoration. ⊠ *Hwy. 1, north of Quang Ngai across the Tra Khuc Bridge,* ☎ *055/842–985,* FAX *055/842–980. 70 rooms. Restaurant, bar, air-conditioning, minibars, massage, tennis court. MC, V.*

Qui Nhon

❷ *180 km (112 mi) south of Son My.*

Qui Nhon, which lies 238 km (148 mi) north of Nha Trang and 280 km (174 mi) south of Hoi An, is a good place to break your trip along the coast. It's also a good spot from which to begin a trip to the central-highland towns of Pleiku and Kontum (☞ *below*). The beaches here are pleasant, although not spectacular, and there are interesting **Cham towers** in town (take a right at 906 Tran Hung Dao Street onto Thap Doi Street) and 26 km (16 mi) north of Qui Nhon on Highway 1.

Lodging

$ ⊞ **Hai Au Hotel.** Located right on the beach, the Hai Au is the most pleasant hotel in town. Rooms are clean, though basic and somewhat run-down. Half of them overlook the sea. The restaurant, which also overlooks the beach, serves good seafood; the attached circular bar is a popular hangout. Staff members are friendly, helpful, and have a good command of English. This is a popular spot for tour groups. ⊠ *489 Nguyen Hue St.,* ☎ *056/846–473,* FAX *056/846–926. 50 rooms. Restaurant, bar, air-conditioning, massage, business services, travel services, car rental. No credit cards.*

En Route Those making the trip to Pleiku via Highway 19 should stop and visit the **Quang Trung Museum,** which is dedicated to Nguyen Hue, later crowned as Emperor Quang Trung, one of the leaders of the Tay Son Rebellion. Beginning in 1772 as a peasant uprising, the Tay Son Rebellion was an expression of deep discontent in rural Vietnamese society that eventually led to the temporary overthrow of the Nguyen rulers in Hanoi. The brief Tay Son era was notable for land and tax reform and for a resurgence of indigenous Vietnamese culture. For more information on the rebellion, *see* Vietnam at a Glance: A Chronology in Chapter 8. ⊠ *From Hwy. 1 head west 30 km (19 mi) on Hwy. 19; museum is 5 km (3 mi) north off Hwy. 19.* ☎ *10,000d.* ☉ *Daily 9–12 and 2–5.*

Pleiku and Kontum

Pleiku is 140 km (87 mi) west of Qui Nhon; Kontum is 41 km (25 mi north of Pleiku.

❸ ❹ The central-highland towns of **Pleiku** and **Kontum** and their surroundings are becoming increasingly popular as the infrastructure and tourist facilities in the area improve. Both towns are good bases from which to stage trips to the mountains and forests of the hinterland. Pleiku the larger of the two towns with about 50,000 residents, has more i the way of accommodations and dining options; sleepy Kontum has much less bustle.

The regions surrounding Pleiku and Kontum were major battlegrounds during the Vietnam War. In the most heavily bombed areas, only now has the vegetation, including coffee trees, begun to recover from the napalm and defoliants rained on this area during the war.

The best reasons to come to Kontum and Pleiku are to visit the region's remaining forests and the villages of the many hill tribes that live nearby. The Bahnar and Jarai, two of the largest hill-tribe groups in the area, possess a fascinating culture with traditions that stretch back for centuries. Join them in drinking the *ruou can* (rice wine) for which this region is famous. Of particular cultural interest are the wood carvings made by the Bahnar tribe to adorn the graves of their departed. Meant to keep the dead company and to make them laugh, these vary from stern-looking American and French soldiers to amorous couples. The strong animistic religious beliefs of the Jarai tribe are expressed through traditional musical instruments, such as the wind flute and gongs with which they produce ethereal and entrancing hymns. Day hikes in the surrounding forests and multiday treks with overnight stays in the homes of hill-tribe villagers can be arranged through local hotel tour agencies (☞ Lodging, *below*). You can also arrange for guided tours of the numerous former battlefields from the Vietnam War.

Lodging

¢–$ 🏨 **Dakbla Hotel.** This lime-green hotel lies just over the bridge that leads you into Kontum from Pleiku. The rooms are clean and have satellite TVs, and the staff speaks English. Inside the Dakbla there's a branch of the Kontum Tourist Company, which can arrange treks and visits to the Jarai and Bahnar villages in the area. ⊠ *2 Phan Dinh Phung St., Kontum,* ☎ *060/863–333,* ℻ *060/863–336. 30 rooms. Restaurant, air-conditioning, minibars, laundry service, travel services. No credit cards.*

¢–$ 🏨 **Hung Vuong Hotel.** Convenient and relatively modern, the Hung Vuong is on the main road as you enter Pleiku on Highway 19. The hotel houses the Gia Lai Tourist Company, which can arrange treks and other guided tours of the surrounding area. ⊠ *215 Hung Vuong St., Pleiku,* ☎ *059/824–270,* ℻ *059/827–170. 20 rooms. Restaurant, air-conditioning, minibars, travel services. No credit cards.*

North of Nha Trang A to Z

Arriving, Departing, and Getting Around

BY CAR

Son My and Qui Nhon, right on the coast along Highway 1, are easily accessible. Pleiku and Kontum are easy to get to by car or motorbike as the roads are in relatively good condition and are uncrowded by local standards. To get to Pleiku, take Highway 19, which begins 10 km (6 mi) north of Qui Nhon. Highway 14 connects Pleiku to Kontum; the highway continues on from Kontum to Danang and other points north, but it's a rough ride.

For information on renting cars from Nha Trang to Pleiku, Kontum, Son My, or Qui Nhon, *see* Arriving and Departing *in* Nha Trang A to Z, *below;* to rent a car from Danang, *see* Danang and Environs A to Z *in* Chapter 4.

Reaching the more interesting destinations outside of the towns, such as hill-tribe villages or the remaining old-growth forests of the region, requires some determination and, in certain cases, a four-wheel-drive vehicle or an agreeable elephant. Your travel agency can make the arrangements.

Vietnam Airlines (⊠ 55 Quang Trung St., Pleiku, ☎ 059/845–9823) flies three times a week (Sunday, Wednesday, and Friday) from both Hanoi and Saigon to Pleiku. There are also direct flights from Danang. Kontum is then a short 41 km (25 mi) drive north from Pleiku on the well-kept and relatively uncrowded Highway 14.

Contacts and Resources

TRAVEL AGENCIES

To arrange tours to the hill-tribe villages near Pleiku and Kontum, contact the Kontum Tourist Company in the Dakbla Hotel or the Gia Lai Tourist Company in the Hung Vuong Hotel (☞ Pleiku and Kontum, *above*). You don't have to be staying at the hotels to use the travel services.

NHA TRANG

A bustling city with a long stretch of developed beachfront, Nha Trang is not an idyllic, deserted hideaway. Older hotels share the waterfront with an assortment of flashy, new, Western-style joint-venture establishments. But the beachfront still retains its charms: swarms of high school students bike to and from classes, and hordes of teenagers play soccer in the few waterfront lots that have not been turned into tourist sights. Recreational attractions include swimming, scuba diving, snorkeling, and boat trips to neighboring Mieu, Tam, and Monkey islands—lush enclaves with isolated beaches and groves of palm trees.

Exploring Nha Trang

The easiest way to get around town is by bicycle or cyclo. They're not hard to find; in fact, they'll probably find you first. Another way to see Nha Trang is by motorbike—with or without a driver. A third option is to hire a car and driver.

❺ The beautiful **Long Son Pagoda,** built in the late 19th century and reconstructed a number of times since, is the town's most famous pagoda. A giant Buddha beckons you up a flight of stairs, at the top of which is a panoramic view of Nha Trang. The entrance to the pagoda itself is down below. The resident monks happily give guided tours of the main sanctuary. To reach it from town, follow Yersin Street (on foot, by bike, or by motorbike) inland about 2 km (1 mi) from the coast. When you come to No. 15 on 23 Thang 10 Street (called Thai Nguyen Street as you get closer to the water), make a right (continuing inland) to get to the pagoda. ⊠ *About 550 yards west of railroad station, opposite No. 15 on 23 Thang 10 St.* 🎟 *Free.* ☉ *Daily 8–noon and 2–4.*

Nha Trang is home to one of the better preserved Cham ruins in Vietnam, the **Po Nagar Cham Towers** (Nha Trang Huu Duc), also known
❻ as the Mother Goddess or Lady of the City Towers. The towers were originally a site of Hindu worship dating from the 2nd century; the present buildings were constructed between the 7th and 12th centuries. Today it is still an active shrine for Vietnam's remaining Cham community and for Chinese and Vietnamese Buddhists. Of the original eight towers, four remain in various states of preservation. The North Tower (Thap Chinh), built during King Harivarman I's reign in AD 817 originally housed a *linga,* a phallic stone. After the linga was stolen and replaced, the stone statue of Uma that you see today was finally substituted for it. Ignore the swarm of hawkers congregating at the bottom of the temples. To reach the towers from the center of town, take Quang Trung Street, which turns into 2 Thang 4 Street (the name of the street, not an address), then cross the Cai River twice over the Ha Ra and Xom Bong bridges. Here there are colorful vignettes of post

Nha Trang

card-perfect fishing-boat activity. As you cross the second bridge, you'll see the impressive towers jutting up from the hill on the left-hand side. The walk here is not that pleasant, so consider taking a cyclo or a motorbike. ⊠ *On north side of Cai River over Ha Ra and Xom Bong Bridges.* 🖭 *6,000d.* ⊘ *Daily 8–5.*

❼ The **Hon Chong Promontory,** on the same side of the river as the Po Nagar Cham Towers (☞ *above*), provides good views of the coastline and the surrounding islands. Climb up the promontory for a view of Nha Trang and Hon Rua (Tortoise Island), both to the northeast. Look northwest to see Nui Co Tien (Fairy Mountain), said to look like a reclining fairy. To get here from the Po Nagar ruins, head north on 2 Thang 4 Street (the name of the street, not an address) and take a right on Nguyen Dinh Chieu Street. ⊠ *About ¾ km (½ mi) from intersection of Nguyen Dinh Chieu and 2 Thang 4 Sts.* 🖭 *10,000d.* ⊘ *Daily 8–4.*

No visit to Nha Trang would be complete without a boat trip to the surrounding **islands,** such as Mieu Island (Tri Nguyen Island), Mun Island, and Tam Island. Boat trips can be arranged through any number of hotels and travel agencies (☞ Contacts and Resources *in* Nha Trang A to Z, *below*) or directly at the port on the south end of town. Both Mieu and Tam islands have bungalows where you can spend a quiet night away from the bustle of Nha Trang. **Mama Hahn's Boat Trips** to these islands are said to be the most fun, with music and a bohemian atmosphere that may not be entirely appropriate for families with small children. These tours can be booked at any tourist office or hotel in town. Almost all boat trips to the islands include an impressive feast of seafood for lunch as well as an array of exotic fruits, all included in the $7 price.

About 16 km (10 mi) outside of Nha Trang on Highway 1 is Dao Khi, otherwise known as **Monkey Island,** which is popular with the tourists during the day but wonderfully deserted at night. There are clean but simple bungalows available for $15 a night and one restaurant that serves good seafood and Vietnamese dishes. To get here, hire a car and driver or take a 15-minute boat ride from the pier in the south part of town.

Forty kilometers (25 miles) north of town is the relatively isolated and largely undeveloped **Doc Let Beach.** The beach here is clean, with white sand and fewer tourists than in Nha Trang. This is a good spot for a day trip, but there are accommodation options for those wishing to stay overnight; your best bet is one of the spartan bungalows next to the beach, which go for $6 a night. To get here it's best to hire a car and driver or simply catch a cab from Nha Trang.

En Route   The beaches in and around the town of **Dai Lanh** (83 km [51 mi] north of Nha Trang) are breathtaking and completely devoid of tourists. There are no accommodations in Dai Lanh, but this is a perfect place to spend a few hours on the trip down to Nha Trang.

Dining and Lodging

$$ ✕ **Ngoc Suong.** This establishment a block from the beach serves the
★ best and the freshest seafood in town. It also has a friendly waitstaff. Fish salad, made from marinated local seafood, is the specialty. The rather daunting and rambling English-language menu also includes wild-boar testicles, but you're better off sticking with fish. ⊠ *16 Tran Quang Khai St., not far from Tran Phu St.,* ☎ *058/954–516. No credit cards.*

$$ ✕ **Nha Trang Sailing Club.** The most happening of all the seaside
★ cafés–restaurants in town, the Sailing Club is popular with expats, locals, and tourists. It's the place to go if you're looking for something other than Vietnamese food: burgers, pizza, and sushi are all on the menu. Westerners come for breakfast, lunch, and dinner. Diving trips can be arranged through the office just behind the restaurant. ⊠ *72–74 Tran Phu St.,* ☎ *058/826–528. No credit cards.*

$ ✕ **Lac Canh.** Here's your chance to hang out with locals. At each table in this smoke-filled restaurant is a charcoal grill on which you can make your own cheap and delicious marinated seafood and meat dishes. Just be prepared for one odd habit: the diners pile empty beer bottles and other leftovers on the floor after they're done with them. ⊠ *11 Hang Ca St.,* ☎ *058/821–391. No credit cards.*

$ ✕ **Louisiane Cafe.** The perfect counterpart to the more adult-oriented Sailing Club (☞ *above*), the cheerfully decorated Louisiane Cafe is a great place to bring the family. Inside the restaurant are a pool and a dizzying array of pastries. More substantial fare includes sandwiches, salads, and dishes you might typically find in a French café. The beach chairs outside are free, and there's a bar should mom and dad prefer something a little stronger than ice cream. ⊠ *Tran Phu St., across from airport,* ☎ *058/812–948. No credit cards.*

$ ✕ **Omar Khayyam's.** An unexpected treat for those wishing for a break from Vietnamese fare, Omar Khayyam's serves up delicious northern Indian cuisine. The atmosphere is decidedly basic, but the staff is as friendly as it gets. Be sure to try the *bhindi masala* (spicy okra served with rice) and the garlic nan. ⊠ *24C Nguyen Thien Thuat St.,* ☎ *058/821–426. No credit cards.*

¢ ✕ **Banana Split.** This small sidewalk café serves ice-cream sundaes, as well as Western-style dishes such as omelets, chicken, and burgers. Open for breakfast, lunch, and dinner, it's a destination for homesick Western travelers looking to meet other people. Boat trips and other travel arrangements can also be made here. ⊠ *58 Quang Trung St.,* ☎ *058/829–115. No credit cards.*

¢ ✕ **Thanh The.** Locals and Vietnamese tourists pack this restaurant specializing in seafood and traditional Vietnamese fare. ✉ *3 Phan Chu Trinh St.,* ☎ *058/821–931. No credit cards.*

¢ ✕ **Vietnam Restaurant.** This family-run Vietnamese restaurant serves excellent seafood at low prices. Tasty unnamed fried fish is a specialty. ✉ *23 Hoang Van Thu St.,* ☎ *058/822–933. No credit cards.*

$$$ 🏨 **Ana Mandara Nha Trang Resort.** Completed in 1997, this beach-
★ front resort is the classiest and most comfortable place to stay in Nha Trang. Reminiscent of Balinese- and Thai-style resorts, the hotel has private thatched cottages, some of which are only footsteps from the ocean. Local arts and crafts are highlighted in the decor. Cottages have IDD phones. There is also a small pool with a bar. ✉ *60 Tran Phu St.,* ☎ *058/829–829,* 𝐅𝐀𝐗 *058/823–629. 68 cottages. Restaurant, air-conditioning, in-room safes, minibars, room service, pool, bicycles, motorbikes, library, dry cleaning, laundry service, meeting rooms, travel services. AE, MC, V.* ☜

$$ 🏨 **Nha Trang Lodge Hotel.** Rooms at this hotel across the street from the ocean are perfectly clean and comfortable and have IDD phones; some have views of the sea. The lobby, unfortunately, is incredibly tacky, and the decor is reminiscent of roadside motels across the United States. But it's still a comfortable place to stay. ✉ *42 Tran Phu St.,* ☎ *058/810–500,* 𝐅𝐀𝐗 *058/828–800. 124 rooms. Restaurant, air-conditioning, in-room safes, minibars, room service, dry cleaning, laundry service, travel services. AE, MC, V.*

$$ 🏨 **Yasaka Saigon–Nha Trang Hotel.** Unwieldy name aside, this brand-new hotel across the street from the beach is the nicest accommodation in town short of the Ana Mandara (☞ *above*). The second-floor pool is the best you'll find in the area. Rooms are spacious and tastefully decorated and have wide-screen TVs and IDD phones. The lodging market in Nha Trang is tight these days, so don't be afraid to bargain a bit as this hotel is still trying to establish its reputation. ✉ *18 Tran Phu St.,* ☎ *058/820–090,* 𝐅𝐀𝐗 *058/820–000. 174 rooms. 2 restaurants, tennis court, exercise room, dance club. AE, MC, V.*

$-$$ 🏨 **Haiyen Hotel.** Although it caters to large cruise ships full of Asian tourists, this big waterfront hotel looks like it has not been touched since the '70s. Nonetheless, rooms are passable—meaning they are reasonably clean and have basic amenities such as TVs. ✉ *40 Tran Phu St.,* ☎ *058/822–828,* 𝐅𝐀𝐗 *058/821–902. 107 rooms. 2 bars, dining room, lobby lounge, outdoor café, air-conditioning, fans, minibars, refrigerators, room service, pool, beauty salon, massage, sauna, dance club, dry cleaning, laundry service, meeting room, travel services, car rental. MC, V.*

$-$$ 🏨 **Vien Dong Hotel.** One of the first large hotels in Nha Trang, the Vien Dong is a hub of tourist activity. Although it's a popular place for Westerners to stay because it's close to the beach and has a pool, the hotel is slightly run-down and overpriced, and the staff tends to be excessively impersonal. On the other hand, the travel service is very good, and you can use it even if you're not staying at the hotel. ✉ *1 Tran Hung Dao St.,* ☎ *058/821–606,* 𝐅𝐀𝐗 *058/821–912. 86 rooms. Restaurant, bar, air-conditioning, fans, minibars, refrigerators, pool, massage, laundry service, travel services, car rental. AE, MC, V.*

$ 🏨 **Nam Long Hotel.** The Nam Long is in the center of town, not too far from the beach. Rooms are clean and nondescript. ✉ *7 Le Thanh Ton St.,* ☎ *058/827–714,* 𝐅𝐀𝐗 *058/824–991. 25 rooms. Air-conditioning, fans, minibars, refrigerators, laundry service, travel services. No credit cards.*

$ 🏨 **Seaside Hotel.** A relatively plush minihotel just south of town on the coast, this place has some of the most tastefully decorated rooms in Nha Trang; a number even have ocean views. No services are offered, however, and the staff sleeps in the lobby at night. Nonetheless, it is one of Nha Trang's best in its price category. ⊠ *96 Tran Phu St.,* ☎ *058/821–178,* FAX *058/828–038. 15 rooms. Restaurant, air-conditioning, fans, laundry service. No credit cards.*

¢ ⊡ **Sao Mai.** If you're looking for a cheap but clean establishment, Sao Mai may be for you. The rooms are basic, a fact that is reflected in the price. The family that runs this lodging is genuinely nice and eager to please. ⊠ *99 Nguyen Thien Thuat St.,* ☎ *058/827–412. 12 rooms. Air-conditioning, fans, bicycles, motorbikes, travel services. No credit cards.*

¢ ⊡ **Thanh Thanh Hotel.** This efficient, brightly lighted minihotel overlooks the water and is just south of town. ⊠ *98A Tran Phu St.,* ☎ *058/ 824–657,* FAX *058/823–031. 18 rooms. Restaurant, air-conditioning, minibars, refrigerators, room service, laundry service, travel services. No credit cards.*

Nightlife and the Arts

People tend to congregate on the beach or at beachfront bar-cafés like the **Rainbow Bar** (⊠ Tran Phu St., behind the small amusement park). The **Nha Trang Sailing Club** (⊠ 72–74 Tran Phu St., ☎ 058/826–528) attracts homesick travelers and expatriates. You can hang out until dawn dancing, drinking, playing pool, and speaking English. It also acts as a surrogate gallery for a brilliant and friendly local photographer named Long Thanh, who works out of his home. The beachside **Huong Duong Center Bar/Discotheque** (⊠ Tran Phu St., ☎ 058/823–914), a hangout for Vietnamese teenagers, is a good place to get away from other travelers.

Outdoor Activities and Sports

Nha Trang has all kinds of water-related activities, including snorkeling, jet skiing, scuba diving, and boating. The **Blue Diving Club** (⊠ 40 Tran Phu St., Coconut Grove, ☎ 058/825–390, FAX 058/824–214), a very well-run Professionally Approved Diving Institute (PADI) center, offers beginning instruction in English and French and arranges guided excursions for all diving levels.

Nha Trang A to Z

Arriving and Departing

BY BUS

The Sinh Café (☞ Travel Agencies *in* Ho Chi Minh City A to Z, Chapter 6) bus links Nha Trang with Danang (190,000d).

BY CAR

Nha Trang is 448 km (278 mi) north of Ho Chi Minh City along Highway 1 (nine hours by car) and 1,250 km (775 mi) south of Hanoi. Dalat is 200 km (124 mi) southwest of Nha Trang (seven to eight hours by car). Danang is 541 km (335 mi) north of Nha Trang (11 hours by car). A car and driver can be hired from hotels and from private and state-run travel agencies (☞ Contacts and Resources, *below*).

BY PLANE

The easiest way to get to Nha Trang is by plane. **Vietnam Airlines** (⊠ 12B Hoang Hoa Tham St., Nha Trang, ☎ 058/822–135) flies between Nha Trang and Ho Chi Minh City (55 minutes; $50; two to three times daily), Hanoi (1½ hours; $100; once a day), and Danang (70 minutes; $35; three times a week).

BY TRAIN

Nha Trang is served three times daily by both express and local trains from Hanoi and Ho Chi Minh City. A soft sleeper to Ho Chi Minh City costs $25–$35; to Hanoi it costs $80–$100, depending on whether you take the express or the local train. The express train (12 hours) between Ho Chi Minh City and Nha Trang is considerably faster than the local train (22 hours); from Hanoi to Nha Trang the express takes 24 hours and the local 32 hours. Note that the ticket office at **Nha Trang Railway Station** (⊠ 17 Thai Nguyen St., ☎ 058/822–113) is open between 7 and 2 only.

Getting Around

BY BICYCLE

One of the best ways to get around Nha Trang is by bicycle. You can rent one at any travel agency (☞ Travel Agencies, *below*) and at most hotels for about 10,000d a day. A deposit may be required.

BY BOAT

Most hotels and travel agencies (☞ Travel Agencies, *below*) can organize boat trips, including the popular Mama Hahn's Boat Trips.

BY CAR

Hiring a car and driver is one option for getting around Nha Trang, but is unnecessary unless you want to go to one of the beaches outside of town. You can make arrangements at any of the travel agencies (☞ Travel Agencies, *below*) in town.

BY CYCLO

The easiest way to get around Nha Trang is by cyclo, which you can find all over town. For about 10,000d you can go just about anywhere you want. Be sure to bargain to get the best rate.

BY MOTORBIKE

Renting a motorbike, with or without a driver, is one way to see Nha Trang and the surrounding areas. You can rent them at any travel agency (☞ Travel Agencies, *below*) and at most hotels for about 70,000d a day. A deposit may be required.

Contacts and Resources

CURRENCY EXCHANGE

Vietcom Bank (⊠ 17 Quang Trung St.) exchanges money, as do many hotels. Cash advances on credit cards can be done at Vietcom Bank or at Sinh Café (☞ Travel Agencies, *below*).

EMERGENCIES

Contact your hotel in case of emergency.

POST OFFICE

The **main branch** (⊠ 4 Le Loi St.) sells stamps, as do many hotels. It also has a separate office across the road at No. 2 Le Loi Street that provides Internet access.

TRAVEL AGENCIES

Ha Phuong Tourist Cafe (⊠ 5A Tran Hung Dao St., ☎ 058/827–814) arranges bus trips to points north and south of Nha Trang as well as boat trips to nearby islands. They can also arrange visits to the Ede hill-tribe villages in the southern central highlands. The staff is particularly friendly and helpful.

Sinh Café (⊠ 10 Biet Thu St., ☎ 058/811–981) provides bus service to all points north and south of Nha Trang. They also do cash advances and arrange tours to the islands and other points of interest in and around Nha Trang, including Ede villages in the area.

THE CENTRAL HIGHLANDS

Part of the southern end of the Truong Son range, Vietnam's centra
highlands is a region of rugged mountains, clear streams, dense forests
and gushing waterfalls spread over the provinces of Lam Dong, Da
Lac, Gia Lai, and Kontum. The area also includes the towns of Pleik
and Kontum (☞ North of Nha Trang, *above*). With the increasing de
velopment of coffee plantations and rice farms, the region is rapidl
becoming an agricultural center. Long inhabited primarily by Vietnam'
ethnic minority hill tribes, the central highlands has only recently see
significant settlement by lowland Vietnamese. Although developmer
and years of warfare have reduced the once large areas of pristine for
est and abundant wildlife here, much remains for the determined vi
itor to enjoy. This is one of the few parts of the country where it :
cool enough to wear a sweater, even in summer.

Difficult to get to, the western part of the central highlands is hom
to a large population of ethnic minorities. Known as Montagnards, fror
the French for "mountain people," these people live in tribal village
Some of the tribes have lived in Vietnam for thousands of year; othe
came from neighboring Thailand several centuries ago. These tribe
of largely nomadic farmers, who live an isolated existence, are culturall
and linguistically distinct from each other and from the ethnic Vie
namese who make up the majority of the country's population.

The mountain resort of Dalat is the principal town of the southern ce
tral highlands region. It has an abundance of natural beauty, with
good measure of kitsch thrown in.

Dalat

*308 km (191 mi) north of Ho Chi Minh City; 205 km (127 mi) sout
west of Nha Trang.*

Named for the "River of the Lat Tribe," after the native Lat peopl
Dalat was "discovered" in the early part of this century by Dr. Alexar
dre Yersin (1863–1943), a protégé of scientist Louis Pasteur. It quick
became a vacation spot for Europeans anxious to escape the infern
heat of the coastal plains, the big cities, and the Mekong Delta. Du
ing the Vietnam War the city, oddly, served as the favorite nonpar
san resting spot for both high-ranking North and South Vietname
officers, before it capitulated to the North Vietnamese on April 3, 197

Dalat today is a favorite of Vietnamese honeymooners, and attemp
are being made to transform it into an international tourist destin
tion. An 18-hole golf course is already in place, new hotels have a
peared, and old colonial villas are being converted into guest house

Dalat bears a vague resemblance to a small French town and is bless
with lovely weather. For those who like kitsch, Dalat offers it up
unspoiled, unselfconscious abundance. The endless flora and fauna a
mocked by plastic versions decorating the white cars of the weddi
processions that pass two or three times a day. Panoramic views of m
jestic mountains and placid lakes are often interrupted by an inco
gruous Vietnamese dressed as an American cowboy offering a ride a
a photo opportunity.

Exploring Dalat

Dalat's prime sight is its market, which ranks among Vietnam's be
Several places outside downtown Dalat are worth a visit, however.
these are spread out across hilly ground, it's a good idea to hire a c
with a driver and a guide. Decide what you want to see and leave t
exact itinerary to your guide.

⑧ Dalat lies northwest of the dam-generated **Xuan Huong Lake** (Ho Xuan Huong), named for a 17th-century Vietnamese poet known for her daring attacks on the hypocrisy of social conventions and the foibles of scholars, monks, mandarins, feudal lords, and kings. Circumscribed by a path and abutted by a beautiful 18-hole golf course, the lake is a hub of leisurely activity (including paddleboating). Although there's traffic nearby, the lake provides a pleasant place to walk and bike.

⑨ The official center of Dalat is the picturesque **Central Market,** with its small collection of restaurants. Locals come here to buy and sell chickens, fruits and vegetables, and specialties such as dried strawberries. The market is usually open from dawn until nightfall. ⊠ *Nguyen Thi Minh Khai St.*

⑩ **Bao Dai's Summer Palace** (Biet Dien Quoc Truong), on the south side of Xuan Huong Lake, is a wonderfully preserved example of modernist architecture—a yellow cement structure built in 1933. The palace houses the original 1930s French furnishings of Emperor Bao Dai, the last emperor of the Nguyen dynasty, who ruled from 1926 to 1945 with the support of the French. Stroll through the rooms and sit behind the emperor's desk. Your guide will no doubt have you pick up Bao Dai's phone and insist on taking your picture. The family sitting room holds military maps and family portraits, as well as chairs designated for each family member (as detailed on the description card). The room has a tactile immediacy, as if it were untouched and suspended in time. ⊠ *Le Hong Phong St., 500 yards southeast of the Pasteur Institute,* ☎ *063/822–125.* ▭ *5,000d.* ☉ *Daily 8–5.*

⑪ An offbeat experience is to be had at the unofficial **art gallery at Hang Nga Guesthouse,** west of Bao Dai's palace. In a strange building made out of a tree, the hotel and gallery are a fairy tale landscape with life-size wood carvings of animals and fantastical creatures. It looks like Salvador Dalí meets the *Swiss Family Robinson.* Its Vietnamese owner and designer, Dang Viet Nga, studied architecture in Russia and has decorated the main dining room with a collection of photos of herself. Each room has its own wacky theme (☞ Dining and Lodging, *below,* for information on staying here). ⊠ *3 Huynh Thuc Khang St.,* ☎ *063/ 822–070.* ▭ *Free.* ☉ *Daily 7 AM–8 PM.*

⑫ The **Lam Ty Ni Pagoda** is the home of the multitalented, multilingual resident monk Vien Thuc, known as the Mad Monk of Dalat. An artist, poet, landscape architect, craftsman, and religious scholar, Vien Thuc is a living legend. He will happily escort you through his rooms of watercolor paintings and may wrap up a picture even before you've agreed to buy it. Keep in mind that it is very hard to bargain with a monk. ⊠ *2 Thien My St.* ☉ *Daily 9–5.*

⑬ One of Dalat's smaller waterfalls, lovely **Cam Ly Falls** is unfortunately crowded with tourists and kids selling gum and dried meat, a local Dalat treat.

⑭ If you love gardens, go to the European-style **Dalat Flower Garden** (Vuon Hoa Dalat), on the northeast side of Xuan Huong Lake. In January and February, around the time of Tet (the lunar new year), its wide variety of *hoa lan* (orchids) are in full bloom. At other times, you'll see all kinds of flowers, including hydrangeas and fuchsias. ⊠ *2 Phu Dong Thien Vuong St.,* ☎ *063/822–151.* ▭ *4,000d.* ☉ *Daily 7–5.*

⑮ If you're a train buff or just want to see what Dalat was like in the first half of the century, visit the **Crémaillère Railway** (Ga Da Lat), to the east of the lake. A movie-set quality pervades this picturesque train station built in the 1920s. From 1928 to 1964 Dalat was linked by train

170

to the small town of Phan Rang–Thap Cham and to then-Saigon. Regular service was suspended in 1964 when Vietcong attacks forced it to shut down. These days the train goes only to **Trai Mat**, a small ethnic minority village 8 km (5 mi) east of Dalat. Falsely advertised as a steam-train ride, the trip is only worth doing if you're with a group: large groups, of up to 20 people, pay as little as $3 per person, but small groups of about five, or solo travelers, have to pay $15 for a whole train car. On the ride to Trai Mat you can get a closer look at the area's bountiful fields full of strawberries, cabbage, flowers, avocados, and rambutan. ✉ ½ km (⅓ mi) east of Xuan Huong Lake. 🎟 10,000d to view station itself. ⏱ Daily 8–5; trains leave for Trai Mat daily at 8 AM.

16 One of Dalat's most famous and popular monuments is the Chinese **Thien Vuong Pagoda** (Chua Tao Thien Voung), southeast of town, atop a steep mountain with great views of the surrounding area. The dirt path leading up to the pagoda is lined with stalls selling candied fruits—a local specialty—and souvenirs. The pagoda was built in 1958 by the Chaozhou Chinese congregation. Dominating the pagoda are three large, Hong Kong–made gilded-sandalwood sculptures—in the third of the three buildings. From left to right are Dai The Chi Bo Tat (an assistant of A Di Da, the Buddha of the past), Thich Ca Buddha (Sakyamuni, the historical Buddha), and Quan The Am Bo Tat (Avalokiteçvara, the Goddess of Mercy). Peaceful gardens surround the pagoda. ✉ About 3 km (2 mi) southeast of center of town, following Khe Sanh St. 🎟 Free. ⏱ Daily 9–4.

17 The **Chu Linh Phong Pagoda**, also known as the Su Nu Pagoda, is a serene Buddhist convent built in 1952. Out of respect, avoid visiting during lunchtime, when the nuns (who traditionally shave their heads) sing their prayers. ✉ 72 Hoang Hoa Tham St. 🎟 Free. ⏱ Daily 9–

18 A favorite of Vietnamese honeymooners is **Prenn Falls** (Thac Prenn). In the crowded park surrounding the falls you can frolic over rope bridge and under the falls themselves. You can also hike up the short path to a makeshift zoo, where a few monkeys and birds sit in small cages. ✉ *South of Dalat on Hwy. 20; look for Prenn Restaurant.* 🗺 *6,000d.* ☉ *Daily 8–4:30.*

⑲ The **Valley of Love** (Thung Lung Tinh Yeu) is another pilgrimage site for Vietnamese honeymooners. Once named the Valley of Peace by Emperor Bao Dai, the valley now has a name reflecting its transformation from a serene setting with lovely vistas into a magnet for newlyweds. On a walk around the lovely green valley you can see Vietnamese couples being photographed with locals on horseback dressed as cowboys. Rest on a heart-shape bench, chewing some of the dried deer meat sold everywhere, and you'll fit right in. ✉ *Approximately 3 km (2 mi) north of Xuan Huong Lake, following Phu Dong Thien Vuong St.* 🗺 *6,000d.* ☉ *Daily 7:30–4.*

⑳ Evoking the story of the lovers Hoang Tung and Mai Nuong, the **Lake of Sighs** (Ho Than Tho), northeast of town, is populated by Vietnamese dressed like cowboys, and a slew of paddleboats. According to the *Romeo and Juliet*–like legend, Hoang Tung joined the army, but Mai Nuong thought she had been abandoned. Out of despair, she killed herself by jumping into the lake. On discovering her body, her lover did the same. ✉ *About 5 km (3 mi) northeast of Dalat, following Phan Chu Trinh St.* 🗺 *5,000d.* ☉ *Daily 8–5.*

Dining and Lodging

$$$ ✕ **Le Rabelais.** Imagine being a guest in a fabulous French country estate complete with chandeliers, period furniture, 3-ft-high floral arrangements, and a portrait gallery—you can almost believe it's true at the beautiful Rabelais. Flawless service and an impressive wine list make it worth dining in this restaurant. Unfortunately, the French-influenced food, although decent, doesn't live up to the setting. ✉ *Sofitel Dalat Palace, 12 Tran Phu St.,* ☎ *063/825–444. AE, MC, V.*

$$ ✕ **Thanh Thanh.** If you're desperate for white tablecloths and napkins, this pleasant though unspectacular Vietnamese restaurant is one of the few formal establishments in Dalat. Because it's recommended by most of the local guides and hotel concierges, it's generally filled with Western tourists. One of the better dishes on the menu is the tasty sugarcane shrimp. ✉ *4 Tang Bat Ho St.,* ☎ *063/821–836. No credit cards.*

$ ✕ **Lyla Restaurant.** A self-proclaimed family restaurant, Lyla, with both European and Vietnamese fare, is one of the better dining choices in Dalat. Try the *xa lat tron thit bo* (mixed salad with beef), a surprisingly tasty dish. Set on a hill, this restaurant overlooks the Central Market. ✉ *18A Nguyen Chi Thanh St.,* ☎ *063/834–540. No credit cards.*

$$$$ 🏨 **Sofitel Dalat Palace.** Reminiscent of a French château, with 15-ft ★ ceilings, ornate fireplaces, and huge public rooms, the Sofitel is one of the best hotels in Vietnam. Spacious rooms with tasteful antique reproductions, original moldings, and unobtrusive modern conveniences, combined with impeccable service, make this a great place to stay. Overlooking Xuan Huong Lake, the exquisite Dalat Palace Golf Club has been renovated to recapture the grandeur and elegance of its original 1922 French design. ✉ *12 Tran Phu St.,* ☎ *063/825–444,* 📠 *063/825–666. 43 rooms. Restaurant, café, lounge, piano bar, pub, in-room safes, minibars, no-smoking rooms, room service, 18-hole golf course, 2 tennis courts, mountain bikes, shops, baby-sitting, dry cleaning, laundry service, concierge, business services, meeting rooms, travel services, airport shuttle. AE, MC, V.* ✎

$$$ 🏨 **Novotel Dalat Vietnam.** A sister hotel of the tonier Sofitel Dalat Palace (☞ *above*), the Novotel Dalat offers first-class, if somewhat

small, rooms within walking distance of town and the golf course. The modern rooms have comfortable beds and are tastefully decorated. ✉ *7 Tran Phu St.,* ☎ *063/825–777,* ℻ *063/825–888. 144 rooms. Restaurant, bar, café, tennis court, mountain bikes, playground, business services. AE, MC, V.*

$$ 🏨 **Golf 3 Hotel.** Located right in the center of town, the Golf 3 offers excellent, spacious, and fairly inexpensive rooms; having said that, the rooms are a bit on the kitschy side. The enormous sunken tubs in the deluxe rooms are reason enough to stay here. If the Golf 3 is full, its sister hotels, the nearby Golf 1 and Golf 2, are other options, though they are less posh than the Golf 3. ✉ *4 Nguyen Thi Minh Khai St.,* ☎ *063/826–042,* ℻ *063/830–396. 72 rooms. Restaurant, bar, café, beauty shop, massage, dance club, business services, travel services, airport shuttle. AE, MC, V.*

$ 🏨 **Hang Nga Guesthouse.** Choose from 18 unique rooms, each with its own offbeat theme, at this small guest house close to the center of town. The Bear Room has a life-size bear with eyes that light up when you turn on the lights and a small fireplace in his belly. Funky, too, are the Ant and Tiger rooms; the latter has a tiger with red-lightbulb eyes that stare you down in the middle of the room. This wacky architectural monument is a cheerful alternative to the more traditional hotels in town, although the rooms are quite small. ✉ *3 Huynh Thuc Khang St.,* ☎ *063/822–070. 18 rooms. Restaurant, travel services. No credit cards.*

Nightlife and the Arts

Barring a few bohemian-type cafés, there isn't much to do at night unless you like karaoke, which you can find everywhere. **Café Tung** (✉ 6 Khu Hoa Binh St.) is a tiny spot where you can get coffee in the evening and swap travel tales. The small **Stop 'n Go Café** (✉ Kiosk 6 Hoa Binh Sq., ☎ 063/821–512), open until 10, is popular with travelers for meeting and exchanging information.

Outdoor Activities and Sports

Dalat's hilly terrain makes it a great place for gentle hikes. The Lake of Sighs (Ho Than Tho) and the Valley of Love (Thung Lung Tinh Yeu) are ideal places to spend an afternoon wandering—it is possible to escape the cowboys and honeymooners.

Dalat Tourist/Lamdong Tourist Company (☞ Travel Agency *in* Central Highlands and Dalat A to Z, *below*) has information on hiking in the Valley of Love and around the Lake of Sighs; it also arranges guided tours of these areas. The pristine **Dalat Palace Golf Club** (✉ Phu Dong Thien Vuong St., ☎ 063/821–201) has an 18-hole course overlooking Xuan Huong Lake. Fees are $65 for Sofitel Dalat Palace guests; nonguests pay $85. You can rent **paddleboats** from stands along Xuan Huong Lake for 20,000d an hour.

The Southern Central Highlands

En route from Dalat to Ho Chi Minh City is the southernmost portion of the central highlands, an unspoiled landscape dotted with ethnic minority villages and religious complexes. There are several Ede villages in the area; visits can be arranged through tourist agencies Dalat and Nha Trang.

★ ㉑ Don't miss the **Po Klong Garai Cham Towers,** west of Dalat on Highway 20, just beyond the semiarid twin cities of Phan Rang–Thap Cham. These four well-preserved Hindu temples are remnants of a 13th century Cham temple built during the reign of the Cham king Jaya Simhavarman III, one of the emperors of the Kingdom of Champa, which ruled this part of Vietnam from the 2nd to 15th centuries. According to legend, King Simhavarman built these towers in honor of King Po Klong Garai, a figure revered by the Cham people for his efforts in leading the resistance against outside invaders of the Cham kingdom. Over the entrance to the tallest tower is an intact carving of a dancing Shiva. Inside the entrance is a statue of the bull Nadin, a symbol of agricultural riches. Excavations around the towers by the French and later by the Vietnamese unearthed a number of gold and silver bowls and other artifacts. Vietnam's Cham community continues to use the towers for their religious and cultural celebrations. ⊠ *Off Hwy. 20.* 🖾 *20,000d.* ⊘ *Daily 8–5.*

㉒ Steep, slippery steps lead to excellent views of the 300-ft **Dambri Falls.** The falls are about 75 km (47 mi) southwest of Dalat and 233 km (144 mi) northeast of Ho Chi Minh City. 🖾 *10,000d.* ⊘ *Daily 7–5.*

㉓ Often inaccessible due to poor road conditions, **Nam Cat Tien National Park,** 250 km (155 mi) northwest of Ho Chi Minh City, shelters the endangered Javanese rhino, as well as monkeys, elephants, tigers, and several bird species. *See* Side Trips from Ho Chi Minh City *in* Chapter 6 for more information.

Approximately 100 km (62 mi) north of Ho Chi Minh City along Highway 20, **Langa Lake** supports a number of floating fishing villages. Although these may sound exotic, they are nothing more than several groups of low-end houseboats. There may or may not be a roadside food stand open if you're in need of a snack.

Central Highlands and Dalat A to Z

Arriving and Departing

BY BUS

Dalat Tourist/Lamdong Tourist Company (⊠ 4 Tran Quoc Toan St., Dalat, ☎ 063/822–125; ⊠ 21 Nguyen An Ninh St., District 1, Ho Chi Minh City, ☎ 08/823–0227) runs daily minibus service from Dalat to Ho Chi Minh City, 308 km (191 mi) south. The trip costs $7 and takes six to seven hours. Try to go to the office one day in advance to reserve a seat.

Sinh Café Travel (⊠ 246–248 De Tham St., District 1, Ho Chi Minh City, ☎ 08/836–9420) sells an open bus ticket that connects Dalat to Ho Chi Minh City heading south and Dalat to Nha Trang heading north. The open-ended ticket allows you to get on the bus any day of the week. The daily trip between Dalat and Ho Chi Minh City takes about seven hours and costs $7; for an open ticket from Ho Chi Minh City to Hanoi, you pay $38 and can get on and off the bus any day you choose (☞ Bus Travel *in* Smart Travel Tips A to Z for more information).

BY CAR

Driving to Dalat from Ho Chi Minh City or Hanoi costs too much, takes too long, and is too complicated; you're better off taking either a plane, a bus, or a minibus.

BY PLANE

Vietnam Airlines has daily flights from Dalat's Lien Khuong Airport (30 km [19 mi] south of town) to Ho Chi Minh City (one hour, $40). There are no direct flights from either Hanoi or Nha Trang. For ticket confirmation and reservations, go to Dalat's **Vietnam Airlines office** (San Bay Lien Khuong; ⊠ 5 Truong Cong Dinh St., ☎ 063/822–895).

Getting Around

BY CAR

The best way to get around Dalat is by car with a hired driver and guide. Be prepared for narrow, hilly, and hazardous roads; along the roadside are small shrines to motorists who have been killed. Drivers, however, are usually good.

Langa Lake, on Highway 20, is hard to miss as you cross a bridge over it when traveling between Dalat and Ho Chi Minh City. Dambri Falls, 16 km (10 mi) off Highway 20, is just north of the town of Bao Loc. Look for signs on Highway 20. The Po Klong Garai Cham Towers are also off Highway 20.

To travel around Dalat or visit the attractions of the region, you can hire a car and driver from Dalat Tourist/Lamdong Tourist Company (☞ Contacts and Resources, *below*).

Contacts and Resources

CURRENCY EXCHANGE

Exchange money at the **Agriculture Bank of Vietnam** (✉ Nguyen Van Troi St.) and at most hotels.

EMERGENCIES

Contact **Sofitel Dalat Palace Hotel** (☞ Dining and Lodging, *above*) if you need assistance.

POST OFFICE

For stamps, go to the **main branch** (✉ 14 Tran Phu St.) or ask at your hotel.

TRAVEL AGENCY

Dalat Tourist/Lamdong Tourist Company (✉ 4 Tran Quoc Toan St., ☎ 063/826–027, ℻ 063/833–956) arranges cars with drivers and tours of the city. You can also arrange for trips to the hill-tribe villages in the area.

6 HO CHI MINH CITY

Ho Chi Minh City—Saigon to most—is a vibrant, bustling city that reflects Vietnam's past and its future. Its broad colonial boulevards leading to the Saigon River and its stucco villas are remnants of the French colonial presence. Cholon, the city's Chinatown, is a reminder of the Chinese influence on the country. And the new office towers and international hotels changing the skyline overnight are symbols of tomorrow's Vietnam.

By Andrew
Chilvers

ARRIVING IN HO CHI MINH CITY can be a bewildering experience. At the airport the endless customs paperwork can be confusing, and the throngs of taxi drivers competing for business outside can be jarringly disorienting when you're jet-lagged. But don't be put off—confusion and chaos are at the very heart of the city. If at first you feel like you are on a breathtaking roller-coaster ride moving at breakneck speed, you soon you get used to the feeling and may even grow to like it.

Once romantically referred to by the French as the Pearl of the Orient, Ho Chi Minh City is still called Saigon by almost everyone who lives here (both names are used interchangeably throughout this book). The city has a more cosmopolitan feel than Hanoi, although much of the old French colonial city is vanishing beneath the rapidly rising skyline and the sheer weight of recent history.

History, however, has bequeathed the city a kaleidoscopic melting pot of styles. Only in Saigon can you get a ride in a '50s French Citroën, a '60s Ford Mustang, a '70s Russian Volga, or a brand-new Toyota. For dinner you have your choice of not only Vietnamese food but also hamburgers, fine French cuisine, or black caviar at one of the city's Russian restaurants. Afterward you can head to one of the new, sleek bars that have opened in the past few years.

At the teeming markets tropical fruits, king cobras, barbecued dogs, and a hundred other such items are for sale; the sidewalks are crammed with noodle stands, cafés, and vendors selling fresh glasses of *bia hoi* (beer) for as little as 25¢. The roads are often gridlocked with motorbikes, scooters, bicycles, cyclos, buses, and an increasing number of cars. All kinds of people travel around by bicycle or motorbike: women dressed in traditional *ao dais* (straight-cut silk gowns worn over flowing pants), long gloves, and conical hats; and whole families—mother, father, and two children—all squeezed on one seat. Everyone seems to be going somewhere, no matter what time of day. And even if people have nowhere to go, they simply cruise around until it's time to go to sleep.

Meanwhile, far above the din of street life, a new city is emerging amid the screech of jackhammers and pile drivers working on the newest Asian skyline. Since economic reforms—known as *doi moi*—were adopted more than 10 years ago, Ho Chi Minh City has witnessed on-and-off growth. In the early '90s, Ho Chi Minh City's economy expanded at the startling rate of 15% a year. Things have since slowed down due to the onset of the regional economic crisis of the late 1990s, but predictions are being made that Vietnam's economy will pick up again in the early years of the 21st century.

Unfortunately, many are being left behind in the struggle for self-enrichment. Homeless children roam the downtown streets, sometimes earning a living by shining shoes or by begging or pickpocketing. Limbless war veterans hobble behind wealthy tourists badgering them for small change. Women desperate for tourist dollars carry comatose infants and endlessly shuffle through the streets like specters. And after twilight prostitutes cruise downtown on their Hondas, prowling for foreign customers.

Ho Chi Minh City encompasses a large region, stretching all the way north to Cu Chi, in Tay Ninh Province, and south to the upper reaches of the Mekong Delta. The part of the city known as Saigon is actually made up of only two of the 14 districts in Ho Chi Minh City: Districts 1 and 3. Bordered by the Thi Nghe Channel to the north, the Ben Nghe

Channel to the south, and the Saigon River to the east, the city has served as a natural fortress and has been fought over by countless people during the past 2,000 years. The ancient empire of Funan used the area as a trading post, and the Khmer kingdom of Angkor transformed Prey Nokor, as Saigon was called, into a flourishing center of trade protected by a standing army. By the 14th century, while under Khmer rule, the city attracted Arab, Cham, Chinese, Malaysian, and Indian merchants. It was then known as the gateway to the Kingdom of Champa, the sister empire to Angkor.

In 1674 the lords of the Nguyen clan in Hue established a customs post at Prey Nokor to cash in on the region's growing commercial traffic. Saigon, as the Vietnamese called it, became an increasingly important administrative post. The building in 1772 of a 6-km (4-mi) trench on the western edge of old Saigon, in what is now District 5, marked the shift in control in the south from Khmer rule to Nguyen rule from Hue. Further Vietnamese consolidation came in 1778 with the development of Cholon, Saigon's Chinese city, as a second commercial hub in the area that is presently District 5.

In 1789 the Nguyen lords moved their power base from Hue to Saigon, following attacks by rebels from the village of Tay Son. Unhappy with the way the Nguyen lords had been running the country, the rebels massacred most of the Nguyen clan and took control of the government—briefly. In 1802, Prince Nguyen Anh, the last surviving heir of the Nguyen dynasty, defeated the Tay Son ruler—with French backing—regaining power and uniting Vietnam. He moved the capital back to Hue and declared himself Emperor Gia Long.

In quelling the Tay Son rebels, Gia Long's request for French assistance, which was readily provided, came at a price. In exchange for their help, Gia Long promised the French territorial concessions in Vietnam. Although the French Revolution and the Napoleonic Wars temporarily delayed any French claims, Gia Long's decision eventually cost Vietnam dearly. In 1859, the French, tired of waiting for the Vietnamese emperor to give them what they felt they deserved, seized Saigon and made it the capital of their new colony, Cochin China. This marked the beginning of an epoch of colonial-style feudalism and indentured servitude for many Vietnamese in the highlands.

The catastrophe that was to overtake Saigon and the rest of Vietnam during the latter half of the 20th century was a direct result of French colonial interference. Despite France's role, however, to this day the Vietnamese people, both north and south, maintain deep sentimental ties with French culture and art, as is apparent across the country.

Today, without the threat of colonial interference or war, the Saigonese are living life to the fullest—and trying to make money. Saigon is the most Western of all the cities in Vietnam, with the greatest range of international cuisine and Western-style high-rises. But reminders of the past still poke through the headlong rush into capitalism. The Hotel Continental, immortalized in Graham Greene's *The Quiet American,* continues to stand on the corner of old Indochina's most famous thoroughfare, the rue Catinat (known to the American GIs as Tu Do Street and renamed Dong Khoi Street by the Communists). The city still has its central opera house and its old French City Hall, the Hôtel de Ville. You can still see the spires of Notre Dame Cathedral from the decks of the new cruise liners sailing up the Saigon River. And the city is still dotted with the bunkers and watchtowers of its more recent violent past.

Pleasures and Pastimes

Ho Chi Minh City is a modern city by Asian standards and has been under firm Vietnamese control for only a little more than 200 years. Consequently, there are few historic monuments or ancient sights to see. The city's character remains essentially French—with wide boulevards, colonial villas, and a café society—and resolutely Asian. Combined with a vivacious street life, the French influences have bred a charm all their own. But it is the people even more than the city that you will remember most.

Art

Nowhere is the French cultural influence clearer than in the works of Vietnamese artists. Ho Chi Minh City has countless art galleries, with many new ones opening each month, showcasing a gamut of European-influenced art movements. The most common type of artwork you'll see throughout downtown Saigon is Impressionist knockoffs. Galleries are chock-full of copies of Monets and van Goghs, although some of the upscale galleries carry more serious works. Many of the tremendously talented artists represented in these galleries are French trained and are only now exhibiting their work to the world—and the world is beginning to take notice. So if you want to buy some art, now is the time, while the prices are still (relatively) low.

Cafés

In Ho Chi Minh City life is at its most colorful on the street, and the city's café society is at the center of this vivid spectacle. It is from a seat at one of the city's small cafés that you will really see the variety of urban life pass by. Order a strong, slow-filtered coffee or hot green tea, and spend an hour simply watching the street. It's hypnotic: you'll see market-bound cyclos crammed with dead pigs; chickens and ducks piled five deep and draped over the handlebars of bicycles; women selling noodle soup from bamboo baskets balanced on poles over their shoulders, singing their own distinctive tunes to attract customers; and young women wearing white ao dais riding motorbikes to school. You may also find that people are most relaxed and most sociable at the cafés, so don't be surprised if someone asks to join you for a drink.

Dining

Ho Chi Minh City has a plethora of Vietnamese and international restaurants, local cafés, and sidewalk noodle stalls. The French had a major influence on the city's cuisine, which means you can find many superb French-Vietnamese restaurants. In more recent years other types of international fare have appeared: Italian restaurants, Swiss eateries, American burger joints, fast-food spots, and even tapas bars. But most Vietnamese simply eat at street stalls serving noodles, rice dishes, satays, kebabs, *pho* (soups), and other foods that are often as delicious and varied as at any of the more upscale establishments—at a fraction of the price. Note that the farther from the road (literally!), the more hygienic the establishment is likely to be. Although the city's air-conditioned restaurants are not always the most authentic places to eat, they are usually the most pleasant places to escape the heat.

Most international restaurants are in and around Districts 1 and 3, though there are several fine international restaurants in the city suburbs. You can also find some good, inexpensive cafés serving Vietnamese and international cuisine along Pham Ngu Lao and De Tham streets in District 1. Most places are open for lunch and dinner but close in between, except cafés, which stay open all day and into the night. Most menus have English translations.

Meals are serious business, and between 11:30 AM and 2:30 PM the city shuts down to enjoy its collective repast and a postlunch siesta, a tradition rooted in the French presence here. It's considered the height of bad manners to interrupt one of these naps. If your guide suddenly decides to sleep for an hour, it's advisable to let him be. It could make the difference between a good and a bad trip. Dinner is generally served any time between 6 PM and 1 AM.

Lodging

Ho Chi Minh City has had something of a hotel boom during the last few years, and new accommodations continue to open. Some of the grimmer state-run hotels have been replaced by new international joint-venture hotels, more of which are opening every month. Many "minihotels" have also opened; these family-run guest houses are excellent alternatives to the bigger hotels. Often only a third of the price of larger establishments, they are generally in good condition, are more sensitive to guests' needs, and have their own restaurants. The minihotels, however, lack the facilities and services provided by international hotel chains.

A third option is to stay in one of the famous old colonial establishments that Saigon Tourist, the state tourism agency, has renovated. Although these old hotels certainly have their charms and some modern conveniences (IDD phones, fax machines), their renovations are often shoddy, and service is sometimes lacking. If you're looking for service and amenities, you're better off staying at one of the international hotels—although it will cost you. (But, as with everything in Vietnam, you can get better deals if you are prepared to negotiate.) Keep in mind that despite the number of facilities and conveniences at these newer hotels—fax machines, photocopiers, computer centers, health clubs, cable TVs, minibars, and marble bathrooms—the level of service will still probably not be what you've come to expect elsewhere. Vietnam's service industry is still in its infancy and often requires patience. Note that all hotels charging more than $10 a night have air-conditioning.

You may want to stay in Districts 1 and 3—the center of old Saigon—where most of the museums, galleries, restaurants, bars, and nightclubs are found. Most old colonial hotels are in Districts 1 and 3, as are many newer international hotels, although some are also in District 5 and in the Phu Nhuan District near the airport. Lower-price accommodations are clustered around Pham Ngu Lao, De Tham, and Bui Vien streets in District 1.

Find out if your hotel offers complimentary airport pickup—most hotels, including minihotels, can arrange a driver for you. Call ahead and arrange to have someone from the hotel pick you up. If you've never been to Saigon, you may be overwhelmed by the general chaos of arriving and the crush of taxi drivers vying for your business. When you're jet-lagged, this is not a pleasant way to start your visit.

Assume guest rooms in hotels listed below have private bathrooms unless otherwise noted. Most hotels and guest houses listed also have IDD phones and satellite TVs.

Museums

Several museums are peppered around the city, most housed in old colonial palaces. Many were set up primarily to promote Communist Party propaganda, and the displays are less than memorable. Nevertheless, most are worth a visit, particularly the harrowing War Remnants Museum. The former presidential palace is also worth a visit: here, on the grounds, is what is said to be the tank that battered down the gates when the Communists took over Saigon in April 1975. (Another tank in Ban Me Thuat in the central highlands and a tank at the Army Museum in Hanoi lay the same claim to fame. For the victorious Communists, these relics are sometimes more symbols than the real McCoy, so don't take them too literally.)

Shopping

In Ho Chi Minh City you can find all kinds of souvenirs of Vietnam—such as woodcarvings, lacquerware, paintings, ceramics, and T-shirts—as well as idiosyncratic items such as imitation GI cigarette lighters. You can also get well-made designer gear at a fraction of the price of even Bangkok's markets and some of the most up-to-date electronic hardware at a steal. Be sure to spend an hour or two at the old colonial Ben Thanh Market in the city center and the Binh Tay Market in Cholon, where you can sample the city going about its daily business and buy a wide variety of items.

EXPLORING HO CHI MINH CITY

Ho Chi Minh City is not noted for its tourist attractions. Although there are several sights that shouldn't be missed, the particular appeal of the city is in its street life. From early morning to late at night, the streets and sidewalks are home to a startling range of activity—from street hawkers and barbers to noodle sellers and street artists. It's a kaleidoscopic maze, where Western-style commercial activity takes place alongside traditional practices.

The city has 14 districts, but most areas of interest are in either District 1 (downtown Saigon) or District 5 (Cholon). In District 1 major arteries such as Le Loi Boulevard, Ham Nghi Boulevard, and Pham Ngu Lao Street converge at the Ben Thanh Market, an important commercial and transportation hub. Northeast of the central market, at the intersection of Le Loi Boulevard with Nguyen Hue Boulevard and Dong Khoi Street, is a cluster of French colonial–style public buildings—the Hôtel de Ville (now the Ho Chi Minh City People's Committee) the Opera House (once again serving its original purpose after housing the former South Vietnam's National Assembly); and hotels like the Rex, the Continental, and the Caravelle, built by the French and made famous during the Vietnam War.

Saigon's waterways have traditionally served as a means of commercial transport as well as a natural moat. District 1 is bounded on the east by the Saigon River and on the south by the Ben Nghe Channel. Not only do the rivers provide an alternative way of getting around, they also serve as convenient landmarks. The city's rather daunting layout and chaotic traffic tend to discourage leisurely walking. The intermittent taxi, cyclo or motorbike ride—ranging 6,000d–10,000d—is an unavoidable but enjoyable alternative. Any of the walks below could also be done as a cyclo ride, an option particularly recommended on hot days.

Numbers in the text correspond to numbers in the margin and on the Ho Chi Minh City, Cholon, and Ho Chi Minh City Environs maps

Great Itineraries

IF YOU HAVE 1–2 DAYS

With one day you can see many of the city's major sights, although you have to be selective, especially if you want to visit a museum. Having a cyclo or taxi will allow you to see the city more quickly. After you've seen the main sights on the first day, you'll have to go farther afield to find areas of interest. If on the first day you hired a cyclo driver you liked, you should use him again.

With four days you can see all the city's sights, go to one or two markets, and take a day trip—or even two—to surrounding areas including the Mekong Delta, the Cu Chi Tunnels, and the Caodai Holy See. Make arrangements for these excursions with one of the city's tourist agencies, or hire a car and driver (and maybe a guide) and go on your own.

When to Tour Ho Chi Minh City

The best time to visit the city is during the dry season, roughly between November and April, especially if you want to go down to the Mekong Delta. The rainy season runs from about May through October, during which time outlying areas can become very flooded.

Central Saigon (Districts 1 and 3)

District 1 is the center of old Saigon. The broad Nguyen Hue and Le Loi boulevards converge at the Hôtel de Ville (now the People's Committee building), the historic Opera House, and the Hotel Continental. Dong Khoi Street, toward the eastern edge of District 1, is the neighborhood's historic main thoroughfare; it runs down to the Saigon River from Notre Dame Cathedral and the Central Post Office. Known as rue Catinat during the French colonial era, Dong Khoi Street might be more easily recognized as Tu Do Street, its moniker when it was Saigon's red-light district in the 1960s and '70s. Since then, shops and restaurants have replaced the bars. Ben Thanh, an old colonial covered market, is on the western edge of District 1, and the former presidential palace (now called the Reunification Palace) is on the northern boundary of the area.

Numbers in the text correspond to numbers in the margin and on the Ho Chi Minh City map.

A Good Walk

Although slightly away from the center, the provocative **War Remnants Museum** ① makes a good starting point for this walk. From here head northeast on Vo Van Tan Street toward tree-lined Nam Ky Khoi Nghia Street. When you come to Nguyen Thi Minh Khai Street, you will see the grounds of the modern **Reunification Palace** ②. Directly behind it is the old French sports club, the Cercle Sportif, now known as **Cong Vien Van Hoa Park** ③; to enter the park, turn right off Nguyen Du Street, which is a one-way road running alongside the palace. Walk through the park into the grounds of the palace; turn left onto Le Duan Boulevard, the street that intersects Nam Ky Khoi Nghia Street at the palace entrance. After passing Pasteur Street, you'll see the back of **Notre Dame Cathedral** ④, with its pink spires. On Le Duan Boulevard, just a couple of blocks past Hai Ba Trung Boulevard, is the site of the former U.S. Embassy, now the **U.S. Consulate,** which is worth a visit only for its historical associations. Proceed about 1,000 ft down Le Duan Boulevard to get to the sprawling grounds of the **Zoo and Botanical Garden** ⑤ and the **History Museum** ⑥.

With your back to the main entrance of the complex, make a left onto Nguyen Binh Khiem Street and follow it to the intersection with Le Thanh Ton Street. Make a right, then take the first left at Ton Duc Thang Street, which runs along the Saigon River. Along the waterfront you can see the late-19th-century **Hotel Majestic** ⑦, at the intersection of Ton Duc Thang and Dong Khoi streets. The hotel's rooftop bar provides magnificent views of the Saigon River and the Thu Thiem swamp district opposite. Turn right at Nguyen Hue Boulevard and make the first left onto Hai Trieu Street, also known as Whiskey Row. Take a right on Ham Nghi Boulevard, where a bunch of international food stores (No.

Ho Chi Minh City

0   400 yards

0   400 meters

PHU AN DISTRICT

Dinh Tien Hoang

Nguyen Van Thu

Mac Dinh Chi

Phung Khac Khoan

Hai Ba Trung

Pham Ngoc Thach

Nguyen Binh Khiem

Du

Ton Duc Thang

Nguyen

Le Thanh Ton

U.S. Consulate

Nguyen Dinh Chieu

Pasteur

Nam Ky Khoi Nghia

Dong Khoi

Thai Van Lung

Le Duan

DISTRICT 3

Nguyen Thi Minh Khai

DISTRICT 1

Hai Ba Trung

Dong Khoi

Ly Tu Trong

Saigon Tourist

Nguyen Thi Minh Khai

Nguyen Du

Le Thanh Ton

Nam Ky Khoi Nghia

Le Loi

Ton Duc Thang

Truong Dinh

Ly Tu Trong

Le Thanh Ton

Le Loi

Ton That Thiep

Nguyen Hue

Dong Khoi

DISTRICT 10

Coch Mang Thang Tam

Le Thi Rieng

Pham Hong Thai

Huynh Thuc Khang

Pasteur

Ton That Dang

Ham Nghi

Hai Trieu

Ton Duc Thang

Nguyen Trai

Le Lai

Pho Duc Chinh

Ton Duc Thang

Pham Ngu Lao

Tran Hung Dao

Nguyen Thai Binh

Ben Chuong

SEE CHOLON DETAIL DISTRICT 5 (CHOLON)

Saigon River

64 is a good one) are jam-packed with Western specialties. Make a right onto Ton That Dang Street, where you can find everything from live eels to laundry detergent at the market that continues along intersecting Huynh Thuc Khang Street, a kind of electronics arcade. Continuing a block past Huynh Thuc Khang Street, you come to Ton That Thiep Street, in what has historically been the Indian quarter.

Make a right onto Ton That Thiep Street, crossing Nguyen Hue Boulevard, and turn left onto **Dong Khoi Street.** Along Dong Khoi Street is the **Hotel Caravelle** ⑧, once a favorite haunt of war correspondents at cocktail hour. Opposite the Caravelle is the **Hotel Continental** ⑨. Although a shadow of its former self, it's still worth a visit. Sandwiched between the two at the end of Le Loi Boulevard is the **Municipal Theater** ⑩, recognizable by its inverted dome. Farther up Dong Khoi Street, past the Continental, is the main branch office of **Saigon Tourist,** on the corner of Le Thanh Ton Street. Next comes Notre Dame Cathedral—the front of the church this time. The beautiful French colonial **Central Post Office** ⑪ is on the right side of the square that opens up in front of the cathedral.

With your back to the cathedral, walk toward Nguyen Du Street, make a right, then take the first left onto Pasteur Street, and the first right onto Ly Tu Trong Street to get to the neoclassic **Museum of the Revolution** ⑫, or Army Museum. Return to Pasteur Street, then proceed down to Le Thanh Ton Street to get to the **Ho Chi Minh City's People's Committee** ⑬, built by the French as the Hôtel de Ville (City Hall). Follow Le Thanh Ton Street southwest, away from the People's Committee, and make a right on Truong Dinh Street. In the middle of the block between Ly Tu Trong and Le Thanh Ton streets is the **Mariamman Hindu Temple** ⑭, the last functioning Hindu house of worship in the city. With your back to the temple, make a left on Le Thanh Ton Street where the busy **Ben Thanh Market** ⑮ spills out onto the surrounding street.

TIMING

The walk could take a day or more, depending on how much time you want to spend in the museums. Start in the morning and take lots of breaks in the small sidewalk cafés along the way. Consider splitting the walk into two parts, with a break after the History Museum. Be careful not to overexert yourself, and remember to drink a lot of bottled water: walking around Saigon can be hot and tiring.

Sights to See

★ ⑮ **Ben Thanh Market** (Cho Ben Thanh). Every imaginable product of the Vietnamese economy is sold here—look for a cheap meal, a hat, even live snakes. The building that houses most of the market was constructed in 1914 by the French, who called it Les Halles Centrales (the Central Market Halls). The best time to visit the market is first thing in the morning, when stocks of produce are piled high and vendors are hustling. ⊠ *At circular intersection of Le Loi Blvd., Pham Ngu Lao St., and Ham Nghi Blvd., District 1.* ☉ *Daily 7–7.*

★ ⑪ **Central Post Office** (Buu Dien Truing Tam). Be sure to go inside to check out the huge map of old Indochina in this classic French colonial building, completed in 1891. Besides the usual mail services, there are phones and fax machines. To mail letters you need to use the entrance to the less romantic, Soviet-era expansion at 117 Hai Ba Trung Street. ⊠ *At the top of Dong Khoi St. opposite Notre Dame Cathedral, District 1.* ☉ *Daily 7:30–7:30.*

Ⓒ ❸ **Cong Vien Van Hoa Park.** Huge tamarind trees line the road leading up to this park, which resembles a botanical garden. A wide variety of flora is lush and teems with deafening cicadas. Known as the Cercle Sportif to the French, this park was the elite sporting club of the French bourgeoisie in colonial times. Vietnamese people were actually barred from entering. Today there is still a sports club, with tennis courts, a swimming pool, a gym and weight room, and a colonial clubhouse. Use of the facilities will cost you no more than a dollar. These days the club is frequented mostly by young Vietnamese students eager to practice their English with any tourists who wander in. Midday, the park tends to be a base for siestas; you'll see plenty of people catching forty winks. ⊠ *Entrance on 115 Nguyen Du St., District 1.*

Dong Khoi Street. Once named rue Catinat, Dong Khoi Street was the Fifth Avenue or Rodeo Drive of Saigon in the French colonial era. During the Vietnam War this road was the center of the infamous red-light district and was known as Tu Do Street. These days most of the old-time bars have been replaced by restaurants and shops (☞ Shopping, *below*). The street remains the center of the old city, but this is the new Dong Khoi: most shops are now geared toward tourists.

NEED A   The **Paris Deli** (⊠ 31 Dong Khoi St., District 1, ☎ 08/829–7533), a Eu-
BREAK?   ropean-style café, serves excellent cappuccinos and pastries.

❻ History Museum (Vien Bao Tang Lich Su). Although the front door leads you right to a statue of the ubiquitous "Uncle Ho" (as Ho Chi Minh is known), this museum is dedicated to Vietnamese history from the earliest inhabitants to 1930, when the Communist Party was established. Half the museum covers the history of the nation as a whole, whereas the other half focuses on the art and artifacts of southern Vietnam; the ethnography section is particularly interesting. The neo-Vietnamese structure was built by the French in 1929, and much of the current collection was compiled by the French Far Eastern Institute. ⊠ *2 Nguyen Binh Khiem, District 1,* ☎ *08/829–8146 or 08/829–0268.* 🎟 *10,000d* ⏱ *Mon.–Sat. 8–11:30 and 1:30–4:30, Sun. 8:30–11:30.*

⓭ Ho Chi Minh City's People's Committee. Built by the French between 1901 and 1908 to be Saigon's Hôtel de Ville (City Hall), this yellow-and-white colonial-style building now houses the city's main governing body. Unfortunately, the building is not open to the public, so you can't get a peek at its ornate interior. ⊠ *Intersection of Le Thanh To St. and Nguyen Hue Blvd., District 1.*

❽ Hotel Caravelle. Most of the foreign correspondents stayed at this hotel during the Vietnam War. During the 1968 Tet Offensive, several U.S. Marines were killed here; journalists filmed the battle from the rooftop. For information about staying here, *see* Lodging, *below.* ⊠ *19–25 Lam Son Sq., District 1,* ☎ *08/234–4999.*

★ **❾ Hotel Continental.** In French colonial days, the Hotel Continental's open terrace (now simply a sidewalk), shaded by broad tamarind trees, was the town's most sought-after lunch spot. During the Vietnam War, journalists and diplomats met on the terrace to discuss the latest events; Graham Greene's *The Quiet American* was set here. For information about staying at the hotel, *see* Lodging, *below.* ⊠ *132–134 Dong Khoi St., District 1,* ☎ *08/829–9201.*

★ **❼ Hotel Majestic.** Built in the late 19th century, the Majestic was one of the first French colonial hotels, and it still has the elegant decor to show for it. Go to the rooftop bar for an excellent view of the Saigon River. For information about staying here, *see* Lodging, *below.* ⊠ *1 Dong Khoi St., District 1,* ☎ *08/829–5514.*

⓮ Mariamman Hindu Temple (Chua Ba Mariamman). Vivid statues and colorful floral offerings at this temple, the last functioning Hindu ho-of worship in the city, create a microcosm of India in the streets of Saigon. Before the temple was returned in the early '90s to the Hindu community, the government used it as a factory for making joss sticks (incense) and processing dried fish. Today it serves a congregation of only 60 Tamil Hindus, but some Vietnamese and Chinese locals also revere it as a holy space. ☒ *45 Truong Dinh St., District 1.* ☉ *Daily 7–7.*

⑩ Municipal Theater (Nha Hat Thanh Pho). This colonial-style theater was built by the French in 1899 as Saigon's opera house. Later it housed the National Assembly of South Vietnam, the congress of the South Vietnamese government. After 1975, when South Vietnam ceased to be, it became a theater again. For information on performances held here, *see* Nightlife and the Arts, *below.* ☒ *Intersection of Le Loi Blvd. and Dong Khoi St., District 1,* ☎ *08/829–1249.*

⑫ Museum of the Revolution (Bao Tang Cach Mang). Constructed in 1886 as the residence for the French governor of Cochin China, the building is now a museum dedicated to the Vietnamese struggle against the French and Americans. Displays focus on famous marches, military battles, and anti-French and anti-American activists. Exhibits include photos of historical events, uprisings, student demonstrations, and the self-immolation of the monk Thich Quang Duc as a protest against the war. The collection also has a lot of American GI paraphernalia—badges, lighters, helmets, and such—as well as a model of the Cu Chi Tunnels, the huge underground complex built by the Vietnamese Communists that allowed them to survive massive U.S. bombings and military sweeps (☞ Side Trips from Ho Chi Minh City, *below*). The displays are in Vietnamese, but you'll easily get the message. The building itself is as interesting as many of the exhibits inside: a neoclassic design, it has huge columns outside and high-ceilinged ballrooms from the 19th century inside. Beneath the building are concrete bunkers and tunnels connecting to the Reunification Palace (☞ *below*). It was here that President Ngo Dinh Diem (1901–63) and his notorious brother Ngo Dinh Thuc hid before being caught and eventually executed in 1963, three weeks before the assassination of President John F. Kennedy. Outside on the grounds are Soviet tanks, a U.S. helicopter, and antiaircraft guns. ☒ *65 Ly Tu Trong St., District 1,* ☎ *08/829–9741.* ▣ *10,000d.* ☉ *Tues.–Sun. 8–4:30.*

④ Notre Dame Cathedral (Nha Tho Duc Ba). A prominent presence on the Saigon skyline, this neo-Romanesque cathedral was built by the French in 1880 on the site of an old fort. Spanish, Portuguese, and French missionaries introduced Catholicism to Vietnam as early as the 16th century. Today there are approximately 9 million Catholics in Vietnam, the largest Christian population in Asia after the Philippines. The Mass celebrated at 9:30 AM on Sunday is quite a spectacle, as hundreds of faithful converge on the church and stand in the surrounding square. The service also includes short sections in English and French. ☒ *Top of Dong Khoi St., District 1.*

② Reunification Palace (Hoi Truong Thong Nhat). This modern palace— the symbolic center of the South Vietnamese government—was the scene of the dramatic seizure of Saigon by the National Liberation Front in 1975, when tanks smashed down the gates and an NLF flag was draped over the building's balcony.

Ngo Viet Thu, a European-influenced modernist architect, designed the classic '60s building when South Vietnamese president Diem decided he had an "image problem" after his own air force tried to assassinate him by bombing the old French palace. Another assassination attempt succeeded a year later, so Diem never saw the palace finished. The former building on the site was called Norodom Palace and was the home of the French governor-general of Cochin China. The present building still sits on large grounds, where there is a somewhat romanticized model of Ho Chi Minh's home.

There isn't much to see except the palace rooms: the cabinet room, the assembly room, the president's office, the war command room with maps and multicolored telephones, the dining rooms, the private quarters, and a bar-and-games room. You also get a look at the network of tunnels to which the government of South Vietnam would retreat in difficult times and the helicopter that bombed the building in 1975. It all sounds more interesting than it is, since there really isn't much in the rooms except some furniture. But the palace is worth a visit, if only to see a vestige of Vietnam's past. Be sure to stand out on the balcony for a view of the city down the long, tree-lined boulevard created by the French. Although tours are free to Vietnamese, foreigners must pay. ⊠ *Visitors' entrance on 106 Nguyen Du St., District 1.* ☎ *10,000d.* ⊙ *Daily 7:30–10:30 and 1–4.*

Saigon Tourist. This government-run travel service provides all kinds of visitor information and services (☞ Visitor Information and Travel Agencies *in* Ho Chi Minh City A to Z, *below*). ⊠ *49 Le Thanh Ton St., District 1,* ☎ *08/823–0100.* ⊙ *Daily 7:30–6:30.*

U.S. Consulate. The new U.S. Consulate stands on the site of the former American Embassy, which was the scene of running battles during the 1968 Tet Offensive and was finally seized by the Vietnamese with the capture of Saigon in April 1975. The U.S. Embassy was the site of one of the most memorable images of the war: the U.S. ambassador, an American flag clutched to his chest, rushing into a helicopter waiting on the roof, while marine guards pushed back mobs of South Vietnamese who had been assured evacuation. The original building remained untouched after its evacuation in 1975; it was only recently demolished to make way for the consulate. ⊠ *Intersection of Le Duan Blvd. and Mac Din Chi St., District 1.*

❶ **War Remnants Museum** (Nha Trung Bay Toi Ac Chien Tranh Xam You may instinctively shy away from this museum, which is dedicated to publicizing the horrors perpetrated by U.S. armed forces during the Vietnam War. You'll probably come away with mixed feelings about the one-sided propaganda—ashamed of the U.S. actions, angry about the Vietnamese inaccuracies in depicting them, or both. Nevertheless it's worth a visit.

Photographs, the majority of the items on display, accurately depict the horrors and details of the war; their presentations range from poignant to dull to obviously slanted. Along with these photos are gruesome displays documenting the effects of Agent Orange, napalm, and other weapons of mass destruction, as well as a mannequin of a rather dissolute looking American soldier (smoking Marlboros, of course) and a replica of a Con Dao prison cell.

Although the museum has toned down slightly by changing its name from the Museum of American War Crimes to the War Crimes Museum and to, more recently, the War Remnants Museum, its coverage continues to be skewed. Conspicuous in its absence, for instance, is a mention of the division of the country into South Vietnam and North Vietnam throughout the Vietnam War. (The Communist government tends to overlook this division; instead it claims a puppet government backed by American imperialists illegally ruled in the South against will of the people.) There are, however, photos of captured spies who attempted to infiltrate and overthrow the Communist regime.

Also missing is information about some of the horrors perpetrated by the National Liberation Front, particularly the 14,000 people massacred in Hue during the 1968 Tet Offensive. There is little information about civilian protests in Vietnam and in America against U.S. military actions, except for a few photos of antiwar demonstrators. ⊠ *28 Vo Van Tan St., District 3,* ☎ *08/829–5587.* ⊠ *10,000d.* ⊙ *Daily 7:30– 11:45 and 1:30–4:45.*

🖐 ❺ **Zoo and Botanical Garden** (Thao Cam Vien). The fauna here does relatively well, and the flora thrives in its natural subtropical niche. In addition to the lackluster array of live animals, visit the eerie "taxidermy-go-round," where you can ride stuffed animals. As if this were not enough, the gardens have been filled with additional carnival-like attractions—a rather unfortunate addition, as the gardens were one of the first French building projects in Vietnam and once one of the finest such parks in all of Asia. ⊠ *Nguyen Binh Khiem St. at Le Duan Blvd., District 1.* ⊠ *2,000d.* ⊙ *Daily 8–5:30.*

Circling Old Saigon

This tour covers the sights around the periphery of Old Saigon. South of District 1, on the broad waterfront along the Saigon River, is a less palatial section of the old city where the old docks and customs houses used to be. This was also the old banking district, and you can still see the colonial-era Hong Kong and Shanghai Banking Corporation, and Banque d'Indochine buildings. Most museums in this area are housed in the former customs houses and colonial buildings and predominantly contain collections dedicated to famous figures and moments in Vietnamese history. You might want to hire a cyclo to take you to some of the sights in this area.

Numbers in the text correspond to numbers in the margin and on the Ho Chi Minh City map.

A Good Walk or Tour

Start at the **Ho Chi Minh Museum** ⑯, in a converted French customs house on Saigon Port. From the museum follow Nguyen Tat Thanh Street across the bridge over the Ben Nghe Channel. Take your first left after the bridge, following the channel along Ben Chuong Street until you get to Pho Duc Chinh Street. Take a right to get to the **Art Museum** ⑰, in a grand old colonial building. After you've seen it, return to Ben Chuong Street and continue back the way you came until you reach Ton Duc Thang Street and the **Ton Duc Thang Museum** ⑱, dedicated to the first president of North Vietnam and later united Vietnam. From the museum take a cyclo along Ton Duc Thang Street, which turns into Dinh Tien Hoang Street, which leads to Dien Bien Phu Street. Take a left and proceed to No. 20; turn left onto Mai Thi Luu Street and follow it to the lovely **Emperor Jade Pagoda** ⑲. After looking around the pagoda, head right down Nguyen Binh Khiem Street and take another right along Nguyen Thi Minh Khai Street (you must use this route if going by cyclo because other roads are one-way or don't allow cyclos). This will bring you to the top of Dong Khoi Street (☞ *above*). Here you can either walk down the street toward the river or continue in your cyclo.

TIMING

Whether you travel by foot or cyclo, exploring this part of Saigon will probably take a day, including visiting the museums and the pagoda and browsing along Dong Khoi Street. All museums are open daily except Monday.

Sights to See

⑰ Art Museum (Bao Tang My Thuat). The Art Museum was designed in a classic French-Vietnamese architectural style (European-type stucco and Asian designs), once common to those edifices built for rich French and Vietnamese families and officials. But considering its grand colonial setting, this museum—aside from the third floor—is something of a disappointment. The best reason to visit the museum is on the third floor, where you'll find antique statues and other relics of the pre-Vietnamese south. Also here are objects from the ancient Funan and Khmer civilizations as well as some of the best examples of Cham art outside the central highlands. The collection on the first and second floors covers propaganda art of the Soviet socialist-realist variety—soldiers and peasants marching arm in arm to battle. At first it's interesting, but after a while you may start to feel bombarded by the number of images of war, Uncle Ho, and defeated foreign armies. ✉ *97A Pho Duc Chinh St., District 1,* ☎ *08/822–2577.* ☞ *10,000d.* ☉ *Tues.–Sun. 7:30–11:30 and 1:30–4.*

★ ⑲ Emperor Jade Pagoda (Chua Ngoc Hoang or Phuoc Hai Tu). Also known as the Tortoise Pagoda, this structure—the finest Chinese pagoda in Saigon—was built by the Cantonese community in 1909. A mixture of Taoist, Buddhist, and ethnic myths provides the sources for the pagoda's multitude of statues and carvings—everything from the *King of Hell* to a *Buddha of the Future.* Slowly strolling around the interior to view them may be preferable to attempting to decipher the significance of each of the numerous, distinct deities. Take a moment to note the main altar, the side panel's depiction of hell, and in the side room the miniature female figures who represent the range of human qualities. ✉ *73 Mai Thi Luu St., District 3.* ☞ *Free.*

⑯ Ho Chi Minh Museum (Khu Luu Niem Bac Ho). The building itself, nicknamed the "Dragon House" (Nha Rong) for its architectural design, which meshes Vietnamese and French styles, is actually far more interesting than most of the displays inside "Uncle Ho's Museum." It was constructed in 1863 as the original French customs house; any individuals coming to colonial Saigon would have had to pass through the building once they docked at the port. Ho Chi Minh (1890–1969) passed through here in 1911 on the way to his 30-year sojourn around Europe and America. Inside are some of his personal belongings, including his journals, fragments of his clothing, and his rubber sandals. Ho Chi Minh was an ascetic type of guy, known for only wearing sandals made from tires; these are now scattered at museums around the country (☞ Close-Up box: Meet Uncle Ho *in* Chapter 2, for more information on Ho Chi Minh's life). ✉ *On Saigon Port at 1 Nguyen Tat Thanh St., by quayside on Ben Nghe Channel at far end of Ham Nghi Blvd., District 4,* ☎ *08/829–5740.* ☞ *10,000d.* ☉ *Tues.–Sun. 8:30–11:30 and 1:30–4.*

⑱ Ton Duc Thang Museum (Bao Tang Ton Duc Thang). This unremarkable museum celebrates the life and times of President Ton Duc Thang (1888–1980), who succeeded Ho Chi Minh as head of North and later unified Vietnam after Ho Chi Minh's death in 1969. Inside are artifacts that Ton Duc Thang used in everyday life as well as photos of him taken during his incarceration by the French on Paulo Condor (now Con Dao Island) and propaganda pictures of him exhorting the people of Vietnam to fight the French and Americans. Housed in a characterless Soviet-era building on the waterfront by the Vietnamese naval barracks, this museum is unremarkable compared to the other museums in the city. ✉ *5 Ton Duc Thang St., District 1,* ☎ *08/829–46* ☞ *Free.* ☉ *Tues.–Sun. 8:30–11:30 and 2–7.*

Cholon (District 5)

Southwest of central Saigon is Cholon, a Chinese sister city, otherwise known as District 5. Cholon was and still is the center of Chinese culture in Vietnam and a commercial mecca. The French supported the Chinese in Vietnam because of their success in commerce and their apolitical outlook, seldom supporting Vietnamese nationalist struggles. The Communists, on the other hand, saw Cholon as a bastion of capitalism, and the area suffered greatly after 1975. Later, in 1979, during the war between Vietnam and China, Cholon was again targeted since it was considered a potential center of fifth columnists (pro-Chinese agitators). Many of the first boat people to flee Vietnam were Chinese-Vietnamese from Cholon. (Now, after having made money in Australia, Canada, and the United States, many have returned to Saigon and are among the city's wealthiest residents.)

Negotiate a price of about 55,000d with a cyclo driver to take you on a tour of the pagodas concentrated around Nguyen Trai Street and Tran Hung Dao Boulevard in Cholon. Bright blue, yellow, red, orange, and gold cover the pagodas in a dazzling display that would put mating peacocks to shame. Pagodas are seldom shut to the public, and most monks begin their prayers early in the morning, so you are generally welcome to enter a pagoda at any time of day. There are no admission fees, but it is traditional to put a donation of about 10,000d or so in the box at the altar in front of Buddha. Monks never hassle you for money, but they do look a little upset if you don't donate. When you've seen enough (the pagodas may start to look the same after a while), alert your guide or cyclo driver so you won't have to see every single one in the area.

Spend the rest of the day exploring Cholon's streets, markets, shophouses (stores that double as the owners' homes), and restaurants, with their distinctive Chinese appeal. Walk down the hundreds of small side streets, where the neighborhood is at its most colorful. And be sure to enter one of the many traditional medicine shops, which sell everything from herbal remedies being packaged for export to animals' hoofs, antlers, and tails to sea horses and snake wine. What makes Cholon so special are the sights and sounds of its streets.

Numbers in the text correspond to numbers in the margin and on the Cholon map.

A Good Walk

Begin at the bustling **Binh Tay Market** ⑳, on Phan Van Khoe Street. Take a left out of the market and walk along Phan Van Khoe Street until you get to Phung Hung Street; take a left and follow it until you reach the **Ong Bon Pagoda** ㉑, where you can pay your respects to the guardian of happiness and virtue. Exiting the pagoda, take Hai Thuong Lan Ong Boulevard east until you reach the old colonial **Post Office** ㉒. Head north on Chau Van Liem Boulevard to Tran Hung Dao Boulevard, the center of Cholon, with its street markets and old, small shophouses (and some newer, taller ones).

Keep walking straight ahead until you reach Nguyen Trai Street; take a right to get to Cholon's pagoda district. Continue on Chau Van Liem Boulevard until you come to small Lao Tu Street, on your right, and the **Quan Am Pagoda** ㉓, which is known for its elaborately decorated scenes. Walk south down Luong Nhu Hoc Street to the **Ha Chuong Hoi Quan Pagoda** ㉔, at No. 802, one of the many temples devoted to the goddess of the sea. Take a left on Nguyen Trai Street and walk along until you come to the **Thien Hau Pagoda** ㉕, at No. 710, where sailors used to come before they went out to sea. Farther along, past the in-

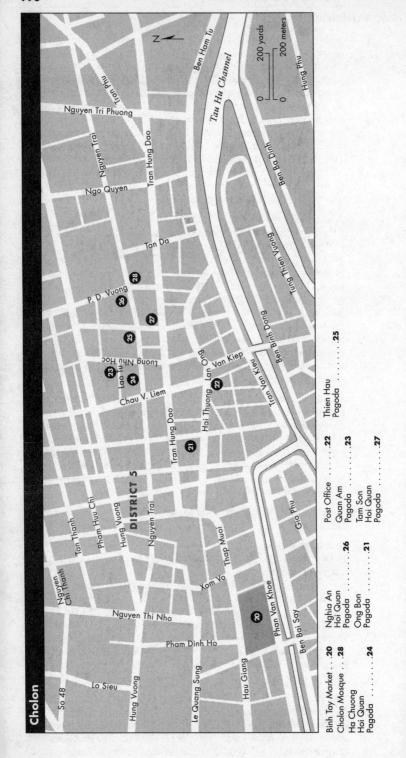

Cholon

Ben Ham Tu

Tau Hu Channel

Hung Phu

200 yards

200 meters

Nguyen Tri Phuong

Tran Phu

Ben Ba Dinh

Nguyen Trai

Tran Hung Dao

Ngo Quyen

Tan Da

Tung Thien Vuong

P. D. Vuong

Luong Nhu Hoc

Lao Tu

Chau V. Liem

Lan Ong

Van Kiep

Ben Binh Dong

Hai Thuong Lan Ong

Tran Van Kieu

Tran Hung Dao

Tan Thanh

Pham Huu Chi

Hung Vuong

Nguyen Trai

DISTRICT 5

Xom Vo

Thap Muoi

Gia Phu

Nguyen Chi Thanh

Nguyen Thi Nho

Pham Dinh Ho

Phan Van Khoe

Ben Bai Say

So 48

Lo Sieu

Hung Vuong

Le Quang Sung

Hau Giang

Binh Tay Market . . . **20**
Cholon Mosque . . .**28**
Ha Chuong
Hoi Quan
Pagoda **24**

Nghia An
Hoi Quan
Pagoda **26**
Ong Bon
Pagoda **21**

Post Office **22**
Quan Am
Pagoda **23**
Tam Son
Hoi Quan
Pagoda **27**

Thien Hau
Pagoda **25**

tersection of Trieu Quang Phu Street, on the left at No. 678 is the **Nghia An Hoi Quan Pagoda** ㉖, famous for its detailed woodwork, and on the other side of the street, at No. 118, is the **Tam Son Hoi Quan Pagoda** ㉗, dedicated to the goddess of fertility. Keep going straight on Nguyen Trai Street, past the intersection of Ly Thuong Kiet Boulevard, until you reach the **Cholon Mosque** ㉘, used by Saigon's Muslim community. Go back to Ly Thuong Kiet Boulevard and turn right onto Tran Hung Dao Boulevard. Take this to Luong Nhu Hoc Street, turn left, and you'll be back at the post office.

TIMING

Depending on how interested you are in pagodas, this walk could take up to three or four hours. If you have an interest in Chinese medicine, be sure to take time to explore the many stores along the small back streets surrounding the Binh Tay Market.

Sights to See

㉕ Binh Tay Market (Cho Binh Tay). Cholon's main market is in a colonial-era, Chinese-style building. The street outside is a frenzy of activity; inside can be a little calmer, although you have to wend your way through very narrow aisles. A variety of items are sold, including dried shrimp and fruit, aluminum kitchenware, baskets, plastic goods, barrettes, straw hats, and food. ⊠ *On Hau Giang Blvd., District 6.* ☉ *Daily, 5 AM–8 PM; hrs vary.*

㉘ Cholon Mosque. Built in 1932 by Tamil Muslims, the Cholon Mosque now serves Saigon's Indonesian and Malaysian Muslim community. Notice the difference in architectural styles between mosques and pagodas. Mosques have simpler domes and spires as compared to the exuberant ornamentation and bright colors that characterize pagodas. Most pagodas are decorated with dragons, lions, a wide variety of Buddhas, and other representations of spirits and deities, whereas mosques are generally far more restrained. In the Islamic tradition it is strictly forbidden to represent God or any animal or human. Hence decoration takes the form of abstract images and calligraphy. ⊠ *641 Nguyen Trai St., at Ly Thuong Kiet Blvd., District 5.*

㉔ Ha Chuong Hoi Quan Pagoda. Like many pagodas built by Fujian congregations, this one is dedicated to Thien Hau, goddess of the sea and protector of fisherfolk and sailors. It has four stone pillars encircled by painted dragons; these were brought from China when the pagoda was constructed in the 19th century. Also note the scenes in ceramic relief on the roof and the murals next to the main altar. ⊠ *802 Nguyen Trai St., District 5.*

㉖ Nghia An Hoi Quan Pagoda. Built by the Chaozhou Chinese congregation in 1872, this pagoda is worth seeing for its elaborate woodwork. There are intricately carved wooden boats and a large figure of the deified Chinese general Quan Cong's sacred red horse, as well as representations of Quan Cong himself with two guardians. A festival dedicated to Quan Cong is held every year on the 13th of the first lunar month. ⊠ *678 Nguyen Trai St., District 5.*

★ **㉑ Ong Bon Pagoda** (Chua Ong Bon or Nhi Phu Hoi Quan). Many deities are represented at this pagoda, but the main attraction is Ong Bon himself, the guardian of happiness and virtue. Ong Bong is also responsible for wealth, so people bring fake paper money to burn in the pagoda's furnace in his honor, hoping the year ahead will bring financial rewards to their families. The centerpiece of the pagoda is an elaborately carved wood and gold altar and a finely crafted statue of Ong Bon. Look for the intricately painted murals of lions, tigers, and dragons. ✉ *264 Hai Thuong Lan Ong Blvd. (parallel to Tran Hung Dao Blvd.), at Phung Hung St., District 5.*

㉒ **Post Office.** This modernist building was constructed by the French in the 1920s. ✉ *Intersection of Hai Thuong Lan Ong Blvd. and Chau Van Liem Blvd., District 5.* ☉ *Daily 7:30–7:30.*

㉓ **Quan Am Pagoda.** Dating from 1816, this pagoda was built by a congregation of Fujian refugees from China. It is notable for its busy array of scenes in lacquer, ceramic, gold, and wood illustrating traditional Chinese stories. Many legendary and divine beings, some dressed in elaborately embroidered robes, are portrayed, as are some simple rural scenes representing the birthplaces of the original members of the congregation. Be prepared for a stifling cloud of incense when you enter—this is still one of Cholon's most active pagodas. ✉ *12 Lao Tu St. (parallel to Hung Vuong Blvd. and Nguyen Trai St.), District 5.*

㉗ **Tam Son Hoi Quan Pagoda** (Chua Ba Chua). The Chinese Fujian congregation built this lavishly decorated pagoda dedicated to Me Sanh, the goddess of fertility, in the 19th century. Women—and some men—pray to the goddess to bring them children. Many other deities are represented here as well: Thien Hau, the goddess of the sea and protector of fisherfolk and sailors; Ong Bon, the guardian of happiness and virtue; and Quan Cong, the deified general, depicted with a long beard and his sacred red horse. ✉ *118 Trieu Quang Phuc St., District 5.*

㉕ **Thien Hau Pagoda** (Chua Ba). Built by the Cantonese congregation at the beginning of the 19th century, the pagoda is dedicated to Thien Hau, the goddess of the sea and protector of fisherfolk and sailors. Sailors used to come here to be blessed. On the main dais are three statues of the goddess, each flanked by two guardians. Note also the figure of Long Mau, guardian of mothers and babies. The turtles living on the grounds are considered sacred animals and are a symbol of longevity. ✉ *710 Nguyen Trai St., District 5.*

DINING

Central Saigon (Districts 1 and 3)

American/Casual

$$ ✕ **Café Mogambo.** A quirky restaurant-cum-burger-bar with an African theme, Mogambo is run by an American expat and his Vietnamese wife. The restaurant is a favorite for returning Vietnam War veterans and other Americans homesick for a good, inexpensive home-style meal. ✉ *20 Thi Sach St., District 1,* ☎ *08/825–1311. MC, V.*

Eclectic

$$ ✕ **Sapa.** This airy Swiss-run bar and restaurant is best known for its breakfasts, which include fine bacon and eggs and hash browns. The Vietnamese-style chicken curry is also delicious. ✉ *26 Thai Van Lung St., District 1,* ☎ *08/829–5754. No credit cards.*

French

$$$$ ✕ **Le Camargue.** One of the most romantic and tastefully done restau-
★   rants in Saigon, the French-influenced Le Camargue is an exciting culinary forum. The cuisine is a mix of East and West—with a good wine list to go along—and is very good, even by other cities' standards. Dine on the elegant, plant-filled terrace of a restored villa or indoors in the warmly lighted dining rooms. Sample dishes include pan-roasted sea bass on a bed of wasabi mashed potatoes, and tamarind-glazed crab cake; the menu changes depending on what's available. The duck is also excellent (Vietnam is the number two exporter of ducks in the

Ho Chi Minh City Dining

'A' The Russian
Restaurant **1**

...ugustin **20**

...i Bi **7**

...lue Ginger **22**

...odhi Tree II **23**

...afé Mogambo . . .**11**

...e Camargue **14**

...e Caprice **10**

...hao Thai **6**

La Fourchette **18**

Legros **8**

Lemongrass **21**

Liberty **16**

Marine Club
Restaurant **5**

May Ngan
Phuong **3**

Pho Hoa **4**

Restaurant 13 . . . .**17**

Ristorante
Pendalesco **2**

Sakura **15**

Sapa **13**

Sawaddee **9, 25**

Sunshine
Restaurant **24**

Thi Sac Street
Cafés **12**

Vietnam House . . .**19**

world). A small, popular bar and nightclub were recently added downstairs. ⊠ *16 Cao Ba Quat St., District 1,* ☎ *08/823–3148. Reservations essential. AE, DC, MC, V. No lunch.*

$$$$ ✕ **Le Caprice.** Stodgy but run like a Swiss timepiece, this landmark provides Saigon's expat elite with unoriginal but fine French cuisine, passé but well-maintained hotel decor, and a beautiful view of the Saigon River. If you don't actually get around to eating here, it's worth stopping by just to have a drink and take in the view. ⊠ *Landmark Bldg., 15th floor, 5B Ton Duc Thang St., District 1,* ☎ *08/822–8337. AE, DC, MC, V.*

$$$ ✕ **Augustin.** Small, intimate, and filled with comfortably solo expats reading the newspaper at the bar, Augustin serves tasty French-bistro food to a predominantly international crowd. ⊠ *10 Nguyen Thiep St., District 1,* ☎ *08/829–2941. AE, DC, MC, V. No lunch Sun.*

$$$ ✕ **Bi Bi.** An excellent new addition to the city's French culinary set, Bi Bi is the type of intimate establishment you'd expect to find on a Parisian backstreet. This is more than just a restaurant or café: people come here to eat, gossip, play cards, drink pastis, and snack on oysters flown in each day from Brittany. The steak, served with French fries, is a popular dish here. ⊠ *8A/8D2 Thai Van Lung St., District 1,* ☎ *08/829–2747. AE, DC, MC, V.*

$$ ✕ **La Fourchette.** A small and extremely intimate affair, La Fourchette, with only six tables, is more a café than a restaurant. The cuisine is good, not great, but its friendly atmosphere more than compensates. ⊠ *9 Ngo Duc Khe St., District 1,* ☎ *08/829–8143. AE, DC, MC, V.*

$$ ✕ **Legros.** Outstanding, authentic French cuisine is cooked by a French chef who may offer you a liqueur on the house if you rave enough about his food. In fact, this place is so French that the menu is not in Vietnamese or English. However, this small show of nationalism is more than compensated for by the cuisine, which is as fine as any found in France. ⊠ *267–269 Le Thanh Ton St., District 1,* ☎ *08/822–8273. MC, V. No lunch Sun.*

Indian

$ ✕ **Sunshine Restaurant.** The outdoor seating in the heart of Saigon's budget travelers' district and the very cheap and delicious Indian fare make up for the poor service. ⊠ *236 De Tham St., District 1,* ☎ *08/ 835–6154. No credit cards.*

Italian

$$$ ✕ **Ristorante Pendalesco.** Most dishes here are Italian, but the restaurant also caters to other cuisines for the international crowd. This is slightly off the beaten path in District 3, but its fine cuisine and intimate atmosphere are always popular, so it's a good idea to book ahead. ⊠ *142B Vo Thi Sau St., District 3,* ☎ *08/820–3552. AE, DC, MC, V.*

Japanese

$$$$ ✕ **Sakura.** This has fast become the most popular sushi bar in town. With all the ingredients flown in fresh every day, Sakura is expensive by local standards, but worth it nonetheless. ⊠ *40 Mac Thi Boi St., District 1,* ☎ *08/822–2182. AE, DC, MC, V.*

Pizza

$$$ ✕ **Marine Club Restaurant.** Although more of a happening nightspot than a food mecca, the Marine Club has the only wood-burning pizza oven in Saigon. Expats gather here for the great piano bar and nautical paraphernalia and the hip and friendly management. ⊠ *17A4 Le Thanh Ton St., District 1,* ☎ *08/829–2249. AE, DC, MC, V.*

Russian

$$ ✕ **'A' The Russian Restaurant.** This is Saigon's premier Russian establishment, catering to the remaining members of the once-mighty Rus sian community, left behind after the collapse of the Soviet Union. Off the main road in an old villa complex, the restaurant has surprisingly good food—Siberian *pelmeni* (dumplings), kebabs from Uzbekistan, beef Stroganoff, and black and white caviar with black bread—at very reasonable prices. Also served are sweet Russian champagne and endless amounts of vodka. The frozen lemon vodkas are particularly good, but be sure to order them in advance. If you're with a group (from 3 to 15), you can hire out one of the two theme rooms for the night: one is designed like a Siberian hunting lodge, replete with moose heads and balalaikas; the other is like an aristocratic dining hall, modeled on 19th-century St. Petersburg. Almost everyone who dines here has a loud, raucous, and often drunken evening. ⊠ *361/8 Nguyen Dinh Chieu St., District 3,* ☎ *08/835–9190. MC, V.*

Thai

$$–$$$$ ✕ **Chao Thai.** This sensational restaurant serves the finest Thai food in the city. The cuisine is equal to the setting: a mock Thai longhouse decorated with *apsara* dancers and wood carvings. If you love spicy Thai food you won't be disappointed, and if you don't, you can request milder dishes. ⊠ *16 Tai Van Lung St., District 1,* ☎ *08/824– 1457. AE, MC, V.*

$ ✕ **Sawaddee.** Saigon has two Sawaddee locations, both of which are well run and have simple, pleasant decor and authentic Thai dishes at good prices. ⊠ *29B Don Dat St., District 1,* ☎ *08/832–2494;* ⊠ *252 De Tham St., District 1,* ☎ *08/822–1402. No credit cards.*

Vegetarian

¢ ✕ **Bodhi Tree II.** Bodhi serves delectable vegetarian delights in a quaint alley just off Pham Ngu Lao Street, next door to another unrelated vegetarian restaurant. The eggplant sautéed with garlic, the vegetable curry, and the braised tofu in a clay pot are superb. Don't miss out on the fresh-fruit shakes, which are like meals in themselves. ⊠ *175 Pham Ngu Lao St., District 1,* ☎ *08/839–1545. No credit cards.*

Vietnamese

$$$ ✕ **Blue Ginger.** Dine on excellent Vietnamese cuisine in an elegant set-
★ ting with an international clientele. At night traditional music shows are performed at 7:30. ⊠ *37 Nam Ky Khoi Nghia St., District 1,* ☎ *08/829–8676. AE, DC, MC, V.*

$$$ ✕ **Lemongrass.** An expat and tourist favorite, Lemongrass serves ex-
★ cellent Vietnamese food in a French-bistro atmosphere. Almost everything on the short menu is delicious, but the spicy mixed-seafood soup deserves special praise. ⊠ *4 Nguyen Thiep St., District 1,* ☎ *08/822– 0496. AE, DC, MC, V. No lunch.*

$$$ ✕ **Liberty.** This spot combines a great Vietnamese menu (pricier Chinese and Western menus are also available) with a kind of *Star Search* live-entertainment ambience. It's definitely worth a visit, if only because of how kitschy it is. ⊠ *80 Dong Khoi St., District 1,* ☎ *08/829–9820. AE, DC, MC, V.*

$$$ ✕ **Vietnam House.** Very popular with travelers and expats, Vietnam House serves a wide selection of hearty noodle dishes and other Vietnamese standards in a glossy Eurasian-style dining room. Performances of live traditional music are held every night upstairs. ⊠ *93 Dong Khoi St., District 1,* ☎ *08/829–1623. MC, V.*

$ ✕ **Restaurant 13.** This local and expat hangout, on a quiet road just off Dong Khoi Street, serves delicious traditional food in a no-nonsense setting. ⊠ *11–17 Ngo Duc Ke St., District 1,* ☎ *08/829–1417. No credit cards.*

$ ✕ **Thi Sac Street Cafés.** Thi Sac Street is a must if you love seafood: here you can get great freshwater and saltwater fish. From 5 PM onward the top part of Thi Sac Street where it borders Le Thanh Ton Street is literally impassable with street restaurants. Best bets are the steamboat (boiling broth in which seafood is cooked at your table), freshwater crabs, and colossal tiger prawns. On a balmy Saigon evening, with the cacophony of street life carrying on all around, eating here can be a truly memorable experience. ⊠ *Thi Sac St., District 1.*

¢   ✕ **May Ngan Phuong.** This very local, hole-in-the-wall Vietnamese eatery has delicious food and traditional live music performances. Be prepared to point at whatever looks good at the next table, or bring a phrase book, as this place doesn't see many foreigners. ⊠ *205 Nguyen Van Thu Si St., District 3, ☎ 08/835–7322. No credit cards.*

¢   ✕ **Pho Hoa.** If you're not quite game for the sidewalk-food-stall eating experience, this open-air noodle kitchen is the next best thing. The homemade noodles and the vegetable and meat stocks are fresh and delicious. Just say "chicken," "beef," or "pork," or point to whatever looks good at the next table. ⊠ *260C Pasteur St., District 3, ☎ 08/ 829–7943. No credit cards.*

LODGING

Central Saigon (Districts 1 and 3)

$$$$ 🏨 **Hotel Continental.** If it's history you're after, stay at the French-colo-
★   nial-style Continental. Graham Greene's classic *The Quiet American* was set here; it was also once the most sought-after lunch spot in colonial Saigon and the meeting place of journalists and diplomats during the Vietnam War. The hotel has a unique outdoor courtyard garden and dining area that dates from the late 19th century. The courtyard is a superb place to while away a couple of hours with a beer below the frangipani trees, in which ong birds swing in cages hung on the branches. However, the Continental is only a shadow of its former self—the decor and finishing lack the finesse and expert renovations of the hotel's international counterparts. The bar, although a little dead, features a very fine cellist. Rooms facing the street are very noisy; ask for one overlooking the inner courtyard. ⊠ *132–134 Dong Khoi St., District 1, ☎ 08/829–9201, FAX 08/829–9252. 87 rooms. 2 restaurants, lobby lounge, air-conditioning, in-room safes, minibars, no-smoking rooms, refrigerators, room service, dry cleaning, laundry service, concierge, business services, meeting rooms, travel services. AE, DC, MC, V.*

$$$$ 🏨 **New World Hotel Saigon.** The New World's central location—across the street from the Ben Thanh Market—makes it very popular particularly with tour groups and businesspeople. The front foyer can seem somewhat sterile, with its somnolent-looking pianist, but if you're jet-lagged or just back from an exhausting day out at Cu Chi, it can seem like heaven. The Chinese restaurant is excellent, but the Western buffet is lackluster. ⊠ *76 Le Lai St., District 1, ☎ 08/822–8888, FAX 08/823–0710. 541 rooms. 3 restaurants, bar, lobby lounge, air-conditioning, in-room safes, minibars, no-smoking floor, refrigerators, room service, pool, sauna, massage, driving range, tennis court, exercise room, motorbikes, nightclub, piano, baby-sitting, dry cleaning, laundry service, concierge, business services, meeting rooms, travel services, airport shuttle, car rental. AE, DC, MC, V.*

$$$$ 🏨 **Riverside Renaissance.** For the tired traveler, drinking a cocktail while
★   watching the bustle of the waterfront is a good way to relax. This new chain hotel has a lovely location overlooking the river. The Riverside Renaissance offers all the comforts you'd expect of an international hotel, but it lacks the colonial flair of some of the older hotels in the city. ⊠ *8–10 Ton Duc Thang St., District 1, ☎ 08/822–0033, FAX 08/ 823–5666. 349 rooms. Restaurant, bar, lobby lounge, air-conditio*

Ho Chi Minh City Lodging

PHU NUAN DISTRICT

DISTRICT 3

DISTRICT 1

DISTRICT 4

DISTRICT 5 (CHOLON)

Zoo and Botanical Gardens

Saigon River

Central Post Office

Notre Dame

Reunification Palace

Hôtel de Ville

Municipal Theater

Cong Vien Van Hoa Park

Ben Nghe Channel

Ben Chuong Channel

400 yards

400 meters

rc En Ciel otel **25**

sian Hotel **6**

am Minihotel **22**

ong Khanh otel **24**

arden Plaza otel **1**

and Hotel **13**

tel Caravelle

lta **10**

Hotel Continental **9**

Hotel Equatorial . . **26**

Hotel Majestic . . . **16**

Kimdo International Hotel **18**

Mercury Hotel . . **23**

Mogambo Guest House **8**

Mondial Hotel **12**

New World Hotel Saigon **21**

Norfolk Hotel **20**

Omni Saigon Hotel **2**

Palace Hotel **14**

Phuong Duong Hotel **4**

Prince Hotel **27**

Rex Hotel **19**

Riverside Renaissance **17**

Saigon Hotel **11**

Saigon Prince Hotel **15**

Sofitel Plaza **5**

Sol Chancery Saigon **3**

Spring Hotel **7**

ing, in-room safes, minibars, no-smoking rooms, refrigerators, room service, massage, sauna, exercise room, dry cleaning, concierge, business services, meeting rooms, travel services. AE, DC, MC, V.

$$$$ 🏨 **Saigon Prince Hotel.** Entering the Saigon Prince is like stepping out
★ of Vietnam—for better or worse. Rooms are more spacious and have higher ceilings and finer finishing touches than many other hotels in the city. But, unfortunately, it has fewer facilities. The staff is competent and pleasant, and the lobby bar is a nice spot for a calm mid-afternoon break. ⊠ *63 Nguyen Hue Blvd., District 1,* ☎ *08/822–2999,* FAX *08/824–1888. 203 rooms. Dining room, lobby lounge, sushi bar, air-conditioning, in-room safes, minibars, no-smoking rooms, refrigerators, room service, hot tub, massage, sauna, steam room, exercise room, nightclub, dry cleaning, laundry service, concierge, business services, meeting rooms, travel services. AE, DC, MC, V.*

$$$$ 🏨 **Sofitel Plaza.** A high-ceilinged, spacious lobby leads to the first
★ floor and the Aromasia, a restaurant serving Western and Asian cuisine. The Sunday brunches are the best value in the city. There's also a pool bar here. ⊠ *17 Le Duan Blvd., District 1,* ☎ *08/824–1555; 08/824–1666 in the U.S.,* FAX *08/823–2333. 280 rooms, 12 suites. 3 restaurants, 2 bars, air-conditioning, pool, massage, sauna, health club, laundry service, business services, meeting rooms. AE, MC, V.*

$$–$$$ 🏨 **Hotel Caravelle Delta.** The recently restored and expanded Caravelle,
★ where many foreign correspondents stayed during the Vietnam War, may offer the best value of all the upscale hotels in town. Centrally located in the bustling heart of the city, it has luxurious, well-appointed rooms with spectacular views. The ninth-floor Saigon Saigon bar is a great place to unwind. An excellent buffet of Asian and Western food is served for lunch and dinner in the Port Orient Restaurant. ⊠ *19 Lam Son Square, District 1,* ☎ *08/823–4999,* FAX *08/824–3999. 335 rooms. 2 restaurants, bar, café, in-room data ports, in-room safes, in-room VCRs, minibars, pool, massage, sauna, exercise room, concierge, business services, meeting rooms. AE, DC, MC, V.*

$$$ 🏨 **Hotel Majestic.** The Majestic, on the waterfront overlooking the Saigon
★ River, is one of Vietnam's truly great colonial hotels. The hotel lacks the service expertise of the international chains, but its charm and location more than make up for that. Be sure to have a gin and tonic in the rooftop breeze bar overlooking the river. Rooms, with high ceilings and the original wooden trim, strike a delicate balance between airy and intimate. ⊠ *1 Dong Khoi St., District 1,* ☎ *08/829–5514,* FAX *08/829–5510. 122 rooms. 2 restaurants, 2 bars, lobby lounge, outdoor café, air-conditioning, in-room safes, minibars, no-smoking rooms, refrigerators, room service, pool, massage, sauna, exercise room, piano, dry cleaning, laundry service, concierge, business services, meeting rooms, travel services. AE, DC, MC, V.*

$$$ 🏨 **Kimdo International Hotel.** The spacious rooms at the elegant and central Kimdo have high ceilings and exquisite French and Chinese antique reproductions that provide a warmth lacking in many modern luxury hotels. The staff seems somewhat inexperienced but is eager to please. ⊠ *133 Nguyen Hue St., District 1,* ☎ *08/822–5914,* FAX *08/822–591 135 rooms. Dining room, lobby lounge, outdoor café, air-conditioning, in-room safes, minibars, no-smoking rooms, refrigerators, room service, massage, exercise room, nightclub, dry cleaning, laundry service, concierge, business services, meeting rooms, travel services. AE, DC, MC, V.*

$$$ 🏨 **Mercury Hotel.** This modern hotel combines warmth and elegance with modern conveniences. Rooms are reasonably sized and are neatly decorated in a luxurious yet utilitarian and unoriginal style. The hotel is closer to the budget traveler's haven—Pham Ngu Lao Street—than to the congregation of upscale hotels and restaurants around Le

and Nguyen Hue boulevards. ✉ *79 Tran Hung Dao Blvd., District 1,* ☎ *08/824–2525,* FAX *08/822–3312. 104 rooms. 2 restaurants, bar, lobby lounge, air-conditioning, in-room safes, minibars, no-smoking rooms, refrigerators, room service, massage, health club, baby-sitting, dry cleaning, laundry service, business services, meeting rooms, travel services. AE, DC, MC, V.*

$$$ 🏨 **Rex Hotel.** The Rex stands as a monument to Saigon's recent history. Originally a French garage, it later became a hotel and then the base for American operations during the Vietnam War. Its conference room was the scene of the daily press briefings to journalists, or "five o'clock follies," as they were called. In 1976 the announcement by the former North Vietnam of the unification with South Vietnam was announced in the same room. Today the hotel is filled with kitsch: stuffed animals, statues, and lamp shades shaped like crowns (the Rex's symbol). Even if you don't stay here, go up to the rooftop bar, which is an ideal setting to take in the view of downtown and have a drink amid statues, songbirds, topiary animals, and decorative lights. You're best off skipping the restaurants. ✉ *141 Nguyen Hue Blvd., District 1,* ☎ *08/829–2185,* FAX *08/829–6536. 207 rooms. 2 restaurants, lobby lounge, air-conditioning, in-room safes, minibars, no-smoking rooms, refrigerators, room service, pool, beauty salon, massage, sauna, steam room, nightclub, dry cleaning, laundry service, concierge, business services, travel services. AE, DC, MC, V.*

$$$ 🏨 **Sol Chancery Saigon.** This all-suites hotel run by Grupo Sol of Spain has a kind of nouveau-French facade and many amenities. Rooms, although comfortable and neat, are afflicted with low ceilings and pastel, no-wood, antiseptic decor. It's not too far from the War Remnants Museum and other points of interest. ✉ *196 Nguyen Thi Minh Khai St., District 3,* ☎ *08/829–9152,* FAX *08/825–1464. 96 suites. Restaurant, lobby lounge, air-conditioning, in-room safes, minibars, no-smoking rooms, refrigerators, room service, massage, sauna, exercise room, dry cleaning, laundry service, concierge, business services, meeting rooms, travel services. AE, DC, MC, V.*

$$ 🏨 **Asian Hotel.** In the midst of the Dong Khoi shopping district, this no-frills hotel has small but tidy rooms. ✉ *146–150 Dong Khoi St., District 1,* ☎ *08/829–6979,* FAX *08/829–7433. 47 rooms. Bar, dining room, lobby lounge, air-conditioning, in-room safes, minibars, room service, dry cleaning, laundry service, business services, travel services. AE, DC, MC, V.*

$$ 🏨 **Grand Hotel.** Although more modest than the Majestic or the Continental hotels, this pleasant old colonial establishment evokes a bygone era of Francophone Saigon in the heart of the old rue Catinat. Unfortunately, like the other colonial-era hotels here, the Grand is state owned and suffers accordingly compared to some of the international chains. The rooms are light and airy, with real character. But the service is indifferent, and the dining room should be avoided. Still, as locations go, this is as central as you can get. ✉ *8 Dong Khoi St., District 1,* ☎ *08/823–0163,* FAX *08/823–5781. 135 rooms. Dining room, air-conditioning, in-room safes, massage, health club, laundry service, business services. AE, DC, MC, V.*

$$ 🏨 **Mondial Hotel.** The renovated Mondial has small, tidy standard rooms. In the lobby are various large bas-relief wooden sculptures of dragons and mythical Vietnamese warriors. The hotel's Skyview restaurant has traditional Vietnamese dancing and music nightly. ✉ *109 Dong Khoi St., District 1,* ☎ *08/829–6291,* FAX *08/829–6273. 40 rooms. Restaurant, lobby lounge, air-conditioning, in-room safes, room service, nightclub, dry cleaning, laundry service, travel services. AE, DC, MC, V.*

$$ 🏨 **Norfolk Hotel.** This superslick establishment is conveniently situated between the Ben Tranh Market and the Hôtel de Ville (Ho Chi

Minh City People's Committee) in central Saigon. White and chrome dominate, making it look like a cross between a cruise ship and a space ship. Rooms are impeccable and comfortable, if small and simple. Facilities are oriented primarily to businesspeople; there is even a resident interpreter. ⊠ *117 Le Thanh Ton St., District 1,* ☎ *08/829–5368,* FAX *08/829–3415. 109 rooms. Restaurant, bar, sports bar, lobby lounge, air-conditioning, in-room safes, minibars, massage, sauna, health club, baby-sitting, dry cleaning, laundry service, business services, meeting rooms, travel services. AE, DC, MC, V.*

$$ 🏨 **Palace Hotel.** The views of central Saigon are excellent from this pleasant but standard no-frills Vietnamese hotel in the center of town. One drawback is the slightly unfriendly front-desk staff, but a plus is the breakfast included in the room rate. ⊠ *56–66 Nguyen Hue Blvd., District 1,* ☎ *08/829–2860,* FAX *08/824–4230. 130 rooms. Restaurant, lobby lounge, outdoor café, air-conditioning, in-room safes, minibars, room service, pool, beauty salon, massage, sauna, steam room, nightclub, dry cleaning, laundry service, business services, meeting rooms, travel services, airport shuttle. AE, DC, MC, V.*

$$ 🏨 **Saigon Hotel.** At the Saigon you can get a clean room overlooking the center of the city. The hotel betrays a '60s aesthetic despite modern black-lacquer furniture accents. ⊠ *41–47 Dong Du St., District 1,* ☎ *08/824–4982,* FAX *08/829–1466. 103 rooms. Restaurant, café, lobby lounge, air-conditioning, in-room safes, minibars, room service, nightclub, dry cleaning, laundry service, business services, meeting rooms, airport shuttle. AE, DC, MC, V.*

$ 🏨 **Cam Minihotel.** In a cluster of family-run minihotels, in an alley be-
★   tween Pham Ngu Lao and Bu Vien streets, this place stands out because it's run with care compared to other budget hotels. It has a 24-hour gate post; mandatory shoe removal at the door; and simple, spotless, and well-maintained rooms. The extended family and friends who run the hotel are very friendly and helpful and speak English. ⊠ *40/31 Bui Vien St., District 1,* ☎ *08/832–4622. 12 rooms. Air-conditioning, fans, refrigerators. No credit cards.*

$ 🏨 **Mogambo Guest House.** This minihotel above the restaurant of the same name (☞ *Dining, above*) is run by an American and is very popular with—guess who?—Americans. Like most of these small establishments, the Mogambo is unexceptional looking, but has clean rooms that are suitable for a good night's sleep. ⊠ *20 Thi Sach St., District 1,* ☎ *08/825–1311. 10 rooms. Restaurant, air-conditioning. MC, V.*

$ 🏨 **Phuong Duong Hotel.** Another one of the city's minihotels, this one too, is bare bones but comfortable and clean. ⊠ *55B Nguyen Van Thu St., District 1,* ☎ *08/822–2437,* FAX *08/822–1346. 10 rooms. Restaurant, air-conditioning. MC, V.*

$ 🏨 **Spring Hotel.** In the hub of a major dining and nightlife area in District 1, this cozy, family-run minihotel has squeaky-clean rooms with new moldings and fixtures made to look old. Some rooms have nice views of the street below, but the standard ones have no windows at all and are a lot less expensive. ⊠ *44–46 Le Thanh Ton St., District 1,* ☎ *08/829–736... * FAX *08/821–1383. 38 rooms. Bar, dining room, lobby lounge, air-conditioning, in-room safes, room service, travel services. AE, DC, MC, V.*

Cholon (District 5)

$$$$ 🏨 **Hotel Equatorial.** This newer four-star hotel is in an odd location on the edge of Cholon, about 15 minutes from the downtown area. To date, bookings have been somewhat scarce because of this, so the doormen seem to scramble when the sporadic guest arrives through the front entrance. Nonetheless, the hotel is one of the best in town. It also has Vietnam's nicest health club, with Jacuzzis, saunas, a v...

good gym, and a half-Olympic-size swimming pool with a poolside lounge area. In addition, the hotel has three fine restaurants, one serving Japanese, another Chinese, and a third with an international buffet. ⊠ *242 Tran Binh Trong St., District 5,* ☎ *08/839–7777,* FAX *08/839–0011. 333 rooms. Bar, café, lobby lounge, air-conditioning, minibars, refrigerators, room service, pool, health club, nightclub, piano, dry cleaning, laundry service, business services, meeting rooms, travel services, car rental, free parking. AE, DC, MC, V.*

$$ 🏨 **Arc En Ciel Hotel.** This neon-clad hotel is done up in a mishmash of modern, '60s, and Chinese interior decor, with accommodations on the higher end of utilitarian. But overall it's a good deal—if you're interested in staying in Cholon. The hotel has a pleasant rooftop garden café. ⊠ *52–56 Tan Da St., District 5,* ☎ *08/855–0332,* FAX *08/855–2424. 91 rooms. Restaurant, bar, lobby lounge, outdoor café, air-conditioning, in-room safes, room service, beauty salon, massage, sauna, exercise room, nightclub, dry cleaning, laundry service, concierge, business services, meeting rooms, travel services. AE, DC, MC, V.*

$$ 🏨 **Dong Khanh Hotel.** In the heart of Cholon, the Dong Khanh sees mostly businesspeople from Hong Kong and Taiwan. Although staff members speak little English, they know enough of the language to help you get by. The Chinese decor—wooden furniture with characteristic inlaid lacquerware and wall hangings with designs depicting dragons and landscapes—is bold but elegant. ⊠ *Tran Hung Dao B Blvd., District 5,* ☎ *08/835–2410,* FAX *08/835–2411. 81 rooms. 2 restaurants, bar, café, lobby lounge, air-conditioning, in-room safes, minibars, no-smoking rooms, refrigerators, room service, massage, exercise room, nightclub, dry cleaning, laundry service, business services, meeting rooms, travel services. AE, DC, MC, V.*

$ 🏨 **Prince Hotel.** Not to be confused with the Saigon Prince in District 1, this small-time "royal" lodging in the middle of Chinatown provides charm and efficiency cheaply. Unlike many hotel restaurants, the Prince's dining room actually serves good food. ⊠ *29 Chau Van Liem St., District 5,* ☎ *08/855–6765,* FAX *08/856–1578. 25 rooms. Restaurant, bar, lobby lounge, outdoor café, air-conditioning, in-room safes, minibars, refrigerators, room service, travel services. AE, DC, MC, V.*

Phu Nuan District

Phu Nuan District, in the north part of the city, is a favorite for businesspeople and those looking to stay close to the airport.

$$$$ 🏨 **Garden Plaza Hotel.** Only about 10 minutes from the airport, this international establishment is one of the best. Its sunken lobby and accompanying swimming pool are a departure from the hotel architecture usually seen in Vietnam. In fact, the hotel's style is more Thai or Balinese than Vietnamese. Its location could be a drawback for you (a good 15–20 minutes from downtown Saigon), but it's a boon if you're a businessperson eager to settle into town quickly. ⊠ *309 Nguyen Van Troi St., Phu Nhuan District,* ☎ *08/842–1111,* FAX *08/842–4370. 157 rooms. Restaurant, lobby lounge, pub, air-conditioning, in-room safes, minibars, no-smoking rooms, refrigerators, room service, pool, massage, sauna, exercise room, motorbikes, shop, dry cleaning, laundry service, concierge, business services, meeting rooms, travel services, airport shuttle, car rental. AE, DC, MC, V.*

$$$$ 🏨 **Omni Saigon Hotel.** Built out of the former CIA headquarters in Saigon with walls so thick cellular phones fail to work, the Omni is one of the city's finest hotels. It has the essence of French elegance mixed with a hint of glitz and a touch of '60s bunker architecture. More importantly,

it's one of the few international hotels to have sent its staff abroad for training, and its service is some of the best in town. The restaurants serve first-class Japanese, Chinese, and international cuisine. Even if you don't stay here, come for the Sunday brunch, a bacchanalian frenzy of Belgian waffles and omelets. ⊠ *251 Nguyen Van Troi St., Phu Nhuan District,* ☎ *08/844–9222,* 𝔽𝔸𝕏 *08/844–9198. 248 rooms. 3 restaurants, lobby lounge, pub, air-conditioning, in-room safes, minibars, no-smoking rooms, refrigerators, room service, pool, beauty salon, massage, sauna, exercise room, motorbikes, nightclub, piano, baby-sitting, dry cleaning, laundry service, concierge, business services, meeting rooms, travel services, airport shuttle, car rental. AE, DC, MC, V.*

NIGHTLIFE AND THE ARTS

Saigon's thriving nightlife is a constant headache to the city's Communist leaders because most of it revolves around the kind of decadence they once promised to stamp out. Still, the city lacks the sort of entertainment that you take for granted in other large cities. There are no multiplex cinemas, for instance: for ideological reasons, authorities tend to view contemporary films as containing polluted materials. The only movies available are videotapes of terrible quality, pirated from Bangkok. There are a few theaters, but the plays and operas presented are often dull, propaganda-filled discourses and are frequently incomprehensible to foreigners. Live theater is just now beginning to change, albeit slowly.

Rock music, too, is still very much in its infancy. Any rock band—local or international—wishing to perform in Vietnam has to go through endless red tape and even has to submit lyrics to the Ministry of Culture for approval. Over the last few years Sting, Air Supply, and an obscure but incredibly popular Danish group, Michael Learns to Rock, performed in Vietnam to lackluster receptions (probably because tickets were far too expensive for the average Vietnamese). Incidentally, Sting's song "Russians" was rejected by the Ministry of Culture for ideological reasons. Classical concerts are more common but still infrequent.

For the most part, the city's nightlife revolves around drinking at one of the many bars and discos—frequented predominately by expatriates—that have opened in the last few years. This may still be communist Saigon, but many of these bars are as raucous as their counterparts in Hong Kong, Manila, and Jakarta. Nonetheless, nightclubs in Saigon are subject to the erratic rules laid down by the authorities. One week they are open, and the next they are classified as social evils and are all shut down. But nightclub owners take this all in stride and just wait for the right moment to start up again. Most expatriate bars are open throughout the night and only close their doors when everyone has left (Local bars tend to close around midnight.) Check in the weekly English-language supplement, "Time Out," in the *Vietnam Investment Review* for information about what's going on around town.

Nightlife

Bars and Clubs

Apocalypse Now (⊠ 2C Thi Sach St., District 1), one of the oldest clubs in Saigon, is loud, fun, and always packed with a cross section of expatriates and foreign tourists. It's the after-hours place to go in the city, and it's now bigger than ever after recent renovations. Amiable pimps and local prostitutes shoot pool while hordes of foreigners drink tequila and vodka and dance until dawn. But remember these words of warning: always take a taxi, not a cyclo, back to your hotel (cabs line up outside); cyclo drivers have been known to steal from drunken foreigners.

Also, you should leave any jewelry, including watches, at your hotel; there are pickpockets at this nightspot.

Bar Rolling Stones (⊠ 177 Pham Ngu Lao St., District 1), in the backpacker area of town, is a rattan bar serving cheap beer. The place spills out onto the street with loud music. If you sit outside, be sure to hold your bag in your lap or wind the straps around your ankles. The children hanging around the bar are magicians at spiriting things away from right under your feet.

Café Latin (⊠ 25 Dong Du St., District 1) is a multilevel tapas bar with constructivist decor that looks like something out of *The Jetsons,* and fine Australian and French wines.

Café Mogambo (⊠ 20 Thi Sach St., District 1), run by an American expat and his Vietnamese wife, is a kind of self-parodying Reno-style roadside stop where you can get good draft beer in a kitschy environment all dressed up with African decor (statues, headdresses, and wall hangings).

Le Camargue (⊠ 16 Cao Ba Quat St., District 1), although really more of a French-influenced restaurant (☞ Dining, *above*), also has an excellent terrace bar where you can have a drink outside among tropical palms and creepers. It's an ideal first stop on your way to a night on the town. Vasco's, a small bar and nightspot, was recently added below the restaurant; it's popular with both foreigners and locals and tends to get very busy on weekends.

Globo (⊠ 6 Nguyen Thipe St., District 1, ☎ 08/822–8855) was designed by the same people who did the Café Latin (☞ *above*), thus the constructivist decor made out of metal—iron stairwells, relief art, and even a burnished metallic toilet. The small place looks like it could be in Paris, and it is very popular with the city's fashionable French set. Good French food is served, and there is often live music on Friday nights.

Hard Rock Café (⊠ 24 Mac Thi Buoi St., District 1), although not official, does a booming business. It is particularly popular late at night with young foreign tourists and expats, especially the French. Occasionally there are late-night jazz band sessions.

Long Phi (⊠ 163 Pham Ngu Lao St., District 1) is one of the few bars in town to attract expats, Vietnamese, *and* backpackers. It's a rattan affair—wicker armchairs and wicker tables—that spills out onto the street, with music blaring until dawn. There's also a pool table. As always, be sure to look after your valuables if you're sitting out on the street. A recently added upstairs restaurant sells good, cheap French-country food.

Number 5 Bar (⊠ Ly Tu Trong St., District 1), on the edge of the downtown area, is one of the latest favorites with expats and tourists. Located in an old French bungalow, it's partly open to the outside and is a good place to start the night on balmy tropical evenings. You can also shoot pool and munch on snacks here.

Sheridan's Irish House (⊠ 19 Le Thanh Ton St., District 1), in the downtown area, is a traditional Irish pub serving Guinness and, oddly, dim sum. It's often busy and is a nice retreat from the heat and dust of the Saigon streets in the hot season.

Dance Clubs and Karaoke

Catwalk (⊠ 76 Le Lai St., District 1), in the New World Hotel, has private karaoke dens where you can sing to your heart's delight and a dance floor where dry ice creates a moody atmosphere.

Cheers (⊠ 257 Pham Ngu Lao St., District 1) is a trendy Singaporean-run nightspot in the Vien Dong Hotel. It's popular with Vietnam's young nouveaux riches as well as the city's Asian expats. There are private karaoke rooms and a regular Filipino band that plays covers of American hits.

Europa (✉ 43 Truong Son St., Tan Binh District), in the Saigon Superbowl (☞ Outdoor Activities and Sports, *below*), is a Singaporean-run club that fills up on weekends with locals. The place looks like a hamburger . . . or the bridge from the Starship Enterprise. Captain Kirk would have been quite at home, but other foreigners aren't so sure about it. It's also a long trip from the center of town—20 minutes by taxi—which you may not want to bother with.

Queen Bee (✉ 104 Nguyen Hue Blvd., District 1) is right in the heart of downtown. A Singaporean DJ is sprucing up the outdated dance tunes. It's especially popular with expat men, who come to meet young Vietnamese women. Like many clubs, it gets closed down from time to time.

Hotel Bars

A more civilized alternative to Saigon's bar scene is one of the many rooftop establishments at the city's hotels. Although drinks are more expensive than those at other places, you often get a panoramic view of the city for your money. Particularly noteworthy hotel bars include those in the **Caprice Hotel** (✉ Landmark Bldg., 513 Le Ton Duc Thang St., District 1) and the **Hotel Majestic** (✉ 1 Dong Khoi St., District 1); the fifth floor veranda at the **Rex Hotel** (✉ Khach San Ben Thanh St., District 1); the piano bar at the **Saigon Prince** (✉ 63 Nguyen Hue Blvd., District 1); and **Saigon Saigon** at the Hotel Caravelle Delta (✉ 19 Lam Son Sq., District 1).

The Arts

Music and Theater

The **Conservatory of Music** (Nhac Vien Thanh Pho Ho Chi Minh; ✉ 112 Nguyen Du St., District 1, ☎ 08/839–6646) is the only regular venue in town for classical music performances. The theater's main season is from September through June; it's generally closed in summer except when there are special concerts of visiting orchestras. Look in the daily *Vietnam News* for information on upcoming events.

Hoa Binh Theater (Nha Hat Hoa Binh; ✉ 14,3 Thang 2 Blvd., District 10, ☎ 08/865–5199), an ugly Soviet-era palace, is mostly used for local Vietnamese dramas, circus acts, and the occasional fashion show.

Municipal Theater (Nha Hat Thanh Pho; ✉ intersection of Le Loi Blvd and Dong Khoi St., District 1, ☎ 08/829–1249), built in 1899 by the French as an opera house, was later used as the home of the National Assembly of South Vietnam. It became a theater again in 1975. Most performances now are family shows with Vietnamese singers and dancers although occasionally an international opera singer performs here.

OUTDOOR ACTIVITIES AND SPORTS

Parks and Farms

In and around Ho Chi Minh City's urban bustle, there are very few spots where you can find green, open spaces and enjoy the outdoor One nice place in the city for a stroll, however, is **Cong Vien Van Ho Park,** on the other side of the Reunification Palace. The **Zoo and Botanical Garden** (✉ Nguyen Binh Khiem St. at Le Duan Blvd., District 1) is another good place for a walk.

You might also consider a short escape outside the city, where orchid farms with thousands of plants and varieties abound. Ask your driver or get a taxi to take you to the **Artex Saigon Orchid Farm** (⊠ 5/81 Xa Lo Vong Dai Hwy., which is better known as Xa Lo Dai Han, or the "Korean Highway" because it was built by the Koreans during the Vietnam War), 15 km (9 mi) outside the city. It's open daily, and there is a 20,000d admission.

Participant Sports

Bowling

☻ **Saigon Superbowl** (⊠ 141, A43 Truong Son St., Tan Binh District, ☎ 08/885–0188), the biggest entertainment complex ever to hit Vietnam, opened in late 1996. Not only does it have state-of-the-art bowling facilities and an electronic games arcade—another one of the entertainments occasionally shut down for being a social evil—it also has a mall (with overpriced clothes from the West) and a Kentucky Fried Chicken. If you intend to go bowling here, you'll have to be patient: all the alleys are in constant use, and you often have to wait some time before getting to play. When you do get to play, be prepared for the crowds that may swarm around you—analyzing your bowling style and technique. The place opens at 7:30 AM and only closes when the last person leaves. Foreigners pay 55,000d per game, which is not cheap.

Golf

There are two 18-hole golf courses outside Saigon. **Vietnam Golf and Country Club** (⊠ Ap Gian Dan, Long Thanh Mi Ward, District 9, ☎ 08/825–2951), in the outlying district of Thu Duc, 10 km (6 mi) north of Saigon, costs about $50 a day for a game. **Song Be Golf Resort** (⊠ 254B Nguyen Dinh Chieu St., ☎ 06/585–5802) is 20 km (12 mi) outside the city. The club's facilities include swimming pools, tennis courts, restaurants, and television rooms where family members can hang out while they wait for their links-playing relatives. The cost for a day is $50.

Health Clubs and Swimming Pools

If it's fitness you're after, the city has some good health clubs, usually based in the newer hotels. It simply depends on how much you're willing to pay.

Cercle Sportif (⊠ In Cong Vien Hoa Park, District 1) was once an elite French club but is now open to all. It has tennis courts, a swimming pool, and a gym with a weight room. You can use the facilities for less than $1.

Hotel Caravelle Delta (⊠ 19 Lam Son Sq., District 1, ☎ 08/823–0163) has a new gym, an outdoor swimming pool, sauna and steam rooms, and massage.

Hotel Equatorial (⊠ 242 Tran Binh Trong St., District 5, ☎ 08/839–7777) has the best gym in town, with a half-Olympic-size pool, stationary bikes, a rowing machine, a step machine, a treadmill machine, and weights. The cost is $15 for the day.

Hotel Majestic (⊠ 1 Dong Khoi St., District 1, ☎ 08/829–5514) has a small pool and gym, both available for use even if you're not a guest, as long as you order something from the bar.

New World Hotel Saigon (⊠ 76 Le Lai St., District 1, ☎ 08/822–8888) charges $12 for use of its small pool and standard gym.

Rex Hotel (⊠ 141 Nguyen Hue Blvd., District 1, ☎ 08/829–2185) has a small rooftop pool, which you can use for $2.

Jogging

Saigon isn't really a good city for jogging; it's generally too hot, too crowded, and too polluted, even in the parks. Some Vietnamese do, however, go out jogging in the streets in the very early morning (around 5) before the traffic begins. They also head for the parks and squares in the wee hours of the morning to do stretching exercises and play badminton. If you're set on running during your visit, contact the **Hash House Harriers running club,** which meets every Sunday outside the Century Hotel (⊠ 68A Nguyen Hue Blvd.; ☎ 08/845–3886 for information).

Spectator Sports

Horse Racing

Pho Tho Racetrack (⊠ 2 Le Dai Hanh St., District 11, ☎ 08/855–1205), built in 1900, was once an exclusive center of French colonial life. The track was shut down the day Saigon fell, on April 30, 1975—gambling was deemed a frivolous capitalist social evil by Hanoi—and wasn't reopened until 1989. After years of neglect, the building and track had fallen into disrepair and were only made suitable for racing again in 1994. They are still in fairly poor condition. Nonetheless, a weekend spent placing 5,000d bets can be a lot of fun. People go crazy when the racing starts: to get a grandstand view, they climb onto everything, including tops of buildings, telegraph poles, and even each other's shoulders. Most of the ponies racing are about half the size of racehorses you're probably used to seeing. They are a special type introduced by the French in the 19th century and are still being bred in villages outside Saigon. Notice how small the jockeys are, even compared to those in the West—that's because their average age is 9 or 10 years old. Watching these children racing tiny horses cheered on by thousands of spectators crowded onto nearby rooftops might just be one of your most memorable experiences in Saigon. Occasionally motorbike racing is also held at the track. It's open weekends from 1 PM on, and there's no admission. Check in the daily *Vietnam News* for more detailed schedule information.

SHOPPING

Ho Chi Minh City is a good place to have casual clothes made or to have designer apparel copied. In addition, the city is famous for its lacquerware (boxes, trays, etc.) and its wood carvings of all kinds.

Continuing a tradition first true when it was French Saigon's main shopping thoroughfare, Dong Khoi Street (formerly Tu Do Street and before that rue Catinat), between Le Loi Boulevard and the river, is lined with art galleries and shops selling jewelry, antique watches (or look-alikes), lacquerware, wood carvings, and other souvenirs mostly for tourists (which doesn't mean there aren't good finds). The galleries have some works by fine local artists, although you may end up paying more than you expected for something you love.

Ready-to-wear Western-style clothes and shoes are available near the central Ben Thanh Market, on Le Thanh Ton and Ly Tu Trong streets in District 1. Both the Ben Thanh Market in the center of the city and the Binh Tay Market in Cholon have all kinds of stuff for sale: clothes, wood carvings, shoes, plastic goods, kitchenware, food, and more. No matter where you shop, even if a place says it has fixed prices but you are purchasing a large number of items, be sure to bargain; it is part of shopping in Vietnam. But be polite: the debate over prices is expected to be a very civil and friendly process. Also, as is the case all over the country, most shops will either take dollars or dong and will often list prices in dollars only.

Department Stores

Nam Hai Yuan Shopping Plaza (✉ 39 Nguyen Trung Truc St., District 1, ☎ 08/823–1988), an enclosed mall, has vendors specializing in jewelry, wood carvings, and lacquerware; it primarily caters to Chinese tourists.

On the ground floor of the huge **Tax Department Store** (Cua Hang Back Hoa; ✉ intersection of Nguyen Hue St. and Le Loi Blvd.) you can find all kinds of souvenirs as well as a place to change traveler's checks. On the two upper floors you'll find the best bargains in Vietnam. Many designer clothes and sneakers, made in China but redirected to Vietnam on the black market, end up here at unbeatable prices. There are also nice and very inexpensive bags made of Chinese, Vietnamese, and Cham fabrics, as well as tailors who can make you clothes in 24 hours. Curiously, a lot of the clothing here is for cold weather, so if you need to pick up a Gore-Tex anorak or a ski suit at absurdly cheap prices, this is the place to come. It's also good for electronic items. The latest video equipment, digital cameras, and minidisk players are on sale here.

Markets

Clothing, shoes, bags, wood carvings, lacquerware, food, and more are available at the large **Ben Thanh Market** (Cho Ben Thanh), at the intersection of Tran Hung Dao, Le Loi, and Ham Nghi boulevards in the heart of District 1. Keep careful watch of your belongings; pickpockets have been known to strike in the narrow aisles here. But don't let this stop you from exploring this busy market.

Cholon's **Binh Tay Market** (Cho Binh Tay), on Hau Giang Boulevard in District 6 (near District 5), has all kinds of wholesale items that can be purchased in small amounts by anyone: kitchenware, baskets, plastic goods (barrettes, magnets, toys, shopping bags, wigs, you name it), hats (traditional conical, straw, baseball caps, etc.), shoes, and food.

The charming open-air market on **Ton That Dam Street,** between Huynh Thuc Khang Street and Ham Nghi Boulevard in District 1, has everything from fish and produce to plastic toys and cleaning products for sale.

On the north side of **Ham Nghi Boulevard,** between Ho Tung Mau and Ton That Dam streets in District 1, you can find imported cheese, olive oil, and just about any international food at the tiny, jam-packed European-style specialty food shops.

pecialty Shops

Antique Replicas

Unless you have permission from the Ministry of Culture (☞ Shopping *in* Smart Travel Tips A to Z), it's against the law for you to take antiques out of Vietnam, and anyone found carrying antiques at the airport has to hand them over to the authorities. Vietnamese law specifies that any object more than 21 years plus one day old is an antique. This creates a vast gray area of what is and isn't an antique, and often it's up to the whims of individual customs officers to decide. If you buy a fake article that looks like an antique, be sure to get a receipt in Vietnamese with the shop owner's signature guaranteeing the object is not genuine. Without it, you'll run into big trouble at customs. If you do decide to spend big bucks on the real thing (genuine antiques don't come cheaply in Vietnam), be sure you know what you're buying. It's very difficult to distinguish between genuine and fake items, especially on Dong Khoi Street, where both sell at comparable prices. In particular, beware of restored antique timepieces, which often have a 1950s Rolex face, for example, covering the much cheaper hardware of a '70s Seiko.

Nguyen Freres (⌧ 2A Le Duan Blvd., District 1, ☎ 08/821–3716) sells antique replicas, including prints of old colonial Saigon.

Art

Taking fine art out of the country isn't as problematic as taking antiques out of the country, but have a receipt for your purchase to show customs just in case. Many art galleries can be found on Dong Khoi Street and the surrounding area. Paintings and lacquerware by master artists Do Xuan Doan, Bui Xuan Phau, Quach Dong Phuong, and Truong Dinh Hao are available at a wide variety of galleries. Many of these artists base their work on French postimpressionist styles, and their work is generally apolitical (still lifes and pastoral scenes, for instance). Canvases fetch as little as $30 and as much as $15,000. Following is a list of suggested galleries.

Anh (⌧ 135 Nguyen Hue Blvd., District 1, ☎ 08/821–3716) sells ethnic folk art and material.

ATC (Art Tourist Services; ⌧ 172 Nam Ky Khoi Nghia St., District 3, ☎ 08/829–6833; ⌧ 29B Dong Khoi St., District 1, ☎ 08/829–2695; ⌧ 2 Cong Truong Quoc St., District 3, ☎ 08/829–6833) is a national art organization.

Dong Phuong Gallery (⌧ 135 Nam Ky Khoi Nghia St., District 1, ☎ 08/822–1716).

Fine Arts Museum (⌧ 97A Pho Duc Chinh St., District 1, ☎ 08/821–0001).

Galerie Lotus (⌧ 43 Dong Khoi St., District 1, ☎ 08/829–2695).

Hong Hac Art Gallery (⌧ 9A Vo Van Tan St., District 3, ☎ 08/824–3160).

Saigon Art Gallery (⌧ 77 Mac Thi Buoi St., District 1, ☎ 08/822–6048)

Clothing

Linh Phuong Maison de Couture (⌧ 38 Ly Tu Trong St., District 1, ☎ 08/824–2985) is very reliable for custom-made clothing for adults an children. Although the English- and French-speaking staff specialize in creating Vietnamese and Japanese silk items, the store carries wide variety of imported and domestic cottons. They copy designe clothes cheaply and very well.

Tropic (⌧ 73A Le Thanh Ton St., District 1, ☎ 08/829–7452) carrie contemporary and traditional clothing as well as some home-furnis ing items.

Zakka (⌧ 23 Dong Khoi St., District 1, ☎ 08/829–8086), next to t Hotel Majestic, sells fabric and beautifully designed clothing, shoe and bags (with a Western influence). Although items are expensive co pared to other shops in the city, you may not mind paying extra f the quality. You can also get clothes made for you in three days. No however, that you can get some things cheaper elsewhere.

Housewares

Home Zone (⌧ 41 Dinh Tien Hoang St., District 1, ☎ 08/822–80₂ sells stylish silverware, furnishings, and other housewares.

Mai Huong (⌧ 73 Le Thanh Ton St., District 1, ☎ 08/829–6233 the place to go for beautifully embroidered tablecloths, napkins, ₄ bedspreads, all made in Saigon.

Q Home (⌧ 65 Le Loi Blvd., 2nd floor, District 1, ☎ 08/821–48 has brightly colored, Western-style ceramics made in Vietnam.

Paris, France.

Paris, Texas.

When it Comes to Getting Local Currency at an ATM, Same Thing.

Whether you're in Yosemite or Yemen, using your Visa® card or ATM card with the PLUS symbol is the easiest and most convenient way to get local currency. For example, let's say you're in France. When you make a withdrawal, using your secured PIN, it's dispensed in francs, but is debited from your account in U.S. dollars. This makes it easy to take advantage of favorable exchange rates. And if you need help finding one of Visa's 627,000 ATMs in 127 countries worldwide, visit **visa.com/pd/atm**. We'll make finding an ATM as easy as finding the Eiffel Tower, the Pyramids or even the Grand Canyon.

It's Everywhere You Want To Be.®

SEE THE WORLD
IN FULL COLOR

Fodor's Exploring Guides bring all the great sights vividly to life with hundreds of photographs, fascinating historical background, and colorful anecdotes. Detailed maps and practical information keep you headed in the right direction.

Pair a **Fodor's** Exploring Guide with your trusted Gold Guide for a complete planning package.

Lacquerware

There are a number of galleries that sell lacquerware on Dong Khoi Street (from No. 137 to No. 145) and in the Phu Nhuan District on Nguyen Van Troi Street (and on its continuation, Cong Hoa Street).

Heritage (⊠ 53 Dong Khoi St., District 1) has beautiful contemporary-looking lacquerware, outstanding replicas of antique Buddhas and statuary, silver jewelry, and ao dais made from traditional fabrics.

Tay Son (⊠ 198 Bo Thi Sau St., District 3, ☎ 08/820–2524) is a large lacquerware distributor with a wide selection and good prices.

Musical Instruments

On the north side of Ham Nghi Boulevard between the circular intersection to the west and Nam Ky Khoi Nghia Street to the east are shops selling fake Fender Stratocasters and other cheap acoustic guitars that are actually not all that bad.

Shoes

Tran Van My (⊠ 95 Le Thanh Ton St., District 1, ☎ 08/822–3041) sells ready-made, custom-made, embroidered, and leather shoes and sandals. The cobblers are quite adept at copying other shoes, but some of their own designs are also very nice. The quality of workmanship is very high, and the prices are low.

Wood Carvings

Not too far from the airport, in the Phu Nhuan District on Nguyen Van Troi Street and on its continuation, Cong Hoa Street (between Nos. 72 and 306), there are a number of shops where you can buy wood carvings (as well as lacquerware, rattan, etc.) and see the craftspeople at work.

SIDE TRIPS FROM HO CHI MINH CITY

When you find yourself ready to escape Ho Chi Minh City—or when you just want to see some of the countryside—make a short excursion outside the city. Some of the destinations around Ho Chi Minh City can be visited as day trips; others may take a few days. Some excursions are more rugged, adventurous trips through forests and islands; others will take you to sandy beaches and new seaside resorts. The easiest way to plan a trip outside Ho Chi Minh City is to do it through a travel agency or one of the "tourist cafés" that organize tours (☞ Travel Agencies *in* Ho Chi Minh City A to Z, *below*); almost all organize trips to various points in the region.

Numbers in the margin correspond to points of interest on the Ho Chi Minh City Environs map.

u Chi Tunnels

❶ *65 km (40 mi) northwest of Ho Chi Minh City via Hwy. 22.*

The Cu Chi Tunnels—a 250-km (155-mi) underground network of field hospitals, command posts, living quarters, eating quarters, and trap doors—stand as a symbol of the Vietcong's ingenuity in the face of overwhelming odds. (A note about the use of the term Vietcong: Vietcong is used throughout this book to refer to the opposition movement in the South because it is the term that is probably most familiar. However, Vietcong—which means, loosely, Vietnamese "Commies"—was the name given by the Americans and the Republic of South Vietnam to this opposition movement. The National Liberation Front [NLF] was the official name of the group fighting the southern government. For more history of these terms, *see* Vietnam at a Glance: A Chronology *in* Chapter 8.) First used in the late '40s to combat the French, the tunnels made it possible for the Vietcong in the '60s not only to withstand massive bombings and to communicate with other distant Vietcong enclaves but to command a sizable rural area that was in dangerous proximity (a mere 35 km [22 mi]) to Saigon.

After the Diem regime's ill-fated "strategic hamlet program" of 1963, disenchanted peasants who refused to move fled to Cu Chi to avoid the aerial bombardments. In fact, the stunning Tet Offensive of 1968 was masterminded and launched from the Cu Chi Tunnels nerve center, with weapons crafted by an enthusiastic assembly line of Vietcong-controlled Cu Chi villagers. Despite extensive ground operations and sophisticated chemical warfare—and even after declaring the area a free-fire zone—American troops were incapable of controlling the area. In the late '60s B-52 bombing reduced the area to a wasteland, but the Vietnamese Communists and the National Liberation Front managed to hang on.

The guided tour of the Cu Chi Tunnels includes a film that documents the handiwork of "American monsters" (with, of course, no mention of South Vietnamese involvement) and an array of booby traps demonstrated by former Vietcong soldiers. If you are prone to claustrophobia, you might consider skipping the crawl through the hot, stuffy, and tight tunnels (although sections have been expanded to allow room for tourists' bigger bodies). Amazingly, in these very same tunnels many Vietnamese survived for months and even years.

The easiest and best way to visit is on a tour arranged through one of the travel agencies or tourist cafés (☞ Travel Agencies *in* Ho Chi Minh City A to Z, *below*), since every agency—state-run and private—does the identical trip. A day trip, which will run you about $40 per person, will generally combine the tunnels with a visit to the Caodai Holy See, in neighboring Tay Ninh.

Tay Ninh

❷ *95 km (59 mi) northwest of Ho Chi Minh City via Hwy. 22.*

★ The town of Tay Ninh is home to Caodaism, an indigenous hybrid religion, and its impressive and brightly colored temple, the **Caodai Holy See.** Caodaism incorporates elements of the major Eastern and Western religions—Buddhism, Confucianism, Taoism, Vietnamese spiritualism, Christianity, and Islam. Founded in 1926 by a mystic named Ngo Minh Chieu, Caodaism is a fusion of a Mahayana Buddhist code of ethics with Taoist and Confucian components. Sprinkled into the mix are elements of Roman Catholicism, the cult of ancestors, Vietnamese superstition, and over-the-top interior decoration that encompasses a fantastic blend of Asian and European architectural styles.

Caodai has grown from its original 26,000 members to a present-day membership of 3 million. Meditation and communicating with spiritual worlds via earthly mediums or seances are among its primary practices. Despite its no-holds-barred decorative tendencies, Caodaism emphasizes abstinence from luxury and sensuality as well as vegetarianism as a means of escaping the reincarnation cycle. Although the priesthood is strictly nonprofessional, clergy must remain celibate.

Perhaps most important, the Caodaists believe the divine revelation has undergone three iterations: God's word presented itself first through Lao Tse and other Buddhist, Confucianist, and Taoist players; then through a second set of channelers such as Jesus, Muhammad, Moses, Confucius, and Buddha. Whether because of the fallibility of these human

Ho Chi Minh City Environs

agents or because of the changing set of human needs, the Caodaists believe the divine transmission was botched. They see themselves as the third and final expression, the "third alliance between God and man." Since anyone can take part in this alliance, even Westerners like Joan of Arc, Victor Hugo, and William Shakespeare have been added to the Caodai roster.

It's worth noting that Caodaism's presence wasn't always so tolerated. Although it quickly gained a large following after its founding, including Vietnamese officials in the French administration, it soon became too powerful for some. By the 1930s the Caodaists had begun consolidating their strength in the region and recruiting their own army. Eventually the area became a minikingdom under the domain of the Caodaists. Needless to say, this didn't make the government very happy, and it did all it could to take away power from the region.

During World War II, the Caodaists were armed and financed by the Japanese, whom the sect saw as also fighting the government. After the war, the Caodaists gained the backing of the French in return for their support against the Viet Minh. This collusion with the French, however, was not always so peaceful, and skirmishes often occurred between the Caodaists and the French. After the French left in the late '50s, the South Vietnamese government made a point to destroy the Caodaists as a military force, which caused many members of the sect to turn to the Communists, and the area became an anti–South Vietnamese stronghold. But when the Communists came to power in 1975, they repossessed the sect's land, and Caodaism lost most of its remaining power. Today the religion is tolerated but is not involved in politics as it once was.

The noon ceremony (others are held at 6 AM, 6 PM, and midnight) at the Caodai Holy See is one of the most fascinating and colorful religious vignettes to which you will ever be privy as a tourist. A finely tuned hierarchical procession of men and women of all ages parades through the temple's great hall, where great painted columns twined with carved dragons support sky-blue arched vaults; panels of stained glass with a cosmic-eye motif punctuate the walls. You are permitted to watch and take snapshots from the mezzanine. Ignore any feeling of complicity in what appears to be a collective voyeuristic sacrilege the ceremony goes on as though you were not there.

Generally a visit to Tay Ninh is part of a day trip to the Cu Chi Tunnels (☞ *above*) arranged through one of the travel agencies in Saigon. A guide will accompany you, explain the history of the Caodai sect, and take you through the temple.

Can Gio

❸ *60 km (37 mi) southeast of Ho Chi Minh City.*

Officially a district of Ho Chi Minh City and only one hour from the city proper by car, Can Gio is an area the size of Singapore covered by a young 30-ft-high mangrove forest. The old forest was destroyed by aerial bombing and defoliants—primarily Agent Orange—during the Vietnam War. The forest had been a regular hiding place for the Vietcong who would fire mortars at the supply ships on the Saigon River. Residents of the area were forced to leave, and it wasn't until 19?? that surviving Can Gio families returned, replanted the forest, and gradually resettled. Surprisingly, the area's wild animals also returned, and today there are monkeys, wild boars, deer, leopards, and even the odd crocodile. Can Gio is a maze of channels, inlets, and tiny fishing hamlets hidden among the swamp and forest.

Vung Tau

❹ *130 km (81 mi) southeast of Ho Chi Minh City.*

Known as Cap St-Jacques during colonial times, Vung Tau was a popular beach resort for the French; some rundown, old colonial buildings still remain. During the Vietnam War it became a major U.S. and Australian army base. The area was later taken over by the Soviet Union as a concession for helping Hanoi win the war. The Soviets used the Vung Tau port as a navy base and drilled for oil off the coast. Many of the Stalinist-style concrete monstrosities dotting the town are a reminder of those postwar years. Following the collapse of the Soviet Union, many Russians left, although Vung Tau is still home to 2,000—a fairly large amount compared to the 200 remaining Russians in Ho Chi Minh City.

Vung Tau's beaches are the closest to Ho Chi Minh City, although they are not some of the country's nicest. But this is beginning to change—for better and worse—as the area is cleaned up for tourism and new hotels are built. There are a number of beaches in the town. The most popular, **Back Beach,** has had a face-lift and is now a very acceptable beach that stretches for miles up the coast. A part of this makeover is a half-finished Disneyland-style park called Paradise, complete with the requisite turrets and posters of Mickey Mouse and Pluto. There is a golf course of sorts to play on, but nothing as good as the greens elsewhere in Southern Vietnam (☎ 06/485–9687 for information). Back Beach is at its best during the week when it is quieter; on weekends it gets very crowded. Be prepared to encounter beggars here.

Bai Dau is a cramped beach below the huge Ha Long Street. It's certainly not a place you would travel miles to see—it's fairly rocky and not ideal for swimming—but it is an acceptable tropical beach and the most secluded one in Vung Tau. Avoid **Front Beach,** the worst of them all; it's a dirty little beach strewn with fishing tackle and oil flotsam from the nearby rigs.

Worth visiting is the **White Villa** (✉ 12 Tran Phu St.), which at different times was the French governor's residence, the home of Emperor Bao Dai (1913–97), and the South Vietnam presidential summer house. The villa, now a museum showing the opulence of the old regime, is a beautiful example of French colonial architecture, with classical columns, busts, and stucco decorations. Other sites of interest are the two small mountains crowned with pagodas and a giant statue of Jesus that overlook the town on a headland above. Interestingly, this hill is currently the site of a club of Japanese hang gliders, based in Saigon, who come here every weekend to fly the local skies. You can get a guide to take you along the mountain circuit around Vung Tau; the trip takes about four hours.

The best way to get to Vung Tau is by the new regular hydrofoil service from Saigon, which takes only about 45 minutes (☞ Getting Around by Boat *in Ho Chi Minh City, below*).

Lodging

$–$$ 🏨 **Petro House Hotel.** Surprisingly, this hotel is not bad at all, considering so few foreign tourists go to Vung Tau. It's a modern building, but it has an elegant, colonial feel to it. ✉ *89 Tran Hung Dao Blvd.,* ☎ *064/852–014,* 🕾 *064/852–015. 57 rooms. Restaurant, bar, lobby lounge, pool, laundry service, business services, meeting rooms. AE, DC, MC, V.*

Long Hai

❺ *170 km (105 mi) southeast of Ho Chi Minh City; 30 km (19 mi) northeast of Vung Tau.*

This beach is about a two-hour drive from Ho Chi Minh City and 40 km (25 mi) up the coast from Vung Tau, but it feels like it's worlds away. Local authorities recently designated Thuy Duong, just outside Long Hai, an international tourist resort and built a complex on the beach called the **Thuy Duong Resort**. The result is surprisingly tasteful, although you probably would just want to visit it for the day. Small kiosks and restaurants dot the bright, sandy beach, which runs for miles up the coast. Sit on the beach, which is equipped with deck chairs and umbrellas, and a waiter will take your order for fresh seafood.

Lodging

$$ 🏨 **Anoasis Beach Resort.** Long Hai's first international-style hotel has wonderful views of the coast. A bamboo beach bar serves snacks and hosts barbecues on the beach. ✉ *Domain Ky Van, Ba Ria-Vung Tau,* ☎ *064/868–227,* FAX *064/868–229. 22 rooms. Restaurant, pool, tennis court, beach, laundry service, business services, meeting rooms. AE, DC, MC, V.*

Ho Coc

❻ *190 km (118 mi) southeast of Ho Chi Minh City; 36 km (22 mi) east of Long Hai.*

Three hours from Ho Chi Minh City and farther up the coast from Long Hai is Ho Coc, the most beautiful beach in the area. It's a splendid retreat for anyone desperate to get away from the chaos of the city. The area is very remote, and consequently no public transportation reaches it. To get here, you need to hire a car and driver in Ho Chi Minh City. The only place to stay is the Ho Coc Guest House (☞ Lodging, *below*). There are a few small sidewalk cafés, but you're best off bringing your own food from Ho Chi Minh City.

Lodging

¢ 🏨 **Ho Coc Guest House.** This bare-bones but clean guest house has only five rooms, each sleeping two people. The bathrooms are basic—just a shower with cold water only and a toilet. But remember: you're not coming here for luxury but to enjoy the beautiful, secluded beach. ✉ *Ask for directions in town,* ☎ *no phone. 5 rooms. No credit cards.*

Binh Chau Hot Springs

❼ *150 km (93 mi) southeast of Ho Chi Minh City; 50 km (31 mi) nor of Long Hai.*

About half an hour's drive from Ho Coc are the Binh Chau Hot Springs (Suoi Nuoc Nong Binh Chau), famous among the Vietnamese for their therapeutic properties. A veritable industry of acupuncture, massage, and other healing methods has grown up around the springs. People suffering from rheumatism or backaches come here to take the water. The springs are okay to use, although they can get very crowded on weekends and holidays. There are a few pho stands and some small cafés serving Vietnamese food. To get here, hire a car and driver or make arrangements with a travel agency in Ho Chi Minh City.

Lodging

¢ 🏨 **Binh Chau Hotel.** The only worthwhile accommodation in town this very basic hotel. This may change in the next few years, but with few hotels now being built, this is probably it for the time being.

Ask for directions in town, ☎ *064/871–131,* FAX *064/871–130. 24 rooms. No credit cards.*

Phan Thiet

❽ *192 km (119 mi) northeast of Ho Chi Minh City.*

Phan Thiet is a lovely place to visit: lush, tropical palm forest surrounds miles of empty sandy beaches interrupted only by the odd lone fisherman. **Mui Ne Beach** is a particularly beautiful and pristine spot. The town itself has a large fishing industry and is known for its *nuoc mam,* the ubiquitous fish sauce served with most Vietnamese food. Dividing the town is the Phan Thiet River; the harbor is filled with small, colorful fishing boats. In the colonial era the French built homes on the north bank of the river, and everyone else lived on the south bank. Until 1692 the area was controlled by the Cham, and some of the present-day population are their descendants.

Make arrangements to get to Phan Thiet through one of the travel agencies in Ho Chi Minh City.

Dining and Lodging

$$ ✕⊡ **Co Co Beach.** A Swiss-run venture that opened in 1995, Co Co Beach has become one of the most popular destinations for Saigon's expats. It's regularly booked up weeks in advance, so call ahead to make reservations. The resort is made up of 20 bungalows on stilts, each with a bathroom and a sitting room. The restaurant serves steaks, freshly caught seafood, and more. ⊠ *Hai Duong Resort Ham Tien,* ☎ *062/848–401 or 062/848–402,* FAX *06/284–8493. 20 bungalows with bath. Restaurant, pool. MC, V.* 🏖

$$ ✕⊡ **Novotel Ocean Dunes Resort.** This recently renovated hotel, 11 km (7 mi) outside of Phan Thiet City, has its own private beach and adjoining golf course (☞ Outdoor Activities and Sports, *below*). This is an international-standard hotel, with air-conditioning and TVs in the rooms. The restaurant serves international cuisine with a focus on French food. ⊠ *1 Ton Duc Thang St., Phan Thiet,* ☎ *062/825–393,* FAX *062/825–682. 123 rooms. Restaurant, air-conditioning, pool, massage, tennis court, exercise room, beach, laundry service. MC, V.*

$$ ✕⊡ **Victoria Resort.** This very popular place, about 5 km (3 mi) down the beach from Co Co Beach, is made up of 50 bungalows on stilts, built in Thai style. It's always a good idea to book in advance, especially during Christmas and Tet. The swimming pool and tennis courts are additional pluses. Beware, though: the staff has had little contact with the outside, so patience is required. But the resort itself is worth it. ⊠ *Victoria Resort Phu Hai, Phan Thiet, Binh Thuan,* ☎ *062/848–437, 062/848–438, or 062/848–439,* FAX *062/848–440. 50 bungalows. Restaurant, pool, tennis court. MC, V.*

Outdoor Activities and Sports

At the **Ocean Dunes Golf Club** (Novotel Ocean Dunes Resort, ☎ 08/824–3729), the Nick Faldo–designed course has a magnificent setting on the edge of the South China Sea, which is peppered with small boats and fishing junks. Games start at $60.

Nam Cat Tien National Park

❾ *250 km (155 mi) northwest of Ho Chi Minh City.*

Often inaccessible due to poor road conditions, Nam Cat Tien National Park, northwest of Ho Chi Minh City and close to the Cambodian border, shelters the endangered Javanese rhino, as well as monkeys, elephants, tigers, and several bird species. The park also has one of

Vietnam's only banyan forests. With the encouragement of the regional tourist agency, Dong Nai Tourism, this national park is fast becoming the most popular adventure-travel location in the country. From Ho Chi Minh City, you may be able to arrange a two- to four-day jungle trip through one of the tourist agencies such as Vidotours (☞ Travel Agencies *in* Ho Chi Minh City A to Z, *below*). Dinner comes in your backpack, and accommodations are on a hammock—so this is only for you if you're a hardy traveler.

Con Dao Island

100 km (62 mi) off southern tip of Vietnam; about 40 mins by plane from Ho Chi Minh City.

One of the most fascinating areas in Vietnam but also one of the most isolated, Con Dao Island (or Poulo Condore, as the French called it) is actually an archipelago of 14 islands. Although it's closer to the Mekong Delta region (☞ Chapter 7), Con Dao Island is most easily accessible by plane from Ho Chi Minh City.

The largest of the islands, known as Con Dao or Con Son, was the Devil's Island of the South China Sea: it was used as a penal settlement by the French for more than 100 years. You can still see the solid French prison, with its infamous open "tiger cages"—where the guards would stand above the cells watching the prisoners pacing (if there was enough room) below—and the communal cells where sometimes more than 100 prisoners were manacled to the walls. Most of the prison is now surrounded by creeping jungle.

The South Vietnamese took over the prison in 1954, incarcerating their own political prisoners. The Americans, with the South Vietnamese, built a prison camp here during the Vietnam War. Today there is only a rotting reminder of the camp next to the old French prison, with its iron watchtowers corroding with age. All told, thousands of people died miserable deaths on Con Dao—Nationalist and Communist prisoners as well as revolutionary insurgents and criminals from all over the French empire. Only one of Con Dao's cemeteries still exists; it alone has 20,000 graves, victims of the struggles from the 1940s to the 1970s. The population of the island currently stands at about 1,000—including many local fishermen and their families.

The attractive French town of Con Dao has been left intact, with the prison officers' quarters now occupied by Vietnamese fishing families. The prison governor's mansion is now a museum. Hours depend on when you show up—they'll open it especially for you if no one else is around. Along the rotting seafront boulevard are the remains of old crumbling French villas where Saigon's wealthy used to fly in for weekend visits in the shadow of the gulag.

The island itself is a dream, with its beautiful but empty beaches, glistening coral in the water, and forests teeming with wildlife. Unfortunately, at present the only feasible means of transportation to the island is an expensive (Russian-made) helicopter charter from VASCO (☞ Arriving and Departing by Plane *in* Ho Chi Minh City A to Z, *below*), the domestic arm of Vietnam Airlines. The only other transportation option to the island is by boat, a 14-hour ride from Vung Tau, with departures just twice a week. But this is not advised, as the boats are generally in bad shape and the trip is extremely unpleasant, especially during the rainy season.

Lodging

¢ 🏨 **Con Dao Guest House.** Presently the only place to stay on the island (although this may quickly change as the island is developed as tourist destination), this guest house, next to the museum in the town of Con Dao, is very run-down. Rooms are communal, as is the one shower, and there is no air-conditioning. As a foreigner and a tourist, you will probably be charged an outrageous $25 a night for the barest of accommodations. But there is no alternative if you want to stay on Con Dao. ⊠ *Ask for directions in the town of Con Dao,* ☎ *no phone.*

ngkor Wat Complex, Cambodia

10 km (6 mi) from Siem Reap, and 260 km (161 mi) from Phnom Penh, which is about 300 km (186 mi) from Ho Chi Minh City.

Only a couple of hours by plane from Ho Chi Minh City is the famous Angkor Wat Complex in Cambodia, built in the 7th–14th centuries by the Kingdom of Angkor for Hindu worship. Here you will find not only the stunning Angkor Wat but also the ancient palace of Angkor Thom, the Bayon Temple, the Terrace of the Elephants, and the Terrace of the Leper Kings. Spend a day exploring the complex, then drive up the Phnom Bakheng hill to watch the sun set over Angkor Wat—one of the most magnificent sights in the world. At the very least, you need two whole days to see the complex.

Getting to the temple takes some planning—and some flexibility. The political situation in Cambodia is not always very stable, and you may not be able to go when planned. From Ho Chi Minh City you will need to fly into Phnom Penh on Vietnam Airlines and then continue on to Siem Reap on Royal Air Cambodge. Visas for Cambodia are granted at the airport, although you can certainly arrange to get one beforehand. You need a visa to get back into Vietnam; this can sometimes take a few days or more (and sometimes only 24 hours), so you might consider flying to Bangkok after visiting the temple and not returning to Vietnam.

You may want to—or have to—spend a day or two in Phnom Penh, and two or three days in Siem Reap, depending on how much time you want to spend at the temple. Siem Reap is the jumping-off point for getting to the temple complex, but there is a lot more to see and do in Phnom Penh. Your hotel can arrange for a car with a driver and a guide to take you around the complex; or you can make arrangements with a travel agency in Ho Chi Minh City before you leave.

Lodging

PHNOM PENH

$$$ 🏨 **Intercontinental.** Be sure to reserve ahead for this international luxury hotel, one of the best in Phnom Penh. ⊠ *Regency Square, 296 Mao Tse Toung Blvd.,* ☎ *023/720–888,* 𝔽𝔸𝕏 *023/720–8850. 354 rooms. Restaurant, bar, pub, air-conditioning, pool, dry cleaning, laundry service, business services. AE, MC, V.*

$$$ 🏨 **Sofitel Cambodiana.** This classy hotel is right on the bank of the Mekong River at Sisowath Quay. A popular choice in town, it is frequently booked. Rooms are large and modern, although a bit overpriced for what you get. ⊠ *Sisowath Quay,* ☎ *023/426–288,* 𝔽𝔸𝕏 *023/426–392. 267 rooms. 2 restaurants, bar, air-conditioning, pool, tennis court, health club, casino, business services. AE, MC, V.*

SIEM REAP

$$$$ ✕🏨 **Grand Hotel d'Angkor.** This grande dame, built in 1930 and long fallen on hard times, was occupied by Khmer Rouge guerillas and then by the Vietnamese army. It's since been rejuvenated and is open for business, complete with gorgeous Taj Mahal–inspired gardens, silken fabrics, and Oriental carpets throughout. It's the most expensive hotel in Angkor—to the point of ridicule by the locals (basic rooms start at $360

and climb up to $2,000 for a suite). Most rooms have balconies that overlook either the swimming pool or the (developing) countryside. Dinners often are disappointingly buffet-style. *1 Vithel Charles de Gaulle,* ☎ *063/963–888,* FAX *063/963–168. 150 rooms. Restaurant, pool, travel services. AE, MC, V.*

$–$$ 🏨 **Angkor Village.** The Angkor Village consists of traditional wooden houses built on stilts. Siem Reap's best hotel and well known by many, this place is often booked. Be sure to make reservations in advance. Rooms are small but pleasant. ⊠ *Ask for directions in town,* ☎ *063/ 963–563. 20 rooms. Restaurant, bar, air-conditioning, fans. MC, V.*

HO CHI MINH CITY A TO Z

Arriving and Departing

By Bus

Traveling by bus around Vietnam is not recommended. They are usually overcrowded, hot, and uncomfortable, and they often break down. Schedules, too, are arbitrary. You're better off taking one of the minibuses that leave from the bus stations, and even preferable is going on a bus organized by one of the travel agencies or tourist cafés (☞ Travel Agencies, *below*). But if you do plan on taking the bus, Ho Chi Minh City has a number of bus stations:

Cholon Station (⊠ Close to the Binh Tay Market on Tran Hung Dao B Blvd., District 5) serves routes to the Mekong Delta. **Mien Dong Station** (⊠ National Hwy. 13, Binh Thanh District) serves points north of Ho Chi Minh City. **Mien Tay Station** (⊠ Off Hung Vuong St., Binh Chanh District) also serves towns in the Mekong Delta. **Tay Ninh Station** (⊠ Le Dai Hanh St., Tan Binh Station), near the airport, is where you catch buses to Tay Ninh and Cu Chi. **Van Thanh Station** (⊠ 72 Dien Bien Phu St., Binh Thanh District) services Dalat and Vung Tau.

By Car

One of the best ways to travel around Vietnam is by a car with a driver (☞ Car Rental *in* Smart Travel Tips A to Z). Most hotels and high-end travel agencies such as Saigon Tourist and Vietnam Tourism (☞ Travel Agencies, *below*) rent private air-conditioned cars (Mercedes Benzes, Mazdas, Renaults) with a driver for about $35 a day (less than 100 km [62 mi]; extra kilometers cost more). At budget agencies like Ann's Tourist and Sinh Café (☞ Travel Agencies, *below*), you can hire a car and driver for about $20–$30, depending on the season. You may want to be driven to sights around Saigon, although you will need car mainly for excursions outside the city.

By Minibus

You should make reservations for minibus trips in or out of the city day in advance through your hotel concierge, a travel agent, or a travel café.

By Plane

Major international airlines with flights to and offices in Ho Chi Minh City include **Air France** (⊠ 130 Dong Khoi St., District 1, ☎ 08/829 0981); **British Airways** (⊠ Jardine House, 58 Dong Khoi St., District 1, ☎ 08/829–1288), which has an office in Ho Chi Minh City, although it doesn't yet fly directly here; **Cathay Pacific Airways** (⊠ Jardine House, 58 Dong Khoi St., District 1, ☎ 08/822–3203); **China Airlines** (⊠ 132–134 Dong Khoi St., District 1, ☎ 08/825–1388); **Emirates Airlines** (⊠ 17 Han Thuyen St., District 1, ☎ 08/865–6575); **EVA Air** (⊠ 32 Ngo Duc Ke St., District 1, ☎ 08/822–4488); **Japan Airlines** (⊠ Sun Wah Tower, G/F Nguyen Hue St., District 1, ☎ 08/821–909

KLM Royal Dutch Airlines (⊠ 2A–4A Ton Duc Thang G/F St., ☎ 08/823–1990 or 08/823–1991); **Lufthansa** (⊠ 132–134 Dong Khoi St., District 1, ☎ 08/829–8529); **Qantas Airways** (⊠ 65 Le Loi Blvd., Saigon Centre, District 1, ☎ 08/821–4660); **Royal Air Cambodge** (⊠ 343 Le Van Sy St., Tan Binh District, ☎ 08/844–0126); **Singapore Airlines** (⊠ Saigon Tower, Suite 101, 29 Le Duan Blvd., District 1, ☎ 08/231–1588); **Thai Airways** (⊠ 65 Le Loi Blvd., 5th floor, District 1, ☎ 08/821–4660); **United Airlines** (⊠ Jardine House, 58 Dong Khoi St., District 1, ☎ 08/823–4755), which has an office in Ho Chi Minh City, although it doesn't yet fly directly here.

Vietnam Airlines (⊠ 116 Nguyen Hue St., District 1, ☎ 08/823–0696), the Vietnamese national carrier, has international flights from Ho Chi Minh City as well as domestic flights to the following destinations: Buon Ma Thuot, Cantho, Dalat, Danang, Haiphong, Hanoi, Hue, Nha Trang, Phu Quoc, Pleiku, and Qui Nhon. Prices for domestic flights range from $60 to $150. It's best to book several days in advance and to reconfirm your flight; you can always change your reservation at branch offices all over the city.

For information about helicopters run by **VASCO,** the domestic arm of Vietnam Airlines, inquire at the Vietnam Airlines office(☞ *above*) or at Vidotours (☞ Travel Agencies, *below*).

AIRPORT

Tan Son Nhat Airport (⊠ Hoang Van Thu Blvd., Tan Binh District, ☎ 08/844–3179), 7 km (4 mi) from central Saigon, is small and navigable. Depending on the officer behind the counter, getting through passport control is intermittently hassle-free. The airport tax on a domestic flight is 20,000d or $1.50 (you can pay in either currency); internationally it's 80,000d or $6.

BETWEEN THE AIRPORT AND DOWNTOWN

Take advantage of the complimentary hotel shuttle service provided by many of the middle to high-end hotels. Otherwise you will have to deal with the throngs of taxi drivers outside the city airport, all trying to get your business. But don't be put off if you do have to take a taxi: just choose an official-looking one and be on your way. From Ho Chi Minh City's airport, fixed-price and metered taxis are the best ways to get into the city center. Despite the advent of taxi meters, you should still try to negotiate a price before getting into the cab: about $5–$10 (you can pay in dong or dollars), depending on the number of passengers and pieces of luggage. The ride takes 10 to 20 minutes depending on traffic.

By Train

From Ho Chi Minh City there is local train service to Nha Trang, Qui Nhon, and Hue. The faster train (if only by a little), the Reunification Express, goes to many of the larger coastal towns north of Ho Chi Minh City, from Phan Rang–Thap Cham all the way north to Hanoi (☞ Train Travel *in* Smart Travel Tips A to Z). This is not the fastest way to go or always the most comfortable, but it certainly is one of the most interesting modes of getting around the country.

Trains connecting Ho Chi Minh City with coastal towns to the north arrive and depart from the **Saigon Railway Station** (Ga Saigon; ⊠ 1 Nguyen Thong St., District 3, ☎ 08/846–8704), about 1 km (½ mi) from central Saigon. It's best to ask a travel agent to call for ticketing and information, although you could try contacting the **Saigon Railway ticketing office** (⊠ 275C Pham Ngu Lao St., District 1, ☎ 08/832–3537) yourself instead of having an intermediary do it; it's open daily 7:15–11 and 1–3. Note that Saigon Tourist does not provide any train service information.

Getting Around

By Bicycle

Hotels often rent out bicycles or can at least suggest where to rent dcent ones. Those available from shops on the street are generally unreliable.

By Boat

Boats touring the Saigon River start at 50,000d an hour and are available at the riverside on Ton Duc Thang Street, between Ham Nghi Boulevard and Me Linh Square. Choose any of the boats lining the river almost all are family owned, and you must negotiate an exact price with the owners before boarding the boat. They will take both individuals and groups. Ask at travel agencies for advice about which a the best trips.

The **hydrofoil to Vung Tau** departs from the waterfront opposite Nguy Hue Boulevard (for information: ⊠ 6A Nguyen Tat Thanh St., ☎ 0 825–3888, FAX 08/825–3333) at 6:30, 8, and 2:30. The returning hydrofoleaves from Vung Tau for Ho Chi Minh City at 1, 4, and 5:30. The times may change depending on demand, so check with a travel agen If you are traveling on a weekend, be sure to book your ticket a day so in advance. On Friday and Saturday the hydrofoil is usually filled w Vietnamese going to Vung Tau's resorts. The hydrofoil also now travels down to the Mekong Delta (☞ Chapter 7), making visits to the gion far less time-consuming. One-way fare to Mytho is $12, to Cant $14, to Vinh Long $16, to Chau Doc $28, and to Vung Tau $10.

By Bus

Public buses are the cheapest way to get around town, although n the fastest, most convenient, or most pleasant way to travel. Service often erratic and painfully slow, and the buses generally have no a conditioning and are crammed full of people at busy times. You're b ter off taking a cyclo or a taxi, either of which is faster, more efficie and not too expensive. If you do decide to take a bus, it is importa to know about the Saigon–Cholon line, which you are most likely use; it starts in Me Linh Square at the Tran Hung Dao intersection a ends up at Cholon's Binh Tay Market. Tickets, available on board, c 2,000d. The Mien Dong–Mien Tay line offers transportation betwe these two bus stations for 4,000d. The Van Thanh–Mien Tay line tra els between the Van Thanh eastern bus station and the Mien Tay we ern bus station. You can pick up all these buses at Me Linh Square at stops marked XE BUYT (bus stop).

By Car

Renting a car with a driver and even a guide makes the most sense day trips outside Ho Chi Minh City (☞ Arriving and Departin *above*). To get around the city, use taxis or cyclos.

By Cyclo

Although cyclos, or pedicabs, are supposed to charge only 2,000d p kilometer, 5,000d–10,000d is a decent rate (this includes the tip) for j about any destination within the same district. Going to districts in outer suburbs obviously will cost you more. Cyclo drivers, often f mer South Vietnamese soldiers, frequently speak English very well a can provide informative city tours for a small price (a generous ha day rate is about 30,000d–55,000d)—bargaining is advised. Drivers v wait for you when you visit sights; just don't leave any valuables in cyclo. If you are happy with your cyclo driver, you can make arran ments to have him pick you up the next day; he will certainly ask if y would like him to do so. Although cyclos are slower than taxis (☞ *belo* they are an excellent way to experience Saigon's street life.

By Motorbike

One of the quickest ways around the city is riding on the back of a motorbike taxi, known as a *Honda om* or a *xe om*. This service usually costs about 20,000d. Motorbike drivers are everywhere—they'll just drive up alongside you and ask where you're going and if you're interested in a ride. It's relatively safe to travel on motorbikes; unfortunately, the same can't be said for the roads, especially at rush hour.

You can also rent your own motorbike from any number of cafés, restaurants, and travel agencies, especially Sinh Café and Ann's Tourist. Daily rates usually start at about 50,000d–100,000d. But beware: don't part with your deposit until you are convinced the place is legitimate. Legitimate establishments usually have a line of motorbikes for rent and a standard ticket they give to all customers.

By Taxi

Taxis are available in front of all major hotels. Many cluster around the Hotel Continental; at the intersection of Le Loi Boulevard and Nguyen Hue Street, near the Rex Hotel and Hotel Caravelle Delta; along Pham Ngu Lao Street; and outside the New World Hotel, near the Ben Thanh Market intersection. Nowadays most taxis have meters, and most drivers speak a little English. An average journey across town starts at 30,000–60,000d. The best taxi companies are **Saigon Taxi** (☎ 08/844–8888) and **Vina Taxi** (☎ 08/811–0888), which is run by a British company with a French manager; it's a good idea to book their taxis in advance. Other recommended taxi companies include **Airport Taxi** (☎ 08/825–4250); **Giadinh Taxi** (☎ 08/822–6699); and **Saigon Tourist** (☎ 08/822–2206).

Contacts and Resources

Consulates

Australia (✉ 5B Ton Duc Thang St., District 1, ☎ 08/829–6035). **Canada** (✉ 203 Dong Khoi St., District 1, ☎ 08/824–2000, ext. 1209). **New Zealand** (✉ 41 Nguyen Thi Minh Khai St., District 1, ☎ 08/822–6905). **United Kingdom** (✉ 21 Le Duan Blvd., District 1, ☎ 08/823–2604). **United States** (✉ 4 Le Duan Blvd., District 1, ☎ 08/822–9433).

Currency Exchange

Although they don't always offer the best exchange rate, hotels are usually the easiest places to change money; they can also change traveler's checks. Banks usually have better rates.

Major banks in Ho Chi Minh City include **ANZ Bank** (Australia New Zealand Bank; ✉ 11 Me Linh Sq., District 1, ☎ 08/829–9316); **Citibank** (✉ 8 Nguyen Hue St., District 1, ☎ 08/824–2118); **Standard Chartered Bank** (✉ 203 Dong Khoi St., District 1, ☎ 08/829–8383); and **Vietcom Bank** (✉ 29 Chuong Duong St., District 1, ☎ 08/823–0310). **ATMs** can be found at ANZ Bank and Hong Kong Bank in the New World Hotel Saigon (☞ Lodging, *above*).

Doctors and Hospitals

Round-the-clock medical treatment is available at **SOS International Assistance** (✉ Han Ham Bldg., 65 Nguyen Du St., District 1, ☎ 08/829–8520), a clinic run by Western doctors who treat minor illnesses and injuries, do dental work, and take care of emergency evacuations. **Cho Ray Hospital** (✉ 201B Nguyen Chi Thanh St., District 5, ☎ 08/554–4137 or 08/554–4138) has regular and 24-hour emergency treatment. **Emergency Centre** (✉ 125 Le Loi Blvd., District 1, ☎ 08/829–0898) can help you with emergency medical care.

Emergencies
Ambulance (☎ 15). **Police** (☎ 13).

If you have lost your credit cards, contact **Vietcom Bank** (☎ 08/829–3068 or 08/822–5413), which is affiliated with Western banks. For passport problems, contact your consulate (☞ Consulates, *above*).

English-Language Bookstores
There are a few bookstores in Ho Chi Minh City that sell English-language books. Many traveling street vendors are also well equipped with English–Vietnamese phrase books and dictionaries, as well as travel guides, Graham Greene's *The Quiet American*, and other books on Vietnamese culture and history.

Quoc Su (✉ 20 Ho Huan Nghiep St., District 1), occupying a tiny space off Dong Khoi Street, not too far from the river, is jam-packed with lots of photocopied bootleg political literature. It also sells guides to Southeast Asian cities dating from the '20s and '30s. French translations abound, but English-language literature is scarcer.

Xuan Thu (✉ 185 Dong Khoi St., District 1, ☎ 08/822–4670), Ho Chi Minh City's first foreign-language bookstore, is definitely lacking in the English literature department, but it sells quite a few international newspapers and periodicals. You can also get Vietnamese–English phrase books and dictionaries here.

Xunhasaba (✉ 76E Le Thanh Ton St., District 1), the largest foreign magazine and newspaper distributor in town, doubles as a tailor shop. Nice, cheap art books and some novels (mostly classics) in English are also available.

Guided Tours
Guided tours that cover only Ho Chi Minh City itself are virtually nonexistent, which is just as well. Since no one travels to Ho Chi Minh City just for its sights, but rather for the whole cultural experience, the few half-day major-sight tours, which cost around $35–$50, are ultimately not that worthwhile. Furthermore, although advertised as "English speaking," guides are often unintelligible in that language. You're better off exploring the city on your own or hiring an English-speaking cyclo driver (just make sure you can understand *his* English first).

On the other hand, do take advantage of the guided tours outside the city. For excellent tours to the Mekong Delta and the Cu Chi Tunnels and for various customized trips—some for as little as $5 per day with lunch included—check itineraries and schedules at the Saigon Tourist budget office or at any number of cafés and small travel agencies on Pham Ngu Lao Street (☞ Travel Agencies, *below*).

Late-Night Pharmacies
My Chau Pharmacy (✉ 389 Hai Ba Trung St., District 1, ☎ 08/822–2266) comes recommended by the Travel Medical Consultancy. The pharmacy is open daily 7:30 AM–10 PM.

Post Office
The **Central Post Office** (✉ 2 Cong Xa Paris St., District 1), next to Notre Dame Cathedral, is open daily 7:30–5:30. Here you can buy stamps, send faxes, and use the phones.

Precautions
As with other major cities, you need to be aware of what's going on around you in Ho Chi Minh City. Don't wear flashy jewelry, and keep a firm grip on your bag. Not only are there pickpockets, but robbers on motorbikes have been known to drive by and grab bags from peo

ple walking down the street. It's relatively safe to walk around the city at night—even for women—but, of course, you need to stay on guard and avoid walking down dark, deserted streets.

Travel Agencies

All these agencies can help you organize tours of Ho Chi Minh City as well as trips to sights such as the Cu Chi Tunnels, the Caodai Holy See, and the Mekong Delta (☞ Chapter 7), a few hours from the city.

Ann's Tourist (⊠ 58 Ton That Tung St., District 1, ☎ 08/833–2564, FAX 08/832–3866) could very well be your only tourist-information stop. The company arranges tours both around Ho Chin Minh City and throughout the entire country, rents cars, makes flight arrangements, handles visa extensions, and provides all the historical, cultural, and orientation material you could ever possibly need. Besides offering a wide array of travel services, Ann's also has a great story behind it: after the fall of Saigon in 1975, Tony and his brother were separated from their mother, Ann, and removed to the United States. Ann founded Ho Chi Minh City's first privately run travel agency with the intention of finding her sons. Reunited as a family, they became a professional unit; Tony now runs the company full time. It's open Monday–Saturday 8–6, and Sunday 9–11.

Exotissimo (⊠ 28 Dinh Tien Hoang St., District 1, ☎ 08/825–1723, FAX 08/825–1684) is an upscale, international tour operator headquartered in Hanoi but with an office in Saigon. It's run by a helpful Frenchman.

Peregrine Tours (⊠ 24/9 Pham Ngoc Thach St., District 3, ☎ 08/829–6086 or 08/822–8464, FAX 08/829–6158), run by Australian John Powell, specializes in adventure tours as well as the more common package trip.

Saigon Tourist (main office: ⊠ 49 Le Thanh Ton St., District 1, ☎ 08/823–0100, FAX 08/822–4987; **budget office** in Café Apricot: ⊠ 187 Pham Ngu Lao St., ☎ 08/835–4535), a government-run travel service, owns an enormous number of luxury hotels, restaurants, and tourist attractions in and around Ho Chi Minh City. It can arrange tours and accommodations in Ho Chi Minh City and throughout the country; provide maps, brochures, and basic tourist information; book domestic and international flights on Vietnam Airlines; and arrange car rental. A word about Saigon Tourist: the company basically operates as two separate agencies—one for budget travel and the other for standard or first-class excursions. Besides the price, the only difference seems to be the size of the bus; the main office arranges for large groups to cruise on colossal buses for five times the cost. Although many budget touring companies will cancel a trip if they haven't filled their bus, Saigon Tourist's budget division has a no-cancellation policy (just on their end—you are permitted to cancel), so a minibus will depart on schedule even if you are the only passenger. It's open daily 7:30–6:30.

Vidotours (⊠ 41 Dinh Tien Hoang St., District 1, ☎ 08/829–1438, FAX 08/829–1435), a successful, privately run Vietnamese tour company, specializes in package and individual trips all over the country. It is one of the most upscale of the Vietnamese tour operators and consequently one of the most expensive. But Vidotours provides excellent personal service and English-speaking guides with an intimate knowledge of Vietnam.

Other offices and agencies include **Getra Tour Company** (⊠ 86 Bui Vien St., District 1, ☎ 08/835–3021); **Thanh Thanh Travel Agency** (⊠ 205 Pham Ngu Lao St., District 1, ☎ 08/836–0205); and **Vietnam Tourism**

(✉ 234 Nam Ky Khoi Nghia St., District 3, ☎ 08/829–0776, FAX (829–0775).

Kim's Cafe (✉ 272 De Tham St., District 1) organizes inexpensive tri to regions such as the Mekong Delta.

Sinh Café Travel (✉ 246–248 De Tham St., District 1, ☎ 08/835–56 or 08/836–9420), specializing in budget travel, is by far the best tour café in Saigon. This agency has Vietnam's greatest travel deal: a $3 $38 open-ended ticket good for bus travel the length of the count (☞ Bus Travel *in* Smart Travel Tips A to Z). The café is open daily AM–11 PM. It also serves food, although you're better off eating at Kin Café nearby.

7 THE MEKONG DELTA

The Mekong Delta is a patchwork of waterways, tropical fruit orchards, mangrove swamps, and brilliant green rice-paddy fields that run their way into the emerald-colored South China Sea. It's a land touched by ancient and modern cultures, from the Funanese to the Khmer, Cham, and Vietnamese. If you're looking for wild frontiers, head south to the farthest reaches of the Mekong Delta—it doesn't get much more isolated than this.

By Andrew
Chilvers

LUSH, BEAUTIFUL, AND FLAT, the Mekong Delta, Vietnam's southernmost region, is just 6 to 20 ft above sea level. The result is that the region is often flooded during the rainy season. Rivers and canals cross the land, functioning as waterways that transport people and goods.

In the northern part of the delta region, fruit grows in abundance: orchards full of mangoes, jackfruit, lemons, custard fruit, dragon fruit, pineapples, durians, and papayas make the area Vietnam's Garden of Eden. The climate, which is hot and humid year-round, is ideal for cultivating tropical fruit. Rice also grows throughout the region. In the Mekong's southern section, steamy mangrove swamps and thick palm forests thrive on the flat, flooded delta, making the area difficult to navigate.

Slicing through the heart of the delta is the Mekong River, also known as Song Cuu Long, or River of the Nine Dragons. Every second the river carries with it from 2,500 to 50,000 cubic yards of fertile soil deposits; this flow of soil created the delta and continues to extend it out into the South China Sea. Descending from the Tibetan plateau, the Mekong River runs through China, separates Burma from Laos, skirts Thailand, passes through Cambodia, and flows through Vietnam into the South China Sea. As it enters Vietnam, the river divides into two arteries: the Tien Giang (Upper River), which splinters at My Tho and Vinh Long into several seaward tributaries; and the Hau Giang (Lower River), which passes through Chau Doc, Long Xuyen, and Can Tho to the sea. The river is filled with islands that are particularly famous for their beautiful fruit gardens and orchards.

Fifteen million people live in the Mekong Delta's 11 provinces. Most subsist by fishing or rice farming. Dotting the endless fields of rice paddies, poor peasant farmers, shadowed by their limpet-shape hats, evoke the classic image of Vietnam. These days enough rice is produced to feed the country *and* to export abroad. Vietnam is now the world's third-largest rice exporter, after the United States and Thailand—a remarkable feat considering that less than 10 years ago the country was importing rice.

Centered around Can Tho and My Tho is the northern delta, with its fruit farms and rice fields, which is far more accessible than the remote southern delta. Encompassing the Ca Mau Peninsula that juts into the sea from Soc Trang, the lower delta is wild country. Isolated fishing communities live along the tributaries running through the area. In the southernmost province of Minh Hai, the ancient mangrove forests are home to monkeys, wildcats, boars, and even crocodiles. Around U Minh on the Ca Mau Peninsula, is Vietnam's only large cajeput forest, which can only be seen by boat.

Over the centuries the Mekong Delta has provided refuge to people fleeing wars and chaos farther north. The region was first mentioned in Chinese scholarly works as a part of the ancient kingdom of Funan or the Oc Eo civilization, which had its capital near the modern-day city of My Tho. The Funan civilization was influenced by Hindu and Buddhist cultures and flourished between the 1st and 5th centuries AD. It was well known by Malay, Arab, and Chinese traders and was even large enough to warrant Chinese ambassadorial status. However, in the 6th century the Funan kingdom inexplicably disappeared. The Mekong Delta was settled by the Cham and the Khmer in the 7th century and was annexed by the Khmer civilization based at Angkor between the 9th and 10th centuries. Some Vietnamese settlers lived the area even under Khmer rule, but with the defeat of the Cham the late 15th century, more Vietnamese moved south. In the 17th ce tury some of the Chinese fleeing one of the many northern dynastic autocrats appeared in the Mekong Delta. The Tay Son Rebellion and the Lords of Hue retributions in the late 18th century brought even more Vietnamese into the region.

The Mekong Delta's modern borders were drawn up by the French in 1954. Under the French, Indochina was a fairly loosely administered region comprising Laos, Cambodia, Cochin China, Annam, and Tonkin (now northern Vietnam) under one governor-general based in Hanoi. Allegiances were based on ethnicity—Cham, Khmer, Vietnamese, and so on—rather than on nationality. And there was feuding: the Khmer believed that over the centuries the Vietnamese had taken away their land, and they wanted it back.

French colonialism briefly put a stop to the disputes—and later contributed to them. The French encouraged the Vietnamese and the Chinese, who were much more commercially driven than the Khmer, to continue settling here. As more Vietnamese moved south, more Khmer left. Uncertainty over who would have sovereignty over the Mekong Delta lasted until 1954, when the French bequeathed the area to the new country of South Vietnam. Under Pol Pot's rule in Cambodia, the Khmer again laid claim to the delta as their ancestral land, and there were frequent skirmishes between Khmer Rouge and Vietnamese soldiers along the border.

Other social upheavals over the last 50-some years have also contributed to the region's further settlement. During the Japanese occupation of Vietnam in the 1940s, colonial French and Vietnamese families fled from towns and villages farther north to avoid the fighting. But the fighting eventually spread to the Mekong Delta, and these refugees were forced to fan out into the previously uninhabited mangrove swamps, hacking them down as they went.

Today the Mekong Delta is still populated with a variety of cultures. The majority of people living in the area are Vietnamese, with the Khmer comprising the second-largest ethnic group. Nearly 2 million Khmer people live in the vicinity of the city of Soc Trang and on the Cambodian border, and the Mekong Delta is still often referred to as Khmer Krom by Cambodians. A small number of Cham also live close to the Cambodian border, but these Cham, unlike their counterparts in the central highlands, are not Hindu but Muslim. The southern Cham were converted to Islam by Malay and Javanese traders who skirted the coast several hundred years ago. The northern Cham contemptuously call the southern Cham the "New Cham," and the groups don't really mix with each other.

leasures and Pastimes

Dining

For a region that produces so much fruit (which you can sample at one of the area's many orchards), the Mekong Delta has the least varied cuisine in Vietnam. Not surprisingly, rice is the diet staple and is usually accompanied by fairly bland boiled or grilled chicken, pork, or beef. Stick to a diet of plain boiled rice and grilled chicken or pork, or French bread and pâté, which you can bring with you from Saigon or buy in larger towns in the delta. The best places to eat throughout the Mekong Delta are restaurants in hotels or guest houses—the seafood there should be fine (at least in the northern delta). You can also get some satisfactory meals in bigger towns such as My Tho and Can Tho.

If in doubt, ensure that vegetables are properly boiled before eating them; many local vegetables are sprayed with toxic insecticides and are often washed only in local tap water. Watch your food being prepared, if necessary. In addition, avoid some of the local fish, particularly catfish and shrimp, especially in the far reaches of the southern delta—they tend to be raised on human and other excrement in small trenches below farmers' houses.

If you're adventurous, try more exotic dishes—snake (usually cobra or python), turtle, deer, monkey, and even rat, more readily available in the southern delta.

Lodging

It can't be overemphasized that much of the Mekong Delta is a remote, undeveloped region, which means it has some of the most primitive accommodations in Vietnam. It's possible to find cheap rooms in most towns, but they're often so basic that you may want to pay more for the best hotel in the area or go to the nearest town with better hotels. Recently, however, the lodging scene has improved slightly with the addition of international-standard hotels. Around Can Tho, for example, hotel standards are improving because of the growing number of tourists, although this doesn't mean accommodations are as nice as they are elsewhere in Vietnam. Keep in mind that the least expensive rooms probably won't have air-conditioning or adequate fans—and you'll definitely want a cool room after a scorching day outside. All hotels and most guest houses in the delta are state owned, which means prices are fixed and generally far too expensive for what you get. But for $30 or more per night, you can usually get an adequate room with air-conditioning and a private bathroom. Rooms vary in grade from standard (which often have a fan and a communal bathroom) to deluxe (which generally have air-conditioning and a private bathroom), so be sure to make your request known when you book your room. Check the different options around town—new hotels and guest houses are opening all the time—before you make a decision.

Exploring the Mekong Delta

The Mekong Delta stretches from the Plain of Reeds in the northern reaches to the wet mangrove forests of Ca Mau at the southernmost tip. A sprawling region, much of it isolated and totally undeveloped, the Mekong Delta can be somewhat difficult to travel around. Can Tho is the capital of the Mekong Delta and the best base for visiting the northern part of the region. Southeast of Can Tho is Soc Trang, the center of Khmer culture, and northwest is Long Xuyen, famous for it relics from the Funan kingdom. Farther north is the Plain of Reeds marshlands controlled throughout the French-Indochina War and the Vietnam War by the Vietminh and the Vietcong and by the Hoa Hao religious sect. (A note on the term Vietcong: Vietcong is used throughout this book to refer to the opposition movement in the South because it is the one that is probably the most familiar. However, the history of this term is a complex one; see Vietnam at a Glance: A Chronology in Chapter 8 for further explanation.)

On the Cambodian border is the center of Cham culture, Chau Doc. The highest peak in the Sam mountain range is also just a few miles from the border. Farther down the coast is the Mekong's only resort town, Ha Tien, although you would be hard pressed to call it a real resort. Along the southernmost tip are remote fishing villages, which are often cut off from the main roads and rivers much of the year because of flooding and so are difficult to visit. Few tourists venture this far into the lower delta, but if you do, the journey can be rewarding. Most likely you will visit the region with a tour arranged through a travel agent in Ho Chi Minh City; many of these include prepaid boat trips.

Numbers in the text correspond to numbers in the margin and on the Mekong Delta map.

Great Itineraries

You can spend anywhere from 1 to 10 days in the Mekong Delta. For example, it's possible just to take a day trip from Ho Chi Minh City to My Tho, in the Tien Giang Province, and go on a boat trip to an island orchard. Or you can travel around the region for longer.

IF YOU HAVE 2-3 DAYS

My Tho ① is only two hours from Saigon, so it's possible to make a day trip of it or to visit as part of a longer tour. While in My Tho, go to both the Island of the Coconut Monk, where the island's namesake set up a religious sanctuary, and Tan Long Island, to see some of the area's orchards. Just outside My Tho, on the road back to Saigon, is the Dong Tam Snake Farm, which probably won't take you more than a half hour to see. That evening, head to ⊞ **Can Tho** ②. Go to the Floating Market at the crack of dawn, then take a ride through the channels surrounding the city. Stop in at the Munirangsyaram Pagoda, a Khmer temple. The next day, make an excursion to **Vinh Long** ③, a river island with abundant fruit gardens and orchards, and the large Chinese Van Thanh Mieu Pagoda.

IF YOU HAVE 4-6 DAYS

After covering the upper and lower Mekong River areas around **My Tho** ① and ⊞ **Can Tho** ②, head west to ⊞ **Long Xuyen** ④, once a center of Fu-nanese civilization. The Long Xuyen Catholic Cathedral, one of the largest churches in the Mekong Delta, is worth seeing. From Long Xuyen travel up through Dong Thap Province to the Plain of Reeds and explore the area by boat. On the fourth day, head down to ⊞ **Chau Doc** ⑤, one of the more cosmopolitan towns in the Mekong Delta. Spend a morning visiting the Chau Giang Mosque, the religious center of the local Cham community, and go to shrine-covered Sam Mountain. You can see Cambodia from its peak when the weather is good. From Chau Doc drive down to the coastal city of ⊞ **Ha Tien** ⑥ to relax on the beach.

IF YOU HAVE 10 DAYS

A visit to the lower delta—Minh Hai and U Minh—takes more time. You could go to this area on a separate journey or tack it onto a trip to the upper and western delta regions around ⊞ **Can Tho** ②. About an hour and a half southeast of Can Tho is the Khmer city of **Soc Trang** ⑦, where there are many beautiful pagodas, a museum of Khmer culture, and a large Catholic church. Spend a day in Soc Trang, then travel to ⊞ **Ca Mau** ⑧, the last big town on the southernmost tip of Vietnam. Use Ca Mau as a base for getting to the bird sanctuaries in Dan Dai, where you can see exotic feathered creatures, and for exploring the large U Minh Cajeput Forest and the Minh Hai Mangrove Forest. On the second day in Ca Mau, take a boat down the Ngang River to ⊞ **Nam Can** ⑨, the last town in Vietnam before the sea.

When to Tour the Mekong Delta

The best time to tour the Mekong Delta is during the dry season, from October to May. During the rainy season, from May to September, a large portion of the region is under water and inaccessible.

---

y Tho

❶ *70 km (43 mi) south of Ho Chi Minh City.*

My Tho is the only port city along the upper Mekong River and the first ferry stop in the Mekong Delta. It's a good place to stop for lunch if you're coming from Ho Chi Minh City for a day of touring along

The Mekong Delta

Hồ Chí Minh City

CAMBODIA

LONG AN

5 Chau Doc

Sam Mountain

DONG THAP

TIEN GIANG

6 Ha Tien

AN GIANG

4 Long Xuyen

Mekong

1 My Tho

Ben Tre

3 Vinh Long

VINH LONG

BEN TRE

Rach Gia

Can Tho **2**

CAN THO

Song Co Chien

Vinh Rac Gia

KIEN GIANG

Song Hau Giang

TRA VINH

Soc Trang

7

Gulf of Thailand

SOC TRANG

BAC LIEU

U Minh Cajeput Forest

Bac Lieu

South China Sea

8 Ca Mau

CA MAU

N

0 40 miles
0 60 km

Con Dao (Son Island)

9 Nam Can

one of the Mekong River's tributaries by boat (with a stop at one of the tropical fruit orchards on the river islands). With a population of about 150,000, it's one of the largest cities in the delta and one of the least attractive. Houses in My Tho are of the ugly, modern, concrete variety that are all over Vietnam—long, thin, and without windows on the side, they're often called tube houses. To find quaint wooden longhouses and cottages on stilts you have to travel farther south.

My Tho was the center of the ancient civilization of Funan from the 1st to 5th centuries AD, and then the culture disappeared—no one really knows what happened. Today Funan relics are still being unearthed. The modern-day city was established by Chinese refugees fleeing Taiwan (then known as Formosa) in the 17th century. During the Vietnam War My Tho was one of the centers of operations for American and Australian troops. The largest battle in the Mekong Delta was fought in 1972 at Cai Lai only 20 km (12 mi) outside the city. My Tho is now known for its fruit and fish markets, a major food source for Ho Chi Minh City.

About 2 km (1 mi) from My Tho, on the Mekong River, is Phung Island (Con Phung), better known as the **Island of the Coconut Monk** (Or Dau Dua). A religious sanctuary before the war, the island once had a garish, eclectic complex in a style similar to the Caodai Holy See at Tay Ninh (☞ Chapter 6). It was built in the 1940s by a monk named Nguyen Thanh Nam, who was nicknamed the Coconut Monk by locals because he was reputed to have once lived for years on nothing but coconuts. The monk presided over a small community of followers, teaching a religion that was a mix of Buddhist and Christian beliefs. He was imprisoned repeatedly, first by the Saigon regime and later by the Communists for antigovernment activities; he died in 1990. All that is left of the monk's utopian dreams are some dragons and gargoyles and columns with mythic creatures wrapped around them. *Take boat from Trung Trac St., next to Mekong tributary.*

☝ Like many of the islands in the Mekong River and its tributaries, **Tan Long Island** is covered with fruit gardens and large orchards. A pretty island with little walkways and paths, it's a haven of peace and tranquility only a few minutes from the bustle of My Tho's docks. You're likely to be invited into someone's house for refreshments. The island is usually a stop on tour itineraries. ✉ *Take boat from Trung Trac St., next to Mekong tributary.*

☝ The **Dong Tam Snake Farm,** 10 km (6 mi) northwest of My Tho, is on an old U.S. military compound that lay deserted for years until a northern Vietnamese general decided to take over the land and develop it into a for-profit snake farm. The farm specializes in cobras, which are prodded and poked for reactions by delighted Vietnamese youths. The most dangerous are the king cobras, which, according to the farm, still have their venom sacs—hard to believe, but if in doubt, keep your distance. There's also a bunch of relatively docile pythons and a selection of rather miserable animals—many of them rare—such as monkeys, bears, wildcats, and pangolins, locked in tiny cages. These animals, too, suffer from the prodding of visiting children. Animal lovers will definitely want to stay away. The restaurant on the farm, which not surprisingly mostly serves snake dishes, is extremely popular with Vietnamese families on weekend day trips from My Tho. ✉ *On road between My Tho and Vinh Long.* 🎫 10,000d. ⊘ *Daily 8–5.*

an Tho

❷ *170 km (105 mi) southwest of Ho Chi Minh City, 108 km (67 mi) southwest of My Tho.*

Can Tho is the capital of the Mekong Delta and the region's gateway. Residents of Can Tho are quick to label themselves the friendliest and most helpful people in Vietnam, and judging by the relaxed atmosphere of the city, they may be right. Can Tho retains a French cosmopolitan feel—it was once one of the largest French colonial trading ports. Elegant villas can still be found throughout the city and along the shores of the surrounding river islands. Many have been renovated and are now occupied by rich Vietnamese merchants, although others are falling to pieces. During the Vietnam War Can Tho was almost constantly surrounded by hostile Vietcong forces, but the city itself stayed loyal to the Saigon regime and many U.S. and South Vietnamese troops were based here. It was the last city to fall to the North Vietnamese army, on May 1, 1975, a day after the fall of Saigon, as North Vietnamese forces moved south.

For a great daylong excursion from Can Tho, take a boat trip around the tiny islands in the river and canals surrounding the city. You can rent boats of various sizes from the quay along Hai Ba Trung Street; all come with a captain and a guide. Negotiate the price yourself, or let your tour guide do it for you.

Markets in the port and on the nearby rivers sell produce from the delta—mainly for markets in Ho Chi Minh City and for export. Can Tho has several floating markets—where people buy and sell from boats all jostling each other—but the **Floating Market at Phung Hiep,** 7 km (4 mi) southeast of the city by boat, is the largest and most picturesque. A bridge overlooking the market gives you a good view of the whole scene. Trading begins at dawn and carries on for much of the day. Goods are tied to poles to indicate what's for sale. A mango seller, for instance, will attach a mango to the top of his pole; others put grapes, pineapples, and other fruits on their poles.

One of Can Tho's highlights is the **Munirangsyaram Pagoda,** a Khmer temple built in the 1940s to serve and provide spiritual well-being to

Can Tho's dwindling Khmer community. The pagoda is an emblem of one of the numerous ethnic groups that live side by side in the Mekong Delta. Unlike many of the elaborately decorated, almost gaudy Vietnamese pagodas, this temple reflects the more spare Khmer sensibility. ⊠ *36 Hoa Binh St.* ☎ *Free.*

Lodging

$$$ 🏨 **Saigon-Can Tho Hotel.** Clean, good-size rooms and an elevator are the highlights of this otherwise ordinary hotel. Being a state-run affair, the Saigon is nothing spectacular, but it's certainly one of the better hotels in the delta. Rooms have the usual borderline-tacky Formica furnishings, and its view—of the street—is not the most appealing. Rooms also have IDD phones and satellite TVs. The restaurant serves an evening buffet of acceptable Vietnamese food, as well as burgers and fries. There is also karaoke nightly. The hotel is next to the main market and downtown shopping area. Ask about ongoing special offers, such as tours of the area or shopping trips, when you book. ⊠ *55 Phan Dinh Phung St.,* ☎ *071/825–831 or 071/822–318,* FAX *071/823–288. 46 rooms. Restaurant, air-conditioning, travel services. MC, V.*

$$–$$$ 🏨 **Victoria-Can Tho Hotel.** Without a doubt, the recently opened Victoria is the best hotel in the Mekong Delta. Some rooms offer panoramic views of the bustling activity of the picturesque Hau River. Rooms have IDD phones and satellite TVs. The building itself is a beautiful 1930s colonial-style hotel. This is an ideal starting point for a trip around the islands of the Mekong River. ⊠ *Con Cai Khe Tourist Center,* ☎ *071/ 810–111,* FAX *071/829–259. 92 rooms. Restaurant, bar, air-conditioning, pool, business services, meeting rooms, travel services. MC, V.*

$$ 🏨 **Cuu Long Hotel.** Just off the waterfront and overlooking the main street is your basic state-run hotel, with nylon bedspreads and curtains, gaudy furnishings, pictures of castles and landscapes in the lobby, and the pervasive smell of dampness. Service is terrible, as it is in most state-run places. Nonetheless, this hotel is clean and one of the few options in Can Tho. Only the deluxe rooms have air-conditioning; the others have fans. ⊠ *52 Quang Trung St.,* ☎ *071/820–300,* FAX *071/826–15. 100 rooms. Restaurant, travel services. MC, V.*

$ 🏨 **Ninh Kieu Hotel.** This hotel on the corner of a street overlooking small boat jetty has the best views of the river. Rooms vary in grade from standard to deluxe, as in most hotels in the area; only those in the upper ranges have private baths and air-conditioning. To get the best views of the bustling waterfront, try to book ahead and be sure to ask for a room overlooking the river. These come with balconies which are a great place to unwind after a long day. ⊠ *2 Hai Ba Trung St.,* ☎ *071/821–171 or 071/825–285,* FAX *071/821–104. 30 rooms, with bath. Restaurant, travel services. No credit cards.*

$ 🏨 **Quoc Te (International) Hotel.** The Quoc Te is one of the best of many hotels along the waterfront. It touts itself as an international hotel, which it definitely is not, but it's clean and has good river views. Top and middle range rooms have private baths and air-conditioning. The restaurant serves Vietnamese food. ⊠ *10–12 Hai Ba Trung St.,* ☎ *071/ 822–079 or 071/822–080,* FAX *071/821–039. 40 rooms, 18 with bath. 2 restaurants, travel services. No credit cards.*

¢–$ 🏨 **Hau Giang Hotel.** Built in 1996, the Hau Giang is basic but comfortable. It's popular with budget travelers, although there are cheaper rooms in town. Only the superior and deluxe rooms have private baths, and only the deluxe rooms have air-conditioning. Stay here if every other place in town is booked. In the evenings there is karaoke. ⊠ *34 Nam Ky Khoi Ngia St.,* ☎ *071/821–851 or 071/821–139, 071/821–806. 34 rooms, four with bath. Restaurant, travel services. No credit cards.*

Vinh Long

❸ *34 km (21 mi) northeast of Can Tho; 170 km (105 mi) southwest of Ho Chi Minh City.*

Lushly draped with thick palm forest and fruit orchards, Vinh Long, the best known of all the river islands in Can Tho Province, is a beautiful place to explore by boat along its canals and tributaries. On much of the island's coast are crumbling—and some newly renovated—French villas, which were abandoned in the late 1940s as the Vietminh overran the territory south of Saigon. The locals are so hospitable that almost everyone will offer you tea and fruit at no expense if you happen to dock near their home. The most popular stop on tours of the island is at the **Binh Thuan hamlet**, where you eat lunch among the bonsai trees and fruit orchards of an eccentric old Francophone artist named Nguyen Thanh Gia. The fruit orchards and gardens are the island's main attraction. **Vinh Long** is also the name of the island's main town, but the town is not attractive enough to warrant a special visit.

Five kilometers (3 miles) from the town of Vinh Long is the **Van Thanh Mieu Pagoda,** a large Chinese Confucian temple built in the mid-19th century. It's decorated with multicolor dragons and statues of Confucius, which is odd because the monks here practice Buddhism. Added to the original structure is a different style of hall built in honor of a local fighter against colonialism, Phan Tanh Gian, who committed suicide in the 1930s rather than submit to French rule. Often the locals refer to the temple by his name, so try both names if the boat guide seems confused.

Long Xuyen

❹ *190 km (118 mi) southwest of Ho Chi Minh City; 62 km (38 mi) northwest of Can Tho.*

Long Xuyen, like My Tho, was founded by the ancient Funanese, or Oc Eo, civilization. Until 1975 it was also the center of the Hoa Hao Buddhist sect, which, like the Caodai, had its own standing army to protect its interests against other sects and armies of the time. The Hoa Hao Buddhists often refer to themselves as Vietnamese Buddhists (that is, practicing a version of Buddhism distinct to Vietnam). Hoa Hao are very proud and fiercely independent people; during the 1950s and '60s they fought both the Saigon regime and the Vietcong with their own army. They were disarmed after the reunification of Vietnam. Their faith lives on, however, in communities like Long Xuyen.

The city is noteworthy for another reason: as Communists here will eagerly remind you, Long Xuyen was the birthplace of Ton Duc Thang (1888–1980), North Vietnam's president after Ho Chi Minh's death and the first president of the unified country after 1975.

Long Xuyen is home to one of the largest cathedrals in the Mekong Delta. The **Long Xuyen Catholic Cathedral** is a relatively new church—it was completed only in 1973. Its most distinguishing feature is its huge bell. ✉ *2 Nguyen Hue St., at Tran Hung Dao and Huong Vuong Sts.*

The **Plain of Reeds** (Rung Tram) is the main reason to come to Long Xuyen. Swamp and marshlands interspersed with clumps of mangrove forest—much of which is impassable—cover the region on either side of the Dong Thap and Long An provinces. The area is also home to the **Tam Nong Nature Reserve,** famous for its rare wild birds. It's a great place to visit if you're an avid bird-watcher. If you want to see the rare herons, note that many migrate out of the region for much of the rainy season. The Plain of Reeds and the reserve are 45 km (28 mi)

from Long Xuyen and Cao Lanh (east of Long Xuyen), an utterly for-
gettable, newly built modern town, and accessible from either. Tours
of the area include the nature reserve and the Plain of Reeds; have the
guide who has accompanied you from Ho Chi Minh City or from your
hotel in the Mekong region organize the trip for you. Be aware that
there are mosquitoes carrying many types of dangerous diseases, including dengue fever, malaria, and Japanese encephalitis; take precautions
like using mosquito repellent and wearing long-sleeve shirts and pants.

Lodging

$$ 🏨 **Mekong Hotel.** You won't get silver service at this state-run hotel,
but it's still the best in town. You'll find the standard nylon curtains
and bedspreads and the smell of dampness that come with Mekong
Delta accommodations. But this place is about as comfortable as you're
going to get in this very rural region. Request one of the top-end
rooms; they are the most comfortable. ⊠ *21 Nguyen Van Cung St.,*
☎ *076/841–265,* FAX *076/843–176. 18 rooms. Restaurant, air-condi-
tioning. No credit cards.*

$ 🏨 **Long Xuyen Hotel.** At this state-tourist-authority-operated hotel,
rooms are comfortable but no-frills. The lower-end rooms are ex-
tremely cheap and come only with a fan and the use of communal toi-
lets. Ask for one of the deluxe rooms—these come with private toilet
and shower and air-conditioning. ⊠ *17 Nguyen Van Cung St.,* ☎ *076/
841–927. 35 rooms. Restaurant, travel services. MC, V.*

$ 🏨 **Thai Binh Hotel.** Rooms are surprisingly comfortable at this inex-
pensive hotel favored by backpackers. Upper-range rooms have air-con-
ditioning. There is karaoke in the room behind the lobby. Only breakfast
is served at the restaurant. ⊠ *12–14 Nguyen Hue St.,* ☎ *076/841–184.
27 rooms. Restaurant, travel services. No credit cards.*

Chau Doc

❺ *245 km (152 mi) west of Ho Chi Minh City; 119 km (74 mi) north-
west of Can Tho.*

Chau Doc is a port town on the Hau Giang River only a few miles from
the Cambodian border. It is well known for its ethnically mixed pop-
ulation, made up of Chinese, Cham, and Khmer minority groups, as
well as Vietnamese. Each ethnic group has built its own distinctive tem-
ples—Khmer wats, Cham mosques, and Vietnamese and Chinese pago-
das. Chau Doc has large populations of Hoa Hao, Catholics, Buddhist,
and Muslims, all coexisting peacefully together. In the late 1970s the
town was notorious as a target of brutal border raids by the Khmer
Rouge under the guise of seeking to reclaim land. There haven't been
any raids in a long time, but if you're hoping to use Chau Doc as a
jumping-off point to Cambodia, forget it. Not only are the Vietnamese
military border posts unsympathetic to travelers, but the Cambodian
side is still rife with dangerous bandits and smugglers.

The religious center for the local Cham community is the **Chau Giang
Mosque.** As with other mosques in Vietnam, this one is starkly sim-
ple, with only some minarets and colonnaded entrances as embellish-
ment, in contrast to the many brightly decorated Buddhist pagodas and
temples. The mosque is on the riverbank opposite Chau Doc, so you
have to take a ferry (⊠ Ferry terminal: Tran Hung Dao St.) to get here.

South of Chau Doc is shrine-covered **Sam Mountain** (Nui Sam), which
is touted as the region's highlight. In fact, visiting is somewhat anti-
climactic: this is more like a hill than a mountain. Nonetheless, it's worth
seeing as long as you understand it will be a little less magical and a
little tackier than claimed. At the base of the mountain are cafés and

food stalls, as well as street children begging for money. The walk up to the summit skirts several pagodas and a park with—oddly—plastic scale models of dinosaurs. The **Tomb of Thoai Ngoc Hau** is the most interesting shrine on Sam Mountain. Built in the early 19th century for Thoai Ngoc, an official of the Nguyen dynasty, the tomb is one of the few still-existing precolonial structures put up by the Vietnamese in the Mekong Delta. The tomb also served as the last resting place of various other lesser functionaries of the time. When you reach the top of the mountain, you'll see splendid views into Cambodia—on a good day. Let your guide organize an excursion to Sam Mountain.

Lodging

$$ 🏨 **Victoria-Chau Doc Hotel.** The newest and best hotel in Chau Doc, the colonial-style Victoria caters to foreign tourists; it has a degree of quality not found elsewhere in this part of the delta. Rooms have IDD phones and satellite TVs. A cocktail at the Tam Giang Sky Bar overlooking Sam Mountain is the best way to relax after a hot, busy day touring the southern delta. ⊠ *32 Le Loi St.,* ☎ *076/865–010,* FAX *076/ 865–020. 93 rooms. Restaurant, 2 bars, air-conditioning, pool, massage, sauna, business services, travel services. MC, V.* 🍴

$ 🏨 **Chau Doc Hotel.** Consider this no-frills, cheap backpacker hotel a place to stay, and no more. There isn't much difference in price between the nicest and the shabbiest rooms, although the least expensive ones don't have private bathrooms or air-conditioning; be sure to ask for the most expensive. All, however, come with standard-issue nylon bedspreads and curtains. Make sure the hotel staff supplies you with a mosquito net if your room doesn't have one. ⊠ *17 Doc Phu Thu St.,* ☎ *076/866–484. 33 rooms, 6 with bath. Restaurant, fans, travel services. No credit cards.*

Ha Tien

❻ *206 km (128 mi) northwest of Can Tho; 306 km (190 mi) west of Ho Chi Minh City.*

This resort town has untouched stretches of beach and limestone formations. The coastal area is a pleasant diversion from the flatness of the rest of the delta and is a good place to spend a day or two just relaxing. The water is crystal clear, and the beaches are a brilliant sandy white. You can go snorkeling, diving, and fishing here, although you have to bring your own gear.

With its crumbling French colonial villas and busy waterfront, the town is surprisingly charming. Today fishing is the main enterprise. Under Khmer rule the town was a thriving port; in the 17th century the Nguyen lords gave it to a Chinese lord, Mac Cuu, as a private, protected fiefdom. For the next 40 years the Khmer, Siamese, and Vietnamese all struggled for control of the port and the trade that would come with it. Ha Tien finally became an outpost of the Vietnamese Lords of Hue in 1780. The town's most famous site is the grave of the original Chinese lord, Mac Cuu, and his ancestors.

Lodging

$ 🏨 **Dong Ho Hotel.** This no-frills establishment, run by the local state tourist agency, is a typically adequate and clean state-run hotel, with nylon bedspreads, pictures of European castles, and small rooms that smell damp. Only the more expensive rooms have air-conditioning and private bathrooms, so you probably want to request one of these. ⊠ *Tran Hau St.,* ☎ *077/852–141,* FAX *077/862–111 (c/o Kien Giang Tourist). 19 rooms, 7 with bath. No credit cards.*

$ 🏨 **Hon Trem Hotel.** Very basic but comfortable and clean, this small state-owned minihotel is good enough for an overnight stay. Only the

higher-price rooms come with air-conditioning. ⊠ *Nga Ba Hon St.,
Binh An,* ☎ *077/845–331,* ℻ *077/862–111 (c/o Kien Giang Tourist).
13 rooms, 3 with bath. Restaurant. No credit cards.*

Soc Trang

❼ *63 km (39 mi) southeast of Can Tho.*

Soc Trang is the center of Khmer culture in Vietnam. Many inhabitants are either Buddhist monks or—oddly enough—Catholic nuns. It
was once a provincial capital of the Angkor Empire, which covered
much of Indochina from the 9th to the 15th centuries. Vietnamese settlers did not appear here until the 17th century; later, in colonial times,
they were encouraged to come by the French, who sought to develop
agricultural production in the region. Even though there is a fairly large
Vietnamese population, Khmer culture is still very much present. Soc
Trang's architecture is a mix of French colonial and Khmer styles. Many
buildings are dilapidated, but still impressive. Note that many roads
in the town have no names, and inquiring about them only produces
puzzled stares from passersby. However, the town is so small that
finding your way around is not a problem.

On November 15 the town's Khmer community takes to the water to
race traditional Khmer boats—long, slim rowing vessels, often with a
half-man, half-bird figurehead—during the Ghe Ngo Water Festival,
a celebration of fertility. In April the Khmer New Year is celebrated
with another water festival.

One of the most beautiful Khmer structures in Vietnam is the **Kleang
Pagoda.** The pagoda and nearby communal longhouse and meditation
center are off the road behind graceful palm groves and huge banana
trees. Originally constructed in the 16th century, the pagoda was rebuilt in the French-Khmer style at the turn of the 20th century. It's an
almost ethereal photo opportunity if you can persuade monks to pose
in the foreground—a request they're willing to comply with once convinced. Watch out for their enthusiasm, though: local Khmer monks
are often so delighted to see you that they may drag you to the nearby
monastic school to introduce you to their friends and have you teach
them a little English. ⊠ *Nguyen Chi Thanh St.*

The **Khmer Museum** is housed in a large stucco French-Khmer colonial-style building with classical colonnades, Khmer flutes and eaves
around the roof, and half-man, half-beast Khmer figures on the walls
and stairways leading to the entrance. The structure was originally built
as a Khmer school in the 19th century. During the French-Indochina
War the building was the headquarters for the local French militia, and
during the Vietnam War it was a headquarters for American troops.
The museum's collection includes Khmer statues and clothing, antique pots and utensils, and two long racing boats painted in vivid green
and reds. Across the street from the museum are Khmer religious
schools. ⊠ *Nguyen Chi Thanh St.* ⊠ *Free.* ⊙ *Tues.–Sun. 8–4:30.*

Built early in the 20th century, the large, active **Catholic church** and nearby
convent are classic examples of French colonial neoclassical architecture. The church is the largest structure in town and can be seen from
everywhere. ⊠ *Hai Ba Trung St.*

The **Clay Pagoda** (Dat Set Pagoda) is a vibrantly decorated Vietnamese
temple built entirely out of clay. Even the statues, dragons, and gargoyles inside are fashioned from clay and painted bright colors. This
is the most popular temple with the town's Vietnamese population. Inside are candles so big and so broad—each about 40 ft high and

wide that two people extending their arms around it can barely reach each other—that they can burn continuously for 30 to 40 years. ⊠ *Hai Ba Trung St.*

The **Matoc (Bat) Pagoda,** 6 km (4 mi) from Soc Trang, is the most interesting of the hundreds of Khmer temples and wats in the countryside around the town. Legend has it that about 400 years ago Khmer monks constructed the pagoda to honor the big bats that live in the mango trees surrounding it. In the Buddhist religion bats are considered sacred and, above all, lucky. Despite the effects of war in the region, these bats survived. Strangely, the bats don't eat the fruit of the trees on which they live but feed on fruit from forests several miles away. Many Chinese from the Cholon district of Ho Chi Minh City make two-day pilgrimages to the pagoda to gather good fortune from the bats. The best time to see these night creatures is dawn or dusk. After visiting the pagoda, take a walk through the surrounding Khmer villages. The first village is about 55 yards from the pagoda, hidden by a small copse of fruit trees. The next village is nearby. People in the villages live isolated lives, but are friendly, and may invite you to have a cup of tea with them. ⊠ *Hai Ba Trung St.*

Twelve kilometers (7 miles) outside town, in the village of Dai Tan, is the **China Bowl Pagoda** (Xa Lon), the largest Khmer pagoda and religious school (for novice monks) in the area. The original pagoda was destroyed during the Vietnam War and was rebuilt using China clay ceramic tiles, hence the name.

Lodging

$$ 🏨 **Khanh Hung Hotel.** Although not the best in town, the Khanh Hung is a basic, relatively comfortable place to spend a night or two. Don't be put off by the overlighted and rather bleak-looking lobby; the better rooms are large, bright, and airy. Be sure to ask for one of the eight rooms with shower and private bathroom; the cheapest ones share a toilet down the hall, though they do have their own showers. ⊠ *15 Tran Hung Dao St.,* ☎ *079/821–026 or 079/820–099. 55 rooms, 8 with bath. Restaurant, air-conditioning. No credit cards.*

$$ 🏨 **Phuong Lan Hotel.** This hotel is Soc Trang's best; it's in the center of town and is fairly comfortable. Rooms are large and have the standard uninspired state-run-hotel decor of nylon curtains and bedspreads. The hotel also has karaoke rooms. ⊠ *124 Dong Khoi St.,* ☎ *079/821–619 or 079/821–993. 20 rooms. Restaurant, air-conditioning. MC, V.*

En Route After leaving Soc Trang, on the way to Ca Mau (☞ *below*), you will pass through the village of **Vinh Loi** (20 km [12 mi] away), where incense is made. It's easy to spot the village from the road—you'll see thousands of incense sticks drying along its sides.

⬛ Mau

❽ *179 km (111 mi) southwest of Can Tho, 350 km (217 mi) southwest of Ho Chi Minh City.*

On the Dai Dong River at the Phung Hiep Canal, some 50 km (31 mi) from the South China Sea, Ca Mau is the heart of Vietnam's version of the Wild West. An isolated, rough-and-tumble kind of territory, it evokes what the American West must have been like long ago. People even wear beat-up old hats that look like cowboy hats. But everyone is very friendly, even if they do unabashedly stare at you. Most of the population of about 40,000 subsists on fishing. Tourists seldom come to Ca Mau because it's not very easy to get here, although it's worth a visit. The town is inaccessible for much of the year because of the monsoons (during which time no flights are available), and the old U.S. air base that now serves as an airport is sometimes hazardous, even in the dry season. Although the airport advertises two flights a week to and from Saigon, the solitary ground staff has no idea when the next flight will actually arrive.

But it's worth trying to get here, whether by boat, by car, or bus from Can Tho or all the way from Saigon (a 13-hour trip). The town has an almost medieval atmosphere, with its chaotic collection of wooden houses leaning over the Dai Dong River, 20 ft below. Also running through the town are tributaries and canals that feed off the river. Along the riverbanks are lush mangrove forests and palm groves with a fascinating panoply of river life: people fishing, sleeping, working, washing, and drinking. Boat trips from Ca Mau's waterfront cost about $70 a day on a private boat and $100 a day on a state-owned boat. Have your guide—either the person you've brought from Ho Chi Minh City or someone from a local hotel—ask around about boats. They range in size from small ones for a few people to larger ones for up to 20.

One of the highlights of a trip to Ca Mau is the **U Minh Cajeput Forest,** 35 km (22 mi) from town and reachable only by boat. This forest of pearl-white cajeput trees is in a swamp, so the boat has to wind its way through the sometimes thick undergrowth. The journey through the forest is quite breathtaking and eerily quiet. But beware of mosquitoes. The U Minh Forest can be approached from Ca Mau or Nam Can (☞ *below*). Let your guide or hotel make boat arrangements.

A daylong boat trip from Ca Mau will take you to the **Minh Hai Mangrove Forest,** one of the largest mangrove forests in the world and a truly primeval experience. The growth is so dense that it's almost unnavigable, but the boats manage to weave their way around the outskirts of the forest or to take wide channels through it. Often the most accessible areas are bordered by lone military outposts on the rivers and estuaries flowing to the sea. Most local soldiers live on their own or with their families in wooden houses above the wash on the muddy banks. Arriving tourist boats combat boredom, and often for no fee these soldiers will take you along the edge of the forest and, if possible, into the interior. Watch out for marauding monkeys and the odd crocodile.

Forty kilometers (25 miles) west of Ca Mau by boat is a series of riverine settlements called **Dan Dai.** The area is well known for its privately owned bird sanctuaries on 2 to 120 acres of small mangrove reserves. Not only can you see rare birds, but you can also find wildcats, monkeys, and deer. Beware: the owners of the reserves often ask for money *after* the fact, sometimes as much as $100, so be sure to negotiate a fee before you enter (you shouldn't pay more than $2 per person). To get to the sanctuaries, take a small boat from Ca Mau.

Lodging

$ 🏨 **Ca Mau Hotel.** Considering the town's frontierlike atmosphere, the quality of this hotel is surprising. In fact, it's actually one of the better hotels in the Mekong Delta. Rooms have many amenities, including air-conditioning, IDD phones, private showers, and satellite TV. There's also karaoke. ⊠ *20 Phan Ngoc Hien St.,* ☎ *078/834–88* 30 rooms. Restaurant, air-conditioning, travel services. MC, V.

$ 🏨 **Phuong Nam Hotel.** A pleasant surprise in Ca Mau, the Phuong a large and rather busy hotel filled with Vietnamese tourists. It has small ornamental rock pool and spacious rooms with balconies, IDD phones, and satellite TVs. Request one of the deluxe rooms, as there is a variety of cheaper and more basic accommodations. ⊠ *91 P*

Dinh Phung St., ☎ *078/831–752,* FAX *078/834–402. 39 rooms. Restaurant, air-conditioning, travel services. MC, V.*

Side Trip to Nam Can

❾ The best part of a trip to **Nam Can,** 45 km (28 mi) mi south of Ca Mau by boat along the Dan Dai River, is actually the return journey to Ca Mau up the Ngang Canal, which is without doubt one of the most beautiful and exotic stretches anywhere in the delta region. Thick palm and mangrove forests line the water's edge, and tiny fishing and fruit hamlets sell goods from boats along the route.

Nam Can is the last settlement of any size in Vietnam before the sea. About 5,000 people live in the town, which consists of a series of lean-tos and old, abandoned boats used as homes. Although there is some fishing here, the town exists mainly to smuggle in commodities from all over, including consumer goods, fish, and rice. Many of the Vietnamese boat people, who left the country between 1975 and 1979, departed from Nam Can, and they bought many of the wretched vessels they used for their escape right here in town. The locals are very friendly.

There isn't much to do in town, but there is a fascinating daily market on the riverfront, with caged rats, as well as chickens, dogs, and cats, for sale as food, shellfish, vegetables, household goods, and clothing.

THE MEKONG DELTA A TO Z

Arriving and Departing

There are three ways to get to the Mekong Delta, all of which must be arranged from Ho Chi Minh City: you can participate in an organized tour, use the hydrofoil service, or hire a private car with driver and guide through a travel agency. All guides speak English. A private car can be expensive ($300–$500), but it enables you to plan your own trip and go farther into the Mekong Delta than you might be able to on a tour. Guides can make all necessary travel arrangements, including boat trips. **Vidotours** (☞ Travel Agencies, *below*) organizes trips for individuals, and many of its tours and treks can take you to the most far-flung places.

Getting Around

By Boat

The most scenic parts of the Mekong Delta are accessible only by boat. Boat trips can be prearranged by your tour company, hired by your guide, or arranged through your hotel for as little as $2 an hour at every dock in every town. Be sure to keep an eye on your bags and valuables during your trip. Can Tho is the departure point for riverboat trips to the river islands.

By Car

Private cars with drivers and tours can be arranged only in Ho Chi Minh City.

By Guided Tour

Group tours that travel via tour bus and boat are available through the Sinh Café or Kim's Café (☞ Travel Agencies, *below*), as well as through more upscale (although not necessarily better) state-run agencies such as **Saigon Tourist. Vidotours** is the best agency for tours of the region.

By Motorbike

If you want to see the Mekong Delta by motorbike, rent one from the **Sinh Café** (☞ Travel Agencies, *below*) in Saigon; there are special discount rates if you rent one for longer periods. Be sure to ask for the motorbike's documents, and try to get a newer Honda. Many of the scooters rented here—such as older Lambrettas from the '50s and '60s—break down almost immediately. Take your motorbike for a test drive before you venture on your way with it.

Contacts and Resources

Currency Exchange

It's a good idea to bring cash, although if you need to change dollars or traveler's checks your hotel can probably do so.

Precautions

If you're planning to travel in the Mekong Delta for 10 or more days, make sure you're adequately prepared. There are malaria-carrying mosquitoes all over the delta and in some of the forests. Other mosquitoes carry diseases such as Japanese encephalitis (or Japanese B). Typhus, which is waterborne, is also a major health problem. However, it's almost unheard of for a tourist to contract any of these diseases; nevertheless, take precautions. Bring along mosquito coils and mosquito repellent for longer stays; malaria pills are generally a waste of time. Hotels usually provide mosquito netting. Try to cover your body at all times by wearing long-sleeve shirts and pants—day and night—and never drink anything but bottled or boiled water. *See* Health *in* Smart Travel Tips A to Z for more information on health precautions.

Travel Agencies

IN HO CHI MINH CITY

The following agencies arrange private and group tours from Ho Chi Minh City to the Mekong Delta:

Kim's Café (⊠ 272 De Tham St., District 1). **Saigon Tourist** (Main office, ⊠ 49 Le Thanh Ton St., District 1, ☎ 08/823–0100, FAX 08/822–4987; budget office, in Café Apricot, ⊠ 187 Pham Ngu Lao St., ☎ 08/835–4535). **Sinh Café Travel** (⊠ 246–248 De Tham St., District 1, ☎ 08/835–5601 or 08/836–9420). **Vidotours** (⊠ 41 Dinh Tien Hoan St., District 1, ☎ 08/829–1438, FAX 08/829–1435).

IN THE MEKONG DELTA

Can Tho Tourist (Cong Ty Du Lich Can Tho; ⊠ 20 Hai Ba Trung St., Can Tho, ☎ 071/821–853, FAX 071/822–719). **Tien Giang Tourist** (Cong Ty Dy Lich; ⊠ On riverfront at intersection of Rach Gam and Trung Trac Sts., My Tho, ☎ 073/872–154 or 073/872–105).

8 PORTRAITS OF VIETNAM

VIETNAM AT A GLANCE: A CHRONOLOGY

Early History

ca. 1300 BC   The Dong Son, the earliest recorded civilization in what is now Vietnam, emerge in the Red River Delta in the region that would later become Hanoi. This far-reaching culture is known for its elaborate bronze kettledrums, which have been discovered as far away as Sumatra, Bali, and Australia.

208 BC   The loosely organized feudal lords, the Lac Viet, of the Red River Delta are conquered by a renegade Chinese general who claims the title of Nam Viet (emperor of the Viet people in the south). The region north of Champa is called Dai Co Viet.

111 BC   The Han Chinese invade and conquer Tonkin and Annam (what is now northern Vietnam). Through about 100 BC, the Han dynasty pursues a policy of administrative and cultural incorporation of Tonkin and Annam into the Chinese empire.

AD 40   The Trung Sisters lead a successful rebellion against the Chinese: After the Chinese execute a high-ranking Vietnamese feudal lord, the lord's widow and her sister mobilize the disorganized Vietnamese chieftains against the Chinese governor. After a quick victory the sisters are proclaimed queens of the newly independent Vietnamese state.

AD 43   Chinese forces reconquer the new Vietnamese state. The Trung sisters choose to commit suicide rather than accept defeat.

AD 100–500   The Funan Kingdom rules the southern part of Vietnam (later known as Cochin China). This Indianized kingdom has major trading centers in the region near what is today Kien Giang. Archaeologists have found evidence of trade links between Funan, China, Indonesia, India, and Persia. Discovery of a Roman medallion in Funan dating from AD 152 indicates the Funanese may have had trade networks extending as far as ancient Rome. Although not much is known about this kingdom, many believe it was either the progenitor of or sister state to the later Khmer Empire.

ca. AD 100   The Champa Kingdom emerges near present-day Danang in southern Annam. Like the Funan Kingdom, the Kingdom of Champa was based on strong trade links with India. The Cham culture adopted Indianized art forms and architectural styles as well as written Sanskrit. The Cham ruins in central Vietnam today are evidence of these influences.

AD 166   The first documented direct contact between Vietnam and the West occurs when Roman travelers arrive in the Red River Delta.

Early Dynasties

939–70   The Annamese Ngo dynasty, under Ngo Quyen, ousts the Chinese and establishes an independent state in the Red River Delta.

967–80   Dinh dynasty: Emperor Dinh Bo Linh ascends the throne and renames the independent state Dai Co Viet.

980–1009   Early Le dynasty: The Dinh dynasty is overthrown by Le Dai Han.

1010–1225   Ly dynasty: Emperor Ly Thai To establishes this dynasty. Thang Long, the City of the Ascending Dragon, becomes the capital and will later come to be known as Hanoi. This dynasty is known for promoting a Chinese-style mandarin education system, symbolized by the construction of Van Mieu, the Temple of Literature, in Hanoi. The dynasty is also known for promoting Mahayana Buddhism over Confucian values and for expanding the Vietnamese state's territory southward into Cham lands through the promotion of agricultural development and the creation of Vietnamese villages. The mandarin Ly Thuong Kiet maintains the dynasty's independence by defeating successive Khmer, Chinese, and Cham army incursions.

1225–1400 First Tran dynasty: This dynasty is known for increasing the nation's population and its cultivated land. Its most celebrated single achievement is the repulsion of Kublai Khan's invading Mongol forces in the mid-13th century. In a brilliant naval victory in the Bach Dang River, Tran Hung Dao lured a superior Mongol fleet into the mouth of the estuary. He patiently held the Mongols at bay, positioning them in a vulnerable area in which their ships were impaled on steel-tipped poles planted by Vietnamese forces and the crews massacred when low tide arrived.

1400–06 Ho dynasty: In 1400 Tonkinese leader Ho Quy Le overthrows the Tran. Tran loyalists and the Cham, who had been fighting their Tonkinese northern neighbors, encourage the Chinese to intervene and reinstate the Tran.

ater Dynasties

1407–13 Later Tran dynasty: After being reinstated with Chinese assistance, the Tran reign briefly.

1413–28 The Chinese Ming Empire reconquers Vietnam and occupies the country, forcing further taxes, servitude, and Chinese culture on the Vietnamese.

1428–1786 Later Le dynasty: The Chinese officially recognize Vietnam's independence following the Lam Son uprising, a revolt led by Emperor Le Loi, who establishes the Le dynasty. It lasts until 1786.

1460–98 Under the rule of Emperor Le Thanh Tong, a comprehensive legal code is introduced and Vietnamese domination extended farther southward into Cham territory. Laos and the Khmer region become a vassal territory of Vietnam.

1516 Portuguese traders land in the port of Danang and set up trading posts alongside their Japanese and Chinese predecessors in the port of Fiafo, the site of present-day Hoi An.

1527 Dominican missionaries from Portugal arrive in Danang to gain converts among the people living there.

1545 As Le rulers' authority weakens, civil strife splits the country for nearly two centuries. The Le dynasty continues its official rule, but warring lords who accept Le rule operate largely independent of the emperor. Much of the conflict is between the Trinh lords, who dominate the north from Tonkin, and the Nguyen lords, who rule from Hue to the south. Although neither achieves dominance, the Nguyen establish control over the Khmer areas of the Mekong Delta and populate the area with Vietnamese settlers.

1580 Franciscan missionaries from the Philippines begin proselytizing in central Vietnam.

1613 English attempts at establishing trade links with Vietnam are thwarted with the murder of an East India Company representative in Hanoi.

1615 French Jesuit missionaries expelled from Japan arrive in Vietnam.

1627 Alexandre de Rhodes, a French Jesuit missionary, adapts spoken Vietnamese to the Roman alphabet, leading to the current Vietnamese script. He creates a Vietnamese dictionary in 1651, six years after being expelled from Vietnam for entering without permission.

1637 Dutch trade is established in North Vietnam.

1700 The country splits into the Trinh dynasty north of Hue and the Nguyen dynasty, which includes Hue and lands to the south. During the mid-17th century, Cambodia becomes a vassal territory of Vietnam.

1771–1802 Tay Son Rebellion: After years of a weak central government and warring factions, a rebellion starts in the village of Tay Son, near present-day Qui Nhon in south-central Vietnam. Led by the three sons of a wealthy merchant, the Tay Son rebels capture central and southern Vietnam by 1783, sending the surviving Nguyen lord, Prince Nguyen Anh, into exile in Thailand. In retaliation, Prince Nguyen Anh asks the French for their assistance in his return to Vietnam to defeat the Tay Son rebels. Meanwhile, the Tay Son conquer the Trinh in the north and pledge allegiance to the weak Le dynasty. The Le emperor, however, asks the Chinese to help him control the Tay Son. Mobilizing popular support against the Chinese, one of the Tay Son brothers proclaims himself Emperor Quang Trung and leads the Vietnamese in an overwhelming defeat of the Chinese forces near Hanoi in 1789. But soon after, Prince Nguyen Anh, with support from French-trained forces, returns to southern Vietnam and moves north against the Tay Son.

French Influence

1802–1945 In 1802 Prince Nguyen Anh proclaims himself Emperor Gia Long, officially beginning the Nguyen dynasty. When Gia Long captures Hanoi from the Tay Son rebels, it marks the first time in 200 years that Vietnam is united, with Hue as its capital. French missionary activity begins to spread, as the Nguyen develop a mutually tolerant relationship with the French.

1847 The first clash occurs between Emperor Thieu Tri, successor to the Nguyen throne, and the French, after the French attack Danang Harbor in retaliation for a Vietnamese crackdown on Catholic converts. Also in this year Nguyen emperor Tu Duc ascends the throne and continues the struggle against the French.

1861 French colonial forces win the battle of Ky Hoa and take Saigon. Defeated, Tu Duc's forces disband. But unhappy with the prospect of French rule, local elites continue resistance, using anti-French guerrilla tactics in the south.

1862 Emperor Tu Duc negotiates a treaty with the French, giving broad religious, economic, and political concessions: permission for missionaries to proselytize throughout the country, the opening of ports to French and Spanish trade, surrender of the three eastern provinces of Cochin China, and payment of a large indemnity to French.

1863 The French expand into Cambodia.

1867 The French name the southern part of the country Cochin China and take over its administration after a final French offensive breaks Vietnamese resistance.

1872 French gunrunner Jean Dupuis is held under siege in Hanoi after attempting to deliver munitions to Yunnanese warlords up the Red River. The French dispatch gunboats under the command of Francis Garnier to retrieve Dupuis and restore order. Garnier instead overtakes the Hanoi Citadel, establishes it as his garrison, and demands tribute from Vietnamese vanguards along the Red River. In response, the Co Den (Black Flag), made up of H'Mong, Chinese, and Vietnamese pirates, fight to retake the citadel. Garnier is eventually captured and beheaded at the Cao Gia Bridge. Dupuis escapes with the returning gunboats. The Co Den terrorize Red River villages, and the first systematic purging of missionaries begins.

1883 After Tu Duc's death, French forces take the Imperial City in Hue and impose the Treaty of Protectorate on the Imperial Court. The French give protectorate status—as an independent government subject to French policy—to the north, which they designate Tonkin, and central Vietnam, which they designate Annam. Cochin China remains a colony administered directly by France.

1887 The French create the Indochinese Union in order to end Vietnamese expansion into Cambodia and Laos, thereby officially ending a unified Vietnamese state. The Union includes Tonkin, Annam, Cochin China, Cambodia, and the Port of Qizhouwan in China.

1890 Ho Chi Minh is born as Nguyen Sinh Cung in Nghe An Province in north-central Vietnam.

1893 France further extends its colonial influence by moving into Laos.

1911 Ho Chi Minh leaves Vietnam and begins his world travels. Over the next 30 years he works in France and spends time in Moscow, becoming involved with the growing communist movement.

1919 Ho Chi Minh petitions American president Woodrow Wilson, at the Versailles peace conference held at the end of World War I, for self-determination for Vietnam and is refused.

1920 Ho Chi Minh joins the French Communist Party.

1930 Ho Chi Minh and his colleagues form the Indochinese Communist Party in Hong Kong, where they are free from French repression.

1932 Bao Dai, the nominal emperor of Vietnam, returns from his education in France to take over the Nguyen dynasty throne under French guidance.

1940 Rather than risk a full-scale confrontation, the Nazi-backed, French Vichy government peacefully capitulates to Japanese troops' invasion of Vietnam. The Japanese leave the French administration in place as the most efficient way of controlling the region.

1941 Ho Chi Minh returns to Vietnam and forms the Vietnamese Independence League, commonly known as the Vietminh nationalist movement, to resist both the Japanese and the French.

1944 General Vo Nguyen Giap forms the Vietminh army in the north with military funding and arms from the U.S. Office of Strategic Services (OSS) to fight the allied Japanese and French.

1945 In March, as a major Vietminh military offensive gets started, the Japanese take over by force the administration of Indochina from the French. Backed by Tokyo, Emperor Bao Dai proclaims Vietnam an independent state under Japanese auspices. In August, as Japan's war machine crumbles, the Vietminh takes over large portions of the country. During that month the Japanese also transfer control of Indochina to Vietminh forces under Ho Chi Minh and Vo Nguyen Giap. Bao Dai abdicates in an attempt to maintain some national unity. Ho proclaims the area north of the 18th parallel the Democratic Republic of Vietnam; south of the parallel is declared an associated state within the French union by the allies, with Bao Dai as supreme counselor. Japanese policies of planting industrial crops and requisitioning rice to feed the Japanese army as well as bad flooding combine to cause famine throughout the north, killing 2 million of the north's 10 million inhabitants.

The French-Indochina War and the Vietnam War

1946 In March the French and Vietminh reach a peace accord, determining that Vietnam will be a "free state" within the French Union. In June the French violate the agreement by proclaiming a separate government for Cochin China. In November, as tensions grow, the French navy bombs Haiphong. Vietminh forces withdraw from Hanoi in December after attacking the French garrison, retreating to build their movement in rural areas. The French-Indochina War begins. Bao Dai flees to France as hostilities increase.

1947 In France Bao Dai reaches an understanding with the French on recognizing limited Vietnamese independence.

1949 Bao Dai returns to Vietnam after three years of self-imposed exile in France to designate Vietnam as an "associated state" of France. France retains control of defense and finances but grants administrative authority to the Vietnamese.

1950 Ho declares that the Democratic Republic of Vietnam is the only legal government. The Democratic Republic of Vietnam is recognized by the Soviet Union and China. The United States and Britain join the French in recognizing Bao Dai's government as legitimate. The Chinese begin to supply weapons to the Vietminh. U.S. president Truman authorizes $15 million in military aid to the French in Indochina to fight the Vietminh.

1953 Laos and Cambodia gain greater independence from France. French forces occupy Dien Bien Phu. The Vietminh pushes into Laos. Ho says he is ready to discuss peace with the French.

1954 The Vietnamese defeat the French at Dien Bien Phu, marking the end of the French-Indochina War. Bao Dai selects Ngo Dinh Diem, who has strong ties to the American government, as prime minister. Agreement is reached among France, Britain, the United States, and the Soviet Union as part of the Geneva Accords to cease hostilities Indochina and to divide Vietnam temporarily at the 17th parallel until national elections determine a single government. The country is divided into the Democratic Republic of Vietnam in the north and the Republic of Vietnam in the south. Seeing a threat to his power, Bao Dai denounces the agreement. As part of the agreement, French forces leave Hanoi. The U.S. government affirms support of Prime Minister Diem with a pledge of $100 million in aid. Hundreds of thousands of refugees, mostly Vietnamese Catholics worried that religious tolerance will not be practiced in the Vietminh-controlled north, flee to the south with U.S. Navy assistance.

1955 The United States begins to provide direct aid to the Saigon government and to train the South Vietnamese army. Diem rejects the Geneva Accords and refuses to participate in nationwide elections. He becomes president of South Vietnam and begins cracking down on suspected Vietminh members in the south. The Vietminh begins to show communist tendencies as it promotes social upheaval and radical land reforms in the north.

1957 The Soviet Union proposes the permanent division of Vietnam at the 17th parallel. Southern-based Vietminh Nationalists and northern communists strengthen ties in their opposition to the southern regime.

1959 As the Vietminh Nationalists from the south and the communists from the north continue to strengthen ties, Diem increases repression against suspected communists and dissidents in the south.

1960 The remaining southern Vietminh members change the name of their movement to the National Liberation Front (NLF), known to the South Vietnam government and the Americans as and popularly called the Vietcong. (The term Vietcong is generally used throughout this book in reference to the opposition movement in the south because it is probably the most familiar term. However, Vietcong—which means, loosely, Vietnamese communists—was the name given by the Saigon government and the Americans to this opposition movement. As Diem's public popularity wanes, southern army officers stage an unsuccessful coup against him.

1961 Close advisers to U.S. president John F. Kennedy visit Vietnam and recommend American military intervention disguised as flood relief on behalf of the weak southern regime. Kennedy rejects the idea but provides military "advisers" and more equipment. Indirect American military support increases over the next few years.

1963 Thich Quang Duc, a Buddhist monk from Hue, is the first of many monks to commit suicide through self-immolation in Saigon, protesting Diem's repressive tactics. With American support, Saigon generals murder Diem. By this time American aid is up to approximately 15,000 military advisers and $500 million.

1964 American-backed general Nguyen Khanh seizes power in Saigon. North Vietnam increases support for the southern revolutionaries. An unconfirmed attack on U.S. destroyers in the Tonkin Gulf prompts passage of the Gulf of Tonkin resolution in Congress, permitting the Americans to respond by bombing North Vietnam for the first time. Years later it is determined that the incident may have been staged by the U.S. government.

1965 The first American combat troops arrive in Danang. Sustained bombing of North Vietnam by American planes begins. Nguyen Cao Ky takes over the weak southern government. By the end of the year, 200,000 American troops are in Vietnam.

1966 President Charles de Gaulle of France calls for U.S. withdrawal from Vietnam. U.S. president Johnson escalates American involvement in Vietnam; the number of U.S. troops reaches 400,000.

1967 Nguyen Van Thieu is elected president of South Vietnam, and Nguyen Cao Ky becomes vice president. Americans begin to fortify Khe Sanh, a hamlet in the central highlands, in preparation for a major North Vietnamese assault. After heavy fighting at Khe Sanh, U.S. troops withdraw from the area, leaving the battle-scarred hillsides bare. Later the United States realizes that Khe Sanh was a ploy to divert U.S. forces from the Tet Offensive. By the year's end American forces number 500,000.

1968 During the Tet Offensive southern insurgents and northern forces orchestrate coordinated attacks on southern towns and cities. Although tactically a failure, the offensive proves that South

Vietnam and U.S. strategists have seriously underestimated the strength of the NLF. American troops massacre South Vietnamese civilians in My Lai. In part because of the Tet Offensive and My Lai, opposition to the war in Vietnam by the American public and politicians increases. American forces number 540,000.

1969 Paris peace talks, which began in 1968, expand to include the Saigon government and NLF representatives. The U.S. government, under President Nixon's administration, begins the secret bombing of Cambodia to root out suspected NLF bases there. In response to growing domestic opposition and military frustrations, the American government says it will "Vietnamize" the war and begins withdrawing troops. Ho Chi Minh dies of natural causes in Hanoi.

1970 U.S. national security adviser Henry Kissinger begins secret talks with Le Duc Tho, the acting North Vietnamese foreign minister. President Richard Nixon announces that U.S. forces have attacked NLF sanctuaries in Cambodia, provoking a major upsurge of antiwar action in the United States. American troops in Vietnam number 280,000 at year's end.

1971 South Vietnamese forces enter Laos in an attempt to cut off the Ho Chi Minh Trail. This network of supply roads stretching from North to South Vietnam, a critical lifeline for the NLF, winds through the mountainous areas on the border between Vietnam, Laos, and Cambodia and is very difficult for Saigon troops to control. The number of American troops is reduced to 140,000.

1972 Nixon announces that Kissinger has been in secret negotiations with North Vietnam. Northern forces cross the 17th parallel. Americans resume the bombing of the north and mine Haiphong Harbor. Kissinger and Le Duc Tho make progress on a peace agreement, but South Vietnamese president Thieu resists a cease-fire.

1973 Kissinger and Tho sign a cease-fire agreement in Paris in January. The last American troops leave Vietnam in March. The United States halts the bombing of Cambodia.

1974 Thieu declares a continuation of war. The NLF further builds up supplies and troops in the south.

1975 North Vietnamese and NLF forces each capture key strategic town Thieu flees Vietnam for Taiwan before settling in Britain. The remaining Americans and their key Vietnamese colleagues in Saigon are evacuated in April. Images of the last overpacked U.S. helicopters lifting from the American Embassy in Saigon are emblazoned in the public mind as the United States—after 30 years in Vietnam—makes a hasty retreat. Communist forces capture Saigon on April 30 and accept the surrender of the government of South Vietnam, thereby unifying the north and the south. The U.S. government does not recognize the legitimacy of a reunified Vietnam. The U.S.-led economic embargo of North Vietnam, in place since the '60s, is extended to the whole of reunified Vietnam. The Soviet Union increases support for the newly unified country.

The Post–Vietnam War Years to the Present

1977 U.S. president Carter commences talks between the United States and Vietnam about official recognition of Vietnam by the U.S. government. Due to the increasing links between Hanoi and Moscow, these talks eventually grind to a halt until the early '90s.

1978 Vietnam joins COMECON (the Soviet-influenced Eastern Europe economic community). Relations among Vietnam, Cambodia, an its Chinese benefactor deteriorate as skirmishes along the Vietnamese-Cambodian border increase. Hanoi signs a friendship pact with the Soviet Union. Following Khmer Rouge border incursions at Chau Doc and the growing China-Cambodia alliance, Vietnam responds and is involved in armed conflict with Cambodia until 1989, effectively ending the "killing fields," the brutal murder of more than a million Cambodians by the Pol Pot regime.

1979 In partial retaliation for Vietnam's conflict in Cambodia, China invades Vietnam. The Chinese Red Army penetrates as far as Vinh Yen, only 60 km (37 mi) north of Hanoi, but is quickly repulsed within two weeks by the People's Army of Vietnam.

1986 Hanoi selects reform-minded Nguyen Van Linh as general secretary of the Communist Party of Vietnam, signaling a cautious opening to the West. Vietnam commits to *doi moi*, the reform of socialist economic policies into a more market-oriented system.

1989 Vietnamese forces withdraw from Cambodia, ending a 50-year period of almost continuous war between the two countries.

1991 Ailing general secretary Linh is replaced by Prime Minister Do Muoi, who vows to continue the economic reforms begun by Linh. The Politburo and the Central Committee of the Vietnamese Communist Party undergo a major shift; aging, conservative leaders are replaced by younger, more liberally oriented members. Prime Minister Vo Van Kiet and Do Muoi visit Beijing in an attempt to heal relations.

1992 Chinese prime minister Li Peng visits Hanoi to further improve strained relations between Vietnam and China.

1994 The United States ends its economic embargo on Vietnam, which helps the country begin to rebuild its economy and infrastructure through International Monetary Fund (IMF) and World Bank loans and greatly increased foreign investments.

1997 The beginning of normalization of relations between Vietnam and the United States occurs. The U.S. Embassy officially opens in Hanoi, a U.S. consulate opens in Ho Chi Minh City, and the Vietnamese Embassy officially opens in Washington.

1998 General Le Kha Phieu assumes the top position of the Vietnamese Communist Party from General Secretary Do Muoi. In an effort to further normalize trade relations between the United States and Vietnam, the U.S. Congress waives the Jackson-Vanik Treaty, which had effectively prohibited trade between the two countries.

1999 Vietnam signs U.S. trade agreement in principal in July. U.S. secretary of state Madeleine Albright visits Vietnam.

2000 Bill Clinton visits Vietnam to discuss trade relations and other issues; he is the first U.S. president to visit the country since the end of the Vietnam War. The country celebrates the 25th anniversary of the "Fall of Saigon," which signaled the end of the Vietnam War. Fourteen years after committing to the doi moi reform process, Vietnam enters the 21st century with limited political and business reforms in place. The U.S. signs the U.S.–Vietnam trade agreement.

— By Jim Spencer

— Updated by William Richardson

RIDING THE DREAM

THE FIRST THING about Vietnam that struck me was how familiar it seemed. The second was how unique it was. The third thing that struck me was a Honda Dream motorbike—carrying a family of four through the chaos of midday traffic. Vietnam is a little surprising like that.

You, too, may find Vietnam oddly familiar, perhaps because you spent years glued to TV images of U.S. helicopters skimming over rice paddies in the Mekong Delta, American soldiers creeping through the thick jungles of the central highlands, and Vietnamese refugees passing trucks bringing GIs to the front; or maybe because you saw Hollywood's version of these events in movies like *Apocalypse Now* and *Platoon*; or maybe you even went to Vietnam yourself. The images of a familiar past may come flooding back to you as you approach the airport in Hanoi over a landscape speckled with craters left by U.S. bombs, or touch down at the airport in Saigon, where American-built tarmac and hangars are still in use.

The desire to come looking for remnants of the war is understandable, especially for those of us from countries whose histories are linked with Vietnam's. And as someone who grew up in New York with a Vietnamese mother educated in America and an American father, surrounded by Vietnamese culture, I had yet another reason for wanting to understand how and why the United States became involved with Vietnam. On my first trip to Vietnam in 1990, I went to discover all I could about what life was like during the Christmas bombing of Hanoi in 1972, and what it was like living in the Vinh Moc underground tunnels. I visited the rooftop bar at the Rex Hotel to see where wartime journalists gathered nightly to reflect on the day's events.

What I found were only a few visible remnants of the war and its aftermath: Soviet-style memorials and cemeteries; towns where famous battles were fought; airplanes, helicopters, and artifacts on display in museums; and underground tunnel systems like those at Cu Chi, which are now open to tourists. The bomb craters at the Hanoi airport have been made into fish ponds, and the hangars at Saigon's have become storage sheds.

I also discovered that although many people are willing to talk with foreigners about the war, they are more often interested in reviewing the finer points of the latest American music videos, price fluctuations of the Toyota Camry, or the semi-automatic clutch on their new Honda Dream motorbikes—the latest in Vietnamese conspicuous consumption—than they are in rehashing the Battle of Khe Sanh. Others are understandably reluctant to talk about this painful history.

Younger people especially have little time for reflections on what they increasingly see as grandpa's old war stories. After years of strife and isolation, they are ready for greater economic and cultural opportunities. The economic reforms instituted in 1986, *doi moi*, have been one of the major factors in bringing Vietnam out of isolation and onto a global stage where it once danced with the world's most powerful nations.

Until the early '90s Vietnam was under the influence of the Soviet bloc and was severely crippled by the U.S.-led economic embargo. As a result, the country has only been able to chart an independent course for a very short time. And for better or worse, the Vietnamese have decided that the road ahead lies with a free-market economy. As the country begins the journey toward becoming the next Southeast Asian "tiger"—a status that former Vietnamese foreign minister Nguyen Co Thach cautioned had to be preceded by becoming a "small cat"—Vietnam is at a critical point in its history. To comprehend why you must first understand something about its history of conflict and synthesis.

As a crossroad of global trading, Vietnam has for more than 2,000 years been an object of desire of the major European and Asian powers. From the early Chinese, Cham, and Khmer empires competing for a piece of what is currently Vietnam right up to the French, Americans, and Soviets vying for political and cultural influence

Vietnam has been a contested land. All who have come have left their mark on the country, resulting in a culture that is an amalgamation of many foreign elements yet one that is uniquely Vietnamese. There are markedly few places in the world where you can find Catholic church spires poking out of the tropical rain forest, indigenous hill-tribe leaders speaking French and English, and farmers piling their Japanese and East German motorcycles high with Chinese-made dishes on their way home from the market.

It would be a mistake, however, to say that Vietnam has compromised its identity by assimilating elements of these invading cultures. This paradox is best summed up by the comments of an aging revolutionary who graciously welcomed me into his home when I first visited the country. Once a high-ranking member of the diplomatic team that negotiated the peace agreement with the Americans in 1973, he had been without question a thorn in the side of both the French and American governments. Strangely, though, on numerous occasions, while sipping French Cognac after dinner, he looked me in the eye and—in impeccable French—made sure I understood one thing: "*Je ne suis pas un Francophile, mais je suis vraiment un Francophone*" (I am not a Francophile, but I am very much a Francophone). Although he felt no lost love for his former colonizers, he did celebrate that he was himself a product of French culture. This kind of cultural adoption predates the French and has come to define a Vietnamese culture of adaptation.

The Conquering Chinese, and the Cham and Khmer Empires

From about 200 BC to AD 1428, Vietnam was subject to heavy Chinese influence, and consequently made a national pastime of kicking out invaders from the north. For centuries Hanoi and Beijing danced in a cycle of liberation and domination until the Chinese were finally kicked out for good in the early 15th century.

The Chinese invaders influenced every aspect of Vietnam, from agriculture to architecture to education to cuisine, particularly in the north. In the 3rd century BC, the Chinese began to promote intensive rice paddy farming in the Red River Delta, replacing nonintensive dryland crops. Over the centuries this system spread throughout the country and eventually came to symbolize the Vietnamese way of life. The Chinese also established an educational system in Vietnam modeled on the Chinese mandarin system. The system was embraced by the Vietnamese and thrived in Vietnam long after the Chinese had abandoned it in their own country.

Other Chinese elements include temples replete with dragons, words in the Vietnamese language, and, more recently, a taste for monosodium glutamate, which rumor has it was imported during wartime from China to add flavor to spare diets. Mahayana Buddhism and Confucianism, too, came to Vietnam from the north, and you can readily see their influence in today's Vietnam. These influences, however, never overshadowed the most Vietnamese form of religious practice in the country: *ban tho,* the altar to family ancestors that graces almost every Vietnamese home from Saigon to Son La to San Jose.

The influence of the Chinese wasn't as strong in the south, where they had competition. Beginning around AD 100, the Funan Kingdom ruled what is now southern Vietnam, and the Kingdom of Champa controlled the central region. Both Indianized kingdoms have had a major impact on this part of Vietnam and contributed to some of the regional differences found there.

Although attempts have been made to claim only one history for Vietnam, many believe these regions have as much in common with Cambodia, Thailand, the Philippines, and Indonesia as they do with China. Many point to the stronger social and economic roles of women, a warmer disposition, and a less regimented way of life in the south and central regions as vestiges of this earlier period. Since the Cham and Khmer were not as meticulous at imposing and institutionalizing social norms, their influences have not survived as well as those imported from China. Instead, the Indianness of *Indo*-China is mostly felt in the old Cham towers that pepper the central coast with images of Vishnu and Shiva, the Khmer temples in the Mekong Delta, and names of places such as Sadec, Kontum, and Daklak, which harken back to non-Chinese origins.

The Paternalistic French

The Chinese, the Khmer, and the Cham were merely the first to come. Centuries later the French burst onto the scene with their French bread, espresso coffee, and *"mission civilisatrice"* (civilizing mission), in an effort to mold the Vietnamese after themselves. As with the Chinese before them, the French had their own policies of domination and integration, and they saw Vietnam as fertile ground for the expansion of French culture.

For better or worse, the French administration took quite seriously the task of making Vietnam an economically productive Southeast Asian province of France. In doing so, the French extended the tentacles of their complicated educational system into the tropics. Under this system, throughout the early part of the century elite young Vietnamese traveled to France and other French colonies, gaining exposure to Western ideas, culture, and people. In addition, the Vietnamese elite were educated at French lycées in Vietnam. Ironically, at the Marie Curie School in Saigon, for instance, young Vietnamese girls were taught Vietnamese as a foreign language. And although many were impressively knowledgeable about which French province produced the finest French wine, they were unable to say which Vietnamese province grew the best rice.

Both Ho Chi Minh, the Nationalist-turned-Communist revolutionary, and his monarchist-counterpart Bao Dai, the dilettante last emperor of Vietnam, spent many of their early years in France absorbing the culture that would later influence their politics. Perhaps because both ends of the political spectrum of this generation of leaders were educated under the French, elements of French culture have survived Vietnam's tumultuous past few decades: the mildewed colonial villas lining the boulevards of both Hanoi and Saigon, the beret gracefully sported by the occasional man over 50, the excellent French bread hawked on almost every street corner, and the cafés serving espressolike coffee.

The Americans Arrive

Although most people associate U.S. involvement in Vietnam with the time the first marines landed in Danang in 1965, the American government had been interested in Vietnam since the end of World War II. In 1945 the U.S. government sent agents from the Office of Strategic Services (OSS) to collaborate with the British Special Air Service (SAS) in order to gather information in northern Vietnam on the transfer of power following the withdrawal of the Japanese from Southeast Asia. During the mission, code-named Deer, OSS agents and SAS soldiers went to live in Ho Chi Minh's camp in the northern highlands. Finding Ho on death's door, plagued by malaria and dysentery, the Americans and British treated him and probably saved his life.

The OSS officers were so impressed with Ho that they supplied him with arms and other materials, ultimately recommending that the United States back his Nationalist forces against the French. Ho, in turn, also had respect for the Americans. This relationship, no doubt, prompted Ho to have OSS officers by his side when he signed the declaration of independence of the Democratic Republic of Vietnam in Hanoi's Ba Dinh Square on September 2, 1945.

For political reasons, however, Washington chose to back its long-standing allies, the French, instead of Ho. Rather than alienate Paris by siding with the Vietnamese Nationalists, President Truman supported President Charles de Gaulle's efforts to regain Vietnam. From 1945 to 1954 the U.S. government provided substantial military aid to the French and set the stage for a protracted American presence in Vietnam that would splatter across headlines for the next 20 years.

After the French were officially defeated in 1954, the U.S. government continued its anticommunist efforts by contributing military advisors who trained and sometimes fought alongside South Vietnamese troops. But it wasn't until 1965 that Uncle Sam's troops landed in Vietnam, bringing billions of dollars in military hardware, thousands of American GIs, and a robust dose of '60s culture. This time, however, the Americans were not there to support the Nationalist forces, but rather Ho Chi Minh's archival Ngo Dinh Diem, president of a struggling southern regime based in Saigon.

Remnants of the American presence survive today in many forms, even if these don't always inspire the same nostalgic enthusiasm from the Vietnamese as do Fren bread and espresso. In the south, Zippo lighters still spark cigarettes among the elite, and GMC trucks form the basis of the Vietnamese trucking industry—although mostly only the engines are left; the bodies have long since been rebuilt and repainted with "GMC," "Desoto," or "Ford." Even more apparent today is the inundation of contemporary American culture, especially in Saigon: for instance, videos of American movies and compact discs of American bands are sold in shops; and American-style bars and restaurants have replaced some of the less competitive noodle shops.

But there is yet another side to America's relationship with Vietnam: throughout the war both Nationalist and Communist Vietnamese leaders always recognized that the United States comprised both a government and a people. To this day they often speak with great appreciation about the Americans who protested the war. Less controversial yet perhaps more telling is that during a 35-year-plus era of strained and nonexistent official relations, American and Vietnamese people-to-people organizations have had long, respectful relationships. These positive legacies of an American influence on Vietnam are what many Vietnamese appreciate and remember. Today, too, they are more than happy to put the past behind them and to begin a new relationship with America.

The Eastern-Bloc Years

After the last overloaded helicopter took off from the roof of the U.S. Embassy in Saigon in 1975, another superpower stepped in: the Soviet Union. For the next 5 years Vietnam was overrun with Volgas—the boxy Russian-made cars—and thousands of Soviet advisers, engineers, and tourists.

This Soviet influx was part of a multibillion-dollar aid package to build up Vietnam's infrastructure and provide education for Vietnamese in Eastern-bloc countries. But the Soviet Union's efforts to help develop Vietnam were largely negated by the drain of two more wars. In 1979 Vietnam invaded Cambodia in response to numerous Khmer Rouge border incursions, and the People's Army of Vietnam effectively ended Pol Pot's reign of terror and the cultural genocide that had claimed more than a million Cambodian lives.

China, an ally to the Khmer Rouge, sent the Red Army into the north of Vietnam as a human wave; the People's Army of Vietnam quickly repulsed the Chinese. Tensions festered until Vietnamese forces pulled out of Cambodia in 1989. The period of peace that ensued had lasted only two years, when in 1991, with the disintegration of the Soviet Union and the rest of the Eastern bloc nearly complete, Soviet aid dried up, and the Vietnamese were left to rebuild their war-torn economy with no major benefactor. Despite this withdrawal and the financial vacuum it has left, Hanoi's leaders can be relieved that doi moi, their version of perestroika, has not led to the kind of social upheaval that the Soviets faced.

The Soviets have left Vietnam, and Vietnamese children have stopped shouting "*Lien Xo*" (the Vietnamese word for Soviet person)—as they did with me when I first visited in 1990—at any passing Westerner. Nevertheless the Eastern bloc has left a legacy of its own. Thousands of young Vietnamese—educated in everything from civil engineering to commercial banking in Moscow, Budapest, and Havana—speak Russian, Hungarian, and Spanish. Their expertise and international experience have been an important and undervalued tool for helping Vietnam rebuild its infrastructure, schools, and economy after 40 years of devastation. The most visible remnants of the Soviet contribution, however, are the dour, concrete-block apartment buildings in neighborhoods around Hanoi and Saigon. Although probably the least appreciated foreigners to visit Vietnam this century, the Soviets have also contributed to the current culture that is Vietnam.

The Vietnamese Melting Pot

With its history of invasions, perhaps it was inevitable that Vietnam would end up reflecting a mélange of cultural influences. But by incorporating these foreign elements without compromising its identity, the country has created a culture that is uniquely Vietnamese.

An excellent way to get a sense of this melting pot is simply to explore the country. Walk through the streets of Hanoi and Saigon past the French colonial villas, American- and Russian-built monoliths (most notably the old U.S. Embassy in

Saigon and the Viet Xo Cultural Palace in Hanoi), Chinese-style pagodas, and shiny, new, glass-fronted high-rise office buildings. Take a trip to Hue to see the old Imperial City, the former home of the Vietnamese emperors. Although it was modeled on the Forbidden City in Beijing, it is actually relatively new: it was built in the early 19th century by the French architect Olivier de Puymanel, who was influenced by that greater builder of French forts, Vauban. Go to Dalat and wander through Emperor Bao Dai's French colonial–style summer palace. The last emperor of Vietnam, Bao Dai (1914–97) had a reputation for dilettantism matched only by his love of French culture—an attitude reflected in this Dalat retreat.

The most distinctive example of Vietnam's cultural syncretism is to be found at the temple of the Caodai sect, in Tay Ninh Province northwest of Saigon. The sect was founded in the Mekong Delta in the 1920s by Ngo Minh Chieu, a civil servant for the French, who claimed to receive revelations from God. Through the French, Chieu was exposed to a variety of Western philosophies. Caodaism was his attempt to create a universal religion based on the major Eastern and Western religions—a fusion of Buddhism, Confucianism, Taoism, Vietnamese spiritualism, Christianity, and Islam.

By the 1950s and '60s the sect had become so strong that it provided an alternative to both the National Liberation Front or the American-backed Saigon regime. As the Caodai strived to maintain its control over the western part of the Mekong Delta, it grew increasingly politically active and heavily armed. After the war, however, the Caodai took on a lower profile and declined in both numbers and firepower. Today the Caodai faithful are concentrated mainly at the home of their Holy See in Tay Ninh, although temples can be found throughout the Mekong Delta and even in the United States and France.

Decorated in a wild array of colors, the massive structure has towering ceilings like those found in a cathedral. But the tile floors, no-shoes policy, and monks in white robes give it a distinctly pagodalike feel. The most telling sign of Caodai's syncretic nature, however, greets you in the bright, open, main room: a mural of the Caodai pantheon, which includes such diverse notables as Buddha, Jesus Christ, Muhammad, Sun Yat-sen, Victor Hugo, Joan of Arc, and others. The Caodai believe these leaders have all made great contributions to world culture, and that their religious, political, and literary traditions have all been unified in a religion that is neither contradictory nor faddish.

Another example of this mélange of cultures is reflected in the Vietnamese language itself. A history of foreign influences is revealed: wherever you go, look at the signs. For example, many inscriptions on buildings are written in Chinese, as are many of Vietnam's oldest history books. Vietnamese began as a distinct language, with its own indigenous vocabulary and sentence structure but no widespread written form. With the coming of the Chinese and the mandarin educational system, Chinese characters came to be the dominant written language. Throughout this period many Chinese words (known as *Han Viet* or words derived from Chinese) were integrated into the Vietnamese language (known as *Nom Viet,* those words derived from indigenous Vietnamese roots).

In 1627 a French missionary named Alexandre de Rhodes adapted spoken Vietnamese to Roman script in order to facilitate the conversion of the Vietnamese to Catholicism. Rhodes's system took hold, so Vietnam, unlike most of its neighbors, uses a Roman-based alphabet. But don't be fooled: although the language is recognizable to Westerners, spoken Vietnamese is based on a tonal system not easily reflected in the Roman script. Tones are denoted by accents, which are placed above or below words and provide clues to pronunciation. Be careful: a recognizable script doesn't make learning to say words correctly any easier, and you still may end up insulting someone's mother. For example, the different tones applied to a seemingly simple word like "ba" can have many meanings: daddy, three or third, grandmother or lady, poisoned food, a lure or bait, waste or residue, an embrace or hug, a fold in one's arms, a panacea, tasteless or devoid of nutrition, and exhausted.

Today the language continues to change; most recently there have been efforts to "Vietnamize" Vietnamese. But the difficulty in doing so is manifest in the tenacity of such words as *tam biet,* the Han Viet word for *chao* in Nom Viet (good-bye in English).

and *banh ga-to,* the Vietnamese word for Western-style cake, which is derived from the French words for bread and cake—*pain* and *gâteau.* These words reflect the unique synthesis now a part of the Vietnamese language.

One word that is universally understood, however is *ca phe,* from the French word, café, or coffee. Unlike most other countries in Asia, good coffee is ever-present in Vietnam, served espresso-style in almost every café. A tradition adopted from the French, the café takes different forms in Vietnam—both the familiar French indoor-outdoor style and a Vietnamized version—tables on the sidewalk surrounded by small plastic stools.

Although Vietnamese coffee is reminiscent of the strong, dark brew found in Paris, its method of preparation is uniquely Vietnamese. Order a *ca phe den* (black coffee) and you'll get a filtration device perched on top of a small espresso cup. You must then patiently wait for the coffee to drip through the filter into your cup until you are left with a rich, dark brew. An even better choice is a *cafe sua,* the Vietnamese version of a cappuccino (although the iced version is more like a shake)—coffee mixed with sweet, condensed milk.

While you sip your coffee, watch people go by—elderly women heading to market weighed down by poles bearing baskets filled with fruit; old men on bicycles sporting green pith helmets, remnants of the North Vietnamese army uniform and originally introduced by the French colonialists; and young women on motorbikes wearing T-shirts and jeans, long gloves, and conical hats or traditional *ao dais* (pronounced "ow zai" in the south and "ow zai" in the

north), the elegant, straight-cut silk gowns worn over flowing pants.

A hybrid of the old and the new, this gown is the perfect emblem for Vietnamese culture. It is said that it was adapted from a Chinese dress called the *cheong sam,* which was modernized in the 1930s by two Vietnamese painters, Cat Tuong and Le Pho, who were influenced by French styles. Tailors took their paintings and produced this new style of gown. The gloves, too, are a Western influence: they came into style in the late 1950s after Madame Ngo Dinh Nhu, the sister-in-law of then President Diem, started wearing them.

It is this ability to synthesize what has been forced upon it that has made Vietnam so resilient. Now, after such a long history of conflict and hardship, the Vietnamese are welcoming the chance to chart their own course. This is why people fantasize about the future so readily, and why, finally, they are more excited about their Honda Dreams than they are about revisiting a painful history. Although only time will tell, there is little doubt that they will be able to adapt this time around as well.

—Jim Spencer

An amateur anthropologist and international development consultant, Jim Spencer has researched the consequences of Agent Orange in Vietnam, looked at the effects of environmental policy in the Mekong Delta, and worked with NGOs in Vietnam, Cambodia, and Laos. His preferred research methods include slurping a bowl of soup at a streetside noodle stand, enjoying a post–soccer game beer with Vietnamese friends, and test-driving Honda Dream motorbikes.

BOOKS AND VIDEOS

Books

Some of the most comprehensive histories of the Vietnam War are David Halberstam's *The Best and the Brightest,* Stanley Karnow's *Vietnam: A History,* Neil Sheehan's *A Bright Shining Lie,* and George C. Herring's *America's Longest War: The United States and Vietnam, 1950–1975.* Marilyn B. Young's *The Vietnam Wars: 1945–1990* and Frances FitzGerald's *Fire in the Lake* provide histories of the war from both the American and Vietnamese perspectives. Other insightful accounts of the war include Jonathan Schell's *The Real War* and Michael Herr's *Dispatches.* Nayan Chanda's *Brother Enemy: The War After the War* looks at the close of the Vietnam War and Vietnam's emerging conflicts with both Cambodia and China throughout the 1980s.

A number of moving personal narratives (some fictionalized) have been written about the war, including *A Rumour of War* by Philip Caputo, *In Pharaoh's Army* by Tobias Wolff, *Nam* by Mark Baker, *Fields of Fire* by James Webb, *Chickenhawk* by Robert Mason, and *The Things They Carried* and *Going After Cacciato* by Tim O'Brien. A more recent account of the war is Robert McNamara's *In Retrospect: The Tragedy and Lessons of Vietnam. From Both Sides Now: The Poetry of the Vietnam War and Its Aftermath* includes poems by both Americans and Vietnamese. *The Vietnam Reader* is an anthology of fiction, nonfiction, poetry, and more relating to the Vietnam War. An in-depth treatise on how the Vietnam War uprooted the American psyche is found in *Apocalypse Then: American Intellectuals and the Vietnam War* by Robert Tomes. For images of the war look for *Requiem,* a moving collection of war pictures by photographers who died at work in Indochina between 1954 and 1989.

Tom Mangold's *The Tunnels of Cu Chi* describes the Vietcong movement based in the tunnels around Cu Chi. *PAVN: People's Army of Vietnam* by Pike Douglas is a history of the war from the North Vietnamese point of view. Michael Lanning's

Inside the VC and the NVA is a look at the workings of the North Vietnamese army and the Vietcong. *When Heaven and Earth Changed Places* is Le Ly Hayslip's story of her life before, during, and after the Vietnam War. Truong Nhu Tang's *A Vietcong Memoir* is a narrative of the war as told by a former member of the Vietnamese National Liberation Front. Bao Ninh's novel, *The Sorrow of War,* chronicles hardships endured by a North Vietnamese soldier. Diem Bui's *In the Jaws of History* offers insight into how the Vietnamese saw Americans. Kiem Do's *Counterpart* brings to light little-known events of the South Vietnamese role at the end of the Vietnam War.

For a history of the French role in Vietnam, read Bernard Fall's *Street Without Joy* and Roy Jules' *The Battle of Dienbienphu.* Graham Green's literary classic *The Quiet American* is a prophetic tale of America's involvement in Vietnam. *The Lover,* by Marguerite Duras, is a fictionalized autobiographical tale of a French girl coming of age in 1930s Indochina.

Joachim Schliesinger's *Hill Tribes of Vietnam* gives insight into Vietnam's hill tribes. Recently translated into English, *Among the Tribes of Southeast Vietnam and Laos* records French explorer Captain P. Cupet' encounters with hill tribes at the end o the 19th century.

To learn more about contemporary Viet nam read Henry Kamm's *Dragon As cending: Vietnam and the Vietnamese* an Neil Sheehan's *After the War Was Over Hanoi and Saigon.* Robert Templer's *Shac ows and Wind* examines Vietnam's cultura transition through the '90s into an emerg ing economy under doi moi. *The Sacre Willow,* by Duong Van Mai Elliot, fo lows four generations of the author's fan ily, beginning with her great-grandfathe a mandarin in the Imperial Court. Loo for an account of traveling through Vie nam by train in Paul Theroux's *The Gre Railway Bazaar.* For a sense of Vietna before you go, take a look at the stunni *Passage to Vietnam: Through the Eyes Seventy Photographers*; there is also CD-ROM version.

Two literary anthologies that address postwar Vietnam are *The Other Side of Heaven: Postwar Fiction by Vietnamese and American Writers,* and John Edgar Wideman; and *Aftermath: An Anthology of Post-Vietnam Fiction.* Robert Olen Butler's Pulitzer prize–winning *A Good Scent from a Strange Mountain* is a collection of short stories about Vietnamese living in America.

Videos

Apocalypse Now is Francis Ford Coppola's powerful look at the Vietnam War based on Joseph Conrad's *Heart of Darkness*; it stars Martin Sheen, Marlon Brando, and Dennis Hopper. Oliver Stone's *Platoon* is a harrowing, first-person tale of a young soldier's experience in the war. Stone's *Born on the Fourth of July* is the stirring story of Ron Kovic, played by Tom Cruise, a gung ho soldier who is paralyzed during the war and becomes an antiwar activist. Brian de Palma's *Casualties of War* focuses on two soldiers in the same platoon, Michael J. Fox and Sean Penn, who battle over moral issues. *The Deer Hunter* is a Michael Cimino film about three steelworkers from Pennsylvania who go off to fight in Vietnam; it stars Robert De Niro, Christopher Walken, and Meryl Streep. Stanley Kubrick's *Full Metal Jacket* is an unblinking look at the realities of the Vietnam War from the perspective of a U.S. army journalist. *The Green Berets* is a clichéd but classic movie with John Wayne as a Green Beret. *Hamburger Hill,* a John Irvin film, follows a group of infantrymen from training to combat.

Barry Levinson's *Good Morning, Vietnam* is a more humorous look at the Vietnam War era, with Robin Williams as a U.S. Army Radio DJ. *Heaven & Earth,* another Oliver Stone film about Vietnam, portrays the odyssey of a young Vietnamese woman, Le Lyn, from 1953 through the war and after in America. Eric Weston's *The Iron Triangle,* starring Beau Bridges, attempts to show the conflict from both the Vietnamese and American sides.

For an inside look at the making of *Apocalypse Now,* see the documentary *Hearts of Darkness: A Filmmaker's Apocalypse.* Bill Couturie, in his documentary about the Vietnam War, *Dear America: Letters Home From Vietnam,* uses newsreels, amateur footage, and letters read by Robert De Niro, Sean Penn, and others to portray soldiers' experiences. The *War at Home* is a documentary about the antiwar movement. Barbara Sonneborn's *Regret to Inform* documents the tragedy of war as seen from the viewpoint of Vietnamese and American women.

Martin Scorsese's disturbing *Taxi Driver* stars Robert De Niro as Travis Bickle, an alienated Vietnam veteran. *Birdy,* a film by Alan Parker, stars Nicholas Cage and Matthew Modine as a Vietnam veteran suffering post-traumatic stress disorder. Emilio Estevez stars in his directorial debut, *The War at Home,* as a son pitted against his father (real-life father Martin Sheen), a Vietnam veteran haunted by his memories. *Alamo Bay,* a Louis Malle film starring Ed Harris, is a revealingly candid story of a Vietnam veteran whose livelihood is threatened by immigrant Vietnamese fishermen on the Texas Gulf Coast. In Hal Ashby's *Coming Home,* Jane Fonda is a career soldier's wife who falls in love with a wheelchair-bound veteran played by John Voight.

The Quiet American is Joseph L. Mankiewicz's cinematic portrayal of Graham Greene's classic. *The Lover,* a Jean-Jacques Annaud film based on the Marguerite Duras book, is the tale of a young French woman coming of age in colonial Vietnam and her relationship with her Vietnamese lover. Régis Wargnier's *Indochine,* starring Catherine Deneuve, is another film set in Vietnam during the French colonial era; it showcases the beautiful scenery of North Vietnam.

Postwar Vietnam and the story of people coping with the ruin at home is the focus of Michael Rubbo's *Sad Song of Yellow Skin.* Le Manh Thich and Do Kanh Toan's *Returning to Ngo Thuy* pays tribute to the spirit of the women of Ngo Thuy 30 years after they fought in the war. Le Duc Tien's *A Quiet Town* pokes fun at hypocrisy and greed.

Contemporary French-Vietnamese filmmaker Tran Anh Hung's cinematographically beautiful *The Scent of Green Papaya* follows the life of a young serving girl in Saigon. For a look at present-day Ho Chi Minh City, see Tran Anh Hung's *Cyclo* or *Three Seasons,* American-Vietnamese writer-director Tony Bui's first film.

VIETNAMESE VOCABULARY

In the mid-17th century, the Vietnamese language, which had been based on Chinese characters, was Romanized by the French Jesuit, Alexandre de Rhodes. This change made the tonal language easier for Westerners to read, but not much easier to pronounce. Vietnamese has six tones, which can significantly change the meaning of a word spelled the same way. Within a certain context, however, Vietnamese people will understand what you are trying to say even if you get the tones wrong. A bit of body language also helps get your point across.

Keep in mind that vocabulary and pronunciation vary from region to region. For example, a spoon in northern Vietnam is a *thìa* but it is a *muỗng* in the south. The soft "d" and soft "gi" are pronouced like a "z" in the north but change to "y" in the south.

Also remember that there is an "honorific" system of address, so what you call people depends on their relation to you. There are many specific titles of address, but the five listed below are all you need in a pinch. Use *ông* for an older man, *anh* for a younger man, and *em* for a boy. Use *bà* for an older woman, *cô* for a younger woman, and *em* for a girl.

Words and Phrases

	English	Vietnamese	Pronunciation
Basics			
	I	Tôi	doy
	We	Chúng tôi	choong doy
	Yes/No	Có/Không	caw/kawm
	Please	Làm ơn	lamb un
	Thank you	Cám ơn	cam un
	That's all right	Không có chi	kawm caw chee
	Excuse me, sorry	Xin lỗi	seen loy
	Hello	Xin chào	seen chow
	Goodbye	Tạm biệt	tom be-it
	Mr. (older man)	Ông	awm
	Mrs. (older woman)	Bà	bah
	Miss (younger woman)	Cô	co (like co-op)
	Mr. (young man)	Anh	ine / un(s)
	Young person	Em	em
	Pleased to meet you	Hân hạnh được gặp (ông)	haan hine dook gup (title)
	How are you?	(Ông) có khoẻ không?	(ông) caw Kway kawm?
	Very well, thanks	Khoẻ, cám ơn	kway, cam un
	And you?	Còn (ông)?	cawn (ông)?
Numbers			
	one	một	moat
	two	hai	hi
	three	ba	bah
	four	bốn	bown

five	năm	num
six	sáu	sow (like cow)
seven	bảy	by
eight	tám	tom
nine	chín	chin
ten	mười	moy
eleven	mười một	moy moat
twelve	mười hai	moy hi
thirteen	mười ba	moy bah
fourteen	mười bốn	moy bown
fifteen	mười năm	moy num
sixteen	mười sáu	moy sow
seventeen	mười bảy	muoi by
eighteen	mười tám	moy tom
nineteen	mười chín	moy chin
twenty	hai mươi	hi moy
twenty-one	hai mốt	hi moat
thirty	ba mươi	bah moy
forty	bốn mươi	bown moy
fifty	năm mươi	num moy
sixty	sáu mươi	sow moy
seventy	bảy mươi	by moy
eighty	tám mươi	tom moy
ninety	chín mươi	chin moy
one hundred	một trăm	moat chum
one thousand	một nghìn (n)	moat nyin
	một ngàn (s)	moat nyan
one million	một triệu	moat chew

Colors

black	đen	den
blue	xanh	sine
brown	nâu	no
green	xanh lá cây	sine la kay
orange	cam	cahm
pink	hồng	hawm
purple	tím	teem
red	đỏ	daw
white	trắng	chaang
yellow	vàng	vang

Days of the Week

Sunday	chủ nhật	chu nyat
Monday	thứ hai	two hi
Tuesday	thứ ba	two ba
Wednesday	thứ tư	two tu
Thursday	thứ năm	two num
Friday	thứ sáu	two sow
Saturday	thứ bảy	two by

Months

January	tháng một	tang moat
February	tháng hai	tang hi
March	tháng ba	tang ba

April	tháng tư	tang tu
May	tháng năm	tang num
June	tháng sáu	tang sow
July	tháng bảy	tang by
August	tháng tám	tang tom
September	tháng chín	tang chin
October	tháng mười	tang moy
November	tháng mười một	tang moy moat
December	tháng mười hai	tang moy hi

Useful Phrases

Do you speak English?	(Ông) có nói tiếng Anh không?	(ông) caw noy ting ine kawm?
I don't speak Vietnamese	Tôi không biết nói tiếng Việt	doy kawm byet noy teng Viet
I don't understand	Tôi không hiểu	doy kawm hue
I understand	Tôi hiểu	doy hue
I don't know	Tôi không biết	doy kawm byet
I'm American/British	Tôi là người Mỹ/Anh	doy la noy mee/ine
What's your name?	Tên (ông) là gì	ten (ong) la zee (southern=yee)
My name is . . .	Tôi tên là . . .	doy ten la . . .
How old are you?	(Ông) bao nhiêu tuổi	bow nyoo toy
What time is it?	Mấy giờ rồi?	may zuh zoy (n) may yuh roy (s)
How?	Bằng cách nào?	bong cack now?
When?	Bao giờ?	bow zuh? (n) bow yuh? (s)
Yesterday	Hôm qua	home kwa
Today	Hôm nay	home ny (like hi)
Tomorrow	Ngày mai	ny my
This morning/ afternoon	Sáng nay/ trưa nay	sang nye chewa nye
Tonight	Đêm nay/tối nay	dem nye/doy nye
Why?	Tại sao?	tie sow (like cow)
Who?	Ai?	eye
Where?	Ở đâu	uh doe
Where is	. . . ở đâu?	uh doe
Train station	Ga tàu Ga xe lửa	gah tow (n) gah say luh-ah (s)
Bus station	Bến xe	ben say
Bus stop	Trạm xe buýt	chum say boot
Airport	Sân bay	sun bye
Post office	Bưu điện	boo dien
Bank	Ngân hàng	nun hang
Hotel	Khách sạn	kack san
Temple	Chùa	chew-a
Restaurant	Nhà hàng	nya hang

Store	Cửa hàng	kua hang
Market	Chợ	chuh
Museum	Bảo tàng	bow taang
Art museum	Bảo tàng mỹ thuật	bow taang me twut
Gallery	Phòng tranh	fowm chine
Theater	Nhà hát	nya hat
Movie theater	Rạp cine	zap see-nay
Beach	Bãi biển	bye be-in
Lake	Hồ	hoe
Park	Công viên	cowm vee-in
Street	Phố (n)/Đường (s)	foe/dooahng
Hospital	Bệnh viện	ben vee-in
Telephone	Điện thoại	dee-in twai
Restroom	Nhà vệ sinh/toilette	nya vay sing
Here/there	ở đây/đằng kia	uh day/dang kee-uh
Left/right	trái/phải	chy/fye (as in 'bye')
Is it far?	Có xa không	caw sah kowm
Go	Đi	dee
Stop	Dừng lại	zoong lie
Slow	Chậm chậm	chum chum
Straight ahead	Thẳng	tang
I'd like . . .	Tôi muốn . . .	doy mun . . .
a room	một phòng	moat fong
the key	chìa khóa	cheah kwa
a newspaper	tờ báo	tuh bow
magazine	tạp chí	tup chee
a stamp	con tem	cawn tem
I'd like to buy . . .	Tôi muốn mua . . .	doy mun moo-a . . .
cigarettes	thuốc lá	twook la
matches	diêm (n)	zee-im
	bật lửa (s)	but luh-ah
dictionary	từ điển	tuh dien
soap	xà phòng/xà bông (s)	sa fong/sa bowm
city map	bản đồ thành phố	ban doe tine foe
envelopes	phong bì	fawm bee
writing paper	giấy viết thơ	zay vee-it tuh
		yay vit tuh (s)
postcard	bưu thiếp	boo tip
How much is it?	Bao nhiêu?	bow nyew
Expensive/cheap	Đắt/rẻ	dut/zay /ray (s)
A little/lot	ít/nhiều	eat/nyew
More/less	Nhiều hơn/ít hơn	nyew huhn/eat huhn
Too much/enough	Nhiều quá/đủ rồi	nyew kwa/
		doo zoy
		doo roy (s)
Too expensive	Đắt quá	dut kwa
Change money	Đổi tiền	doy tee-in
I am ill	Tôi bị ốm	doy be awm

Call a doctor	Gọi bác sỹ	goy back see
Help!	Cứu tôi!	ku doy
Stop!	Dừng lại!	zoong lie
Fire!	Cháy nhà!	chay nyah
Caution!/look out!	Coi chừng!	coy chung

Dining Out

A bottle of	Chai	chye
A glass of	Cốc (n)/Ly (s)	cup/lee
Bill/Check please	Tính tiền	ting tee-in
Bowl	Bát (n)/Tô (s)	baht/toe
Bread	Bánh mỳ	bine mee
Breakfast	Ăn sáng	ahn sang
Butter	Bơ	buh
Chopsticks	Đũa	doo-a
Delicious	Ngon	nawn
Dinner	Bữa tối	booa doy
Eat	Ăn cơm	ahn come
Fork	Dĩa	zee-a
Hot/cold	Nóng/lạnh	nawm/line
Thirsty	Khát nước	cat nooc
Fish sauce	Nước mắm	nooc mum
Knife	Dao	zow
Lunch	Ăn trưa	ahn chewa
Menu	Thực đơn	took duhn
Napkin	Giấy ăn	zay ahn/yay ahn (s)
Pepper	Tiêu	tyew
Plate	Đĩa	dee-a
Please give me . . .	Cho xin . . .	chaw seen . . .
Rice	Cơm	come
Salt	Muối	moo-ee
Shrimp paste	Mắm tôm	mum tome
Spicy	Cay	kai (as in eye)
Too spicy!	Cay quá	kai (as in eye) kwa
Spoon	Thìa (n)/Muỗng (s)	tee-ah/moong
Sugar	Đường	dooahng
Sweet	Ngọt	naught
Bon appetit	Chúc ăn ngon	chook ahn nawn
Bottoms up!	Trăm phần trăm	chum fun chum
I am a vegetarian	Tôi ăn chay	doy ahn chai (as in eye)
I am hungry	Tôi đói	doy doy
I cannot eat . . .	Tôi không biết ăn . . .	doy cawn bee-it ahn . . .
To your health	Chúc sức khoẻ	chook soo kway

MENU GUIDE

Vietnamese	English

Soups

Canh	Soup, broth
Canh chua	Sour soup
Bún	Round rice noodles
Bún Riêu	Freshwater crab soup
Cháo	Congee, or rice porridge
Cháo cá	Congee with fish
Phở	Flat rice noodle soup
Phở bò	Beef noodle soup
Phở gà	Chicken noodle soup
Phở xào	Fried rice noodles
Miến	Vermicelli
Miến lươn	Vermicelli eel soup
Miến gà	Vermicelli chicken soup
Mỳ ăn liền	Instant noodles

Salads/Các loại gỏi

Gỏi đu đủ xanh	Green papaya salad
Gỏi ngó sen	Lotus stem salad
Nộm hoa chuối	Banana flower salad

Fish and Seafood/Đồ biển

Cá	Fish
Cá chép	Carp
Cá thu	Cod
Cá trê	Catfish
Cua	Crab
Ếch	Frog
Lươn	Eel
Mực	Squid
Tôm	Shrimp
Tôm hùm	Lobster

Meat/Thịt

Bít tết	Beefsteak
Bò	Beef
Chả	Grilled meat patties
Chó	Dog
Dê	Goat
Giò	Processed meat roll
Heo(s)	Pork
Lợn (n)	Pork
Ốc	Snail
Rắn	Snake
Sóc	Squirrel
Sườn	Pork ribs

Poultry/Chim

Chim cút	Quail
Gà	Chicken
Trứng	Egg

ốp-la/rán	fried
ốp lếp	omelet
luộc	boiled
Vịt	Duck

Vegetables/Các loại rau

Bắp cải	Cabbage
Cà chua	Tomato
Cà pháo	Baby eggplant
Cà tím	Eggplant
Đậu đũa	String bean
Đậu phụ (n) Tàu hũ (s)	Tofu
Giá	Bean sprouts
Gừng	Ginger
Hành	Onion
Khoai	Potato
Lạc	Peanuts
Măng	Bamboo shoots
Nấm	Mushroom
Ớt	Chili pepper
Rau cải	Mustard greens
Rau dền	Amaranth
Rau muống	Water convolvulus
Su hào	Kohlrabi
Súp lơ	Cauliflower
Tỏi	Garlic
Xả	Lemongrass

Methods of preparation

Chiên	Fried
Hấp	Steamed
Kho	Braised, with caramelized sauce
Kho tộ	Claypot
Lẩu	Steamboat
Luộc	Boiled
Nhúng dấm	Dipped in hot vinegar
Nướng	Grilled
Quay	Roasted
Rút xương	Filleted
Sống	Raw
Xào	Sauteed
Xốt	Sauce

For example: Gà xào nấm = chicken sauteed with mushrooms
                    Cá hấp bia = fish steamed with beer
                    Đậu phụ xốt cà chua = tofu with tomato sauce

Fruit/Hoa Quả

Cam	Orange
Chanh	Lemon
Chôm chôm	Rambutan
Chuối	Banana
Đu Đủ	Papaya
Dưa hấu	Watermelon
Dừa	Coconut

Dứa	Pineapple
Khế	Starfruit
Măng cụt	Mangosteen
Mít	Jackfruit
Na	Custard apple
Nhãn	Longan
Sầu riêng	Durian
Táo	Apple
Thanh Long	Dragon Fruit
Vải	Lychee
Vú Sữa	Milkfruit
Xoài	Mango

Miscellaneous delicacies

Bánh chưng (n)/Bánh tết (s)	Stuffed sticky rice cake
Bánh cuốn	Rice noodle crepe
Bánh xèo	Meat & shrimp crepe
Gỏi cuốn	Summer rolls
Nem (n)/Chả giò (s)	Spring rolls
Xôi	Sticky rice

Drinks/Đồ uống

Bia	Beer
Có đá	With ice
Không đá	Without ice
Nước cam	Orange juice
Nước chanh	Lemonade
Nước dừa	Coconut milk
Nước khoáng	Mineral Water
Nước	Water
Rượu Vang	Wine
Rượu	Alcohol
Sinh tố	Smoothie
Sô-đa chanh	Soda-water lemonade
Sô-đa	Soda
Sữa tươi	Fresh milk
Chè/Trà (s)	Tea
Trà đá	Iced tea
Cà phê	Coffee
Cà phê đen	Black coffee
Cà phê sữa	Coffee with sweetened milk
Cà phê đá	Iced coffee

Dessert/Tráng Miêng

Bánh flan/kem caramen	Flan
Bánh ngọt	Sweet cakes
Chè đậu đen	Black-bean compote
Chè đậu xanh	Green-bean compote
Chè thập cẩm	Assorted compote
Kem	Ice cream
Kẹo	Candy
Sữa chua	Yogurt

266

INDEX

Icons and Symbols

★ Our special recommen-
dations
✕ Restaurant
🏠 Lodging establishment
✕🏠 Lodging establishment
whose restaurant war-
rants a special trip
👋 Good for kids (rubber
duck)
☞ Sends you to another
section of the guide for
more information
✉ Address
☎ Telephone number
🕐 Opening and closing
times
💰 Admission prices
🖱 Sends you to
www.fodors.com/urls
for up-to-date links to
the property's Web site

Numbers in white and black
circles ③ ❸ that appear on
the maps, in the margins, and
within the tours correspond
to one another.

A

A Dong Hotel 1 🏠, 135
A Dong 2 Hotel 🏠, 135
'A' The Russian Restaurant
✕, 194–195
Air Force Museums, 28
Air travel. ☞ Plane travel
Al Fresco ✕, 46
Am Phu ✕, 133
Ambassador's Pagoda, 28
Ana Mandara Nha Trang
Resort 🏠, 165
Angkor Village 🏠, 218
Angkor Wat Complex, 217–
218
Anoasis Beach Resort 🏠,
214
Antique shops, 207–208
Arc En Ciel Hotel 🏠, 201
Architecture, 5–6, 123–124
Army Museum, 34–35
Art, 6–7
Art galleries and museums.
☞ Museums
Art Museum (Ho Chi Minh
City), 188
Art shops
Hanoi, 65–66
Ho Chi Minh City, 208
Artex Saigon Orchid Farm,
205
Asian Hotel 🏠, 199

Assembly Hall of the
Cantonese Chinese
Congregation, 148
Assembly Hall of the Fujian
Chinese Congregation,
148–149
Assembly Hall of the Hainan
Chinese Congregation, 149
Au Lac Café ✕, 43, 46
Auberge Hotel ✕🏠, 117
Augustin ✕, 194

B

Ba Be Guest House 🏠, 109
Ba Be Hotel 🏠, 109
Ba Be Lakes, 108–109
Ba Vi Mountain, 70–71
Bac Ha, 118
Back Beach, 213
Bai Dau, 213
Bamboo Green ✕, 143
Banana Split ✕, 164
Bangkok-Hanoi ✕, 48
Banh Beo Ba Cu ✕, 133–134
Banh Khoai ✕, 134
Bao Dai's Summer Palace,
169
Bao Tang Cach Mang
(Hanoi), 30
Bao Tang Cach Mang (Ho
Chi Minh City), 185
Bao Tang Ho Chi Minh, 36,
38
Bao Tang Lich Su, 29
Bao Tang My Thuat (Hanoi),
35
Bao Tang My Thuat (Ho Chi
Minh City), 188
Bao Tang Quan Doi, 34–35
Bao Tang Thanh Pho Hai
Phong, 94
Bao Tang Ton Duc Thang, 188
Bars and pubs
Haiphong, 97
Hanoi, 60–61
Ho Chi Minh City, 202–203,
204
Basketball, 61
Bat Pagoda, 237
Beaches, 7
China Beach, 144–145
Ho Coc, 214
Lang Co, 140
Long Hai, 214
Nha Trang, 156, 163–164
Phan Tiet, 215
Tra Co, 103
Vung Tau, 213
Ben Thanh Market, 182
Bi Bi ✕, 194
Bicycling
Haiphong, 97
Hanoi, 62, 78
Ho Chi Minh City, 220
Hoi An, 153
Hue, 138

Nha Trang, 167
Northern Vietnam, 119
Biet Dien Quoc Truong, 169
Binh Chau Hot Springs, 214–
215
Binh Chau Hotel 🏠, 214–
215
Binh Minh (Hue) 🏠, 135
Binh Minh Hotel (Mong Cai)
🏠, 103
Binh Tay Market, 191
Binh Thuan, 233
Blue Ginger ✕, 195
Boat travel
Halong Bay, 99–100
Hanoi, 62
Ho Chi Minh City, 220
Hoi An, 153
Hue, 138–139
Mekong Delta, 239
Nha Trang, 163, 167
Northern Vietnam, 105–106
Bodhi Tree II ✕, 195
Bong, 74
Books on Vietnam, 257–258
Bookstores. ☞ English-
language bookstores
Botanical Garden (Hanoi),
35
Bowling, 62, 205
Brother's Cafe ✕, 51
Buffalo Fighting Festival, 13,
98
Bun Bo Hue ✕, 134
Bus travel
Dalat, 173
Hanoi, 76, 77
Ho Chi Minh City, 218, 220
Hue, 138
Nha Trang, 166
Northern Vietnam, 104–105
Buu Dien Truing Tam, 183

C

Ca Mau, 237–239
Ca Mau Hotel 🏠, 238
Café Can ✕, 151
Café des Amis ✕, 151
Café des Arts de Hanoi ✕,
46
Café Moca ✕, 31, 46
Café Mogambo ✕, 192
Cafe Que Huong ✕, 51
Café 252 ✕, 46
Cafés, 17
Cam Ly Falls, 169
Cam Minihotel 🏠, 200
Cambodia, 217–218
Camellia II Hotel 🏠, 54
Cameras and photography,
xvi–xvii
Camillia Restaurant ✕, 117
Can Gio, 212
Can Tho, 231–232
Caodai Holy See, 210, 212